MYCENAEAN GREECE

MYCENAEAN GREECE

by

RICHARD HOPE SIMPSON

NOYES PRESS

PARK RIDGE, NEW JERSEY

Published in the United States of America by
NOYES PRESS
Mill Road, Park Ridge, New Jersey 07656

Library of Congress Cataloging in Publication Data

Simpson, R. Hope.
    Mycenaean Greece.

    Bibliography: p.
    Includes indexes.
    1. Civilization, Mycenaean. 2. Greece--An-
tiquities. 3. Excavations (Archaeology)--Greece.
I. Title.
DF220.S52   938   81-14180
ISBN 0-8155-5061-8   AACR2

PREFACE AND ACKNOWLEDGEMENTS

This study is partly based on fieldwork in Mainland Greece and the Islands during the period 1955 to 1975. Its main focus is on the Mainland and the Aegean Islands (excepting Crete). The only sites in Epirus, Macedonia, and Western Asia Minor listed are those where material alleged to be of Mycenaean type has been found. The present publication is intended both as a revision of, and as a replacement for, my former *Gazetteer and Atlas of Mycenaean Sites* (1965), which has long been out of print. I here incorporate results from several important recent surveys, *i.e.*, of Achaea by Åström (1964), Euboea by Sackett *et al.* (1966), Southwest Peloponnese by McDonald, Hope Simpson and others (1961, 1964, 1969, and *MME*), and Eastern Arcadia by Howell (1970). Also incorporated are the results of some travels in the Dodecanese published by Hope Simpson and Lazenby (1962, 1970, and 1973). Much is owed also to two important studies by D.H. French, one for Central Macedonia (1967) and one for Central Greece (1972). He is currently preparing another for Thessaly, and P. Halstead has provided some further information on this province. K.A. Wardle has given much help on Northwest Greece, and C. Renfrew, R. Barber and J. Cherry have generously provided information on the Cyclades in advance of their own publications. Asia Minor has been well covered by regular reviews presented by M.J. Mellink in *American Journal of Archaeology,* D.H. French in *Anatolian Studies* and by J.M. Cook and others periodically in *Archaeological Reports* (by the Society for the Promotion of Hellenic Studies in conjunction with the British School of Archaeology in Athens). There is also now a very good summary by C. Mee (1978).

Among the various colleagues, both past and present, to whom I am indebted, I should like to record my special gratitude to the following: Miss S. Benton, Miss A. Burford, Mrs. E. French, Miss L.S. Garrad, Miss V.R. Grace, Miss D.H.F. Gray, Mrs. A. Demako-poulou-Papantoniou, The Hon. Mrs. Vronwy Hankey,

Mrs. Th. Karageorga, Miss L.H. Jeffery, Miss L. Parlama, Miss A. Romiopoulou, Miss L. Talcott, Lady Helen Waterhouse, Miss I. Zervoudakis, Messrs. A. Andrewes, P. Åström, R. Barber, Y. Béquignon, J.L. Bintliff, C.W. Blegen, G. Cadogan, J.L. Caskey, H.W. Catling, W. Cavanagh, J. Chadwick, S.J. Charitonides, J. Cherry, A. Choremis, Ch. Christou, J.N. Coldstream, J.M. Cook, P.E. Corbett, S.I. Dakaris, V.R. d'A. Desborough, O.T.P.K. Dickinson, D.R. Dicks, C. Doumas, T.J. Dunbabin, C.W.J. Eliot, J.M. Fossey, P.M. Fraser, D.H. French, N.G.L. Hammond, P. Halstead, R.A. Higgins, T. Hodge, E.J. Holmberg, M.S.F. Hood, R.J. Hopper, R.J. Howell, A Hunter, R.W. Hutchinson, G.L. Huxley, S. Iakovidis, T. Jacobsen, M.H. Jameson, I. Kontis, G. Konstantinopoulos, G.S. Korres, J.F. Lazenby, D. Levi, W.A. McDonald, C. Mee, R. Meiggs, G. Papathanasopoulos, V. Petrakos, P. Petsas, H.W. Pleket, M. Pope, C. Renfrew, C.M. Robertson, J. Rutter, L.H. Sackett, M. Sakellariou, J. Servais, J.W. Shaw, A.M. Snodgrass, F.H. Stubbings, Lord William Taylour, R.A. Tomlinson, E.G. Turner, N. Valmin, E. Vanderpool, A.J.B. Wace, K.A. Wardle, P.M. Warren, T.B.L. Webster, F.E. Winter, J.R. Wiseman, and N. Yalouris.

My work in Greece began in November 1955, and from 1956 to 1958, as School Student of the British School of Archaeology at Athens, I continued the survey of Prehistoric Laconia begun by Lady Helen Waterhouse (née Helen Thomas) in 1936-1938. During this period I received advice and encouragement from the late Professor A.J.B. Wace, and from M.S.F. Hood and R. Meiggs, among others.

From spring 1958 to summer 1961 I collaborated with J.F. Lazenby in the investigation of the topography of Mycenaean Greece in relation to the Homeric Catalogue of the Ships. In summer 1958 I travelled in Central Greece in the company of Miss D.H.F. Gray and of my wife, and in 1959 my wife and I travelled extensively in the Peloponnese. (My wife was accompanied on separate occasions also by Miss A. Burford and Miss L.S. Garrad.) From 1959 onwards I collaborated with W.A. McDonald and others in the survey of Southwestern Peloponnese, and in 1960, 1967-68, and 1970 Lazenby and I completed our reconnaissance of the Dodecanese. In 1970-71 and in 1974-75 I carried out some supplementary fieldwork, specifically with a view to completing the autopsy of Mainland Greece necessary for the present work.

I am very grateful to the Managing Committee and officials, both past and present, of the British School of Archaeology at Athens, to the University of Birmingham, where I was a Research Fellow from 1960 to 1963, to University College London, to the Institute of Classical Studies in the University of London, to the University of Minnesota, and to Queen's University at Kingston, Ontario, Canada. I received welcome support from the Oxford University Craven Fund during the period from 1957 to 1961, from Mr. and Mrs. W.B. Weigand (during the same period), from the University of Birmingham in 1961 and 1962, from the Leverholme Trust in 1962 and 1963, and from the University of Minnesota at various times since 1959. In 1970-71 I was awarded a Leave Fellowship by the Canada Council, and I am also indebted to the Council for Research grants for the work in the Dodecanese in 1967, 1968, and 1970, and for work on this present project in the summers of 1974 and 1975. I also gratefully acknowledge support from the Research Fund of Queen's University at Kingston in 1967, 1968, 1972, 1973, and 1977.

Since 1969, I have collaborated with O.T.P.K. Dickinson in an archaeological and topographical study of the Bronze Age sites on the Greek mainland and islands (excepting Crete). The results have recently been published in P. Åström's series, Studies in Mediterranean Archaeology, as *A Gazetteer of Aegean Civilisation in the Bronze Age, Vol. I: The Mainland and Islands (SIMA vol. 52, 1979).* I wish to express my deep gratitude both to my colleague, Dr. Dickinson, and to Dr. Åström, who have given me permission to make use of, and to summarise here, the information on Mycenaean sites included in that work.

All the photographs used here were taken by myself in the field, and I have also myself produced all the maps and other figure illustrations. Nevertheless, several of these illustrations have appeared in previous publications (of which I have been the author or co-author). I am most grateful to the following persons and institutions for permission to reproduce these here: Lady Helen Waterhouse, Professor W.A. McDonald, Mr. J.F. Lazenby, The Oxford University Press, The University of Minnesota Press, The British School of Archaeology at Athens, and The Archaeological Institute of America.

I have been greatly assisted in the production of the maps, figures, and plates by Dr. H.W. Castner of the Department of Geography of Queen's University at Kingston, together with Mr. R.W. Hough (cartographer) and Mr. G.E. Innes (photographer) of the Department. Mr. R. Eastman also assisted Mr. Hough in the production of the End Paper, "Mycenaean Sites in Mainland Greece and the Aegean". The typescript was prepared at Kingston by Miss A. Mann, Mrs. A. Hunt, and Mrs. W.J. Hope Simpson, to all of whom I am most grateful for their patience and perseverance. I record my thanks also to all the other members of the Classics Department of Queen's University at Kingston, and also to our former Chairman, Professor S.E. Smethurst, for their support.

Finally, I wish to express my special thanks to the publisher, Robert Noyes, to the editors Sarah Jones and Mildred Schumacher, and to the staff at Noyes Press. Their advice and assistance is deeply appreciated.

R. Hope Simpson
June 1981

Kingston, Ontario, Canada

ABOUT THE AUTHOR

R. Hope Simpson is a Professor of Classics at Queen's University, Kingston, Ontario, Canada, and a Life Member of the British School at Athens. Since 1955 he has undertaken extensive fieldwork in Greece, principally with a view to locating prehistoric settlements, particularly the Mycenaean. He has worked with several colleagues, including Professor (Emeritus) William A. McDonald, of the University of Minnesota, and Mr. J.F. Lazenby, of the University of Newcastle upon Tyne. He is currently engaged (with others) in the publication of the Nichoria Excavations (directed by Professor McDonald), and, together with Professor J.W. Shaw, of the University of Toronto, is acting as a coordinator of the Archaeological Survey of the Kommos Area in southern Crete.

CONTENTS

LIST OF FIGURES

LIST OF PLATES

INTRODUCTION

MYCENAEAN GREECE: THE CURRENT STATE OF EXPLORATION

The number of Mycenaean sites already discovered is impressive, and the amount of excavated material is now substantial. But few Mycenaean settlements have been fully, or even adequately, excavated. Most of the sites are either tombs, usually found by chance, or settlement sites found in surveys. The excavations have tended to focus upon the major centres, where richer rewards are to be expected. And most survey work has been of the "initial" or "pilot" type, whose chief purpose was often to find sites suitable for excavation. Such surveys may be termed "extensive", since they cover a wide terrain, using selective techniques; and their main purpose is to discover as many sites as possible in the time available, usually in areas previously unexplored. It has been suggested recently that these surveys have failed to discover the "smaller and satellite" settlements that can (supposedly) be predicted on geographical grounds, and that they have deliberately concentrated on the "upper hierarchy" of settlements. I will be arguing (below) that this is not true as regards at least some parts of the Euboea, Laconia, Messenia, and Arcadia surveys. The surveys in South-east Argolid, of the Peneios Barrage area in Elis, and the "Systematic Random Transect Survey" on Melos, are all of an "intensive" variety, involving laborious coverage (ideally) of every square metre of surface area. It is presumed by the proponents of such survey methods that substantially more settlements and other sites will be found than in "extensive" surveys, and that they will reveal a hitherto unrecognized wealth of smaller sites interspersed among the larger and more obvious sites.

While the new techniques and the new zeal are to be welcomed, it must be pointed out that there are obvious limitations inherent in *all* survey work, especially when not accompanied by excavations. Some areas are covered by modern structures (roads, houses, etc.),

others have suffered from agricultural disturbance, such as deep ploughing, or are now totally obscured by natural vegetation (especially in cases where cultivation has recently been discontinued). The somewhat random results of erosion and/or deposition further distort the surface patterns. Thus even "intensive" surveys may not succeed in giving a true reflection. Such surveys are, of course, extremely expensive, both as regards time and resources. In Greece, as elsewhere, the pace of modernisation is hectic. Much of Attica, for instance, especially along the coast, is now heavily covered by buildings. In Athens and Piraeus and their suburbs archaeological work is now mainly confined to salvage operations. Outside Attica most of the damage to ancient sites is caused by modern agriculture, and by the use of the bulldozer in particular. This instrument can, of course, assist in the discovery of sites, but too often such discoveries are not reported. And it is often difficult even to keep pace with the reported occurrences, despite the valiant efforts of the Greek Archaeological Service and others.

There are still vast areas of Greece which have never been surveyed even "extensively". Without such initial surveys, we can not determine which areas should be selected for "intensive" survey. For it should be realised that not all areas are worth surveying intensively. Some are covered by relatively recent alluvial fill or other deposition. Others may never have been inhabited, or at least not until recently. I have observed, in Messenia and elsewhere, quite considerable areas of cultivable land, which appear to never have been used by man. In Mycenaean times, much of the land may still have been virgin forest or woodland, as is suggested, for instance, by the considerable quantity of deer bones found in Mycenaean levels at Nichoria. Other regions may have remained as swamps or marshes.

The geography and climate of Greece were, of course, major factors in determining the patterns of prehistoric settlement. The two most important necessites were a fertile and *easily* cultivable soil (*i.e.* amenable to primitive ploughs) and a *perennial* water supply. Since Greek rivers are few and mainly with only a seasonal flow, greater reliance would have to be placed on spring and well water. This factor, together with the primitive need for defence, and for natural drainage, usually gave rise to the location of the main settlements on hills or slopes on the edges of fertile plains or valleys, since it is here that the springs usually emerge. Sometimes the hills chosen resemble the "acropolis" type; but suitable hills of this kind are more rare than the low rounded hills or hillocks, or even mere rises in the ground. Few important Mycenaean sites were situated in the middle of plains, unless an especially fine "acropolis" site was available (*e.g.* Athens).

The most suitable soils for prehistoric cultivation were those derived from the early worked marls (*i.e.* those classed as "Neogen") and sandstones formed during the Pliocene period. The red earth ("terra rossa") which is formed far more slowly (at a rate of erosion over ten times as slow as that for the "Neogen") from the hard limestones tends to be shallower in depth and much less fertile. The heavy alluvial loam in the plains must have presented considerable problems to the early settlers, both because of the difficulty of ploughing with primitive instruments and also because of the drainage problem. The comparative lack of good drainage would have imposed some restriction on Mycenaean agriculture. The earliest form of agriculture would indeed have been (as in the medieval period) that of *terrace cultivation* (and the importance of Mycenaean Messenia may have depended very largely on this factor). But, while lower terraces, especially on the edges of the plains, were intensively cultivated, there seems to have been little penetration into, let alone exploitation of, the higher and more rugged terrain. There are, indeed, a few possible exceptions, e.g. the sites with tombs of tholos type at Arkines on the slopes of Mt. Taygetus and near Spilia on the slopes of Mt. Ossa; but, in general, there appears to have been no such system as the Upper and Lower (Ano- and Kato-) villages of medieval and modern Greece. The mountain areas appear to have been used sparingly, and probably only for short seasonal periods, presumably for grazing and hunting.

Recent environmental studies in Greece must, of course, be considered in relation to the distribution of the Mycenaean settlements. The fullest treatment of this relationship is that given by J.L. Bintliff, *Natural Environment and Human Settlement in Prehistoric Greece* (1977). It has not been possible to examine all the implications of Bintliff's detailed arguments, but I have added some discussions of these at the end of the relevant chapters (Maps A, E, and F) and in the summary. Bintliff repeatedly emphasizes the preference shown for the Pliocene marls and conglomerates in the siting of prehistoric settlements; and he stresses the association of the sites with the more fertile components of the Neogen, *i.e.* the soil most favourable for the cultivation of dry-farmed cereals and olives. He also reminds us that we must exclude from consideration all "recent" (*i.e. post*-Classical) alluvium in relation to the positioning of prehistoric settlements. It is indeed most gratifying to find that our previous insistence on these factors was correct [*BSA* 55 (1960) 69, 87].

It is also useful to be reminded of the manner in which a surface survey should (ideally) be conducted. Unfortunately, archaeologists also have other commitments, including excavations, and are not always able to allot sufficient time to surface survey work. Indeed the ideal, fully intensive and inter-disciplinary, type of survey is a luxury normally confined to the immediate vicinity of an excavated site. And editors normally insist that articles dealing with survey work should concentrate on giving as concise an account as possible of the *positive* results derived from a survey. Failure to find surface evidence is, of course, an unreliable guide, since this may be partly due to the ground cover or to the state of deposition/erosion in the area concerned. Such failure may also be partly due to the actual state of preservation of the artefacts on the surface.

THE MYCENAEAN SETTLEMENTS

A main objective of excavation and survey work is, of course, to identify as closely as possible the exact periods during which an ancient site was occupied. The evidence for Mycenaean habitation on *settlement* sites is derived mainly from surface potsherds. This is true of almost all of the smaller sites in particular. There is, however, often great difficulty in diagnosing with any accuracy the date of such potsherds, which are usually much fragmented, heavily worn, and often lacking most or all of their original surfaces. In many cases we have to rely on shape alone. The most easily recognized Mycenaean shapes are the kylix and deep bowl. On some sites these or other fine ware sherds may be found, but usually they are heavily outnumbered by the coarse wares, which are seldom closely identifiable. In areas where the soil is more alkaline, and the pottery less well made, as in most of the western Peloponnese, the difficulties of identification are even greater.

In general we may reasonably assume that Mycenaean culture was predominant in the Peloponnese and in most central Greece, even if some of the local pottery is of "provincial" nature. But in the outlying "fringe" areas of Mycenaean Greece it is sometimes difficult to distinguish between true Mycenaean settlements and sites where Mycenaean finds are probably to be regarded as merely objects of trade on otherwise "native" Late Bronze Age settlements. This difficulty is particularly evident in Epirus, Macedonia, Western Asia Minor, and in some of the Aegean Islands. I have here attempted to follow what I take to be the "majority opinion" in such cases.

Another important objective is to determine the *size* of the settlements in the period(s) of occupation. If a site is well defined, either by man-made enclosures or by natural features, or by a combination of both, the problem becomes easier; although we can seldom be certain of the absence of contemporary settlement immediately beyond the defined area. In many cases, however, erosion has removed large portions of a settlement (as for instance at the Menelaion site in Laconia). Conversely, on some other sites the spread of surface potsherds may be considerably greater than the actual extent of the settlement (as may be the case at the Vaphio site). And, without excavation, we have no means of ascertaining what part of the area indicated was actually covered by structures of the period(s) indicated. The results of man-made disturbances, such as ploughing, are not uniform, and neither are the effects of natural erosion and/or deposition. Often the search for Mycenaean sherds is made on sites occupied in later periods; and the scarcity of Mycenaean surface sherds on these may be deceptive. Even in the case of excavated sites, we rarely have more than a rough idea of their total size. And only in the case of sites more fully excavated, such as Mycenae, Tiryns, and Malthi-Dorion, can we begin to make any proper estimate of the *density* of the ancient habitation.

In view of these and other considerations, scholars should be warned that the assessments made here of the size of Mycenaean settlements are to some extent conjectural and must remain entirely provisional. In particular, it would be extremely unwise to attempt to analyse (especially by computer) any "raw data" presently available concerning the size of the settlements or their observed distribution. The results of any such analyses would only reflect the inadequate and subjective judgements upon which the assessments depend. In my opinion, the use of the computer for *analysis* of archaeological finds should at present be restricted entirely to data obtained from *excavated* material found in *stratified* deposits. (But there is, of course, no great danger of distortion inherent in a simple recording of survey finds and observations in a data bank.)

With the above warnings, and with considerable hesitation, I have decided to attempt a size classification for the Mycenaean settlements. This is to some extent arbitrary, and based almost entirely on subjective observations. The actual field data are of varying degrees of reliability, and can provide only a very rough guide as to the actual size of the settlements. The estimates are mainly based on the observed distribution of the surface sherds; but common sense and personal experience, and some degree of guesswork have also been employed.

Mycenaean settlements were of small size compared to modern Greek villages. Most range from about half a hectare (5,000 m²) to two hectares (20,000 m²). Large settlements are relatively rare, and fewer still are of palatial type. The provisional table below is, I consider, the most appropriate, although it may, of course, require modification in the future:

"small"	= up to 5,000 m²
"small to medium"	= 5,000 m² to 10,000 m²
"medium"	= 10,000 m² to 15,000 m²
"medium to large"	= 15,000 m² to 20,000 m²
"large"	= over 20,000 m²
"very large"	= over 40,000 m²

There is a great variety in the size of the areas enclosed within the walls of the known Mycenaean fortresses. This is illustrated here by a diagram (Fig. 15) consisting of sketch plans of the major fortresses drawn to the same scale. The classification of certain other sites as "major" is to some extent subjective and arbitrary.

Major Excavated Sites

In the commentaries on important excavated sites, I have not attempted to give full summaries of the significant finds, since such summaries are regularly presented elsewhere. Both in the text and in the references given I have concentrated on the topography of the sites, and particularly on the extent and the density of habitation in the Mycenaean period. In practice most excavations of Mycenaean settlements have concentrated on buildings of the *later* Mycenaean periods (LH IIIA2 to LH IIIC). Few major buildings of *earlier* Mycenaean periods (LH I to LH IIIA1) have been found, principally because such are usually covered over by, or obliterated by, the important later structures, which excavators normally do not remove. Thus far more earlier Mycenaean tombs have been uncovered than dwellings. It follows that it is seldom possible to gauge the extent and density of *earlier* Mycenaean settlement on the habitation sites. We are more fortunate as regards the *later* Mycenaean periods, especially LH IIIA2 and LH IIIB; but we must always bear in mind the many factors (outlined above) which limit the interpretation of the evidence. The picture is far from clear or complete even in the case of the excavated sites.

Minor Excavated Sites or Sites Not Yet Excavated

Many Mycenaean sites have been revealed only by means of surface indications. At others only limited excavations have taken place. I have tended to give reasonably full summaries of the discoveries at such sites, since they are relatively less well known. It is important also to try to counteract the natural impression that excavated sites are in all cases more important than those not excavated. If an excavated site is revealed to have been of lesser importance, or of a restricted use or purpose, this evidence will help to indicate the varieties of Mycenaean sites that we may expect. It will also assist in our assessments of the size of, and density of settlement at, similar but not yet excavated sites.

It must, however, be admitted that it is extremely difficult to interpret evidence given by surface finds alone. Apart from the attempts made here to gauge the size of the settlements, I have tried to indicate the apparent geographical groupings of the sites, and to estimate their relative importance. There is, of course, no guarantee that any such geographical groupings reflect actual Mycenaean *political* combinations. And in those areas where little or no exploration has been carried out, the known pattern is unbalanced or even distorted. I have tried (in the summary below) to point out the major "gaps" in our knowledge of Mycenaean Greece.

The Major Monuments

The achievements of the Mycenaeans are exemplified by monuments almost as magnificent as those of the Egyptians and the Hittites. Their repertoire of architectural forms was somewhat limited, but included some distinctive techniques of construction, particularly the "Cyclopean" walling of the main fortresses, the special Mycenaean "arch", and the elaborate stone corbel vaulting of the tholos tombs. The principles employed in the construction of Mycenaean tholos tombs have been well described elsewhere [especially by Mylonas, in *Mycenae and the Mycenaean Age* (1966) 118ff.]. The doorways of several well preserved examples demonstrate both the post-and-lintel system (for the doorway itself) and the Mycenaean "vaulted" arch (used in the "relieving triangle" above the doorway, *e.g.* Plate 3a and Plate 28a). The Mycenaean arch, however, is not a true arch, but is formed simply by inclining the upper parts of the walls until they meet at the highest point. The Mycenaean arch was employed for several purposes, usually in conjunction with "Cyclopean" walling. The "galleries" of Tiryns and the passages leading to the Spring chambers of Tiryns and Mycenae (Plate 3c) are among the most spectacular examples. The arch was also used in some of the larger road culverts or "bridges" (*e.g.* Plate 6a and Plate 9, with Figs. 2 and 3). The characteristic "Cyclopean" walling of Mycenae and Tiryns has been well described by Mylonas (*op.cit.* 16), "The walls . . . are built of large limestone blocks of different sizes, roughly dressed with the hammer or completely unwrought, and piled on top of one another with their interstices filled with clay and small stones. These large stones, however, form but the inner and outer faces of the wall; the space between them the width or thickness of the wall, is filled in with smaller stones and earth". The fortification walls of Tiryns range in width from 4.50 m. to 17 m., and in many places average 7.50 m. Those of Mycenae average 5 m. in width, but in places are up to 8 m. wide.

Exactly the same system of retaining walls with stone and earth fill was used for the Mycenaean roads in the Argolid (Plates 2b, 6, 8, and 9, with Figs. 2 and 3, *cf.* Mylonas, *op.cit.* 86ff.) The actual width of the roadway itself was normally little more than 2 m., although 2.50 m. or more on the tops of the larger culverts (Plate 2b and Plate 9, with Fig. 3). The main examples come from the network of roads radiating from Mycenae, but there is now fresh evidence for a Mycenaean road linking the Tiryns area with that of Epidauros (see under A 28 below). The only other roads which can be reliably assigned to the Mycenaean period are those leading from the gates of the citadel of Gla in Boeotia (C 7 below). The claims for Mycenaean built roads near Corinth (see under A 55), near Livadostro in Boeotia (see under C 41), in Phocis, and in Messenia have not yet been substantiated.

It appears that the first major fortifications at Mycenae, Tiryns, and Gla were constructed in the LH IIIA2 period. But most other major Mycenaean fortifications, including those at Midea (A 8), Eutresis (C 39) and Araxos (G 6) belong to LH IIIB, at which time the citadels of Mycenae and Tiryns were greatly enlarged and strengthened. To this period also belong the known Mycenaean roads in the Argolid, and a remarkable fortification wall designed to cross the Isthmus of Corinth from the Saronic Gulf to the Corinthian Gulf (see under A 61). Other exceptional defence measures taken at this time include the provisions taken to ensure water supply in times of siege for the citadels of Mycenae, Tiryns, and Athens. In all three cases the elaborate shafts, access tunnels, or staircases involved considerable engineering skill. Both at Mycenae and at Pylos the water supply was further assisted by aqueducts leading from neighbouring springs. Even more remarkable is the evidence, albeit not yet quite conclusive, for the diversion by the Mycenaeans of a stream near Tiryns, by means of a dam and canal, and for dykes and canals constructed by them for the partial drainage of Lake Copais in Boeotia.

All these feats of structural engineering will be discussed below in their topographical contexts, and with due emphasis on the relative weight of evidence for (or against) a Mycenaean date for each of them severally. It is also important to realize that not every example of so-called "Cyclopean" walling need necessarily belong to the Mycenaean period. In general, the evidence for Mycenaean engineering skill is impressive enough not to require gratuitous exaggeration.

CONVENTIONS USED IN THE GAZETTEER OF MYCENAEAN SITES

The Maps

The locations of sites on Maps A to K and M to N are, it is hoped, reasonably accurate. The maps themselves are partly based on the 1:200,000 series produced by the Statistical Service of Greece in 1963. Conventions for Maps A to K are indicated on Maps A and

C, and conventions for Maps M and N are indicated on Map N.

Conventions Used in the Text

For the spelling of the place names a compromise has been adopted between the so-called "phonetic" and the traditional. In doubtful cases, the more usual spelling has been adopted, in the hope of avoiding confusion. Normally the town or village name is given first, followed by the toponym or other identification.

References to periodicals will be to the first relevant page of discussion, without the author(s)' name(s). References to books will give the author(s)' name(s) in the select bibliography; and thereafter normally only by surname and year of publication (*e.g.* "Wace 1949"), unless a special abbreviation is used.

Symbols used in the Gazetteer

* = A site where excavations have been made.
\# = A site visited by the author.

Abbreviations for Archaeological Periods

N	= Neolithic	BA	= Bronze Age
EH	= Early Helladic	EM	= Early Minoan
MH	= Middle Helladic	MM	= Middle Minoan
LH	= Late Helladic	LM	= Late Minoan
EB	= Early Bronze Age	MB	= Middle Bronze Age
LB	= Late Bronze Age		

(N.B. "Late Helladic" is here regarded as synonymous with before Mycenaean")

GP = Grotta-Pelos (as in Renfrew 1972)

KS = Keros-Syros (as in Renfrew 1972)

Phyl I = Phylakopi I (as in Renfrew 1972)

(the terms Early, Middle and Late Cycladic will not be used)

SMyc = Sub-Mycenaean

PG = Protogeometric of Attic Type

"PG" = Protogeometric not of Attic Type

DA = Dark Age

G = Geometric

A = Archaic

C = Classical

H = Hellenistic

LH I/II indicates early LH material not closely assignable to either LH I or LH II

LH III(A-B) indicates material probably within the LH IIIA-B range (similarly LH III(A2-B), LH III(B-C)

LH IIIA-B indicates material probably of both LH IIIA and LH IIIB

LH I-IIIB (or similar) indicates material probably covering the whole range of LH I to LH IIIB.

It is emphasized that dates assigned purely on the basis of surface finds must be considered as provisional. Although I have attempted to record both *pre-*Mycenaean and *post-* Mycenaean material on the sites listed, there is no guarantee that such listings are complete, and commentaries on periods other than Mycenaean will be abbreviated or omitted in most cases. Prehistoric and other sites where no material of Mycenaean type has been claimed are *not* included.

The Description of Tombs

Chamber Tomb—A tomb usually cut into soft rock, and consisting of an open passage (dromos) leading into a chamber hollowed out in the rock, often through a narrow covered doorway (stomion).

Tholos Tomb—This term will be confined to stone-built Mycenaean tholoi of substantial size and wealth. The elements of the true Mycenaean tholos are as follows:

The tholos: a chamber almost always of circular plan and domed.

The dromos: similar to that of chamber tombs, but often lined with stone.

The stomion: this is always walled and covered over with one or more large lintel slabs.

Tholos tombs are normally sunk into a hill slope or level ground up to the level of the lintel-slabs, and the projecting dome is covered with an earth mound.

Cist Grave—A rectangular pit cut in earth or soft rock, lined with stone slabs or walls, and roofed with a stone slab or slabs.

Pit Grave—A pit normally rectangular but sometimes oval or shapeless, cut in earth or soft rock and unlined, but usually roofed in the same way as the cist grave.

The term "shaft grave" will be confined to those graves at Mycenae and Lerna which have the characteristic deep shaft *above the roof.*

PROVISIONAL CHRONOLOGICAL TABLE

It is always difficult, and to some extent undesirable, to attempt to assign dates to periods defined mainly on the basis of changes in pottery style, even when these changes are well supported by evidence from stratified deposits. Even in the case of the relatively well documented Late Bronze Age, the evidence for *absolute* chronology is still somewhat deficient. The available evidence has been well assembled, and the outstanding problems defined, by V. Hankey and P.M. Warren, in *BICS* 21 (1974) 142-52. In the table below, however, I adopt a simplified form of the scheme favoured by my colleague, O.T.P.K. Dickinson. It should be emphasized that it mainly represents a *relative* chronology, and should not be regarded as definitive. Since I do not consider myself sufficiently qualified to present full arguments concerning the table, I confine my commentary to a few explanations.

The dotted lines used in the table indicate a greater degree of uncertainty about the dating of a division than that conveyed by the continuous lines. Euboea is included under "Mainland". The ending of LH IIA before that of LM IB is deliberate, since it is based on the presence of LH IIB in the LM IB destruction deposits at Ayia Irini on Kea. "LB I-II" in the Cyclades includes the phases Phylakopi II:1-2 and Kea G and H. Kea J is roughly contemporary with LH IIIA1, but its beginning can not be securely dated, since there may be a break (of unknown duration) in the occupation of Ayia Irini after the end of Kea H. Although we must await the full publication of the Kea excavations and the new Phylakopi excavations, it is already clear that from LH IIIA1 onwards, the mainland style becomes steadily more dominant in the Cyclades and the Dodecanese. But subsequently there is considerable local variation throughout Greece in the LH IIIB period. And after the catastrophes at the end of LH IIIB, the following LH IIIC styles become increasingly diverse.

Provisional Dates for the Late Minoan and Late Helladic Periods

LM IA	1575 - 1500	LH I	1550 - 1500
LM IB	1500 - 1440	LH IIA	1500 - 1450
LM II	1440 - 1405	LM IIB	1450 - 1405
LM IIIA1	1405 - 1375	LH IIIA1	1405 - 1375
LM IIIA2	1375 - 1320	LH IIIA2	1375 - 1320
LM IIIB	1320 - 1200	LH IIIB1	1320 - 1250
		LH IIIB2	1250 - 1200
LM IIIC	1200 - 1100	LH IIIC	1200 - 1100
Sub Minoan from 1100		Sub-Mycenaean and later LH IIIC	1125 - 1050
(+ PG from 1000)		(Attic PG from 1050)	

Suggested Provisional Dates for Some Major Destructions

Akrotiri on Thera c. 1500	Pylos (Ano Englianos) c. 1225
Ayia Irini on Kea c. 1450	Mycenae (citadel) c. 1200
Thebes (Kadmeia) c. 1300	Tiryns (citadel) c. 1200
	Mycenae (Granary) c. 1150

Provisional Chronological Table for the Greek Middle and Late Bronze Ages and Early Dark Age

KEY TO MAPS
OF MAINLAND GREECE

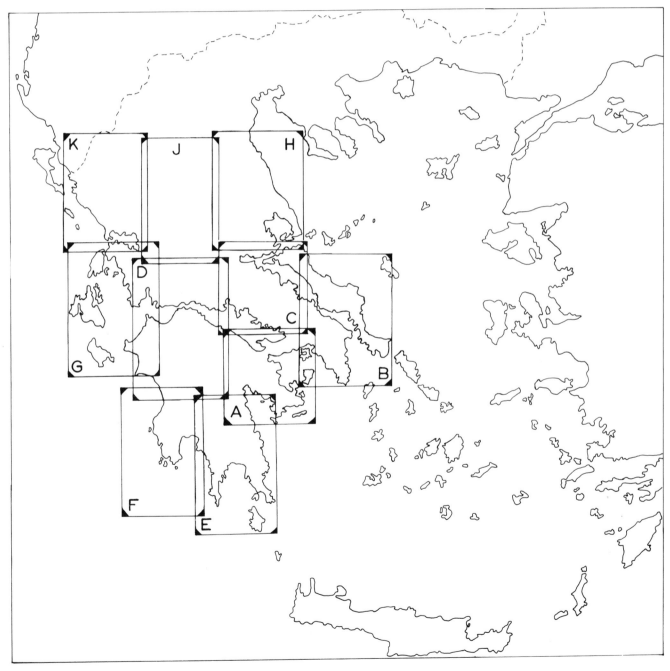

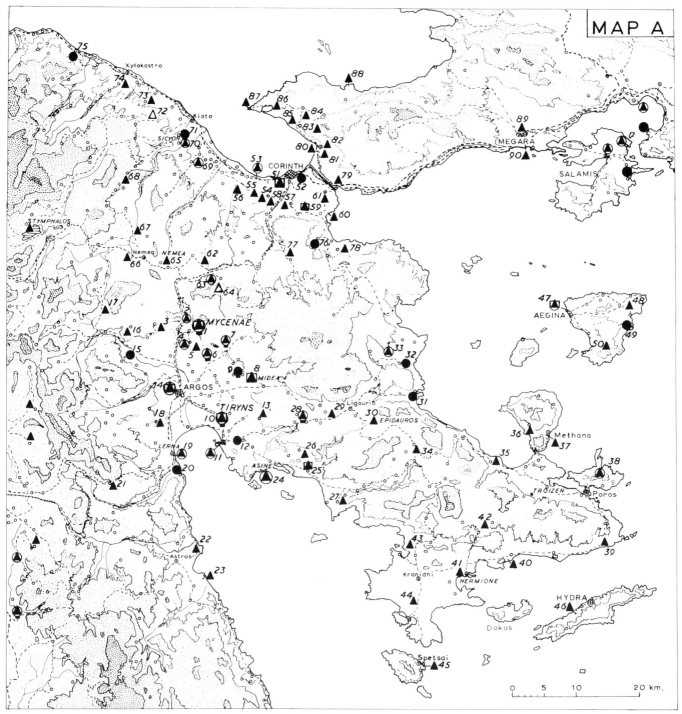

MAP A

SALAMIS

MEGARA

Xylokastro

Kiato

SICYON

STYMPHALOS

Nemea   NEMEA

CORINTH

AEGINA

MYCENAE

ARGOS

MIDEA

TIRYNS

Ligourió

EPIDAUROS

LERNA

ASINE

Methana

TROIZEN   Poros

Astros

Kranidhi

HERMIONE

HYDRA

Dokos

Spetsai

0   5   10   20 km.

Symbols used for marking Mycenaean Sites		Key to Conventions used on Maps A to K
▲ Settlement (except major)	⬢ Fortified settlement	Modern City or Large Town..
● Tomb site (only)	⬤ Settlement with tomb(s)	Small Town or Large Village ...⊙
⬤ Tholos tomb(s)	⬤ Settlement with tholos tomb(s)	Smaller Villages, and Hamlets..o
△ Mycenaean finds not related to Mycenaean sites		Modern motor roads ....
		Railways.... Lakes......
⬤ Major settlement site	⬛ Fortified Major site	Rivers, Streams etc. ....
⬤ Major site with Tholos Tomb(s)		Land above 200 m. a.s.l. ...
		Land above 600 m. a.s.l. ...
Ancient Place Names ... MYCENAE NEMEA etc.		Land above 1000 m. a.s.l. ...
Modern Place Names ... CORINTH Astros etc.		Spot Heights (in metres)... 24˙07 etc.

(MAPS COMPILED AND DRAWN BY R. HOPE SIMPSON)

THE ARGOLID   THE MEGARID
CORINTHIA   AEGINA

MAP A

The Argolid, and the Argos plain in particular, was the chief centre of Mycenaean Greece, as is demonstrated by the disproportionate number of major Mycenaean monuments concentrated here. The known Mycenaean settlements in the Argolid and Corinthia are numerous and often large. Unfortunately, our understanding of the political reasons for the special degree of Mycenaean power in the Argolid, and the measure of its control over the Corinthia also, is almost entirely dependent on archaeological evidence in default of any relevant written documents. I discuss below (in the Appendix to Map A) a recent attempt by J.L. Bintliff [in *Natural Environment and Human Settlement in Prehistoric Greece* (1977)] to explain the data purely on the basis of the agricultural potential of the region. In view of the obvious phenomena, any such attempt is doomed to failure, and is, in any case, methodologically unsound. Geography alone can not determine politics or history.

Of the various regions in Map A, few have received adequate attention from archaeologists. Even in the plain of Argos search has not been systematic. There are large gaps in exploration elsewhere, particularly in the valleys between the Argolid and Corinthia. An unpublished "intensive" survey in part of southeast Argolid has revealed a density of prehistoric settlement much higher than expected (see below under A 39-46), in an area of only moderate fertility.

For convenience, I have divided the Mycenaean sites on Map A into several groups which are roughly defined geographically, and each group will be introduced separately. But in view of the importance of the region, a general introduction is also required. The geography of the Argos plain has been summarised most recently by J.L. Bintliff (*op.cit.* 271-369, *cf.* 689-699), and by J.C. Kraft, S.E. Aschenbrenner, and G. Rapp [in *Science* 195 (1977) 941-7]. Their studies have confirmed that the ancient shore of the Gulf of Argos lay much further north than the present shore, and that much of the lower (southern) part of the Argos

plain consists of recent alluvium. Thus Tiryns (A 10) and Argos (A 14) were much closer to the sea in Mycenaean times, and much of the most fertile modern land in the plain was not then in existence. The effects of deforestation, erosion, and alluviation elsewhere in the plain since the Mycenaean period are harder to determine. But some areas, that of Mycenae itself for example, may have been more fertile than at present. Other areas have probably always been productive, especially around Tiryns, Lerna, Asine, Sikyon, and Corinth, and parts of the Nemea and Cleonae valleys. The plains of Troizen and Megara were evidently also fertile. All these regions supported separate states in historic times, and most are known to have been important in the Mycenaean period also. In the Argos plain the prehistoric sites tend to be placed near the edges of the plain, often on prominent hills of the "acropolis" type. Other sites in the Argolid are spaced along the coasts and in the inland valleys. In the Corinthia a chain of sites was established along the foothills which form the southern boundary of the Corinthian plain, while others were on low hills or ridges close to the south coast of the Corinthian Gulf.

By the beginning of the Mycenaean period, Mycenae had outstripped other possible rivals, such as Tiryns, Argos, Lerna (A 19), and Asine (A 24), and had become the single most important site in the whole area. Mycenae could only have acquired such a position either by overcoming its rivals or in the absence of opposition. And to maintain its power it must have controlled at the very least the Argos plain and a secure access to the sea on the Gulf of Argos. The early tholos tombs at Prosymna (A 6), Berbati (A 7), Dendra (A 9), and Kasarma (A 28) reflect an early prosperity, but not necessarily independence. Tiryns and Dendra, in particular, although important, must be considered as having been either dependent on Mycenae or closely allied to it, at least in the LH IIIA2 and LH IIIB periods. Neither they nor Mycenae could have prospered so greatly if they had been forced to compete for domina-

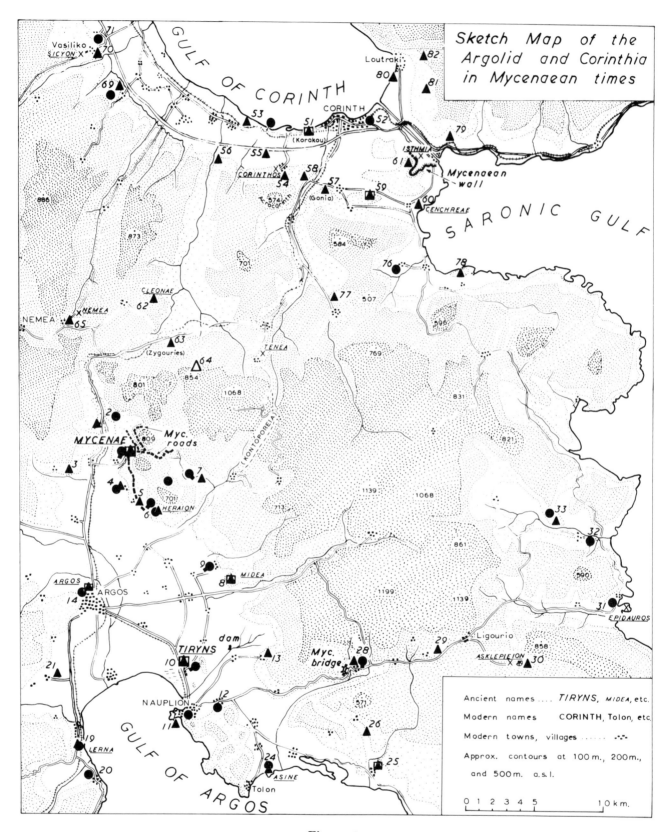

Figure 1

tion over the Argos plain. Tiryns obviously held a special position, being the only other site in the Argolid to have produced a palace and Linear B documents, and to have had fortifications apparently as old as those of Mycenae. It was probably the capital of a major administrative area, either under Mycenae or associated with it, and would also have served as the main port of Mycenae. The built roads radiating from Mycenae, obviously designed for swift horse transport, together with the Isthmus fortification wall (see under A 61), are surely the work of a major power.

The security of the region depended on a combination of static and mobile defence, which could only be maintained by the cooperation (whether willing or not) of all the regions concerned. The Argos plain was well served by the main fortresses, Mycenae, Midea (Dendra), Tiryns, and Argos, and was linked by roads to Epidauros (see under A 28) and the Corinthia (see under A 1, A 55, A 56, and A 62). The fortified settlements of Korakou (A 51) and Perdikaria (A 59) were also presumably part of this system. The importance of the sites of ancient Cleonae (A 62) and Zygouries (A 63), together with the evidence for a probably Mycenaean road at Mylos Cheliotou (A 55, and *cf.* under A 56), strongly suggest that one of the Mycenaean highways leading north from Mycenae ran down the Longopotamos valley, past Zygouries, Cleonae, and Aietopetra (A 56), into the Corinthian plain. Another Mycenaean highway may have used the Kontoporeia pass [Fig. 1, and *cf.* A.J.B. Wace, *Mycenae* (1949) 3, 47, and Ill. 7], and thence preceeded north *via* the Tenea valley. The highway system and the Isthmus fortification wall belong to the later part of the LH IIIB period, to the time when major additions were made to the walls of Mycenae and Tiryns. In the LH IIIA2 and LH IIIB periods there was evidently a large population in the Argolid and Corinthia, attesting an unprecedented prosperity in the region. Population seems to have been especially dense in the neighbourhood of Mycenae, but several other sites, Tiryns, Argos, Dendra, and Asine in particular, had "lower towns" of considerable size. Before the end of the LH IIIB period this prosperity was obviously under threat, and, it appears, particularly from the north. It came to an end when disaster, involving destruction by fire and/or desertion of many settlements, overtook the area at the end of the period.

Several of the most important sites, Mycenae, Tiryns, Argos, Nauplion (A 11), Asine, and Korakou, survived as major centres. All of these, in fact, with the exception of Korakou, continued to survive throughout the Dark Age, although Mycenae seems to have lost all importance after the middle of the LH IIIC period. Some other important sites, however, such as Prosymna, Berbati, Dendra, and Zygouries, and many smaller sites, were not reoccupied after the disaster, and there is sufficient evidence for a major depopulation in the region as a whole at the end of the LH IIIB period. Some of the survivors seem to have concen-

trated at Argos and Asine, in addition to Tiryns. Others may have migrated to other parts of Greece, especially the islands, on some of which there appears to have been an increase in population at least in the earlier part of the LH IIIC period [see below on Naxos (Map M) and *cf.* the introduction to Map N, the Dodecanese)]. A comparable prosperity at this time was enjoyed by some sites in Achaea (see introduction to sites D 22-47) and in the Ionian Islands (see introduction to sites G 7-33). The situation in central Greece is more complex (see especially under Perati (B 30) and Lefkandi (B 67), *cf.* introductions to sites B 1-44 and to sites B 45-80).

THE PLAIN OF ARGOS (A 1-14) (FIG. 1)

The geography of the plain and its environs has been well summarised by Bintliff (1977, pp. 271-356). Although it is obvious that further survey and excavation are needed here (as is vividly demonstrated by the recent finds at Argos), we can now begin to determine the probable pattern of the Mycenaean "hierarchy" in the plain. It is obviously very likely that the sites (A 1-7) in the immediate neighbourhood of Mycenae were "satellite" settlements under her control, at least in the LH IIIA2-B period. The tholos tombs at the Heraion site (A 6) and at Berbati (A 7) are both of early Mycenaean date. The Berbati settlement was not large, and there is no indication that the Mycenaean settlement at the Heraion ever attained a size or importance remotely comparable to that of Mycenae. Tiryns, which was clearly second only to Mycenae in size and importance, probably controlled the whole of the fertile southeast sector of the plain (including the territory around sites A 11-13). Midea (A 8) and Argos (A 14) probably dominated the east and west sides of the plain respectively. As we know, much of the present south central part of the plain, at the head of the Gulf of Argos, was in Mycenaean times either sea or marsh, which was filled in by alluvium in a comparatively recent period.

A 1 MYCENAE * # (Figs. 2, 15; Plates 1-3, 28a)
N EH I-III MH LH I-IIIC SMyc PG G A C H

H. Schliemann, *Mycenae* (1878); G. Schuchhardt, *Schliemann's Excavations* (1891) Chapter V; *BSA* 25 (1921-3) *passim*; A.J.B. Wace, *Mycenae, an Archaeological History and Guide* (1949); G.E. Mylonas, *Ancient Mycenae* (1957); G.E. Mylonas, *Mycenae and the Mycenaean Age* (1966); G.E. Mylonas, *Mycenae, A Guide to its Ruins and its History* (1973); E. French, H. Wace, and C.K. Williams, *Mycenae Guide* (1971); Schoder (1974) 145; Bintliff (1977) 294.

1. The Citadel and its History

The acropolis hill of Mycenae (Fig. 15, Plates 1-2) has a well defined upper citadel, with a flat top and steep or precipitous sides. The area enclosed by the Mycenaean fortifications at the time of their maximum extent (in the LH IIIB period) is estimated to have been about 38,500 m². The steep Chavos ravine provided a natural defence on the southeast side, and the north side of the acropolis is steep in most places. The southwest side was more vulnerable.

The earliest extant fortifications on the upper citadel are of LH IIIA2 date (Wace 1949, 132). The earliest surviving palace is of the same date [*BSA* 25 (1921-3) 147, cf. *MMA* 58], although it is likely that a "mansion" of some type stood on the same site at the time of the Shaft Graves (Wace 1949, 87). During the LH IIIB period the fortifications were greatly extended on the southwest, and the famous Lion Gate was constructed, to defend the sector most vulnerable to attack. This southwest extension of the citadel was probably made mainly for the sake of enclosing the Shaft Grave Circle A, whose grave markers (stelai) were at this time apparently re-positioned, and it was provided with a new supporting terrace and elaborate enclosure wall. The northeast extension was obviously designed primarily to incorporate a concealed entrance to an underground water supply, derived ultimately from the Perseia spring [*AJA* 38 (1934) 123].

The whole citadel appears to have been destroyed by fire at the end of the LH IIIB period, although there are few traces of this in the eastern part. It was at least partly reoccupied during the LH IIIC period, especially in the area of the northeast extension and on the southwest slope.

2. The Buildings Within the Citadel

a) *The Palace:* PAE (1886) 59; *BSA* 25 (1921-3) 147; Wace 1949, 69; *MMA* 58.

b) *The Eastern Terraces:* PAE (1965) 87; *Hesperia* 35 (1966) 419.

c) *The House of Columns:* Wace 1949, 91; *PAE* (1967) 7; G.E. Mylonas, *Mycenae's Last Century of Greatness* (1968) 11.

d) *Buildings Gamma and Delta:* PAE (1966) 105, (1967) 14.

e) *South House, "Granary", Citadel House etc.:* Schliemann 1878, 99, 130; *BSA* 24 (1919-21) 200, 25 (1921-3) 1; *BSA* 50 (1955) 177, 64 (1969) 261, 68 (1973) 297; *MT III* 35; *AR* (1959-60) 9, (1960-61) 30, (1962-3) 12, (1964-5) 10, (1966-7) 8, (1968-9) 11, (1969-70) 11; *AAA* 3 (1970) 72; *Antiquity* 44 (1970) 270; *AJA* 75 (1971) 266.

f) *Tsountas' House and Area:* Wace 1949, 66; *JHS* 71 (1951) 254; *AR* (1959-60) 31; *PAE* (1886) 74, (1967) 107, (1968) 9, (1970) 118, (1971) 146, (1972) 116, (1973) 99, (1974) 89; *Ergon* (1975) 90; G.E. Mylonas, *The Cult Centre of Mycenae* (1972).

g) *The Northeast Extension:* AJA 38 (1934) 123; *AE* (1962) 142; *PAE* (1964) 74, (1965) 85.

h) *The North and Northwest Slopes:* Wace 1949, 68; *BSA* 49 (1954) 254; *PAE* (1959) 144, (1961) 155, (1962) 61, (1963) 99, (1964) 68, (1968) 5.

The structures attributed to the Palace occupied the upper citadel and terraces to the east, over which it probably expanded progressively during LH IIIA2-B. The oldest part appears to have been on the summit. The surviving megaron complex seems to be a later addition, and was built on a fill supported by the forti-

fications. The "grand staircase" is probably also a late addition. The "domestic quarter" on the summit has been almost totally eroded. The buildings on the east terraces probably included workshops and storage areas. In some places there is evidence of an upper storey, but the whole area has been much disturbed by Hellenistic buildings. The "House of Columns", on the easternmost terrace, and against the fortification wall, seems to have been built in the LH IIIB2 period. Its monumental character has suggested that it was part of the main palace (*MMA* 72), but it was much eroded and produced few finds, although these included an inscribed stirrup-jar. It was partly reconstructed in the LH IIIC period. Two other buildings, Gamma and Delta, built in the LH IIIB period, flanked the court to the north. Here also there are signs of LH IIIC occupation.

In the LH IIIB1 period many large buildings were constructed on the southwest slope, within the expanded fortifications. In the areas of the Citadel House and of Tsountas' House a remarkable group of shrines and altars, together with the finds from the Rhyton Well, indicate that this was an important cult centre at this time; although substantial buildings to north and some ordinary houses to the south have no obvious religious connections, and there is evidence for workshops in the area of the shrines, perhaps connected with their use. Much debris from the LH IIIB2 destruction collapsed onto these buildings from higher up, including fragments of Linear B tablets and of fine frescoes. This debris was levelled up to provide a basis for LH IIIC buildings, including the "Granary", and the LH IIIC strata are very deep here. A further destruction in the middle of the LH IIIC period seems to have been followed by a desertion of this area, until its use as a cemetery in the Sub-Mycenaean and Protogeometric periods.

The buildings in the northeast extension were presumably constructed after the fortifications were extended here late in the LH IIIB period. There are traces of at least three buildings, whose storage areas, containing pottery, lead receptacles, a stone mortar, and some fine ivories, had survived. The walls of the northeast extension are well preserved, and feature a "sally-port" or "postern window" (Plate 3b) and the famous vaulted passage (Plate 3c) through the thickness of the wall down to a cistern which was fed by an aqueduct from the Perseia spring (*MMA* 87).

On the north and northwest slopes a series of buildings, passages, courts, and terraces has been uncovered. This whole area was built over by the LH IIIB2 period, and chambers were constructed within the fortification wall itself, in the manner of the Tiryns "galleries". The contents of Building M include many lead vessels and a faience plaque with the cartouche of Amenophis III. Other important finds are a bronze hoard near a staircase, and a large and fine female figurine, together with vases and jewellery. Objects which had probably fallen from a storeroom include several ivories, a Linear B tablet, and a headless stone figurine. Traces of the LH IIIB2 destruction are widespread here, and some LH IIIC was also found.

3. The Prehistoric Cemetery on the Southwest Slope etc.

a) *The Prehistoric Cemetery etc.* (general): *BSA* 45 (1950) 204, 48 (1953) 5, 49 (1954) 232, 50 (1955) 190, 51 (1956) 106, 52 (1957) 207, 61 (1966) 216, 64 (1969) 71; O.T.P.K. Dickinson, *The Origins of Mycenaean Civilisation* (1977).

b) *Grave Circle A and Area:* G. Karo, *Die Schachtgräber von Mykenai* (1930-33); *BSA* 25 (1921-3) 103, 39 (1938-9) 65, 49 (1954) 244; *MMA* 94.

c) *Grave Circle B:* G.E. Mylonas, *Ho Taphikos Kyklos B ton Mykenon* (1973).

The erection of fortifications along the southwest slope of the acropolis in the LH IIIB1 period divided the Prehistoric Cemetery into two parts. Grave Circle B originally stood on a separate knoll. It was founded late in the Middle Helladic period, and ceased to be used in LH I, although Tomb Rho was inserted in its eastern half in LH IIA. Near the end of the Middle Helladic period, Grave Circle A was founded. It was presumably the burial place of the ruling family of Mycenae until at least the end of the LH I period (Grave I contained at least one burial of early LH IIA date). Its area was not disturbed, and the southwest slope was apparently not occupied by any other construction, until the LH IIIB period; although burials were made elsewhere in the Prehistoric Cemetery area until LH IIIB. The "Golden Treasure" [*BSA* 39 (1938-9) 65] found just south of the Circle, was probably looted from a rich tomb of LH IIA or LH IIB date. And there are traces of buildings of a time prior to LH IIIB beneath the Ramp House [*BSA* 25 (1921-3) 75, 59 (1964) 242].

The next evidence for use of the Prehistoric cemetery area belongs to the time of construction of the Tomb of Clytaemnestra, whose chamber wall cut into the northeast section of Circle B. To judge from the radius of the Great Poros Wall, which apparently retained the mound covering the Tomb of Clytaemnestra, this mound would have wholly covered Circle B. A LH IIIA2 or early LH IIIB1 floor in the Prehistoric Cemetery area extends up to the Great Poros Wall [*BSA* 64 (1969) 72 n. 9]. There is other evidence of LH IIIB1 habitation in the area and also LH IIIB2 deposits. Some LH IIIC habitation is reported to east of the Tomb of Clytaemnestra [*PAE* (1954) 268], and occasional LH IIIC sherds and a late LH IIIC or Sub-Mycenaean infant's burial were found [*BSA* 49 (1954) 258, 58 (1963) 50, 61 (1966) 233] and some Dark Age burials.

4. Habitation Outside the Citadel.   A. The "Lower Town"

Settlements which may originally have been independent of the Mycenae acropolis were established in the neighbourhood from an early date. The earliest appears to have been that on Kalkani hill. In Mycenaean times most of the population probably lived in these settlements which were scattered over a considerable area (at least 250,000 m²), as the distribution of chamber tombs indicates. The slopes closest to the citadel were probably covered by a "Lower Town", and buildings of considerable importance have certainly been found here. This "Lower Town" may have been mainly abandoned after the destruction in the LH IIIB1 period, since a scatter of sherds in surface layers indicated only limited continuing occupation, which continued into the Dark Age. The "Lower Town" comprised at least the areas immediately west and northwest of the Lion Gate, in addition to the Prehistoric Cemetery area discussed above. The main excavated building areas are listed below.

a) *The Cyclopean Terrace Building Area: BSA* 25 (1921-3) 403, 48 (1953) 15, 49 (1954) 267, 56 (1961) 81, 88.

b) *Petsas' House and Area: PAE* (1950) 203, *BSA* 60 (1965) 171 [*cf. PAE* (1972) 116 for recent excavations in the vicinity].

c) *The House of the Oil Merchant, The House of Shields, The House of the Sphinxes, The West House, and Area: BSA* 48 (1953) 9, 49 (1954) 235, 50 (1955) 180, 51 (1956) 107, 60 (1965) 183, 63 (1968) 149; *PAE* (1958) 157, (1959) 146, (1961) 161, (1962) 81, (1963) 107; *MT II* 3, *III* 13.

The excavated buildings in the "Lower Town" comprise two main groups, the northern (a) and (b) and the southern (c). On the north-facing terraces to west and northwest of the Lion Gate, important finds have been made [groups (a) and (b)]. There is evidence for habitation as early as the LH IIA period, but the earliest major buildings excavated are of the LH IIIA2 period. These comprise a number of storerooms containing large amounts of unused pottery (Petsas' House) and the "House of the Wine Merchant". These were apparently destroyed by fire. The Cyclopean Terrace Building was constructed in the LH IIIB1 period, and there was widespread occupation on other terraces here at this time. The importance of the area is indicated by various finds including fragments of a fresco, a Linear B tablet, and part of a gold vessel.

Not far to south of the Tomb of Clytemnaestra, and close to the modern road, traces of occupation were found, extending back to the Middle Helladic period. In late Mycenaean times a major road to the acropolis ran through this area, flanked by substantial buildings on both sides. The surviving buildings [group (c)] are of LH IIIB date, but it is clear from excavations in the terraces in and around them that they succeeded equally substantial LH IIIA2 buildings, some decorated with frescoes. Of the four major structures, little more than the basements survive, although they contain some material fallen from upper floors. The oldest, the West House, seems to have been an ordinary house, with a kitchen and much household pottery. The others may have been partly used as stores for produce and various artefacts, including precious vessels and inlaid furniture or boxes, but the presence of Linear B tablets in all four houses suggests that they were also used as "offices"; and the whole group may have been a single unit, under the charge of an important official. All were destroyed by fire, at some time within the LH IIIB period. A few LH IIIB2-C sherds from surface layers may represent later re-occupation on a reduced scale.

5. Habitation Outside the Citadel. B. The Panayitsa (Makry Lithari) Ridge, and Kalkani Hill

The lower hills and ridges to southwest of the acropolis were inhabited from early times. Kalkani hill was settled in the Early Helladic period [A.J.B. Wace, *Chamber Tombs at Mycenae* (1932) 19]. It lies close to two good wells, the Epano and Kato Pigadhia, which are also close to the southern part of the Panayitsa ridge. Middle Helladic pottery found along this ridge and in the dromoi of tombs dug into it probably indicates habitation [Wace 1932, 44; *BSA* 25 (1921-3) 291, 320, 59 (1964) 2, 244, 60 (1965) 174]. Early Mycenaean has also been found on the ridge; and the "Bothros Deposit", through which the dromos of the Treasury of Atreus was cut, contained LH IIIA1 domestic material, including fresco fragments [*JHS* 59 (1939) 211, *BSA* 59 (1964) 241]. The LH IIIA2 deposit in the dromos of Tomb 505 [*BSA* 60 (1965) 174] is probably also domestic; and there is widespread evidence for LH IIIB1 habitation, both on the top of the ridge [*BSA* 51 (1956) 119, including the "House of Lead"] and on the eastern slope, to north of the Treasury of Atreus [*PAE* (1962) 65, (1963) 104, (1964) 68, (1965) 94, (1966) 111, *MMA* 83], where several buildings of this date have been uncovered. The many tombs cut into the sides of the Panayitsa ridge and of the Kalkani hill also indicate the size and importance of the Mycenaean settlements here [cf. also *AE* (1896) 1 for evidence of habitation as far south as the Kato Pigadhi area]. There is widespread evidence in these settlements for a destruction in the LH IIIB1 period. Some of the houses on the east slope of the Panayitsa ridge are reported to have been occupied in the LH IIIB2 period, and LH IIIB2 or LH IIIC sherds have been found on the summit [*BSA* 58 (1963) 50, 60 (1965) 183 cf. Plate 52b]. Some of the tombs also continued in use or were reused in the LH IIIC period (especially Tombs 502 and 515).

6. Habitation Outside the Citadel. C. Other Areas

At Plakes, about 150 m. northeast of the Postern Gate, an important building has been found [*Ergon* (1975) 95; *PAE* (1975) A 158]. It contained LH IIIB pottery, fresco fragments, and other finds. The presence of three bodies in the cellars and other evidence suggests that it was destroyed by earthquake. To east of the Perseia spring, a house with several rooms was discovered, associated with copious LH IIIA2 pottery [*BSA* 48 (1953) 18, where the pottery is wrongly attributed to the LH IIIB period].

7. The Tholos Tombs of Mycenae (Plates 3a, 28a)

General Discussions: Wace 1949, 16; A.W. Persson, *The Royal Tombs at Dendra near Midea* (1931) 140 (appendix by A.J.B. Wace); *MMA* 111.
The Cyclopean Tomb: *BSA* 25 (1921-2) 287.
The Epano Phournos Tomb: *BSA* 25 (1921-3) 292, 48 (1953) 69.
The Tomb of Aegisthus: *BSA* 25 (1921-3) 296, 50 (1955) 207; *PAE* (1955) 218.
The Panayia Tomb: *BSA* 25 (1921-3) 316.
The Kato Phournos Tomb: *BSA* 25 (1921-3) 320.
The Lion Tomb: *BSA* 25 (1921-3) 325, 50 (1955) 180.
The Tomb of the Genii: *BSA* 25 (1921-3) 376.
The Treasury of Atreus: *BSA* 25 (1921-3) 338; *Antiquity* 14 (1940) 233, Wace 1949, 119; *MMA* 120; *BSA* 63 (1968) 331.
The Tomb of Clytaemnestra: *BSA* 25 (1921-3) 357, 48 (1953) 5, 50 (1955) 194, 209; *MMA* 122.

The order in which the tombs are here listed is probably that of their construction. The first six all contain fragments of "palatial" LH IIA jars, which provide the best indication of the date of construction. The Tomb of the Genii (Plate 28a) produced some LH IIB-IIIA1 pottery. The dates of the Treasury of Atreus and of the Tomb of Clytaemnestra are harder to determine. The Treasury of Atreus (Plate 3a) can be no earlier than the end of the LH IIIA1 period, since its dromos cut through a deposit of that phase [*BSA* 59 (1964) 241]. The figurines found in the dromos fill and beneath a large block in the dromos wall suggest that it was not much later [*BSA* 66 (1971) 177]. The LH IIIB2 sherds from beneath the threshold are too late to give a reliable indication, and must belong to a period of reuse of the tomb during which the threshold would have been disturbed [*BSA* 58 (1963) 46 n. 29]. The Tomb of Clytaemnestra is generally considered to be slightly later than the Treasury of Atreus on architectural grounds. But, since very similar gold ornaments and stone vase fragments were found in both, the interval may not be great, and a *terminus ante quem* for the Tomb of Clytaemnestra seems to be provided by the LH IIIB1 material from the Prehistoric Cemetery (see under item 3. above).

All the tholos tombs had been thoroughly robbed, probably during the Dark Age, since Geometric material was found in almost all of them.

8. The Chamber Tombs

PAE (1887) 65, (1888) 28, (1890) 36, (1892) 56, (1893) 8, (1895) 24, (1896) 30, (1897) 27, (1899) 102; *AE* (1888) 136 (Tombs 1-52), (1891) 1 (Tomb 70), (1896) 1 (The Kato Pigadhi tombs); *JHS* 24 (1904) 322 (Tomb 102); *AD* 5 (1919) *Parartema* 34, 20 (1965) B 160 (Gourtsoulia); A.J.B. Wace, *Chamber Tombs at Mycenae* (1932) (Tombs 502-33, mainly Kalkani); *AR* (1958) 8; *PAE* (1952) 465, (1953) 207 (beside Circle B), (1962) 67, (1963) 111, (1964) 68 (Gourtsoulia), (1972) 114 (Panayitsa, Vlachostrata, Kapsala) (1974) 92 (Kalkani).

The Mycenaean type of chamber tomb was almost certainly introduced in the LH I period. Although the only material from the Mycenae chamber tombs which can be considered LH I is that from Tomb 518 (Wace 1932, Plate 42:5, 7-9), LH I pottery has been found in chamber tombs elsewhere, especially at Prosymna (A 6). The wide distribution of the cemeteries around Mycenae must indicate that many belong to outlying "satellite" settlements. The richest and most important tombs are those nearest the centre. The tombs of the Panayitsa and Kato Pigadhi areas are especially notable (particularly Tombs 2, 5, 24-7, 49, 52-5, 70, 78, 81, 88, 81, and 102-3), but their pottery has mainly not been published. Most of these are likely to be of LH IIIA-B date. Their contents, many of which are displayed in the National Museum of Athens, include quantities of gold jewellery, sets of bronzes, fine seal stones, and many ivory objects. These finds far surpass those from almost all Mycenaean chamber tombs elsewhere, and provide a striking proof of the exceptional wealth and importance of Mycenae.

Several tombs continued to be used and even constructed [*cf. PAE* (1964) 68] in the LH IIIC period at some distance from the acropolis (*e.g.* at Kalkani, Alepotrypa, and Gourtsoulia), but the finds are not remarkable, and consist mainly of pottery.

Mycenae: Summary

Although both the Citadel of Mycenae and the "town" outside it were of capital status and size by the LH IIIA2 period at least, they evidently reached their fullest extent in the LH IIIB period. The LH IIIC reoccupation appears everywhere to have been on a reduced scale, although still widespread. There was considerable construction, and even some new construction, within the Citadel at this time; but the character of the LH IIIC remains is generally inferior to that of the LH IIIB, and they are not even sufficient to prove a continued capital importance of the site. Nevertheless, it is evident that the Citadel continued to serve as a centre, and there are even some modest signs of physical, and perhaps also of cultural, revival, especially in the areas of the "Granary" and of the House of Columns.

The Mycenaean Roads in the Area of Mycenae (Figs. 1-2; Plates 2b and 6)

H. Steffen, *Karten von Mykenai* (1884); A.J.B. Wace, *Mycenae* (1949) *passim;* S.E. Iakovidis, in *AE* (1961) 180-196; W.A. McDonald, in *Mycenaean Studies* (1964) 217-240; G.E. Mylonas, *Mycenae and the Mycenaean Age* (1966) 86-87; J.M. Balcer, in *AJA* 78 (1974) 148-9.

The network of ancient roads radiating from Mycenae was thoroughly surveyed over a considerable area by Hauptmann Steffen, whose descriptions and excellent map still remain our chief source of information. Later studies include a preliminary report of some survey and test excavation carried out by Mylonas (*loc.cit.*), but this does not provide any further maps or plans. My own sketch maps are partly adapted from illustrations by Steffen and Wace. I have, however, omitted the conjectural lines included in Wace's map (Wace 1949, Ill. 7). I have included some descriptions, illustrations, and discussion based on autopsy, but I do not claim to have made a thorough, or even an adequate, examination of the roads. My account mainly depends on the work of others, particularly Steffen and Mylonas, to whom we are indebted for most of the primary fieldwork. I am also most grateful to my companions with whom I visited the monuments at various times, and principally to J.E. Fant, D.K. Hagel, J.F. Lazenby, and W.A. McDonald.

It is virtually certain that the roads were constructed at a time late in the LH IIIB period, since Mylonas found sherds of this date in his two trial trenches dug to determine the nature of the construction of Steffen's Road No. 1 (*MMA* 87). This road, which runs eastward from Mycenae, is the best preserved, and incorporates all the main features of Mycenaean road construction. The road began at the Lion Gate, and ran below the north wall of the citadel. Where it passed below the vicinity of the postern gate there are wheel ruts in the rock, 1.03 m. apart, according to Mylonas' measurement. The road passed close by the Perseia spring and thence to the head of the Chavos ravine, which it crossed by means of the Dragonera bridge (at Point B on Fig. 2), whose Mycenaean arch culvert is still partly preserved. Between Dragonera and the monumental Lykotroupi bridge (at Point F on Fig. 2), the road climbs gently around the contours of the Agrilovounaki hill. Great care was taken by the builders to ensure gradients as gentle as possible (Steffen 1884, 11). The road and its massive retaining walls are well preserved in places in this sector (especially at Point C on Fig. 2, *cf.* Plate 6a). Many culverts had to be constructed over the numerous small gullies (*e.g.* at Points D and E on Fig. 2). For these culverts a simple "post and lintel" system sufficed. The Lykotroupi bridge, however, required an arched culvert. It is an excellent example of the "Cyclopean" construction employed (Plate 6b), and much resembles the Arkadiko bridge near Kasarma (A 28) described below. The Lykotroupi bridge is about 5.20 m. wide, including the retaining wall, but the roadway itself on the bridge is only about 2.40 m. wide. Mylonas (*loc.cit.*) estimates that Road No. 1 averaged 3.50 m. in width, but it is clear that this estimate includes the main (outer) retaining wall on the Agrilovounaki slope. The actual road surface seems to have varied in width here from about 2.10 m. to about 2.40 m., although it must be admitted that the inner retaining wall of the roadway is hard to detect, let alone measure, in most places. We must also await the publication of the test excavations by Mylonas, which may include more reliable measurements. Mylonas reports as follows on the composition of the road: "Its understructure is made up of a fill of stones and earth of a depth varying in accordance with the slope. On it was laid a

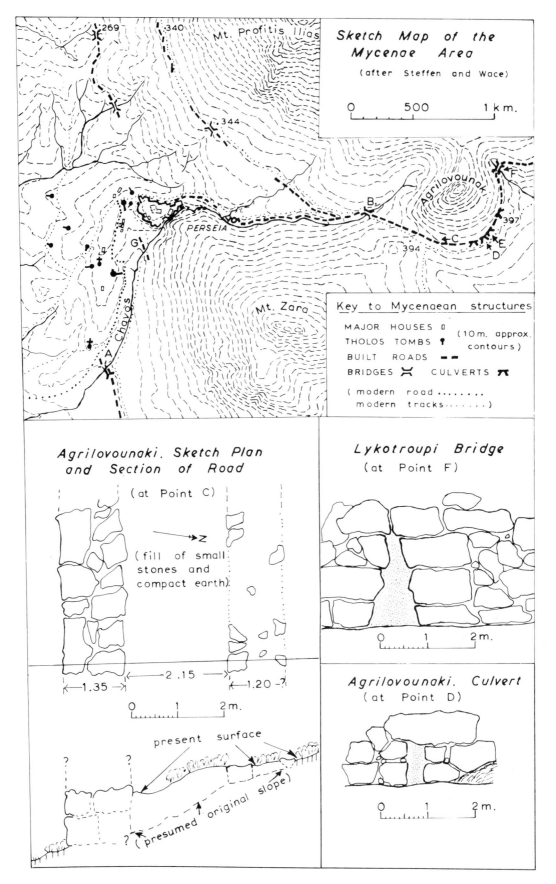

Figure 2

layer of earth with small stones averaging 25 cm. in thickness and this supported the pavement, apparently of well-packed earth, clay, pebbles and sand" (*MMA* 86).

Other roads in the Mycenae area, *i.e.* Steffen's Nos. 2, 3, and 4, are not so well preserved, but there is enough evidence to show that the same care was taken to bridge over the gullies and to avoid steep gradients. Steffen (*op.cit.* 11) records gradients of 1 in 18 to 1 in 19 for part of Road No. 2, which winds around the west slope of Mt. Profitis Ilias, and of 1 in 14 to 1 in 15 for part of the lower Road No. 3. The gradients for Road No. 4, which ran to the south at least as far as the Prosymna site (A 6), posed no problems; but at least five Cyclopean bridges were needed on this road, in addition to the famous bridge across the Chavos ravine at Ayios Yeoryios (at Point A on Fig. 2, *cf.* Plate 2b). Less than half of this bridge survives (the culvert and its presumed arch are missing). It is preserved to a height of 3.79 m., and is 5.84 m. wide at its southeast end. In the central part, however, it was apparently only about 4.40 m. in width. It is not of typical "Cyclopean" construction, since it employs courses of masonry, fairly well shaped, in which rows of longer stones alternate with rows of more square-shaped stones. But the stones are certainly of "Cyclopean" size; and a Mycenaean date for the bridge is also probable on general grounds.

On the other hand, it may seem curious that a second road was apparently constructed for the same route to Prosymna. Traces of this second road (found by Mylonas, *loc.cit.*) include a much ruined bridge over the Chavos ravine below the southwest corner of the citadel (at Point G on Fig. 2). Indeed a surprising feature of the roads in the Mycenae area is their number, and apparent duplication. It is perhaps hard to understand why three separate roads would be needed to the north and two more or less parallel roads to the south. Roads Nos. 2 and 3 also run parallel at the beginning of their course. It had previously been assumed that Road No. 1 was designed to link Mycenae with the "Kontoporeia" pass (*cf.* Wace 1949, Ill. 7, following the suggestion made by Lolling in Steffen *op.cit.* p. 8). But Mylonas (*MMA* 86), as a result of further fieldwork, believes that Roads Nos. 1 and 2 joined together at the Mavroneri pass into the Ayios Vasilios valley (running into the valley at a point near A 63 on Fig. 1). In any case, as Mylonas comments (*MMA* 87), the luxury of so many roads was possible only at a time of "great prosperity and strength".

Guard posts or forts were built along the line of the roads (*MMA* 86), including one on the summit of Mt. Profitis Ilias (Wace 1949, 47 and s.v. Hagios Elias); and there can be little doubt that the main purpose of the roads was military, *i.e.* to serve as part of an "early warning system" in case of attack and as a means of rapid deployment of mobile forces, presumably including chariots. The need for such rapid deployment

(and for avoidance of congestion in a time of emergency?) may in fact be the reason for the "luxury" of so many roads (apparently at least five) leading from Mycenae. The Pylos tablets suggest similar provisions for the defence of the Pylos area.

The extent of the system of Mycenaean roads in the Argolid and Corinthia can not yet be fully determined. The evidence (outlined above in the introduction to Map A) is sufficient to demonstrate that it extended as far as the Epidauros vicinity (see under A 28), and it seems probable that some at least of the roads leading north from Mycenae had been completed as far as the Corinthia. But the labour involved was immense, and some sections may not have finished before the onset of the disasters at the end of the LH IIIB period.

It is surprising that no full study of the structure and design of the Mycenae area roads and of their bridges and culverts has yet been made. The observations so far made in the field invite several interesting questions. The roads were provided with massive "Cyclopean" retaining walls, especially on the bridges. Were these walls sufficiently high to prevent chariots from slipping off the roadway and plunging down a slope or into a ravine? If so, then the labour involved would have been even greater. Were the surfaces of the roads properly maintained? (N.B. wheel ruts in the rock are more likely to occur when maintenance has ceased.) The width of the roadway on the Lykotroupi and Arkadiko bridges is only about 2.40 to 2.50 m. If the gauge of the chariots was about 1.10 m. or 1.20 m. (a reasonable exterpolation from Mylonas' measurement of 1.03 m. between the wheel ruts), was there in fact room for two chariots to pass? A conceivable explanation of the number and the apparent duplication of the roads in the Mycenae area could be that they were designed primarily for one way traffic.

These and other questions about the nature and purpose of the Mycenaean roads can not yet be answered. Meanwhile, however, the monuments themselves should be fully mapped and planned by archaeologists in combination with qualified surveyors and experts in transport engineering. Some parts of the roads have already been destroyed (*e.g.* much of Steffen's Road No. 2, *cf.* *MMA* 86), and they are being progressively eroded.

A 2 PHYCHTIA: BOLIARI *
LH IIIA2-C

AD 19 (1964) B 118, 21 (1966) B 125; Bintliff (1977) 292.

About 3 km. northwest of the acropolis of Mycenae, and about a kilometre to east of the main road to Corinth, a chamber tomb was found. The site is the hillock marked "Pera Sphalaktra" on Steffen's map. The tomb contained LH IIIA2-C pottery. About a kilometre to southwest, near the 37 mark on the main road, Mycenaean sherds and obsidian were found.

A 2A   PHYCHTIA   *   (Not marked on Map A)
LH IIIA-B

AA (1931) 262; *Alin* 36; Bintliff (1977) 290.

A chamber tomb excavated near Phychtia is said by Ålin to have produced LH IIIA and LH IIIB pottery. Bintliff claims that a Mycenaean settlement was found near the village, but this is not confirmed.

A 3   PHYCHTIA: AYIOS YEORYIOS
LH III(A-B)

AD 21 (1966) B 125; Bintliff (1977) 293.

Surface sherds, including some attributed to the LH IIIB period, were said to have been found near the chapel of Ayios Yeoryios, described as one hour to west of Phychtia. The exact location has not yet been made clear, and the position marked on Map A is therefore only approximate (the position marked on Fig. 1 here is probably about 2 km. to southeast of the real location).

**A 4   MONASTERAKI (formerly PRIPHTIANI):
MAGOULA   * #**
LH IIIA1-B

AD 5 (1919) *Parartema* 34, *AE* (1952) *Parartema* 19; Alin 37; Bintliff (1977) 290.

Six Mycenaean chamber tombs have been excavated in various locations around Monasteraki village. Remains of Mycenaean settlement have been found both on the Magoula hill 200 m. to southwest of the village and on the east side of the village. A small Mycenaean community seems indicated.

A 5   VRESERKA   #
LH I? LH IIA-IIIB

AE (1888) 123; *PAE* (1916) 91; *RE* Suppl. VI (1935) 605; Bintliff (1977) 289.

A Mycenaean settlement occupied gentle slopes facing south and southwest, on the southern flank of the hamlet of Vreserka, which lies on the Mycenaean road from Mycenae to the Argive Heraion. To judge from the spread of surface sherds observed in 1960, the area of the Mycenaean settlement was about 200 m. east to west by 100 m. The site is probably identical with the "Eleutherios" (named after the bed of the old river Eleutherios nearby) from which R.W. Hutchinson collected some LH II-III sherds (now in the BSA collection). Chamber tombs were noted here by Tsountas (*AE loc.cit.*) and two were investigated by Arvanitopoullos (*PAE loc.cit.*). There is a copious spring issuing from the southeast foot of the Vreserka hill.

**A 6   PROSYMNA: THE ANCIENT ARGIVE
HERAION   * #**
N   EH II-III   MH LH I-IIIB   G   A   C   H

1. The Prehistoric Settlement

C. Waldstein. *The Argive Heraeum* (1902) 71; C.W. Blegen, *Prosymna* (1937); *AJA* 43 (1939) 410; *Hesperia* 21 (1952) 165; R.A. Tomlinson, *Argos and the Argolid* (1972) index s.v. "Heraion"; Schoder (1974) 89; Bintliff (1977) 285.

The topography of the site has been well described and illustrated by Blegen (*cf. Prosymna* Fig. 1). The sanctuary occupied the middle and lower terraces of a conical hill on the northeast side of the Argos plain. On the summit and on the upper and middle west and south slopes was a prehistoric settlement, about 150 m. northeast to southwest by 100 m. This was apparently first occupied in the EH II period and thereafter continued without a break until late in the LH IIIB period. There are also traces of EH, MH and LH habitation in the surrounding area, including widely scattered groups of late MH graves, and there are Neolithic remains on slopes adjoining the hill to the northwest. On a small hill named Kephalari about 350 m. to the west of the sanctuary, a LH IIIB house was found. This hill was named after a spring at its foot, which has dried up. Mycenaean pottery was also found in the area of the Archaic shrine, well to the northwest, beyond the tholos tomb.

Bintliff (*loc.cit.*) follows Blegen's arguments for the importance of Prosymna, emphasizing the number of Mycenaean houses and streets, and a building "with all the hallmarks of a megaron", as well as "possible traces of a fortification wall and a gateway, bits of which looked Mycenaean". And he concurs with Blegen's view that the "missing palace of Mycenaean date" was probably centred on the platform of the early historic temple. Unfortunately, the massive constructions in the later sanctuary have obscured or obliterated most of the centre of the Mycenaean settlement, and the actual Mycenaean settlement remains are not nearly as impressive as Bintliff's description would suggest, although the site is fairly large. Bintliff is at pains to bolster his arguments for "palace" status of the Heraion with considerations of an entirely hypothetical nature, involving deductions from the observed intervals between *known* Mycenaean palaces in the Argolid [Bintliff (1977) 289, *cf.* 689 ff.). And there is certainly no evidence whatsoever of a cult of Hera at Prosymna in the Mycenaean period. The site appears to have been abandoned in the later part of the LH IIIB period, and its earliest reuse, this time as a cult centre, does not seem to have been prior to the Geometric period.

2. The Chamber Tombs

C.W. Blegen, *Prosymna* (1937); *AE* (1956) *Parartema* 10; *AD* 25 (1970) B 156.

A large cemetery of Mycenaean chamber tombs extends over the slopes to north and northwest of the sanctuary hill. It is the largest cemetery of Mycenaean date to have been fully published. Over fifty tombs were examined, including two cist graves. The earliest tombs (Nos. 25, 26, and 52) are of the LH I period, and the latest of the LH IIIB period, and they also contained a wide range of finds other than pottery. Late Geometric deposits, possibly connected with cult, were found in several tombs.

3. The Tholos Tomb

AM 3 (1878) 271; *BSA* 25 (1921-3) 330; Wace 1949, 16.

About a kilometre to west of Prosymna, by the track to Vreserka, is a tholos tomb, the largest (diameter 9.5 m.) in the Argolid outside Mycenae. The small amount of pottery found in the tomb all seems to be of the LH IIA period. Although robbed, it contained the remains of some rich goods, including several fragments of stone and bronze vases and of gold jewellery etc. The dromos faced towards the line of the Mycenaean road from Mycenae to the Heraion discussed above.

A 7 BERBATI: KASTRAKI or MASTOS *
N EH I-III MH LH I-IIIB2 G

1. The Prehistoric Settlement

AA (1936) 139, (1938) 552, *BCH* 78 (1954) 117, G. Säflund, *Excavations at Berbati 1936-7* (1965) Part I; *MycCon I* 48; Bintliff (1977) 305.

The settlement is centred on a small but conspicuous acropolis with a conical formation of hard limestone at its summit. It completely dominates the Berbati valley, and is well situated to control both the Kontoporeia pass to the northeast, and the route northwest to Mycenae. Early Helladic remains were excavated on the south slope, and on the east slope a Middle Helladic settlement and cemetery were succeeded by a potter's establishment of early Mycenaean times, which included a kiln. A larger building of LH IIIA2-B date was surely also a potter's establishment, although no kiln was found. Large deposits of "wasters", ranging from the end of the Middle Helladic to the LH IIIB period, were found, including many fragments of "Pictorial Style". The settlement appears to have been abandoned late in the LH IIIB period. It is difficult to assess the status of this Mycenaean settlement, since relatively little has been excavated; but it does not seem to have been very large, although the position is strategic, and some importance is demonstrated by the tholos tombs and chamber tombs nearby.

2. The Tombs

AA (1935) 200, (1936) 140; *ILN* (15/2/1936) 276 (the tholos tomb), Säflund 1965, Part II.

About a kilometre to northwest of Kastraki is a tholos tomb (diameter 8 m.). It had been robbed, but contained much LH IIA to LH IIIA1 pottery and some other finds, especially fragments of a gold-rimmed sil-

ver cup. Beyond it, in the slopes of the hills on the west side of the valley, is a chamber tomb cemetery, mostly plundered, in which seven tombs were excavated, one of which produced more than 50 Mycenaean vases and LH IIIA and LH IIIB figurines. The cemetery spanned the LH IIA to LH IIIB periods, and the finds were mainly pottery.

A 8 DENDRA: PALAIOKASTRO (ANCIENT MIDEA) * # (Fig. 15; Plate 4)
EH II-III MH LH I-IIIB2 G? C or H

A.W. Persson, *The Royal Tombs at Dendra near Midea* (1931) 73, *New Tombs at Dendra near Midea* (1942) 3, 61; *OpAth* 4 (1962) 79, 7 (1967) 161; *MycCon I* 54 [*cf. AD* 20 (1965) B 134]; Bintliff (1977) 283.

The acropolis of ancient Midea comprises the summit (about 220 m. northwest to southeast by 160 m.) and north and west slopes of a high limestone hill of conical shape. This was one of the chief Mycenaean fortresses in the Argolid. The Cyclopean walls, built during the LH IIIB period, enclosed an area comparable to that of the acropolis of Mycenae (Fig. 15). On the northeast side (Plate 4b) they are as massive as those of Tiryns. An important building may have stood on the summit (Persson 1942, 7), as indicated by systematic rock cuttings; and a fresco fragment is reported [*OpAth* 7 (1967) 174 n. 14]. The acropolis settlement was apparently destroyed by fire at the end of the LH IIIB period. Mycenaean settlement, marked by sherds and house foundations, was widespread on the acropolis and its slopes, especially the northwest, and on the southeast slopes of the hill adjacent on the northwest, as is shown both by limited excavations and by detailed surface survey [*OpAth* 4 (1962) 79]. There is a good spring at the northwest foot of the acropolis, well situated between it and the adjacent northwest hill. This was obviously a key factor in the location of the Mycenaean settlement (whose "lower town" is now known to have been concentrated on both sides of the spring), although Bintliff underestimates its significance [Bintliff (1977) 285].

It is important to note that the Mycenaean finds in the area of the villages of Manesi and Dendra are associated only with the Mycenaean tombs there. There are no certain traces of Mycenaean *habitation* in this area [marked XII on *OpAth* 4 (1962) 81 Fig. 1], despite Bintliff's assertion to the contrary [Bintliff (1977) 283, relying on a vague and unsupported conjecture by Persson 1931, 73]. For abundant traces of Early Helladic settlement in this area, see under A 9 below.

A 9 DENDRA VILLAGE *
N EH II(-III?) MH? LH IIA-IIIB LH IIIC? G A? C? H

Persson 1931, 1942; *AD* 16 (1960) B 93, 18 (1963) B 63; *MMA* 127; *OpAth* 4 (1962) 79; *AM* 82 (1967) 1; P. Åström et al., *The Cuirass Tomb and Other Finds at Dendra* (1977).

On the gentle slopes to southwest of the linked villages of Manesi and Dendra [cf. OpAth 4 (1962) 81 Fig. 1] and to northwest of Dendra, there are extensive traces of an EH II settlement (Persson 1931, 27, 29, 31; Persson 1942, 17, 20, 51, 63), which may have continued into the EH III and MH (Persson 1931, 91). This later became the site of a very important Mycenaean cemetery, of which one tholos tomb and fourteen chamber tombs have been excavated. There are, however, no traces of a Mycenaean *habitation* site here [cf. OpAth 4 (1962) 87], and (as has been stated above) it is evident that the Mycenaean settlement was confined to the Palaiokastro acropolis and its slopes and the adjacent hill (above Dendra village) to northwest of it.

The earliest material from the cemetery is LH IIA (Tomb 6), but the most spectacular finds are of the periods between the end of LH IIA (to which belongs the coffin burial in Tomb 8) and LH IIIA1. Some finds in Tomb 2 may be rather later, since the pottery appears to range from LH II to LH IIIA2 (Persson 1931, Fig. 64). The tholos tomb is rather small (diameter 7.3 m.) and poorly built, but the intact burials in Pit I below the floor were accompanied by extremely rich goods. There was little pottery left in the tomb to suggest a date, but the bronze vessels and other objects are mainly of types found in LH IIB-IIIA1 contexts elsewhere, although some could be "heirlooms" from an earlier phase. A burial in Pit III, provided with gold jewellery, and human bones found in Pit II and in the floor could well be later (the bones surely represent burials rather than human sacrifices), but there is nothing to suggest that use of the tomb continued much beyond the end of the LH IIIA1 period. Some of the chamber tombs contained ordinary burials of LH IIA-IIIB date. The only later remains are an amphoriskos [attributed to the LH IIIC period by Desborough (1964) 77], found beneath the collapsed roof of the tholos, a burial accompanied by an Early Geometric pyxis high in the fill of the tholos doorway, and Geometric and later pottery from the area.

A 10   TIRYNS   * #   (Fig. 15)
N EH I-III   MH   LH I-IIIC   SMyc   PG   P   G   A   C   H

H. Schliemann, *Mycenae* (1878) chapter 1; H. Schliemann and W. Dörpfeld, *Tiryns* (1886); *AM* 38 (1913) 329; *AA* (1927) 365; Guides by G. Karo (1934), W. Voigtländer (1972), U. Jantzen (1975); *Tiryns I-VIII; Alin* 25; Schoder (1974) 229; Bintliff (1977) 276, 337.

Special Finds: AM (1930) 119 ("The Tiryns Treasure"); *AE* (1956) *Parartema* 5; *AD* 20 (1965) A 137 (The LH IIIB "Epichosis" outside the West Gate), cf. also *Tiryns VI* 241; *AD* 21 (1966) B 130, *AAA* 6 (1973) 306, 7 (1974) 25, *BCH* 101 (1977) 229 (Linear B finds); *AAA* 6 (1973) 158 (stone vase fragment); *AA* (1977) 123 (LH "pebble-mosaic" in the "Lower City").

1. The Citadel

Schliemann and Dörpfeld 1886, *Tiryns III; AD* 19 (1964) B 118 (the Ramp area).

Excavations in the Lower Citadel: AD 18 (1963) B 66, 19 (1964) B 108; *AA* (1967) 92, (1969) 1; *AAA* 4 (1971) 398; *Tiryns V passim; Tiryns VIII* 55; *AR* (1977-8) 26, (1978-9) 16 (especially plans on p. 17).

The Citadel of Tiryns occupied a long and low oval-shaped limestone outcrop, of maximum dimensions about 300 m. north to south by 100 m. About 22,000 m.² were enclosed within the walls. The Citadel is composed of three sections, termed the Upper, Middle and Lower Citadels, of which the first (comprising the southern half of the hill) was always the most important. In the EH II period the whole Citadel may have been covered with buildings, but after the EH II destruction there was apparently little occupation outside the Upper Citadel for a considerable time, and the Lower Citadel seems to have remained unoccupied from the end of the EH II until the LH IIIB period.

A long sequence of Middle Helladic strata, including several substantial buildings, has been revealed by tests below the LH III Palace. But both the Middle Helladic and the earlier Mycenaean remains are poorly documented. Nevertheless, a series of plaster floors, in some cases associated with column bases and fresco fragments, were found below Court 16 in front of the "Little Megaron", which appear to indicate that this was the site of a series of palatial buildings as far back as early Mycenaean times (*Tiryns III* 77).

The Upper Citadel was probably first fortified in the LH IIIA2 period, at about the same time as Mycenae. The eastern approach and entrance were developed progressively, and other additions (including the famous "galleries") were made, of which only the latest, the extension of the wall to include the Lower Citadel, and the construction of tunnels through the walls to an underground water supply, can be closely dated, to a late phase of the LH IIIB period. The LH III Palace, whose construction may have begun in the LH IIIA2 period, had expanded by the time of its destruction to cover almost all the Upper Citadel; but finds in the Palace area were few, although some storage areas were identified.

Traces of LH III habitation and a kiln of the same date have been found on the Middle Citadel. Houses were built in the Lower Citadel after its fortification, some of which were quite substantial. Recent investigation of the Lower Citadel has concentrated on the LH IIIB2 and LH IIIC phases [*AR* (1978-9) 16, with excellent plans on p. 17 Fig. 20]. A bone from the foot of a lion was found here in the LH IIIB2 context (It is presumably not possible to estimate whether the beast to whom the bone belonged was imported or indigenous).

Beneath the Palace and in the area of the main entrance on the east there are traces of a destruction by fire which appears to have preceded that of the end of the LH IIIB period, which affected the whole Citadel. Large deposits found outside the West Gate have been regarded as material from this destruction (the "Epichosis"). The best evidence for LH IIIC reoccupation is from the Lower Citadel, where a free-standing shrine of LH IIIC date has recently been found [*AR* (1977-8) 26]. In the LH IIIC period the site was reorganised and enlarged beyond the Citadel both to north and south. A further destruction identifiable in the Lower Citadel should probably be correlated with the destruction at Mycenae in the middle of the LH IIIC period. It was apparently followed by the collapse of a mudbrick superstructure of the west side of the fortification wall, which sealed lower layers.

2. Settlement Outside the Citadel

Tiryns V 1; *VIII* 7, 137; *AAA* 2 (1969) 344, 7 (1974) 15; *AA* (1977) 123; *AD* 25 (1970) B 156.

On level ground surrounding the Citadel, widespread Early and Middle Helladic remains were found. In Mycenaean times the inhabited area extended to north of the Citadel, an area apparently not occupied previously. Excavations in the "Lower City", especially to west and southeast of the Citadel, have yielded important finds, including Linear B tablets. The LH IIIC settlement outside the Citadel included the substantial megaron W in Area H on the southeast, and Protogeometric house remains have also been found near the Citadel. The Tiryns Treasure, a hoard apparently hidden on the site of a destroyed Mycenaean house, includes several objects which must be attributed to the LH IIIC period or the early Dark Age. They provide a striking proof of surviving wealth at Tiryns in this obscure period (*cf.* the similar evidence at Mycenae, Argos, and Asine in particular).

3. The Tombs

The Tholoi: AA (1939) 251; *Tiryns VIII* 1.
The Chamber Tombs: Tiryns VI 23.
Sub-Mycenaean to Geometric Graves: Tiryns I 127; *AM* 78 (1963) 1; *AD* 22 (1967) B 180, 24 (1969) B 104.

The hill of Profitis Ilias, about 800 m. to east of Tiryns, was the site of a large Mycenaean chamber tomb cemetery, dug into its east slope, and of at least two tholos tombs, dug into its west slope. The excavated tholos (diameter 8.5 m.) was found empty as regards prehistoric finds, and had probably been robbed in Geometric times. The architecture suggests a date in the LH III period for its construction. The fine early Mycenaean rings and jewellery among the Tiryns Treasure might have come from this or another tholos, as might two gold head-bands reported to have been found on the northwest slope of Profitis Ilias [*AA* (1940) 220]. The chamber tombs range from the LH IIA to the early LH IIIC period. Their contents consist mainly of pottery. Dark Age cist and pithos burials, found at various points around the citadel, provide the best evidence for continuity of habitation at Tiryns. Some of the burials, especially the Sub-Mycenaean "Warrior Grave", were accompanied by relatively rich finds.

Tiryns: Summary

As at Mycenae, both the Citadel of Tiryns and the "town" around it appear to have attained their fullest extent and density of habitation in the LH IIIB period. As in the case of Mycenae, it is difficult to estimate the actual size of the town. But we already have evidence that it was widespread, and quite densely inhabited in the LH IIIB and LH IIIC periods at least. The LH IIIC re-occupation, and especially the entirely new alignment of buildings in the Lower Citadel, suggests continued importance at this time, either under conquerors or as a centre for refugees, or some combination of both. The degree of LH IIIC occupation outside the Citadel appears to have been proportionately greater than the corresponding re-occupation outside the Mycenae Citadel, on present evidence. But no firm conclusion may yet be made on this point; and in particular we must remember that the LH IIIC (and other) remains outside the Mycenae Citadel were more liable to erosion, being on ridges and hill slopes, whereas those outside the Tiryns Citadel, in flat ground, were generally better preserved under alluvial and other deposits.

The Ancient Dam Near Tiryns (Figs. 1 and 3; Plate 7)

AA (1930) 112; *AJA* 38 (1934) 126; *AM* 78 (1963) 5 n. 4, Beil I, Taf. II; *AJA* 78 (1974) 141; Bintliff (1977) 280, 337, 339.

About 4 km. east-northeast of Tiryns, and about 700 m. north of Ayios Adrianos, are the remains of an ancient dam, constructed in order to divert a seasonal stream which originally flowed into the vicinity of Tiryns. The location is marked by the eikonostasis of Ayios Demetrakis, beside the track from Kofini, a village about 2 km. to the west. I here record some results from autopsy in 1973 (with my colleague D.K. Hagel) and in 1974. My provisional sketch maps (Fig. 3) are based partly on those published by Verdelis (*AM loc.cit*) and Balcer [*AJA* 78 (1974) 146]; and I here attempt to correlate my own surface observations with those made by others, principally Gercke, Balcer, and Bintliff (*op.cit*. 280).

The dam (Plate 7a and 7b) was constructed of earth, stones, and gravel, retained by inner and outer stone walls built in Cyclopean style. The artificial bank thus formed was at least 100 m. in length and 10 m. in height (as preserved to southwest of point A on Fig. 3). At the same time (*i.e.* between two annual flood seasons) the stream bed to east of the dam was connected with another stream bed a considerable distance to the southwest by means of a deep channel [up to 8 m. deep at one point, *cf. AJA* 78 (1974) 148], which is clearly artificial since it cuts across several natural contours. The outer (eastern) retaining wall of the dam is discernible in three places (B, C and D on Fig. 3, *cf.* Plate 7c and d). The position of the inner (western) retaining wall can not be exactly determined by surface examination, but its course is roughly shown by a

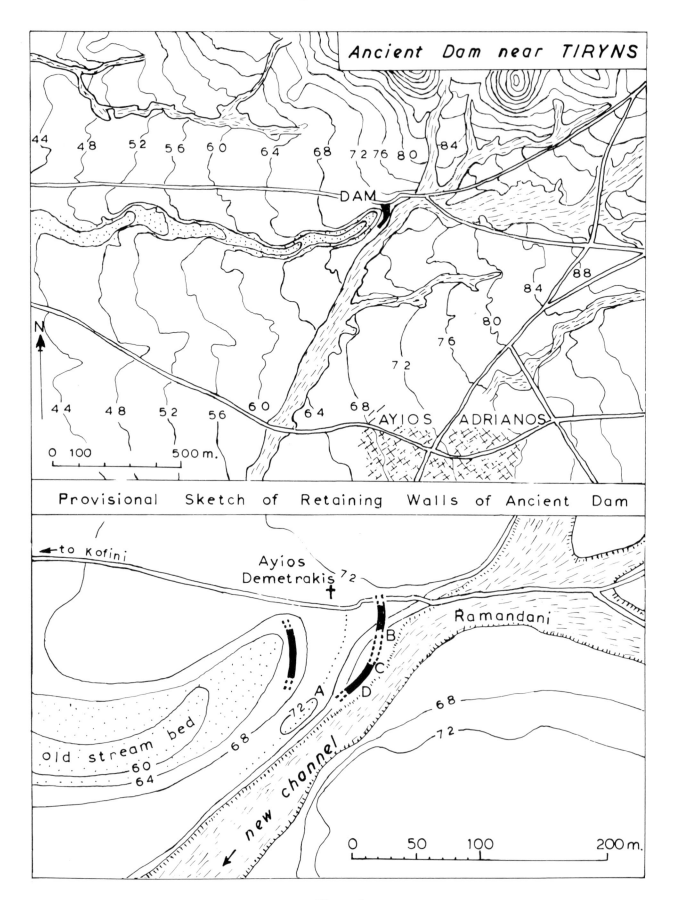

Figure 3

ragged line of dislodged stones. Thus, although the exact width of the dam can not yet be measured in any place, it is already apparent that there was a variation in width between the northern section, apparently about 80 m. wide, and the southern section, apparently about 50 m. wide.

It was, of course, the northern section which was the most crucial, since it is at this point that the course of the stream had to be diverted from a westerly into a southwesterly direction, eventually ending at or near the sea about a kilometre to north of Nauplion (Fig. 1). The outer wall of the dam, where it could be measured (seen in section at point B on Fig. 3), was 3.50 to 4.0 m. in width, being composed of the customary stone facings and rubble fill of Cyclopean masonry. A stretch of about 20 m. of this northern part is observable sporadically. After a gap of about 25 m. to south of it, a more or less continuous stretch may be discerned (between points C and D on Fig. 3), although the face of the wall is only fully apparent at two places (i.e. at point C and point D) where three courses of Cyclopean masonry are visible. At one place (point C) the stones preserved are obviously at or near the base of the wall.

The construction of the dam and of the artificial channel (in one season) must have involved a considerable labour force. Although it has been assumed by some that the motive was to prevent flooding of the Tiryns area, a more plausible reason [as suggested by Bintliff (1977) 339] is to prevent the silting up by deltaic fill of the harbour at Tiryns. It is, of course, generally assumed that the dam and the channel were the work of the Mycenaeans. So far, however, there is no definite proof of this. We are told [AJA 78 (1974) 147 n. 40] that surface sherds are rare in the area of the dam (we saw nothing recognizable either in 1973 or in 1974). According to Bintliff (op.cit. 281), on his visit with Gercke Mycenaean sherds were observed "between the dam upper stones". It is not clear what is meant by this observation, and the sherds themselves have not been described. If they are in fact Mycenaean, and if they are from *within* the dam itself, they would provide a *terminus post quem* for its construction. But it appears that in this case, as so often, we are confronted by the limitations of surface survey, and only excavation can provide conclusive evidence.

A 11 NAUPLION: ANCIENT NAUPLIA *
N EH LH I/II-IIIC SMyc PG G A C H

Athenaion 7 (1878) 183, 8 (1879) 411; *AM* 5 (1880) 142, 36 (1911) 37; *PAE* (1892) 52, (1953) 195; *RE* Suppl. VI (1935) 605; *BCH* 78 (1955) 238 Fig. 11; *Alin* 46; *AD* 24 (1969) B 104, 28 (1973) B 90; R. Hägg, *Die Gräber der Argolis I* (Boreas 7:1, 1974) 71; Bintliff (1977) 308.

Some Mycenaean sherds have been found on the acropolis of ancient Nauplia, and in the area of the present town [*AM* 36 (1911) 37 and *RE loc.cit.*]. Obsidian and prehistoric sherds have also been noted below the acropolis on the north slope, and part of a wall which may be Cyclopean (*AD loc.cit.*). The acropolis was presumably the site of the main Mycenaean settlement here, although it seems very unlikely that it covered the whole of this large area (about 500 m. east to west by 200 m.). A very extensive chamber tomb cemetery has been found on the northeast slope of the Palamidi hill and in its neighbourhood. Thirty-six tombs were excavated up to 1954, and thirty-three recently [*AD* 28 (1973) B 90]. The contents are mainly of the LH IIIA and LH IIIB periods, but LH I-II is reported from the group most recently excavated; and one or two LH IIIC vases [Desborough (1964) 80, *cf. BCH loc.cit.*] and some Sub-Mycenaean pit graves suggest that occupation was continuous into the Dark Age.

A 12 ARIA *
LH II-IIIA

BCH 79 (1955) 244; Bintliff (1977) 311.

Two small chamber tombs were excavated here, at the north foot of the range of hills to east of Nauplion. They were reported to be of unusual shape. They contained LH II-IIIA vases [*BCH* 79 (1955) 243 Fig. 30 is probably no later than LH IIA] and an early animal figurine [*BSA* 66 (1971) 153, 179].

A 13 PROFITIS ILIAS *
LH II-IIIB A

AR (1962-3) 16; *BCH* 87 (1963) 748; *AD* (1963) B 65; *AJA* 78 (1974) 149; Bintliff (1977) 307.

The small village of Profitis Ilias is about 3 km. east of Ayios Adrianos, in foothills to east of the Argos plain. The chapel of Profitis Ilias, on the steep hill to north of and above the village, overlies the remains of an Archaic temple, near which, on a terrace just below the summit, was an *apothete* full of votives, also Archaic. Some Mycenaean material, including house foundations, was found *beneath* the pit which contained the votives. On the south slope remains of a Cyclopean wall were found and Mycenaean and Archaic sherds nearby. A thick scatter of such sherds was also noted on the southeast slope. The top surface of the Profitis Ilias hill measures only about 60 m. north to south by 40 m., but the lower east and northeast slopes, and the south side of the lower ridge adjoining the hill on the southeast, were also covered in Mycenaean sherds, indicating a total spread of about 200 m. northwest to southeast by 150 m. Surface sherds observed in 1971 included part of the rim of a LH IIB "Ephyraean" goblet and some other splaying rims of cups or goblets either LH II or LH IIIA1, but pithos and LH IIIA2-B kylix fragments predominated. The Archaic sherds seemed to be confined to the hill of Profitis Ilias itself.

Balcer (*AJA loc.cit.*) conjectures that Mycenaean roads from Dendra and Tiryns may have converged near Profitis Ilias, identified by some as the site of ancient Lessa, which Pausanias (II 25, 9) mentions as having a temple to Athena and as being on the road from Tiryns to the Asklepieion at Epidauros. Bintliff remarks that the land in the vicinity of Profitis Ilias is not very fertile, and, perhaps because he was unable to observe the full extent of the Mycenaean surface pottery, prefers to accord to the site the status of a "Peak Sanctuary". There is, however, no evidence to support this conjecture, and the indications are of a *normal* Mycenaean habitation site of slightly greater than average size.

A 14   ANCIENT ARGOS   * #   (Plate 5b)
N EH II(-III?) MH LH I-IIIC SMyc PG G A C H

1. *The Larisa: Mnemosyne* 56 (1928) 315, 323; *BCH* 54 (1930) 480, 90 (1966) 932; *OpAth* 5 (1964) 179; N.C. Scoufopoulos, *Mycenaean Citadels* (1971) 29, 33.

2. *The Aspis and environs: BCH* 30 (1906) 5, 31 (1907) 139, 99 (1975) 707, 100 (1976) 755, 101 (1977) 667, 102 (1978) 661; *Orlandos Charisterion II* 239; *AD* 19 (1964) B 122, 26 (1971) B 76, 80, 27 (1972) B 198, (1973) B 97.

3. *The Deiras:* J. Deshayes, *Argos: Les Fouilles de la Deiras* (1966); *BCH* 28 (1904) 364, 77 (1953) 59, 93 (1969) 574; *AD* 26 (1971) B 76.

4. *The Agora: BCH* 77 (1953) 263, 78 (1954) 164, 80 (1956) 207.

5. *The South Quarter: BCH* 78 (1954) 176, 79 (1955) 312, 80 (1956) 370, 81 (1957) 678, 96 (1972) 157.

6. *Sector Delta: BCH* 92 (1968) 1021 ff., 93 (1969) 986, 94 (1970) 765, 95 (1971) 736, 66 (1972) 883, 886, 98 (1974) 761, 99 (1975) 696.

7. *Other Excavations: BCH* 83 (1959) 755, 90 (1966) 932, 91 (1967) 808, 92 (1968) 1040; *AD* 18.(1963) B 61, 19 (1964) B 122, 21 (1966) B 127, 22 (1967) B 172, 23 (1968) B 127, 26 (1971) B 74, 27 (1972) B 201; 28 (1973) B 94; *AAA* 8 (1975) 259.

8. *General Commentaries:* R.A. Tomlinson, *Argos and the Argolid* (1972), especially 15-27; Schoder (1974) 25; Bintliff (1977) 326.

9. *Recent Discoveries: AD* 28 (1973) B 94; *AR* (1978-9) 13.

The Argos of the historic period incorporated two citadels within its walls (Tomlinson *op.cit.* p. 16 Fig. 2). The highest, the Larisa, is a high conical hill (Tomlinson *op.cit.* Pl. 4), whose summit was ringed by a Hellenistic circuit wall (now covered by mediaeval fortifications). C.W. Volgraff (*Mnemosyne loc.cit.*, and *cf.* bibliography cited by Scoufopoulos *op.cit.* 29) claimed Mycenaean fortification walls here, including a lintel and threshold of a gate (*cf. OpAth* 5 *loc.cit.*). But the "Cyclopean" blocks were all found either loose and out of position or built into later walls, and all may have been brought from elsewhere. Some prehistoric pottery, including MH and LH III (the latter in the American School collection) has been found on the Larisa. It is unlikely, however, that it was a centre of habitation, and more likely that it served mainly as a watch-tower (like Profitis Ilias above Mycenae) in Mycenaean times, if not earlier.

The Aspis (Plate 5b) is a low and broad limestone hill, whose upper part is a small plateau, about 200 m. northeast to southwest by 150 m.). This was probably the main citadel and centre of the Mycenaean and ear-

lier settlement. Volgraff [*BCH* 30 (1906) 43 and 31 (1907) 141, Plan V] claimed two circuit walls on the Aspis, and attributed them to successive phases of the Middle Helladic period. But recent investigations have failed to confirm the existence of either wall. In any case, the claimed "Cyclopean" character of the second wall (said to be 2.60 m. thick) would suggest a Mycenaean, rather than a Middle Helladic, date.

Middle Helladic and Mycenaean habitation is now known to have been widespread, as has been recently revealed in a dramatic manner by a water main trench along the length of Heracles Street, which revealed Mycenaean occupation levels throughout its length, on both sides [*AD* 28 (1973) B 94, *cf. AR* (1978-9) 13]. A LH III well, containing many human and animal bodies, was found earlier near the Aspis [*AD* 27 (1972) B 198]. It is thus now known that the Mycenaean settlement covered a very considerable area in the LH IIIA-C periods. Fragments of fine frescoes are among the latest finds, and the quality and quantity of the recent material should serve to allay any doubts as to the size and importance of Mycenaean Argos. We must, however, await fuller publication of the Mycenaean finds, and a map showing their distribution is also a priority.

Most of the Mycenaean tombs have been found on the slopes of the Deiras hill, between the Larisa and the Aspis. They are mainly chamber tombs; but one rectangular built tomb containing burials of LH IIA to LH IIIA2 date was found on the east slope of the Aspis, and some pit graves containing single burials are closely associated with the Deiras chamber tombs. The earliest chamber tomb is on the Larisa slope of the Deiras hill. It contained LH IIA pottery and gold ornaments [*AD* 26 (1971) B 76]. Few of the other tombs are rich, although Tombs 6 and 7 contain important finds. A very fine stone-lined dromos (Tomb 10) was presumably intended for a tholos tomb, but this was not completed. Some chamber tombs continued in use into the early part of the LH IIIC period. Others were re-used in the Late LH IIIC and/or Sub-Mycenaean periods. But none of the tombs have an uninterrupted LH IIIC sequence. Groups of cists and pits of Dark Age date have been found in various parts of the modern town. The earliest of these is in the group on Tripolis Street [*AAA* 8 (1974) 259], and appears to be of late LH IIIC date.

THE INACHOS VALLEY (A 15-17)

This wide and fertile valley has been given relatively little attention. Investigations have mainly concentrated on the problem of the location of ancient Lyrkeia, and on the ancient route from Argos to Mantineia which led along the valley *via* Lyrkeia towards the Klimax pass [*cf. BSA* 65 (1970) 87 and refs., *AAA* 3 (1970) 117].

A 15 SCHOINOCHORI: MELICHI *
EH MH LH I/II-IIIA2

AM 36 (1911) 24; *JHS* 22 (1912) 386 and refs.; Fimmen (1921) 11; *BCH* 44 (1920) 386, 47 (1923) 190; *Alin* 43; *CMP* 53, 57, 62; *AAA* 3 (1970) 117; Bintliff (1977) 331.

Five small and poorly constructed chamber tombs were excavated [*BCH* 47 (1923) 190] on the small hill of Melichi (also known as "Melissi" or "Skala") between Schoinochori and the river Inachos. The cemetery was established early in the Mycenaean period, as is shown by the Vaphio cup fragment, probably LH I, from Tomb E (it is surely not intrusive, *pace CMP* 53). A pre-historic settlement between the tombs and the village of Schoinochori, is said by Ålin to have produced Early, Middle, and Late Helladic finds (*cf. BCH loc.cit.*). Classical and Hellenistic remains have also been found near the village, and traces of an ancient road, reinforcing the view that ancient Lyrkeia was situated at Schoinochori (*AAA loc.cit.*).

Mycenaean finds were also claimed (*AM loc.cit.*) at the ancient fort (Palaiokastro) near Skala, the village opposite Schoinochori on the north side of the Inachos river. But recent investigations [*AD* 26 (1971) B 82] have revealed only a quantity of obsidian and Hellenistic and Roman finds, and Mycenaean habitation is not confirmed (*pace* Bintliff *loc.cit.*).

A 16 MALANDRINI
MH? LH

RE Suppl. VI (1935) 606; Bintliff (1977) 331.

A Mycenaean and "vormykenishe" site was reported by Karo near Malandrini, on the north side of the Inachos valley, about 15 km. northwest of Argos.

A 17 GYMNO: KASTRO
MH LH II-IIIB C H?

AR (1961-2) 31; *CSHI* 66, Pl. 6a.

About 3 km. south-southeast of Gymno, to east of the road to Sterna and Argos, is a steep and rocky hill, on whose top is a tower, about 3 m. by 3 m., of which three courses of isodomic masonry are preserved. It is probably of the Classical period, and some 5th or 4th century B.C. sherds were found nearby. The top surface of the hill measures about 170 m. east to west by 55 m. Copious Mycenaean sherds and a few Middle Helladic were found here in 1961. The site is on the height of the pass between Phlious and the Inachos valley and may be the site of ancient Orneai.

SOUTHWEST ARGOLID AND THE THYREATIS (A 18-23)

The Mycenaean sites discovered are mostly on or near the coast. The interior part of this region has been neglected, but it is unlikely that any major Mycenaean

settlement existed here [Bintliff (1977) 689 ff. *contra*].

A 18 KEPHALARI: MAGOULA
N EH II-III MH LH IIIB A C H

PAE (1916) 79; *AA* (1939) 271; Bintliff (1977) 325.

The hamlet of Magoula (part of the community of Kephalari) is centred on a prehistoric mound, to west of the Argos-Tripolis road, and about 5 km. south of Argos. Recent excavations here are not yet published, but Bintliff (*loc.cit.*) has released certain details of them. Burials of the MH/LH transitional period are said to have been found below a "pure" Mycenaean level. The size and relative importance of the Mycenaean settlement have not been determined. (N.B. on Fig. 1 this site has been wrongly labelled as "21".)

A 19 MYLOI: ANCIENT LERNA *
N EH II-III MH LH I-IIIB PG G A C H

1. *The site: Hesperia* 23 (1954) 3, 24 (1955) 25, 25 (1956) 147, 26 (1957) 142, 27 (1958) 125, 28 (1959) 202, 29 (1960) 285; *AJA* 72 (1968) 313; Schoder (1974) 127; J.L. Caskey, *A Guide to Lerna* (1977); Bintliff (1977) 317.
2. *Associated Tombs: AE* (1955) *Parartema* 1, (1956) *Parartema* 12, *AD* 22 (1967) B 182.

Lerna is a large site (about 150 m. in diameter) of "low mound type", close to the sea on the south side of the village of Myloi. It is famous mainly on account of the Early Helladic palace complex, the "House of the Tiles". The late Middle Helladic and Mycenaean remains have been mostly eroded. Two shaft graves, emptied of their original contents in the LH I period, may have contained burials of important persons, but there are no signs that Lerna was of any importance in later Mycenaean times. It was apparently abandoned at some time in the LH IIIB period.

Two cist tombs in Myloi contained burials of LH I-II date (*AE* 1955 *loc.cit.*), and a group of eight cist graves of late MH and LH I date was found subsequently in the village (*AD loc.cit.*). About two kilometres south of Myloi, near the junction of the Argos Tripolis road and the road to Kiveri, a LH III chamber tomb was excavated and two others noted [*AE* 1956 *loc.cit., cf. BCH* 82 (1958) 713].

A 20 KIVERI: NEKROTAPHEION *
LH IIIA1-IIIB

AD 22 (1967) B 179; Bintliff (1977) 316.

On the north side of Kiveri, on the east slope of the ridge to south of the village cemetery, seven Mycenaean chamber tombs were excavated. Among the contents were fragments of a number of stone vases. The tombs have long dromoi, inclined towards the top, similar to those at Asine and Dendra.

A 21 ACHLADOKAMBOS: ANCIENT HYSIAI
LH IIIB C H

R.A. Tomlinson, *Argos and the Argolid* (1972) 37 and Pl. 10.

On the east side of Achladokambos, and to south of the main road is a well known fortified site of the historical period (identified by Tomlinson as ancient Hysiai), on a steep spur overhanging the valley to the south up which runs the railway to Tripolis. The surface pottery (observed in 1971) is mainly Classical and Hellenistic, and the surviving circuit walls also belong to one or both of these periods. But a LH III kylix stem and a fragment from a LH IIIB deep bowl with coated interior were also noted.

A 22 ASTROS: KASTRO
MH LH PG C

AA (1927) 365; *BSA* 56 (1961) 131.

The acropolis of ancient Astros is near the sea on the north side of Astros bay, about 3 km. east of the town. A few Mycenaean sherds were found on the southwest side of the hill, and burials of the Middle Helladic and Protogeometric periods on the west side.

A 23 AYIOS ANDREAS: CHERSONISI *
EH II MH LH III(A-B) G A

AA (1927) 365; *BSA* 56 (1961) 131; *BCH* 87 (1963) 759; *AD* 18 (1963) B 89.

On this small promontory, on the south side of Astros bay, prehistoric and later sherds, including Mycenaean, have been found on the surface, and a small trial excavation revealed EH II levels, and some Middle Helladic, Geometric, and Archaic pottery.

A 24 ANCIENT ASINE * # (Plate 5a)
EH I-III MH LH I-IIIC SMyc PG G A C H

O. Frödin and A.W. Persson, *Asine* (1938); *OpAth* 8 (1968) 87, 11 (1975) 177; *AD* 25 (1970) B 157, 26 (1971) B 113, 27 (1972) B 231; *AAA* 4 (1971) 147, 8 (1975) 151; *AR* (1971-2) 9, (1972-3) 14, (1974-5) 10; I. and R. Hägg, *Excavations in the Barbouna Area of Asine I* (Boreas 4:1, 1973); *Archaeology* 28 (1975) 157; W. Brett, *Asine II: Results of Excavations to East of the Acropolis 1970-74* (1976); Bintliff (1977) 312.

Ancient Asine is centred on a rocky acropolis, on a peninsula at the southwest edge of a fertile coastal plain. The Mycenaean remains on the acropolis have been much disturbed by later constructions, and the fortifications which remain here are of the Classical or Hellenistic period. The prehistoric settlement spread not only over the terraced slopes of the acropolis, but also onto the "lower town" immediately below to the northwest, and onto the south slopes of the Barbouna hill further to north, and to the plain below on the east.

By the end of the Middle Helladic period the settlement was spread over an area of about 60,000 m². The Mycenaean settlement was evidently of comparable size, extending at least 100 m. to northwest of the acropolis and 200 m. to east. The chamber tombs excavated on the slopes of the Barbouna hill are mostly large and rich, and their contents include pottery of all Mycenaean periods, especially LH IIIA and LH IIIC.

The LH IIIB period is not well represented in the tombs or on the acropolis, and few remains earlier than LH IIIC have been found. The LH IIIC remains include substantial buildings in the "lower town", one of which contained a shrine. Sub-Mycenaean pottery is reported from mixed strata to the east, and habitation seems to have continued without a break into the Dark Age.

A 25 KANDIA: KASTRO *
EH II-III MH LH I/II-IIIC G H

AA (1927) 365, (1939) 287, (1940) 220; *AR* (1944) 82; *AD* 20 (1965) B 157; *Tiryns VI* 214, 215 n. 41.

Kastro is a low hill about 200 m. north of the hamlet of Kandia, on the edge of a narrow valley which stretches inland for about 3 km. The summit, crowned by the chapel of Ayia Eleousa, has a top surface of only about 80 m. east to west by 50 m. It is enclosed by remains of fine Cyclopean walls, which have been attributed variously to the LH IIIB and/or the Geometric periods. It seems likely that the walls were originally constructed in Mycenaean times, and possibly repaired in the Geometric period, when there was evidently substantial occupation of the site.

The Mycenaean settlement spread over the summit and also over the steep southern terraces. Fine Middle Helladic and Mycenaean sherds, especially LH IIIB, are abundant on the upper terraces, and on the lower terraces fine Geometric pottery is apparently connected with house foundations here [*cf. OpAth* 6 (1965) 132]. Material from trial excavations indicates continuous habitation from the EH II period until late in the LH IIIC period. The site may have been abandoned from this time until the Geometric period. Despite the fortifications, the site does not seem to have been either large or important.

A 26 SYNORO *
EH II LH I-IIA

AA (1939) 293, (1940) 221; *Tiryns VI* 195.

On a small rocky hill further up the valley from Kandia (A 25) trial excavations produced evidence for habitation in Early Helladic and early Mycenaean times. This site appears to have been small and unimportant.

A 27 IRIA: KASTRO TOU KAPETANOU etc. *
N EH II MH LH I-IIIC G A? C H

AA (1938) 561, (1939) 294, (1940) 221; *Alin* 50; *AD* 21 (1966) B 130; *Tiryns VI* 127, 221.

At the Kastro hill, overlooking the village of Ano Iria and a small fertile coastal plain, Early Helladic, Mycenaean and Classical sherds have been found. Below the village, and nearer to the sea, is a low hill with two summits. Excavation on the west side of the western summit uncovered a Mycenaean building and associated cistern, which was partly filled with debris from a destruction by fire. The examination of the pottery suggests that this destruction took place at the very beginning of the LH IIIC period, and that the site was abandoned shortly after. Other material found indicates continuous habitation here from the Middle Helladic period, if not earlier.

EPIDAUROS AND VICINITY (A 28-34)

Recent discoveries at the Asklepieion site (A 30) and at Kasarma (A 28) demonstrate the importance of this region in Mycenaean times. In particular, the existence of a Mycenaean road for wheeled traffic between Tiryns and the east coast of the Argolid at Old Epidauros (A 31) is now amply corroborated (see under A 28).

A 28 AYIOS IOANNIS: KASARMA * # (Fig. 4, Plates 8-9)

EH II   MH   LH IIA-IIIB   PG   C   H

AJA 43 (1939) 83; *BCH* 79 (1955) 246, 94 (1970) 961, 95 (1971) 867; *AAA* 1 (1968) 236, 2 (1969) 3; *AD* 22 (1967) B 179, 24 (1969) B 104, 28 (1973) B 94.

The hill of Kasarma above the village of Ayios Ioannis dominates the highest part of the routes from Nauplion and Tiryns to Epidauros. It was fortified in the Classical and/or Hellenistic periods (*AJA loc.cit.*), and its polygonal walls are still well preserved in parts. The hill is strewn with Classical and Hellenistic sherds, but Mycenaean and earlier sherds have also been found, and in 1961 fine quality Middle Helladic and LH IIIA-B deep bowl and kylix fragments were found, the latter extending over most of the summit and also the upper slopes on the south side, over an extent of about 150 m. north to south by 130 m.

About 200 m. east of Ayios Ioannis, and about 10 m. north of the road, a tholos tomb was discovered. It is fairly small (diameter 7.5m.) and badly preserved, but intact burials of LH IIA date were preserved in deep pits below its floor, and a variety of finds, including remains of a pyre, upon the floor. There is also evidence of sacrifice on an altar in the doorway in both Mycenaean Protogeometric times [*AD* 24 (1969) B Pl. 84c to right is Protogeometric].

About 4 m. to west of Ayios Ioannis, to west of the road to Nauplion, is the famous "Arkadiko" bridge (Fig. 4, Plates 8-9). This is of typical "Cyclopean" construction, employing the Mycenaean arch, and much resembling the culverts of the Mycenaean road at Agrilovouno near Mycenae. The width of the roadway where it crosses the ravine is 2.50 m., and the overall width at the top of the bridge (5.55 m.) accords well with that (about 5.20 m.) of the bridge at Lykotroupi (see above under Mycenae). The total height of the arch is about 2.35 m., and the base of the culvert is more or less horizontal, assuring greater stability. It is clear that the stone walls on either side of the roadway were once higher, forming protecting balustrades at the bridge. The fill of small stones and compact earth between them is presumably part of the substructure of the original road, and its composition conforms with that of the section of the Agrilovouno road examined by Mylonas (*MMA* 86). The bridge is evidently part of the main Mycenaean highway from the Argolid plain to the Saronic Gulf at Epidauros [*cf. AJA* 78 (1974) 148]. Remains of three more similar bridges have recently been found in the Kasarma vicinity [noted in a preliminary report in *AD* 28 (1973) B 94, especially Pl. 92B].

It was noted above (under A 4) that the dromos of the tholos tomb near the Argive Heraion faces towards the line of the ancient road from Mycenae [*cf.* Wace (1949) 27, *BSA* 25 (1921-3) 330]. The dromos of the Ayios Ioannis tholos tomb faces south, towards the modern road, which is probably more or less on the same line as the ancient road. A similar juxtaposition of tholos tombs and ancient routes has been observed in Messenia (see below p. 143), although the evidence for actual Mycenaean roads in that region is as yet inconclusive.

A 29 LIGOURIO: ALEPOTRYPES etc. *

LH III(A-B)   C or H

Alin 51; *AJA* 43 (1939) 83; *AD* 27 (1972) B 215.

About 4 km. west of Ligourio, and about 200 m. north of the main road, are the remains of a circular watchtower of the Classical or Hellenistic period (*AJA loc.cit.*) on a limestone knoll named Alepotrypes, about 80 m. east to west by 40 m. Here Åström found a Mycenaean sherd (*Alin loc.cit.*), and obsidian chips and Classical or Hellenistic tiles are plentiful on the surface. Two badly damaged Mycenaean chamber tombs were found within the courtyard of the new gymnasium at Ligourio. Previous Mycenaean finds are also recorded from "Palaio Ligourio" on the road to Ancient Epidauros, and there are further reports of Mycenaean finds on the hills to west of the junction of the roads to the Asklepieion and to Ancient Epidauros (*AD loc.cit.*). A cup and three stirrup-jars, attributed to the LH IIIB period, in the Nauplion museum are also said to have come from Ligourio (*Alin loc.cit.*). The reports require further clarification, but it seems at least one more Mycenaean site in the Ligourio vicinity is indicated in addition to Alepotrypes.

A 30 THE ASKLEPIEION OF ANCIENT EPIDAUROS: THE TEMPLE OF APOLLO MALEATAS *

EH II   MH   LH I-IIIB   G   A   C   H

PAE (1948) 90, (1949) 94, (1950) 197, (1974) 93, (1975) A 162; *Ergon* (1975) 101, (1976) 112, (1977) 98; *RA* (1971) 3.

On the summit of Kynortion hill, and on its upper north slopes there are substantial, although damaged,

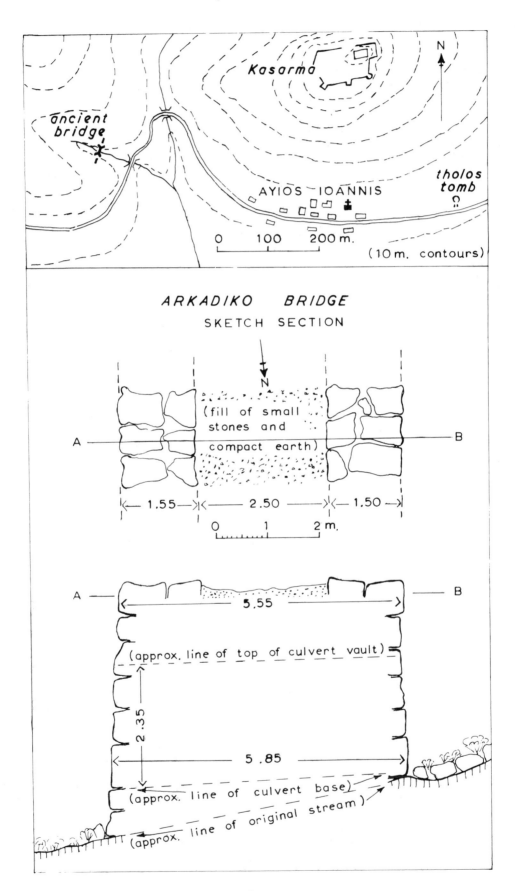

Figure 4

traces of a Mycenaean and earlier settlement of domestic character. These are only about 30 m. distant from an open air Mycenaean "altar" found in levels below those of the later sanctuary of Apollo Maleatas. Material from beneath the sanctuary suggests continuous habitation here from the EH II to LH IIIB periods, but a gap thereafter until the Geometric. It is claimed that there was a Mycenaean shrine here. Figurines found previously have been thought to be votives [*BSA* 66 (1971) 107], and more have been found in the new excavations, including large hollow animal figurines. Unusual finds from the Mycenaean deposit include a stone vase with relief decoration (*RA loc.cit.*), of which new fragments have appeared recently. Mycenaean finds also include much early pottery of fine quality, three sealstones, phi figurines, and bronze axe and spear heads. The recent finds reinforce the evidence for a Mycenaean cult here, but this can not yet be firmly linked with the later cult.

A 31 PALAIA EPIDHAVROS: PANAYIA (ANCIENT EPIDAUROS) *
MH LH IIIA2-C G A C H

AD (1888) 155; *AM* 37 (1911) 29; *Alin* 51; *AD* 29 (1974) A 70; *CSHI* 63.

The site of ancient Epidauros was centred on the headland to southeast of the harbour of the modern Palaia Epidhavros. The acropolis was the steep hill on which stands the Panayia chapel, which is ringed by circuit walls around its upper slopes, where there are widespread Classical and Hellenistic sherds. The earliest finds previously recorded were Geometric, but in 1961 Middle Helladic Grey Minyan ware and obsidian chips were found near the chapel. Seven Mycenaean chamber tombs were excavated on the southwest edge of Palaia Epidhavros on a slope to west of the road and about a kilometre to northwest of the acropolis. Their contents were of the LH IIIA2-B period except for one Close Style stirrup-jar (*cf. MP* 613, 647).

A 32 NEA EPIDHAVROS: PALAIOCHORI
LH IIIB

RE Suppl. VI (1935) 605; *AM* 63 (1938) 558.

Mycenaean tombs were reported at Palaiochori, about 500 m. east-southeast of Nea Epidhavros, on a slope on the south side of the road. In 1959, in the vicinity of a newly dug chamber tomb here, were found fragments of two tankards attributable to the LH IIIB period. The shape of both was similar to *MP* Fig. 25 no. 266, and the decoration similar to *MP* Motives 37 ("Myc. Flower", as on Figs. 14 and 18) and 21 ("Whorlshell", as on Figs. 51 and 23) respectively. It is possible that there was a Mycenaean settlement on the hill on the north side of Nea Epidhavros, where there is a mediaeval fort. Alternatively, the chamber tombs could be connected with the site at Vassa (No. 33 below) about 2.5 km. to the northwest.

A 33 NEA EPIDHAVROS: VASSA
EH II MH LH I/II-IIIB G

AA (1911) 150; *RE* Suppl. VI (1935) 606; *AA* (1938) 559; *Alin* 52 (s.v. "Dimena").

Vassa is a high and rocky ridge, to north of the road which leads inland from Nea Epidhavros to the Dimaina plain. It commands both this route and the route to north from Palaia Epidhavros. The settlement was large (about 200 m. north to south by 120 m. to judge from the sherd distribution), covering the high ridge and the extensive south slopes. The Cyclopean walls are well preserved on the south flank of the summit. Middle Helladic Matt-painted and Grey Minyan wares and obsidian are plentiful in the top area, and there are abundant LH I/II-IIIB sherds and some fragments from Mycenaean figurines both on the top and the west and south slopes (observed in 1959 and 1961). Gebauer [*AA* (1938) 559] mentions also some Mycenaean and Geometric sherds near the chapel of Ayios Leonidas, about 1.5 km. to northwest of Vassa. It was learned in 1959 that many Mycenaean tombs had been found at Prinias Ktima, near the chapel. It seems likely that this was the main Mycenaean cemetery for the Vassa settlement. Ålin (*loc.cit.*) mentions LH IIIA vases from Dimaina in the Nauplion museum.

Gebauer also mentions obsidian found at Kastraki, about 3 km. to the west, on the west side of the Dimaina plain, which suggests a separate prehistoric site here.

A 34 TRACHIA
LH

AA (1927) 365; *RE* Suppl. VI (1935) 605.

A Mycenaean site was reported near the village of Trachia, on the route between the Asklepieion at Epidauros and Troizen.

TROIZEN, METHANA, AND POROS (A 35-38)

This part of southeast Argolid was described by G. Welter, *Troizen und Kalaureia* (1941). The main fertile area is the Troizen plain itself, although there are some patches of good land on the Methana peninsula and on Poros. It is likely that there were other Mycenaean settlements in the Troizen area, particularly at the site of ancient Troizen itself (No. 35B).

A 35 KALLONI: AYIOS YEORYIOS
LH IIIA-B C

CSHI 62 n. 8.

The isolated hill of Ayios Yeoryios lies at the southeast end of the fertile coastal plain of Lessia, on the route from Troizen to Ancient Epidauros (A 31), and at the northeast end of the pass to Choritsa (see under A 35A below). The hill is conspicuous, being fairly high, with a flat top measuring about 110 m. east to west by 50 m. Beside the chapel of Ayios Yeoryios on the top of the hill, Mycenaean sherds were observed in 1959 in the spoil heaps of a number of modern graves recently dug. The Mycenaean pottery was of good quality. Some Classical sherds were also observed, on the south slope, where there is an abundant spring.

A 35A KASTRO CHORITSA (Not marked on Map A)
LH?

AA (1927) 365.

A tower between Ortholithion and Choritsa was identified as a Mycenaean watchtower. This is presumably the same as the tower described by Gebauer [*AA* (1938) 561] as "zwischen Lessia und Karatza". But the evidence for a Mycenaean date has not yet been presented.

A 35B ANCIENT TROIZEN *
EH II LH? G A C H

AM 36 (1911) 33; G. Welter, *Troizen und Kalaureia* (1941) 10; *Klio* Beiheft 49 (1944) 46; *CSHI* 62.

No Mycenaean remains have yet been found in the vicinity of Ancient Troizen. The tombs from the garden of Paspati [*AD* (1889) 163], formerly reported as Mycenaean, are in fact of the Geometric period (*AM* and *Klio loc.cit.*). Early Helladic sherds were found on the broad and low spur of the Asklepieion site, on the south side of the plain of Troizen, and not far to west of the centre of the ancient city. This site in particular, and the vicinity of a large spring (which used to work a water mill) to northwest of the historic centre should both be investigated further. In general, it is very difficult to believe that this area would have been neglected by Mycenaean settlers.

A 36 METHANA: MEGALOCHORIO (ANCIENT METHANA)
EH LH III(A-B) G A C H

AM 36 (1911) 35; Welter 1941, 10.

Early Helladic and Mycenaean sherds are among the finds reported from the small acropolis hill of ancient Methana, about a kilometre to southwest of Megalochorio.

A 37 LOUTRA METHANON: VROMOLIMNI etc.
EH II LH C H

Alin 52.

A Mycenaean and later settlement was reported at a site by the plain of Throni and near the village of Vromolimni, on the northern outskirts of Loutra Methanon. And in 1959 Early Helladic sherds and obsidian were observed on the promontory to south of Loutra Methanon.

A 38 POROS: THE TEMPLE OF POSEIDON AT KALAUREIA *
EH II LH III(B) G A C H

AM 20 (1895) 297, 39 (1911) 35; *Arch.Zeit.* (1886) 260 Pl. A3, 4; Welter 1941, 10, 50, Taf. 28.

The temple site is one of a range of hills to northeast of the town of Poros. There is a small fertile upland plain to the north of the hills. Early Helladic sherds were found both at the temple site and on a slope to east of the chapel of Ayios Stathis, which lies to east of the path from Poros to the temple. A chamber tomb, probably Mycenaean, was also found to east of the same path (*Arch.Zeit. loc.cit.*). A deposit between the temple contained LH III (probably LH IIIB) pottery and jewellery; and an early Eighteenth Dynasty scarab was found just above this deposit [J.D.S. Pendlebury, *Aegyptiaca* (1930) 67]. The main Mycenaean centre, however, may have been the hill of "Polis" to southwest of the Temple (*cf.* Welter 1941 Taf. 28).

HERMIONE, KRANIDHI, SPETSAI, HYDRA, AND DOKOS (A 39-46)

In the southern part of southeast Argolid the districts of Hermione and Kranidhi are somewhat isolated from the main part of the Argolid by some barren highland country to the north of it. There is, however, a circuitous connection with Poros along the coast, and Ancient Eileoi (A 42) lies on a pass to Troizen. Until recently there had been relatively little exploration of this part of the Argolid. An intensive and interdisciplinary survey has now been made in the Kranidhi vicinity by the Universities of Indiana and Pennsylvania under T.W. Jacobsen and M.H. Jameson. A preliminary report of primary investigations into the palaeoecology of part of the region has been presented by J.L. Bintliff (1977) 173-270. This, however, is based on an unpublished report of the archaeological survey by J.A. Dengate, which is extant only in cyclostyled form, and which in any case provides no detailed account of the finds made in the survey and no full topographical indications. It has therefore proved impracticable to add the Mycenaean sites found to Map A here, and it would be premature to estimate their type and status in many cases. We must await publication of the full archaeological report. Other work in progress includes a survey of the islands of the Hydra-Spetsai group by S.E. Iakovidis and other, and investigations in the Hermione area by E. Deilaki [*AD* 28 (1973) B 87].

A 39 PHOURKARIA
LH H

AA (1927) 365; *RE* Suppl. VI (1935) 605; Welter 1941, Taf. 1 (shown as "Tourkaria"); *Alin* 52 (s.v. "Phurkaria").

This was apparently a small coastal settlement, at the edge of a plain which is shut in by rounded hills on the east and west.

A 40 THERMISI
LH III(A-B)

RE Suppl. VI (1935) 606.

The description of this site reads as follows: "Thermisi, nordöstlich des gleichnamigen Kaps, auf einem Felsvorsprung über Salzwerken, byzant. Festung and Spätmyk. Scherben (Mitt. Heurtleys)". A small Mycenaean site seems to be indicated in this remote coastal plain.

A 41 HERMIONE: KASTRI
EH II-III MH LH II-IIIB

PAE (1909) 175; *AM* 36 (1911) 37; *CSHI* 62.

The low promontory called Kastri or Magoula lies about 500 m. west-southwest of the modern town of Hermione, and to south of the hill named Gron, the necropolis of the historic Hermione. To west and southwest of Kastri is a fertile coastal plain, where grain, olives, vines, oranges, and cypresses are cultivated. The promontory is fairly small (the top surface of the hillock measures about 127 m. northeast to southwest by 55 m.), but fine surface pottery was abundant, including Middle Helladic Grey Minyan and Matt-painted and polychrome (purple and white), and some early Mycenaean. The latest Mycenaean piece recognized was part of a "Panel Style" deep bowl with decoration similar to *MP* Motif 50: 22. The autopsy in 1959 shows that the theory (*AM loc.cit.*) that this was the site of a Mycenaean cemetery must be discarded. This was clearly a Mycenaean and prehistoric settlement site of moderate size.

A 42 EILEOI: ILIOKASTRO (ANCIENT EILEOI) *
EH II MH LH III(A-B) C H

PAE (1909) 182; *AM* 36 (1911) 35; Fimmen (1921) 13; *Alin* 52 (s.v. "Karakasi"); *AJA* (1964) 231.

The hill of Iliokastro is about 2 km. northeast of Eileoi (formerly Karakasi), on the left of the track to Troizen. The hill is identified as the site of ancient Eileoi, as is indicated by the Classical and/or Hellenistic circuit walls, which enclose an area about 350 m. north to south by 150 m. Late Mycenaean vases were found in cist tombs at the south foot of the hill (see especially Fimmen and *Alin loc.cit.*). Some LH III sherds found on the south slopes of the hill in 1959 probably demonstrate a Mycenaean settlement here, and Mid-dle Helladic Grey Minyan and Matt-painted sherds are also attested (*AJA loc.cit.*). It is, however, unlikely that the prehistoric settlement occupied the whole area enclosed by the historic circuit walls.

A 43 KOILADHA: AYIOS IOANNIS
LH (including LH IIIB) C

RE Suppl. VI (1935) 606; *Klio* Beiheft 49 (1944) 48; *Alin* 52 (s.v. "Keladi"); *CSHI* 63.

A small low rocky promontory, about 2 km. north of Koiladha, and about 2.5 km. west of the main road from Kranidhi to Nauplion, is marked by a chapel of Ayios Ioannis. The promontory is narrow and the ancient settlement here, marked by Mycenaean and some Classical and later sherds, was obviously small. Immediately to the north is a small fort of the Classical or Hellenistic period named Pyrgo.

It should be pointed out that the site at Ayios Ioannis is now only one of several Mycenaean sites found in the Kranidhi district, mainly by the team from the universities of Indiana and Pennsylvania. Earlier reports include a mention of a discovery by Heurtley of remains of Mycenaean walls (presumably Cyclopean) on a hill (near Koiladha) described as about 3 km. left of the road to Hermione (*RE loc.cit.*). Burr (in *Klio loc.cit.*) pointed out that there directions do lead us (although in a roundabout way) to the vicinity of the bay of Koiladha. Mycenaean sherds have recently been found in a well near Fourni [*AD* 28 (1973) B 87]; and others were found on the surface in and around the Franchthi cave [*Hesperia* 42 (1973) 45, 253].

A 44 PORTO-CHELI and vicinity
N EH MH LH III PG G A C H

LAAA 4 (1912) 128; *AD* 18 (1963) B 73; *Hesperia* 38 (1969) 318.

M.S. Thompson (*LAAA loc.cit.*) recorded "Myc. (LM III) remains near Porto-Kheli opposite Spetsia". It is presumed that the site in question would be at or near that of ancient Halieis. In the excavations on and around the acropolis of Halieis Neolithic and possibly EH I material has been found, but the next period represented (by unstratified finds) is the Protogeometric. The symbol on Map A refers to a site described (*AD loc.cit.*) as about 3 km. to north of Porto-Cheli, where Early and Middle Helladic and Mycenaean sherds were reported.

A 45 SPETSAI: AYIA MARINA *
EH II(-?III) LH I/II-III(A-B)

AD 26 (1971) B 84; *AR* (1973-4) 13.

On the low promontory of Ayia Marina, on the east coast of Spetsai, Early Helladic buildings were excavated. One LH I/II and several LH III sherds were also reported.

A 46 HYDRA: CHORIZA
    LH III(A-B)   G C H

AM 36 (1911) 38; *AD* 20 (1965) B 130.

The hill of Choriza is about 2 km. southwest of the town of Hydra, and opposite the islet of Ayios Ioannis tou Theologou. It is about 75 m. a.s.l., with cliffs on the south side, and less steep slopes on the northwest leading down to the Gulf of Vlichos. On the north and northwest slopes many LH III sherds and the head of a Mycenaean figurine were found, together with sherds of later periods.

A 46A DOKOS: SKINDOS BAY
    EH II LH H

AAA 9 (1976) 17.

On the east side of the small bay of Skindos on the north coast of the island of Dokos, obsidian and flint blades and chips and sherds of Early Helladic, Mycenaean, Hellenistic and mediaeval date have been found on the surface. A shipwreck of the EH II period was discovered near the northern arm of the bay.

THE ISLAND OF AEGINA (A 47-50)

Only four Mycenaean sites are known on the island, and no systematic survey has yet been undertaken on Aegina. The main settlement was at Kolonna (A 47).

A 47 AEGINA: KOLONNA (THE TEMPLE OF APHRODITE) * #
    N EH II-III MH LH I-IIIC PG G A C H

AE (1895) 234, (1910) 172; *AA* (1925) 4, 317, (1938) 510; *AD* 22 (1967) B 147, 24 (1969) B 146, 25 (1970) B 136, 26 (1971) B 61, 27 (1972) B 183; J.P. Harland, *Prehistoric Aigina* (1925) 11; G. Welter, *Aigina* (1938) 7; *Alin* 114; S. Hiller, *Alt-Ägina IV 1:Mykenische Keramik* (1975).

Kolonna is a "low mound" site, on the promontory to north of modern Aigina and its harbour, and accessible only from the southeast. The prehistoric settlement occupied an area about 250 m. by 100 m. The original excavations here have never been fully published, but important information has been yielded by the new excavations. There was already a substantial settlement here in the Early Helladic period, with a large tiled building and a fortification wall. This settlement continued to expand and was provided with successive fortifications until late in the Mycenaean period [*cf. AD* 26 (1971) 61 and Pls. 54-55]. It seems to have been an important trading centre, resembling Cycladic towns such as Ayia Irini on Kea and Phylakopi on Melos. Early Helladic wells and bothroi, early Mycenaean cist or pit graves, and LH III chamber tombs have been excavated on a hill to the east. The "Aegina Treasure" in the British Museum was found in one of the chamber tombs. It is quite different in character from ordinary Mycenaean jewellery, and it is sug-

gested that it is a cache of Middle Minoan jewellery looted in modern times from Crete, perhaps from Chrysolakkos at Mallia [*BSA* 52 (1957) 42].

The recent publication (Hiller *op.cit.*) of the best Mycenaean pottery from the original excavations shows the high quality of local production, especially in the LH II period, when there seems to have been local "palatial style" workshop. It also provides further corroboration of continued occupation in the area in the LH IIIC period, by adding two further whole stirrup-jars (in the Aigina Museum), now recognized as LH IIIC, to the solitary LH IIIC "Close Style" stirrup-jar (in the British Museum) previously recognized [Desborough (1964) 119]. The amount of published LH III material from the settlement is, however, very slight, and includes nothing certainly of the LH IIIC period. Since the next recognizable material is late Protogeometric, there may have been an evacuation of the main settlement at the end of the LH IIIB period [*cf. AJA* 82 (1978) 118].

A 48 AEGINA: THE TEMPLE OF APHAIA * #
    N LH IIIA-B LH IIIC? G A C H

G. Furtwaengler, *Aegina: das Heiligtum der Aphaia* (1906) 369, 434, 471; Welter 1938, 7; *Alin* 115; Schoder (1974) 16.

Some LH III sherds were found near and below the temple terrace, together with fragments of figurines and a few other objects probably of Bronze Age date. The figurines apparently range from LH IIIA2 to LH IIIB at least, and may be a votive deposit [*BSA* 66 (1971) 107]. But such a deposit need not be of Mycenaean date, and there is no necessity to assume that this was a Mycenaean cult centre. One sherd from the site might be LH IIIC (Furtwaengler 1906 Pl. 127:5), and one of the figurines also seems to be of this period [*BSA* 66 (1971) 137].

A 49 AEGINA: KILINDRA
    LH IIIA2(-B?)

Furtwaengler 1906, 435; *CMP* 41, 58.

Several whole Mycenaean vases are reported to have come from a grave near this small hamlet, which lies on a hill above and to north of the village of Portes, near one of the few beaches on this rocky east coast of the island.

A 50 AEGINA: MT. OROS
    MH? LH IIB or IIIA1 LH III(A-B) C H

Furtwaengler 1906, 473; Fimmen (1921) 9; Harland 1925, 27; Welter 1938, 26; *BSA* 35 (1934-5) 132; *AJA* 67 (1963) 151.

Prehistoric house foundations were found immediately below the summit of Mt. Oros, and near the chapel of Ayios Ilias. The position suggests that it may have been a refuge site. Four coarse ware sherds may have been erroneously classed as Middle Helladic Matt-painted, since the bulk of the material seems to be late Mycenaean. But one sherd (in the collection of the Department of Ancient History and Archaeology at Birmingham) from the site is earlier. It is decorated with "Scale Pattern" (*MP* Motif 70) and must be LH IIB or LH IIIA1. Other finds reported to be from the site include a fragment of a Type F sword (*AJA loc.cit.*) and a bronze arrowhead (*BSA loc.cit.*).

THE CORINTHIAN PLAIN AND ITS ENVIRONS (A 51-61) (Plate 10a)

The Corinth area was famous in antiquity for its fertility, and parts of it are still extremely fertile, and it remains a major centre for currant production. The Mycenaean settlements discovered are relatively numerous, but this is clearly due in large measure to the excellent work in this area by the American School of Classical Studies at Athens. The "extensive" pioneer survey by C.W. Blegen [in *AJA* 24 (1920) 1-13] was followed by selective excavations, principally at Korakou (A 51). The importance of the area in Mycenaean times is underscored by the size of some of the settlements, *i.e.*, Korakou, Aietopetra (A 56), Gonia (A 57), and Perdikaria (A 59). Korakou and Perdikaria were fortified; and the Corinthia as a whole was apparently protected by a fortification wall at Isthmia (A 61), which ran in a northwesterly direction from the Saronic Gulf towards the Corinthian Gulf. The brilliant discovery of this wall and its careful excavation by O. Broneer have provided an eloquent testimony of Mycenaean power and engineering achievement, the implications of which will be discussed below.

A 51   KORAKOU   * #   (Plate 11a)
EH I-III   MH   LH I-IIIC   A   C

C.W. Blegen, *Korakou* (1921); J.B. Rutter, *The Late Helladic IIIB and IIIC Periods at Korakou and Gonia* (Ph.D. thesis, Pennsylvania 1974); *BSA* 67 (1972) 103; *AJA* 79 (1975) 1.

Korakou is a low but conspicuous oval mound (about 260 m. east to west by 115 m.) on a bluff overhanging the coast road, about 2 km. west of the outskirts of modern Corinth. There was a substantial settlement here (over an area of about 225,000 m²) from the Early Helladic period to well into the LH IIIC period. The well preserved stratified deposits provided the first reliable guide for the sub-divisions of the Bronze Age on the Greek mainland. The site seems to have been important in the LH III period, to which belong remains of a circuit wall, probably a fortification, and of substantial buildings. Further indications are provided by a massive threshold block and a fresco fragment. Several of the buildings excavated belong to the LH IIIC phase, during which the site seems to have suffered a disaster. Reoccupation after this was followed by a final, and perhaps hasty, abandonment.

The importance of Korakou may have been due largely to its location near the most suitable beaches

for a harbour (near the historic harbour of Lechaion). Such a harbour may have been needed as a base for defence against attack from the north by sea (see also under A 53 below).

A 52   MODERN CORINTH   *
EH II   LH II-IIIB   SMyc?   PG

Hesperia 1 (1932) 63, 36 (1967) 26 n. 22; *AA* (1933) 223; *AR* (1938-9) 9; *AJA* 58 (1954) 232.

Traces of prehistoric habitation in the eastern part of modern Corinth include an EH II cemetery reported near the Corinth Canal [*Hesperia* 36 (1967) *loc.cit.*] and a large tomb on the terrace of the hill immediately south of the railway station (*AJA loc.cit.*). The tomb contained LH IIIA and LH IIIA2/B vases. An unpublished tomb group consisting mainly of LH II vases is in the Corinth Museum (the group, items C 63/23-30, is to be published by Miss H. Palaiologos of the Greek Archaeological Service, who has kindly given permission for this advance mention). Earlier reports (*AR loc.cit.*) cite Protogeometric and possible Sub-Mycenaean finds.

A 53   AYIOS GERASIMOS   *
EH I-II   EH III?   MH   LH I/II-IIIB   C

AJA 24 (1920) 4, 27 (1923) 160; *AD* 26 (1971) B 68.

The chapel of Ayios Gerasimos stands on a slight rise near the shore, about 1.5 km. west of ancient Lechaion. Limited excavations have revealed Early Helladic structures. Surface sherds observed on a visit in 1957 included fine Mycenaean wares of LH I/II-IIIB range. This site, together with Korakou, commands the area of the later Corinthian harbour of Lechaion, which lies between the two sites. The chief Mycenaean harbour in Corinthia also appears to have been in the same area [*cf. AJA* 24 (1920) 4, 9]. A Mycenaean chamber tomb excavated in the vicinity of ancient Lechaion [*BCH* 78 (1954) 112] may be associated either with Ayios Gerasimos or Korakou.

A 54   ANCIENT CORINTH   *
N   EH I-II   MH?   LH IIIB-C   SMyc   PG   G   A   C   H

AJA 1 (1897) 313, 24 (1920) 1, 27 (1923) 161, 40 (1936) 207; *Hesperia* 17 (1948) 197, 18 (1949) 148, 20 (1951) 292, 29 (1960) 240, 39 (1970) 12, 41 (1972) 144, 291, 42 (1973) 1, 43 (1974) 398, 44 (1975) 7; *AD* 26 (1971) B 94; Schoder (1974) 110.

It is evident that most of the traces of Mycenaean habitation at ancient Corinth have been destroyed by later constructions. Earlier levels have in places escaped this destruction. There is widespread evidence for Neolithic and Early Helladic habitation, especially from the Temple of Apollo site. T.W. Allen [*The Homeric Catalogue of the Ships* (1921) 64] records a statement by Wace that a few Mycenaean sherds had also been found in the excavations at the Temple of Apollo, although later remains had evidently removed all traces of Mycenaean structures here [*AJA* 24 (1920) 3].

Later excavations behind the Julian basilica [*Hesperia* 18 (1949) and 20 (1951) *loc.cit.*] revealed good quality LH IIIB pottery, including a "Chariot Krater" [a single fine sherd is published by J.L. Benson in *Horse, Bird, and Man* (1971) 116 Pl. 41:7, and other scattered fragments have been reported]. LH IIIC material has been found more recently beneath the Sanctuary of Demeter and Kore on the slopes of Acrocorinth [*Hesperia* for 1970 and following years; and *cf. AJA* 77 (1975) 24 n. 1 for an unpublished fragment]. Sub-Mycenaean pit graves, and a group of Sub-Mycenaean or early Protogeometric vases found near a hearth, appear to indicate continuity into the Dark Age. The Mycenaean remains cover a wide area, and may represent separate settlements, *i.e.*, one perhaps centred on the Temple of Apollo site and the other on the slopes of Acrocorinth. There is as yet no evidence for an important Mycenaean settlement at ancient Corinth, although one seems likely, as does a fort, or at least a watchtower, on Acrocorinth itself.

A 55 MYLOS CHELIOTOU *
N EH I-III MH LH I-IIIB G A C H

AJA 24 (1920) 3, 27 (1923) 159, 34 (1930) 403; *Hesperia* Supplement 8 (1949) 415; C.W. Blegen, *Korakou* (1921) 116; *Corinth XIII* (1964) Part I; *AD* 21 (1966) B 121.

This site is a small oval hillock, on the northern edge of the upper plateau to south of the main coastal plain. It stands about 30 m. above the level of the plain, overlooking the new motorway which runs below on the north side. The area of settlement, comprising the top and the upper slopes, was roughly 85 m. north to south by 75 m. The remains excavated are mainly of the Early and Middle Helladic periods, but most of the surface pottery is Mycenaean. In 1957 several fine ware sherds of the LH IIIA2-B periods were noted. Recently a Mycenaean highway has been claimed, on the basis of associated LH IIIA2 sherds, running east to west, and parallel to a road of the Archaic period (*AD loc.cit.*). These remains are about 100 m. to northeast of the site, on the south side of the new motorway.

A 56 AIETOPETRA
N EH I-III MH LH II-IIIB LH IIIC?

AJA 24 (1920) 3, 27 (1923) 160.

Aietopetra, about 3 km. west of Ancient Corinth, is an oval hill with steep cliffs, at the mouth of a deep ravine leading south through the hills on the south side of the Corinthian plain, over which it commands an excellent view. Over the flat top surface, about 225 m. north to south by 100 m., surface pottery is abundant. In 1959 fine Mycenaean sherds of the LH II-IIIB periods were observed, and some possibly of early LH IIIC. Blegen [*AJA* 24 (1920) 3] surmised that "one

of the Mycenaean highways conjectured by Steffen must have come down this ravine, passing just below the site". And the probability of a Mycenaean highway in the ravine is strengthened by the evidence of an important Mycenaean site at Cleonae (A 62) and by the investigations of Mylonas (*MMA* 86) of Steffen's Roads 1 and 2 (*cf.* Wace, 1949, Ill. 7), which appear to have converged at the pass of Mavroneri, to south of the valley of Ayios Vasilios in which lies the site of Zygouries (A 63, *cf.* Fig. 1). The route from Mavroneri *via* the Ayios Vasilios valley and Cleonae to Aietopetra is indeed the most direct way from Mycenae to the Corinthia (see also under A 62 below).

A 57 GONIA *
N EH I-III MH LH I-IIIB C H

AJA 24 (1920) 6; *Metropolitan Museum Studies* 3 (1930-31) 55; Rutter 1974 (see under A 51 above).

Gonia is a broad and rather irregular plateau, about 350 m. east to west by 250 m., with mainly steep sides, about a kilometre to east of the old road from Corinth to Argos, and about 2 km. north of Examilia. The site may have been occupied continuously from the Middle Neolithic to the LH IIIB periods. According to Rutter, occupation did not continue beyond the middle of the LH IIIB period. To judge from surface pottery of the LH II-IIIB periods observed on the surface in 1957, the Mycenaean settlement appears to have extended over the whole plateau. Yet, despite the size of the site, extensive trial trenches produced nothing to suggest any particular importance. The Mycenaean remains, however, were often found to be much eroded.

A 58 ARAPIZA
EH II MH LH IIIA-B

AJA 24 (1920) 5, 27 (1923) 159.

This rather small site lies just west of the old main road from Corinth to Argos, at the northern end of a thin ridge of soft white rock. Sherds found here in 1959 included LH IIIA and LH IIIB.

A 59 PERDIKARIA
EH II MH LH III(A-)B

AJA 24 (1920) 7, 27 (1923) 160.

About 2 km. east of Examilia, on the south side of the road to Cenchreae, is an oval hill with a rather steep north side. The top of the hill measures about 100 m. east to west by 60 m., but sherds, mainly MH and LH IIIB, were noted in 1959 extending over the north terraces also for a further 150 m. east to west by 130 m., indicating a fairly large prehistoric settlement. On an upper slope on the north side a section of Cyclopean wall is preserved for a length of about 30 m., and to a maximum height of about 3 m. Perdikaria is in a strategic position at the junction of routes from

Cenchreae (A 60) and Isthmia (A 61), and may be part of a defensive network based on the Isthmia wall.

A 60   ANCIENT CENCHREAE   *
EH II   MH   LH IIIB   C   H

AJA 24 (1920) 7, *AA* (1939) 269.

The prehistoric site seems to have been small, and confined to the hill above the northeast mole of the harbour. In 1959 Early and Middle Helladic and a few LH IIIB sherds were noted on the surface, among far more abundant Classical and Hellenistic. But the extensive later occupation may have obscured or removed some of the evidence for Mycenaean settlement, and the harbour may have been of some importance in Mycenaean times.

A 61   ISTHMIA   *
EH I-II   MH   LH IIA-B   LH III(A2-)B   PG   G   A   C   H

AJA 24 (1920) 8; *Hesperia* 24 (1955) 142, 35 (1966) 346, 37 (1968) 25; *Antiquity* 33 (1959) 80; *AD* 24 (1969) B 84, 26 (1971) B 105; *BCH* 95 (1971) 843; O. Broneer, *Isthmia II* (1973) 6; Schoder (1974) 97.

At the Isthmia sanctuary slight traces of Mycenaean habitation were found, and some LH II pottery; and on the eroded spur of Rachi, to southwest of and above the sanctuary, prehistoric sherds were found, including Mycenaean. More important, however, are the remains of a fortification wall of Cyclopean style, 3.60 m. to 4.00 m. in width where measurable, which ran in a roughly northwest direction from the Saronic Gulf at least as far as the Isthmia sanctuary. The wall has tower-like projections at regular intervals on its northern (outer) side, and it is sited wherever possible in such a manner as to force attackers from the north to approach over steeply sloping ground. Indeed a very wide (and expensive) loop was made in the central part of its preserved length (*cf.* Fig. 1), adding about 2 kilometres of "extra" walling, obviously in order to maintain the desired elevation and to take advantage of the steep slopes. The wall follows the contours of the hill slopes in a manner so closely resembling that of Mycenaean highways that one scholar has (mistakenly) conjectured that it was not a fortification wall but a retaining terrace for a road [*AAA* 4 (1971) 85].

The material found in the fill of the wall is LH IIIB of advanced style, and Broneer argues convincingly that the wall was designed to meet an impending threat from the north at the end of this period. Because of later constructions, especially the Justinian wall, it has not proved possible to ascertain whether the Mycenaean wall had in fact been continued further to the northwest. But it was presumably the intention of the builders to complete the wall all the way from the Saronic Gulf to the Gulf of Corinth, whether or not it was ever actually finished.

THE VALLEYS OF ANCIENT CLEONAE, NEMEA, AND PHLIOUS (A 62-68)

Fieldwork in this interior district between the Argolid and Corinthia has been selective and spasmodic. The only Mycenaean sites of any importance are Ancient Cleonae (A 62) and Zygouries (A 63). The chief Mycenaean site in the Phlious valley, for instance, has yet to be found. And, in general, a much greater density of Mycenaean habitation is to be expected here, since some parts of the valleys are extremely fertile.

A 62   ANCIENT CLEONAE
EH II   MH   LH I/II-IIIB   A   C   H

Frazer, *Pausanias* III 82; *AA* (1913) 114, (1939) 271; *CSHI* 66.

The site of the historic Cleonae lies about 4 km. northwest of Ayios Vasilios, in the Longopotamos valley, along which probably ran one of the Mycenaean roads to the Corinthian plain (*cf.* Wace 1949, 47 and Ill. 7; and see under A 56 above). The highest and westernmost of the three hills which formed the acropolis of ancient Cleonae was the centre of an important Mycenaean settlement, which apparently extended about 300 m. north to south by 250 m. The hill is steep on the west and northwest, but slopes more gently on the south, and on the east it connects with the lower hill on which are the remains of the Temple of Athena. Fine surface sherds found in 1960 included Middle Helladic Grey and Yellow Minyan Ware, LH IIB "Ephyraean", and LH IIIA and LH IIIB from kylikes and deep bowls.

A 63   AYIOS VASILIOS: ZYGOURIES   *
EH I-III   MH   LH I-IIIB1   G

C.W. Blegen, *Zygouries* (1928); *BSA* 64 (1969) 265 n. 18; *Alin* 58.

Zygouries is a conspicuous "low mound" site, on the southwest edge of the village of Ayios Vasilios. It measures about 170 m. northeast to southwest by 90 m., and is much eroded on the top and partly disturbed by Byzantine buildings. It was probably inhabited without a break from EH I to early LH IIIB. The periods of its greatest importance were EH II and LH IIIB, when habitation spread to the level ground below the hill. Both these phases ended with destruction by fire. The "Potter's Shop" is the most substantial LH IIIB building, and it was probably the basement of a mansion belonging to a local magnate. On a hill about 500 m. to west of the site were found EH II, MH, and LH IIIB graves. The latter are chamber tombs whose contents may be a little later than those of the "Potter's Shop" (*BSA loc.cit.*).

A 64   AYIOS VASILIOS: AYIA TRIADHA
LH IIIA2-B

AA (1913) 116; *Alin* 37.

The chapel of Ayia Triadha is about 4 km. southeast of Ayios Vasilios railway station, on the southeast slopes of Mt. Daphnias. About a hundred Mycenaean figurines of Phi and Psi types were found here, and a male figurine.

A 65 HERAKLION: TSOUNGIZA *
N EH I-III MH   LH I-III(A-)B   C or H

AJA 31 (1927) 436, 32 (1928) 69; *Hesperia* 44 (1975) 150, 45 (1976) 174.

The Tsoungiza ridge projects northward from the west end of Heraklion village, and overlooks the Nemea valley to its north. A neolithic deposit and remains of a Bronze Age settlement were partially excavated but never published. The "House of the Arrowmaker" on a terrace seems to have contained a LH IIB floor deposit. More recently, Neolithic and LH IIIB material has been found at a point about 100 m. south of the previous excavation site. Mycenaean finds are also reported from the area of the Sanctuary of Zeus, over 500 m. to the east [*Hesperia* 44 (1975) 157, 161, 168].

A 66 MODERN NEMEA: AYIA IRINI
LH IIIA-B

AR (1961-2) 31; *CSHI* 67

About 2.5 km. west-northwest of Modern Nemea (formerly Ayios Yeoryios) is a very low hill named Ayia Irini, on the west bank of the Asopos river, and on the south side of the road to Stymphalos. The hill lies at the foot of higher hills bounding the western side of the plain of ancient Phlious. The hill is heavily eroded, and the surface sherds found in 1961 were small and worn, but LH IIIA and LH IIIB were represented by fragments from kylikes and deep bowls. The total area of Mycenaean settlement does not seem to have been more than about 150 m. north to south by 100 m.

A 67 ANCIENT PHLIOUS *
N EH II LH III(A-B) PG G A C H

Hesperia 38 (1969) 443.

On the low mound to west of the acropolis of ancient Phlious evidence of Neolithic and Early Helladic settlement was found. The only evidence for Mycenaean settlement in this vicinity consists of one kylix stem fragment and a steatite whorl. It seems likely, however, that later building activities on the site, especially in the Hellenistic period, may have removed evidence of Mycenaean habitation.

A 68 GONOUSSA: AYIOS TRYPHON (ANCIENT TITANE)
EH II LH III(A2-B) C H

Frazer, *Pausanias* III 69; E. Meyer, *Peloponnesische Wanderungen* (1939) 11; *CSHI* 68.

The chapel of Ayios Tryphon lies on a spur projecting from the west into the Asopos valley, about a kilometre to southeast of Gonoussa (formerly Lopesi) and about 500 m. northeast of Titane (formerly Voivonda). The fine isodomic walls (of ancient Titane) are Classical or Hellenistic. Within the area they enclosed (about 100 m. east to west by 60 m.) a few Early Helladic sherds and part of the stem of a Mycenaean tall kylix were found in 1959.

THE SIKYON AREA AND NORTHWEST CORINTHIA (A 69-75)

The coastal region in the vicinities of Sikyon (Kiato) and Xylokastro is as fertile as the Corinthian plain, of which it is (geographically) a continuation. Some extensive search was carried out here by Gebauer [*AA* (1939) 272 ff.], but many more prehistoric sites are to be expected, especially in the foothills on the south side of the coastal plain.

A 69 KRINES: BRAIBEY *
EH I-III MH LH IIIA2-B

AD 21 (1966) B 123, 22 (1967) B 163.

The prehistoric settlement occupied the eastern tip of a long and low rounded hill, about 250 m. east-northeast to west-southwest by 100 m., called Litharakia. This is in the district named Braibey, about a kilometre south of Krines village and about 200 m. south of the new Corinth-Patras motorway, near the point where the old road from Krines to Tarsina passes over it. The site is on a line of low ridges at the south end of the plain of Sikyon. A Mycenaean chamber tomb about a kilometre to southwest, near the hamlet of Ellinochori, contained LH IIIA2-B pottery.

A 70 SIKYON (formerly VASILIKO) * # (Plate 10b)
MH LH I/II-IIIB

AJA 24 (1920) 10; *AA* (1939) 272; *CSHI* 67.

The prehistoric site is a hillock of "high mound" type on the east end of a spur projecting from the plateau on which lies the village of Sikyon. The hillock itself is small (about 85 m. northwest to southeast by 30 m.), but Mycenaean sherds were found in 1960 at least 100 m. down the slopes to north and northwest, and along the ridge on the west and southwest. Good Middle Helladic Matt-painted, one LH I/II, and fine quality LH IIIA and LH IIIB sherds were collected. The site overlooks the most fertile part of the Sikyon plain, and also a small fertile valley to the northwest. The soil in the vicinity of the site is formed from white marl, in contrast to the infertile soil of the plateau to south, on which Hellenistic and Roman Sicyon was built.

Gebauer (*AA loc.cit.*) claimed that the hill with the

mediaeval castle named Xerokastelli, to south of ancient Sicyon, was the site of a Mycenaean "Wachtstelle". He also noted a Mycenaean grave nearby.

A 71 MOULKI
LH III(A-B)

JHS 68 (1948) 60 n. 22.

Mycenaean tombs have been reported at Moulki, about 1.5 km. north of Sikyon. These may either belong to the site at Sikyon (A 70) or else represent a further Mycenaean settlement on the edge of the coastal plain.

A 72 LALIOTI
LH   C

AA (1939) 272.

Gebauer reported obsidian and Classical sherds from Ayios Ioannis, about a kilometre north of Lalioti. He was shown a Mycenaean vase apparently found near Lalioti.

A 73 MELISSI and THOLERON
EH II   MH   LH

AA (1939) 275.

Between Melissi and Tholeron, and closer to Tholeron, Gebauer discovered a site described as about 200 m. in diameter, occupied in the EH, MH, and LH periods. Two other EH sites were also found in this area, to north and south respectively.

A 74 MERTEIKA
EH II   LH

AA (1939) 287.

Gebauer noted fine EH and LH sherds on a site near the village of Merteika, which is about 3 km. southwest of Xylokastro. The site is apparently on the slopes of a hill near the northern exit of the valley which runs inland to southwest of Xylokastro. But Gebauer's directions are insufficient.

A 75 PITSA
LH I   A   C

AA (1935) 197; *Alin* 61.

In a cave near Pitsa Archaic and Classical terracottas were found and a Mycenaean sherd. There is also an unpublished LH I tomb group in the Corinth Museum from the vicinity of Pitsa. It will be published by Miss H. Palaiologos of Greek Archaeological Service, who has kindly given permission for this advance mention.

SOUTHEAST CORINTHIA (A76-78)

This is a district of lesser importance. But "exten-

sive" search by Gebauer [*AA* (1939) 270] demonstrates that more Mycenaean sites are to be expected. Unfortunately, in several cases the surface pottery could not be definitively attributed to specific prehistoric periods. Gebauer's reports must accordingly be assessed with caution, and some of his sites are therefore not marked on Map A.

A 76 GALATAKI   *
LH IIA-IIIA1   A   C

AE (1956) *Parartema* 8; *PAE* (1958) 135; *AD* 16 (1960) B 81; *Archaeology* 15 (1962) 184; *AA* (1939) 270.

On a low hill about 300 m. southwest of Galataki five Mycenaean chamber tombs were excavated. They had been disturbed in later times, and in one of the chambers there was a deposit of some 1,000 vases and 50 figurines, ranging from "Sub-Geometric" to the early 5th century B.C. An archaic sanctuary was later found about 50 m. to the north, but the absence of late Mycenaean and Dark Age finds make it unlikely that there was any cult here previously. There is no clear evidence for a Mycenaean habitation site on the hill, but reported finds of obsidian suggest prehistoric settlement. Gebauer (*AA loc.cit.*) reported traces of a Mycenaean site at an unspecified location near Galataki, and Early Helladic finds on the hill of Brielthi just before Mertesa on the road from Galataki. He surmised that Brielthi was also a Mycenaean site. In default of precise evidence, these reports require confirmation.

A 77 ATHIKIA: AYIOS NIKOLAOS etc.
LH   C

RE Suppl. VI (1935) 606; *AA* (1939) 270; *Alin* 58.

Mycenaean and Classical sherds were found by Gebauer (*AA loc.cit.*) near Ayios Nikolaos, on the saddle by Athikia (where the "Apollo of Tenea" was found). He also found Mycenaean and later traces on the west side of Dyovouna, the ridge which separates the plains of Athikia and Alamanou, and Bronze Age sherds at Alamanou (*cf. RE loc.cit.* for Mycenaean finds from a cult cave here). Ålin (*loc.cit.*) separates the three sites (as "Dyovuna", Alamanu", and "Ayios Nikolaos"), but it is not clear whether or not the Mycenaean traces represent more than one settlement in this area.

A 77A KLENIES: AYIA PARASKEVI (Not marked on Map A)
LH?   A   C   H

AA (1939) 271.

Gebauer reported Bronze Age sherds in the vicinity of ancient Tenea (*cf.* Fig. 1 here), at Ayia Paraskevi near Klenies, on the ridge to south of the plain.

A 78 KATAKALI: MALLIA TUMSA
LH   C

AA (1939) 271.

Gebauer reported a Classical site at Ayios Antonios near Katakali and Vlaseika, and Mycenaean sherds on the low hill of Mallia Tumsa nearby.

A 78A SOPHIKON: AYIA PARASKEVI (Not marked on Map A)
LH?

AA (1930) 270.

Prehistoric sherds, possibly Mycenaean, were reported by Gebauer from the hill of Ayia Paraskevi, about 2.5 km. east of Sophikon.

A 78B KORPHOS: PANAYIA and PROFITIS ILIAS (Not marked on Map A)
EH LH?

AA (1939) 270.

Gebauer reported Early Helladic sherds from the vicinity of the chapel of Panayia, overlooking the sea, and about 3.5 km. east-northeast of Korphos. He also marked another site, at Profitis Ilias about 2.5 km. east of Korphos, as possibly Mycenaean.

THE LOUTRAKI AREA AND THE PERACHORA PENINSULA (A 79-87)

This district was probably subordinate in Mycenaean times to the Corinth and Isthmia areas, to which it is most closely linked by both land and sea communications. Fieldwork by the British School of Archaeology at Athens in the Perachora vicinity and by Gebauer in the Loutraki area has revealed several Mycenaean sites, but none of them appear to have been of importance. Much of the land, especially in the Perachora peninsula, is marginal.

A 79 KALAMAKI
EH II MH LH III(A-B)

Corinth I 114; *Alin* 60.

A prehistoric settlement was found on the hill above the village of Kalamaki, about 1.5 km. northeast of the southeast end of the Corinth canal.

A 80 DAMARI
LH III(A-B)

AA (1939) 269.

A Mycenaean site was recorded by Gebauer about 50 m. west of the road at a point about a kilometre to south of Loutraki.

A 81 LOUTRAKI: ASPRA CHOMATA
EH II MH LH

AA (1939) 69.

Aspra Chomata is described as a small hill, about

halfway between Loutraki and Loutraki railway station, and more than a kilometre to east of the road from Corinth.

A 82 LOUTRAKI: AYIA KYRIAKI
EH II MH LH IIIC

AA (1939) 269.

Gebauer reported a small Mycenaean site on a high hill about 2 km. east of Loutraki, near the chapel of Ayia Kyriaki. Sherds from here in the BSA collection include Middle Helladic and LH IIIC.

A 83 LOUTRAKI MOUNTAIN
LH A

H. Payne *et al.*, *Perachora I* (1940) vii, 17; *Corinth I* 114 n. 1.

On the slopes immediately below the pointed summit of Loutraki mountain Dunbabin noted Mycenaean and Archaic sherds.

A 84 MODERN PERACHORA: AYIOS DEMETRIOS
EH II LH III(A-B)

AA (1939) 269.

EH II and LH III sherds were noted by Gebauer on the low saddle between the hills of Magoula and Ayios Demetrios, to south of Perachora village.

A 85 LOUTRAKI: (SITE TO NORTHWEST)
LH

Perachora I 20.

A Mycenaean stirrup-jar was found at a location described as halfway between Loutraki and the Cape Perachora lighthouse. This would appear to be about 5 km. northwest of Loutraki, but the exact position needs to be confirmed.

A 86 PERACHORA: LAKE VOULIAGMENI (east side)
MH? LH A

Perachora I 9, 20.

On a path from modern Perachora village to the Heraion at Cape Perachora (A 87) some Mycenaean and Archaic sherds were found near the eastern end of Lake Vouliagmeni. Some distance to east of the lake were traces of rock-cut pit graves, possibly Middle Helladic.

A 87 THE HERAION AT CAPE PERACHORA *
N EH I-II MH? LH IIIB-C G A C H

Perachora I 9, 20, 51.

During the excavations of the sanctuary of Hera Akraia at Cape Perachora some prehistoric material was found. EH I-II and LH IIIB-C are certainly represented, and one sherd (*Perachora I* Pl. 10:16) may be late MH. But the evidence did not suggest anything more than a small fishing community here in prehistoric times.

A 88 SCHOINOS
LH C

AA (1939) 270.

Mycenaean and Classical sherds were reported from the peninsula northeast of Schoinos harbour.

A 89 MEGARA # (Plate 11b)
EH II MH LH I? LH III(A-B) G A C H

MV 83; Fimmen (1921) 9; *Alin* 114.

Before the acropolis of ancient Megara (in the centre of the modern town) was completely built over. EH, MH, and LH sherds and Cyclopean walling were observed. The site is well placed to command both the small coastal plain and the fertile valley stretching inland to the northwest. The Mycenaean settlement here was probably important.

A 90 MEGARA: PALAIOKASTRO * # (Plate 11b)
EH II MH LH I/II-IIIB C

AM 29 (1904) 94; *BSA* 19 (1912-13) 70; *PAE* (1934) 50; *Alin* 114 s.v. "Nisäa".

This prominent hill of "high mound" type, near the shore, is crowned by the ruins of a small mediaeval fort. According to Highbarger [*The History and Civilization of Megara* (1927)], this site is not that of ancient Nisaia. It has been equated with ancient Minoa (*BSA loc.cit.*), and this identification seems the more likely, since the site may once have been an island (*cf.* Pausanias I 44, 3), in view of the marsh now around it. The top surface of the hill is small (only about 90 m. in diameter), but Mycenaean and earlier fine sherds have been found (some of which are in the BSA collection). All the Mycenaean periods are represented except LH IIIC, but LH IIIA and LH IIIB sherds predominate. Trial excavations suggest almost continuous occupation from the EH II to the LH IIIB periods.

Little exploration has been carried out in the remainder of the Megarid. Sherds in the BSA collection from the acropolis of Pagai, on the north coast near Kato Alepochorion, include EH II-III and MH (*CG* Figs. 10-14); and cist tombs, apparently of the late MH period, have been found at Moulki, near Ayioi Theodhoroi on the south coast [*AD* 24 (1969) B 103]. Mycenaean settlement appears likely at both locations.

APPENDIX TO MAP A

THE MYCENAEAN SETTLEMENTS IN THE ARGOLID AND CORINTHIA: GEOGRAPHY, POLITICS, AND HISTORY.

A long discussion of the prehistoric sites in and around the plain of Argos and of their environment has recently been presented by J.L. Bintliff [Bintliff (1977) 271-369, 689-703, and *passim*]. Bintliff is an excellent field worker, and his explorations have added greatly to our understanding of the geology and geography of the region. He is also an ardent disciple of Vita-Finzi, and indeed far exceeds his master in proseletyzing zeal. As an apostle of geographical determinism, he is at pains to demonstrate that the position and relative size of prehistoric settlements depends almost entirely on their local land resources, and owes little or nothing to political or strategic considerations. This theory or rationale is at least partially tenable as regards the Early Helladic period, but less so for the Middle Helladic period, while for the Mycenaean period, where "incipient urbanisation" is observable, it is quite inadequate.

The obvious phenomena of the fortresses of Mycenae and Tiryns, and of some other major Mycenaean monuments, constitute for Bintliff an embarrassing dilemma, as does the network of Mycenaean roads in the Argolid and Corinthia. He largely ignores or suppresses the evidence (especially that set out in *MMA* 86-88) for the Mycenaean roads, and embraces outmoded arguments for a later date for some of the "Cyclopean" bridges [Bintliff (1977) 287, 294, *cf.* 304]. Yet he assumes without hesitation a Mycenaean date for the Tiryns dam, although there is as yet no definite proof of this date. In this particular case, the evidence revealed by its construction, and that of the canal dug to accommodate the diverted stream, is seemingly crucial to his simplified analysis (alluvial deposits are usually organised by Bintliff to conform either to an "Older Fill" or to a "Younger Fill") of the geological history of the area.

Despite Bintliff's somewhat strained arguments to the contrary, Mycenae is obviously an excellent choice as a site for a fortress. And the hard limestone, so insistently declared by Bintliff to be unsuitable for settlement sites, was frequently chosen by the Mycenaeans for its excellect properties, both to provide good building stone and to serve as a stable base for their fortification walls and house foundations. And, since such elaborate measures were taken by the Mycenaeans to ensure a permanent water supply for Mycenae, Tiryns, Athens, and Pylos, it is surely perverse to argue that this consideration was of minor concern to them.

Bintliff's analysis of Mycenae (*op.cit.* 294-305 and 345-7) involves a particularly unsuccessful attempt to make the archaeological data fit the theory of geographical determinism, and results in a compromise, which finally admits the strategic importance of Mycenae, and is thus inconsistent with the previous arguments concerning the (supposed) inferiority of the Mycenae citadel site. In the case of Tiryns, Bintliff more readily admits that "Tiryns is archaeologically more important than its land resources would suppose, and this must almost certainly relate to its role as the chief marine site for the region" (*op.cit.* 698).

There is perhaps a need to remind some archaeologists and historians of the relevance of geographical factors, but there is at the same time no need to ex-
aggerate their importance. Bintliff's detailed field
observations are, fortunately, more valuable than
some of the conclusions which he derives from them;
and all that is required, to maintain the proper balance
between geographical and political considerations, is
the exercise of a little common sense.

The most hypothetical part of Bintliff's analysis is
contained in an appendix (*op.cit.* 689 ff.), in which he
superimposes on the observed (and incomplete) data a
rigid pattern of territorial divisions or "cells". These
are manufactured from conjectured "Thiessen Polygons", based on a combination of observed spatial relationships between discovered sites and a calculation
of the land resources that would have been available
in their vicinities. The resulting "maps" (*op.cit.* Appendix 1a to 2e) reflect by their artificiality the arbitrary
nature of the criteria employed. They also involve considerable distortion of the detailed and cautious observations made by those (including Bintliff) who recorded the data in the field.

As might be expected, the sites included within
the arbitrary "cells" do not conform to any special pattern. Some of the "cells" have very large or "capital"
sites as their nuclei, others have no sites at all. In some
cases we may expect a geographical reason for the differences, since fewer sites, let alone sites of importance,
are to be expected in the mountainous areas surrounding the Argos plain, for instance. In other cases, however, it is obvious that the explanations are largely
social or political. In the Early Helladic period it is apparent that there were fewer large centres. But by Mycenaean times a considerable measure of synoecism is
evident. Thus even in the more fertile parts of the ancient plain of Argos no uniformity of site distribution
or size is to be expected.

Since few areas of Mycenaean Greece have been
adequately explored, it is not possible to present a detailed refutation of some of Bintliff's more radical assertions concerning "settlement hierarchy" and similar analyses. But readers should be warned that "Peak
Sanctuaries", for instance, should be identified only
on the basis of *suitable* finds, such as statuettes or
hoards of figurines, which may reasonably be associated with a "cult" (kylix and cup fragments, for example, are so ubiquitous on Mycenaean sites that they
alone can not be used as evidence for cult).

Above all, it should be remembered that land
available for agriculture has not always been used for
that purpose. And the actual position of settlements is
not always determined by a (supposed) priority need
to be as close as possible to the land to be cultivated.
Reasons for the choice of a particular site may indeed
include an assured water supply (either from perennial springs or from reliable wells), a good supply of
building stone, a firm base for foundations, and de-
fensibility. The Mycenaeans, in particular, evidently
had good reason to be preoccupied with defensive
measures, as is dramatically illustrated by the vast
scale of their defence preparations and by the overwhelming evidence for man-made destructions and
disruptions at the end of the LH IIIB period.

ATTICA
SALAMIS

SOUTHERN EUBOEA
EASTERN BOEOTIA

MAP B

ATTICA AND SALAMIS (B 1-44)

Attica is separated from central Greece by Mt. Parnes, and the major plains of Attica are separated from one another by the ranges of Mt. Hymettos, Mt. Pendeli, and Mt. Aigaleos. The best land in Attica lies in the eastern Mesogaia plain, beyond Pendeli and Hymettos; and this area may have been better watered in antiquity before wholesale deforestation. Elsewhere in Attica, Mycenaean settlement was predominantly coastal.

In the early part of the Mycenaean period, the tholos tombs at Thorikos (B 22) and Marathon (B 41) suggest that Athens had not yet attained control over the rest of Attica. And, if the rich tombs at Menidi (B 10) and Spata (B 35), for instance, are to be taken as indications of independent major sites, synoecism under Athens may not have been complete even in the LH IIIB period. The numerous chamber tomb cemeteries, especially near the southwest and east coasts, demonstrate a considerable population at this time; and the extremely large LH IIIB2-C cemetery at Porto Rafti (B 30), together with the LH IIIC and Sub-Mycenaean tombs on Salamis (B 16-8), show a continuing, or increased, prosperity in some regions even after the LH IIIB disruptions. Athens itself also survived the disasters, and became the leading site in Attica in the Dark Age.

B 1 ATHENS: THE ACROPOLIS and ENVIRONS * # (Fig. 15)

N EH I-II MH LH I-IIIC SMyc PG G A C H

1. The Acropolis and the North Slope

S. Iakovidis, *He Mykenaike Akropolis ton Athenon* (1962); Desborough (1964) 113; *Hesperia* 2 (1933) 356, 4 (1935) 109, 6 (1937) 539, 8 (1939) 317; *OpAth* 4 (1962) 31; *AD* 24 (1970) A 174, B 25, 26 (1971) B 29; *Agora XIII* 1, 51, 112, 261; Schoder (1974) 28.

Middle Helladic material is abundant on the sum-

mit and on the North Slope of the Acropolis. Fragments of "palatial" LH IIA vases give the impression that Athens was already a centre of some importance by this time. Traces of a system of terraces which could have supported a palace have been identified in the central part of the Acropolis, and some house remains on the north and south. But the most impressive Mycenaean remains are the "Cyclopean" fortifications, which enclosed an area about 280 m. east to west by 120 m. (maximum dimensions). The walls were up to 5.20 m. thick, and there are remains of massive gateways on the southwest and northeast, both protected by bastions resembling that of the "Lion Gate" at Mycenae. On the north slope a shaft was cut to enlarge and extend an opening in the rock leading to a spring chamber or "fountain" [*Hesperia* 8 (1939) 317]. The shaft reached a depth of 34.50 m. below ground surface, and a Mycenaean stairway of eight flights was constructed to provide access to the water supply. The shaft seems to have been cut late in the LH IIIB period, at which time houses appear to have been built over a stairway leading to a postern gate on the north.

Excavations on the North Slope yielded important evidence of houses outside the citadel which were abandoned in the same period. To this evidence of troubled times may be added the hoard of bronzes hidden in the wall of a house on the south of the acropolis, probably also at the end of the LH IIIB period. On the other hand, the rubbish thrown into the "Fountain", and material from the Acropolis, indicate a fairly substantial settlement in the LH IIIC period. The latest remains include fourteen cist burials, mostly of children, which are attributable to the Sub-Mycenaean phase [*AJA* 69 (1965) 176]; and a vase from a cutting in the Klepsydra area is probably also of this period (*Agora XIII* Pl. 64:482).

2. The Agora and Adjacent Slopes

Agora XIII passim; AR (1972-3) 4, (1973-4) 4; *Hesperia* 44 (1975) 375; Schoder (1974) 28.

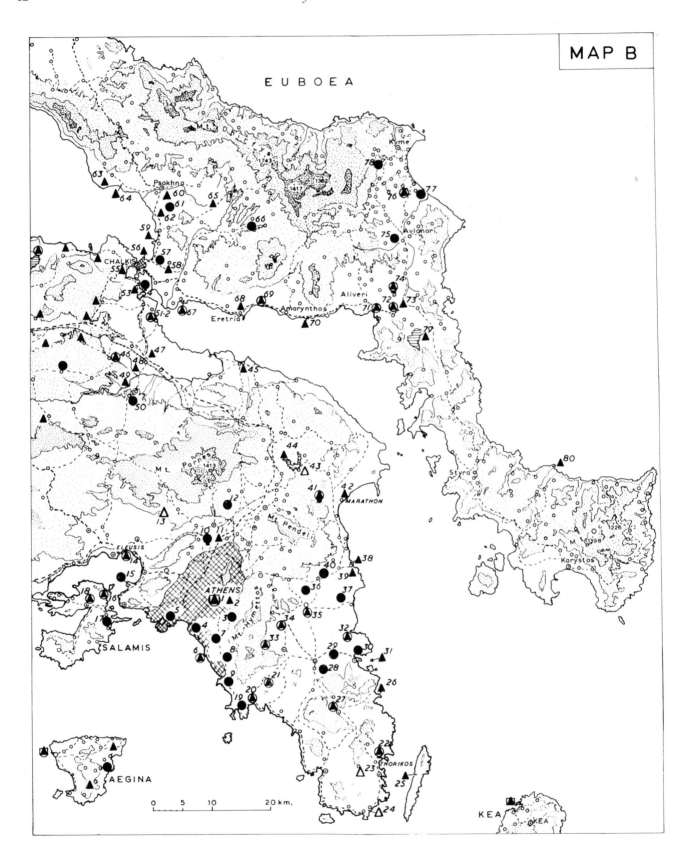

The area of the Agora was apparently the chief cemetery for Mycenaean Athens. Several chamber tombs were dug into the slopes of the surrounding hills, the richest being those on the Areopagus slope (Tombs I and III). Groups of graves including chamber tombs, cists and pits were found in the west, centre, and especially the east and northeast parts of the Agora. The earliest burial can be assigned to the LH IIA period (*Hesperia loc.cit*), but most are of LH IIIA1-2 date, the richest being almost entirely LH IIIA1. Only a few burials are later, and LH IIIC material is notably rare (Tomb VI is probably of this phase, as may be the latest burials in Tomb VII). This could indicate a move to a new burial ground. An important find, however, is a fragment of a LH IIIC "Octopus stirrup-jar" (*Agora XIII* 266, no. 503). Little Mycenaean domestic material has been found in the Agora. Only two small wells of the period have been found (*Agora XIII* 11). Graves and another well (*Agora XIII* 112, 261, well U26:4) are attributed to the Sub-Mycenaean phase, and the area continued in use without a break after this period.

3. The North and Northwest Areas

The Kerameikos: Kerameikos I, IV 32; *AM* 32 (1907) 157, 558, 78 (1963) 148: *AA* (1936) 197; *Hesperia* 30 (1961) 174; *AD* 19 (1964) B 42.

The Odos Kriezis Cemetery: AD 22 (1967) B 92, 23 (1968) B 67; *AAA* 1 (1968) 20.

The Acharnian Gate: AM 18 (1893) 77 (*cf. Kerameikos I* 132).

The Academy: AJA 41 (1937) 138; *AA* (1937) 117; *PAE* (1955) 56, (1956) 53; *AD* 16 (1960) B 33, 18 (1963) B 41, 21 (1966) B 63; Schoder (1974) 38.

In the Kerameikos area, over a kilometre to northwest of the Acropolis, pottery which may represent a LH IIIB-C settlement has been found (*Kerameikos I* 109); but the most important remains from this area are the Sub-Mycenaean and later cemeteries. A complete LH IIIC "Octopus stirrup-jar" from near the Dipylon Gate may have been removed from a looted tomb and reburied, like the stirrup-jar in Tomb PG 1. One tomb (Tomb 106) has been attributed to late LH IIIC, but might be later. Sub-Mycenaean graves were found to north and south of the Eridanos stream, most being on the north in the area of the later Pompeion. Although badly disturbed, this group consisted of over one hundred graves, often arranged in regular rows. Other Sub-Mycenaean graves have been found in the Odos Kriezis cemetery further north, including two cremation burials with weapons, and a single grave was found near the Acharnian Gate. Finds in a small settlement on the site of the Academy, over 2 km. northwest of the Acropolis, include Mycenaean.

4. South Athens *cf.* M. Pantelidou, *Hai Proistorikai Athenai* (1975).

The South Slope of the Acropolis and Vicinity: AJA 9 (1894) 113; *AE* (1902) 123; *AM* 35 (1910) 35; *Ann.* 13-14 (1930-1) 411; *Hesperia* 5 (1936) 20; *AD* 17 (1961-2) A 85, 90, 18 (1963) B 14,

19 (1964) A 62, B 24, 20 (1965) B 26, 21 (1967) B 36; (*cf. Agora XIII* 53 for discussion).

The Muses' Hill: AD 19 (1964) B 49 (*cf. Agora XIII* 113).

The Olympieion Area: BCH 64-5 (1940-1) 238, 84 (1960) 634; *AR* (1960-1) 3; *AD* 17 (1961-2) B 10, 20 (1965) B 90, 21 (1966) B 83; (*cf. Agora XIII* 54, 114 for discussion); Schoder (1974) 36.

Odos Erechtheiou (Tombs): PAE (1955) 43; *AD* 21 (1966) B 71, 23 (1968) B 55.

Odos Demetrakopoulou (Tombs): AD 21 (1966) B 85, *AAA* 3 (1970) 171; *AD* 25 (1970) B 55 [*cf. Hesperia* 35 (1966) 55 n. 2].

Other Tombs: AA (1931) 213; *AD* 22 (1967) B 73, 112, 23 (1968) B 48, 73, 24 (1969) B 68, 73, 25 (1970) B 44, 70, 71; *AAA* 4 (1971) 433.

There is considerable, although sporadic, evidence for habitation south of the Acropolis, particularly in Mycenaean and Sub-Mycenaean times. Graves of all periods from LH I/IIA [*AD* 24 (1969) B 68] to Sub-Mycenaean have been found. There are some rich LH IIB-IIIA1 graves [*AA* (1931) 213; *AD* 25 (1970) B 44], and a LH IIIC stirrup-jar probably from a grave, and Sub-Mycenaean vases from a chamber tomb [*AD* 25 (1970) B 71]. It seems probable that Mycenaean settlement to south of the Acropolis was as extensive as that to north of it (*cf. Agora XIII* 113).

In general, Mycenaean Athens appears to have been comparable in size to Mycenaean Tiryns, although the exact extent of the "Lower Town" of both is hard to gauge.

B 2 KAISARIANI MONASTERY
EH LH III(A2-)B C

JHS 87 (1967) 183.

Some Mycenaean sherds (now in the BSA collection) were found on the saddle of the ridge to south of, and above, the monastery, on the left of the track to Ayios Markos.

B 3 MT. HYMETTOS *
EH II MH LH IIIA1? LH IIIA2-B PG G A C H

AJA 44 (1940) 1; *BSA* 42 (1947) 57; *PAE* (1950) 158; *Bulletin Antike Beschaving* 48 (1973) 91.

One Early Helladic and one Mycenaean sherd were found in the area of the Sanctuary of Zeus to north of the summit of Mt. Hymettos, together with Protogeometric and later material. Mycenaean is also reported from a cave at the foot of the mountain (*PAE loc.cit.*), and goods appear to have come from chamber tombs on the west side. An unusual vase of ritual appearance is also reported to be from a cave on Mt. Hymettos. It may be of the LH IIIA1 period [*BSA* 42 (1947) 57].

B 4 PALAION PHALERON *
LH IIIA2 G

Fimmen (1921) 8; *CVA* Karlsruhe I Pls. 1:8, 2:1, 5; *AA* (1943) 303; *BSA* 42 (1947) 8.

Chamber tombs have been found in the neighbourhood of Old Phaleron, some at Kalamaki. Some rich contents are reported.

B 5   PEIRAEUS: CHARAUGI
LH IIIA2-B

AD 21 (1966) B 106; *PAE* (1935) 159; Schoder (1974) 176.

Remains of a Mycenaean burial were found in the Charaugi area of Peiraeus, and a tall-stemmed kylix and a bridge-sprouted jar were recovered. Mycenaean sherds were apparently found on the slopes of the hill to southwest of Munychia harbour. But these finds are not confirmed, and the area is now built over.

B 6   AYIOS KOSMAS *
EH II-III   MH   LH IIA-IIIC

G.E. Mylonas, *Aghios Kosmas* (1959); Desborough (1964) 18.

The low promontory of Ayios Kosmas is close to Athens Airport, on the southwest coast of Attica. It was originally more extensive on the south side, where the prehistoric remains are now under water. The settlement seems to have been more important in the Early Helladic period than later. But there are remains of LH IIA structures and graves of similar date at the southwest end, and extensive though fragmentary remains of LH III structures. A krater from House T is probably LH IIIA1, and other pottery from this house and House S is LH IIIA2-B. Mycenaean children's graves were widespread. A wall along the south and east edge of the site may be part of a fortification. Two vases were found in its entrance area, a LH IIIB stirrup-jar, and a deep bowl almost certainly LH IIIC. While the presence of whole vases in the houses might suggest hasty desertion at some time in the LH IIIB period, this deep bowl appears to show some later use of the site.

B 7   TRACHONES
EH II   LH IIIB   G   A   C

MV 37; *BSA* 42 (1947) 4; *AR* (1951-2) 25; Mylonas (1959) 4.

Mycenaean vases, apparently found in chamber tombs, are reported from this suburb near Athens Airport, but no precise location is given.

B 8   PYRNARI
LH III(A-B)

MV 37; *BSA* 42 (1947) 4.

Some Mycenaean vases are reported from this district, but the exact location is not known. They presumably came from chamber tombs.

B 9   VOULA: ALIKI *
EH?   LH IIA-IIIC   PG   G

MV 37; *BSA* 42 (1947) 4; *PAE* (1954) 72, (1955) 78, (1957) 29.

Chamber tombs have been identified here on two occasions. Furtwaengler (*MV loc.cit.*) reported that Aliki was the source of various Mycenaean vases on the market; and fourteen chamber tombs were later excavated (*PAE loc.cit.*). The latter are on the east side of the road to Sounion, near the seaside resort of Voula. They were dug in the soft rock of gentle slopes. Large numbers of burials and vases (predominantly LH IIIA-B) were found in the tombs, but few other goods. Further burials were often found in niches and pits in the dromoi.

B 10   ACHARNAI: THE MENIDI THOLOS TOMB
* #   (Plate 28b) (Fig. 5)
LH III(A2-B)   G   A   C

MV 39; H.G. Lolling *et al.*, *Das Kuppelgrab bei Menidi* (1880); *JdI* 14 (1899) 114; *BSA* 53-4 (1958-9) 293.

This famous tholos tomb, at Lykotrypa about 2 km. south of Acharnai, had an unusually long dromos (26.5 m.) and, instead of the normal "relieving triangle", a series of horizontal slabs with spaces between them (Plate 28b). The chamber (diameter 8.35 m.) had a stone bench built against the wall. The remains of six burials were recorded, accompanied by much pottery, including four "Canaanite" amphorae, jewellery, finely carved ivories, stone vases, bronze arrowheads, and boar's tusk plates for helmets. The Mycenaean pottery, which is mostly plain or worn, may belong mainly or entirely to the LH IIIB period.

B 11   NEA IONIA: NEMESIS #   (Fig. 5)
N   MH?   LH IIIA(1?)-B   C

BSA 53-4 (1958-9) 292.

The low hill named Nemesis lies only about a kilometre to southeast of the Menidi tholos tomb (Figure 5). Its top surface now measures about 160 m. northwest to southeast by 120 m., but the hill has been heavily eroded, especially on the west and southwest edges, so that its original size was probably considerably larger than at present, perhaps about 30,000 m². Mycenaean sherds were found over the whole area, though mainly in the eroded parts on the west and southwest, where remains of rubble walling were observed in association with the sherds. The remains were particularly noticeable in the sides of the steep cliffs formed by erosion here. In one place the Mycenaean deposit appeared to be over a metre in thickness. On the top of the hill, however, the total depth of earth is often less than one metre, and the natural rock protrudes in several places. No traces of ancient buildings were observed here, and there were fewer recognizable sherds. Military trenches (from World War II) on the edges of the hilltop have created further disturbance.

The Mycenaean remains are not by themselves impressive but an exhaustive search in the vicinity of the Menidi tomb (B 10) for at least 2 km. in every direc-

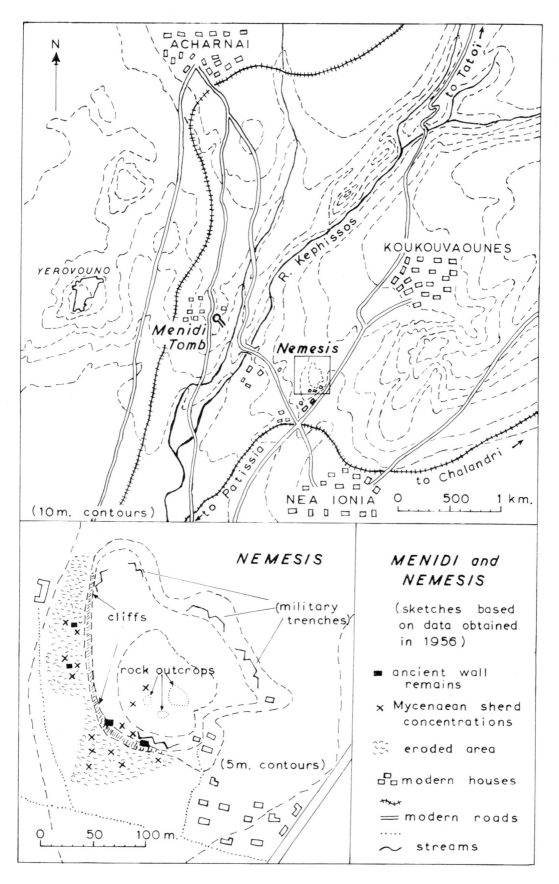

Figure 5

tion revealed no trace of any other Mycenaean settlement. A LH IIIA1 vase (*CVA* Karlsruhe I Pl. 2:3) is said to have been found at Koukouvaones, about a kilometre to the northeast, but this is probably from a tomb. Since the Nemesis settlement has been badly damaged by erosion and construction, it is difficult to determine whether or not it would originally have been sufficiently important to have been the seat of the "dynasty" for whom the Menidi tomb was presumably constructed.

B 12　DEKELEA: TATOI
LH IIIA2-B

MV 41.

A Mycenaean stirrup-jar is said to have been found in this district, near the lower slopes of Mt. Parnes.

B 13　CHASIA: THE CAVE OF PAN
MH　LH III(C?)　C

AE (1906) 100; *Alin* 111.

In the Cave of Pan on Mt. Parnes, about 4 km. north of Chasia, MH Matt-painted and Mycenaean sherds were found. It has been deduced from the description (*AE loc.cit.*) that the Mycenaean sherds belong to the LH IIIC period (*Alin* 112 n. 3).

B 14　ANCIENT ELEUSIS　*
EH II-III　MH　LH I-IIIB　PG　G　A　C　H

1. The Settlement

AE (1889) 187, (1898) 51, (1912) 2; *AD* 13 (1930-31) *Parartema* 2, 15 (1933-5) *Parartema* 23; *AJA* 36 (1932) 104, 37 (1933) 271, 40 (1936) 415; *PAE* (1952) 55; G.E. Mylonas, *Proistorike Eleusis* (1932), *The Homeric Hymn to Demeter and her Sanctuary at Eleusis* (1942), *Eleusis and the Eleusinian Mysteries* (1961) Chapter II; Schoder (1974) 62.

The site of Eleusis is now surrounded by an industrial area, and the acropolis itself has been ruined by quarrying. It was previously heavily eroded on the top; and it is difficult to estimate the size of the prehistoric settlement, since the remains, found on the south and east slopes, were mostly disturbed and/or covered by later buildings. The earliest preserved structures are Middle Helladic. In the south area these were succeeded by an early Mycenaean building. The main periods represented by building remains are LH IIA and LH IIIA2-B. The latter are best preserved in two areas. The first is near the top of the acropolis, where walls 0.90 m. thick, associated with LH IIIA2 pottery and figurines, may have been foundations of terrace walls for retaining important buildings. The other area is on the east slope, below the later Telesterion. Here there seems to have been a building of megaron type, surrounded by an enclosure wall, in front of which was a raised platform.

Very little evidence for dating was found. Sherds from either side of the megaron and the enclosure wall have suggested a date at the end of the LH II period, while pottery from a later structure founded partly on the megaron and partly on the platform is assigned to LH IIIB, although two Geometric fragments were found 0.05 m. above the final floor (Mylonas 1961, 37). A fresco fragment was found in this area (Mylonas 1961, 43). The argument that these buildings had a religious purpose is not well supported by the remains; and there is no evidence for continuity of occupation or use in the area between the end of the LH IIIB period and the beginning of the 8th century B.C., the date of the first remains of a Telesterion.

Remains of the LH III and Geometric periods are also reported from the Kallichoron area [*PAE* (1952) 55, *cf. Archaeology* 5 (1952) 249, Mylonas 1961, 45], and a patch of a LH III floor below the Lesser Propylaea. An inscribed stirrup-jar was found on this, with pottery that has been assigned to the LH IIIC period (Mylonas 1961, 49), but is not published. With the exception of this pottery, whose date appears doubtful, nothing has been reported from Eleusis of a date later than the LH IIIB or earlier than the late Protogeometric period [Desborough (1964) 114].

The remains of Mycenaean settlement at Eleusis suggest that it was then a place of some importance, but it cannot be assumed to have been fortified merely on the basis of the Homeric *Hymn to Demeter*. Eleusis itself may have been abandoned for a considerable time after the end of the LH IIIB period; although occupation may have continued somewhere else in the Eleusis plain, which has not yet been searched by archaeologists.

2. The Tombs

G.E. Mylonas, *To Dytikon Nekrotapheion tes Eleusinos* (1975); *cf.* also preliminary reports in *PAE* (1938) 40, (1950) 127, (1952) 58, (1953) 77, (1954) 50, (1955) 67, (1956) 57; *AE* (1953-4) I 35.

A number of cist tombs, of dates ranging from the Middle Helladic to the LH IIB periods, were found on the site, but most of the excavated prehistoric graves were found in a cemetery on the north slopes of the acropolis hill, about 750 m. northwest of the Telesterion. They covered a wide area (over 300 m. in length). Later graves and constructions may have destroyed many prehistoric graves, but over 130 have survived, ranging from the late Middle Helladic to the LH IIIB periods. All except four were stone built, progressing from Middle Helladic cists to large rectangular built graves with an entrance (presumably intended as family tombs), which were developed by the end of the Middle Helladic period and continued to be built and used in Mycenaean times. Four graves were earth-cut chamber tombs, used in the LH IIIA2-B periods but no later (bronzes from tomb CT 11 might be LH II). None of the graves was particularly rich in goods. The area was not used again for burials until the Early Geometric period. The lack of evidence for use in the LH IIIC period seems to strengthen the argument (expressed above) that the settlement itself was not inhabited at this time.

B 15 PEIRAEUS: SKARAMANGA
LH III(A-B)

AA (1943) 303.

Two Mycenaean chamber tombs were reported near the suburb of Skaramanga, in the industrial district north of the Peiraeus, on a promontory opposite Salamis.

B 16 SALAMIS: THE ARSENAL *
LH IIIC? SMyc

MV 41, 83; Fimmen (1921) 9; *AM* 35 (1910) 17; *OpAth* 4 (1962) 103; Desborough (1964) 17, 37, 231, 252, 278 and *passim.*

A large Sub-Mycenaean cemetery was found here, of over one hundred graves, laid out in seven parallel rows. All except two were cists; the other two were pithos burials, one of which contained a cremation. The contents of the graves were mainly pottery, and most of this is Sub-Mycenaean, although a few vases may be slightly earlier (especially nos. 3614, 3632, and 3665). Some jewellery, and a plain bronze bowl, were also found.

Fimmen (*loc.cit.*) recorded part of a "Cyclopean" circuit wall above the arsenal, which may indicate a Mycenaean (or Sub-Mycenaean) settlement here.

B 17 SALAMIS: AMBELAKIA *
LH III(B-C?)

AR (1961-2) 7, (1963-4) 5; *AD* 17 (1961-2) B 39, 23 (1968) B 113, 27 (1972) B 179.

Mycenaean chamber tombs have been excavated at Ambelaki, and an intact chamber tomb at Limnionas, about a kilometre to the south, is reported to have contained cremations in addition to inhumations. It is assigned to the LH IIIB period. A "Submycenaean tholos tomb" reported from Kamini nearby seems more likely to be a chamber tomb and to be of the LH IIIC period. This also is reported to have contained both inhumations and cremations. Other pottery and bronzes evidently from tombs here have been handed in. None of this material has yet been published, and the dates therefore require confirmation. Further finds made at Kamini [*AD* 27 (1972) *loc.cit.*] seem to indicate a Mycenaean settlement here, near the historic centre of Ancient Salamis.

B 18 SALAMIS: Modern SALAMIS (formerly KOULOURIS) *
EH MH LH IIA-IIIC SMyc

AE (1916) 8, (1948-9) 114 n. 4; *AA* (1940) 183; *AJA* 54 (1950) 1; *AR* (1952) 27; *Hesperia* 33 (1964) 235; *AD* 20 (1965) B 125; *CVA* USA 4 Pls. 8:3, 9:2-5.

On the slopes of hills above the modern town of Salamis Early and Middle Helladic and Mycenaean sherds have been found (some of which are in the BSA collection). At Ayia Kyriaki on the east slopes of the hill of Profitis Ilias, to east of the town, is a large chamber tomb cemetery. Excavated vases have produced a range of pottery from the LH IIIA1 to the Sub-Mycenaean periods [*AD* 20 (1965) B Pls. 98-9]. It may also be the source of various vases (*e.g. CVA loc.cit.*) which were said to come from Salamis, and which include some of the LH II period. The Mycenaean settlement and cemetery here appear to be the most important on the island.

B 19 VOULIAGMENI
EH II MH LH IIB LH III(A-B) G

OpAth 6 (1950) 262 n. 1; *Alin* 106; *AA* (1962) 212.

Vases of the LH IIB and LH III periods have been recorded as from Vouliagmeni, apparently from separate tombs. The Vouliagmeni promontory was formerly strewn with prehistoric sherds, including EH II, and obsidian throughout its length, until the site was ruined by the enlargement of the resort. It is, however, uncertain whether this was also a Mycenaean site. Middle Helladic sherds were found at Mikro Kavouri nearby, and Geometric is also reported there [J.N. Coldstream, *Greek Geometric Pottery* (1968) 403, where the site is identified as Halai Aixonides].

B 20 VARI—VARKIZA: KAMINI * and AYIOS IOANNIS
EH II LH II-IIIB G A C H

BSA 42 (1947) 4; *BCH* 78 (1954) 110; *Antiquity* 24 (1960) 266; *AD* 16 (1960) B 39; *Alin* 106; *AAA* 1 (1968) 110, 7 (1974) 422.

A Mycenaean cemetery has been partly investigated on the lower part of the northeast slope of Kamini hill at the north edge of Varkiza [*cf.* the map on *AAA* 7 (1974) 428-9]. Various chamber tombs and pit graves have been excavated or plundered here. The pottery on show in the National Museum in Athens ranges from the LH IIA to the LH IIIB periods. The finds include a LM II vase and a gilded seal-ring. The LH IIA vase from "Vari" in the Robinson Collection (*CVA* USA 4 Pl. 8:2) and the LH IIIA2 vase from "Vari" in the British Museum (*CVA* BM IIIA Pl. 10:25, *cf. Alin* 106) are probably also to be attributed to the Kamini cemetery, since the coastal suburb of Varkiza is a recent development, and this area was formerly part of the territory of Vari.

The Vari-Varkiza area is identified as the ancient Attic deme on Anagyrous. At Ayios Ioannis, the ridge by the sea at the west end of the plain of Vari, EH II and LH III sherds were found together with later material. A Mycenaean site was formerly claimed at "Lathouresa" [*AA* (1970) 178, *cf. Alin* 106], but the walls found there are now assigned to the 5th or 4th century B.C. [C.W.J. Eliot, *Coastal Demes of Attica* (1962) 45, *cf. Hesperia* Suppl. XI (1966) 28, Fig. 6].

B 21 VARI: KITSI and VOURVATSI *
EH II   MH   LH IIIA1-C   C   H

AD 11 (1927-8) *Parartema* 65; *BSA* 42 (1947) 7; Desborough (1964) 112.

Kitsi is a prominent hill at the southwest edge of the Mesogaia plain, controlling the route into it from Vari. The small knoll on the top (about 60 m. east to west by 30 m.) and the upper west and northwest terraces (which extend about 150 m. northwest to southeast by 100 m.) are covered in sherds, mainly prehistoric, suggesting a total area of settlement of about 20,000 m². Mycenaean sherds (LH IIIA-B) were found, although not in quantity, both on the top and the terraces. Some thick wall foundations on the northwest may possibly be the remains of fortifications. The site is about 4 km. northeast of Vari, and about halfway between Koropi and Vari, so that it must presumably be the hill referred to by Kyparissis as lying above the Mycenaean cemetery at Vourvatsi, which is also described as being about halfway between Koropi and Vari.

Kyparissis investigated seven chamber tombs in a hill slope here, whose exact position is apparently no longer known. The cemetery was large, but most of the tombs had been plundered. The bulk of the pottery recovered is of the LH IIIA2-B periods, but some is of the LH IIIC period (Desborough, *loc.cit.*).

B 22 ANCIENT THORIKOS *
NH   EH II   MH   LH I-IIIB   PG   G   A   C   H

PAE (1893) 12; *AE* (1895) 229; *MMA* 383; *Thorikos I* 27, *III* 20, *IV* 53, *V* 21; *AR* (1973-4) 4; H. Mussche, *Thorikos, a Guide to the Excavations* (1974).

Ancient Thorikos has a high conical acropolis (Velatouri hill) overlooking two harbours on either side of the promontory of Ayios Nikolaos. Prehistoric remains are scattered over the hill, and especially the extensive south and east slopes, within an area about 500 m. in diameter. Material of the transitional period from Middle Helladic to Mycenaean is reported to be particularly widespread (*Thorikos IV* 68 n. 7); and, to judge from the discovery of litharge in a late Middle Helladic layer, silver was already being extracted from the Lavrion ores at this time. In the same area, on the saddle between the two summits of Velatouri, were three oval built tombs. One was large (9.0 m. by 3.0 m.) and domed like a tholos. It may have been built in the LH I period, and was certainly in use in the LH IIA period. Two smaller tombs of similar type had been robbed, but a LH IIA pyxis and jewellery were found in one of them. On the east slope was a tholos of more normal type (diameter 9.15 m.), built in the LH IIA period but also used later. This also had been robbed. These tombs show that this was an important centre in early Mycenaean times. Later Mycenaean remains are less impressive, although fine LH IIIA and LH IIIB sherds have been observed on the surface. There is as

yet no material from the site which can be certainly dated to any time between the LH IIIB and late Protogeometric periods.

B 23 LAVRION: KITSOS CAVE *
N   EH   MH   LH III(A-B)   C   H

AD 26 (1971) B 42, 27 (1972) B 183; *BCH* 97 (1973) 413; *AAA* 7 (1974) 8.

The Kitsos cave is about 5 km. west of Lavrion, on the east slope of Mikro Ripari hill near the village of Kamareza. It is important mainly for its Paleolithic and Neolithic deposits; but some Bronze Age sherds, including Mycenaean, were also found in the excavation.

B 24 SOUNION
LH

MV 39.

Mycenaean vases were reported from a location described as on the way from Sounion to Lavrion.

B 25 MAKRONISOS: LEONDARI
N?   EH II   MH   LH III(B-C)   C

BCH 96 (1972) 873; *AAA* 6 (1973) 1.

Leondari is a heavily eroded promontory on the west coast of Makronisos island, to south of the village of Ayios Yeoryios, and opposite Lavrion. Extensive but scattered traces of prehistoric settlement, including remains of walls and cists, were discovered by surface exploration over an area about 120 m. northwest to southeast by 30 m. They include Mycenaean sherds of the LH IIIB period or later (*i.e.*, coated deep bowls).

B 26 KAKI THALASSA: AYIOS PANDELEIMON
EH II   MH   LH   G   C

AA (1963) 458 and Pl. opposite p. 496; Fimmen (1921) 7; *CG* Fig. 14.

Kaki Thalassa is a small and steep promontory about 5 km. east-northeast of Keratea. The chapel of Ayios Pandeleimon on the top was the centre of a small prehistoric settlement, perhaps mainly important in the Early Helladic period (represented in the BSA collection). Some Middle Helladic is recorded (*CG loc.cit.*), and Mycenaean sherds both here and in a nearby cave (Fimmen, *loc.cit.*).

B 27 KERATEA: KEFALI
EH II   MH   LH III(A-B)   LH IIIC   G

AA (1916) 142, (1926) 400; *CVA* Karlsruhe 1 Pl. 1:1-2, 3 Pl. 2:4; *BSA* 42 (1947) 8, *AA* (1963) 457 and Pl. opposite p. 496.

Surface traces of prehistoric settlement were found by M.S.F. Hood in 1962 on Kefali hill, a low saddle about 1.5 km. northwest of Keratea, on the north side of the road, opposite the church of Ayia Triadha. Sherds were found of the EH II, MH, and LH III periods. But the "wahrscheinlich mykenische

Burg" claimed on the high ridge to the south [*AA* (1963) *loc.cit.*] must be discounted, since the ridge bears no trace whatever of Mycenaean habitation. Three vases of the LH IIIC period were found near Keratea (*CVA loc.cit.*), two of which were said to have come from a cave (*BSA loc.cit.*). One of them is an "Octopus stirrup-jar" of Perati type. Two Mycenaean chamber tombs have been reported in the neighbourhood [*AA* (1916), (1926) *loc.cit.*]; and it seems more likely that all the vases originally came from tombs.

B 28 MARKOPOULO: KOPREZA *
LH IIB-IIIC

AE (1895) 210; *BSA* 42 (1947) 6.

Twenty two chamber tombs were excavated at Kopreza, about 2 km. southeast of Markopoulo. The pottery includes many LH IIIC vases. An alabastron of the LH IIB period is said to have come from Markopoulo, and is presumably also from the Kopreza cemetery.

B 29 MARKOPOULO: LIGORI etc. *
LH IIIB-C

AE (1895) 210; *AD* 11 (1927-8) *Chronika* 59; *BSA* 42 (1947) 6.

Stais (*AE loc.cit.*) excavated ten rather small chamber tombs at Ligori, which apparently lies about halfway on the road from Markopoulo to Porto Rafti. A chamber tomb was later excavated by Kyparissis (*AD loc.cit.*) at a point described as being near the 33rd km. stone on the road from Athens to Porto Rafti, to north of the road. Stubbings (*BSA loc.cit.*) believed that this tomb was part of the Ligori cemetery, which appears to be approximately 4 km. east-northeast of Markopoulo. The Ligori tombs contained some pottery of the LH IIIB period, but more of the LH IIIC period. The tomb excavated by Kyparissis contained only LH IIIC vases.

B 30 PORTO RAFTI: PERATI *
LH IIIB2-C

AE (1895) 149; *AD* 19 (1964) B 87; *AAA* 1 (1968) 184; S. Iakovidis, *Perati: to Nekrotapheion I-III* (1969-70); *OpAth* 11 (1975) 129.

An unusually large chamber tomb cemetery of over 220 tombs has been completely excavated here, in hill slopes on the north side of Porto Rafti bay. It seems to have been founded before the end of the LH IIIB period, but its main period of use was the LH IIIC period, when it provides clear evidence for an important site in the neighbourhood. Widespread overseas connections are indicated by imports from Egypt and the Levant. Distinctive features are a few iron objects, a number of cremations, and "Octopus stirrup-jars". Some bronze fibulae have suggested a chronological overlap with the Sub-Mycenaean period, although the most distinctive Sub-Mycenaean vase types of Attica

are not found here. This overlap may be disputed, but there can be no doubt that the cemetery continued in use until late in the LH IIIC period [*cf. BSA* 66 (1971) 349]. No Mycenaean settlement has yet been found near the tombs on the mainland, but there are traces of a road leading to the tombs [*PAE* (1954) 91], and these seem to suggest a site to the west of the tombs. Unfortunately, much of the area has now been built over.

B 31 PORTO RAFTI: NISOS RAFTIS
LH IIIC

JHS 70 (1950) 4; *Acta Musei Nationalis Pragae* 20 (1966) 171; Iakovidis 1969-70, 4.

Some LH IIIC sherds "and nothing that need be earlier" were found on Nisos Raftis, the larger of the two islands at the mouth of Porto Rafti bay; and it has been assumed that the island was used at this time as a refuge, in the manner documented for the 6th and 7th centuries A.D. It has also been conjectured that it may have been the site of the settlement to which the important Perati cemetery belonged. But the rich LH IIIC finds at Perati, together with the long duration of its use surely indicate a habitation site on the mainland, with a settled, and presumably agricultural basis for its economy.

B 32 ANCIENT BRAURON (AYIOS YEORYIOS)
* # (Plate 11c)
N EH I-II EH III? MH LH I-IIIB G A C H

AE (1895) 196; *PAE* (1948) 83, (1950) 188, (1955) 119, (1956) 77; *Ergon* (1962) 34; *AD* 21 (1966) B 98, 22 (1967) B 131; 25 (1970) B Pl. 87b; *AAA* 1 (1968) 184; Fimmen (1921) p. 7 Abb.1.

Ancient Brauron is at the head of a small bay which gives easy access to the Mesogaia plain. It was presumably a harbour town (*cf.* Fimmen *loc.cit.* for a sketch of the area). The acropolis is a fairly low hill (Plate 11c) with a ridge along the north side of its summit, above a spring and the chapel of Ayios Yeoryios at its north foot. Most of the prehistoric settlement was on the broad south and east slopes, which extend about 160 m. east to west by 80 m. An excavation at the northeast tip of the hill (preparatory to the construction of the museum) revealed massive retaining walls; and there were remains of a large house near the summit, attributed to the Middle Helladic period. The reported "fortification" [*PAE* (1956) 79], however, may in reality be part of a retaining wall for a terrace. It is attributed to the late Middle Helladic or early Mycenaean period. The excavations revealed very little LH IIIB material and no LH IIIC, but there is no lack of LH IIIA-B sherds on the surface, and one LH IIIB house was found (*Ergon loc.cit.*). Surface sherds appear to indicate that most of the available space on the acropolis was in use throughout the Bronze Age periods indicated, giving an estimated size of approximately 16,000 m².

Chamber tombs have been excavated at "Lapoutsi",

on the slopes of the adjacent hill of Chamolia, about 200 m. east of the acropolis (*AE loc.cit., AAA loc.cit.*). Their contents were mainly of the LH IIIA and LH IIIB periods, but one vase [*AA* (1974) 3 Fig. 2]. seems to be no later than the LH IIA period. The tombs at "Chamolia", further to east along the same hill, include some which are large and relatively rich. Their pottery seems to be no later than the LH IIIB period, despite arguments to the contrary [*e.g. BSA* 42 (1947) 72].

The apparent lack of settlement both here and at Thorikos (B 22) in the LH IIIC period seems strange in view of the ample evidence of prosperity at this time at the similar east coast harbour of Perati (B 30). But it would be unwise to make speculations on the basis of such "negative" evidence.

B 33　KOROPI:　AYIOS CHRISTOS　#
MH　LH I/II　LH IIIA-B　G　C

AM 16 (1891) 220; Fimmen (1921) 7; *AR* (1935-6) 14; *PAE* (1950) 165; *Alin* 106; *CG* Fig. 14.

Ayios Christos or "Kastro tou Christou" is an acropolis hill about 3 km. west-northwest of Koropi, near the west edge of the Mesogaia plain. A monastery named "Bethlehem" has recently been built on the east side of the hill, just above the chapel of Ayios Christos. The flat upper part of the hill, an area about 200 m. east to west by 90 m., was surrounded by "Cyclopean" walls (*AM* and Fimmen *loc.cit.*) and mediaeval. This area and the terraced south slopes (a further 200 m. east to west by 100 m.) are strewn with prehistoric and later sherds. Sherds from the site in the BSA collection include Middle Helladic (*CG loc.cit.*), and a LH I/II jug was reported (*AR loc.cit.*). Robbed chamber tombs were noted on the northwest slope (*PAE loc.cit.*), and sherds beside plundered tombs on the northeast slope include one kylix fragment attributed to the LH IIB or LH IIIA1 period. In a cave about 200 m. to northwest of the site, between it and Profitis Ilias on the east slope of Mt. Hymettos some Mycenaean sherds were found [*PAE* (1950) 159 Fig. 12 and 165 Fig. 18].

B 34　PAIANIA (formerly LIOPESI):　KARELIA
LH

AA (1916) 142; *BSA* 42 (1947) 8; *Alin* 106.

A Mycenaean grave was found to south of Paiania, and some Mycenaean sherds on a tumulus at Karelia, between Paiania and Koropi.

B 35　SPATA:　MAGOULA　*
EH II　MH　LH IIIA1-B　LH IIIC?　G

Athenaion 6 (1877) 167; *AM* 2 (1877) 82, 261; H. Schliemann, *Mycenae* (1878) xli; *BCH* 2 (1878) 185; *MV* 35; *AA* (1926) 400; *BCH* 89 (1965) 21, especially 22 Fig. 1 (sketch plan).

On the low rounded hill of Magoula, on the south side of the village of Spata, prehistoric sherds, includ-

ing Mycenaean, were observed thinly spread over much of the surface, for an extent of about 200 m. northwest to southeast by 100 m. The two famous excavated chamber tombs were cut into the southwest foot of the hill, and other tombs are reported here. The more important of the excavated tombs had three chambers leading off one another, and a long dromos. It had been robbed, but some rich finds survived, mostly in front of the doorway, including jewellery, ivories, boar's tusk plates for helmets, stone vase fragments, and an agate stamp-seal. The pottery has a wide range: a piriform jar is of the LH IIIA1 or possibly the LH IIB period, other vases are of the LH IIIA2 and LH IIIB periods, and one or two are probably of the LH IIIC period (*cf. CMP* 70, 76). Some of the material may have come from the smaller tomb excavated nearby or have been washed down from the settlement above, so that the precise duration of use of the main tomb remains obscure. Its contents bear comparison with those of the Menidi tholos tomb (B 10), and strongly suggest a local dynasty here.

B 36　CHARVATI
LH IIIB

BCH 73 (1949) 521 Fig. 3 and Pl. 39:2; *Studies Presented to David M. Robinson I* (1951) 108 Pl. 4-5; *Alin* 110.

Some Mycenaean figurines (now in the Stathatos collection) were found in a chamber tomb about 3 km. south of Charvati.

B 37　VELANIDEZA:　AYIOS SOTIROS　*
LH IIIB-C

AD 11 (1927-8) *Parartema* 64; *BSA* 42 (1947) 7; *Alin* 110.

On a hill slope to north of the chapel of Ayios Sotiros near Velanideza five robbed chamber tombs were cleared. The vases recovered span the LH IIIB and early LH IIIC periods.

B 38　RAPHINA　*
EH II　EH III?　MH　LH II-III(A-B)

PAE (1951) 77, (1952) 129, (1953) 105, (1955) 116; *Neon Athenaion* 1 (1955) 287.

The centre of the prehistoric settlement at Raphina seems to have been the low hill on the north side of the bay and to west of the harbour, but house remains have also been found along the shore. The settlement was apparently most important in the Early Helladic period. The Middle Helladic and Mycenaean periods are represented by sherds only, and the structural remains have apparently been entirely removed, presumably by erosion.

B 39　RAPHINA:　ASKITARIO　*
EH I-II　LH II-IIIA2

PAE (1954) 104, (1955) 109; *AE* (1953-4) III 59.

About 2 km. south of Raphina is a hill roughly triangular in shape, and about 5000 m² in area, which was largely if not entirely built over in the Early Helladic period. A few Mycenaean sherds are the only traces of later occupation.

B 40 PIKERMI *
LH IIIA2-B

AD 11 (1927-8) *Parartema* 70; *BSA* 42 (1947) 7.

Three small chamber tombs were excavated on a small hill about a kilometre to east of Pikermi, on the north side of the road to Raphina. They contained several Mycenaean vases and some steatite whorls.

B 41 MARATHON: AGRILIKI and VRANA *
EH II MH LH I/II-IIIB PG G A

J.G. Frazer and A.W. Van Buren, *Graecia Antiqua* (1930) plan opposite p. 50; *PAE* (1933) 35, (1934) 35, (1935) 92, (1936) 42, (1958) 15, (1970) 9; *AA* (1934) 194; *BSA* 42 (1947) 7, 51 (1956) 88 n. 7; *AAA* 3 (1970) 68, 155, 349; Pritchett (1965) 83, (1969) 1; Schoder (1974) 137.

The high acropolis hill of Agriliki, near the small village of Vrana, lies at the narrow western end of the Marathon plain (*cf.* Frazer and Van Buren, *loc.cit.* and Schoder, *loc.cit.* for illustrations). There is some evidence from the surface for Early Helladic and Mycenaean occupation (*PAE* 1936 *loc.cit.*). Below the acropolis, at the head of the Vrana valley, is a group of four tumuli (about 120 m. to west of the famous "Tumulus of the Plataeans", *AAA loc.cit.*). The earliest, Tumulus I, is of the Middle Helladic period. The other tumuli are Mycenaean. They contained complex stone structures, imitating rectangular and apsidal houses, whose compartments held many burials, accompanied by pottery, obsidian arrowheads, jewellery, and bronze objects. The latest, Tumulus IV, continued in use at least until the LH IIIA2 period.

About a kilometre to the southeast is a tholos tomb, of medium size (diameter 7.0 m.) but with a very long unlined dromos (25 m. in length), in which two horses had been buried in a pit. Within the chamber, reported as found intact, were two cists. In one a gold cup was placed upon the body. The floor was covered with a thin layer of ash and animal bones, and the finds were few, and mostly pottery. A plain flat alabastron [*BSA* 42 (1947) 42] is probably of the LH IIB or LH IIIA1 period, and pottery found during cleaning activities is said to be of the LH IIB period, a date which would fit the parallels for the gold cup. But some LH IIIB pottery is also reported [*BSA* 42 (1947) 7, 72; and a fragment from a stemmed krater cited on p. 39], which may indicate a reuse of the tomb at this time.

B 42 MARATHON: PLASI (near AYIOS PANDELEIMON) *
EH II MH LH III(A-B) G A C H

AAA 3 (1970) 14, 63, 153, 349; *PAE* (1970) 5; Pritchett (1969) 1.

Near the shore, in the centre of the bay of Marathon, and about 300 m. northeast of Ayios Pandeleimon, is a prehistoric site on a low rise. A large Middle Helladic building was found, and a fortification wall which is said to be either Early or Middle Helladic. Many Mycenaean sherds were found; and the site was obviously important at this time. The Marathon "Soros" lies about 1200 m. to the west, and may have been itself originally the site of a prehistoric tumulus [for alleged Mycenaean finds from the Soros *cf.* A.R. Burn, *Persia and the Greeks* (1962) 243 n. 15, 254 n. 42].

B 43 MARATHON: NINOI (the Cave of Pan) *
N EH (I?-)II MH LH I/II? LH III(A-B) C

Ergon (1958) 15; Pritchett (1969) 1.

The cave lies about 3 km. west of modern Marathon on a hill near the spring of Ninoi. It was occupied in the Neolithic period, and Bronze Age material has been found near the entrances. There is, however, no proof of a cult here until the Classical period, which may accord with Herodotus' statement that Pan was introduced into Attica because of his help at Marathon.

B 44 ANCIENT APHIDNA *
MH LH II-IIIB C

AM 21 (1896) 385; *BSA* 42 (1947) 8.

The prominent acropolis hill of Kotroni, on the northwest edge of the lake of Marathon, dominates a route from Attica to Boeotia. Middle Helladic and Mycenaean sherds were found in 1956 all over the large upper surface of the hill. A Middle Helladic tumulus with rich finds, including circlets of gold and silver, was excavated in low ground about 1.5 km. to south-southwest of the acropolis, and similar tumuli were noted nearby. It is possible that some of these may belong to early Mycenaean times, since they are similar to tumuli excavated at Koukounara in Messenia (F 29). There is, in any case, no doubt that Aphidna was an important Middle Helladic and Mycenaean settlement. In view of the published evidence, the assertion [in *Hesperia* Suppl. XI (1966) 82 n. 169] that no Mycenaean remains have been found on the acropolis is entirely erroneous.

EASTERN BOEOTIA AND SOUTHERN EUBOEA (B 45-80)

In Boeotia and the central part of Euboea the Mycenaean pottery, even on the surface, is often of the same high quality as in the Argolid and Corinthia. Euboea has been well surveyed, although as yet mainly in an "extensive" and selective manner, by L.H. Sackett and others [in *BSA* 61 (1966) 33-112, henceforth abbreviated as *Euboea*]. Their publication includes excellent topographical summaries of sites and regions, which will not be repeated here. Areas of importance in central Euboea in Mycenaean times are the Psakhna plain, the Lelantine plain between Chalkis and Eretria, and the Aliveri area. The exploration of Boeotia on the other hand, especially the eastern part, has been only partial and unsystematic. The spectacular recent finds at Tanagra (B 46), for example, clearly indicate considerable prosperity in this region (the lower part of the Asopos valley) in the LH III period.

The Euboean channel, and the Euripos in particular, evidently formed an important line of communication and a focus for trade in Mycenaean times. Several important sites, *e.g.* Dramesi (B 51), Chalkis (B 56-7), and Lefkandi (B 67), are located on the shores of the channel. A considerable number of the coastal Mycenaean settlements on both sides of the channel are known to have survived into the LH IIIC period (*i.e.* B 51, 55, 57, 67, 70, and 71), and Lefkandi in particular was a very important site at this time.

B 45　SKALA OROPOU:　AYIOI ANARGYROI etc.
EH III　MH　LH IIIA-C

AA (1962) 211; B.H. Petrakos, *Ho Oropos kai to Hieron tou Amphiaraou* (1968) 11; *CG* Figs. 11, 14; *AD* 29 (1974) A 95.

Prehistoric sherds have been found on a low mound, about 100 m. in length, about a kilometre to east of Nea Palatia, a suburb of Skala Oropou. The site is described as lying near the edge of the coastal plain and about 500 m. from the sea, at the point where the road from Skala Oropou to Markopoulo cuts a disused mine railway track which runs part the north and east foot of the mound. A few LH III sherds were found with earlier prehistoric pottery.

LH IIIA-C vases have recently been reported (*AD loc.cit.*) from Vlastos near Ayioi Anargyroi, described as 500-600 m. east of Ayioi Taxiarchoi, near a small spring. The site is said to be about 1.5 km. northeast of the Amphiaraion. The exact relationship, if any, between this site and the mound discussed above has not yet been clarified, but they appear to be in the same vicinity.

B 46　TANAGRA:　GEPHYRA and DENDRON　*
LH IIIA1-B　LH IIIC?　C

Alin 120; *JHS* 85 (1965) 125; *AAA* 2 (1969) 20, 3 (1970) 61, 184; *PAE* (1969) 5, (1970) 29, (1971) 7, (1973) 11, (1974) 9, (1975) B 415, (1976) A 61; *Ergon* (1975) 17, (1976) 8, (1977) 14; T. Spyropoulos, *Anaskaphe Mykenaikes Tanagras* (1974).

Two large chamber tomb cemeteries are being excavated at Gephyra, about 400 m. east of modern Tanagra, and at Dendron, about 700 m. southeast of Gephyra. Mycenaean habitation sites have been identified near each cemetery, and have been tested by excavation. The pottery from the settlement at Gephyra spans the LH IIIA2 and LH IIIB periods, and a LH IIIB room in a large house here has been cleared.

Of the two cemeteries, Dendron may be the older, and it certainly extends back to the LH IIIA1 period. It appears richer, since finds here include bronzes and

sealstones. Pottery is plentiful in both cemeteries, and several figurines were found. Of special interest are the larnakes, also found in both cemeteries. These were often decorated with scenes of mourners or other scenes which may have funerary or religious significance. Although these larnakes were originally attributed to the LH IIIC period, no certainly LH IIIC pottery has yet been published from the cemeteries. One or two vases from the Gephyra cemetery might be of this period [*e.g. AAA* 2 (1969) 23 Fig. 6, the deep bowl and the cup]; but the bulk of the published material is of the LH IIIA2 and LH IIIB periods. The cemeteries, which together consist of over a hundred chamber tombs, are evidence for a large population. The larnax burials are unique on the Greek mainland. The Tanagra cemeteries are now known to be the source of some thirty larnakes previously found in illicit excavations [*cf. AR* (1964-5) 16].

B 47　SCHIMATARI:　AYIOS ILIAS　*
N　EH I-III　MH　LH IIIA2-B

BSA 12 (1905-6) 94; *CG* Figs. 9-11, 14.

The hill of Ayios Ilias is about 2 km. to northeast of Schimatari and to east of the road to Dilisi. Surface sherds of most periods of the Bronze Age have been found on the hill, where remains (which included worked blocks) of the foundations of a house were excavated, apparently associated with LH IIIA2-B pottery. Two cists were also discovered. One of these is reported to have contained two cups and two amber beads. Their date is uncertain and could be later than Mycenaean.

B 48　AYIOS THOMAS:　KOKKALI etc.
N　EH I　EH III　LH (III)

CG Fig. 19; *AD* 24 (1969) B 187.

An Early Helladic site was reported by D.H. French (*CG loc.cit.*) at Kokkali, a low isolated hill about 3.5 km. north of the village of Ayios Thomas, and about 750 m. north-northwest of a church of Ayios Thomas, to north of the Asopos river. This is presumably the same neighbourhood as the "Liougo or Kokkali" described (*AD loc.cit.*) as to south of Schimatari, where Mycenaean sherds were said to have been found over an area of about 10,000 m². But more than one prehistoric settlement may be indicated, and the topography needs clarification.

B 49　AYIOS THOMAS:　AYIOS KONSTANDINOS
N　EH II　MH　LH III(A2-B)　A　C　H

AD 24 (1969) B 186.

About 1.5 km. northwest of Ayios Thomas, a prehistoric settlement was found on a high hill, steep on all sides except the northwest where a chapel of Ayios Konstandinos is situated. The sherds on the flat hilltop included some from tall-stemmed Mycenaean kylikes.

B 50 KLIDHI
LH III(A2-B)

AD 19 (1964) B 199.

Mycenaean chamber tombs were found at the southeast edge of the village. Five LH III vases were recovered from one excavated tomb.

B 51 DRAMESI *
N EH I-III MH LH I-IIIC

PAE (1911) 142; *AD* 1 (1915) *Parartema* 55, 20 (1965) B 242; *Hesperia* Suppl. 8 (1949) 39; *AE* (1956) *Chronika* 26.

A large "high mound" site, about 250 m. northeast to southwest by 100 m., lies at the northwest edge of Dramesi (now renamed Paralia Avlidhos). Significant remains of all periods of the Bronze Age have been found in various investigations here, and Mycenaean surface sherds of good quality are numerous. A massive stone built doorway on the west slope has been thought to be that of a tholos tomb [it has now mainly disappeared, *cf. Kadmos* 5 (1966) 142 n. 1]. To the south of this, a cemetery, apparently of cist tombs, yielded pottery and weapons of the Middle Helladic to LH II periods. Traces of a probable fortification wall have been identified. A four-sided stone stele, decorated with incised representations of ships, was recovered from illicit excavations. Blegen (*Hesperia loc.cit.*) conjectured that it may have been a special monument set up in a tomb, possibly in connection with an overseas expedition such as that against Troy. He attributed the stele to the Mycenaean period on the grounds of the similarity of its design to that on a sherd from Tragana (F 6) in Messenia, especially with regard to the "transverse lines to decorate the hull" [*cf.* E. Vermeule, *Greece in the Bronze Age* (1972) Fig. 43b-c].

B 52 PHAROS AVLIDHOS: YERALI
EH LH IIIB

AD 26 (1971) B 218.

A settlement of the Early Helladic and LH IIIB periods, and a cemetery of pit graves and chamber tombs, also dated to the LH IIIB period, were found on a low mound, situated about 700 m. from the sea, about a kilometre to northwest of the Dramesi mound (B 51). In addition to pottery, the chamber tombs contained a considerable amount of jewellery.

B 53 VATHY: NISI *
LH (III?) G A C H

PAE (1959) 32; *Ergon* (1959) 30; Schoder (1974) 42.

Nisi (or Yeladovouni) is the name given to the long ridge which stretches from north to south between the main Aulis bay (Megalo Vathy) and the smaller bay (Mikro Vathy) to the north. Trial excavations on the west slope of Nisi, to east of the Sanctuary of Artemis, revealed Mycenaean pottery associated with a stretch of walling built with large stones. Other traces of Mycenaean settlement were noted about 50 m. north of the chapel of Ayia Paraskevi, near the Sanctuary.

B 54 MIKRO VATHY *
LH IIB-IIIB

PAE (1956) 95, 101, (1960) 48; Schoder (1974) 44.

Mycenaean pottery and weapons were recovered from chamber tombs destroyed during construction of the cement works on the northeast side of Mikro Vathy bay. The tombs are probably to be associated with the settlement at Nisi (B 53).

B 55 CHALKIS: VLICHA
EH I-II MH LH I/II-IIIC PG or G? C

Archeion Euboikon Meleton 6 (1969) 309; *CG* Fig. 9, 10, 14, 16c; *Euboea* 58 Fig. 10 (map); S.C. Bakhuizen, *Salganeus and the Fortifications on its Mountains; Chalcidian Studies II* (1970) 16 Fig. 7.

Vlicha (or Tseloneri) is an isolated hill near the shore, about 2 km. southwest of the bridge across the Euripos at Chalkis, and to north of a shallow inlet crossed by the railway. There was a prehistoric settlement of considerable size here, perhaps about 200 m. north to south by 120 m. Most of the sherds were found on the seaward side. It was apparently occupied throughout the whole of the Mycenaean period, which is well represented in the BSA collection [and *cf. Kadmos* 5 (1966) 142 for a sherd with a painted potmark].

B 56 CHALKIS: KAKI KEFALI
EH MH LH C H

Archeion Euboikon Meleton 6 (1959) 282, 308; *Euboea* 58 (No. 38).

Kaki Kefali is the promontory with a lighthouse on the northern edge of the town of Chalkis. It has a small harbour on the south side and beaches to the northeast. The top surface of the promontory is almost totally eroded, and the Bronze Age sherds were few, including some Mycenaean described as "scrappy" (*Euboea* 58).

B 57 CHALKIS: VROMOUSA (TRYPA) *
MH LH I-IIIC PG G C H

G.A. Papavasileiou, *Peri ton en Euboiai archaion taphon* (1910) 21; *PAE* (1910) 266, (1911) 237; *BSA* 47 (1952) 49; *Euboea* 57 (No. 37).

Twenty Mycenaean chamber tombs were excavated in the area of Vromousa to east of Chalkis, on hill slopes to southwest, north, and east of Ayia Eleousa. Some Middle Helladic and later surface material was also found. The tombs contained about 200 vases, mainly of the LH II-IIIA2 periods, and some figurines, jewellery, and bronze objects. No traces of the tombs themselves now survive.

B 58   DHOKOS: AYIA TRIADHA
MH LH C

Euboea 60 (No. 47).

Some obsidian and surface sherds of Middle Helladic and Mycenaean type were found in the field above and to south of the village, between the church of Ayia Triadha and the village school. The slight scatter of sherds indicates only a small prehistoric settlement.

B 59   CAPE MANIKA *
EH I-III MH LH I-IIIB G C

Papavasileiou 1910, 21; *Archeion Euboikon Meleton* 6 (1959) 292; *Euboea* 56 (No. 35); *AD* 24 (1969) B 202, 25 (1970) B 248, 26 (1971) B 267.

Cape Manika is a low promontory about 5 km. northeast of Chalkis. It is about 500 m. in length. The Early Helladic settlement here was important, but later prehistoric remains are not very significant, although surface sherds of good quality indicate occupation during most of the Mycenaean period. A chamber tomb in the vicinity, near Panayitsa, produced a fine Type C sword and two cylinder seals, together with LH IIIA1-B pottery.

B 60   PSAKHNA: AYIOS ILIAS and PIRGOS
N? EH I-II MH LH IIIA-C G? C

Euboea 54 (Nos. 30-31).

Ayios Ilias, about 1.5 km. southeast of Psakhna, is the most prominent hill in the Psakhna plain, and has commanding views to west, south, and east. Middle Helladic, Mycenaean, and later sherds were found over all its west and south slopes, concentrated particularly on the southwest slopes opposite the mediaeval tower (Pirgos) below. Early and Middle Helladic sherds were found for more than 300 m. to south and 100 m. to west of Pirgos. The authors of the Euboea survey considered that the Ayios Ilias settlement was "a strong and central site of some size and importance in its area".

B 61   PSAKHNA: AYIA PARASKEVI *
LH A C H

AD 19 (1964) B 213; *Euboea* 56 (No. 33).

The church of Ayia Paraskevi is about 2.5 km. south-southeast of Psakhna, and about a kilometre south of Ayios Ilias (B 60). To west of the church, on the opposite side of the road, are several Mycenaean chamber tombs, in the slopes of a ridge. They were in-

vestigated in 1963 by B.H. Petrakos. Some had been already robbed. The tombs were presumably connected with the site at Ayios Ilias.

B 62   PSAKHNA: GLIFAS
EH? MH? LH G C

Euboea 56 (No. 4).

Glifas is a small rounded hill about 3.5 km. south-southwest of Psakhna, about 500 m. to east of the road from Chalkis, on the south edge of the Psakhna plain and above the marshes. Some Mycenaean and later sherds of poor quality were found here, and traces of walling, possibly fortifications.

B 63   POLITIKA: CAPE MNIMA
N EH II MH LH III(A-B) C

BSA 47 (1952) 60 n. 14b; *Euboea* 52 (No. 25).

Prehistoric and later sherds were found scattered over the slopes between Politika and Cape Mnima. The greatest concentration was at a point about 500 m. above and northeast of the beacon. Mycenaean sherds included LH III kylix stems.

B 64   POLITIKA: KAFKALA
EH (II?) MH LH I/II? LH III(A-B) A C

Euboea 53 (No. 26), 104; *AD* 10 (1926) 15, 675.

Kafkala is a low mound about 200 m. from the shore and about 3 km. south-southeast of Politika. On the mound, and in the adjacent fields for over 50 m., Bronze Age and later sherds and other material are widespread. Mycenaean sherds include LH III kylix fragments.

B 65   KATHENI: KRASAS
N? EH I MH LH III(A-B)

Euboea 54 (No. 29); *CG* Fig. 9.

The high flat-topped ridge of Krasas lies on the west side of the road to Chalkis, about 4 km. southwest of Katheni. Prehistoric sherds, mainly Early Helladic, were found over an area about 200 m. by 70 m. on the hilltop. Only one Middle Helladic sherd was recognized, and the only Mycenaean find was a poorly preserved piece of a kylix.

B 66   MISTROS *
LH IIIA2-C PG?

AAA 2 (1969) 30.

During construction of a road from Mistros to Mavropoulon (a village northeast of Mistros) six chamber tombs were found. They are part of an extensive Mycenaean cemetery on the slope, both above and below the road. The tombs had been partly plundered, but a variety of goods and a wide range of pottery were recovered. The latter is presumably a Dark Age or later intrusion.

B 67 LEFKANDI: XEROPOLIS *
N EH II(-III?) MH LH I-IIIC SMyc PG G C

AR (1964-5) 16, (1965-6) 10, (1966-7) 12, (1967-8) 12, (1968-9) 8, (1969-70) 8, (1970-71) 7; *Euobea* 60 (Nos. 48-50); *BSA* 66 (1971) 333; *AJA* 72 (1968) 41; *AAA* 2 (1969) 98; *AD* 25 (1970) B 250, 258, 26 (1971) B 267; M.R. Popham and L.H. Sackett, *Excavations at Lefkandi, Euboea 1964-66* (1968); V.R. d'A. Desborough, *The Greek Dark Ages* (1972) 188.

Xeropolis is a prominent low hill of "high mound" type, with steep sides and a flat top surface about 500 m. east to west by 120 m. It forms a promontory to east of a small harbour, which is sheltered from all except the southwest winds. The hill is severely eroded in parts, but there are deep deposits in some areas, especially the northwest. Excavations have demonstrated continuity of occupation from Final Neolithic onwards. The most important remains on the site are the thick LH IIIC deposits, representing three major phases. They indicate that the settlement, which appears to have covered the whole hill in the early part of the LH IIIC period, was completely destroyed by fire at the end of the first phase and partially destroyed again in the course of the second phase, after which it seems to have declined. While the settlement here may have been wholly abandoned at the end of the LH IIIC period, continuity of occupation in the area is evidenced by the Dark Age cemeteries found to the northwest. The Skoubris cemetery began here in the Sub-Mycenaean period, and the other two cemeteries (Palaia Perivolia and Toumba) in the Protogeometric period.

The area of Mycenaean settlement was apparently not confined to the Xeropolis hill. Mycenaean and earlier sherds were also found on the low promontory which extends to east-southeast of the hill; and other Mycenaean sherds were among those found on the upper south and east slopes of the small but prominent hill of Palaia Perivolia on the northern outskirts of Lefkandi village, and to northwest of Xeropolis.

The importance of Lefkandi in the LH IIIC period, and the evidence for continuity into the Dark Age in its neighbourhood have encouraged speculation that this site may be Strabo's "Old Eretria" (Strabo IX. 403 and X. 448. But Strabo's directions, although vague, seem to place this "Old Eretria" to *east* of the historic Eretria). Others [*e.g.* Themelis in *AAA* 2 (1969) 101] have conjectured that it may rather be the Oechalia in the territory of Eretria said to have been destroyed by Herakles (Strabo X. 448).

B 68 ERETRIA (NEA PSARA): ANCIENT ERETRIA * # (Plate 16b)
EH II(-II?) MH LH IIIA2-B PG G A C H

Euboea 62 (Nos. 56-8); *AAA* 2 (1969) 26; *AE* (1969) 143; *CSHI* 51; P. Auberson and K. Schefold, *Führer durch Eretria* (1972) 16, 59, 137, 156.

The high and extensive acropolis of ancient Eretria lies only about 1.5 km. from its excellent natural harbour, and completely dominates both the harbour and the coastal plain. Earlier reports of Mycenaean finds on the acropolis were formerly rather summarily dismissed by some scholars (*Euboea* 62 and n. 78); and later occupation here has obviously removed or obscured the prehistoric structures. But further Mycenaean sherds have now been found in reasonable quantity at several locations on the acropolis [*cf.* the map in *AE* (1969) p. 155 Fig. 6], together with Early and Middle Helladic, some Protogeometric, and more numerous later sherds, and later buildings (including fortifications of various periods). A Mycenaean figurine and some obsidian fragments were found on the southeast flank of the acropolis, and a decorated sherd (LH IIIA2 or LH IIIB) by the west gate (*AAA loc.cit.*). And, besides other sporadic Mycenaean sherds on the summit, a considerable amount of Mycenaean pottery is said to have been found in the northeast sector, behind Tower h (Auberson and Schefold 1972, 137).

Although the Mycenaean finds are not numerous, their distribution (including some probably Mycenaean from the area of the Temple of Apollo, *cf.* Auberson and Schefold 1972, 16), and the strategic nature of the site, constitute good arguments for its importance. Despite Strabo's assertions concerning an "Old Eretria" elsewhere, prior to the Eretria of the historic period (*cf.* on B 67 above), it is probable that Homeric Eiretria reflects the site here at Nea Psara.

B 69 ERETRIA: MAGOULA
N EH I-III LH III(A-B) C H

Euboea 63 (No. 59).

Magoula is a low mound beside the shore about 5 km. to east of Eretria (Nea Psara), on the road to Amarynthos. Its top is very small, but forms part of a broader sloping hillock. The site is not extensive, and may have been more important in the Early Helladic period than later. But fragments of LH III bowls and kylixes were found; and there are traces of robbed chamber tombs on a ridge to the north.

B 70 AMARYNTHOS: PALAIOCHORIA * # (Fig. 8)
N EH I-II EH III? MH LH I-IIIC PG G? C H

PAE (1898) 15, 95, 100, (1902) 65, (1903) 18; *AE* (1900) 5, (1902) 121; Papavasileiou 1910, 86; *BSA* 47 (1952) 60 n. 14b, 52 (1957) 23; *Euboea* 64 (No. 62); *CG* Figs. 8-10, 13.

Palaiochoria (or Palaioekklisies) is a prominent low hill, about 2.5 km. east of Amarynthos, and at the eastern end of the plain of Eretria. The cliffs on the south side of the site project slightly into the sea, and provide some shelter for the small beach immediately below the site on the east. To the west of the site, flat land and a shelving beach stretch up to the harbour of modern Amarynthos. The hill is crowned by two Byzantine churches and remains of a third, which was constructed partly on ancient foundations. The upper surface of the hill, about 160 m. northeast to south-west by 85 m., is flat and cultivated. Prehistoric sherds are abundant both here and on the upper slopes on the northwest side, indicating a total extent of about 200 m. northwest to southeast by 160 m. Middle Helladic and Mycenaean of fine quality were particularly dense and widespread. Several fine Mycenaean sherds, ranging in date from LH I to LH IIIC, are illustrated (especially in *Euboea* Figs. 25-28, abbreviated AM, and Pls. 16b, 17c-d). Two LH IIIC pictorial sherds are among the finest, and in general the quantity of good LH IIIC surface sherds on the site is particularly striking (*cf. Euboea* 104). The evidence suggests that the site, although not exceptionally large, was important throughout the Mycenaean period.

B 71   ALIVERI: MAGOULA and LIVADHI
EH II   MH   LH IIIA-C   C

Archeion Euboikon Meleton 6 (1959) 311, 313; *AE* (1945-7) 11 and Fig. 12; *Euboea* 68 (Nos. 63-64).

The low mound of Magoula is about 2 km. south-southeast of Aliveri, on the outskirts of the harbour settlement at Karavos (*Euboea* Fig. 11). Sherds and building material are spread over an area about 150 m. by 100 m. There are numerous Middle Helladic and some Mycenaean sherds (some of the latter are decorated), which indicate that this was probably the principal settlement in the area in these periods. And no other comparable site has yet been found further to the south in Euboea. A chamber tomb at Livadhi, on the southern outskirts of Aliveri, is presumably to be connected with the Mycenaean settlement at Magoula.

B 72   VELOUSIA   *
LH (IIIA-B)

PAE (1907) 114; Papavasileiou 1910, 42; *BSA* 47 (1952) 49; *Euboea* 69 (No. 67).

A small built tomb of tholos type (diameter 4.2 m.) was investigated about 500 m. northeast of the village. It is presumably Mycenaean, but had been robbed, and the only finds reported from it are bones and a button of pyrites. Some kylix sherds were apparently also found at the site, but search in the immediate neighbourhood has produced no sign of a Mycenaean habitation site. The nearest known Mycenaean settlement is at Lepoura (B 73) about 2 km. to the northeast.

B 73   LEPOURA: MAGOULA
EH   LH III(A-B)

Euboea 71 (No. 69).

The site is a low rise, about 100 m. by 50 m., at the northwest edge of the small Lepoura plain. It lies about 500 m. southwest of Lepoura, and is cut through by the road to Aliveri. The site is much eroded, and among the thin scatter of prehistoric sherds the only recognizable fragments were one

Early Helladic goblet foot and one Mycenaean kylix stem. The site might possibly have been associated with the tombs at Velousia (B 72) and Katakolou (B 74), but the surface material is too poor to justify making a firm association, and the prospects for excavation are not good. Further exploration in the area is judged to be necessary, before conclusions can be drawn.

B 74   KATAKOLOU: AYIA PARASKEVI   *
LH IIIA2(-B?)   G   C

PAE (1907) 116; Papavasileiou 1910, 39; *Euboea* 70 (No. 68).

A small tholos tomb (diameter 5.6 m.) with a "relieving triangle" was excavated on the southwest slope of a spur, about 2 km. north of Katakolou, and about 250 m. southwest of the spur on which stands the church of Ayia Paraskevi. The contents may have included a kylix in grey ware [*BSA* 47(1952) 59], probably of the LH IIIA2 period. On the spur above, a thin spread of worn sherds with some obsidian was found on the surface. These included a Mycenaean kylix stem and foot.

B 75   AVLONARI: PALAIOKASTRI and ANTIRES   *
N?   EH II   MH   LH   G?   C   H?

PAE (1902) 71, (1941-4) 37; *Archeion Euboikon Meleton* 6 (1959) 309; *Euboea* 71 (Nos. 72-73).

Palaiokastri, about 2.5 km. west-southwest of Avlonari, is a high conical hill, fortified in the Classical or Hellenistic period. Antires is a long low hill, about 300 m. north-northwest to south-southeast by 75 m., to northeast of Palaiokastri and nearer to Avlonari (*Euboea* Fig. 12). Considerable quantities of Early and Middle Helladic sherds were found on both hills, especially on the northeast slopes of Antires. No Mycenaean sherds have yet been found in the Avlonari area, but Mycenaean chamber tombs were reported (although their location has not been verified), and there is a local legend of a tomb on the southeast slope of Palaiokastri, said to have contained much gold, including a mask.

B 76   OXYLITHOS: PALAIOKASTRO, EVRIMA and PARALIA   *
EH   MH   LH IIIA1-B   LH IIIC?   C   H

PAE (1907) 114; Papavasileiou 1910, 24, 29; *Euboea* 73 (Nos. 75, 76, 78).

Palaiokastro is a prominent hill in the valley about 1.5 km. south of Oxylithos (*Euboea* Fig. 13). Early and Middle Helladic and Mycenaean sherds were found here, mainly on the gentle southwest slopes above the church of Ayia Triadha. The site appears to have been the main prehistoric settlement in the valley. The Mycenaean tombs at Evrima, Paralia, and Moni Mantzari (B 77) may all have been associated with it.

At Evrima, about a kilometre to east-northeast of Palaiokastro, a small built tomb of tholos type (diameter 4.6 m.) produced vases of the LH IIIA1-2 periods and LH IIIB(-C?) sherds. To southwest of Paralia, and near the chapel of Ayios Pandeleimon, is the robbed and destroyed tomb of tholos type described by Papavasileiou (*op.cit.* 29). A fine Type E1 dagger, of LH IIIA1, or even possibly LH IIB date, may have come from this tomb.

B 77 OXYLITHOS: MONI MANTZARI
LH IIIA1 LH III(A2-B) C

Euboea 74 (No. 77).

A robbed Mycenaean tomb, which may have been a built tomb of tholos type, was found in 1939 on the top of the hill which lies to east of the hill above Moni Mantzari (*Euboea* Fig. 13). Three vases were recovered, one of which is definitely LH IIIA1 (*Euboea* Pl. 20f). Another (*Euboea* Pl. 20g) is probably LH IIIA1, while a double pyxis (*Euboea* Pl. 20f) is of either the LH IIIA2 or the LH IIIB period. The tomb may possibly have been associated with the Palaiokastro settlement (B 76), although it is over 2 km. distant from it.

B 78 ANDRONIANI *
LH IIIA

Archeion Euboikon Meleton 6 (1959) 313; *BSA* 47 (1952) 60 n. 14b; *Euboea* 75 (No. 80).

A Mycenaean tomb, variously described as a shaft grave or as a chamber tomb, was excavated here. It was reported to have contained fine bronzes, including two swords with gold studs, and sherds of LH IIIA type.

B 79 DYSTOS: The Acropolis
N MH LH III(A-B) C

Euboea 76 (No. 84).

The acropolis of ancient Dystos is an isolated and prominent conical hill on the eastern edge of Lake Dystos, and dominating the Dystos plain (*Euboea* Fig. 11 and Pl. 18b). Obsidian and Neolithic sherds were widespread on the acropolis, and especially at its southeast foot. Middle Helladic and Mycenaean sherds are also recorded, the latter from fields at the eastern foot of the acropolis.

B 80 CAPE PHILAGRA
LH C

BSA 47 (1952) 89; *Euboea* 80 (No. 89).

On Cape Philagra, about 2 km. north of the village of Yiannitsi, is a fortified hill site of the Classical period, commanding the only landfall for miles on a forbidding rocky coastline. A few Mycenaean and Classical sherds were found here.

APPENDIX TO MAP B

SOUTHERN EUBOEA

Apart from the few Mycenaean sherds found at Cape Philagra (B 80), there are no other certain indications of Mycenaean settlement in the southernmost parts of Euboea. There is evidence for a substantial Early and Middle Helladic settlement at Nea Styra (*Euboea* 78), but one sherd possibly of the LH IIIC period (*Euboea* 104) is not sufficient to establish Mycenaean habitation here.

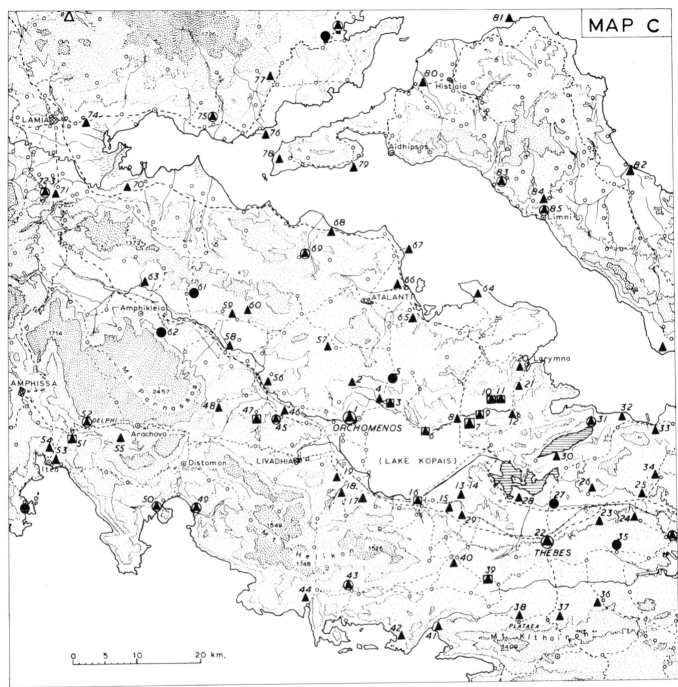

MAP C

Symbols used for marking Mycenaean Sites

▲ Settlement (except major)

● Tomb site (only)

⬤ Tholos tomb(s)

△ Mycenaean finds not related to Mycenaean sites

⬤ Major settlement site

⬤ Major site with Tholos Tomb(s)

⬟ Fortified settlement

⬤ Settlement with tomb(s)

⬤ Settlement with tholos tomb(s)

⬛ Fortified Major site

Ancient Place Names ... *MYCENAE* NEMEA etc.

Modern Place Names ... CORINTH Astros etc.

Key to Conventions used on Maps A to K

Modern City or Large Town ...

Small Town or Large Village .... ⊙

Smaller Villages, and Hamlets .. o

Modern motor roads .... ═══

Railways .... ╌╌╌ Lakes ......

Rivers, Streams etc. ....

Land above 200 m. a.s.l. ...

Land above 600 m. a.s.l. ...

Land above 1000 m. a.s.l. ...

Spot Heights (in metres) ... 24o7 etc.

(MAPS COMPILED AND DRAWN BY R. HOPE SIMPSON)

BOEOTIA   EASTERN LOCRIS
PHOCIS   MALIS
NORTHERN EUBOEA

MAP C

The part of central Greece included in this map is dissected by extensive mountain ranges, especially those of Mt. Parnassos and Mt. Helikon, which separate the coastal regions from the plains in the interior. The main line of communication in the interior is the route from Thebes *via* the south side of Lake Copais, up the Kephissos valley to Lamia and the mouth of the Spercheios river.

Mycenaean habitation along this route was dense, with the greatest concentrations of sites around the former Lake Copais (C 1-19), in the Theban plain (C 22-29), and in the Asopos valley (C 35-40). The Mycenaean settlements seem to thin out in the northwestern part of the Kephissos valley (C 58-63); although it must be admitted that much of Phocis and eastern Locris has not yet been properly surveyed (recent fieldwork in the regions of ancient Doris and Phocis is here discussed under C 63A-B and C 73A-B). In eastern Locris, Malis, and northern Euboea, the Mycenaean sites (C 64-85) have been found mainly on or near the shores of the Euboean channel. The Mycenaean settlements discovered in the Spercheios valley are mostly in the lower (east) part (C 70-74), and this may possibly be linked to the fact that the upper (west) part of the valley is too cold for olive production. On the north coast of the Corinthian Gulf a scatter of sites includes a concentration in southern Phocis (C 51-55), centred on the Amphissa plain. In general, the known Mycenaean sites in this part of central Greece are too few to give an adequate reflection of the actual Mycenaean population. Survey work has been mainly limited to the more accessible areas.

In the LH III period the two major sites in the area were Orchomenos and Thebes, which at this time seem even to have rivalled Mycenae. Other centres of importance at this time were Eutresis (C 39) and Krisa (C 57); while the fortress of Gla (C 7), and the other fortified sites around the Copais Plain are evidence of an exceptional prosperity in this region in the period, presupposing the drainage of at least part of the former Lake Copais in Mycenaean times. In most areas Mycenaean prosperity ended abruptly at the end of the LH IIIB period. In some more remote areas there was a degree of survival into the LH IIIC period (*e.g.* in western Phocis at C 49, 52, and 62; and *cf.* C 69 and 73).

THE COPAIS PLAIN (C 1-19)
(Figs. 6-7; Plate 15)

Lake Copais has now been converted into a plain by a modern drainage scheme. According to tradition (Strabo IX 415; Pausanias I 9, 3, VIII 33, 2 and IX 38, 7) the Minyans of Orchomenos had at one time drained and cultivated Lake Copais. Modern archaeological research indicates, although it can not yet prove, that the main system of ancient drainage canals and dykes in Lake Copais was of Mycenaean construction [Frazer, *Pausanias* V 110 ff; A. Kenny, *LAAA* 22 (1935) 189 ff.]. But the system (discussed below) seems to have been designed not to drain the whole lake, but rather to protect the peripheral land by canalizing the main rivers, especially the Melas and the Kephissos, and leading them to the natural emissaries ("katavothrai") on the north, northeast and east shores of the Lake. The main objective was apparently not to irrigate the area, but to prevent seasonal flooding. It is uncertain whether the shafts sunk in an attempt to construct a tunnel (which was never completed), leading from the northeast corner of the Lake towards Larymna, were designed to be part of the same system. But the argument for a Mycenaean origin of the main canals and dykes rests not only on the evidence of their "Cyclopean" structure and design, but also on the common-sense observation that at no other time were the shores of the Lake so thickly inhabited as in the Mycenaean period. This argument is strengthened by the number and the positions of the Mycenaean fortresses around the northeast shores of the Lake, especially the fortress of Gla (C 7). The only plausible reason for this

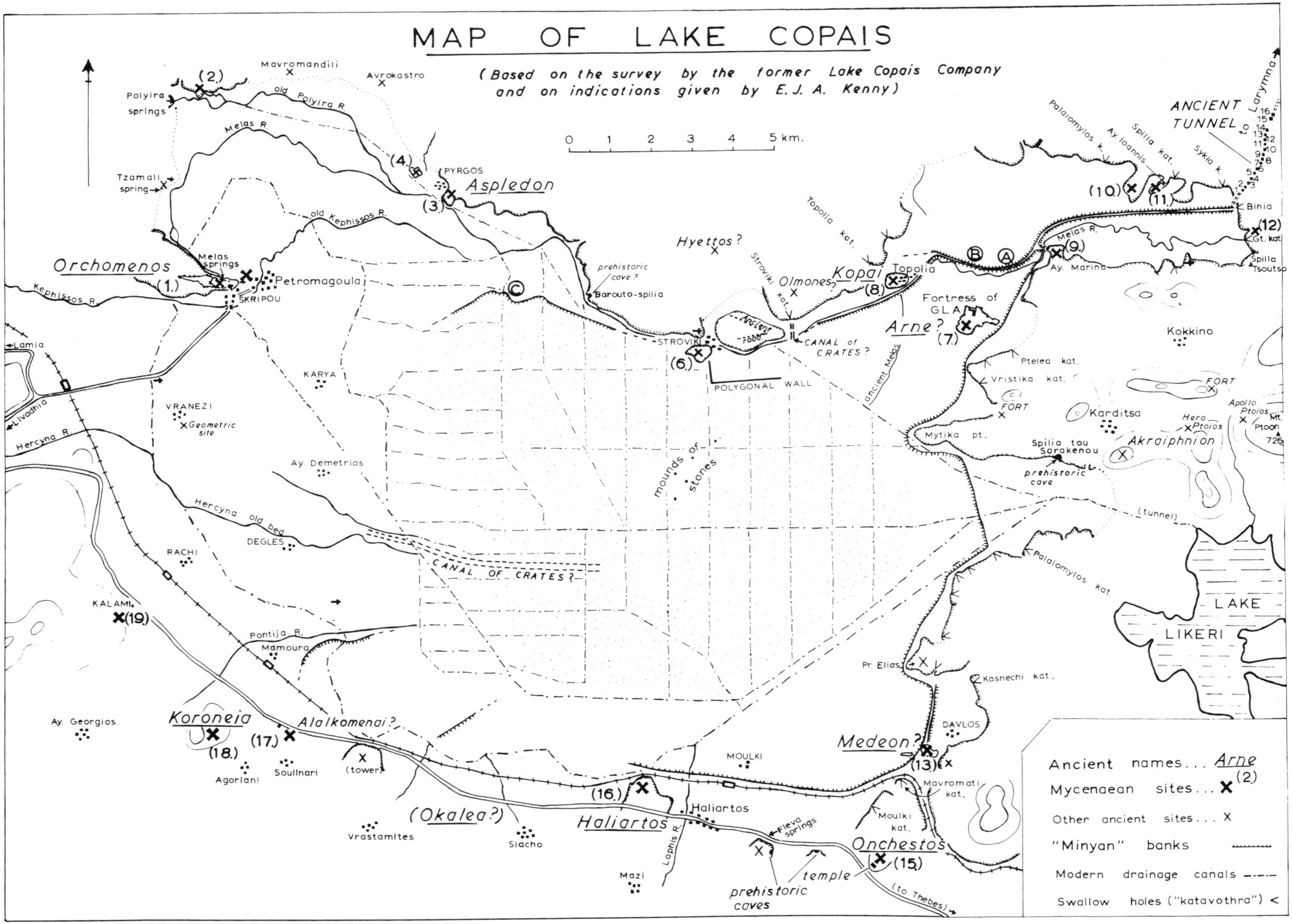

MAP OF LAKE COPAIS

(Based on the survey by the former Lake Copais Company and on indications given by E.J.A. Kenny)

Legend:
- Ancient names .... *Arne*
- Mycenaean sites .... **X** (2)
- Other ancient sites x
- "Minyan" banks
- Modern drainage canals
- Swallow holes ("katavothra")

Figure 6

Map C 61

phenomenon appears to be the need to control the system of drainage, especially near the emissaries. The lack of springs in the northeast bay of Lake Copais would seem to render this area unattractive for normal settlement (there are no permanent villages here at present). Indeed the fortresses in the northeast bay presuppose a source of manpower from elsewhere for their upkeep.

The main result of an effective drainage of even part of Lake Copais (as has been shown by the recently completed modern drainage project) would have been to render more fertile especially the land on the west side of the Lake, in the vicinity of ancient Orchomenos. And Orchomenos was evidently also by far the most important Mycenaean settlement on the shores of the Lake. The existence of Mycenaean roads leading into the Lake from the fortress of Gla presupposes some measure of success in the system of drainage; and the dykes themselves (if we assume that they originated in the Mycenaean period) would presumably have carried roads for wheeled traffic, thereby giving an additional measure of central control. We may therefore be justified in accepting the indications of both tradition and archaeology, and in concluding that the prosperity of Lake Copais in Mycenaean times (at least up to the end of the LH IIIB period) was due to the continuing power and wealth of Orchomenos.

C 1   ANCIENT ORCHOMENOS   * #   (Plate 12)
N EH I-III MH LH I-IIIB LH IIIC? SMyc PG G
A   C   H

JHS 2 (1882) 122; *BCH* 19 (1895) 177; *AM* 30 (1905) 130; *PT* 193; *Orchomenos I-III*; *AD* 1 (1915) *Parartema* 51, 23 (1968) B 223, 24 (1969) B 179, 26 (1971) B 218, 27 (1972) B 312; *AAA* 3 (1970) 263, 6 (1973) 329, 7 (1974) 313; *Alin* 121; *CSHI* 38.

The centre of Mycenaean Orchomenos was the eastern spur of Mt. Dourdouvana (the ancient Akontion), an area at least 500 m. east to west by 200 m. Strata from the Neolithic to the Middle Helladic periods were excavated here, but the Mycenaean remains were largely eroded on the hillside itself. Nevertheless, pottery of excellent quality, ranging from the LH II to the LH IIIB periods, from various parts of the area lies unpublished in Chaeronea Museum (*Alin loc.cit.*). The excavations by De Ridder (*BCH loc.cit.*) yielded good LH IIIA-B pottery from the area of the Asklepieion, and from the "Herakleion" near the eastern source of the Melas river. Schliemann's trenches uncovered Mycenaean wares halfway up the east slope, and in 1959 LH IIIA-B sherds were observed in the spoil of a drainage ditch higher up.

Fresco fragments were found even higher up, and a building containing pottery and fine goods has been discovered in another part of the acropolis. Other fragments of frescoes were found below the acropolis on the east, mixed with burnt brick and lead; and here, in front of Skripou church, large buildings, some of whose rooms were said to be of the LH IIIA2 pe-

riod, have been found on the low hillock. They are interpreted as part of the Mycenaean palace. Many fresco fragments and some plain whole vases of LH III type were found with them.

The "Treasury of Minyas" (diameter 14 m.) was set into the southeast slope of the acropolis spur. It is the finest tholos tomb outside Mycenae, and so closely resembles the "Treasury of Atreus" at Mycenae that it seems probable that both tombs were designed by the same architect. The tomb can not be dated definitively, however, since its contents, with the exception of architectural remains, had been removed long before Schliemann investigated it (*JHS loc.cit.*). Fortunately, the very finely carved stone relief which decorated the roof of the side chamber remained mainly in a good state of preservation (Plate 12c). An extensive chamber tomb cemetery is reported in the neighbourhood; and a structure to the south (*AM loc.cit.*). A necropolis of the transitional MH/LH I period is also noted, to north of the "Treasury of Minyas".

Although Orchomenos was obviously a Mycenaean capital, there is yet no coordinated publication of the Mycenaean remains. The pottery, in particular, has not yet been studied intensely. All that can be said at present is that there is no material which can be certainly attributed to the LH IIIC period. One vase has been considered to be Sub-Mycenaean [*AM* 35 (1910) 35], and there are Protogeometric graves. The site may have suffered destruction during the LH IIIB period and have been abandoned then temporarily. A hoard of bronzes found in a well [*AAA* 3 (1970) 263] may be attributed to the LH IIIB period, and might be a sign of trouble at this time.

The ground level in the plain in the immediate vicinity of Orchomenos is considerably higher than that in the central and eastern parts of Lake Copais. It was thus the least liable to seasonal flooding. On the other hand, even a partial drainage of the lake, if guaranteed all year round, would have greatly increased the amount of arable land around Orchomenos. Indeed Orchomenos would have been by far the greatest beneficiary from any moderately successful flood prevention system in Lake Copais. It follows that there would indeed have been the greatest incentive to the "Minyans" of Orchomenos to construct and maintain such a system. Ancient tradition (Pausanias IX 38, 7) reminds us of the penalty for failure; the plain of Orchomenos was said to have been flooded by the Kephissos river, when "Herakles" blocked the chasm leading below the mountain to the sea.

C 2   POLIYIRA   *
N EH I MH LH I/II? LH III(A-)B LH IIIC? C

Orchomenos I 116, *PT* 196; *CG* Figs. 9, 16a-d; *CSHI* 39 and n. 3.

Poliyira is a low spur on the north side of Lake Copais, near the northwest corner. The hilltop, about 120 m. in diameter, is surrounded by a circuit wall (probably of the Classical or the Hellenistic period) about 2.5 m. thick. Material from test excavations and from surface survey has a wide range, including a sherd in the BSA collection (*CG* Fig. 16d, the piece marked "Tegyra") which is from the LH IIIB-C transitional period. The site is probably that of ancient Tegyra [*CSHI loc.cit.; cf. BCH* 98 (1974) 643].

C 3 PYRGOS * # (Plate 13c)
EH? MH LH IIIA-B A C

Orchomenos I 119; *PT* 196; *AA* (1940) 187; *CG* Figs. 16c-d; *CSHI* 38.

This site (probably that of Ancient Aspledon) is a prominent hill on a spur projecting into Lake Copais from the north (Plate 13c). It lies on the southeast edge of Pyrgos village. The Mycenaean settlement here appears to have been large, since LH III sherds of good quality were found all over the hill (which measures about 250 m. north to south by 150 m.) and over the wide eastern terraces below. Test excavations uncovered a slab-built cist grave in which was a contracted burial. There are remains of circuit walls in "Cyclopean" style on the lower south slope, and there appears to have been an inner ring also around the little mediaeval tower (Pyrgos) at the top. Tombs near the bank of a stream to northwest of Pyrgos village are apparently Mycenaean, and, if so, presumably belonged to the Pyrgos settlement.

C 4 PYRGOS: MAGOULA *
N EH II MH LH I/II? LH III(A-B) C

Orchomenos I 121; *PT* 197; *CG* Figs. 10, 14, 16a-d.

Magoula is an isolated rocky hill, about 120 m. north to south by 60 m., near the northern edge of Lake Copais, and about 700 m. west-northwest of Pyrgos village. Trial excavations produced only Neolithic material, but surface sherds of the Early to Late Helladic periods have been found here, including LH III and possibly early Mycenaean also. The site is small, however, and much of it is too rugged for house foundations. In the Mycenaean period it was probably subsidiary to the Pyrgos site (C 3), which is only a kilometre to the southeast.

C 5 KOLAKA: AYIOS IOANNIS
LH

AD 23 (1968) B 223.

The hill of Ayios Ioannis is described as located about 5 km. south of the village of Kolaka and above the torrent bed Platania. Eighteen medium-sized chamber tombs were discovered here, and another group of 17 robbed chamber tombs on a hill to southeast of Ayios Ioannis. The finds (if any) have not yet been reported, and there is no indication of any ancient habitation site in the vicinity. The location appears to be near the north edge of Lake Copais.

C 6 STROVIKI
N EH II-III MH LH III(A-B) C H

LAAA 22 (1935) 202; *AA* (1940) 186; *AD* 24 (1969) B 179, 26 (1971) B 241; *CG* Figs. 10-11, 14, 16a-d.

On the southwest edge of the village of Stroviki, and near the north edge of Lake Copais, is a low rounded hillock. Surface sherds indicate a substantial prehistoric and later settlement here. Early and Middle Helladic and Mycenaean sherds of good quality, together with some later material, were spread over an area about 200 m. east to west by 150 m. There are remains of the foundations of two circuit walls, preserved mainly on the north side. Slab-built cist graves were observed on the top of the hill in 1959. They had been recently robbed. Some Middle Helladic sherds were in the vicinity, but a Mycenaean date is also possible. Kenny (*LAAA loc.cit.*) recorded an extensive wall of "polygonal" construction, which he nevertheless called "Cyclopean", to southeast of Stroviki, in flat ground within the Lake. It is more likely to be of Classical or Hellenistic date than Mycenaean.

On Tourloyanni, a higher and rather conical hill to northeast of Stroviki, Kenny observed the traces of an ancient road ascending to a levelled surface on the summit. No potsherds were found on this hill in 1959, so that an ancient settlement here seems to be ruled out. The road may have been connected with quarrying activities.

C 7 GLA * # (Figs. 7, 15; Plates 13a, 14, 15c)
MH LH IIIA2-B C or H

BCH 18 (1894) 271, 448; *AM* 19 (1894) 405; *PT* 193; *PAE* (1955) 121, (1956) 90, (1957) 48, (1958) 38, (1959) 21, (1960) 23, (1961) 28; *CG* Figs. 16c-d; Schoder (1974) 78.

The fortress of Gla occupies a strategic position at the northeast corner of the main Copais plain, commanding the access to the smaller connected plain or "bay" on the northeast, and lying at the junction of the routes along the east and north sides of Lake Copais. The site, which is almost entirely enclosed by the fortifications, is an extensive rock outcrop, which has the appearance of a low island. The area within the walls is estimated to be about 235,000 m². The walls are not so thick as those of Mycenae and Tiryns, and the stones used are smaller, but the design is equally elaborate. There are four gateways, one of which (that on the southeast) had a double gate, and there are substantial remains of roads leading from them into the plain. An inner enclosure, about 31,000 m², in the upper central part of the site, consists of the "palace" on the north, and the "agora" to south. The "palace" is composed of multifarious and abnormally small compartments, and the plan of the "agora" much resembles that of a military barracks. The rectangular divisions of the long buildings in the south and east of its courtyard strongly suggest stables; and chariots are of course suggested by the remains of the

Figure 7

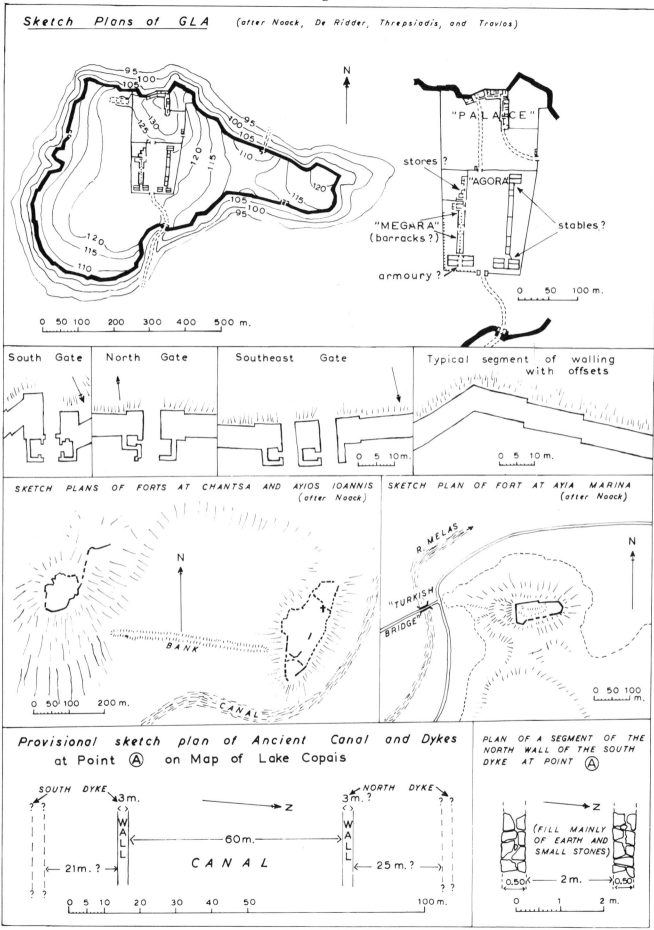

Sketch Plans of GLA (after Noack, De Ridder, Threpsiadis, and Travlos)

"PALACE"

stores ?

"AGORA"

"MEGARA" (barracks?)

stables ?

armoury ?

0 50 100 m.

0 50 100 200 300 400 500 m.

South Gate   North Gate   Southeast Gate   Typical segment of walling with offsets

0 5 10 m.   0 5 10 m.

SKETCH PLANS OF FORTS AT CHANTSA AND AYIOS IOANNIS (after Noack)

SKETCH PLAN OF FORT AT AYIA MARINA (after Noack)

R. MELAS

"TURKISH" BRIDGE

N

BANK

CANAL

0 50 100 200 m.

0 50 100 m.

Provisional sketch plan of Ancient Canal and Dykes at Point Ⓐ on Map of Lake Copais

PLAN OF A SEGMENT OF THE NORTH WALL OF THE SOUTH DYKE AT POINT Ⓐ

SOUTH DYKE   3 m.   →Z   NORTH DYKE   3 m. ?

WALL   ←— 60 m. —→   WALL

←21 m. ?→   CANAL   ←— 25 m. ? —→

0 5 10 20 30 40 50 100 m.

→Z   (FILL MAINLY OF EARTH AND SMALL STONES)

0.50   ←— 2 m. —→   0.50

0   1   2 m.

roads leading from the gates. The "palace" has yielded few signs of luxury, although some fresco fragments were found there.

The earth cover on the site was thin, and finds were relatively few. They include fragments of bronze, lead, and stone objects, and part of a "horns of consecration". The earliest Mycenaean pottery seems to be of the LH IIIA2 period, and the later of the LH IIIB1/2 transitional period [*PAE* (1960) Pl. 7b seems to include LH IIIA2 kylikes, and Pl. 7c part of a LH IIIB1/2 stemmed bowl or krater]. There are traces of destruction by fire at the south and southeast entrances and in the "palace", where signs were found not only on the last floors but under the surviving plaster layer on the walls [*PAE* (1960) 37], which suggests an earlier fire. The site seems to have been abandoned after the LH IIIB period.

Gla is by far the largest Mycenaean fortress discovered (Fig. 15). There must have been a compelling reason for the labour involved in surrounding this barren and rocky "island" with Cyclopean walling over a circumference of about two kilometres (enclosing an area over ten times that of Tiryns). Most scholars agree that Gla must have been the headquarters for the maintenance of a defensive system in the north and northeast parts of Lake Copais, composed mainly of smaller fortresses (C 3, C 6, and C 9-11) and probably also of watchtowers on neighbouring hills, especially Mt. Ptoon (see under C 9 below).

Traces of roads leading to the south and southeast gates of Gla have been found *in the plain* [*cf. AR* (1959-60) 13]. It therefore follows that this area at least was successfully drained by the Mycenaeans. *A fortiori* it is also certain that they must have succeeded in draining a considerable extent of Lake Copais, and in particular the higher land on the west, in the vicinity of Orchomenos. Thus, although we can not yet actually prove that the system of dykes originated in the Mycenaean period, it is hardly possible to doubt this, especially when we consider also the proximity of the Mycenaean fortresses around Lake Copais to the dykes themselves. The evidence for the structure of the dykes, and for repairs made to them in the Roman period, is discussed below.

C 8 KASTRO (formerly TOPOLIA) # (Plate 15a)
N   EH II   LH III(A-B)   G   A   C   H

Frazer *Pausanias* V 131; *AD* 22 (1967) B 243; *CG* Figs. 10, 16b, 16d; *CSHI* 26.

The village of Topolia occupies most of a low rounded hill (the site of ancient Kopai). A few prehistoric sherds, including Mycenaean, and some obsidian fragments have been found on the bare ground on the east side of the village. It was not possible to ascertain whether the prehistoric settlement had extended over the whole hill; and the ancient causeway, rough polygonal wall, and "lower city" on the north side, noted by Frazer (*loc.cit.*), could not be observed in 1959.

C 9 AYIA MARINA # (Fig. 7; Plate 13b)
MH   LH IIIA-B

Frazer *Pausanias* V 129; *AM* 19 (1894) 442, 445 Fig. 9 (plan); *PT* 12; *LAAA* 22 (1935) 189; *AA* (1940) 185.

The Mycenaean fort at Ayia Marina lies on the spur at the corner between the main Copais plain and the northeast bay. The small upper surface of the hill, about 150 m. east to west by 50 m., is surrounded by circuit walls two to three metres thick. On the south side of the enclosure some ruined cist graves were found beside the walls. Mycenaean sherds were observed in 1974 (by the author) over much of the surface of the hill, and their spread indicates that Mycenaean settlement also extended over part of the lower slopes on the southwest.

Ayia Marina was evidently a key site in the system of fortresses in the northeast sector of Lake Copais, because of its central position in the network of communications. In particular, it provides a link between Gla and the forts of Chantsa (C 10) and Ayios Ioannis (C 11) on the north side of the northeast bay. It also lies immediately above the confluence of the two ancient canals which skirted the north and east sides of Lake Copais, and met near the "Turkish Bridge" just below Ayia Marina (Plate 15a). Their waters were subsequently made to combine in one canal leading eastward to the swallow-holes ("katavothrai") at the eastern end of the northeast bay. Ayia Marina would also have been able to receive signals from any observation posts in the Mt. Ptoon area. It is, however, uncertain which, if any, of the ancient forts in this area recorded by Kenny [*LAAA* 22 (1935) 203] were of Mycenaean date; although some Mycenaean sherds labelled as from Mt. Ptoon have long resided in the BSA collection.

The fort on Megalovouno, to northwest of Mt. Ptoon, is described as a round tower 5.50 m. in diameter, standing in an enclosure with a gateway. This structure is apparently Hellenistic, although Mycenaean sherds are claimed here, and in the vicinity of Kokkino (by Kirsten, in Philippson *GL* I 742 nos. 178 and 179). The "round tower of polygonal masonry" (*LAAA loc.cit.*, and Philippson *GL* I 742 No. 176) on Mt. Ptoon is also apparently Hellenistic. The "semi-circular wall on the highest peak of Ptoon, a little to south" (*LAAA loc.cit.*, and Philippson *GL* I 752 no. 177) is also marked as Mycenaean by Kirsten. Two other forts were noted "one on each side of the valley above the temple of Ptoan Apollo" and "remains of another guard-house by the road which runs from Karditsa to Topolia". . . "on the left, where the road comes down into the Copais in the bay north of Mittika Point" (*LAAA loc.cit.*). These ancient forts would have guarded the approaches from Anthedon, Thebes, and Larymna; and, although most of their structural remains are probably of the Classical or Hellenistic periods, it can hardly be doubted that the Mycenaeans would have had a similar network of observation posts in this district.

Map C 65

C 10 CHANTSA # (Fig. 7)
MH? LH III(A-B)

AM 19 (1894) 440, Taf. XIII (plan); *AA* (1940) 185.

Of the three promontories on the north side of the northeast bay of Copais, the western two were fortified. The southern tip of the western promontory, Chantsa, an area about 100 m. in diameter, is surrounded by circuit walls. Mycenaean sherds and obsidian fragments were found in 1959 near the walls on the south side. Apsidal house foundations and a cemetery of cist graves recorded here may be of the Middle Helladic period.

C 11 AYIOS IOANNIS # (Fig. 7)
EH III? MH LH IIB-IIIB PG? G? C

AM 19 (1894) 440, Taf. XIII (plan); *PT* 12; *AA* (1940) 185; *CG* Figs. 11, 16c-d.

The fort at Ayios Ioannis, the central promontory on the north side of the northeast bay, encloses an area about 250 m. north-northeast to south-southwest by 100 m., an amount almost identical to that enclosed by the walls of Tiryns. It is the easternmost of the Copais fortresses, and overlooks the final part of the canal leading to the Binia Katavothra at the east end of the bay. Middle Helladic and Mycenaean sherds are abundant on the surface, and one or two pieces of LH IIB Ephyraean ware have been found. Middle Helladic tombs were also noted (*AM loc.cit.*).

C 12 MEGALI KATAVOTHRA
N? LH IIIB C

AA (1940) 185; *AD* 26 (1971) B 242; *BCH* 98 (1974) 644.

The Megali Katavothra is the main natural swallow-hole at the east end of the northeast bay of Copais, and the Melas river flows into it. Sherds of all periods from Neolithic to Byzantine have been claimed here (*BCH loc.cit.*). But the only finds properly attested are Mycenaean and Classical sherds picked up in 1959 on the rock ledge above the cave mouth. Neolithic habitation is, however, likely, especially since Neolithic has been found at Spilia Tsoutso to the south.

C 13 DAVLOSIS: KASTRAKI
EH II MH LH III(A-B) C H

AM 63-64 (1938-9) 177; *CG* Figs. 11, 14, 16b-d.

Kastraki is a small acropolis on a rock outcrop, overlooking the canals and dykes in the Davlos bay on the east side of Lake Copais. Middle Helladic and Mycenaean sherds are common on the surface, and later sherds occur both on the hill and on the saddle to the east. A Mycenaean cemetery was noted on the west slope of Mt. Sphingion to the southeast opposite.

C 14 DAVLOSIS: KALIMPAKI (Not marked on Map C)
LH?

AM 63-4 (1948-9) 183, Taf. 72, 1; *Alin* 121.

Kalimpaki is a hill about 50 m. in height, on the northwest side of Mt. Sphingion. Polygonal walls here appear to indicate a fort of the Hellenistic period. House remains are recorded, and Mycenaean sherds are claimed (*Alin* 121), but only obsidian and "frühe Scherben" are recorded in the field report (*AM loc.cit.*). The site is, in any case, near Kastraki (C 13), and would appear to have been subsidiary to it.

C 15 ANCIENT ONCHESTOS *
EH I-III MH LH III(A-B) C

Frazer *Pausanias* V 139; *AR* (1961-2) 31; *AD* 19 (1964) B 200, 21 (1966) B 203; *CSHI* 30; *CG* Figs. 9-11, 13-14, 16b-d; *AAA* 6 (1973) 379; *AD* 28 (1973) B 269.

Kasarma is a low rounded hill on the north side of the road from Thebes where this enters the southeast corner of the Copais plain. A ruined building stands on the top of the hill, and Bronze Age sherds, including some Mycenaean, were found in its vicinity, for a radius of about 50 m. in all directions, and extending somewhat further to the southeast. On the south side of the road, opposite the hill, remains of two Classical buildings have been excavated, and are provisionally identified as the Temple of Poseidon and the Bouleuterion of the Amphictyonic and Boeotian Leagues.

C 16 KASTRI (ANCIENT HALIARTOS) *
N EH II MH LH I/II? LH IIIA-B G? A C H

Frazer *Pausanias* V 164; *BSA* 27 (1925-6) 82, 28 (1926-7) 129, 139, 32 (1931-2) 190; *CG* Figs. 11, 14, 16; *CSHI* 28.

The Mycenaean acropolis occupied the higher western part of the extensive ridge of Ancient Haliartos. This area, about 250 m. east to west by 150 m., was originally surrounded by a circuit wall of "Cyclopean" style, of which some remains are well preserved on the south side. A sherd from the fabric of the wall was provisionally dated as "about 1400 B.C.", which would suggest that it was in reality of the LH IIIA period. It certainly provides a LH IIIA-B *terminus post quem* for the wall. Prehistoric sherds found on the surface of the acropolis and its north slopes included several Mycenaean; and a "Mycenaean area" at the east end of the sanctuary produced sherds said to range from the LH II to the LH IIIB periods. It is thus apparent that the Mycenaean site extended to east along the ridge for a considerable distance; and in 1959 some Mycenaean sherds were found at a point 300 m. east of the western end of the ridge. This was therefore a large, and presumably important, Mycenaean settlement, although no pure prehistoric strata or building remains were revealed by the excavations. This area at the south of the Lake would have benefited from an ancient drainage scheme, as it certainly does from the modern.

C 17   KATO AGORIANI
N EH I   MH   LH IIIB

CG Figs. 9 (under "Alalkomenai"), 14; *Euphrosyne* 6 (1973-4) 9 (under Agoriani).

The site is on the east side of the hamlet of Kato Agoriani, on a spur to south of the main road. The prehistoric sherds found in 1959 were mainly on the tip of the spur, over an area about 120 m. in diameter. Mycenaean is well represented.

C 18   ANCIENT KORONEIA
N MH LH A C H

W.K. Pritchett, *Studies in Ancient Greek Topography* II (1969) Pl. 56; *Euphrosyne* 6 (1973-4) 9.

The acropolis of ancient Koroneia is a large and prominent hill about 2 km. east of Ayios Yeoryios village, and not far from the southern edge of the Copais plain. Prehistoric sherds of several periods have been found on the surface recently (*Euphrosyne loc.cit.*), but the building remains observed, including part of a circuit wall, are of the historic period.

C 19   KALAMI
N EH I-III   MH   LH I/II-IIIB   LH IIIC?   C

BSA 26 (1923-4) 42; *AA* (1940) 184, Abb. 37; *CG* Figs. 9-11, 14, 16a-d; *Euphrosyne* 6 (1973-4) 9.

Kalami (or Lioma) is a large mound site on a low hill at the northeast foot of Mt. Granitsa, near the southern edge of the Copais plain. Surface sherds of all prehistoric periods and obsidian are very plentiful on the site. Mycenaean habitation is well attested for almost all periods, although there is no certain indication of habitation in the LH IIIC period (claimed in *CG* Fig. 16d, but none of the sherds from Kalami in the BSA collection are certainly LH IIIC). The Mycenaean settlement here was evidently large and may have been important; but the arguments (*Euphrosyne loc.cit.*) for equating Kalami with the Homeric Mideia are slender.

THE ANCIENT DRAINAGE PROJECTS IN LAKE COPAIS (Figs. 6-7; Plate 15)

Frazer, *Pausanias* 110; *BCH* 16 (1892) 121, 17 (1893) 322; *AM* 19 (1894) 405; *AD* 5 (1919) *Parartema* 34; *LAAA* 22 (1935) 189; *AA* 5 (1937) 1; *AD* 26 (1971) B 239; 27 (1972) B 315; *GRBS* 12 (1971) 221; *AAA* 5 (1972) 16, 6 (1973) 201; *AJA* 77 (1973) 230, 78 (1974) 182; *BCH* 98 (1974) 644.

The main circumstantial arguments for a Mycenaean origin of the main system of ancient dykes and canals in Lake Copais have been set out above. It now remains to summarise the evidence for the extent of this system, and for its design and structures. Also to be examined is its relationship (if any) to the uncom-

pleted ancient tunnel leading from the northeast corner of the lake towards the sea in the direction of Larymna. The first illustrated study of the ancient remains, by Lallier and Kambanis [in *BCH* 16 (1892) and (1893) *loc.cit.*], still remains the main source of evidence, when combined with the further study and critical appraisal by Kenny (*LAAA loc.cit.*). Surprisingly little fieldwork has been carried out since Kenny's survey, despite the abundant opportunities provided during the construction of the most recent (and now successful) modern drainage system.

The evidence is complicated by the fact that the original system of dykes and canals was at least partially altered or repaired at various times during the historical period. According to Strabo, Diogenes Laertius, and Stephanus of Byzantium, Crates of Chalcis (a mining engineer according to Strabo, and a digger of ditches according to Diogenes Laertius) initiated, under the sponsorship of Alexander the Great, an attempt to drain the lake, but was prevented because of dissension among the Boeotians. Strabo merely describes Crates as trying to clear away obstacles, but Stephanus of Byzantium indicates that he cut a canal (or canals?) through the lake. It appears therefore that the scheme involved either the construction of new canals, or the clearing of old canals, or both. Since Strabo at this point mentions the underground chasm near Kopai, which received the Kephissos river and released it in the Larymna area, it would appear that the project may also have involved attempts to clear blocked swallow-holes (katavothrai); and Kambanis argued that Crates was responsible for the spectacular, but unfinished, tunnel attempt.

The remains of the uncompleted tunnel and the sixteen shafts sunk in order to cut it, were measured by the French engineer Moulle, and illustrated by Kambanis and Lallier [*BCH* 17 (1893) *loc.cit.*]. Most of the shafts are now filled in with stones, and many are obscured by bushes. The shafts were cut through the solid rock of the ridge between the northeast bay of Copais and the lower ground to south of Larymna on the other side of the ridge. The upper end of the tunnel would have been close to the Binia katavothra. The deepest of the shafts went down about 65 metres. The tunnel attempt is not specifically mentioned by any ancient writer, and Kenny argued that the "Minyans" (*i.e.* the Mycenaeans) were responsible for it, and that Crates' attempt to drain the lake consisted only of the construction of dykes and canals. He attributed to Crates various traces of ancient canals, principally that noted by Kambanis to southeast of Orchomenos (marked here on Fig. 6 as "Canal of Krates?"), described by Kenny as "the central canal". Unfortunately, the traces of this "central canal", although specifically attested by Kambanis, had apparently disappeared by 1910, as Kenny records. But Lauffer [*AD* 26 (1971) 243] surmised that some remains of an ancient canal near Mytika point, cut into by a modern canal, may be part of this lost "central canal".

Map C 67

The evidence for repair work carried out on the dykes in the Roman period is more reliable. An inscription, dated c. A.D. 40, records that Epameinondas of Akraiphia (or Akraiphnion) contributed a large sum for the purchase of cement to be used in repairing the dyke which protected the land (in the Karditsa bay) which belonged to Akraiphia (*cf.* J.H. Oliver, in *GRBS loc.cit.*). Kenny (*op.cit.* 194 and Pl. LXIIIa) identified traces of these repairs; and Lauffer (*loc.cit.*) confirms the existence of repairs here to a wall of Lesbian masonry (6th century B.C.?) by means of squared blocks bonded with mortar. A well preserved section of the Lesbian masonry can be seen just to south of Mytika point, to south of the main road (N.B. the main road has been omitted on Fig. 6 here, in order to show the ancient remains with greater clarity). Other ancient repairs were also carried out on dykes in the area of ancient Koroneia, in the time of Hadrian [*AD* 5 (1919) *loc.cit.*].

We may now return to the consideration of the main system of ancient dykes and canals in Lake Copais. This consists of two main lines of massive banks and channels, one along the south and east sides of the lake, and the other along the north side. The two lines were joined together near Ayia Marina (C 9) and from there proceeded as one to the Binia katavothra. The total length of the canals was over 50 kilometres. Since very little excavation of the dykes has taken place, the evidence available comes mainly from surface observations, principally those of Kenny. Estimates of dimensions are, of course, mainly very rough, since the canals have all been filled in, and the dykes have been mainly ploughed down and spread out, and hugh quantities of stone have been removed from the original walls. The southern dyke, identified by Kambanis, was no longer observable when Kenny made his survey. The outer bank of the eastern dyke in the Davlos bay (*i.e.* the bank on the west side of the channel) was calculated by Kenny to have been 19 metres thick, and the channel itself 41 metres wide. It is uncertain whether or not there was a dyke on the east side of the channel here, since the land is higher at this point, so that a dyke may not have been necessary. Kenny recorded retaining walls here in both banks of the channel. In both the Davlos and Karditsa bays a line of stone masonry incorporated in the centre of the dykes forms a reinforcing spine along their length.

Of great importance are Kenny's observations of the nature of the western part of the northern dyke (in the neighbourhood of Pyrgos and Stroviki), since the walls which he recorded are not now visible, although the line of the single bank here is discernible for much of its course. Kenny estimated that this bank was about 66 metres wide, and he observed within its thickness two lines of polygonal walls about 2 m. thick and 27 m. apart. A small excavation by Spyropoulos [*AAA* 6 (1973) 201, *cf. AD* 27 (1972) B 315] revealed some details of the structure of one of the walls in this dyke. At Anderas, about 6 km. east of modern Orchomenos and 3 km. southeast of Pyrgos (at point C on Fig. 6), he uncovered a stretch about 10 m. in length of the wall, to a depth of 2.80 m. It is here composed of fairly small stones in a rough polygonal style similar to that of the walls of Gla (Plate 14). It slopes inwards slightly towards the top on both sides, and the width at the top is only about 1.50 m. According to Kenny's interpretation, this wall would not itself have formed the side of the channel, but would have been one of two reinforcing walls within the thickness of the bank. But in any case the coarse Bronze Age pottery found in the excavation, and described as early Middle Helladic, can not be used as evidence to provide a *terminus post quem* for the dyke, since the wall itself was not excavated, and there is no published record of the exact position of the pottery when found.

The most impressive visible remains of the Copais dykes are in the sector between Topolia and Ayia Marina. The longest preserved section is that to west of the "Turkish Bridge" (Plate 15). Here the line of both banks of the ancient canal are apparent. At one point (marked A on Fig. 6), about a kilometre to west of the bridge, it was possible to measure (in 1964 and 1974) the distance between the visible remains of the northern and southern retaining walls. The northern wall, however, has been much disturbed by the plough, and its line is indicated by a broken line of stones and a slight rise in the ground. The southern wall is better preserved, and visible for a much greater length, and up to a height of about 2 m. above the modern ground level in places. The masonry (Plate 15 b-c) is again of the same rough polygonal style, which is here very similar to that of the walls of Gla. The technique resembles "Cyclopean", although the blocks used are not often large. But there is one important difference between this section and that uncovered at Anderas. Here the wall, whose overall width is about 3.0 m., is composed of two small retaining walls, each about 0.50 m. wide, and a fill between them, about 2.0 m. wide, consisting mainly of earth and small stones (Fig. 7). This construction technique strongly resembles that of the Mycenaean roads near Mycenae.

A short distance to the west, however, the style of the wall changes abruptly. Where the modern road (omitted on Fig. 6) from Topolia to the "Turkish Bridge" cuts the bank (at point B on Fig. 6), a short stretch, recently cleared, of the top of the bank (apparently uncovered by excavation, although this is not yet recorded) shows that it is here a *single* stone wall, 2.20 m. wide, and composed almost entirely of large rough blocks. The change in construction may be observed at a point about 1.5 km. west of the bridge (in 1974 this was between an electricity pylon and a telephone post). Such varieties in technique are puzzling but need not necessarily indicate differing dates of construction (*cf.* similar varieties in Hadrian's Wall in north England).

Kenny calculated the width of the canal (*i.e.* the distance between the northern and southern walls) near the Turkish Bridge as 60 m., which exactly coincides with the measurements made in 1964 and 1974 (at this point A on Fig. 6, *cf.* Fig. 7). Kenny, however, who was then able to measure the width of the northern bank also, spoke of a *single* polygonal wall, 3 m. thick, in both banks. And he noted that in this canal the walls acted as both reinforcement and facing for the banks. In 1974 I observed faint traces of the lines of two other stone walls, much ploughed down, about 21 m. to the south and about 25 m. to the north respectively of the walls previously recorded (Fig. 7). These measurements agree remarkably well with the distance (27 m.) recorded by Kenny between the stone walls in the western part of the northern dyke (*i.e.* near point C on Fig. 6).

After the northern and eastern canals merged, at a point near the "Turkish Bridge", the waterway was presumably enlarged. Kenny calculated the width of the channel between this point and the Binia katavothra as about 80 m. since the distance between the top of the north and of the south banks appeared to be about 105 m. The banks are here much ploughed down and spread, and their width (estimated by Kenny as between 40 m. and 50 m.) is uncertain. If the canal was in fact enlarged, there would seem to have been no compelling necessity for increasing the size of the banks. On the other hand, there would appear to have been a special need here for stone facing of the sides of the canals, to protect the dykes from erosion. Indeed such a stone facing was essential whenever the main rivers were actually canalised, and in particular in the northern canal from the vicinity of Topolia eastwards.

We do not yet possess sufficient data for a full understanding of this main drainage system, and the arguments for a Mycenaean origin remain hypothetical. There is an obvious need for a full survey of the dykes and for some thorough excavation at selected points. Excavation should be carried to the *bottom* of the dyke walls, especially in the sector near the "Turkish Bridge" and between here and Binia Katavothra. It is obviously necessary also to determine the minimum depth of the canals (N.B. Kenny observed a shrinking of the land surface in the Copais plain since 1882). At present the only firm *archaeological* basis we possess for dating the main drainage system is the *terminus ante quem* provided by the evidence of the later repair works. On the other hand, the commonsense and circumstantial arguments for a Mycenaean origin can justifiably be termed overwhelming. The techniques used in the walls, particularly in the section between Topolia and the "Turkish Bridge", bear a very strong resemblance to those of monuments known to be Mycenaean. Above all, the existence of the roads (presumably Mycenaean) leading into the plain from Gla presupposes a successful drainage scheme at least in this vicinity in the Mycenaean period. As to the attempted tunnel, this would presumably only have been needed if the katavothrai failed to function properly.

In Arcadia the plains of Pheneos and Caphyai are at present successfully drained by similar swallow-holes, but these are prevented from clogging by iron grills and concrete enclosures. We may here again recall the tradition (Pausanias IX 38, 7) that Herakles caused the Kephissos river to flood the plain of Orchomenos by blocking the "chasm" which led from Lake Copais beneath the mountain to the sea (*cf.* Strabo IX 415). This tradition may be entirely mythical, or it may reflect an actual attack on Orchomenos by (Theban?) enemies, in Mycenaean times or later. In any case, it would have been relatively easy (for a victorious enemy) to block the katavothrai, at least temporarily, simply by digging through sections of the dyke at a time of flood, and allowing debris to be washed in by the floodwaters. Apart from danger from enemies, it would have been essential in any canal scheme to devise a means of filtering the waters sufficiently to prevent such blockage. For this reason alone, it would have been necessary to line the banks of the canals with stone or other durable material. Kenny believed that the "Minyans" (*i.e.* Mycenaeans) were also responsible for the tunnel attempt, and that it was a necessary complement to the system of dykes and canals. But no tunnel would be necessary unless the katavothrai were more or less permanently blocked. This would surely not have been allowed to occur while the canal system was in working order.

Finally, both the construction and the maintenance of this system presuppose a very large source of manpower and a strong central authority. The only period prior to the Hellenistic when such conditions existed in Lake Copais appears to have been the Mycenaean. After the end of the Mycenaean occupation, the dykes and canals evidently deteriorated. Crates of Chalcis was thus faced with restoring a drainage system which had collapsed. He undertook a drastic attempt to remedy the situation. We are told that he was prevented from completing his project, and the uncompleted tunnel is best explained as part of his unfinished work. Since his scheme was not successful, there is no good reason to expect a full record of it in the ancient sources, let alone any accurate topographical information concerning it (although both Strabo and Pausanias knew about the underground "chasm" which led through the mountain).

If we accept the argument that the Mycenaeans were responsible for the main dyke and canal system, it follows that they had in their time solved the major problem, that of protecting the most fertile land in the Orchomenos area from seasonal flooding by the chief rivers, the Kephissos and the Melas. Some of the smaller rivers, particularly the Hercyna, which originates at Livadhia, may have been allowed to continue to flow into the centre of the lake. In any case the banks on the south and east sides of the lake would not have required the same size and strength as those

Map C 69

on the north. They would only have had to be sufficient to withstand encroachment by floodwaters from the centre of the lake and to canalise the flow of smaller rivers and streams along the edges.

The Mycenaeans must presumably have succeeded in draining the land around Gla. According to the survey by the former British Lake Copais Company, this area is about 94.50 m. above sea level, whereas the level in the centre of the dried out lake is recorded as about 91.50 m. above sea level. The roughest calculation is sufficient to indicate that the vicinity of Gla would have been in no danger of flooding, provided that there was no threat from the major rivers, the Kephissos and the Melas. In the western part of the lake the 94.50 m. contour falls in the vicinity of Pyrgos on the north, and from there follows a general line more or less southward, passing about 2 km. to east of Karya and Ayios Demetrios. It curves eastward at a point about 3 km. northeast of Vrastamites. All the land to west and southwest of this contour is, of course, higher, and therefore would seem to have also been drained successfully by the Mycenaeans. The prime land thus rescued from flooding would have comprised perhaps 80 km.[2], not including the smaller parcels of low land on the north, east, and south sides of the lake.

C 20 LARYMNA: KASTRI
MH LH IIIB LH IIIC? PG? G C H

AJA 20 (1916) 32; *AA* (1967) 527.

Ancient Larymna occupied the low headland between the two bays of Larymna harbour. The ancient circuit walls, which have recently been studied in detail (*AA loc.cit.*) enclosed an area about 150 m. northeast to southwest by 80 m. The remains of these walls preserved on the south side are of isodomic construction, and are presumably Classical or Hellenistic. But a longer stretch, well preserved on the northwest flank, is of true "Cyclopean" style, with small stones in the interstices [*cf. AJA* 20 (1916) 38 Fig. 1], and some LH IIIB sherds found within the wall in 1959 give a *terminus post quem* for its construction. Other sherds in the vicinity include one Middle Helladic, and a few other Mycenaean (including one krater fragment possibly of the LH IIIC period), but Classical and Hellenistic predominate. The port of Larymna was probably important to Orchomenos in the Mycenaean period. Oldfather [*AJA* 20 (1916) 41 and Fig. 3] traced part of an ancient road between "Upper Larymna" (at Bazaraki, No. C 21 below) and the sea at Larymna. He pointed out that the depth of some of the wheel ruts (from 0.40 m. to 0.45 m.) indicates a very heavy traffic. He thought that the most likely period for such heavy traffic was a time of "Minyan" control (*i.e.* the Mycenaean period) under Orchomenos. This view is supported by the evidence of LH IIIB habitation at Larymna, and the "Cyclopean" circuit walls, if Mycenaean, would provide a further indication.

C 21 LARYMNA: BAZARAKI
EH LH III(A-B) C

AJA 20 (1916) 41; *CSHI* 37 n. 67.

About 3 km. south of Larymna is a small spur named Bazaraki, commanding the defile which leads from the upper Larymna valley to the lower. It lies to east of the main road, and is connected to higher hills on the east. On the south and north side are terraces which slope gradually down to the upper and lower valleys respectively. The Kephalari spring lies a short distance to the southwest, near the last (no. 16) of the shafts for the uncompleted tunnel. The top of the Bazaraki hill is about 100 m. in diameter. Oldfather (*AJA loc.cit.*), who is almost certainly correct in identifying Bazaraki with the ancient "Upper Larymna", found remains of ancient fortifications here, of which two to three courses were preserved. In 1964 some of these traces still survived, and Early Helladic and Mycenaean sherds, together with much Bronze Age coarse ware and obsidian, were found on the top and the upper terraces, both on the north and on the south side. Some Classical sherds and tiles were also found in the same area. The pottery was all very rough and worn, and it is difficult to estimate the size of the Mycenaean settlement, but it may have been up to 150 m. north to south by 120 m. east to west, to judge from the spread of identifiable Mycenaean surface sherds.

The traces of the ancient road observed by Oldfather (*AJA loc.cit.*) were confirmed in 1964. They are preserved in an outcrop of hard limestone on the west flank of the site. The ruts, which are about 0.12 m. wide at the bottom, are as much as 0.45 m. deep (below the present rock surface). They are about 1.40 m. apart (inner edge to inner edge). The line of the road was traced by Oldfather for some 300 m. It is, of course, impossible to determine whether this road was Mycenaean, or began at a later period, but the ancient route must always have followed its line.

THE THEBAN PLAIN (C 22-29)

The plain of Thebes was always well suited for dry farming, and particularly for wheat production. It was sufficiently watered, and yet not liable to flooding on a large scale. The hill of Thebes, at its southern edge, lies at the cross-roads of the main north to south and east to west routes in Boeotia, and overlooks most of the best land in the plain.

C 22 THEBES *
N EH II-III MH LH I-IIIC SMyc PG G A C H

1. The Kadmeia

AE (1909) 57, (1930) 29; *AD* 3 (1917) 2, 19 (1964) B 192, 20 (1965) B 230, 21 (1966) B 177, 22 (1967) B 226, 23 (1968) B 207, 24 (1969) B 177, 25 (1970) B 211, 26 (1971) B 195, 27 (1972) B 307, 28 (1973) B 274, 30 (1975) 698; *AAA* 1 (1968) 9, 241, 3

(1970) 62, 322, 4 (1971) 32, 7 (1974) 162, 8 (1975) 86; S. Symeonoglou, *Kadmeia I* (*SIMA* 35, 1973); *AA* (1971) 16; *AJA* 78 (1974) 88; *RA* (1977) 79; Schoder (1974) 220.

Special Studies: H. Reusch, *Die zeichnerische Rekonstruktion der Frauenfrieses im böotischen Theben* (1956), *AD* 25 (1970) A 104 (frescoes); *Archaeometry* 8 (1965) 3 (analysis of the inscribed stirrup-jars); *Minos* 10 (1970) 115, and Supplement 5 (1975) (the Linear B tablets).

The Kadmeia, the centre of prehistoric and later Thebes, occupied almost the whole of an extensive hill, whose upper surface is about 800 m. north to south by 600 m. The prehistoric remains are overlaid by those of later periods, which in turn lie under modern Thebes. Full excavation of the Mycenaean buildings has therefore been precluded, and investigation has been piecemeal. Most of the results are still not fully published. There are abundant signs of palatial and other Mycenaean buildings, and these are spread over most of the hill. It has been argued (*e.g.* in *Kadmeia I*) that there were two successive palaces, the first of which was oriented northeast to southwest, and was destroyed either at the end of the LH IIIA2 period or at the beginning of the LH IIIB period [*cf. AJA* 78 (1974) 89, *CG* 40]. The second, apparently more extensive, and oriented north to south, is said to have been destroyed later in the LH IIIB period. But Spyropoulos [*Minos* Supplement 5 (1975) 58, *cf. AJA* and *RA loc.cit.*, reviewing *Kadmeia I*] argues that there was a single complex which underwent various destructions and reconstruction. He points out that the central block of the palace has not yet been found, and may be under the modern square [*AAA* 4 (1971) 32]. Only on the Kordatzis site are two buildings of different orientations directly above one another, and these are only workshops. The question can not be solved until further excavation and full publication of the pottery excavated.

Outside the central area which has been suggested to have been occupied by the palace (or palaces?) and its ancillary buildings, fine frescoes have been found both to the north [*AD* 25 (1970) A 104] and to the south [*AD* 24 (1969) B 180], which may belong to separate buildings. And the workshop on the Koroupolis site is some 50 m. southwest of the Kordatzis site, which has been thought to be at the south boundary of the palace [*AAA* 4 (1971) 33 Fig. 1]. The evidence for a Mycenaean fortification wall around the Kadmeia [*AD* 3 (1917) 14, 20 (1965) B 237, 25 (1970) B 217] is as yet inconclusive. The palace (or palaces?) was obviously substantial, with thick foundations (suggesting at least two storeys), fine frescoes, a treasury, extensive workshop for jewellery, and Linear B tablets and inscribed stirrup-jars. It may have been even larger than the palaces at Mycenae and Tiryns.

Some Mycenaean buildings thought to be subsequent to the LH IIIB palace have been found on the Stavris site. Apart from this, the only published evidence for continued Mycenaean occupation of Thebes after the destruction of the palace comes from the chamber tombs, chiefly those from the Kolonaki cemetery to south of Thebes (see below). Cists found in the southeast part of the Kadmeia may be attributed to the late Sub-Mycenaean or early Protogeometric phases [*AD* 3 (1917) 25, 20 (1965) B 239; *AAA* 8 (1975) 86], so that continuity of occupation is likely. The decline of Thebes after the end of the LH IIIB period recalls the Hypothebai (or "sub-Thebes") of the Homeric Catalogue of the Ships (*Iliad* ii 505), but we have no reliable indications as to where this residual "lower town" may have been located.

2. The Chamber Tombs

Kolonaki: AE (1910) 209; *AD* 3 (1917) 123, 22 (1967) B 227, 23 (1968) B 219, 26 (1971) B 207.
Ismenion: AE (1910) 209; *AD* 3 (1917) 108, 22 (1967) B 227.
Megalo and Mikro Kastelli: AD 3 (1917) 108, 22 (1967) B 227, 23 (1968) B 213, 24 (1969) B 177, 25 (1970) B 218, 22 (1972) B 309, 23 (1973) B 252; *AAA* 4 (1971) 161.

Chamber tomb cemeteries have been found to east, southeast, and southwest of the Kadmeia, at Kastelli, Ismenion, and Kolonaki respectively. Of particular importance are those recently found at the Gerokomeion site on Megalo Kastelli, including one of remarkable size (10.52 m. by 6.24 m.) with two dromoi, and traces of frescoes in the chamber which may originally have covered all the walls of the tomb. It had been robbed, but may well have been a royal tomb (surviving finds include a fine ivory pyxis). At least one other tomb has remains of a fresco [*AA* (1974) 16]. The finds from the Kastelli cemetery span the LH IIIA1 to LH IIIB periods. The Kolonaki tombs, in use throughout most or all of the LH II to LH IIIC periods, were often robbed or disturbed, but remains of some rich goods were found. In all a total of about fifty Mycenaean chamber tombs have now been discovered near the Kadmeia.

C 23   SOULES
LH   C   H

Philippson *GL* I 742 no. 207.

According to Kirsten (*loc.cit.*), a small Mycenaean settlement was found on this low hill on the south edge of the Theban plain, near ancient Teumesos.

C 24   HARMA (formerly DRITSA):   ANCIENT ELEON   #   (Fig. 8)
EH I-III   MH   LH I/II-IIIC   A   C   H

Frazer, *Pausanias* V 63; Fimmen (1921) 6; *RE* Suppl. VI (1935) 609; *CG* Figs. 9-14, 16b-d; *CSHI* 24.

The site is a low but steep-sided hill on the northwest side of the village of Harma, overlooking the east part of the Theban plain. The flat top area, about 200 m. northwest to southeast by 120 m., and the extensive north slopes are strewn with prehistoric surface sherds. Middle Helladic and Mycenaean sherds are abundant and of excellent quality, especially on

Figure 8

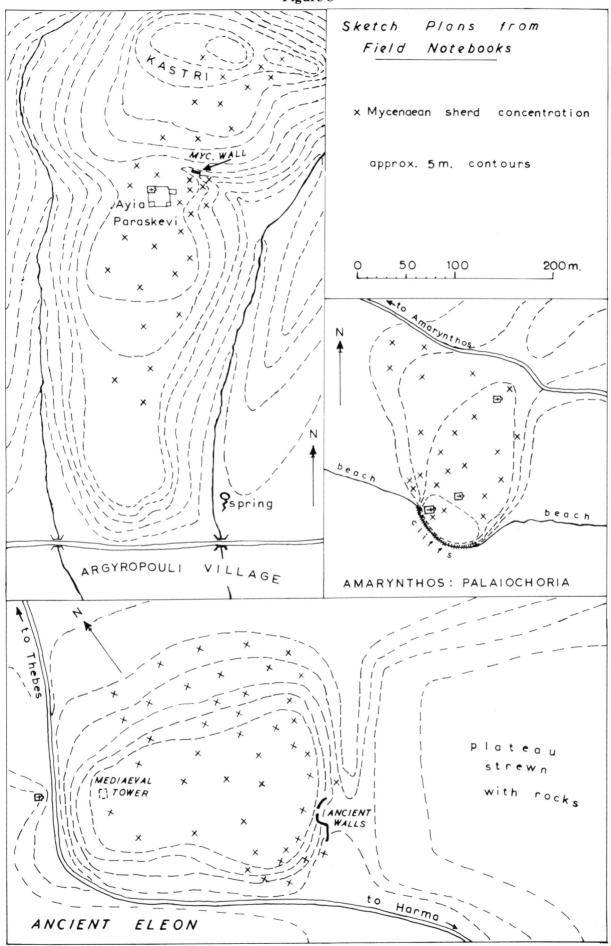

Sketch Plans from Field Notebooks

× Mycenaean sherd concentration

approx. 5m. contours

0   50   100   200 m.

KASTRI

MYC. WALL

Ayia Paraskevi

spring

N

ARGYROPOULI VILLAGE

AMARYNTHOS: PALAIOCHORIA

to Amarynthos

N

beach

cliffs

beach

to Thebes

N

MEDIAEVAL TOWER

ANCIENT WALLS

plateau strewn with rocks

to Harma

ANCIENT ELEON

71

the southeast part of the hill, where obsidian was also found. The site has been identified as ancient Eleon, and there are remains of a fine Archaic defence wall of Lesbian masonry on the east side, but few surface sherds of periods later than Mycenaean. This was undoubtedly a large and important Mycenaean settlement, probably second only to Thebes in the Theban plain.

C 25 KASTRI (LYKOVOUNO)
LH III(A-B) C H

Frazer, *Pausanias* V 62; *CSHI* 23.

This high and barren hill, covered in low scrub, lies to north of the road from Thebes to Chalcis where it begins to ascend towards the Anephorites pass. It is probably the site of ancient Harma (Frazer *loc.cit.*). The extensive summit, about 300 m. north to south by 200 m., is covered with many ancient wall foundations of rough polygonal masonry, including those of a small square tower on the south. At one point there appear to be remains of a circuit wall of large blocks, with a rubble core. But much of the walling seen by Frazer seems to have disappeared (by 1959). Most of the sherds on the top and the slopes were Classical or Hellenistic; but near the top, and on the upper west and south slopes, some Mycenaean sherds and obsidian chips were found. The Mycenaean settlement was probably small, perhaps only about 150 m. by 100 m., and confined to the higher south end of the hill.

C 26 HYPATON (formerly SYRTZI): TOURLEZA *
N EH II MH LH III(A-B) G A C H

Frazer, *Pausanias* V 60; *CSHI* 29; *AD* 25 (1970) B 224.

The small acropolis hill of Tourleza, to northeast of and above Hypaton, projects from Mt. Sagmatas (the ancient Hypaton) at some distance to north of the road from Thebes to Chalcis. It was probably the centre of ancient Glisas. The remains on the small summit (about 80 m. northwest to southeast by 50 m.) are mainly Classical and Hellenistic, but on the extensive southwest slopes some Mycenaean sherds were found, and obsidian fragments are plentiful both here and on the summit, although only one Mycenaean sherd was identified on the latter. Recent excavations have produced evidence of an Early Helladic settlement, and Middle Helladic sherds and a cemetery in use from the Geometric to Classical periods were noted in surface investigations (*AD loc.cit.*).

C 27 VOULIAGMA
LH

AD 22 (1967) B 242.

To north of the motorway from Athens to Thessaloniki, and halfway along the road from Thebes to Mouriki, some robbed Mycenaean chamber tombs were noted, and a possible tholos tomb.

C 28 PYRI: LITHARES *
EH I-III MH LH III(A2-B)

AAA 1 (1968) 140, 2 (1969) 97, 5 (1972) 467, 6 (1973) 371; *AD* 24 (1969) A 28, 27 (1972) 319.

This site is near the south side of Lake Hyliki, a short distance to north of the motorway from Athens to Thessaloniki, and near the village of Pyri. It is a broad tongue of land, cut off by a ravine, and between two hills. An important Early Helladic settlement has been uncovered here. The cemetery, on a slope to the west, consists of small rock-cut chamber-tombs, one of which contained much Middle Helladic pottery. Mycenaean kylix stems are also reported from the area, but it is not clear whether they are from a habitation or a burial site.

C 29 MAVROMATI: PANAYIA
MH LH

CG Figs. 14, 16d, 19.

This site, discovered by D.H. French (*loc.cit.*), lies about a kilometre to north of the road from Thebes to Livadhia, and about 2 km. east-southeast of the Copais plain. It is on the end of a spur jutting to south from the low hills which form a saddle between the Copais and the Theban plains. There is a chapel of the Panayia on its top. Middle Helladic and Mycenaean surface sherds are recorded.

C 30 MOURIKI: KAMELOVRYSI *
MH? LH G A

AD 21 (1966) B 199, 26 (1971) B 215.

This low hill lies near the southeast shore of Lake Paralimni, about 5 km. northwest of Mouriki. Traces of a prehistoric settlement, apparently Middle Helladic, and possibly also Mycenaean, have been observed here, and there are remains of at least five robbed Mycenaean chamber tombs near the foot of the hill on the east side, and robbed Archaic tombs. A tumulus of the Geometric period was excavated here also [*AD* 26 (1971) B 215]. The site lies on the ancient route from Lake Copais to Anthedon. Ancient wheel ruts have been found at intervals along the south shore of Lake Paralimni [*Orchomenos I* Taf. VII, *cf. AM* 19 (1894) 405, Frazer *Pausanias* V 130, *AD* 27 (1972) 316].

C 31 LOUKISIA: ANCIENT ISOS *
EH MH LH IIB-IIIA1 LH IIIA2-B? LH IIIC PG G A C H

AM 19 (1894) 457; *AD* 21 (1966) B 198, 22 (1967) B 243, 24 (1969) B 174, 26 (1971) B 219, 27 (1972) B 316, 28 (1973) B 265; *AAA* 1 (1968) 139, 2 (1969) 96, 4 (1971) 319.

Noack (*AM loc.cit.*) discovered an acropolis hill on the northwest slope of Mt. Ptoon, at the northeast end of Lake Paralimni, and above the northwest shore of the Lake. He reported walls about 2 m. thick and a small section of a "Mycenaean" wall. The recent reces-

Map C 73

sion of the waters of the Lake has revealed ancient structures at many points at the edge of the lake here, and these are described as "an entire town" [*AAA* 4 (1971) 332], probably ancient Isos, at the southeast foot of the acropolis. Many buildings and graves were found in or near the water. Rock-cut tombs at the north corner of the lake are probably Early Helladic, since sherds of that period were found in their vicinity. Two rectangular enclosures containing cist graves are reported to have yielded Middle Helladic, Mycenaean, and Protogeometric finds. Pottery illustrated includes LH IIB-IIIA1, LH IIIC, and Protogeometric, but the vase assigned to the Sub-Mycenaean period [*AAA* 4 (1971) 330 Fig. 16] might be much later than this. Some LH IIB vases were also found in an isolated cist grave. Excavation in the settlement produced much LH III pottery, from rather disturbed levels. There is no specific record as yet of the LH III sub-periods included, and it would be very interesting to know whether the site was occupied in the LH IIIA2 and LH IIIB periods. Later habitation may have been continuous from the Protogeometric to the Hellenistic periods. On the high hill of Chelonokastro to north of this area, Mycenaean, Archaic, and Classical remains have been observed.

C 32 LOUKISIA: ANCIENT ANTHEDON *
EH II MH LH IIIB-C LG A C H

Frazer, *Pausanias* V 92; *AJA* 5 (1889) 78, 443, 6 (1890) 96; *AM* 19 (1894) 457; Desborough (1964) 48 n. 6; *AA* (1968) 21; *CG* Figs. 14, 16c-d; *CSHI* 32.

The acropolis of ancient Anthedon is not very high, but is quite large (about 180 m. northwest to southeast by 160 m. on the top), and has extensive slopes. It commands a small sheltered harbour to the north. Trial excavations on the acropolis [*AJA* 6 (1890) 99] were said to have revealed only "two walls roughly built of small, irregular stones". But some bronze tools and other objects were found elsewhere on the site, including double axe heads [*AJA* 6 (1890) 104 and Pl. XV]. It seems likely that these finds, like other such hoards, belong to the end of the LH IIIB period; although Desborough (*loc.cit.*) argued that a fragment of a tripod rim suggests the possibility of a LH IIIC date. Both the LH IIIB and LH IIIC periods are represented among the abundant surface sherds [*cf. AA* (1968) 25 n. 25]. There are remains of ancient circuit walls, presumably Classical or Hellenistic, on both the north and the southwest sides (*cf.* the important recent study of the site and its environs, in *AA loc.cit.*). The site is impressive, and its harbour may have been of some importance, since it supplies the easiest link with the sea for the Theban plain.

C 33 DROSIA (formerly CHALIA): SOROS *
N EH I-III MH LH I/II LH IIIA-B LH IIIC?

Frazer, *Pausanias* V 91; *AD* 1 (1915) 246, 25 (1970) B 222; S.C. Bakhuizen, *Salganeus and the Fortifications on its Mountains: Chalcidian Studies II* (1970) 6; *AJA* 73 (1969) 246; *BCH* 96 (1972) 709; *CG* Figs. 9-15, 16b-d.

This prehistoric site is a low ridge, on the south side of a small bay about 3.5 km. west of Drosia. The main area of settlement was evidently the upper part at the northwest end. The small knoll of "high mound" type here measures only about 95 m. northwest to southeast by 50 m. A much smaller mound, possibly a burial tumulus, lies about 250 m. to the southeast, at the end of the ridge. This smaller mound in particular may have given rise to the legend of the "Tomb of Salganeus", mentioned by Pausanias as being on the way from Chalcis to Anthedon (*cf.* Frazer and Bakhuizen *loc.cit.*). The results of the earlier excavations [*AD* 1 (1915) *loc.cit., cf. Parartema* 55] were not published. In the recent trial excavations [*AD* 25 (1970) *loc.cit.*] the Early Helladic remains were the most prominent. But fine Middle Helladic and Middle Helladic and Mycenaean surface sherds were found here in 1959. According to the recent excavation report, the site was abandoned at the end of the LH IIIB period or in the early part of the LH IIIC period. Surface sherds in the BSA collection include late LH IIIB, but none certainly later (*pace CG* Fig. 16d). There are also traces of chamber tombs in hill slopes to the east of the site.

C 34 RHITSONA: ANCIENT MYKALESSOS *
LH G A C H

CSHI 22.

The site is a low knoll about 400 m. southwest of Rhitsona and 300 m. west of the road from Thebes to Chalkis. The excavations in the nearby Geometric and later cemetery [*BSA* 14 (1907-8) 216] provide support for the identification of the site as that of ancient Mykalessos; and there are traces of circuit walls and other ancient foundations, including Classical house walls [*cf. AD* 20 (1965) B 243]. The site is now known to have been occupied in the Mycenaean period, since Mycenaean surface sherds have been discovered by J.M. Fossey. The Mycenaean settlement appears to have been confined to the knoll, whereas the historic Mykalessos was certainly more extensive.

THE ASOPOS VALLEY (C 35-40)

This district is not a coherent geographical unit, but consists mainly of low hills with occasional small plateaus and valleys. The land is generally quite fertile, and there is every reason to believe that many more Mycenaean settlements existed here than the few which have been discovered. The most important of the known sites is Eutresis (C 39), which lies on the easiest route between Thebes and the Corinthian Gulf [see under Livadostro (C 41) below].

C 35 KALLITHEA (formerly MOUSTAPHADHES): PYRGARI *
LH IIB-IIIB H

AD 19 (1964) B 199, 20 (1965) B 242, 23 (1968) B 224, 26 (1971) B 213; *AAA* 3 (1970) 328.

A large cemetery of Mycenaean chamber tombs has been discovered at Voros, in the slopes of the hill of Pyrgari at the northern edge of Kallithea village. The pottery from the 15 excavated tombs is of excellent quality, and covers a wide range of periods. Among the other contents is a Type E dagger. The habitation site has not yet been found.

C 36 DAPHNI: AYIOS MELETIOS
LH III(A-B) C H

Frazer, *Pausanias* V 21; *AJA* 61 (1957) 9; W.K. Pritchett, *Studies in Ancient Greek Topography* 1 (1965) 103; *CSHI* 21.

This site is one of three (C 36-38) found in the northern foothills of Mt. Kithairon. It is marked by the ruined Metochi of Ayios Meletios, which lies about 800 m. west of Daphni (formerly Darimari) on the road to modern Erythrai. A small plateau here to north of the road lies at the foot of a spur of Mt. Kithairon. There is a fine spring below on the northeast. Classical and Hellenistic sherds and tiles predominate, but a Mycenaean kylix stem was found here by Vanderpool (Pritchett, *loc.cit.*). The site is probably that of ancient Skolos (but *cf.* Pritchett, *loc.cit. contra*).

C 37 ERYTHRAI: PANTANASSA
LH III(A-B) C H

Frazer, *Pausanias* V 2; Fimmen (1921) 6; *AJA* 61 (1957) 9; *CSHI* 24.

This site, which may be the ancient Erythrai, is a ridge, about 130 m. north to south by 80 m. on top, about 2 km. east of modern Erythrai. It is just to north of the main slope of Mt. Kithairon, and overlooks a wide stretch of the Asopos valley. The two Mycenaean sherds from "Erythrai" found by Bölte (Fimmen *loc.cit.*) were presumably from this site; and in 1961 some fragments of LH III deep bowl handles and part of a LH III animal figurine were found on the surface, among sherds predominantly Classical and Hellenistic.

C 38 ANCIENT PLATAEA *
MH? LH III(A-B) G A C H

PAE (1899) 42; Frazer *Pausanias* V 8; J.G. Frazer and A.W. Van Buren, *Graecia Antiqua* (1930) 136; *RE* 20 (1950) 2255, especially 2282 and plan on p. 2266; *CSHI* 29; Schoder (1974) 178.

Ancient Plataea occupied a broad spur protruding north from Mt. Kithairon, and overlooking the rolling hill country of the upper part of the Asopos valley. The historic site and the topography of the region have been frequently discussed and illustrated in textbooks and articles. Discussion here is mainly limited to the evidence for prehistoric remains of the site itself. Trial excavations by Skias on the uppermost northwestern part of the walled city revealed sherds ranging from "pre-Mycenaean" (a literal translation of the modern Greek description) to Archaic. Mycenaean

sherds and part of a LH III animal figurine are specifically mentioned. In 1959 a Mycenaean and a Geometric sherd were found on the surface in this same northwestern area. This part of Plataea was enclosed separately, and was apparently the inner citadel in the historic period (*Graecia Antiqua* and *RE loc.cit.*), although it was exposed to attack from the south along the line of the spur, which may explain the mining and counter-mining during the famous siege.

C 39 ANCIENT EUTRESIS *
N EH I-III MH LH I-IIIB C H

H. Goldman, *Excavations at Eutresis in Boeotia* (1913); *Hesperia* 31 (1962) 126; *CSHI* 27; *Alin* 123; Desborough (1964) 120; *CG* 39.

Ancient Eutresis is about midway between Thebes and the harbour of Livadostro (C 41) on the Corinthian Gulf. It lies on the edge of the plain of Leuktra, near the village of Parapoungia, on the south side of the road to Thebes. The main part of the site is a broad hill, about 500 m. in length (north-northeast to south-southwest), most of which is like a plateau. It has a higher summit near the north end and a lower eminence on the south. At its west foot is the spring of Arkopodi. The earlier prehistoric levels are the best preserved, and Mycenaean building remains are rare. Few Mycenaean sherds earlier than LH IIIA were found, and the foundations of only three LH III houses were explored.

The most important phase of Mycenaean construction on the site appears to have been the LH IIIB period, to which seem to belong the extensive fortification walls (which, according to tradition, were built by Amphion and Zethos, *cf.* Strabo IX. 411). These enclosed the settlement and a considerable amount of adjacent land, especially on the east and southeast, comprising an area of about 213,000 m². Of this area only about 35,000 m² was occupied by prehistoric buildings. At the southern end a well preserved section of the wall, which is of normal "Cyclopean" type, was 4.60 m. in width; and in the southwest sector there are remains of a gateway with a threshold 3.28 m. long, and apparently some kind of bastion.

The floor deposit in House V (*Eutresis* Fig. 263) probably belongs to the final Mycenaean occupation of the site. This deposit was assigned to an early phase of the LH IIIC period by Furumark (*CMP* 41, 72). But recent commentators (*e.g.* Ålin, Desborough, and French *loc.cit.*) place the pottery firmly in the LH IIIB period. The site was subsequently abandoned (there are no signs of any destruction), and was apparently not re-occupied until the Classical period.

C 40 THESPIAI: MAGOULA *
M EH II-III MH LH III(A-)B C H

Frazer, *Pausanias* V 140; *RE* Suppl. VI (1935) 609; *Hesperia* 20 (1951) 289; *BCH* 76 (1952) 219, 79 (1955) 257; *JHS* 73 (1953) 119; *CG* Figs. 10-11, 16a-d; *CSHI* 22.

Map C 75

To south of modern Thespiai, and on the south side of the road to Domvraina, is a long and fairly low ridge, above the north bank of the stream Kanavari. The higher eastern end of the ridge is called Kastro or Magoula. This was apparently the centre of the historic Thespiai (Frazer, *loc.cit.*). Trial excavations here have partly revealed a Neolithic settlement. A few Early and Middle Helladic sherds have been found, and several Mycenaean, but the extent of the Mycenaean settlement is hard to determine.

C 41   LIVADOSTRO: KASTRO
EH II   MH   LH II-IIIB

BSA 26 (1923-5) 38; Pl. VII; *AD* 24 (1969) B 185; *CG* Figs. 10, 14, 16b-d; Pritchett (1965) 49, especially 52-6, Fig. 4, Pls. 52-57; *CSHI* 27.

Kastro is a low hill, topped by a small mediaeval tower, at the end of the river valley. It is rather small, with an upper surface only about 100 m. northwest to southeast by 70 m., but the quantity and the quality of the surface sherds, which included fine Early and Middle Helladic and some early Mycenaean, were striking. Remains of two cist graves were noted on the top of the hill, and traces of a possible circuit wall on the southwest slope.

On the opposite side of the valley there are extensive remains of an ancient road, which connected ancient Thespiai (C 40) with the ports of Kreusis (opposite Livadostro, on the west side of the coastal plain) and Siphai (near Halike, No. C 42 below). The masonry of the supporting terraces of this road closely resembles "Cyclopean" [Pritchett (1965) Pls. 52-3], and the gradients are made as easy as possible by means of numerous zig-zag bends on the way up the northwest slopes of the valley. On the height of land near Ayios Mamas, overlooking both the Livadostro bay and the plain of Leuktra, there are well preserved wheel ruts in the rock [Pritchett (1965) Pl. 57b] in several places. The ruts (measured in 1961) are about 1.40 m. apart (inner edge to inner edge), *i.e.* of the same gauge as those observed at Bazaraki (C 21) near Larymna. The date of the road is not established, but a Mycenaean origin is not ruled out. It was obviously in use in the classical period, to judge from the tower in isodomic polygonal masonry, about 100 m. east of Ayios Mamas [Pritchett (1965) 55, Pl. 56].

C 42   HALIKE (or ALIKI):   ANCIENT SIPHAI
MH   LH I/II?   LH IIIA-B   C   H

BSA 26 (1923-5) 40, 44; Pritchett (1965) 49, Fig. 4.

The small coastal plain of Aliki is shut in by high mountains. Towards its southern end is a prominent ridge, running east to west, on whose top are the fortifications of Ancient Siphai, which end in a mole projecting about 30 m. into the sea. Siphai was evidently the terminus of the ancient road from Thespiae discussed above (under C 41). Heurtley (*BSA loc.cit.*)

found Middle Helladic and Mycenaean sherds on the south slope of the acropolis, and just below the summit traces of a wall of large blocks which he considered to be probably Mycenaean.

C 43   THISBE: PALAIOKASTRO   #   (Plate 16a)
MH   LH IIIA-B   A   C   H

Frazer, *Pausanias* V 160; *JHS* 45 (1925) 1; *BSA* 26 (1923-5) 41, 44; *AM* 73 (1958) 17; *AD* 25 (1970) B 232; *CSHI* 27.

The hill of Palaiokastro (Plate 16a) lies on the northwest side of modern Thisbe (formerly Kakosi) below Mt. Helikon. The hill tapers as it slopes down to the southeast, towards the village. Its total length (northwest to southeast) is about 300 m., and the width on the top is about 100 m. On its northwest end are remains of a wall corner built of massive blocks, which seems to be the inner face of a "Cyclopean" circuit wall. The top surface of the hill and the extensive slopes are strewn with Mycenaean sherds of very fine quality, and there were few later sherds observed here (in 1961). Indeed it appears that the historic Thisbe was mainly centred on the lower hill named Neokastro, on the south side of the village. This hill is much broader, and has a much flatter top. It has impressive remains of fortifications in good isodomic masonry, including a well preserved tower (*AM loc.cit.*), which must belong to the Classical or Hellenistic period.

At the south foot of Neokastro, and in other slopes in the vicinity, remains of chamber tombs are evident, some of which were Mycenaean (*BSA loc.cit.*). Other tombs were noted to northwest of the village, near Palaiokastro (*cf. AD loc.cit.* for further chamber tombs), and it is perhaps from one of these that the genuine artefacts among the famous "Thisbe Treasure" (*JHS loc.cit.*) were looted. The goods in this "treasure", apart from the rings, appear genuine, and are probably of LH IIIA-B date.

The Mycenaean settlement at Thisbe was obviously important, and it lies at the junction of important routes leading from the harbours at Vathy and Chorsiai (C 44) to Orchomenos (*via* the Steveniko pass and Kalami, No. C 19 above), to Orchomenos (*via* Thespiai). A fertile plain stretches to south of Thisbe, over an extent of about 2.5 km. east to west by 2 km., and the ancient dyke seen by Pausanias (Frazer *loc.cit.*), which divided the plain into two halves, may also have carried the road to the harbour. The area is now being intensively surveyed by teams from Ohio State University and the universities of Cambridge and Bradford.

C 44   CHORSIAI
MH   LH IIIA-B   C

BSA 26 (1923-5) 42, 44.

The fortress of Ancient Chorsiai stood at the south end of a spur of Mt. Helikon, which ends abruptly about 2 km. from the sea in a steep crag, with sheer precipices on its western side. On the slopes above these precipices Heurtley found Middle Helladic and Mycenaean sherds (*BSA loc.cit.*). The harbour at Chorsiai would have provided a link with the Peloponnese, although the harbour at Vathy in the Domvraina bay to south of Thisbe would appear to have been safer [*BSA* 26 (1923-5) 41].

PHOCIS AND DORIS (C 45-63, 63A, 63B)

The Mycenaean sites discovered in the territory of ancient Phocis form two main groups, those to south-west and south of Mt. Parnassos (Nos. C 49-55) and those on either side of the Kephissos river valley (Nos. C 45-48 and C 56-63). The only links between the two regions are the pass to Delphi between Mt. Parnassos and Mt. Helikon and the pass from the Gulf of Itea via Amphissa to the upper part of the Kephissos valley in ancient Doris. Known Mycenaean settlements in the upper part of the valley are sparse, but this picture may be modified when the results of recent survey work are available. A preliminary report of the Phokis-Doris expedition of Loyola University contains brief mentions of Mycenaean finds at three sites in the vicinity of ancient Doris. The exact locations of the sites have not yet been given, so that they can not be marked on Map C, but they are here assigned the numbers C 63B (Paliambela), C 73A (Dhiovouna) and C 73B (Kastro Orias) respectively. The prehistoric site at Lilaia should now also be included (as C 63A), since N. Wilkie and P. Ålin have recently found Mycenaean sherds there (see also Addenda).

C 45   CHAIRONEIA: The Acropolis
N EH LH A C H

MV 84; Fimmen (1921) 5; *AD* 24 (1969) B 179; *Euphrosyne* 6 (1973-4) 10; Schoder (1974) 94.

The acropolis of ancient Chaironeia is strategically placed at the border between ancient Phocis and ancient Boeotia. Modern Chaironeia (formerly Kapraina) lies at its east foot below a long thin ridge (Schoder *loc.cit.*). Sherds both on the acropolis and in the lower city to north and east of it include Neolithic, Early Helladic, and Mycenaean, and remains of a "Cyclopean" circuit wall are claimed on the acropolis [*Euphrosyne loc.cit.*, citing *AM* 28 (1903) 324, Pl. 4]. Two Mycenaean chamber tombs and signs of probable others have been observed on the east slope (*AD loc.cit.*).

C 46 CHAIRONEIA: MAGOULA BALOMENOU *
N MH LH IIIB

AE (1908) 63; *PAE* (1909) 123; *PT* 197; *CG* Fig. 14.

This large mound lies near the south bank of the Kephissos river, and about 2 km. north-northeast of Chaironeia village. From the excavations here only

Neolithic material was reported, but Middle Helladic surface sherds have been found (*CG* Fig. 14), and five LH IIIB sherds in the Chaironeia museum are marked as from the site.

C 47   AYIOS VLASIS: ANCIENT PANOPEUS
MH LH IIIA-B C H

Frazer, *Pausanias* V 215; *CSHI* 42, Pl. 3; *CG* Figs. 16c-d.

The acropolis of ancient Panopeus towers above the village of Ayios Vlasis, which lies at its north foot, on the south side of a broad valley (a tributary of the Kephissos valley), which is bounded on the west by the foothills of Mt. Parnassos. The hill dominates the routes to north and east, and also a small pass through the hills on the south. Fortifications of the historic period are well preserved on the summit, especially on the south side, and there are also remains of a "Cyclopean" circuit wall (in one place three to four courses high, *CSHI* Pl. 3b), running around the southeast slopes about 40 metres below the line of the later walls. At the eastern end of the hill the Cyclopean wall turns to the north, again following the line taken by the later walls, but continuing outside and below them. It appears therefore that the Cyclopean wall once enclosed the whole of the rocky summit (about 250 m. east to west by 80 m.) and much of the upper slopes on the east side.

Middle Helladic and Mycenaean sherds were found in 1961 in the southeast part of the hill, near the Cyclopean wall, and remains of small cist graves, apparently associated with Mycenaean sherds. Obsidian was also plentiful here. The Mycenaean settlement here certainly appears to have been important, and the site certainly would have controlled a wide extent of good agricultural land (*cf. Od.*xi. 581). It was celebrated in legend as the place where Prometheus made the first men (Frazer, *Pausanias loc.cit.*).

C 48 DAVLEIA: ANCIENT DAULIS
EH I MH LH I/II? LH III(A-)B C H

Frazer, *Pausanias* V 222; *MV* 43; *PT* 201; *Alin* 134; *CSHI* 42; *CG* Figs. 16c-d.

The acropolis of ancient Daulis is a massive rounded hill, one of the foothills of Mt. Parnassos, to which it is connected by a narrow ridge on the northwest, where there are the remains of a gateway. This is part of the fortifications of the historic period, of which traces remain elsewhere on the hill, although they are not so well preserved as those of ancient Panopeus (C 47). The top surface of the hill, about 250 m. north to south by 200 m., is mostly covered in dense scrub with a few trees. In 1881 a well was cleared on the acropolis (*MV loc.cit.*). It contained mainly Middle Helladic pottery, but also some Mycenaean sherds (including LH IIIB, according to Alin *loc.cit.*), together with obsidian blades and small stone

Map C 77

whorls. In 1959 some worn LH III sherds were found on the surface and a rim fragment from a stemmed bowl of Yellow Minyan ware which may be Middle Helladic or early Mycenaean.

The site controls a route to south which connects with the pass leading to Delphi. It also commands a pass to the north into the Kephissos valley *via* modern Davleia, which is about a kilometre to the north. There is a copious spring at the north foot of the acropolis, near which are the remains of some disused mills.

C 49 ANCIENT MEDEON *
EH III MH LH IIIA1-C PG G A C H

Hunter 27, 236; *AD* 19 (1964) B 223; C. Vatin, *Médéon de Phocide* (1969).

Ancient Medeon was centred on the low hill of Ayios Theodoros, near the north shore of the Corinthian Gulf, about 3 km. southeast of Paralia Distomou, and opposite Antikyra (C 50). The hill was fortified in historic times, and was also the site of a substantial prehistoric settlement, which apparently began in the EH III period. A number of Mycenaean tombs found here have produced a fine sequence of Mycenaean pottery from the LH IIIA1 to the LH IIIC periods. Some of the tombs were in use throughout this range. The graves included pits and cists, and also built tombs with entrances, mostly rectangular but one shaped like a tholos. Two whole vases of the late Middle Helladic period (*Hunter* nos. 247-8) may have come from earlier tombs, but no diagnostic early Mycenaean material has been found. It seems unlikely, however, that the site was abandoned during this phase. Several of the Mycenaean tombs contained rich goods, and these indicate that the Mycenaean settlement was important. A few graves are attributed to the end of the LH IIIC period, perhaps contemporary with Sub-Mycenaean. Cremation pits of Protogeometric and Geometric date were also found, and an unbroken sequence of burials thereafter up to the Hellenistic period. It seems possible therefore that there was continuity at the site from the end of the Bronze Age onwards.

C 50 ANTIKYRA: KASTRO TOU STENOU
LH IIIB LH IIIC? PG C H

AE (1956) *Parartema* 24; Desborough (1964) 126; *Alin* 132.

Kastro tou Stenou is about 1.5 km. southwest of Antikyra, near Stenon, a group of houses belonging to the village of Desphina. It is a low acropolis hill, steep on all sides except the north. LH IIIB and other Mycenaean sherds were found on the west slopes of the hill (*AE loc.cit.*), and Mycenaean cist graves were discovered a short distance to the southwest, near the chapel of Ayios Sotiros, in the plain between the acropolis and the sea. The site overlooks a small harbour, at the end of the route between Mt. Parnassos and Mt. Helikon, *via* Distomon.

C 51 CHRYSO: ANCIENT KRISA * # (Plate 18a)
MH LH I/II LH IIIA1-B C H

Frazer, *Pausanias* V 459; *RA* (1936) 129; *BCH* 61 (1937) 299, 62 (1938) 110; *BSA* 59 (1964) 242; Desborough (1964) 125; *CSHI* 41.

The acropolis of ancient Krisa, at Ayios Yeoryios on the south side of Chryso village, occupies the tip of a long rocky spur projecting southward from Mt. Parnassos, and ending in precipices overhanging the Pleistos valley. The site completely dominates the Amphissa plain and the Gulf of Krisa, and commands the routes up the Pleistos valley, both the upper one *via* Delphi and the lower one along the bottom of the valley. Fortifications were unnecessary on the precipitous south and east sides, but on the north and west there are remains of extensive Cyclopean circuit walls attributed to the LH IIIB period. They are built of very massive blocks (one recorded by Frazer, *loc.cit.*, was almost three metres in length and about 1.60 m. high), and enclose an area about 350 m. north to south by 300 m.

The site was probably inhabited continuously from the Middle Helladic to the LH IIIB periods (*Kirrha* Pl. 34b is probably LH IIB). Of the four excavated building strata, two are attributed to late Middle Helladic (the second of which is covered by a burnt layer), the third to LH IIIA1, and the fourth to LH IIIB (*BSA loc.cit.*, cf. Desborough *loc.cit.*). The LH III buildings were substantial, some containing column bases. The site appears to have been destroyed and abandoned by the end of the LH IIIB period. Although it was obviously important, and probably the chief site in this region, the Mycenaean settlement, like that at Eutresis (C 39), does not appear to have covered all of the area enclosed by its fortifications, whose line was largely dictated by the lie of the land in both cases.

C 52 DELPHI *
N MH LH IIIA2-C PG G A C H

Fouilles de Delphes II 5, V 1; *RA* (1938) 187; *BCH* 59 (1935) 275, 329, 61 (1937) 707, 85 (1961) 352, 365, 96 (1972) 997; Desborough (1964) 122; Schoder (1974) 45; *CSHI* 40.

The Corycian Cave: *BCH* 95 (1971) 776, 96 (1972) 899.

The main area of Mycenaean settlement seems to have been on the slopes to northeast and east of the Temple of Apollo. The remains of houses are not very extensive, and are mainly of LH III date. The LH IIIB phase was the most important, but the settlement lasted into the earlier part of the LH IIIC period, when it may have been abandoned because of a flood and/or a fall of rocks from the heights above. Some chamber tombs to west and southwest of the Temenos have produced LH IIIB and LH IIIC pottery (mainly the latter). The tombs were roughly circular, cut into the rock, and were mainly without dromoi.

A Mycenaean "cult" is suggested by the quantity of female Mycenaean figurines discovered in various areas, especially the 175 complete or fragmentary "goddess" figurines found in the area of the sanctuary of Athena Pronaia at Marmaria. These were not connected with any remains of settlement, and were probably transferred from elsewhere. The deposit in which they were found appears to have been of the Geometric period [*BCH* 81 (1957) 707]. The area of the Altar of Apollo was thick with Mycenaean sherds, and some figurines were found here also. The Marmaria figurines could have been taken from here or from the area of Mycenaean settlement to the northeast. In any case, they are presumably evidence of a sacred place somewhere in the vicinity.

The main settlement seems to have dwindled after the early part of the LH IIIC period. But some of the pottery from the rich tomb to west of the Temenos is said to be possibly contemporary with Athenian Sub-Mycenaean (Desborough, *loc.cit.*); and there is said to be a "persistance d'une catégorie de céramique domestique locale" (L. Dor *et al.*, *Kirrha* (1960) 17], which appears to follow on traces of fire in one or two places. Burials of early Protogeometric date were found in one tomb in the Museum area. It is therefore likely that there was some habitation at Delphi in the period of transition from the Bronze Age to the Iron Age, if not continuity of occupation.

In the Corycian cave Palaeolithic and Neolithic deposits have been found and there is also some LH III material.

C 53 KIRRHA: MAGOULA XEROPIGADO *
EH II-III MH LH I-IIIB G?

L. Dor *et al.*, *Kirrha, Etude de préhistoire phocidienne* (1960); *JHS* 49 (1929) 89; *Antiquity* 38 (1964) 138; *AAA* 1 (1968) 144, 6 (1973) 70; *BCH* 99 (1975) 35; *CG* Figs. 10-12, 14, 16-b-d; *AD* 28 (1973) B 318.

This is a large site, of "low mound" type, near the coast on the east side of the mouth of the Pleistos river, and less than 2 km. east of Itea. It is centred on the church of the Dormition, but remains of prehistoric habitation have now been identified at least 100 m. to east of the main site. The most substantial finds were late MH buildings and a series of graves ranging from late MH to LH IIB. The graves included large cists containing several burials, sometimes accompanied by weapons or jewellery. There is now better evidence for LH III occupation than was found in the original excavation, including house remains and abundant Mycenaean pottery, although these upper levels have been much disturbed. It appears that the settlement did not continue after the LH IIIB period.

Traces of ancient mining were reported in the neighbourhood of the site (*JHS loc.cit.*), but it is now known that the material sought was certainly not tin (*Antiquity loc.cit.*).

C 54 ITEA: GLA
LH IIIA2-B LH IIIC? "PG"

AD 6 (1920-21) 147; L. Lerat, *Les Locriens de l'Ouest* (1952) 164; *AE* (1956) *Parartema* 24; Desborough (1964) 126.

Gla is a low hill on the west side of the junction of the roads from Itea to Amphissa and to Chryso and Delphi, about a kilometre north of Itea. It is a precipitous rock, accessible only from the west, at the end of a spur projecting from the hills on the western edge of the Amphissa plain. Surface sherds found include fine quality LH IIIA2-B and some probably LH IIIC. A probably Mycenaean cemetery was noted nearby at Keramos, to west of the district called Gonia. This adjoins the hill of Moulki, where chamber tombs were found, reported to be similar to those at Delphi, but larger. Vases from these tombs (Lerat *loc.cit.*) are of the LH IIIB-C and early Protogeometric periods (Desborough *loc.cit.*).

C 55 KASTROULI *
MH LH III(A-B)

L. Dor *et al.*, *Kirrha* (1960) 20.

The site is described as a prominent hill, on the escarpment above the north bank of the Pleistos river. It is about 3 km. southwest of Arachova. Some large Middle Helladic cist tombs and remains of some Mycenaean buildings are reported. The finds are described as rather poor (they remain unpublished) and the site is presumably not significant.

C 56 ANTHOCHORION: LEVENDI
LH IIIA2-B C H

Frazer, *Pausanias* V 418; *CSHI* 44; *CG* Fig. 16d.

The broad hill of Levendi, the site of ancient Parapotamioi, is connected on the east to the ridge which bounds the Chaironeia plain on the north side, and extends eastward to Orchomenos. The hill dominates the defile named Stena between the Chaironeia plain and the broader plain of the main Kephissos valley to the west. The hilltop is only about 40 m. above the level of the valley, but is well defended by steep escarpments on all sides. Below the hill to the northwest, on the other side of the Kephissos river, is the junction of the modern roads to Amphikleia and Atalanti. The flat upper surface of the hill, about 250 m. north to south by 200 m. is rather bare, and surface sherds are relatively sparse. They are mainly Classical and Hellenistic, but some Bronze Age coarse ware and a fragment from a LH IIIB kylix were found in 1959. Walling of masonry resembling Cyclopean was noted on the east side.

C 57 EXARCHOS: ANCIENT HYAMPOLIS
EH I LH IIIB C H

JHS 16 (1896) 291; Frazer, *Pausanias* V 443; *CSHI* 43; *CG* Figs. 9, 16d.

Map C 79

The little valley of Exarchos is enclosed on all sides by rugged hills (on one of which stands the historic fortress of Abae). In the middle of the valley, about 2 km. west of the village of Exarchos, is a flat table-land with steep slopes, whose top is about 30 m. above the level of the valley. This natural acropolis was the site of ancient Hyampolis, fortified in historic times by walls of excellent isodomic masonry, enclosing an area about 200 m. northeast to southwest by 150 m. Due to the thick cover of Classical, Hellenistic, and later material, no prehistoric material was found on the surface within the walled area. But on the eroded slopes outside the walls some Bronze Age sherds, including EH I and one LH IIIB, and obsidian chips were found in 1959. Although one sherd constitutes only slim evidence for Mycenaean occupation, argument for this is supported in this case by other considerations, *i.e.* the suitability of the site and its surroundings for settlement, and its strategic position on the easiest route from Orchomenos to the coastal plain of Atalanti.

C 58 AYIA PARASKEVI: AYIA MARINA *
N EH I-III MH LH IIIA-B LH IIIC?

PAE (1910) 163, (1911) 205; *REG* 25 (1912) 211, 270; *PT* 12; *Hunter* 108; *CG passim.*

The "low mound" site of Ayia Marina lies on the north side of the Kephissos river, about 1.5 km. northeast of Ayia Paraskevi (formerly the Kalyvia of Ayia Marina). The site is not large (about 120 m. east to west by 100 m.), but trial excavations here established a long history of occupation, perhaps continuous from Neolithic. Interest has focussed on the deep early deposits, which have yielded a fine variety of stratified wares. Some Mycenaean pottery was found. It remains unpublished, except for some sherds discussed by Hunter (*loc.cit., cf. CG* Fig. 16d).

C 59 ELATEIA (formerly DHRACHMANI): PIPERI *
N EH I-III MH LH IIA-III(A2-B)

AM 31 (1906) 402; *AE* (1908) 93; *PAE* (1909) 127, (1910) 161; *REG* 25 (1912) 256, 269; *JHS* 35 (1915) 196; *PT* 204; *Hunter* 108; *CG passim.*

About 1.5 km. northwest of Elateia village is the mound known as "Dhrachmani-Piperi" (in various spellings in the publications). Most of the mound consists of Neolithic deposits. Only the top metre contains Bronze Age material. There are some fragmentary remains of the Mycenaean settlement, including foundations of a wall and a "tower" built of undressed blocks, and a pavement. A group of plain LH III whole vases may represent a destruction or an abandonment of the site. They resemble the material from the "House of Kadmos" at Thebes, but there are no certain LH IIIB vases or sherds; so that the settlement may have come to an end either during or just before

the early part of the LH IIIB period. There is no good evidence as to the size of the Mycenaean site.

C 60 ANCIENT ELATEIA *
LH IIIB G A C

P. Paris, *Elatée* (1892) 283, Fig. 21; *MP* 647; *Alin* 134.

One or more sherds were found during the excavations at the site of the Temple of Athena Kranaia at ancient Elateia, about 3 km. northeast of modern Elateia. The one sherd illustrated (Paris, *loc.cit.*) is assigned to the LH IIIB period by Ålin (*loc.cit.*).

C 61 MODION: AVLAKI POURI
LH III(A2-B)

RE 20 (1941) 478.

Three Mycenaean chamber tombs were reported at Avlaki Pouri near Modion. Two stirrup-jars were noted as among the contents.

C 62 AMPHIKLEIA: AYIOI ANARGYROI * # (Plate 17b)
LH III(A-C)? SMyc

AD 25 (1970) B 237, 26 (1971) B 231.

A row of chamber tombs was found about 400 m. south-southeast of the chapel of Ayioi Anargyroi, which is about 4 km. southeast of Amphikleia. The site overlooks the main Kephissos valley (Plate 17b), and is in fact separated from Amphikleia by hills. The tombs, of which eleven were excavated, are on the northeast edge of the pine forest on the lower slopes of Mt. Parnassos, overlooking cultivated terraces above the chapel, which is on a gently sloping spur above the valley. Sherds of coarse ware on the surface near the chapel may include Bronze Age. To judge from the description of the pottery and other objects found in the tombs, the burials may belong mainly to the Sub-Mycenaean phase, although the cemetery is likely to have begun earlier. The tombs are of conventional type, with the usual inclination of the dromoi towards the top. Some had a slab blocking the entrance instead of a wall, and many contained pits in which earlier (and displaced) burials were put. Long pins and fibulae were prominent among the grave goods, and other small bronze objects were found.

C 63 AMPHIKLEIA: PALAIOKASTRO (ANCIENT TITHRONION) # (Plate 17a)
LH III(A2-B) C

AE (1956) *Parartema* 25; *Alin* 133.

Ancient Tithronion [*cf. BSA* 17 (1910-11) 54] was centered on a broad low hill about 4.5 km. north-northeast of Amphikleia. The hill was fortified in the Classical period. The Kephissos river runs past the south foot of the hill, and there is a tributary stream below the steep northwest flank, where some Myce-

naean sherds (said to include LH IIIB) were found on
the surface. Although the site is not large (its top surface is about 180 m. northeast to southwest by 120 m.),
its position is strategic.

C 63A   LILAIA (formerly KATO AGORIANI)   # (Not marked on Map C)
MH LH III C H

CSHI 44; *CG* Figs. 16c-d.

The historic Lilaia occupied a long thin ridge
above and to southeast of the village [*cf.* Frazer,
Pausanias V 410; *BSA* 17 (1910-11) 60]. Not far to north
of the classical fortifications, and only about 400 m. to
east-northeast of the village, is a small pointed rocky
hill, standing about 40 m. above the level of the plain
below. The upper surface of the hill measures about
200 m. north to south by 130 m. On the broad terraces,
mainly those to north and east of the small conical
peak in the centre, many fragments from coarse
Bronze Age vessels were found in 1959, and also some
Grey and Yellow Minyan ware sherds and a fragment
with monochrome paint which appeared to be from a
LH III deep bowl. Further Mycenaean pottery has now
been found at the site by N. Wilkie and P. Ålin (see
Addenda). The site has not been marked on Map C,
but it is located about 7 km. due west of Amphikleia.

C 63B   PALIAMBELA   (Not marked on Map C)
LH III(A-B) G? A? C H

P.W. Wallace, in *Symposium on the Dark Ages in Greece* (1977)
55.

Paliambela lies to southwest of Gravia, in the
vicinity of the pass to Amphissa (which is about 16 km.
to the south). Two Mycenaean kylix fragments are
mentioned among the surface sherds found here by
the Phokis-Doris expedition of Loyola University.

EASTERN LOCRIS (C64-69)

Most of the Mycenaean sites discovered in this
province are near the coast. Only one, at Agnandi (C
69), is inland. The plain of Molos in the northwest
part, and the fertile valleys which lead from it into the
interior, are particularly good targets for search. But
even in the Atalanti plain, for instance, fieldwork has
been quite inadequate. None of the sites found are
particularly large.

C 64   THEOLOGOS: ANCIENT HALAI
N LH C H

AJA 19 (1915) 436; *Hesperia* 9 (1940) 381, 11 (1942) 315; *AM* 71
(1956) 8.

The main excavations here revealed traces of an
acropolis and a harbour, on the southeast side of the
bay named Ayios Ioannis Theologos (after the church

which is a little to southwest of the site). Classical and
Hellenistic finds predominated, but some Neolithic
material was found. Mycenaean sherds were discovered much later (*AM* and *BCH loc.cit.*).

C 65   KYPARISSI: AYIOS IOANNIS
LH III(B?) G A C H

AJA 30 (1926) 401; *CSHI* 47.

On the lower slopes of the foothills on the south
side of the coastal plain of Atalanti, there are signs of a
considerable ancient settlement. These are particularly
evident in the vicinity of the chapel of Ayios Ioannis,
about 1.5 km. south of Kyparissi. The small gullies
and hillocks to south of the chapel are covered in potsherds. At one point, to south of a small ravine and
about 300 m. west of the chapel, erosion had revealed
a deposit of Mycenaean, Geometric, Archaic, and
Classical sherds. Elsewhere, foundations of large
blocks and purple-glazed tiles were observed. This is
presumably the site of the lower town below the citadel of Kastraki or Kokkinovrachos, which was investigated by Blegen (*AJA loc.cit.*), whose summit is about a
kilometre to the southeast, and which may have been
the acropolis of the historic Opous. No prehistoric remains were found at the latter site.

C 66   ATALANTI: SKALA
EH III MH LH IIIB

CG Figs. 12, 14, 16b-d, 19.

This site, discovered by D.H. French, is a very
low mound, which lies about 500 m. to northwest of
the intersection of the National highway and the road
from Atalanti to the Skala of Atalanti, which is about
750 m. to east of the site. The dimensions of the
mound are about 150 m. east to west by 60 m. Mycenaean pottery of the LH IIIB period is recorded among
the surface finds.

C 67   LIVANATES: PYRGOS   #   (Plate 16c)
MH LH IIIA-C G A C H

RE 12 (1925) 29; *CSHI* 47; *CG* Figs. 14, 16c-d; *AD* 25 (1970)
240.

The low hill of Pyrgos (Plate 16c) lies about 2 km.
northeast of Livanates, and only about 30 m. from the
shore. It is a conspicuous "high mound" site with
steep slopes. The top surface, about 130 m. north to
south by 90 m., and the fields below to west and south
are covered in ancient sherds, predominantly Mycenaean, Classical, and Hellenistic. On the hilltop itself
obsidian, fine Middle Helladic wares, and copious
Mycenaean sherds (including a LH IIIC krater fragment with panel-style pattern) were found with later
material. The LH IIIA and LH IIIB fine wares are of
very good quality. A small cist grave (with the skull
still inside) was observed in 1959 near the southeast

Map C 81

end of the hill, and there are apparent signs of others. The remains of a circuit wall on the west and north-west slopes, running just below the crest of the hill, are presumably Classical or Hellenistic, as are probably also the ruins of a small square tower at the north end. The site has been identified as that of ancient Kynos (*RE loc.cit.; cf. CSHI loc.cit.*).

C 68 MELIDONI: KASTRO
EH I EH III MH LH IIIA-B C H

CG Figs. 9, 11, 14, 16c-d.

Kastro is a rocky spur, about a kilometre north-west of the village of Melidoni, towering above the sea, and commanding the eastern end of the coastal plain of Longos. The hill is sheer on all sides except the south, where it is joined to a higher ridge by a low saddle. The top surface, about 150 m. north to south by 100 m., is covered in rough building stones, tiles and sherds. The latter are mainly Classical and Hellenistic, but there were also several prehistoric, especially some good Middle Helladic and Mycenaean. There are remains of a circuit wall in rough masonry on the east side, and this may possibly be Mycenaean. At the northern foot are some Byzantine remains, near a spring named Ayio Nero. The site is probably that of Locrian Alope, the next city after Kynos on the coast of eastern Locris (Strabo IX 4, 3).

C 69 AGNANDI: KASTRI and KRITHARIA *
EH MH LH IIIA-C SMyc or PG? C H

AD 25 (1970) B 235.

The prehistoric settlement was on the steep spur of Kastri about a kilometre to northeast of Agnandi village, overlooking dissected hill country in the interior, separated from the coastal plain by high ridges. There is abundant evidence of Bronze Age and later habitation here. The chamber tomb cemetery at Kritharia, on a slope at the south west edge of Agnandi, was in use from the LH IIIA to LH IIIC periods or even later, to judge from the finds described, which include a jar with semicircles on the shoulder, pins, fibulae, and iron rings. This site is the first to be discovered in the remote inland region of eastern Locris.

THE SPERCHEIOS VALLEY AND MALIS (C 71-77)

Some extensive survey work has been carried out in this region, most recently by the Phokis-Doris expedition of Loyola University. It is obvious, from the discoveries recently made, that many more Mycenaean settlements are to be expected here, especially along the shores of the Malian Gulf. Two newly discovered sites, C 73A (Dhiovouna) and C 73B (Kastro Orias), not marked on Map C, supply further evidence for the importance of the area in the vicinity of ancient Trachis and Herakleia, on the southern side of the Spercheios valley, and on the inland route to the north from Phocis and Doris. There is, however, no evidence for any major Mycenaean site in the region, and claims for Mycenaean roads from Itea *via* Amphissa to the Malian Gulf [*AJA* 77 (1973) 74] have not been substantiated.

C 70 THERMOPYLAI: ANCIENT ALPENOI?
MH LH I/II? LH III(A-B) A C

AR (1961-2) 31.

A prehistoric settlement was found in 1961 on a low spur projecting northward into the marsh at the south side of the mouth of the Spercheios river, about 2 km. east of the modern Thermopylai monument. The new National highway has cut through the south side of the site. The part of the site which remains to north of the highway is about 110 m. east to west by 55 m. Sherds included Middle Helladic and Mycenaean, the latter represented mainly by LH III stemmed bowl and kylix fragments, although one base appears to be of a LH I or LH II goblet. Some Archaic and Classical sherds (one of which was incribed) and many tile fragments, together with the indications in ancient literature, strongly suggest that this is the site of ancient Alpenoi [Herodotus VII 176, 5 and 229, 1; *cf. AJA* 20 (1916) 47].

C 71 ANCIENT HERAKLEIA
LH III(B?) C H

Y. Béquignon, *La Vallée du Spercheios* (1937) 243; *Antiquity* 33 (1959) 103; Pritchett (1965) 81; *CSHI* 128.

On the lowest terraces of the site of ancient Herakleia (which supplanted Trachis in 426 B.C.) three Mycenaean sherds were found in 1958. No signs of prehistoric habitation were found on the upper citadel above.

C 72 RAKHITA
MH LH IIIA2-B LH IIIC?

Antiquity 33 (1959) 103, Pl. XVa.

About a kilometre to west-northwest of the lower slopes of ancient Herakleia (C 71) are similar terraces at the foot of the Trachinian cliffs. Here, on a small projecting tongue of land, about 60 m. east to west by 50 m., and on its north slopes, Middle Helladic and Mycenaean sherds were found in 1958. In the plain below the site two small streams, fed by springs issuing from the foot of the cliffs, unite to flow into the Xerias river. Between Rakhita and ancient Herakleia, on both sides of the Skliphomeli ravine, are remains of tombs cut in the rock. Most of these are Hellenistic or later, but some have a superficial resemblance to Mycenaean chamber tombs.

C 73 VARDHATES *
LH IIIB-C

BCH 63 (1939) 311; S. Marinatos, in *Bericht über die VI. Internationale Kongress für Archäologie* (1939) 334; *Hunter* 117, Desborough (1964) 126; *AD* 25 (1970) B 243.

A rectangular built grave was excavated near Vardhates. According to local information (in 1958), this lay to southeast of Vardhates in the direction of Rakhita (C 72), with which it may in fact be associated. The grave contained several burials with which were found a bronze spear head and some vases. These are normally attributed to the LH IIIC period, but include several which must surely be earlier [e.g. *BCH* 63 (1939) 310 Fig. 21, left]. The mound about a kilometre to northeast of Vardhates, on the track to Moschochori, has recently described as probably prehistoric (*AD loc.cit.*). But it more closely resembles a Thessalian/Macedonian tumulus of the historical period. It is about 30 m. by 25 m. and about 5 m. high.

C 72 and C 73 have been grouped together on Map C, since it does not seem that two separate settlements are indicated.

C 73A DHIOVOUNA: DHEMA (Not marked on Map C)
N EH MH LH IIIA-C PG A C H

P.W. Wallace, in *Symposium on the Dark Ages in Greece* (1977) 55.

This site lies at the northern end of the pass which connects Malis and Doris, and is marked by a massive Byzantine wall, which closed off the pass and climbed the mountains on both sides. The site itself, Dhema, is not described in the preliminary publication, but is said to be near the village of Dhiovouna (see also Addenda).

C 73B KASTRO ORIAS (Not marked on Map C)
LH III(A-B) C H

P.W. Wallace, in *Symposium on the Dark Ages in Greece* (1977) 55.

Kastro Orias is an impressive ancient citadel near the Asopos river, on a route between Doris and Malis. Most of the surface pottery found was of the Classical and later periods, but two Mycenaean kylix stems are reported.

C 74 MEGALI VRYSI: PLATANIA
N EH? MH LH IIIB LH IIIC? G

Antiquity 33 (1959) 102, Pl. XIVb; *AD* (1964) B 242.

About 4 km. east of Lamia, on the old road, is the spring of Platania. To south of the road at this point is a fairly large "low mound" site, about 170 m. northwest to southeast by 150 m., on whose surface Middle Helladic and Mycenaean sherds were found and one Geometric. Neolithic sherds are also reported (*AD loc.cit.*).

C 75 AKHINOS: ANCIENT ECHINOUS
MH LH IIIA2-B C H

Y. Béquignon, *La Vallée du Spercheios* (1937) 299; *AJA* (1942) 500; *Antiquity*, 33 (1959) 102, Pl. XIVa.

The acropolis of ancient Echinous is on a low limestone hill, on the north side of Akhinos village commanding a small fertile coastal plain, which stretches about 5 km. east to west by 2 km. The upper surface of the hill, about 200 m. northwest to southeast by 150 m., is enclosed by fortifications of the Classical period. Most of the surface sherds were Classical or Hellenistic, but a few Mycenaean and one Middle Helladic were also found. The plundered chamber tombs near the hill (*AJA loc.cit.*) are almost certainly Mycenaean.

C 76 RAKHES: FOURNI
N EH I-III MH LH IIIA1-B LH IIIC? C

AR (1961-2) 31; *CG* Figs. 9-11, 14, 16a-d.

Fourni (also known as "Kafki") is a low promontory on the edge of a small coastal plain, about 1.5 km. east of Rakhes in a district called Alopeka. The spread of surface pottery indicates an area of settlement about 120 m. north to south by 100 m., on the promontory and its slopes. Mycenaean sherds include one which must be LH IIIA1 at the latest. The prehistoric sherds were of excellent quality, especially the Mycenaean.

C 77 PELASGIA: ANCIENT LARISA CREMASTE
MH LH IIIB C H

Béquignon (1937) 140; *Antiquity* 33 (1959) 102; *AD* 25 (1970) B 243; *AAA* 5 (1972) 470.

The citadel of Larisa Cremaste lies about 2 km. to north of modern Pelasgia. The site commands a fine view of Euboea and the Malian Gulf, and dominates the route from Lamia to Volos. The historic fortifications are well preserved, especially on the west side. Among the plethora of Classical and Hellenistic surface sherds, two LH IIIB deep bowl fragments were found in 1958.

Two Matt-painted jugs of the Middle Helladic period, found on a tumulus near Pelasgia (*AD* and *AAA loc.cit.*) suggest that there was an important prehistoric settlement here, which may not have been centred on the site of Larisa Cremaste itself.

NORTHERN EUBOEA (C 78-84)

The northern part of Euboea is dissected by several mountain ranges, and the only plain of any size is that of Histiaia. There are smaller strips of lowland at various other points along the coast, especially at Kerinthos (C 82), Rovies (C 83) and Limni (C 84-5). Fieldwork in the area has so far been limited to "extensive" survey, and only one of the sites (Oreoi, No. C

Map C 83

80) has been tested by excavation. The current position has been well summarised by L.H. Sackett *et al.* [in *BSA* 61 (1966) 33-52 and 83-111, cited here as *Euboea*].

C 78 LIKHAS: KASTRI
EH I-III   MH   LH   PG   G   C

PAE (1912) 140; *BSA* 47 (1952) 60 n. 14b; *Euboea* 37 (No. 2); *CSHI* 53.

Kastri is a low hill on the coast about 3 km. west of Likhas. The top area is only about 30 m. by 30 m. Classical and later sherds were found on the lower slopes, and sherds from the Early Helladic to Geometric periods were widely scattered on the higher slopes. The size of the site and its position are said to suggest an important settlement, perhaps to be equated with ancient Dion (*CSHI loc.cit.*).

C 79 YIALTRA: KASTELLI
N   EH I-III   MH   LH I-IIIB(-C?)   PG   G   A?   C   H

PAE (1912) 140; *BSA* 47 (1952) 60 n. 14b (listed as "Athinai Dhiadhes"); *Euboea* 37 (No. 3), 103.

Kastelli is about a kilometre to west-southwest of Loutra Yialtron, on the north side of the road to Lichas. It is a fine natural acropolis with a small summit (about 70 m. north to south by 50 m.) and extensive seaward slopes, thickly scattered with sherds. There is a spring at its south foot. The prehistoric pottery is of particularly good quality, and the Mycenaean sherds are said to compare well with pottery from Chalkis (B 57). The site is probably that of Athenai Diades (Strabo X 446). Traces of the foundations of a large building on the top are indeed suggestive of a temple here, and good surface pottery from the Late Geometric to the Hellenistic periods has been found.

C 80 OREOI: KASTRO *
EH II   MH   LH IIIB   LH IIIC?   PG   G   C   H

Ann. 3 (1921) 276; *BSA* 47 (1952) 60 n. 14b, 93; *Archeion Euboikon Meleton* 6 (1959) 307, 310, 313; *AD* 16 (1960) B 152; *Euboea* 39 (No. 6); *CSHI* 52.

The Kastro of Oreoi must surely be the site of ancient Histiaia (*CSHI loc.cit.*). It is a typical "high mound" site, standing out conspicuously on the east side of the modern town of Oreoi. It is about 30 m. high and its top surface, about 135 m. northeast to southwest by 100 m., is ringed by mediaeval fortification. There is a long extension on the west along the lower continuation of the ridge, and further signs of settlement have been observed on the slopes. Mycenaean sherds have been found on the upper part and the north slopes, and there are indications that the south and southeast slopes may also have been part of the prehistoric settlement, although Geometric and later sherds are predominant here. The total extent of the prehistoric site may have been about 200 m. north-

west to southeast by 160 m. The site has been much disturbed and eroded, and trial excavations revealed only Early and Middle Helladic remains (*AD loc.cit.*).

C 81 GOUVAI: PALAIOKASTRO
EH II   MH   LH III(A-B)   C

Archeion Euboikon Meleton 6 (1959) 307; *Euboea* 41 (No. 10).

This site (also known as Kato Kastro, and marked on some maps as Ormos Vouliki) is a prominent headland with beaches on either side. It is about 5 km. northeast of Gouvai, but only 2 km. north-northeast of Kastri. It is almost sheer on the north and west sides, but slopes gently on the south and east, where there are remains of the Classical period. On the northeast side some prehistoric sherds were found, including Mycenaean. The site is not large, but controls two of the few beaches in this part of northern Euboea where boats can safely land.

C 82 KERINTHOS: KRIA VRISI *
N?   EH   MH   LH III(A-B)   PG   G   A   C   H

Ann. 3 (1921) 276; *Archeion Euboikon Meleton* 6 (1959) 281, 307, 312; *BSA* 52 (1957) 2 n. 8; *Euboea* 43 (Nos. 13-14); *CSHI* 52; *AAA* 8 (1975) 28.

Kastri is a long narrow ridge (about 800 m. west-northwest to east-southeast by 150 m.) at the southeast end of a sandy beach, and above the Voudhoros stream. It is opposite the hamlet of Kria Vrisi, and about 4 km. north-northwest of Mantoudhi, and about 4 km. northeast of Kerinthos. The ancient settlement was mainly confined to the western part of the ridge and the more gentle west and southwest slopes on the landward side. Prehistoric sherds and obsidian are sparse, but halfway down the western slope, near some rough masonry resembling Cyclopean, were a few Mycenaean sherds, and higher up a hand-axe (Neolithic) and some Early and Middle Helladic scraps and obsidian were found.

It is, however, possible that the higher hill of Ayios Ilias, adjacent on the southwest, was the main centre of prehistoric habitation. Middle Helladic sherds have been found on the surface here, and Middle Helladic levels are confirmed by trial excavations. But the Protogeometric and later remains on Kastri may have largely removed or obscured the prehistoric traces there. Trial excavations produced much material of the Protogeometric to Classical periods, but little prehistoric and nothing certainly Mycenaean.

C 83 ROVIES: AYIOS ILIAS and PALAIOKHORI etc.
N   EH II   MH   LH I/II-III(A-B)   PG   G   A   C

Euboea 46 (Nos. 19-20).

Rovies is a small village on the coast about 9 km. northwest of Limni. Some Early and Middle Helladic and later sherds were found near the Frankish tower in the village itself, and also on the hill of Ayios Ilias, near the shore about 800 m. to the northwest. Some sherds, possibly Mycenaean, were recorded at both locations. But the only site in the Rovies area where Mycenaean pottery is definitely certified is that located between Rovies and Palaiokhori, [and this site is therefore shown on the map (as C 83)]. About 1.5 km. east-northeast of Rovies, on the track to Palaiokhori, slopes on both sides of the track are strewn with sherds. A substantial Bronze Age settlement is indicated by those of the Early to Late Helladic periods on the south side of the track. These include early Mycenaean in addition to LH III. To the southeast above are remains of chamber tombs, some of which have been opened.

C 84-85

It should be noted that the position of these sites (which are only about a kilometre apart) is covered by the symbol for C 85 on Map C. The symbol for C 84 is out of position on the map, and should be disregarded.

C 84 LIMNI: KASTRIA
N EH II MH LH III(A-B) G C H

Ann. 3 (1921) 283; *AE* (1960) 53; *BCH* 85 (1961) 758; *Euboea* 49 (No. 21).

The two hills known as Kastria, about 800 m. north of Limni, were inhabited in most periods from the Neolithic onwards, with a possible gap in the Protogeometric. The northern hill, which lies to right of the path to Panayia, was the prehistoric centre. Most of the sherds were found on the north slope. They include some Mycenaean which appear from the description to be of the LH IIIA or LH IIIB periods.

C 85 LIMNI: PANAYIA: PHASOULA etc.
N EH? MH LH IIIA1(-2?) C

Euboea 50 (No. 22), 108, Pl. 22.

Between the Kastria and the church and spring of Panayia, a kilometre to the north, some sherds, obsidian, and flint blades have been found. A small Neolithic site and a Middle Helladic sherd were also reported at separate sites in the vicinity. At the chapel itself no prehistoric finds have been made; but at Phasoula, to northwest of Panayia, a Mycenaean chamber tomb was found, cut in the soft limestone a little below the crest of the hill. Of the eight vases found in the tomb, *Euboea* Pl. 22:c and e might be of the LH IIIA2 period. The rest belong to the LH IIIA1 period, except for the coarse handmade cup, which does not appear in harmony with the rest of the group, and may in fact be Early Helladic.

APPENDIX TO MAP C

The following are sites (within the area covered by Map C) where Mycenaean settlement has been suggested, but not certified.

DISTOMON: THE ANCIENT SCHISTE ODOS *
EH II MH? LH or PG or G

PAE (1907) 110; *AE* (1897) 110 Fig. 1, (1908) 65, 91; *REG* 25 (1912) 262; Frazer, *Pausanias* V 231; *PT* 202; *PPS* 22 (1956) 112; *CG* Figs. 10, 16d.

The small rocky hill (about 6 km. north of Distomon) at the famous Schiste Odos (the "Cleft Way", where the ancient road from Delphi to Daulis met the road from Thebes) is now marked by the monument of Megas (died July 1856). Early Helladic remains were found in excavations here, and some other objects (including terracotta "anchor" ornaments) considered to be contemporary with Orchomenos III (*PT* 202). A sword of the "Naue II" type found here has most recently been considered to be of Geometric date, despite the fact that it is of bronze [A.M. Snodgrass, *Early Greek Armour and Weapons* (1964) 97]. It must in any case be either late LH IIIB or later.

DRYMAIA (formerly GLUNISTA)
EH? MH? LH?

PAE (1909) 130, (1910) 166; *REG* 25 (1912) 259.

The pottery from this prehistoric settlement, near the historic Drymaia, is very rough and coarse. It may include Late Bronze Age wares of non-Mycenaean type, similar to those found at Lilaia (C 63A).

STYLIS: PROFITIS ILIAS
EH? MH? LH? C H

Béquignon (1937) 293.

The remains of a small ancient fort on the rocky conical hill of Profitis Ilias northeast of Stylis were described by Béquignon. In 1958 some worn Bronze Age coarse ware sherds and many obsidian chips were found here. The site is about 15 km. east of Lamia, to north of the main road.

VASILIKA: PALAIOKASTRO
N? EH II LH III(A-B)? A H

Euboea 42 (No. 12).

Palaiokastro is a high hill about 1.5 km. northeast of Vasilika (in northeast Euboea), which dominates the long beach between Mt. Spalathrias and Cape Lefka. Early Helladic sherds were found on the spur which juts out toward the beach, and one sherd from the main historic site, which is between the spur and the walls on the top of the hill, may be from the handle of a Mycenaean kylix.

ARCADIA
ACHAEA
EASTERN ELIS

NORTHERN TRIPHYLIA
WESTERN LOCRIS
EASTERN AETOLIA

MAP D

This map covers several provinces, or parts of provinces, each of which will be discussed separately. The only areas which have received any substantial attention are eastern Arcadia (extensively surveyed by Howell), the Olympia district, and those parts of northern Achaea which are accessible from Patras and Aigion.

EASTERN ARCADIA (D 1-16)

The survey by R.J. Howell [in *BSA* 65 (1970) 79-127, henceforth referred to as *Arcadia*] has added greatly to our knowledge of Mycenaean settlement in eastern Arcadia. The sites found are mainly in or around the main Tripolis plain (comprising the plains of Tegea and Mantinea) and the smaller plains of Caphyai and Orchomenos which adjoin it on the north. This upland region has a climate much cooler than most districts settled by the Mycenaeans, and the plains are surrounded by bleak mountain slopes. Few of the Mycenaean settlements here appear to have been important, and the surface pottery found is generally of poor quality (*Arcadia* 113). It was noted by Howell (*Arcadia* 116) that most of the Mycenaean settlements discovered were on rather steep-sided hills that could easily be defended.

D 1 ALEA: ANCIENT TEGEA, THE TEMPLE OF ATHENA *
LH IIIB PG G A C H

BCH 25 (1901) 256, 45 (1929) 247; Desborough (1964) 87; *Arcadia* No. 26; Schoder (1974) 206.

A few fragments of Mycenaean vases, including parts of two stirrup-jars, were found with later material during the excavation of the Temple. Also from the excavations are a spindle whorl and a Psi figurine [for the latter, *cf. BSA* 66 (1971) 183]. If these finds represent a Mycenaean settlement here, it would have been on flat ground.

D 2 THANAS: STOYIA
MH LH III(A-B)

Arcadia No. 23.

This was a fairly large prehistoric site, extending along the whole of a low ridge about 800 m. southeast of Thanas. Abundant evidence of Mycenaean habitation is recorded.

D 3 VOUNON
MH LH III(A-B)

Arcadia No. 27.

The village of Vounon, on the northeast edge of Lake Taka, lies on a long rocky hill about 20 m. high. In the terraced fields on the upper east and southeast slopes some Mycenaean sherds were found, and it seems that the prehistoric settlement continued under the houses and gardens of the village, so that a fairly large Mycenaean settlement is indicated.

D 4 MANTHYREA: PANAYIA
EH II LH III(A-B) C

Arcadia No. 33.

A scatter of sherds, including some EH and Mycenaean, was observed extending about 200 m. northwest from the church of Panayia, about a kilometre west of Manthyrea.

D 5 ALEA: PALAIOCHORI *
EH? LH I/II-III(A-B) PG C

BCH 45 (1921) 403; *BSA* 56 (1961) 130 n. 119; *Arcadia* No. 32.

The Palaiochori site lies in a gentle depression on the plateau high above the east bank of the Sarandapotamos, about 5 km. south-southeast of Alea and about a kilometre to south of the edge of the Tegea plain. In the hollow to west of the church of Ayia Sotira here Mycenaean and mediaeval sherds were

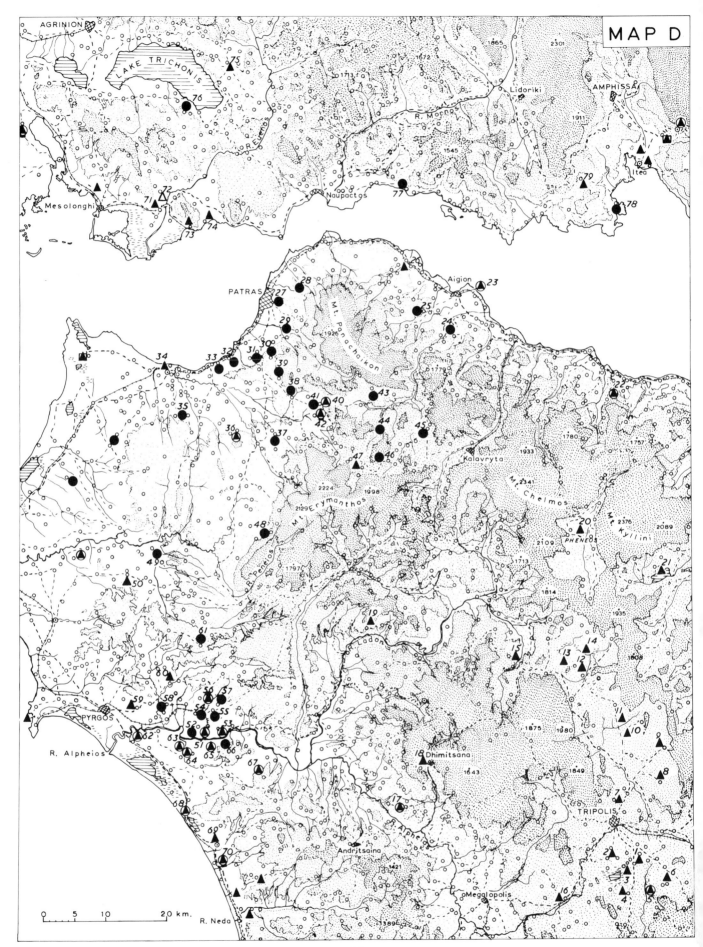

observed over an area about 300 m. in diameter. About 500 m. to southwest of the site, in the east bank of the Sarandapotamos gorge, several small built tombs of tholos type were identified, one of which was excavated. The contents included one LH I/II vase (*BSA loc.cit.*, the piriform jar), and three LH II-III.

D 6 PSILI VRYSI: VATIONA
LH III(A-B)

Arcadia No. 30.

About 200 m. north of the village of Psili Vrysi is a broad depression (or "hollow"), measuring about 400 m. north to south by 200 m., in which grain is grown. It is surrounded on all sides except the east by low hillocks which would have shielded it from view from the plain of Tegea to the north. Several Mycenaean sherds were found in the hollow.

D 7 MERKOVOUNION: AYIOLIAS
N? EH II MH LH III(A-B) C

Arcadia No. 17; Pritchett (1969) 37, Pl. 43.

The chapel of Ayiolias lies on top of the high rounded hill immediately to east of Merkovouni. The hill measures about a kilometre east to west by 800 m. On the top and the upper slopes a thin scatter of prehistoric sherds (and one classical) was found, including a few Mycenaean.

D 8 LOUKAS: AYIOS YEORYIOS
MH LH III(A-B) C H

Arcadia No. 16.

The church of Ayios Yeoryios stands at the north end of the rocky ridge which runs into the Mantinea plain north of Loukas. The church partly incorporates the remains of a Hellenistic tower. Prehistoric and later sherds occur sparsely over most of the ridge, and include several Mycenaean.

D 9 NESTANI: PANIYIRISTRA (ANCIENT NESTANE) # (Plate 19b)
N MH LH I/II C H

Frazer, *Pausanias* IV 177; *JHS* (1895) 80; *AA* (1913) 395; *Arcadia* No. 14.

The village of Nestani (formerly Tsipiana) lies in the small plain known to Pausanias as "The Untilled Plain", to the northeast of the Mantinea plain, with which it is connected by two gaps in the ridge on its west side. On the eastern side of the plain, to northwest of and above Nestani, is the rocky hill of Paniyiristra, the citadel of Ancient Nestane. It has ancient fortification walls in both isodomic and polygonal masonry. At one point, near the well-preserved eastern gateway, the style resembles "Cyclopean", with small stones used in the interstices. Just outside this gateway, some prehistoric sherds were found by

Howell in a road cutting. They included a few Mycenaean fragments, which appeared all to be early Mycenaean. Elsewhere on the hill only Classical and Hellenistic sherds were found. The famous "Klimax" pass, from Mantinea to Argos *via* the Inachos valley, began from the vicinity of the village of Sangas at the north end of the Nestani plain (*Arcadia* 87, with references).

D 10 PIKERNIS: GORTSOULI (ANCIENT PTOLIS) *
EH? MH LH III(A-B) PG? G A C H

Frazer, *Pausanias* IV 201, 221; *BCH* 11 (1887) 49; *AD* 18 (1963) B 88; *Arcadia* No. 11; *CSHI* 92, Pl. 8; Pritchett (1969) 37, Pls. 21-24, 44.

The rounded hill of Gortsouli (*CSHI* Pl. 8a) rises abruptly from the plain a short distance to north of the ruins of Classical Mantinea. The site is almost certainly the "Ptolis" or "Old Mantinea" mentioned by Pausanias, since excavations have demonstrated the existence of a sanctuary and habitation from the Geometric period onwards. Evidence for Mycenaean settlement here is confined to some surface material; and the actual date of the considerable remains of a "Cyclopean" fortification wall visible on the upper eastern flank (*CSHI* Pl. 8b) has not been established. It should be noted that the excavations (which revealed one Early Helladic and some Middle Helladic sherds) were not sufficient in scope to test the extent of Mycenaean occupation of the hill. Mycenaean surface sherds were, however, found near the Panayia chapel on the summit on two separate occasions, together with other ancient sherds and obsidian fragments.

D 11 ARTEMISION: AYIOS ILIAS
LH (II-IIIA1)

Arcadia No. 10.

The church of Ayios Ilias is situated on a low hill to the right of the road from Ancient Mantinea to Artemision. It is about 3 km. southeast of Artemision, and about 2 km. to north of Gortsouli (D 10). It has sometimes wrongly been identified with the ancient Ptolis. The hill is now planted with pine trees, and surface search is therefore difficult, but sherds from the east slope include an early Mycenaean goblet stem.

D 12 ANCIENT ORCHOMENOS *
MH LH III(A-B) G A C H

Frazer, *Pausanias* IV 223; *BCH* 38 (1914) 71; Fimmen (1921) 10; *RE* Suppl. VI (1935) 608; *CSHI* 91; *Arcadia* No. 5; Pritchett (1969) 120.

Ancient Orchomenos occupied a high conical hill, at the eastern end of the chain of hills which separates the plain of Orchomenos from the plain of Caphyai to the north. The village of Kalpaki lies on the southern slopes of the hill, outside the Classical and Hellenistic fortification. The earliest material found in the excavations (*BCH loc.cit.*) seems to have been Geometric. Fimmen (*loc.cit.*) records Matt-Painted ware collected here, and Karo (*RE loc.cit.*) mentions Mycenaean sherds, but gives a reference to Fimmen (*loc.cit.*) for these! The evidence for Mycenaean presence here is thus reduced to a solitary fragment from the foot of a Mycenaean kylix, found near the summit of the hill in 1958.

D 13 VLAKHERNA: PLESSA
EH? MH LH

Arcadia No. 3.

On a terraced slope about 800 m. to west of the hamlet of Plessa near Vlakherna, a few prehistoric sherds, including a Mycenaean goblet or kylix foot, were found scattered over an area about 100 m. by 50 m.

D 14 KANDHILA: BIKIZA
EH? MH LH III(A-B) G A C

Arcadia No. 4.

The deserted hamlet of Bikiza, although belonging to the village of Kandhila, 12 km. distant, is only 4 km. from the village of Limni (formerly Kato Agali). The long rocky spur above the ruins of the hamlet projects from the plateau on the northern edge of the plain of Caphyai. Prehistoric and later sherds, including several Mycenaean, were found on terraces at the southwest foot of the spur, and more sparsely on its south tip.

D 15 KARVOUNION: SFAKOVOUNI
MH LH III(A-B)

Arcadia No. 45.

About a kilometre to east of Karvounion, towards the end of the mountain spur bordering the Karvounion valley on the north, rises the steep hill of Sfakovouni, to east of the plain of Dara. The hill is about 400 m. in diameter. On the rocky top and the terraced slopes ample evidence was found of Middle Helladic and Mycenaean occupation.

D 16 KATO ASEA: PALAIOKASTRO (ANCIENT ASEA) *
N EH I-III MH LHI-IIA LH IIIA2 G H

E.J. Holmberg, *The Swedish Excavations at Asea in Arcadia* (1944); *Arcadia* No. 51.

The rocky acropolis hill of Palaiokastro lies immediately north of Asea railway station, and about 4 km. southeast of Asea village. The Tripolis-Megalopolis road runs close to the foot of the hill. The site is fairly large, with a top surface about 250 m. north to south by 120 m. Mycenaean occupation is represented only by a few sherds, mostly early. One sherd is certainly LH IIIA2, and an askos from a cist grave may also be of the same date. The site lies in a small but fertile plain, but this is remote and isolated. It is difficult to gauge its importance in the Mycenaean period, since the extensive Hellenistic occupation has probably removed any Mycenaean levels which may have existed.

D 17-21

Few Mycenaean sites are known in the rest of Arcadia, but the positions of those already discovered indicate the probability that many more are still to be found, especially in the vicinity of Alpheios and Ladon rivers (*cf.* also the Appendix to Map D for discussion of two prehistoric sites, Aspra Spitia and Trypeti, both near the confluence of the two rivers).

D 17 PALAIOKASTRO: AYIA SOTIRA and PALAIOPYRGOS *
LH IIIC A C H

BCH 80 (1956) 537, 82 (1958) 717; *AAA* 2 (1969) 229; *Arcadia* No. 55; *MME* No. 330.

The village of Palaiokastro lies on a hill at the western end of a range on the east side of the Alpheios. On the summit, just west of the village, are the remains of ancient Bouphagion. Some Mycenaean walls were identified here, and obsidian and Mycenaean sherds were found. Below the hill, at a place called Palaiopyrgos, some distance to the west, is an extensive Mycenaean chamber tomb cemetery. Several of the tombs are large and well cut, and one (Tomb 6) imitates a tholos. It contained fine pottery and weapons, including a Naue Type II sword (*AAA loc.cit.*). The pottery from the six excavated tombs is exclusively LH IIIC, and includes some Close Style, and one or two vases which may be as late as Sub-Mycenaean. The finds appear to indicate a substantial site, which may have begun in the LH IIIC period.

D 18 DHIMITSANA
EH II MH LH III(A-B) G? C

Arcadia No. 47.

The town of Dhimitsana occupies two peaks joined by a saddle, overlooking the Lousios valley. The western peak has a sheer cliff on its west side reaching to the river below. On the east slope of this peak Howell found some prehistoric and later sherds, including at least one Mycenaean. The site is usually identified as that of ancient Teuthis.

D 19 DHIMITRA: TROUPES
N EH II MH LH I/II-III(A-B) PG?

Arcadia No. 43; *BSA* 68 (1973) 193.

The small hill called Troupes lies about 2 km.

northeast of Dhimitra, on the south slopes of Mt. Aphrodision, above the Ladon river valley. During road construction a cutting was dug through a prehistoric settlement here, and Syriopoulos (*BSA loc.cit.*) collected a large quantity of sherds from it, mainly from the eastern slope. Most of this was Middle Helladic coarse ware, but a few sherds were Mycenaean of provincial type. Some LH I/II is recognizable, but the LH IIIC claimed is not certain (*BSA* 68 Pl. 48 b:8 may be Protogeometric), and the LH III sherds are not in general closely attributable to sub-periods.

D 20   KALYVIA: PYRGOS   (ANCIENT PHENEOS)
* #   (Plate 19a)
EH II   MH   LH IIIA2-B   G?   A?   C   H

Frazer, *Pausanias* III 235; *AD* 17 (1961-2) B 60, 20 (1965) B 158; *Arcadia* No. 40; *CSHI* 91, Pl. 76.

The Pyrgos hill lies on the northwest edge of Lake Pheneos, about a kilometre to east of Kalyvia. It is conspicuous by reason of the pyramidical knoll on its higher western end (Plate 19a). Recent excavations have made it certain that this was the centre of the historical Pheneos (*cf.* Frazer, *loc.cit.*). Polygonal walls round the acropolis have been partly cleared; and, at the eastern end of the lower southeast part of the hill, beneath an Asklepieion of the 2nd century B.C. and to north of it, deep soundings have revealed Middle Helladic and Mycenaean strata. Sherds of these periods have also been found over most of the surface of the hill, over an area about 250 m. northwest to southeast by 150 m., and especially on the southeast slopes, among later material. The Mycenaean pottery was of quite good quality, including several fragments from kylikes, angular bowls, and deep bowls. This appears to have been a fairly important Mycenaean settlement, well situated to control the more fertile parts of the Pheneos plain, the southeast part of which was formerly a lake.

D 21   KIONIA: ANCIENT STYMPHALOS   *
LH III(A-B)   A   C   H

Frazer, *Pausanias* IV 269; *RE* IVA (1932) 436; *AM* 40 (1915) 71, especially Taf. XII; *Arcadia* No. 41; *CSHI* 93.

The historic Stymphalos lay on the northwest side of the lake of the same name, about 1.5 km. south of modern Stymphalos (formerly Kionia). The long narrow limestone ridge which forms the acropolis is at the eastern end of a spur from Mt. Kyllini (*cf.* Frazer, *loc.cit.*). It is apparent that the earlier citadel occupied the lower eastern part of the ridge (an area about 250 m. east to west by 50 m.), which is divided from the higher western section (where there are later fortifications, presumably Hellenistic) by a small saddle. On the south side of the lower eastern section are traces of circuit walls in a style resembling Cyclopean. On this eastern area some chips of obsidian and two Mycenaean sherds (from a kylix and an angular bowl re-

spectively) were found in 1958 (*CSHI loc.cit.*). Excavations on the historic town below the acropolis, both to northeast and to south of it, revealed remains from the Archaic to Hellenistic periods.

ACHAEA (D 22-47)

Achaea, like Messenia, abounds in springs. There is some excellent agricultural land between the mountains and the sea, and in the narrow valleys running inland between the main mountain ranges. Apart from the site of ancient Aigeira (D 22), which borders on Corinthia, the Mycenaean sites found fall into two groups, a smaller one around Aigion (D 23-26), and a larger group in the Patras area. An important cluster of sites (D 38-47) lies along the inner circuitous route over plateau land from Patras to Kalavryta *via* Chalandritsa. Most of the discoveries have been of Mycenaean cemeteries, and these show a considerable prosperity in the LH IIIC period, although several are now known to have been in use much earlier (especially D 23, D 27, D 30, D 40, D 42, and D 45), and the LH IIIB period is well represented.

D 22   DERVENI: SOLOS   (ANCIENT AIGEIRA)
* #
LH IIIA1?   LH IIIA2-C   G   A   C   H

Frazer, *Pausanias* IV 176; *ÖJh* 19-20 (1919) Beiblatt, cols. 5-42; *AE* (1956) *Chronika* 11; *OpAth* 5 (1964) 97; *AAA* 6 (1973) 197, 7 (1974) 157, 9 (1976) 162; *CSHI* 68.

The acropolis of ancient Aigeira occupies the upper southern end of the long ridge which stretches down to the coast and formed the city of Aigeira. The upper part of the acropolis is a small gently sloping area, about 140 m. north to south by 120 m. Fine quality Mycenaean sherds of the LH IIIA-C periods were found here, and recent excavations have revealed four building levels assigned to the LH IIIC periods together with two buildings of megaron type. A group of finds reported to have come from Aigeria, presumably from a chamber tomb, include an early figurine [*BSA* 66 (1971) 178], some fine weapons, one of which is a probably early Type C sword, and LH IIIA2-C pottery.

Chamber tombs were found at Psila Alonia, about 1.5 km. to east-southeast of the acropolis, on the opposite side of a deep ravine. Two of these were excavated. They were of unusual type and contained several burial cists, similar to those in some Kephallenian cemeteries [G 18-19, Metaxata and Lakkithra, *cf.* Desborough (1964) 86, 104]. They appear to be of similar date, *i.e.* LH IIIB-C.

D 23   AIGION: PSILA ALONIA SQUARE etc.   *
N   EH II   MH   LH IIA-IIIC   G   H

PAE (1939) 104, (1954) 289; *OpAth* 5 (1964) 89; *AAA* 1 (1968) 136; *AD* 22 (1967) B 214, 26 (1971) B 175; A.J. Papadopoulos, *Excavations at Aigion*, 1970 (1976).

Modern Aigion is on the site of ancient Aigion (*cf.* Frazer, *Pausanias* V 159), a high bluff dominating the coast road and the fertile plains to east and west. Two Mycenaean chamber tomb cemeteries have been investigated, one in Psila Alonia Square on the seaward slope of the town, the other at its edge, beside the road to Patras. This latter is the older, and indeed is the earliest cemetery yet known in Achaea.

D 24   ACHLADIES: ACHOURIA   *
LH III(A2-C)?

PAE (1938) 119, (1939) 103; *OpAth* 5 (1964) 87, 96.

A Mycenaean cemetery is recorded on this steep hill near Achladies, in the foothills to south of the coastal plain. Vases and other goods from chamber tombs here have been mixed with those from tombs at Chadzi (D 25), so that neither cemetery can now be accurately dated. The goods include a stirrup-jar of Sub-Mycenaean appearance [*OpAth* 5 (1964) 93 Fig. 2:1].

D 25   CHADZI: TRAPEZA   *
LH III(A2-C)?   G

PAE (1938) 119, (1939) 103; *OpAth* 5 (1964) 89, 108.

The site is a trapezoidal hill to east of Chadzi, on a spur overhanging a valley. Mycenaean tombs, mainly plundered, were found here, and walls claimed as "Cyclopean" (but *cf. OpAth loc.cit. contra*). The finds were mixed with those from tombs at Achladies (D 24) so that neither cemetery can be accurately dated.

D 26   KAMARAI: XERIKO
EH II   MH   LH III(A-B)

PAE (1934) 114; *OpAth* 5 (1964) 106, 109.

Prehistoric sherds and stone implements were found on this hill near the river Salmeniko. One Mycenaean sherd is recorded.

D 27   PATRAS: AROE, SAMAKIA, LOPESI, and GEROKOMEION   *
LH IIIA2-C

PAE (1933) 92, (1934) 114; *OpAth* 5 (1964) 106; *AD* 22 (1967)B 214.

There were extensive Mycenaean cemeteries of chamber tombs in the hills behind Patras on the east, mainly comprising the groups at Aroe Mesatis, Lopesi-Englukas, and Samakia. Of these, Aroe is about 600 m. to east of Patras castle, and Lopesi a little more than a kilometre to south of Aroe. And recent road construction has revealed chamber tombs near the Gerokomeion monastery, about 2 km. east-southeast of Patras. The contents of an excavated tomb here include LH IIIB and LH IIIC pottery, in addition to a spearhead and a "razor". A group of objects said to be from the Patras area, and now in Yale Museum, includes LH IIIA2 pottery. There must have been an im-

portant Mycenaean settlement somewhere in the foothills behind Patras Castle, if not at the Castle itself.

D 28   ANO SICHAINA: AGRAPHIDHIA   *
LH IIIC

BCH 47 (1923) 512, 48 (1924) 472; *AA* (1925) 334; *AD* 16 (1960) B 137; *OpAth* 5 (1964) 97.

A chamber tomb cemetery was investigated at Agrapidhia, to east of Ano Sichaina, and near the villages of Voudeni and Bala. Many of the tombs had been destroyed. Further ruined chamber tombs were reported in another cemetery, to west of Ano Sichaina. Finds included pottery, jewellery, and a dagger.

D 29   KOUKOURA (near the "Achaia-Klauss" factory)   *
LH IIIB-C

PAE (1936) 95, (1937) 84, (1938) 118; *PPS* 22 (1956) 111; *AJA* 64 (1960) 9; *OpAth* 5 (1964) 104.

A Mycenaean cemetery of well cut and rich chamber tombs was found at the foot of the mountain Koukoura, behind the "Achaia-Klauss" factory. The tombs resemble the best examples in the Argolid, with dromoi sloping inwards towards the top. The pottery seems largely LH IIIC, but probably extends back into LH IIIB; and some "duck-vases" are probably contemporary with Sub-Mycenaean. The other finds include a fine decorated stone pyxis, an ivory comb, glass jewellery, and several weapons. It seems likely that the Mycenaean settlement occupied the same site as the factory, a prominent spur, overlooking the coastal plain.

D 30   KALLITHEA   *
LH IIIA(2)-C

BCH 78 (1954) 124; *JHS* 74 (1954) 157; *PPS* 22 (1956) 112; *AM* 75 (1960) 42; *OpAth* 5 (1964) 102; *AD* 26 (1971) 185; *Ergon* (1976) 105, (1977) 96.

At a site 10 km. south of Patras and about a kilometre north of Ano Kallithea, on the west slope of a spur of Mt. Panachaikon, two chamber tombs were excavated. One had been plundered, but the goods were recovered. The most important finds apparently belong to a single burial in a pit. They comprised a spear, fragmentary bronze fittings from a corselet, and a pair of bronze greaves. They may be dated to the LH IIIC period, since fragments of a stirrup-jar of that date were found in the fill of the pit. The other tomb was found intact, and finds included several bronzes and boar's tusk plates from a helmet. In both tombs LH IIIC and earlier pottery was found.

At another site about 500 m. west of Ano Kallithea more chamber tombs were identified. Those excavated are small but relatively rich in finds, containing many LH IIIA-C vases, sealstones, and tools of bronze and stone. The finds as a whole further indicate the importance of the Patras area in Mycenaean times, although the settlements themselves still remain to be found.

D 31 TSAPLANEIKA *
LH IIIB-C

PAE (1933) 90, (1934) 115, (1935) 70; *OpAth* 5 (1964) 109.

Chamber tombs were found here near the road to Chalandritsa, and others also at Pavlokastro in the southeast foothills of Mt. Panachaikon.

D 32 VRACHNEIKA: AYIOS PANDELEIMON *
LH IIIA2-B?

BCH 78 (1954) 124, 80 (1956) 291; *OpAth* 5 (1964) 109.

A chamber tomb excavated here may be the source of at least two LH IIIA2-B vases [*AJA* 64 (1960) 8 (no. 221), 11 (no. 41)]. The tomb is on the eastern edge of the small fertile valley which runs inland from Vrachneika. A small hill near Ayios Pandeleimon may have been the settlement site, and the vicinity of Dresthena to the southeast is suggested as another possibility (*OpAth loc.cit.*).

D 33 TSOUKALEIKA
LH

BCH 78 (1954) 124; *OpAth* 5 (1964) 109.

Mycenaean chamber tombs have been reported at this village on the north coast, about 14 km. west of Patras and 8 km. east of Kato Achaia.

D 34 KATO ACHAIA: BOUCHOMATA
EH II LH

AD 19 (1964) B 190.

On the low hill of Bouchomata, near the sea and a short distance to northwest of Kato Achaia, abundant Early Helladic and Mycenaean sherds were found, said to be of a quality comparable to those from Teichos Dymaion (G 6).

D 35 FOSTAINA etc.
LH (III)

AR (1961-2) 12.

A "Late Mycenaean" tomb and signs of others were noted about 7 km. southeast of Kato Achaia, in the vicinity of Fostaina, Elaiochorion, and Lousika.

D 36 MITOPOLIS: AYIA VARVARA and PROFITIS ILIAS
LH (III)

PAE (1929) 91, *AD* 17 (1961-2) B 129; *OpAth* 5 (1964) 106.

Three bronze objects and a Mycenaean jar were found in a Mycenaean cemetery at Profitis Ilias near Mitopolis. A Mycenaean settlement was reported on a hill of acropolis type, named Ayia Varvara, one of the three hills of the village of Mitopolis.

D 37 STAROCHORION (formerly LALOUSI)
LH

PAE (1933) 91; *OpAth* 5 (1964) 105.

Mycenaean chamber tombs were noted on hills around this village.

D 38 CHALANDRITSA: AYIOS VASILIOS and TROUMBES *
LH IIIA? LH IIIC G

PAE (1928) 110, 119, (1929) 86, (1930) 81; *AJA* 64 (1960) 5; *OpAth* 5 (1964) 101.

About a kilometre northwest of Chalandritsa, and to south of the road to Patras, is a row of small hillocks called Troumbes, where three built tombs of tholos type were found. Their contents, some pottery and bronze fragments, remain unpublished. At Ayios Vasilios, in fields below Troumbes, some chamber tombs were excavated. Their contents seem to be entirely of the LH IIIC period. A LH IIIA figurine [*BSA* 66 (1971) 180] was found in a tumulus at Troumbes, with material otherwise Geometric, and undatable coarse pottery (which may be Dark Age) at Agrapidhies, to north of the road.

D 39 PLATANOVRYSI (formerly MEDZENA) *
LH (III)

PAE (1930) 88, (1932) 61; *AD* 17 (1961-2) B 129; *OpAth* 5 (1964) 106.

A cemetery of plundered chamber tombs was found here, from one of which four Mycenaean vases were recovered.

D 40 KATARRAKTIS: DRAKOTRYPA *
MH LH IIIA2-C

AE (1919) 98; *AR* (1955) 17; *PAE* (1958) 166; *Ergon* (1957) 69, (1958) 139; *AR* (1957) 11, (1958) 10; *AJA* 64 (1960) 5, 16; *OpAth* 5 (1964) 103.

At Katarraktis (formerly Lopesi) chamber tombs containing LH III pottery and glass jewellery were excavated. At Drakotrypa, a small hill to east of Katarraktis, a settlement was partly investigated. Middle Helladic and Mycenaean strata were revealed, including remains of houses of the LH III period.

D 41 KATARRAKTIS: (Near the 28th km. mark) *
LH G

AE (1919) 98; *PAE* (1952) 400; *OpAth* 5 (1964) 103.

To west of Katarraktis, seven Mycenaean chamber tombs were excavated in 1920 at the foot of the steep hill to south of the road to Patras, at a point described as below the 28th km. mark. The pottery was not published.

D 42 RODHIA: AYIOS ATHANASIOS *
MH LH III(A1-B)

PAE (1956) 193, (1957) 114, (1958) 70; *OpAth* 5 (1964) 103.

Ayios Athanasios is about 2 km. to south of Katarraktis, to east of and above Rodhia. Middle Helladic and Mycenaean strata were tested here, and a building of megaron type is reported. But Mycenaean material was relatively scarce. At Bouga to the north, two tholos tombs were discovered, both plundered. Near the larger of the two (diameter 5.2 m.) a collection of rich goods was found, and in it bones and pottery. The pottery has been dated LH IIIB, but both the pottery and the goods are more likely to be LH IIIA. Parallels for the goods go back to LH IIIA1 (and even earlier for the inlaid dagger).

D 43 LEONTION (formerly GOURZOUMISA): AYIOS ANDREAS etc. *
EH III? LH IIIB-C

PAE (1930) 88, (1931) 71, (1932) 57; *OpAth* 5 (1964) 102.

Near Ayios Andreas chapel, to south of Leontion, below the spring above the village, some chamber tombs were found. Only one was intact, and from it came LH IIIC pottery and a vase assigned to EH III [*AJA* 64 (1950) 4]. Traces of a possible Mycenaean settlement were noted at Ayios Andreas. Near Ayios Ioannis, about 3 km. south of Leontion, and to west of the road, is another chamber tomb cemetery, from which came LH IIIB-C pottery and some jewellery. Destroyed chamber tombs were noted at Koutreika, also in the Leontion area.

D 44 MIKROS BODIAS: LOBOKA etc. *
LH IIIC

PAE (1933) 90; *OpAth* 5 (1964) 105.

Loboka, a summer resort for the villagers of Bodia, is on the bank of the river Selinos, below Mt. Krania. An intact chamber tomb, with LH IIIC contents, and two looted tombs were excavated here. Kyparissis also noted chamber tombs at Mikros Bodias itself. But the pithoi from the so-called tholos tomb at Bartholomio near Mikros Bodias may be of Dark Age date (*OpAth loc.cit.*).

D 45 KATO GOUMENITSA: VRISARION *
LH IIB/IIIA1-B

PAE (1925) 43, (1926) 130, (1927) 52; *AD* 9 (1924-5) *Parartema* 14, 16 (1960) B 138; *AR* (1959-60) 12; *BCH* 85 (1961) 682; *OpAth* 5 (1964) 104; *BSA* 73 (1978) 173.

At the 72nd km. stone on the Patras-Kalavryta road, a short distance beyond Kato Goumenitsa, is a white hill with a levelled top, a little to east of the road. A large number of rock-cut chamber tombs were excavated here, and the goods included many weapons and fine jewellery. Diagnostic pottery includes an early alabastron [*AJA* 64 (1960) Pl. 2; 15-16] and a later rhyton. An early Mycenaean grave containing a vase and a dagger is also reported. Three of the vases from the tombs found in 1959-60 are now published (*BSA* loc.cit.), and are assigned to the LH IIIA2 period, to which are also tentatively assigned three "razors" and a knife.

D 46 MANESI: VROMONERI *
LH IIIC

PAE (1929) 91, (1930) 87; *OpAth* 5 (1964) 106.

At Vromoneri near Manesi a chamber tomb cemetery was explored on a low hill among a chain of limestone hills. All the vases from it which are illustrated belong to the LH IIIC period.

D 47 AYIOS VLASIOS: ANCIENT LEONTION
LH C H

E. Meyer, *Peloponnesische Wanderungen* (1939) Pl. 31, Map VII; *BCH* 79 (1955) 252, 83 (1959) 620; *OpAth* 5 (1964) 100.

Mycenaean sherds were found on the lower part of a hill 3 km. north of Ayios Vlasios, at the foot of Mt. Erymanthos, near the 51st kilometre stone on the road from Patras to Kalavryta. The site is also part of ancient Leontion (*cf.* Meyer, *loc.cit.*).

EASTERN ELIS AND NORTHERN TRIPHYLIA (D 48-70)

Most of the sites discovered in this region are in the Olympia area (*cf. Myc Con I* 176-82). But there is a very large chamber tomb cemetery at Prostovitsa (D 48), on the west slope of Mt. Erymanthos, which indicates the probable importance of this area of Elis also (and *cf.* also under Skoura in the appendix to Map D). And more Mycenaean sites are to be expected in the region of ancient Triphylia, in the district between the Alpheios and Neda rivers. Mycenaean discoveries in Elis have been summarised recently by L. Parlama, in *AD* 29 (1974) A 25-28.

Special Abbreviations for Sites D 48-70

Messenia I = *AJA* 65 (1961) 221-260
Messenia II = *AJA* 68 (1964) 229-245
Messenia III = *AJA* 73 (1969) 123-177

MME = W.A. McDonald and G.R. Rapp, *The Minnesota Messenia Expedition* (1972). (The numbers refer to the list of sites in Register A on pp. 264-309.)

Myc Con I = *Atti e memorie del primo congresso internazionale di micenologia* Vol. I (1968) (referring to the report by N. Yalouris on prehistoric finds in the Olympia area).

D 48　PROSTOVITSA　*
LH IIIC

PAE (1927) 52, (1928) 114; *OpAth* 5 (1964) 107.

Over a hundred chamber tombs were noted a short distance to west of Prostovitsa, on a sandy hillock. The cemetery had been badly robbed, but bronzes and fine jewellery were found in the excavations. The only vase known to have come from the cemetery is LH IIIC [*AJA* 64 (1960) 6 no. 8a].

D 49　AGRAPIDOCHORI:　KOTRONA:　GISA　*
LH IIIA2-C

AE (171) *Chronika* 52; *AD* 27 (1972) B 268.

The village of Kotrona is about 2 km. southeast of Agrapidochori. At a place named Gisa here, on the south slope of a low hill and above a torrent bed, a rock-cut chamber tomb was excavated. It contained LH IIIA2-B inhumation burials and at least one LH IIIC cremation burial, whose pottery seems of advanced style. This burial may indicate a reuse of the tomb. The early appearance of cremation at this remote location is of considerable interest.

D 50　ORAIA:　TSALEIKA:　BOUKA
LH

AR (1967-8) 11; *BCH* 92 (1968) 832; *AD* 23 (1968) B 178.

This site was found in the course of an international cooperative salvage project prior to the construction of the Peneios dam. [The sites are shown on the plan given on *AD* 23 (1968) 175.] A thin scatter of Mycenaean sherds was found on the lower slopes of the ridge Bouka near Tsaleika, about a kilometre south of Oraia. Of interest is a possible LH IIIC sherd from a large artificial mound on the northeast edge of the ridge.

D 51:　OLYMPIA:　DROUVA, THE ALTIS etc.
EH II-III　MH　LH I-IIIC　"PG"　G　A　C　H

AM 36 (1911) 163, 77 (1962) 23; W. Dörpfeld, *Alt-Olympia I* (1935) 73; *BCH* 83 (1959) 655, 84 (1960) 720; *AA* (1962) 198; *Messenia I* 226; *MME* Nos. 315, 317, 321-2; *AD* 16 (1960) B 125, 17 (1961-2) B 105, 18 (1963) B 103, 19 (1964) B 175, 20 (1965) B 309, 24 (1969) B 149, 25 (1970) B 191, 27 (1972) B 268; *Myc Con I* 178; Schoder (1974) 157.

A Mycenaean settlement has been identified here at the south end of the ridge occupied by the village of Drouva, overlooking the Altis and the confluence of the Alpheios and Kladheos rivers. The hilltop here, around the chapel of Ayios Yeoryios, measures about 150 m. east to west by 100 m., and the settlement also extended to slopes on the east below and to the north end of the ridge, where the main part of Drouva is situated. This was probably the main centre of habitation in the area of ancient and modern Olympia in Mycenaean times.

Some Mycenaean pottery has been found in the area of the later sanctuary, but no remains of buildings can be attributed to this period. LH I-IIIB is reported from the north of the Stadion, and a Mycenaean figurine of early type from its eastern edge [*AD* 25 (1970) B 194]. In a Dark Age deposit above buildings of Middle Helladic date a sherd which appears to be LH IIIC and a ringed kylix stem were found [*JHS* 56 (1936) 81 Fig. 1; *cf. AM* 36 (1911) 189, Dörpfeld (1935, 87]. There is no reason to suppose that the site had religious importance in Mycenaean times. A Late Minoan bronze statuette (discussed in *Myc Con I* 179) has no known context and might well be a dedication made after the Bronze Age.

Remains of a Mycenaean settlement have been reported on the Kronion hill to north of the Altis, and a Mycenaean chamber tomb cemetery in the west slope of the hill. Further Mycenaean material has been found in the north bank of the Kladheos river, and a Mycenaean grave about 800 m. east of the new museum and 200 m. north of the Kladheos.

The Mycenaean remains at Olympia are substantial, but neither their quantity nor their quality are in any way outstanding, compared to other Mycenaean sites in the Olympia area in general (*i.e.* D 52-67).

D 52　FLOKA:　The Alpheios Dam
LH III(B?)　C　H

AD 18 (1963) B 103; *MME* No. 316.

An unusual bell-skirted figurine and three Mycenaean vases were found here, presumably from a destroyed tomb.

D 53　MIRAKA:　CHANDAKIA, LAKKOPHOLIA, GOUVA, REMA, and OINOMAOS (PISA)　*
MH　LH II　LH IIIA-B　LH IIIC?　C　H

Messenia I 226; *AD* 21 (1966) B 171, 23 (1968) B 161, 25 (1970) B 180, 193; *MME* Nos. 323-4.

A variety of Mycenaean finds is reported from the vicinity of Miraka. From destroyed tombs at Chandakia come a Type F dagger and a spearhead, probably LH II-IIIA, and LH IIIA2 vases. Other weapons and LH IIIA2 pottery were found in chamber tombs at Lakkopholia. An alabastron from Gouva, attributed to LH IIIA, is perhaps LH IIIB; and two vases from Rema, attributed to LH IIIB-C are perhaps LH IIIA2. A kylix foot in the BSA collection marked "Pisa" is presumed to have come from the site of Oinomaos or "Pisa", a low hill about 1.5 km. east of Olympia on the north side of the road to Tripolis [Fimmen (1922) 10 Abb. 3]. Trial excavations here revealed traces of a Middle Helladic settlement (*Messenia I* 226 with references).

D 54　MAGEIRA:　KIOUPIA etc.　*
MH?　LH III(A-B)　C　H

AD 21 (1966) B 170, 22 (1967) B 211; *AAA* 2 (1969) 248; *AA* (1971) 410; *Myc Con I* 178; *MME* No. 319.

A tumulus excavated at Mageira contained pithos burials, variously attributed to Middle Helladic and late Mycenaean; and Mycenaean sherds are reported from the area. Fragments of large clay statuettes, probably of the LH III period, have been found at Kioupia.

D 55 PLATANOS: TOMBRINO and RENIA *
LH IIIA2-B   A   H

AD 19 (1964) B 177; *MME* No. 318.

A chamber tomb at Renia on the southeast edge of Platanos contained fine jewellery and pottery. Another chamber tomb at Tombrino nearby had been totally plundered.

D 56 KAFKANIA: FENGARAKI and AGRILITSES *
MH   LH (IIIA-B?)   H

AD 16 (1960) B 126, 19 (1964) B 178, 22 (1967) B 209; *MME* Nos. 327-8.

Middle Helladic and Mycenaean surface pottery found at Agrilitses, between Kafkania and Kladheos, indicate a probable habitation site here. Prehistoric tombs, including cists containing faience beads, are reported from Fengaraki nearby, but their date is not clear.

D 57 KLADHEOS: STRAVOKEFALO and TRYPES *
LH IIIA2-C

AD 18 (1963) B 103, 19 (1964) B 177; *Myc Con I* 178; *MME* Nos. 325-6.

Seven chamber tombs, partially destroyed by road works, were excavated at Stravokefalo, near the west bank of Kladheos river. They are part of a large cemetery. The finds were rich, and included a diadem of glass beads found in position on a skull. At least one of the published vases, a hydria decorated with a thick wavy line, appears to be LH IIIC. Another rich cemetery was found at Trypes to north of Kladheos [*AD* 19 (1964) B 177]. The goods from the ten tombs excavated include fine jewellery and objects of bronze and ivory. The published vases show that the cemetery continued to be used in the LH IIIC period.

D 58 STREPHI *
EH II   LH III(A2-B)   "PG"   H

AD 17 (1961-2) B 104, 24 (1969) B 150; *MME* No. 309.

Among finds near Strephi are two Mycenaean chamber tombs on the north side of the village.

D 59 VARVASSAINA: VROMONERI
MH   LH III(A-B)   H

Messenia I 225; *MME* No. 307.

Middle Helladic and Mycenaean sherds were found on the upper slopes of a hill on the north side of the Pyrgos-Olympia road, about 1.5 km. west-north-west of Varvassaina. The sherds were concentrated mainly in an area about 200 m. northeast to southwest by 50 m., to north and northeast of a spring on the hillside. A rather small Mycenaean settlement is indicated.

D 60 LADZOI: ETIA
LH III(A-B)   C   H

Messenia I 226; *MME* No. 320.

About 1.5 km. north-northeast of Ladzoi is a low hill, about 200 m. northeast to southwest by 60 m. Plentiful Mycenaean sherds are concentrated mainly on the high central area which measures about 100 m. by 30 m. The site commands the route northeast up the Lestenitza valley.

D 61 GOUMERO: AMMOULI
LH IIIC?

AR (1959-60) 11; *BCH* 83 (1959) 658.

A vase described as an alabastron was found at Ammouli north of Goumero. It was described as LH IIIC, but is probably earlier, since alabastra are not common in this period.

D 62 EPITALION: AYIOS YEORYIOS *
MH   LH I/II-III(A-B)   LH IIIC?   C   H

Messenia I 227, III 129; *AD* 21 (1966) B 172, 23 (1968) B 170; *AAA* 1 (1968) 201; *MME* No. 303.

The group of four small hills northwest of Epitalion adjoins the delta of the Alpheios river, and controls the north to south coastal route, and a ford across the Alpheios. On the southwestern hill of the group is the chapel of Ayios Yeoryios. Mycenaean sherds were found on this small hilltop and the slopes below over an extent of about 200 m. northwest to southwest by 150 m. On the adjacent southeast hill, named Tou Varkou to Vouno, whose top is only about 50 m. in diameter, a Mycenaean house was partly excavated, and there are indications of ruined chamber tombs in the soft sandy marl of the upper slopes, where several Mycenaean sherds of good quality were found. There is thus evidence for a Mycenaean settlement and cemetery of considerable extent.

D 63 MAKRYSIA: CHANIA *
EH II   MH   LH IIIA2-B

PAE (1954) 295; *Messenia I* 229, III 130; *MME* No. 311.

About 2.5 km. west-northwest of Makrysia, the lowest spur of the ridge west of the Selinounta river projects eastward into the valley, not far south of the Alpheios. Two Mycenaean chamber tombs were excavated in the southeast slope, and remains of at least two more chamber tombs are visible in the vicinity. A prehistoric settlement occupied in the Early and Middle Helladic periods was noted in the same area, but the Mycenaean settlement connected with the tombs may be that at Ayios Ilias (D 64) opposite to the southeast.

D 64 MAKRYSIA: AYIOS ILIAS *
MH LH I-IIA LH III(A2-B) H

Messenia I 229; *AAA* 1 (1968) 126; *AD* 23 (1968) A 284, 25 (1970) B 189; *MME* No. 312.

The church and convent of Ayios Ilias occupy the top (about 100 m. east to west by 80 m.) of a high hill about 700 m. west of Makrysia, dominating the Alpheios valley. The hill and the slopes (which are fairly steep on the north and west) are strewn with sherds, mainly Mycenaean. A small burial tumulus (diameter 4.7 m.) was found here, but was largely destroyed before proper excavation. The material found in it indicates use from late in the Middle Helladic period to LH IIA; and a LH IIA alabastron was found about 50 m. distant from the tumulus. This was obviously an important Mycenaean site, situated across the Alpheios from Olympia; and a river crossing here seems indicated by the small punt now used for ferrying at this point.

D 65 MAKRYSIA: YERAKOVOUNI
MH? LH I/II LH III(A-B) C

Messenia I 229; *MME* No. 313; E. Meyer, *Neue Peloponnesische Wanderungen* (1957) 47.

This small isolated hill, about 2 km. east-northeast of Makrysia, overlooks the Alpheios valley and lies almost opposite ancient Olympia. Mycenaean sherds and Bronze Age coarse ware were thinly spread over the north and west slopes, over a total area about 130 m. north to south by 50 m., comprising a concentration on the upper part and another on the lowest north slope. The site is probably the same as that referred to by Meyer (*loc.cit.*) as about 2.5 km. east of Makrysia. Two LH I/II vases were found at Raza to the east nearby.

D 66 BABES: ARNOKATARACHO *
MH? LH IIB G A C H

BCH 83 (1959) 658; *Myc Con I* 177; *Messenia III* 130; *MME* No. 314; *AA* (1974) 16 Fig. 27.

A town site of the historical period was partly investigated on an acropolis hill about 1.5 km. west of Babes [*cf. PAE* (1956) 186]. A destroyed rectangular built grave here contained vases, of which at least one is of the LH IIB period. A dagger found on the north slope (*AA loc.cit.*) was said to be Mycenaean, but appears to be more similar to Middle Helladic types.

D 67 DHIASELA: KOUTSOCHEIRA *
LH IIIA2-C C

PAE (1955) 243; *BCH* 80 (1956) 287, 81 (1957) 574; *Messenia I* 229; *MME* No. 331.

The site is about 2.5 km. north-northwest of Dhiasela, and about 300 m. northeast of a chapel of Ayios Athanasios. On a low hill, about 130 m. east to west by 100 m., remains of a Mycenaean settlement were discovered. Traces of fortification were also reported, but these are probably of the Classical period or later, and there is some classical surface pottery with the Mycenaean on the upper south slopes. Three collapsed chamber tombs were dug in a cemetery on the south slope. Most of the pottery from these appears to be LH IIIA2-B, but some LH IIIC (including a coated jar that seems to be very late in the period) was found in Tomb C. On the top of the hill are traces of two possible tholos tombs. Although the excavated remains and the distribution of surface pottery are not very impressive, the site may have had some importance, since there are signs that it may have been opposite to a river ford here.

D 68 KATO SAMIKON: KLIDHI * # (Plate 22b)
EH II-III MH LH I-IIIB C

AM 33 (1908) 320; *AA* (1909) 120; *Messenia I* 230; *AD* 20 (1965) A 6, B 210; *MME* No. 302 (with Plates 5-1 and 7-3).

Klidhi is an isolated low hill beside a coastal lagoon, and about 100 m. west of Kato Samikon railway station. (*MME* Pl. 7-3.) The total extent of the hill (now bisected by the railway line) was about 300 m. northnorthwest to south-southeast by 50 m. (cf. *Messenia I* Ill. 4). Surface sherds of all prehistoric periods listed were found, including several fragments of LH IIIA-B kylikes and kraters. Remains of a "Cyclopean" wall reported in 1908 were confirmed in 1954, but appear to have been ruined subsequently. A large tumulus (diameter about 50 m., and height preserved about 5 m., before excavation) was excavated at the north end. It was used for 12 or more burials between the last phase of the Middle Helladic period and the LH IIIB period, and contained some fine pottery but no goods of much value. A stirrup-jar (LH IIIB1?) was also found somewhere on the site.

On the summit to east of Klidhi enclosed by Classical fortifications [*cf. Hesperia* 6 (1937) 525 and *MME* Pl. 5-1) was found the base of a LH III kylix. This may have been the site of a Mycenaean watchtower, combining with Klidhi to control the coast route. In any case, it appears that Klidhi was an important Mycenaean site, despite its moderate size.

D 69 ZACHARO: KAIMENA ALONIA
LH III(A-B)

Messenia II 231; *MME* No. 301.

About 400 m. north of the hill which was formerly the centre of the town of Zacharo is a low ridge, about 300 m. northeast to southwest by 100 m., above a spring. The ridge is much denuded, and the Mycenaean sherds were found mainly on the southeast slopes, down towards the spring. Compared to its neighbour at Kakovatos (D 70), this is a rather unimportant site, but it provides an indication that more Mycenaean sites existed in and around this relatively wide and extremely fertile coastal plain around Zacharo.

D 70 KAKOVATOS: NESTORA *
MH LH I-IIIB

AM 32 (1907) VI, 33 (1908) 295, 34 (1909) 269, 38 (1913) 101; *Messenia I* 230; *MME* No. 300; *GRBS* 11 (1970) 5.

The small acropolis hill (called "Ktiria" before Dörpfeld's excavations) is on the east side of the main highway, about 1.5 km. east-northeast of Kakovatos. It is on the southeast edge of the fertile coastal plain of Zacharo. The hilltop is small, rather thin and elongated (east to west), with steep slopes on the east and south. It is much eroded. Excavation here revealed a large building (called a palace by Dörpfeld), which included storerooms, and a (circuit?) wall of large blocks, both presumably Mycenaean. There was also a fairly extensive Middle Helladic and Mycenaean "lower town" on the north and northwest slopes, marked by some sherds and many stones, indicating an inhabited area of at least 200 m. east to west by 90 m. On a lower ridge, to northeast of the acropolis and connected to it, three tholos tombs were excavated. All were large (diameters 12.12 m., 9.0 m., and 10.35 m. respectively), and contained pottery of LH IIA date, mostly fragments of "palatial" jars, and the remains of rich goods. Tomb A in particular held large quantities of amber beads (*cf. GRBS loc.cit.*) and other jewellery.

This was obviously a centre of considerable importance in early Mycenaean times. Its later history and the date of the buildings on the acropolis are obscure, since the excavation reports (in *AM loc.cit.*) concentrated on the tholos tombs. But a group of sherds from the 1908 excavations and marked "Unterburg" include many typical fragments from LH III deep bowls, stemmed bowls, and kylikes, both painted and plain, of average to good quality. The site may therefore have been the local capital controlling the fertile Zacharo plain throughout most of the Mycenaean period. But is must be admitted that this plain and the surrounding hills have not yet been adequately searched for rival candidates.

EASTERN AETOLIA AND WESTERN LOCRIS (D 71-79)

In the eastern part of Aetolia, Mycenaean civilisation is so far documented mainly around the coastal plain of Mesolonghi (D 71-74). But the examples of Thermon (D 75) and Lithovouni (D 76) show that Mycenaean penetration may be expected also in the more inland areas, especially the fertile shores of Lake Trichonis. In Western Locris there should be several more Mycenaean sites, especially around Naupactos, and in other coastal plains on the north side of the Corinthian Gulf. Little work has been done in Aetolia since W.J. Woodhouse's survey in the 19th century, and both this and the reconnaissance in Western Locris by L. Lerat were in any case mainly concerned with remains of the historical period.

D 71 ANCIENT KALYDON *
LH III(A-B) "PG" G A C H

PAE (1908) 99; *AD* 17 (1961-2) B 183, 20 (1965) B 343, 22 (1967) B 320; Schoder (1974) 105.

The highest and northernmost hill of ancient Kalydon was the Mycenaean acropolis. This hill completely dominates the Mesolonghi plain to west and south, and also commands the route inland up the Euenos river valley on the east. Traces of a possibly Mycenaean fortification wall were found near the west corner of the classical fortifications on the acropolis, and substantial amounts of Mycenaean and Geometric surface pottery have been found in this vicinity. Vases from a cemetery, assigned to the Early and Middle Helladic periods, are more likely to be local Dark Age, and a pithos burial is certainly of this date.

D 72 PSOROLITHI (Near KALYDON)
LH

AD 20 (1965) B 343; *BCH* 92 (1968) 849.

About 2.5 km. northeast of ancient Kalydon, on the west bank of the river Euenos, was a cache of Mycenaean bronzes, including double axes, an arrowhead, sickles, and a dagger.

D 73 KRYONERI
N MH LH II-III(A-B) G C H

BSA 32 (1931-2) 238.

On a low and much eroded terrace projecting from the west foot of Mt. Varassova, and about 600 m. northeast of Kryoneri, is a prehistoric settlement. The top area measures about 150 m. north to south by 100 m. Neolithic, Bronze Age, and Geometric sherds were noted here and house walls which may be Middle Helladic. To the north, at the base of the mountain, are caves which have the appearance of destroyed Mycenaean chamber tombs.

D 74 KATO VASILIKI: AYIA TRIADHA
LH III(A-C) C H

AA (1941) 99; *AD* 22 (1967) B 320.

To east of Kato Vasiliki, and near the north shore of the Corinthian Gulf, is the isolated low hill of Ayia

Triadha (top surface about 170 m. north to south by 120 m.). Bronze Age, Classical, and Hellenistic sherds and obsidian fragments were noted here in 1958; and a Mycenaean bronze double axe and rider figurine were found here later.

D 75 ANCIENT THERMON * # (Plate 18b)
MH? LH I-IIIC "PG" G A C H

PAE (1908) 95; *AD* 1 (1915) 225, 2 (1916) 179, 25 (1970) B 296; Schoder (1974) 211.

The site of ancient Thermon is about a kilometre to south of the village of Thermon, on a fertile plateau about 3 km. east of Lake Trichonis. The site is famous for its early Temple of Apollo, whose remains overlie a series of prehistoric buildings. Some of these appear to have been destroyed in the LH IIA period, since they contain a deposit of whole pots including types derived from the local Middle Helladic tradition together with LH I-IIA vases, both imports and evidently local products. An apsidal megaron and some rectangular structures are apparently later stratigraphically, and may be associated with the considerable quantities of LH III pottery found, as is suggested by K.A. Wardle. The site may have been inhabited continuously from the Mycenaean period through the Dark Age into later times.

D 76 LITHOVOUNI
LH III(B-C)

AD 18 (1963) B 147, 22 (1967) B 318; *BCH* 89 (1965) 761.

At Lithovouni, near the south shore of Lake Trichonis, a small chamber tomb was discovered in the course of road building. It seems to have been without a dromos. Many burials were reported, and finds included Mycenaean sherds and part of a handmade cup, two bronze spearheads, the top of a Type F dagger, and two bronze fibulae. The latter seem to indicate a date late in the Mycenaean period for the contents.

D 77 EUPALION: GOUVA
LH III(A2-B)

PAE (1906) 134; *AM* 31 (1906) 394; L. Lerat, *Les Locriens de l'Ouest* (1952) 102; *AD* 20 (1965) B 243.

At Gouva, near the north shore of the Corinthian Gulf, about 1.5 km. east of Eupalion, two stirrup-jars were found in a chamber tomb. A Mycenaean spear point from Eupalion is mentioned as having been stolen from Thermon museum (*AD loc.cit.*).

D 78 GALAXIDI
EH I-II LH III(A2-B) LH IIIC G

L. Lerat, *Les Locriens de l'Ouest* (1952) 157; *AE* (1956) *Parartema* 22; *BCH* 87 (1963) 937, 88 (1964) 559.

An Early Helladic settlement was cut through by the main road about 800 m. to south of Galaxidi. A stirrup-jar (LH IIIA2 or LH IIIB), an amphoriskos (LH IIIC), and two Geometric vases were reported from tombs in the area.

D 79 PENTEORIOI: PALAIOPANAYIA
MH LH C

AE (1956) *Parartema* 22.

The low hill of Palaiopanayia to south of Penteorioi is surrounded by a fortification of the Classical period. Middle Helladic and Mycenaean sherds were found on the west slopes. The site commands the road inland from Galaxidi.

APPENDIX TO MAP D

The following are locations in Achaea, Elis, and Arcadia where Mycenaean settlement is not yet proved.

AKRATA

OpAth 5 (1964) 100.

A Mycenaean cemetery was presumed at the western foot of the hill above Akrata, near the acropolis of ancient Aigeira (D 22).

DIAKOFTO: KASTRON

OpAth 5 (1964) 102.

A Mycenaean cemetery has been claimed here.

MIRALI

PAE (1930) 87, (1952) 398; *OpAth* 5 (1964) 106.

Two tumuli, one of which contained MH pottery, were found about 1.5 km. southwest of Mirali. Rock-cut tombs, possibly Mycenaean, are reported from Pori nearby (about 26 km along the road from Patras to Kalavryta).

MAMOUSIA

PAE (1938) 119, (1939) 104; *OpAth* 5 (1964) 105.

This village is about 12 km. south-southeast of Aigion, between the rivers Keronitis and Vouraikos. A burial pithos and twelve Geometric vases were found at the foot of the hill where ancient Keryneia is located [*cf. BSA* 48 (1953) 154]; and a Mycenaean cemetery has also been inferred, although not yet tested.

KERINIA: AYIOS YEORYIOS

The village of Kerinia lies about 8 km. southeast of Aigion, in the foothills of Mt. Klokos. A Mycenaean bronze double axe head, seen at Kerinia in 1962 and now in Patras museum, was said to have come from the vicinity of the chapel of Ayios Yeoryios, which lies on a spur to northeast of and above the village, overlooking the coastal plain. On the north slope of the spur, and above the chapel, are remains of ancient circuit walls; and the spur and its slopes are covered with ancient sherds (including Classical) and dislodged building stones. But no Mycenaean sherds were found in the course of a brief visit in 1962.

KOULOURA: PALAIOKAMARES

OpAth 5 (1964) 106.

It is possible that a LH IIIC stirrup-jar [*OpAth* 5 (1964) 90, Fig. 1:4-6] came from this location.

VOVODA

OpAth 5 (1964) 109.

A Close Style stirrup-jar [*OpAth* 5 (1964) 90, Fig. 1:1-3] may have come from the vicinity of this village, about 5 km. south-southwest of Aigion. Tombs were said to have been found at Ayios Ioannis near Vovoda, where an Archaic building and a Geometric cemetery have been noted [*BCH* 84 (1960) 690; *AR* (1960-61) 14].

AKARNES

BSA 32 (1931-2) 238; *OpAth* 5 (1964) 100.

Some sherds which were shown to Miss S. Benton were said to be from this village near Cape Drepanon, about 15 km. northeast of Patras. She described these as "LM I", but LH I/II is presumably indicated (*cf. OpAth loc.cit.*). The location has not been confirmed.

KRINI (formerly VELIZI)

OpAth 5 (1964) 109.

There is a verbal report of Mycenaean tombs near this village in the Patras area.

SKOURA

OpAth 5 (1964) 107.

Some Mycenaean objects brought to Patras museum in 1960 were said to have come from the neighbourhood of this village, which lies to south-southwest of Prostovitsa (D 48), on the west slopes of Mt. Erymanthos.

DAMIZA

RE Suppl. VI (1935) 607.

"Damiza (bei Amalias)" is listed among the Mycenaean chamber tomb cemeteries recorded by Karo in Elis and Achaea. Amalia is about 16 km. northwest of Pyrgos, but the location of Damiza is uncertain, and there is no confirmation of Mycenaean finds here.

ASPRA SPITIA: TOURLA

AJA 46 (1942) 86; *Messenia I* 227; *MME* No. 329.

About 3 km. southeast of and below Aspra Spitia, to northwest of the confluence of the Ladon and Alpheios rivers, is a magoula-shaped hilltop about 45 m. in diameter. The sloping plateau which stretches south from the hilltop down to the Alpheios measures about 150 m. east to west by 120 m. Bronze Age and later sherds are spread sparsely over the hilltop and plateau, covering a maximum area of about 200 m. east to west by 150 m. The position is strategic, and it is unfortunate that the Bronze Age sherds could not be closely dated.

TRYPETI: KASTRO

AJA 46 (1942) 81; E. Meyer, *Neue Peloponnesische Wanderungen* (1957) 40, 69; *Messenia I* 320, *MME* No. 332.

The acropolis of Kastro occupies the summit immediately above and southwest of Trypeti (formerly Bitsibardi). It has extensive and gentle northern and eastern slopes. On the summit (about 150 m. east to west by 25 m.) and east slopes the sherds are predominantly Classical or Hellenistic. But sherds of Middle Helladic and Mycenaean types have been claimed.

KALLIANI

AR (1959-60) 10.

Kalliani is a village in the Gortynia district, about 10 km. north of the confluence of the Alpheios and Ladon rivers. According to a newspaper report, a Mycenaean tomb was found here, near the church of Ayios Yeoryios, but there is no confirmation of this report; and it may indeed be mistaken [*cf. BSA* 68 (1973) 201 n. 28].

VLAKHERNA: PETRA

Arcadia No. 2; Pritchett (1969) 123.

Petra is an isolated rock in the southwest corner of the plain of Caphyai, about 4 km. south of Khotoussa and about 4 km. northeast of Vlakherna. The small top area, only about 35 m. by 20 m. is surrounded by polygonal walls. Much obsidian, some Early Helladic sherds, and coarse wares resembling both Neolithic and Mycenaean types, were found here together with Classical sherds and tiles.

KHOTOUSSA: AYIOS YEORYIOS

Arcadia No. 1.

About a kilometre to southeast of Khotoussa, to south of the road to Limni, is an isolated hill about 300 m. northwest to southeast by 150 m., on top of which is the church of Ayios Yeoryios. Sherds of prehistoric and later periods were scattered over the whole of this area and for a considerable distance to the north. The prehistoric sherds were hard to identify, but may include Early Helladic, Middle Helladic, and Mycenaean.

LACONIA   KYTHERA

MAP E

The main inhabited area of Laconia has always been the Eurotas valley, bounded by the two great mountain ranges of Taygetos on the west and Parnon on the east. The principal known concentrations of Mycenaean settlement are those in or around the inland Sparta plain and the coastal plain of Helos (Fig. 10). Next in importance are the smaller plains of Molaoi and Vatika (Neapolis) in the southeast, and the Vardhounia valley (inland from Gythion) on the west. Other important Mycenaean centres have been found at Epidauros Limera (E 30), Pellanes (E 46), Vourvoura (E 48), and in the upper part of the Leonidhi valley in Kynouria (E 50-52).

There was apparently a considerable increase in the number of LH settlements in Laconia over those of the MH period. The transition from MB to LH in Laconia has recently been investigated by J.B. and S.H. Rutter in *The Transition to Mycenaean [Monumenta Archaeologica* 4 (1976)]*, who discuss a stratified pottery sequence at Ayios Stephanos (E 14). They conclude that there was considerable Minoan and/or Kytheran influence on the pottery of this phase here; and they go so far as to surmise that the earliest LH I pottery may have developed in Laconia and perhaps Messenia rather than in the Argolid. O.T.P.K. Dickinson, who formerly argued the case for the primacy of the Argolid in this respect [*BSA* 69 (1974) 109], now allows the possibility that the origin of Mycenaean pottery may have to be sought in Southern Laconia [O.T.P.K. Dickinson, *The Origins of Mycenaean Civilisation* (1977) 108 n. 2, *cf.* p. 24].

Fine Early Mycenaean pottery has been found at most excavated sites in Laconia and at several not excavated; and this, together with the Vaphio tholos tomb (E 4) in particular, suggests early prosperity. The successive "mansions" of the Menelaion site (E 1) demonstrate its importance in LH IIB-IIIA1, when it may have been the "capital" of the Sparta plain, if not of Laconia as a whole. Although there is no definitive

evidence from excavation of a major centre in Laconia in LH IIIA2-B, the impression given, particularly by the surface finds, is that Mycenaean settlement in Laconia was at this time the most widespread and flourishing. There may have been a considerable degree of survival of settlement into the LH IIIC period, when four of the excavated sites (E 5, E 21, E 30, and E 46) were still occupied; but two of the principal sites, *i.e.* the Menelaion and Ayios Stephanos, were apparently abandoned at the end of the LH IIIB period, or soon after.

Fuller discussions of most of the Mycenaean sites in Laconia have been given in the survey articles in *BSA* 55 (1960) 67-107 and *BSA* 56 (1961) 114-175, here abbreviated as *Laconia I* and *Laconia II* respectively. References given here are therefore selected; and discussion of J.L. Bintliff's commentaries on the sites in the Sparta valley and the Helos plain are relegated to a note at the end of the chapter.

THE SPARTA PLAIN (E 1-13)

The plain is surrounded on all sides by mountains or hills, and is suitably described as "hollow Lacedaemon" (*Iliad* ii. 581). On the southwest is the steep outer range of Taygetos, an impressive limestone formation (Plate 20a). On the northwest are conglomerate foothills extending to the site of classical Sparta, and on the east a similar conglomerate chain, from Aphissou to Skoura. On the south and southeast the hills of Lykovouni and Vardhounia rise more gradually from the edge of the plain. In the centre of the plain a line of low undulating hills of conglomerate or marl stretches from the site of the Amyklaion (E 5) to Ayios Vasilios (E 7). On either side of these hills are belts of alluvium, much of which is "recent". The Mycenaean settlements found in and around the plain are all on either marl or conglomerate.

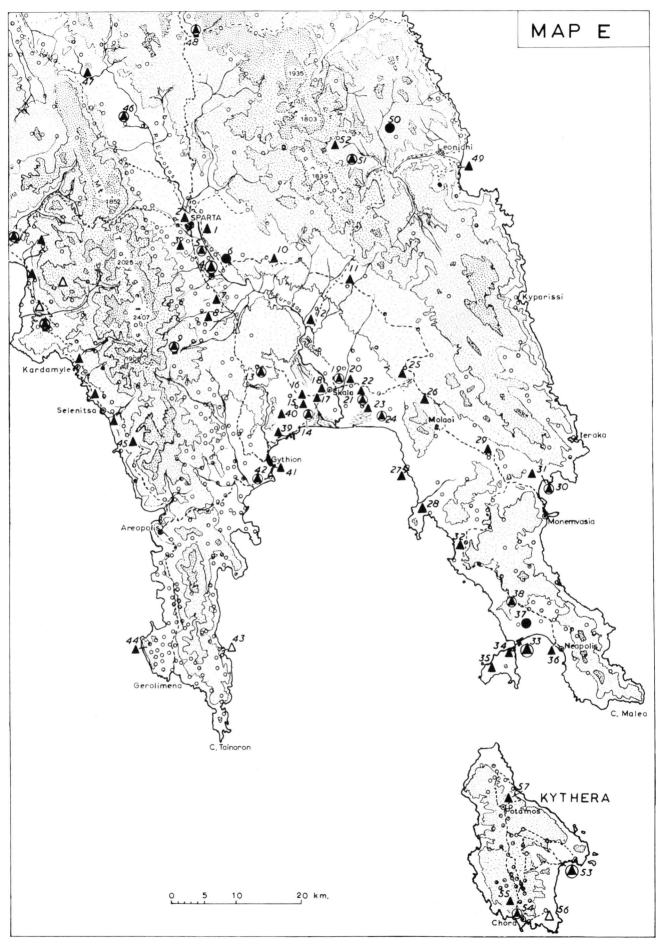

MAP E

Leonichi

Kyparissi

SPARTA

Kardamyle

Selenitsa

Skala

Molaoi

Ieraka

Gythion

Monemvasia

Areopolis

Neapolis

C. Malea

Gerolimena

C. Tainaron

KYTHERA

Potamos

Chora

0   5   10   20 km.

E 1 THE MENELAION *
MH LH I-IIIA1 LH IIIB2 G A C H

Laconia I 72; *AR* (1973-4) 14, (1974-5) 12, (1975-6) 13, (1976-7) 24 (with full references).

The British School, under H.W. Catling, has resumed excavations here. The results have been extremely rewarding, and at times spectacular. The site occupies most of a long conglomerate ridge high above the east bank of the river Eurotas. The area within which Mycenaean building remains and sherds have been found is now known to be about a kilometre north to south by approximately 150 m. (average width of the ridge). But surface sherds on the southern third of this area were sparse (none were found on the lower south slopes of the Aetos hill in an exhaustive search in 1956); and the Mycenaean buildings may have been concentrated mainly on the summits of three hills. These are the Menelaion itself (about 140 m. northeast to southwest by about 40 m.), the hill to north (of comparable size), and the smaller hill of Aetos to the south. The tops of the latter hills are about 300 m. distant from the Menelaion shrine, which marks the approximate centre of the area in which excavations have been made. Remains of Mycenaean structures were found on all three hills, but those from the "North Hill" and Aetos seemed confined to LH IIIB2 or early LH IIIC.

The best preserved structures are those on the northeast arm of the Menelaion hill. This area and part of the "North Hill" were apparently first occupied in late MH times; and the site was apparently already of some importance in LH IIA, to judge from the fine "palatial" jar fragments and some LM IB imports. But the earliest surviving building, the complex designated as "Mansion 1", was constructed in the LH IIB period. This was followed by the even more elaborate "Mansion 2", above the ruins of "Mansion 1", but on a different orientation. This second building was abandoned apparently before the end of the LH IIIA1 period; and it appears that, on this part of the site at least, there was no occupation in either the LH IIIA2 or LH IIIB1 periods. "Mansion 2" was partly repaired and reoccupied in LH IIIB2, and it is clear that this was the time that the Mycenaean settlement was at its most extensive.

The Menelaion was almost certainly a "capital" site during LH IIB and LH IIIA1. But whether it again reached such a status in the LH IIIB2 period can not be decided from the available evidence. Catling notes that, although the site was of considerable importance at this time, its administrative centre may no longer have been in the same place as in the LH IIB-IIIA1 period. A possible "rival" to the Menelaion in the LH IIIB2 period might be the Vaphio settlement (E 4); but of the few Mycenaean surface sherds positively identified there as LH IIIB, none can be definitely attributed to LH IIIB2.

The Mycenaean settlement on the Menelaion site was destroyed by fire; and there are as yet no signs of any occupation or any use of the site (other than possible agriculture) between the LH IIIC period and the Late Geometric (see Addenda for the most recent evidence).

E 2 ANCIENT SPARTA *
LH III(A-B) "PG" G A C H

Laconia I 70.

In the excavations of 1926-7 on the acropolis of ancient Sparta about twenty-five LH III sherds were found, in a mixed deposit. Some distance to southeast of the acropolis, a fragment of a LH III stirrup-jar and other LH III sherds were found by chance; and a few Mycenaean gems were found at the Sanctuary of Artemis Orthia. The indications are that the Mycenaean settlement on the site of the historical Sparta was probably of minor importance. The acropolis is the first in a chain of conglomerate hills which stretch to northwest from Sparta. Search (in 1956-7) of the other hills in this chain for a distance of about four kilometres revealed no further signs of Mycenaean habitation.

E 3 KOUPHOVOUNO *
N EH II LH III(A-B)

AA (1942) 156; *Laconia I* 72.

Kouphovouno is a low rise about 170 m. in diameter, to southeast of the road from Sparta to Ayios Ioannis, and about 2 km. southwest of Sparta. Trial excavations here revealed Neolithic and EH II houses and graves. A few LH III sherds were later found on the surface, together with larger amounts of Neolithic and EH artefacts. The Mycenaean sherds were mainly on the edges of the rise. A minor Mycenaean settlement is indicated here also.

E 4 VAPHIO: PALAIOPYRGI * # (Plate 19c and Fig. 9)
EH II MH LH IIA-IIIB

AE (1889) 136; *Laconia I* 76; *AD* 18 (1963) B 87, 23 (1968) B 152; *BSA* 69 (1974) 219 n. 23.

Palaiopyrgi is the highest point in the chain of conglomerate hills on the west side of the Eurotas river in the centre of the Sparta plain. The Mycenaean settlement here is probably the largest in Laconia, to judge from the spread of surface sherds (over about 200,000 square metres). Most of the sherds were of the LH IIIA-B periods, but some LH IIA have recently been found (*AD* 23 *loc.cit.*). The hill was first settled in EH II, and was probably occupied continuously from MH to LH IIIB.

The famous tholos tomb was dug into the top of the hill adjacent on the northwest. It was large and well constructed. Besides the famous gold cups and the rest of an untouched assemblage of extremely rich

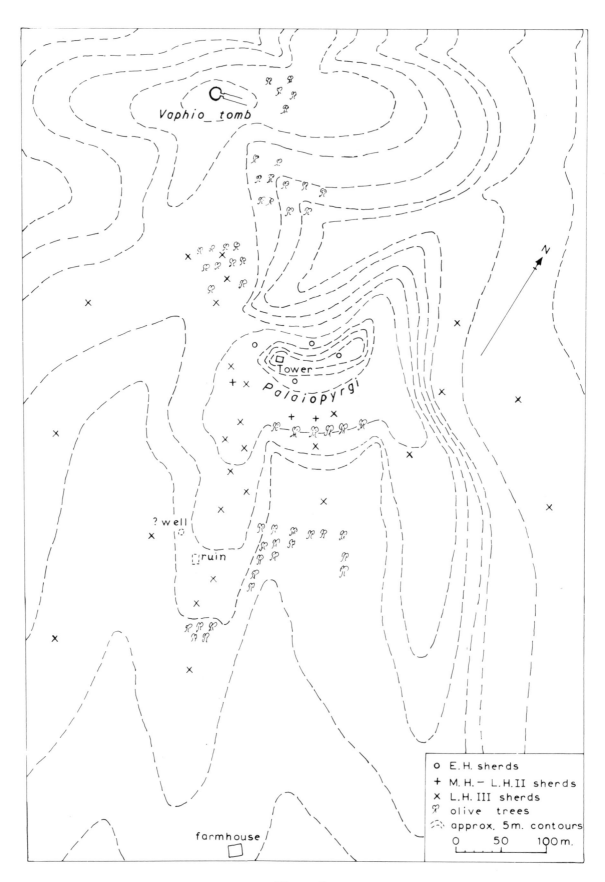

Figure 9

goods in the grave-pit, remains of "palatial" LH IIA jars were found in the dromos. The grave-pit also contained some pottery probably of late LH IIA, and other sherds in the chamber include one apparently LH IIIA1.

As was stated above (under E 1 The Menelaion), it is not possible to determine whether the Palaiopyrgi site flourished in the LH IIIB2 period. But it may indeed have been the "capital" site in Laconia in the periods LH IIIA2-B1 when the Menelaion site was apparently deserted.

E 5 THE AMYKLAION *
EH II MH LH IIA-IIIC "PG" G A C H

AM 52 (1927) 1; *Laconia I* 74; Desborough (1964) 88; *BSA* 66 (1971) 139.

The chapel of Ayia Kyriaki, above the remains of the Amyklaion shrine, is on the northernmost of the chain of conglomerate hills mentioned above (under E 4). Apart from the prehistoric finds on the summit found in the Amyklaion excavations, the spread of potsherds on the southeast slopes and along the ridge stretching to west of the chapel indicates an extent of settlement about 200 m. east to west by 120 m. Habitation was probably continuous from MH, although not all LH phases can be certified. LH IIA "palatial" jar fragments were found, and the elaborate Psi figurines and wheel made animal terracottas seem to indicate a cult in late LH IIIB and LH IIIC. There is, however, no indication of the continuity of such a cult, since the next certain evidence for use of the site is the presence of Laconian Protogeometric pottery.

Two chamber tombs, presumably LH, and a MH (?) pithos burial were observed on the hill to south of the Amyklaion.

E 6 SKOURA: MELATHRIA *
LH IIIA1-IIIB

AD 22 (1967) B 197; *AAA* 1 (1968) 37; *BSA* 66 (1971) 95; *AE* (1977) 29.

About 2 km. to northeast of Skoura, on the west side of the thin valley of Melathria, and to west of the ravine in its centre, is a small hillock named Profitis Ilias. Chamber tombs were dug into the soft marl rock in the south and east sides. Five tombs were excavated, and most were found already robbed. The site is in foothills on the east side of the Sparta plain. The Mycenaean settlement itself has not yet been discovered here.

E 7 AYIOS VASILIOS
EH II MH LH IIIA-B C H

Laconia I 80.

The chapel of Ayios Vasilios lies on the low hill which forms the southern point in the chain of hills which runs south from the Amyklaion down the middle of the Sparta plain. It is above the junction between the Sparta-Gythion road and the side road to Xerokambi. EH II and MH sherds were found concentrated mainly around the chapel itself. Mycenaean sherds (mainly LH IIIB) were more numerous and widespread, upon the chapel hill and part of the adjoining plateau on the southwest, over an area about 250 m. northeast to southwest by 120 m., indicating a medium to large settlement.

About a kilometre to south of the chapel, in the side of a low oval-shaped hillock, are two cuttings in the soft conglomerate rock, which may be the remains of chamber tombs.

E 8 ANTHOCHORION: ANALIPSIS *
LH IIA-IIIB "PG" G A C H

PAE (1962) 113; *AD* 18 (1963) B 86.

The chapel of Analipsis is on a low rise about 2 km. south of Xerokambi, on the road to Goranoi, near the south end of the Sparta plain. Mycenaean and later strata were excavated in flat ground near the chapel. O. Dickinson was able to attribute the Mycenaean pottery to the range LH IIA-IIIB. It was not possible to estimate the size of the Mycenaean settlement.

E 9 ARKINES *
LH III(A-B) C

Laconia II 128.

That the Mycenaeans also penetrated the high mountain cantons of Taygetos is shown by the discovery of two small and poorly constructed tholos tombs in a high, stony and wooded valley just south of the summit of Taygetos, at the head of the Goranoi river. That these were probably not simply the tombs of unfortunate hunters or shepherds is demonstrated not only by the jewellery found in one of the tombs but also by the discovery of a Mycenaean settlement site on terraces opposite. Mycenaean sherds were found here over an area about 200 m. northwest to southeast by 50 m. It must, however, be supposed that occupation here was seasonal.

E 10 GORITSA: LAINA
N EH II MH LH I/II LH III(A-B)

Laconia I 83

A prehistoric settlement occupies a hillock about 2 km. southeast of Goritsa overlooking a plain to the east along the road to Geraki. The site is steep on the south and east, but on the north and west it is connected by a saddle to barren hills on the southeast side of Goritsa. The surface finds, over an area about 200 m. by 180 m., attest a considerable settlement, at least in LH IIIB, to which period belong most of the diagnostic sherds.

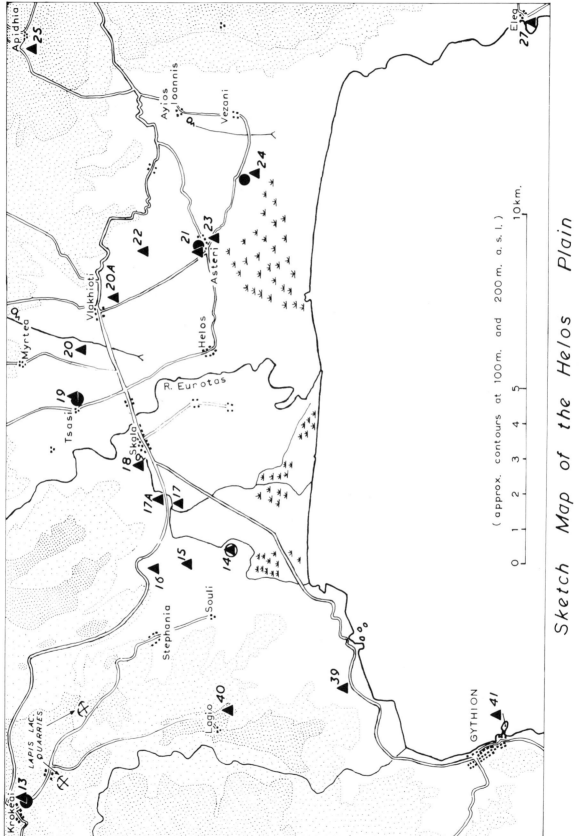

Sketch Map of the Helos Plain

Figure 10

(approx. contours at 100 m. and 200 m. a. s. l.)

0   1   2   3   4   5   10 km.

E 11 GERAKI: ANCIENT GERONTHRAI *
N? EH II MH LH III(A-B)? C H

BSA 15 (1908-9) 163, 16 (1909-10) 72; *Laconia I* 85.

The acropolis of ancient Geronthrai on the summit of the hill above the large village of Geraki was certainly occupied in the EH II and MH periods, as was shown by the trial excavations. The fortifications are of "Cyclopean" type, and so may be Mycenaean, as may also be some figurines, although they would be very late Mycenaean in this case [*BSA* 66 (1971) 139].

E 12 VRONDAMA
LH III(A-B) C H

Laconia I 83.

On the edge of a small plain on the east side of the Eurotas is a small hill of soft poros limestone on whose top surface (about 120 m. north to south by 90 m.) were found a few Mycenaean sherds. Later sherds were far more abundant and spread over a wider area, including the larger terrace on the south side.

E 13 KROKEAI: KARNEAS *
LH II-IIIB C H

Laconia I 103.

On the top surface (about 120 m. northwest to southeast by 60 m.) of the hill Karneas, about 300 m. southeast of Krokeai, several LH III sherds were found. A large rectangular stone built grave was found on the southwest flank, and its contents included LH II-III pottery.

THE HELOS PLAIN (E 14-24) (Fig. 10)

This plain is now the most fertile area in Laconia. But in Mycenaean times it must have been mostly sea or marshland; and any alluvial deposits (brought down mainly by the Eurotas) would then have been difficult to cultivate because of the problem of drainage and the lack of instruments for deep ploughing. The position of the sites (E 14 to E 24) on the low hills immediately bordering the plain, follows the normal pattern, and may also tend to show that the marshland was not extensively farmed, but that the ancient settlers preferred the more easily cultivated hillocks and terraces around the plain.

The settlements are numerous, but mainly small. There can be little doubt that Ayios Stephanos (E 14) was the chief site in the region, and only two other sites, E 16 and E 21, appear to have been of moderately large size. E 18, E 19, and E 24 may have been the other main centres. The rest of the sites around the plain would seem to have been minor and subordinate to these six. Ayios Stephanos lies at the cross roads of the routes from the Sparta plain (*via* Krokeai) and from the Gythion coastal strip. It is also the only site discovered in the region naturally suitable for use as a fortress.

E 14 AYIOS STEPHANOS * # (Plate 21a)
N? EH II MH LH I-IIIB2 C H

Laconia I 97; *BSA* 67 (1972) 205; *AR* (1973-4) 15, (1974-5) 15, J.B. and S.H. Rutter, *The Transition to Mycenaean* (1976).

The site (in the background of Plate 21a) is a low hill, about 25 m. above the level of the plain, steep on the north and east, at the eastern end of a limestone spur projecting from the barren range of hills on the southwest edge of the plain. It was probably a promontory jutting into the sea in Mycenaean times. The Mycenaean settlement occupied an area about 160 m. in diameter, and was continuously inhabited from some time in MH until the end of LH IIIB. The particularly important stratified pottery sequence from MH to LH IIA published by J.B. and S.H. Rutter (*loc.cit.*) has been discussed above. The Mycenaean buildings uncovered in the excavations are neither large nor impressive, although there is possible evidence for a fortification wall. *Lapis Lacedaemonius* from the nearby Psephi quarries was probably being exported *via* Ayios Stephanos before the end of MH, and appears to have reached Crete in considerable quantities by the early part of the Mycenaean period. Many fragments of this stone were found on the site and some implements also. The site appears to have been abandoned at the end of LH IIIB or shortly after (see also Addenda).

E 15 STEPHANIA: LEKAS (SOUTH)
N? EH II MH LH III(A-B) C H

Laconia I 97.

About 1.5 km. north-northwest of Ayios Stephanos is a low mound about 150 m. north to south by 120 m., on the northwest edge of the former marsh. Its top is about 5 m. above the level of the plain. Most of the sherds here were pre-Mycenaean, but two LH III fragments were found and eleven pieces of *Lapis Lacedaemonius*.

E 16 STEPHANIA: LEKAS, PANAYIOTIS # (Plate 21a)
EH II MH LH IIIA-B C H

Laconia I 95.

At the northwest edge of the Skala plain is a range of low undulating hillocks in the district known as Lekas. One prominent hillock, standing about 15 m. above the surrounding fields is marked by a ruined farmhouse named Panayiotis on its top (Plate 21a, in foreground). It lies about 400 m. to south of the Skala Krokeai road, where this begins to climb towards Krokeai.

There is evidence of a considerable Bronze Age settlement here, and there appear to have been two rings of ancient walls round the site (*Laconia I* Fig. 13), whose lines are followed in part by modern field walls. The surface pottery was mainly LH III, and eight fragments of *Lapis Lacedaemonius* were found, including part of a pounder. The sherds were distributed over a wide area, about 250 m. north to south by 180 m., but this spread may be largely due to cultivation and erosion, so that the site should probably be classed as "medium to large" rather than "large". Further traces of MH and LH III settlement were found on a low rise about 200 m. to southwest of the site, in the vicinity of three large pits, in the sides of which walls of mud brick and stone were revealed.

E 17 XERONISI
EH II MH LH IIIA-B

Laconia I 95.

About 2 km. west-southwest of Skala, and to south of the road, is a small low mound, standing only about 5 m. above the former marsh level. In the walls of a ruined mud brick hut, and for a short distance around it were several EH II sherds and some MH and LH III. The site is now largely ploughed away. A few LH III and later sherds were found at Ayios Ioannis on the north side of the road, and opposite Xeronisi.

E 18 SKALA: AYIOS NIKOLAOS
MH LH IIIA-B

Laconia I 94.

The chapel of Ayios Nikolaos lies on a low flat hillock, about 120 m. east to west by 80 m., near the six springs of the Vasilopotamos, about 1 km. west of Skala, on the north side of the road. Several LH III sherds were found in piles of stones cleared from the top surface.

E 19 TSASI *
EH II LH IIIA-B C H

Laconia I 92.

A Mycenaean chamber tomb was discovered on the south slope of a low hill on the northern edge of the Skala plain about 500 m. east of Tsasi. Among the contents of the tomb were two jugs of LH IIIA2 or LH IIIB date, and a few LH III sherds were found in the immediate vicinity. EH II sherds were more abundant and widespread, and it is possible that the LH habitation site here still remains to be found.

E 20 VLAKHIOTI: KOKKINADHA etc.
EH II LH III C H

Laconia I 92.

Sporadic traces of LH III settlement were found on hills bordering the Helos plain both to northwest and to southeast of Vlakhioti, particularly on the west slope of a large red hill named Kokkinadha, about 1 km. to northwest of Vlakhioti.

E 21 ASTERI: KARAOUSI *
N EH II MH LH I/II-IIIC DA? C H

Laconia I 89; *BSA* 67 (1972) 262.

About 200 m. to north of Asteri, on the east side of the road to Vlakhioti, is the prominent flat-topped hillock named Karaousi, whose top surface measures about 160 m. northwest to southeast by 100 m. LH I-III sherds of good quality were plentiful and widely distributed over the hillock, with a concentration on the lower south slopes. The trial excavations, however, showed that the site was badly eroded. The bulk of the pottery found in the trials was Mycenaean, including some LH IIIC. Fragments from LH *alabastra* and other LH sherds were found on the east slopes of a low hill about 300 m. east of the site, near pits which appear to be the remains of collapsed chamber tombs. The evidence demonstrates a site of medium size.

E 22 ASTERI: SITE TO NORTH
LH IIIA-B

Laconia I 92.

A small Mycenaean settlement (about 100 m. north to south by 80 m.) was noted on a low rise about 2 km. north of Asteri among olive groves in a district of small undulating hills.

E 23 ASTERI: DHRAGATSOULA
EH II MH LH III(A-B)

Laconia I 89.

About 500 m. east-southeast of Asteri, to south of the road to Vezani, is a flat-topped hillock about 140 m. by 120 m., on the northern edge of the plain. Sherds here were mainly EH II, and only two LH III were found. The site itself is not impressive.

E 24 AYIOS EFSTRATIOS
N EH (I?-)II MH LH II-IIIB C

The chapel of Ayios Efstratios lies on a low ridge about 3 km. west-southwest of Vezani on the northern edge of the marsh. The LH site is about 1 km. east-southeast of the chapel, on the easternmost hillock of the ridge. The extent of the LH settlement appears to have been about 100 m. east to west by 70 m. At a place named Elitsa about 500 m. to the north there were remains of a very small and poorly built Mycenaean built tomb of tholos type, near which two LH III jug bases were found.

The area to east of the Helos plain was only partially and briefly investigated. Some MH sherds and others possibly LH were found on the top of the hill above Ayios Ioannis village (*Laconia I* 87), and a tumulus was observed near the coast to north of Kokkinia at the fort of Mt. Kourkoula (*Laconia II* 139).

THE REMAINDER OF LACONIA AND KYNOURIA (E 25-52)

E 25 APIDHIA (ANCIENT PALAIA)
N EH II MH LH II-IIIB "PG" C H

Laconia I 96.

Apidhia lies at the southern end of a small valley. An acropolis of moderate size (top surface about 160 m. by 90 m.) rises immediately above the village on its southwest side. Good Neolithic and Bronze Age surface sherds were found. The Mycenaean includes a LH II sherd and several LH IIIB.

E 26 GANGANIA
EH MH LH III(A-B)

Laconia II 139.

Below the monastery of Gangania, and beside the main road about 4 km. northwest of Molaoi is a rocky hill with a profile very like that of the citadel of Mycenae, and precipitous on its eastern side. It commands the northwest approach to the fertile Molaoi plain. Bronze Age sherds were plentiful on the upper slopes, and there are apparent traces of foundations here. The Mycenaean pottery was very shattered, but LH III(A-B) bowl fragments were recognized. Half-way up the adjacent hill to the west two plundered chamber tombs were noted. The site is of moderate size.

E 27 ELEA
EH LH III(A-B) C H

Laconia II 139.

On the south edge of the seaside village of Elea, at the west end of the Molaoi plain, is a rocky hill crowned by a mediaeval tower. The hill is steep on all sides, especially to seaward. EH and LH sherds were found on the upper east slopes over an area about 100 m. in diameter, indicating a small to medium settlement.

E 28 PLITRA: GOULAS # (Plate 21c)
N EH I-II MH LH III(A-B)

Laconia II 139.

Goulas is an acropolis hill of medium size and little height at the southern edge of the Molaoi plain, near the foot of the promontory of Xyli. The flat summit (about 180 m. north to south by 100 m.) is surrounded on all sides by sheer cliffs of soft white limestone. The Bronze Age sherds, which include typical LH III kylix and bowl fragments, were mainly found on this summit, where there are also remains of the foundations of small rectangular buildings.

E 29 SIKEA: ANEMOMYLO
EH II LH III(A-B)

Laconia II 138.

On a gentle rise, about 1.5 km. northwest of Sikea, and on the northeast side of the road to Molaoi, is a ruined tower, once part of a windmill. Within a radius of about 50 m. round the tower EH and LH sherds were found and much obsidian. This small site is near the eastern edge of the Molaoi plain, on the natural route to Epidauros Limera on the east coast.

E 30 ANCIENT EPIDAUROS LIMERA * # (Plate 21b)
N? EH or MH? LH I-IIIC SMyc? C H

PAE (1956) 207; *Laconia II* 136; *AD* 23 (1968) A 145.

The acropolis of Epidauros Limera is a limestone outcrop about 5 km. north of Monemvasia, at the end of a small coastal valley and above a long beach. Some Mycenaean surface sherds were found on the summit and upper slopes (an area about 400 m. north to south by 250 m.) among much greater quantities of Classical and later fragments. The Mycenaean sherds were mainly found within the area of the later fortifications.

Mycenaean chamber tombs of an individual type (some with stepped dromoi) have been excavated at three different locations to south and southwest of the acropolis. One group is nearer to Ayios Ioannis village and site no. E 31 below. The earliest material from the tombs is LM IA or very early LH I, apparently of a local type, independent of the Argolid. Several LH IIIC vases, some of which have clear connections with the Argolid and the Aegean, suggest that this site was an important survivor in LH IIIC.

E 31 AYIOS IOANNIS
EH LH III

Laconia II 137.

About a kilometre to northeast of Ayios Ioannis village and 2 km. west of Epidauros Limera is a small and steep limestone hill (Plate 21b left centre), whose top surface measures only about 60 m. by 50 m. On its upper southeast slope were found a few EH and LH III sherds and some obsidian chips, indicating at most a small settlement.

EH sherds and other Bronze Age sherds, including some probably LH were found on the slopes of a small hill adjoining the Kollyri plateau, about 1.5 km. east of Angelona, overlooking the ravine which leads into the Epidauros Limera valley, and only about 2 km. northwest of the Ayios Ioannis site. Both these small sites were probably subordinate to the prehistoric site at Epidauros Limera.

E 32 DAIMONIA: KASTELLI (ANCIENT COTYRTA)
MH LH IIA-IIIB G C H

Laconia II 141.

The rocky acropolis of Kastelli lies to southeast of Daimonia, midway between the village and the sea, on the edge of a small coastal plain, at the south end of the route from Epidauros Limera, and commanding the coastal route from the Molaoi plain to the Neapolis area. The hill is covered with potsherds and LH sherds are plentiful, including one LH IIA and several LH IIIB, found within an area about 200 m. northeast to southwest by 150 m., indicating a medium to large settlement.

E 33 ELAPHONISI: PAVLOPETRI
EH II   MH   LH I-IIIB   C   H

BSA 64 (1969) 113.

This site, now under two to three metres of seawater, was probably the most important in the Vatika (Neapolis) plain. It is about a kilometre to northeast of Elaphonisi village, and occupies an area at least 350 m. northeast to southwest by 200 m., between what is now the islet of Pavlopetri and the mainland. It is clear that the island of Elaphonisi was at this time a promontory, joined by a low saddle to the rest of the mainland [cf. BSA 64 (1969) 113 Fig. 1].

An extensive plan of the site has been obtained by means of difficult and painstaking underwater survey carried out by students of the University of Cambridge. Conclusions as to the data of the preserved walls can only be tentative, since no excavation has yet taken place. The resulting plan most resembles that of Aegean towns such as Phylakopi, rather than of any Mycenaean settlement hitherto excavated; although there is a superficial resemblance between the "streets" and one found at Nichoria (F 100). And it is likely that the connections of Pavlopetri with the Aegean will prove to have been stronger than those with the mainland in the Middle Bronze Age and early in the Late Bronze Age (cf. E 14 (Ayios Stephanos). A wide range of prehistoric pottery was recovered, both underwater and on Pavlopetri islet. A large cemetery of small rock-cut tombs on the mainland shore may be EB, and two larger tombs appear to be Mycenaean chamber tombs.

E 34 ELAPHONISI VILLAGE
EH II   LH III(A-B)

Laconia II 146.

A series of small sites found near Elaphonisi village may represent only scattered farms or single dwellings. Most surface sherds were EH, and were accompanied by many obsidian fragments. Some LH sherds were found on the north slopes of low hills to south of the village.

E 35 ELAPHONISI: PANAYIA
EH II   LH III(A-B)

Laconia II 147.

A fairly extensive EH II and LH III settlement is indicated by abundant sherds in the vicinity of the church of Panagia on a low hill towards the southwest

end of Elaphonisi. To south and east of the church, sherds were found over a considerable area. In the white cliffs 200 m. to west of the church, and below the slopes of the Pelakidhi hill, are small caves, which may once have been Mycenaean chamber tombs. The slopes immediately to west of and below the church also may conceal chamber tombs. This part and indeed all of Elaphonisi may have had considerably more good agricultural land in prehistoric times, before the rise in sea level [cf. BSA 64 (1969) 113 Fig. 1, noting especially the position of the three fathom contour].

E 36 NEAPOLIS
EH   LH III(A-B)   C   H

Laconia II 142.

About a kilometre to northwest of Neapolis is a low hillock near the shore, to west of the road. Mycenaean sherds were plentiful and extend over an area about 100 m. in diameter. The site may have been considerably larger, since it has been much eroded by the sea here [it was originally inland, cf. BSA 64 (1969) 113 Fig. 1]. There are remains of at least 16 chamber tombs, some of them presumably Mycenaean, cut in the soft limestone slopes of low hills to east of the site.

E 37 AYIOS YEORYIOS
LH

Laconia II 145.

Some plundered Mycenaean chamber tombs, including some with stepped dromoi like those of Epidauros Limera (E 30), were found near the village school of Ayios Yeoryios, towards the western end of the Vatika plain. No settlement site has been found here, but pottery from a well at the hamlet of Ayia Triadha about 1.5 km. to the southwest included coarse ware of LH type, and Bronze Age sherds and obsidian chips were found at two other locations nearby.

E 38 STENA
EH II   LH IIA   LH III(A-B)

Laconia II 141.

On a steep conical hill on the watershed commanding the pass from Elika down to the Vatika plain, a small prehistoric settlement was found. On the upper southern terraces of the hill EH and LH sherds, including one attributed to LH IIA, were found over an area about 120 m. northwest to southeast by 80 m. About 500 m. southeast of the summit, on the east bank of a stream, are two groups of plundered chamber tombs cut in the soft sandstone rock.

E 39 PAIZOULIA
EH   II   MH   LH I/II   LH IIIA-B   C   H

Laconia I 105.

About 4 km. to north of Gythion, on the north side of the road to Skala is a low hill with a top surface of about 170 m. east to west by 60 m. On its southern slopes Bronze Age sherds, mainly Mycenaean, were found over a considerable extent, indicating a settlement of medium size, in a small coastal valley here.

E 40 LAGIO
EH II LH III(A-B)

Laconia I 105.

In the small valley which leads from Lagio down to the shore at Trinasa, is a small low hill, about a kilometre east-southeast of Lagio village. On its top surface (about 110 m. north to south by 80 m.) scant traces of EH and Mycenaean habitation were found. Only two LH sherds were recognized, and the site may only have been a small farm in this period.

E 41 GYTHION: ISLAND OF CRANAE
(Plate 22a)
LH IIIA-B

Laconia II 114.

That Gythion was a major centre in Mycenaean times is suggested by the story of the sojourn of Paris and Helen on the island of Cranae (*Iliad* iii. 443-6). No prehistoric remains have yet been discovered on the acropolis of ancient Gythion on the north edge of the modern town, and this may be due to the overlay of Classical and later sherds on the acropolis slopes. On the island of Cranae itself, however, several LH III sherds, rather worn and of poor quality, were found on the western and central parts, over perhaps half of the surface of the island (which measures in all about 300 m. east to west by 100 m.). There is now little soil left, except in the vicinity of the Turkish fort near the centre.

E 42 GYTHION: MAVROVOUNI
EH II LH IIIB "PG" G C H

Laconia II 114.

An extensive cemetery of Mycenaean chamber tombs has been found on a prominent hill to north of the main road from Gythion to Areopolis, about 4 km. southwest of Gythion, near the shore and on the edge of the rich Vardhounia plain. Several Mycenaean chamber tombs have been carved out of the soft marl rock of the upper terraces, and there are a few EH and LH III sherds on the summit. But the main prehistoric settlement may have been on a lower hill about 300 m. to the northeast, where there are more sherds over a wider area. These include Mycenaean and Classical. EH and LH III sherds were also found in a well at the south foot of the cemetery hill, and later remains, including two vases of local Protogeometric, among the low sandy hills to northeast and east of the site.

E 43 SPIRA
EH LH? C

Laconia II 119; *BSA* 63 (1968) 332.

On the southwest slope of the hill of Spira near Kyprianon, near the southern tip of the Mani, some EH sherds and others probably LH were found. The quarries of Antico Rosso in the mountain slopes above are almost certainly the provenance of the purple and green marble which formed the principal decoration of the facade of the Treasury of Atreus (*cf. BSA loc.cit.*). The traces of prehistoric habitation are slight, and the land here is marginal and unproductive.

E 44 KIPOULA
EH? LH (III?) A C H

Laconia II 123.

On a high limestone ridge above cliffs on the west coast of the Mani, a few worn LH sherds were found. The land in this vicinity is marginal, but some arable soil exists in the plateau below to the east.

E 45 KOUTIPHARI: SVINA (ANCIENT THALAMAI) *
LH III(A-B) DA? A C H

BSA 10 (1904-5) 24, 52 (1957) 232; *AJA* 65 (1961) 251.

Traces of a small LH III settlement were observed on slopes to east of and above the village of Koutiphari, in an elevated position above the west coast, near a fine spring. A LH III vase was found in limited excavations and a male figurine of odd type may be Mycenaean or Dark Age.

E 46 PELLANES: SPILIES AND PALAIOKASTRO *
EH? LH IIIA-C C H

AD 10 (1926) *Parartema* 41; *Laconia II* 125.

In the upper part of the Eurotas valley, about a kilometre to north of Pellanes, two unusual Mycenaean chamber tombs were found, with diameters about 6 m., and shaped like tholos tombs. In one of these fine LH vases of the range LH IIIA1-C were found. The settlement was apparently at Palaiokastro about 700 m. to the south, where a few LH III sherds were found within the mediaeval castle walls, together with Classical sherds. This is almost certainly the centre of ancient Pellana (Pausanias iii. 21. 3).

E 47 BELMINA
EH? MH? LH III(A-B) C

Laconia II 125.

On a small plateau named Kanalaki on the south slopes of Mt. Chelmos, and at Iannakas nearby, some Mycenaean sherds and obsidian were found. The mainspring of the Eurotas river is less than a kilometre to the northwest. The fortifications on the summit, those of the ancient Belmina, are of the Classical or Hellenistic period.

E 48 VOURVOURA: ANALIPSIS *
N MH LH I-IIIB C H

PAE (1954) 270, (1956) 185, (1957) 111, *AA* (1962) 257, *Laconia II* 130; *BSA* 65 (1970) 95.

The hill of Analipsis is about 4 km. west of Vourvoura and 2 km. east of the Sparta-Tripolis road, on the south side of the deep gorge of the Sarandapotamos river. It is about 300 m. in diameter, and is the site of a large Classical settlement. A burnt layer containing LH IIIB pottery is reported (*AA op.cit.* Fig. 49), and Mycenaean kylix fragments have been found on the surface. A large number of tombs was found on the lower hill adjoining the site on the west. One large tholos tomb (diameter 8.65 m.) contained goods of LH IIA-B date, and eight small built tombs imitating tholoi are reported to have contained pottery of a LH I-IIIB range. Another Mycenaean tomb at the foot of the hill contained pottery either late MH or early LH (*AA* Fig. 47). This was clearly an important settlement in early Mycenaean times, but may have become less important later.

E 49 LEONIDHI: PLAKA (ANCIENT PRASIA)
LH IIIA2-B C

Laconia II 131.

The plain of Leonidhi, although small, is fertile and lies at the head of a route along the river valley to the main ridge of Mt. Parnon. The ancient Prasiai (Pausanias iii. 21. 6) lay on the seaward slopes of Plaka, near the port of Leonidhi, and in this vicinity a few LH III sherds and obsidian were found. This was presumably the site of a small port serving the Mycenaean settlements up the valley.

E 50 VASKINA: KOTRONI
LH IIIA2-B

Laconia II 131.

Kotroni is in a barren upland region of hard limestone, about 2 km. northwest of Vaskina, a small kalyvia occupied only in summer. A small elliptical built tomb here was constructed of fairly large field stones, roughly corbelled and capped by a large stone slab. It contained many burials and several Mycenaean vases, some of which are of surprisingly good quality. As at Arkines (E 9), this is further proof that the Mycenaeans penetrated into the upper hill country. No suitable habitation could be located nearby, and it is not easy to understand why the area was ever settled, even if occupation was seasonal. Yet the pottery covers a fairly long period (LH IIIA2-B), suggesting a family tomb; and another tomb like it was said to have been found nearby.

E 51 PALAIOCHORI: KOTRONI etc. *
EH II MH? LH IIA-IIIB

AD 9 (1924-5) *Parartema* 18; *Laconia II* 132.

Other discoveries have been made in upland areas of the Leonidhi valley. Two groups of small ellliptical built tombs were found, one to southeast of the village of Palaiochori on the Sykokis property, and the other on the hill of Mikri Tourla to south of the village. A group of LH IIA-IIIA1 vases, including late LM IB cups, is reported to have come from the former location, where LH IIIB pottery was found in one of the tombs. These tombs, like that at Vaskina (E 50), are corbelled, and suggest connections with Thorikos in Attica.

The Mycenaean settlement was apparently the hill of Kotroni, a rocky hill with a flat top and terraced slopes on the northeast outskirts of Palaiochori. Here the identifiable sherds were EH II, but MH and LH also appear to be represented.

E 52 AYIOS VASILIOS: LYMBIADA
EH II LH III(A-B) C

Laconia II 135.

A small Bronze Age settlement was found on a rocky knoll near Ayios Vasilios, even further up the valley towards the main ridge of Mt. Parnon. Among other Bronze Age sherds are a few LH III pieces. The site may be that of ancient Glyppia (Pausanias iii. 22. 8), and is marked by the derelict monastery of the Palaiopanayia.

THE ISLAND OF KYTHERA
(E 53-57)

E 53 KYTHERA: KASTRI (Kythera) (ANCIENT SKANDEIA?) *
EH I-II EM II-LM IB LH IIIA2-B1 G A C H

Laconia II 152; J.N. Coldstream and G.L. Huxley, *Kythera: Excavations and Studies* (1972).

The promontory of Kastri is at the centre of a broad beach near the east end of Kythera, about 3 km. west of the village of Avlemon. It lies at the southeast end of the Palaiopolis valley, the most fertile area of this rather unproductive island, where ancient Kythera was situated (on the mountain of Palaiokastro). Kastri is almost certainly the ancient Skandeia (*Iliad* x. 268; Pausanias iii. 23. 1). Excavations and surface finds indicate that the Minoan settlement extended at least 250 m. north to south by 150 m., and at least part of this area was densely built upon. In addition, much of the promontory has been eroded by the sea. A small EH settlement on Kastraki, a knoll about 200 m. inland, was superseded by the settlement centred on Kastri to south, apparently founded by immigrants from Crete, at some time in EM II. This settlement grew and prospered until early in the Late Bronze Age, maintaining contact with both Crete and central Laconia (see on E 14 and E 33). Some of its prosperity may have been due to exploitation of the purple dye extracted from the Murex shell. The town was abandoned late in the LM IB period, perhaps after the time of destructions in north and east Crete; and it does not seem to have been reoccupied until LH IIIA2. Apparently it did not survive up to the end of LH IIIB, and was not occupied again until the Geometric period. Many chamber tombs, some with several chambers, have been found in the neighbouring marl slopes, often plundered, or re-used in the Late Roman period, when Kastri was fortified. Prehistoric material from these tombs ranges from MM III to LM IB, with the exception of one which contained a deposit of LH IIIA2-B domestic pottery. A MM pithos buiral is also reported.

Kastri is a site worthy of comparison with Ayia Irini on Kea, Phylakopi on Melos, and Trianda on Rhodes, all of which show similar initial Minoan influence, with subsequent gradually increasing Mycenaean trends in pottery styles, and all of which show signs of a similar break towards the end of the LM IB period. The problem of the relationship between the stratigraphic evidence at Kastri (and other sites) and the Thera eruption is a complex one, which has attracted much speculation. But there can be no doubt that Minoan influence in the Aegean was superseded by Mycenaean not long thereafter.

E 54 KYTHERA: LIONI (Kythera) *
LM IB   LH (IIB-)IIIA1

AD 1 (1915) 191; *Laconia II* 149; Coldstream and Huxley (1972) 263.

About 150 m. to left of the road at a point about 1 km. north of Chora are two chamber tombs, one of which contained LM IB and LH (IIB-)IIIA1 pottery and other goods. On gently sloping terraces about 300 m. to northeast of the tombs and to east of the road sherds of LM I-II type were observed over an area about 200 m. north to south by 100 m., suggesting an undefended site of Minoan type. It is interesting also that the evidence from this tomb demonstrates at least some inhabitation of the island of Kythera at the time when the Kastri settlement was deserted.

E 55 POURKO: AYIOS DEMETRIOS (Kythera)
LH III(A-B)

Coldstream and Huxley (1972) 34.

A small Mycenaean settlement, about 100 m. in diameter, was found on a low spur, in an area of dissected hills at the edge of the central plateau of Kythera. The spur is about 200 m. to northwest of the Pourko churches. Several fragments of long-stemmed kylixes were found here.

E 56 KALAMOS: AYIA SOPHIA (Kythera)
LM I

Laconia II 152.

About 1.5 km. south of Kalamos is a cave in the side of a steep gorge. Miss Benton found a LM I sherd and "polished Bronze Age pottery" here. This evidence, together with the situation, and the stalagmites and stalactites at the back of the cave, suggest a cult here.

E 57 AYIA PELAYIA: VITHOULAS (Kythera)
EH II   LH III(A-B)   C H

Laconia II 149.

This is a small acropolis in hilly country, overlooking the harbour of Ayia Pelayia, which is about 600 m. to the northeast. The prehistoric sherds were distributed over an area about 150 m. by 100 m., on the top and the east slopes. On the upper east terrace a cist grave was found, and LH III sherds of poor quality nearby.

APPENDIX TO MAP E

Some other sites in particular in Laconia and Kynouria may also have been occupied in Mycenaean times: Angelona (*Laconia II* 138), Chrysapha (*Laconia I* 82), Las (*Laconia II* 118), Kotrones (*Laconia II* 119), Oitylos (*Laconia II* 121), Tigani (*Laconia II* 122), Kosmas (*Laconia II* 135), Mari (*Laconia II* 136), Kyparissi (*Laconia II* 136), Ieraka (*Laconia II* 136), and Tyros (*Laconia II* 131). I would also now expect Mycenaean settlement near Koutoumou (*Laconia II* 114). Other districts where I consider that search would be profitable are given in the summary below.

A NOTE ON RECENT FIELDWORK IN LACONIA

The Sparta Valley and the Helos Plain are discussed in a very interesting recent commentary by J.L. Bintliff [*Natural Environment and Human Settlement in Prehistoric Greece* (1977) 371, 699]. In connection with the excavations under H.W. Catling at the Menelaion and under Lord William Taylour at Ayios Stephanos, Bintliff carried out field investigations of both areas; and his conclusions are both valuable and important. Bintliff is an excellent observer, and his extremely detailed and exhaustive study recalls most refreshingly the terrain over which we have so repeatedly trodden.

For the sake of clarity and of economy, in the publication of the Laconia survey we concentrated on giving the *positive* results, and were not always able to indicate exactly which particular districts had been thoroughly searched in vain or (conversely) omitted from the search. Yet, despite the lack of published information on these points, Bintliff is able to surmise that our surveys in the Sparta Valley and the Helos Plain have been "acropolis-oriented", and that we have in general failed to look for the "smaller and satellite" settlements here. I have read Bintliff's field observations on Laconia with great interest, and I am delighted at my own recollection of many of the specific phenomena he describes, although my lack of geographical training precluded articulation in the appropriate technical terms. In response to Bintliff's implied criticism, I take this opportunity of supplementing the published record of the survey coverage in Laconia.

I am able to confirm that I have personally traversed most of the Sparta plain itself, from Aphissou and Magoula in the north to Xerokambi (but no further) in the south. I also walked the hills above the east bank of the Eurotas, from Aphissou to Skoura, occasionally venturing further east, towards Chrysapha. I paid special attention to the conglomerate hills in the vicinities of the Menelaion site and of ancient Sparta and Magoula, and to all hills, hillocks, and even to all low rises or "mounds" observable in the valley centre. Like Bintliff, I largely ignored the Taygetos "piedmont" area, with the exception of the vicinities of Trypi, Mistra, Parori, and Ayios Ioannis in the northwest, and of Xerokambi in the south. I still believe that there were Mycenaean settlements at Trypi and Parori, despite my failure to find them. And, like Bintliff, I believe that there was indeed a Mycenaean settlement, and probably an important one, at Mistra. But later habitation, both here and at Trypi, makes surface search futile. For similar reasons, it was not possible to search in the rich (and often enclosed) gardens and orchards of the suburbs in the Sparta-Magoula area. I usually refrained from searching the more low-lying areas (*e.g.* beside the Eurotas), in the belief (evidently correct) that the surface here would normally consist of the "recent" alluvium or colluvium. Admittedly this coverage was "extensive" rather than "intensive", but much ground was investigated, some of it repeatedly. It is not clear exactly how much of the plain has been covered in Bintliff's travels, but I note that he has had little further luck as regards archaeological surface finds (and one Mycenaean sherd between the Menelaion and Aphissou surely does not constitute sufficient evidence for even a "small and satellite" settlement).

In the Helos plain my coverage was more intensive, although mainly restricted to the edges and immediate environs of the plain. The search in the Stephania-Skala and the Asteri-Vezani areas was particularly thorough and exhaustive, and resulted in the discovery of several small and low-lying sites besides the larger and more prominent hill sites. Even here it is probable that more sites still await discovery. But I do not believe that we should expect a *more important* Mycenaean site in the vicinity of Asteri in particular, in addition to the medium-sized and numerous smaller sites already found here. Conversely, I am not at all disturbed to find two "large" (or medium to large) Mycenaean sites, Ayios Stephanos and Lekas, in close proximity.

I outlined above the suggested (and obvious) "*political*" reasons for the choice of Ayios Stephanos. Here, as at Mycenae and Tiryns, for instance, the Mycenaeans, in defiance of Bintliff's prescriptions, selected a *limestone* base for their (probably fortified) settlement. In this case, as elsewhere, the doctrine of soil preference, a kind of geographical "determinism", has been taken too far, and Bintliff's supposition (*op.cit.* 476) of seasonal migrations between the neighbouring sites of Ayios Stephanos and Lekas is surely put forward in jest. The Mycenaeans, it appears, did not always manage to place their "large" settlements according to the exact spacing required to conform with Bintliff's "Thiessen polygons". In this connection it should be noted that a supposed gap in known prehistoric settlement between Ayios Stephanos and Gythion is in fact adequately filled by site E 39 (omitted by Bintliff), a settlement of moderate size, but quite appropriate to the moderate amount of good land available in its small coastal valley. No doubt more Mycenaean settlements will be discovered in and around the Helos plain, but they will not necessarily conform either in size or location to a rigid predicted pattern.

Occasionally Bintliff adds a sprinkling of antiquarian flavour to the more prosaic geographical discussions. In addition to a catholic mixture of odd legends from sources of varying reliability, he pays considerable attention to the location of places in Laconia mentioned by Homer. In this connection, it is evident that Bintliff was not able to make use of R. Hope Simpson and J.F. Lazenby, *The Catalogue of the Ships in Homer's Iliad* (1970) where much of his discussion, and some of his conjectures, are anticipated. He also attempts to adapt to his geographical theories a notoriously difficult passage in Pausanias (III 20), concerning various place names in the Taygetos foothills and "piedmont". Not only is there a *lacuna* at a vital point in the text of Pausanias in the passage concerned, but it is also extremely likely that Pausanias himself never in fact visited the places listed. At this point certain un-named scholars are mysteriously accused by Bintliff (*op.cit.* 437) of a "misuse" of Pausanias. Readers may judge for themselves whether such a sin has in fact been committed and, if so, who is the culprit.

MESSENIA   SOUTHERN TRIPHYLIA

MAP F

The southwest Peloponnese has been the subject of considerable and prolonged excavation and survey work, much of it particularly oriented towards uncovering the pattern of Mycenaean habitation. Most of Messenia enjoys a fertility far greater than that of the Argolid or Laconia, for instance, partly due to its higher rainfall. It now supports a considerable population, concentrated mainly in the Pamisos and Soulima valleys and in the coastal plains.

Before the formation of the present alluvial plain in the southern part of the Lower Pamisos valley, it would have been considerably smaller and more marshy [Kraft, Rapp, and Aschenbrenner (1975)]. And the soils most easily cultivated with primitive Bronze Age ploughs and implements would, in any case, have been the Pliocene marls of the terraces around the plains. Thus the terraces of the Pylos District (Map F inset), for instance, may have been of relatively greater agricultural importance, as compared to the "bottom land" of the time [i.e. the "Older Fill" as defined by Vita-Finzi (1969)]. When dry farming, especially of cereals, was of greater relative importance, there would probably have been less emphasis on irrigation, and more on drainage and the retention of the *appropriate* amount of rainfall by means of terracing. This would go a long way towards explaining the early prosperity (in MH-LH I) of the Pylos District and of similar districts in Messenia composed mainly of "Neogen" hills and plateaus formed during the Pliocene. But in all parts of Messenia the abundant perennial springs, and lush vegetation around and below them, must have contributed to the successful animal husbandry also vouched for by the Pylos Tablets (*MME passim*, and especially 245 ff.). Many of the Mycenaean settlements in Messenia seem to have been deliberately located near perennial springs [*pace* Bintliff (1977) 115].

In the LH IIIB period, most, if not all, of Messenia may have been controlled from the palace at Pylos (F 1 Ano Englianos). But there are signs that in the earlier phases of the Mycenaean period there may have been several smaller and separate units, independent "kingdoms" more in conformity with the natural divisions of Messenia. The sites of Nichoria (F 100), Peristeria (F 203), Malthi (F 217) and Kambos (F 137), for instance, may have been the centres of such previous independent districts. Evidence from survey strongly suggests a proliferation of new sites in the LH III period and a catastrophic disaster at the end of LH IIIB, marked by the apparent desertion of about 90% of all the sites. The best explanation of such a disaster remains the political, namely a breakdown of the agricultural system following the collapse of the Pylian bureaucracy [*cf.* P. Betancourt, *Antiquity* 50 (1976) 40]. The few survivors seem to have clustered in a few areas, one of which is near Pylos itself (*i.e.* F 2 and F 6) and another a probable "refuge site" near Malthi (*i.e.* F 220).

In the commentary which follows, I have attempted to identify *groups* of Mycenaean sites in Messenia, and to determine which are likely to be the "capital" sites in the various groups. Although the fieldwork in Messenia is far from complete, there are sufficient data to warrant such an attempt, so long as it is realized that any conclusions remain hypothetical. In order to facilitate a fresh look at the data, particularly as regards the apparent groups or "clusters" of settlements, I have adopted a new numbering system (which omits the numbers between F 60 and F 100 and between F 140 and F 200), while still providing cross-references to the *MME* numbers [*i.e.* the numbers adopted in Register A of W.A. McDonald and G.R. Rapp, *The Minnesota Messenia Expedition* (1972) pp. 123-128 and 264-309].

Special Abbreviations for Map F

Messenia I = *AJA* 65 (1961) 221-260.
Messenia II = *AJA* 68 (1964) 229-245.
Messenia III = *AJA* 73 (1969) 123-177.
MME = W.A. McDonald and G.R. Rapp, *The Minnesota Messenia Expedition* (1972).

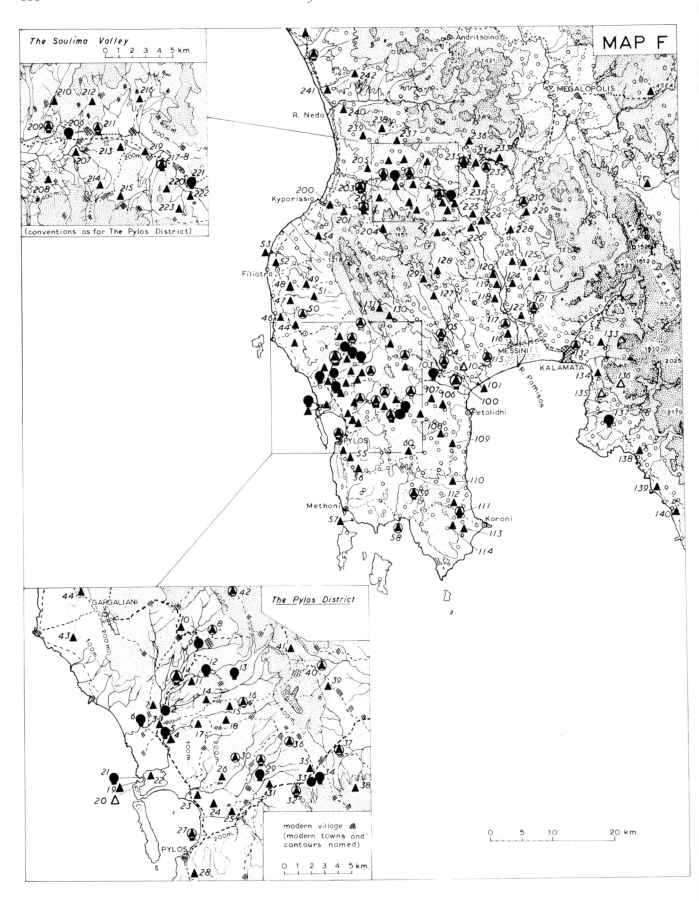

The Soulima Valley

0 1 2 3 4 5 km.

(conventions as for The Pylos District)

MAP F

The Pylos District

GARGALIANI

PYLOS

modern village ✳
(modern towns and
contours named)

0 1 2 3 4 5 km.

0   5   10   20 km.

N.B. The material presented in *MME* is not always repeated or referred to in detail here, and normally only the *MME* site number is given. The details given in *MME*, and in *Messenia I-III* constitute a vital complement to the account given here. Despite the care taken in the presentation of the material evidence in the above works, some corrections and additional observations have occasionally been necessitated; and in several cases it is difficult to decide whether or not a site should be included in the LH category, due to the poor quality and preservation of the surface material. I have tended to give "the benefit of the doubt" in such cases, *i.e.* to include rather than to exclude.

F 1-22

The Palace at Ano Englianos (F 1) and the sites around it (F 2 to F 22) appear to form a distinct group, presumably under direct control of the Palace itself in LH IIIB. Some centres, however, such as Myrsinochori (F 13) and Tragana (F 6), may have been independent in the LH I-IIIA1 periods [as was almost certainly the case with the Koukounara group (F 29) to the southeast]. In the LH IIIA2-B period there may have been subordinate local capitals at Chora (F 8), Iklaina (F 17), Koukounara (F 29-30), and possibly also at Tragana (F 6), Beyler Bey (F 4), and Yialova (F 23), among others.

F 1 CHORA: ANO ENGLIANOS (ANCIENT PYLOS) * # (*MME* No. 1)
MH LH I-IIIB G C or H?

Pylos I-III; J. Chadwick, *The Mycenaean World* (1976); Schoder (1974) 173.

The palace and its "Lower Town" occupy part of a long ridge dominating the north side of the coastal plain and bay of Pylos. The centre of the site is a prominent flat hill-top about 170 m. northeast to southwest by 90 m. (maximum) with steep sides, particularly on the north. The great palace here was preceded by successive settlements from MH to LH IIIA1; and there are traces of fortifications of the LH I-IIA period, including a monumental gateway on the northwest. The site was cleared and levelled at the time of the construction of the palace, whose first phase appears to have been of the LH IIIA2 period (to judge from LH IIIA1 sherds below). The palace was completely destroyed by fire towards the end of the LH IIIB period, when the site was apparently not fortified. The portion of the "Lower Town" which lay to south and southwest of the palace was destroyed at the same time. The full extent of this "Lower Town", and of the "satellite" settlements in the immediate vicinity of the palace is not known. But it was obviously considerable, at least 325 m. northeast to southwest by 200 m., excluding a separate LH III settlement nearby along the ridge to west of the site. And the early Mycenaean "Grave Circle", the successive tholos tombs,

and the chamber tombs, with finds ranging from LH I to LH IIIB, also testify to the continuous importance of the site throughout these periods.

Since the spectacular finds within the palace complex are so well known and so well published, there is no point in repeating any further details here. The documents in Linear B script preserved in the "archives room" of the Palace are presumably copies of some of the records of the final year of the "Pylos Kingdom" (*cf.* J. Chadwick, *op.cit.*). They demonstrate a degree of bureaucratic supervision unsurpassed subsequently in Greece until the Byzantine era. And the number and variety of agricultural and manufacturing commodities and activities under palace surveillance also suggests control over a considerable territory.

Although the palace is not at the centre of Messenia (in contrast to the later historic capital of ancient Messene), it commands the only good harbour on the west coast, and lies on easy land routes to north, south, and east. The Linear B tablets themselves provide clues as to how the problem of controlling northern and eastern Messenia may have been tackled by the rulers in the west (see Appendix to Map F: Part II).

F 2 PISASKION: MAVROUDHIA * # (*MME* No. 2).
LH IIIB-C "PG"

Pylos III 224.

About 3 km. to south of the palace a chamber tomb and a small tholos-shaped built tomb were found, close together and beside the Chora-Pylos road. The chamber tomb contained burials of the LH IIIB-C date with fine pottery and other goods. The preserved half of the built tomb produced vases probably of the late tenth or early ninth century B.C., and fragments of bronze and iron objects.

F 3 KORIFASION: PORTES # (*MME* No. 3)
MH? LH III(A-B) C H

AJA 43 (1939) 559; *Messenia I* 242.

A low mound, about 120 m. east to west by 80 m., is bisected by the Pylos-Chora highway at a point about 400 m. south of the turning to Korifasion village. The sherds, mainly LH, were found mostly to east of the highway, and stone artifacts were also numerous here.

F 4 KORIFASION: BEYLER BEY * # (*MME* No. 4)
LH III(A?-)B

AJA 43 (1939) 559; *PAE* (1960) 197; *Messenia I* 242, III 149.

This low hill, about 200 m. north to south by 150 m., forms the north end of a long ridge at the edge of the plain, and about 1 km. to south of Korifasion village. There was much good surface pottery, but trials showed that the site has been badly eroded.

F 5 KORIFASION: CHARATSARI * # (*MME* No. 5)
MH (late) LH I

PAE (1925-6) 140; *Hesperia* 23 (1954) 158.

The tholos tomb excavated here is the earliest known in Messenia and may indeed be the earliest tholos tomb on the Greek mainland. The pottery included several Late MH Matt-painted vases of local types, and some sherds either LM IA or local imitations.

F 6 TRAGANA: VIGLITSA * # (*MME* No. 11)
MH LH I-IIIA2 LH IIIB? LH IIIC SMyc PG H

AE (1912) 268, (1914) 98; *PAE* (1955) 247, (1956) 202; *BCH* 80 (1956) 285; *AD* 16 (1960) B 113; *AA* (1962) 113; *Messenia I* 240; *Ergon* (1976) 139, (1977) 127; Desborough (1964) 95, (1972) 84.

At the south end of the low ridge on whose north end is the village of Tragana, two tholos tombs were excavated, set back to back. MH and LH I sherds and flint and obsidian found in the fill probably derive from a settlement here. The smaller tomb was disturbed by use as a dwelling in the Hellenistic period, but it contained a pit with two intact cremation burials of the LH IIIA2 period. The larger and better built tomb was in use from LH IIA to LH IIIA, and was reused for a whole series of burials extending from LH IIIC into PG (Desborough, *loc.cit.*). The contemporary settlement site (or sites?) indicated by the tombs has yet to be found.

F 7 TRAGANA: VOROULIA * # (*MME* No. 12)
MH LH I LH III(A-B)

PAE (1956) 202; *AD* 16 (1960) B 114; *Messenia I* 239; *Ergon* (1977) 127.

About 800 m. north-northeast of Tragana, on a steep slope to east of and below the road, traces of habitation, probably continuous from MH to LH III, included a one-roomed building containing about a hundred whole vases of the LH I period and some shells, suggesting cult connections.

F 8 CHORA: VOLIMIDHIA * # (*MME* No. 20)
MH LH I-IIIB G A C H

PAE (1952) 473, (1953) 238, (1954) 299, (1960) 198, (1964) 77, (1965) 102; *Das Altertum* 1 (1955) 140; *Messenia I* 237, III 147; *AD* 25 (1970) B 182, 27 (1972) B 256.

About 800 m. north-northeast of Chora, on the road to the Kephalovrysi spring, is an extensive chamber tomb cemetery. Traces of a LH I-III settlement were found on gently sloping ground about 100 m. south of the tombs, and on the east side of the road. The remains were not impressive, but much of the settlement was hidden beneath vines.

The tombs are large and well cut, with many burials, but are not particularly rich except for pottery finds. Nevertheless they suggest a large community here at least until near the end of LH IIIB. In the Geometric period some tombs were rediscovered and were apparently used for cult purposes.

F 9 CHORA: AYIOS IOANNIS * # (*MME* No. 21)
LH III(A2-B)

PAE (1954) 305.

A small chamber tomb cemetery was found at the southwest edge of the village of Chora.

F 10 AMBELOFITO: LAGOU # (*MME* No. 19)
MH? LH IIIB

Messenia I 237, III 147.

A small settlement about 100 m. in diameter was found on a flat area near the edge of a high spur about 1 km. north-northeast of Ambelofito, about 100 m. east of the main road.

F 11 MYRSINOCHORI: VAIES * (*MME* No. 55)
LH

AD 19 (1964) B 150.

On a ridge parallel to that of Ano Englianos, and about 1 km. to the east of the palace, evidence of a small settlement was found in trial excavations, which uncovered a number of LH sherds near the surface.

F 12 CHORA: KOUKOUYERA # (*MME* No. 56)
LH

Messenia I 240 and Pl. 78b.

A very large mound, about 27 m. by 21 m. and approximately 7 m. high, stands on the crest of a high ridge about 2 km. south of Chora and about 500 m. west of the Chora-Myrsinochori road. This is apparently the site of a large Mycenaean tholos tomb, presumably not collapsed.

F 13 MYRSINOCHORI: ROUTSI * # (*MME* No. 54)
MH? LH IIA-IIIA1 H

PAE (1953) 250, (1956) 203, (1957) 118; *BCH* 78 (1954) 124, 81 (1957) 558; *Antiquity* 31 (1957) 97; *ILN* (6/4, 27/4/1957); *AD* 16 (1960) B 114; *AA* (1962) 272; *Ergon* (1977) 127.

Three mounds and two tholos tombs were excavated on a broad ridge about 1.5 km. northeast of Myrsinochori. At least two of the mounds contained pithoi and are probably MH burial tumuli. The two tholos tombs contained pottery ranging from LH IIA to LH IIIA1, and possibly also including LH I. They were small, and not particularly well built, but contained a variety of weapons and ornaments. The finds suggest a separate dynasty, although perhaps not of the highest rank.

F 14 PLATANOS: LAMBROPOULOU PIYI # (*MME* No. 49)
LH

Messenia II 232.

On the slope of a low hill on the south side of the ravine between Platonos and Myrsinochori is a copious spring, above which a few LH sherds were found. The site is about 1 km. west of Platanos.

F 15 PLATANOS: MERZINI # (*MME* No. 51)
MH LH III(A-)B

Messenia II 232.

On a slope about 800 m. east-southeast of Platanos is a very low mound. Abundant MH and LH sherds were found here, over an area about 150 m. east to west by 120 m.

F 16 PAPOULIA VILLAGE * # (*MME* No. 53)
LH II-III(A-B) A C?

PAE (1954) 315, (1955) 255; *Messenia I* 240, *II* 239.

Within the village of Papoulia and immediately outside it to the west were found three small built tombs imitating tholoi and a rectangular built grave. There were also traces of LH settlement in the western part of the village.

F 17 IKLAINA: TRAGANES and GOUVITSES * # (*MME* Nos. 46-7)
MH LH III(A-B)

PAE (1954) 308; *Messenia I* 241, *III* 149; *AD* 17 (1961-2) B 92.

About 1.5 km. west-northwest of Iklaina is a substantial site (about 200 m. north to south by 150 m.) at the western end of the broad spur named Traganes, overlooking a deep ravine to the west and southwest and with a fine view over the bay of Pylos. Excavations revealed remains of an important LH III building, including massive double walls and two fresco fragments. About 500 m. to the northwest of Traganes some scattered stones and sherds, including one probably LH, were found at Gouvitses on an eroded slope, and there are reports of two collapsed LH tholos tombs at Klarakia nearby. The remains suggest a local capital in the LH III period.

F 18 IKLAINA: PANAYIA
MH? LH III(A-B)

Messenia I 241.

The Panayia chapel is at the east end of a low spur, about 200 m. east to west by 70 m., over a kilometre to northeast of Iklaina. On the heavily eroded surface a few fragments of LH III kylikes were found,

and coarse ware of MH appearance. A very large stone slab lies about 30 m. to the north of the site, and reports of "gold nails" and "plates with pictured animals" also suggest a Mycenaean tholos tomb here.

F 19-22

This group of sites [*cf. Messenia II* Pl. 71 and Plate 20b here; *cf.* Schoder (1974) 1941], centred on the headland of Palaiokastro (the ancient Koryphasion), strongly suggests that the main harbour of Mycenaean Pylos lay on the north side of the Osmanaga Lagoon. The settlement (F 19) on the headland itself would have been very exposed, and was probably chosen entirely for strategic reasons, since it commands the western entrances to the Osmanaga Lagoon.

F 19 PETROCHORI: PALAIOKASTRO (Ancient Koryphasion) * # (*MME* No. 9)
LH III(A-B) "PG" C H

PAE (1958) 184; *Messenia I* 243; *La Parola del Passato* 78 (1961) 225.

The low promontory to north of and below the mediaeval fort of Palaiokastro measures about 200 m. north to south by 70 m. LH III and later remains were found in trial excavations here.

F 20 PETROCHORI: "CAVE OF NESTOR" * # (*MME* No. 10)
N EH II MH LH III(A-B) C

Messenia I 243, *II* 32; *Pylos I* 9.

The spectacular cave on the north slope of the Palaiokastro headland was inhabited in the Neolithic period, and also contains stratified Bronze Age and later material.

F 21 PETROCHORI: VOIDHOKOILIA * # (*MME* No. 8)
LH (IIB-IIIA?)

PAE (1956) 202; *Antiquity* 31 (1957) 97; *La Parola del Passato* 78 (1961) 225; *Ergon* (1975) 139, (1976) 137, (1977) 127.

A small tholos tomb, on the north side of Voidhokoilia bay, was apparently built above ground, founded on rock. The burials appear to be of relatively early date, to judge from those on show in the Pylos Museum, but investigations are not yet complete (see Addenda).

F 22 PETROCHORI: OSMANAGA LAGOON # (*MME* No. 7)
EH II MH? LH III(A-B) "PG" H

Messenia II 232, *III* 149.

The stones and sherds found in the spoil heaps of drainage canals in the Osmanaga Lagoon reveal that its northwest and north banks were inhabited in

EH II and LH III times and later. The finds were distributed over a wide area (*cf. Messenia II* Pl. 21); but some have presumably been washed into the lagoon from the banks (*i.e. Messenia III* nos. 59B and 59E). Finds which appear to be more or less in position (*i.e. Messenia III* nos. 59A and 59C-D) include EH II and LH III sherds.

F 23-28

The small but fertile valley of Pilokambos on the east side of Pylos bay was bordered by sites on the surrounding hills especially on the long ridge of Dappia on the northeast flank. The sites on the north and northeast of the plain (F 23-25) are regularly spaced, while the site on the southwest edge (F 27) is strategically placed, overlooking the south entrance to the bay of Pylos and at a cross-roads of routes to north, south, and east. Sites F 26 and F 28 are peripheral, on routes to northeast and south respectively.

F 23 YIALOVA: PALAIOCHORI # (*MME* No. 42)
LH III(A-)B

Messenia I 242.

At the western end of the Dappia ridge is a prominent acropolis hill overlooking both the Pilokambos valley to south and the small fertile valley of the Yiannousaka river on the north. The site is about 500 m. northeast of Yialova, commanding the north-south route and the good beaches immediately to west and south of Yialova. Mycenaean sherds were abundant on the summit and upper terraces (an area about 150 m. north to south by 120 m.) and more sparse on the lower west terraces, a further 250 m. east to west by 300 m. Possible burial mounds were noted about 500 m. to east along the ridge and on a parallel ridge to the north.

This was clearly an important Mycenaean settlement, possibly the "capital" of a region in LH IIIB.

F 24 PILA: VIGLES # (*MME* No. 41)
EH II? MH? LH III(A-B)

Messenia III 149.

At the east end of the Dappia ridge, about 1.5 km. west of Pila, were considerable traces of Mycenaean settlement, extending at least 200 m. east to west by 125 m., over the summit and the relatively gentle west slopes. Elsewhere the slopes are steep.

F 25 PILA: ELITSA # (*MME* No. 39)
LH III(A-B)

Messenia III 149.

A thin ridge, about a kilometre east to west, overlooks the east end of the Pilokambos valley. A steep

gully separates the site from the village of Pila on the north. An area about 100 m. east to west by 50 m. in the centre of the ridge is sparsely covered with LH sherds.

F 26 SCHOINOLAKKA: KOKKINIA # (*MME* No. 43)
MH? LH III(A-B)

Messenia I 244, *III* 150.

The village of Schoinolakka occupies the western end of a ridge on the north side of the Yiannousaka river, and some distance to north of Pilokambos. On the top of the same ridge, about 250 m. east-northeast of Schoinolakka, some LH III sherds were found over an area at least 125 m. east to west by 100 m. There may have been a prehistoric cemetery at Akona on the slope opposite about 200 m. to the south, where, according to local reports, sherds, pithoi, gems and bronze tweezers have been found.

F 27 PYLOS: VIGLA and MIDHEN # (*MME* No. 44)
N? LH III(A-B)

AJA 43 (1939) 559; *Messenia I* 244.

The small spur named Vigla is immediately above the bay of Pylos, about 1.5 km. northeast of modern Pylos and 700 m. southwest of the junction (named Midhen) of the Pylos-Chora and Pylos Kalamata road. What remains of the Mycenaean settlement at Vigla is a low mound about 50 m. in diameter and 4 m. high. The rest has fallen down the steep cliffs into the bay. Few surface sherds are now visible. About 130 m. to northeast of the road junction are two collapsed tholos tombs, close together. A LH III sherd was found near the southern of the two. About midway between Pylos and Midhen two celts, presumed to be Neolithic, were found during excavation for house foundations.

F 28 PYLOS: AYIOS NEKTARIOS # (*MME* No. 45)
LH H?

Messenia III 154.

Some Mycenaean sherds were found on a low limestone hillock to east of the Pylos-Methoni road, about 1.5 km. south-southeast of modern Pylos. The extent of settlement indicated is no more than c. 120 m. east by 60 m., and the small amount of cultivable land in the vicinity is not very fertile.

F 29-38

There is a rich belt of fertile land on the plateau between the Pylos District and the head of the Messenian Gulf. It is composed mainly of Pliocene deposits with occasional limestone outcrops. The known Mycenaean settlements here are clustered in the most productive areas, Koukounara and vicinity (F 29-31, and F 36), and in the Chandrinou-Mesopotamos area (F 32-35, and F 37), where they are found mostly along the main east-west route.

F 29 KOUKOUNARA: KATARRACHI, GOUVA-LARI etc. * # (*MME* Nos. 35-6)
MH LH I-IIIC G A C H

PAE (1954) 311, (1958) 187, (1959) 174, (1960) 195, (1961) 174, (1963) 114; *AD* 16 (1960) B 115; *Messenia I* 244, *III* 150; *La Parola del Passato* 78 (1961) 223; *AA* (1962) 176; *Ergon* (1974) 78, (1975) 132; *PAE* (1974) 139, (1975) B 431, *BCH* 99 (1975) 626; *AR* (1974-5) 17, (1975-6) 15.

1. Katarrachi and Gouvalari

The hill of Katarrachi, about 800 m. northeast of Koukounara village, is small (about 120 m. north to south by 70 m.) and not very prominent, but it is naturally defended by a deep ravine ("to Potami tou Arapi") on all sides except the north. Remains of MH to LH III habitation here include an apsidal megaron; and a LH IIIC deep bowl of "Granary" type is reported [*AD* 19 (1964) B 164, on show in the Pylos Museum]. Further traces of LH habitation have been found immediately across the ravine to the east, in the Gouvalari area.

Tombs in the Gouvalari group include two tholoi (Koukounara Tomb 4-5), and two groups of mounds containing small built tombs of various types, some imitating tholoi. These latter began in LH I, and some continued in use until LH IIIA2 or LH IIIB. One tomb in the first group appears to contain only LH IIIA and LH IIIB burials; and there was an *apothete* in the vicinity in LH IIIB. The two tholos tombs were in use from LH I to LH IIIA2.

2. Livadhiti, Phyties, Akona, and Polla Dendra

Six other tholoi have been excavated at sites near Koukounara. Koukounara Tomb 1; at Livadhiti, lies to the southeast (and over a kilometre northeast of Stenosia); Tombs 2-3, at Phyties, are about 750 m. northeast of Livadhiti; Tombs 6-7, at Akona, lie about 50 m. northwest of Katarrachi; and Tomb 8, at Polla Dendra, is a kilometre to east of Koukounara. Most of these tholoi were in use in early LH, but tombs 6 and 8 appear to contain only LH III burials. All of the tombs are in the general vicinity of the centre at Katarrachi-Gouvalari, which appears to have been the "capital" of the district; and their number and size indicate a considerable population here.

F 30 KOUKOUNARA: PALAIOCHORIA and PALAIALONA * (*MME* No. 36)
LH III(A2-B) LH IIIC?

PAE (1961) 174, (1962) 90; *Messenia III* 150.

An unusual tomb excavated at Palaiochoria, about 2 km. west of Koukounara, appears to be of the same general type as the built tombs of Gouvalari. It is described as a circular enclosure (diameter about 3-5 m.), with an entrance, and covered by a mound. Pottery with the burials scattered over its floor included a kylix, a stirrup-jar, and a vessel with wavy line (LH IIIC?). About 50 m. to south a large LH III (B?) building was partly uncovered, which contained at least nine rooms. Nearer to Koukounara, at Palaialona, were remains of another LH building. The remains, especially the large building, suggest that this may have been an important centre.

F 31 CHANDRINOU: KOUMBE # (*MME* No. 37)
LH III(A-B)

Messenia I 245.

The Koumbe spring, which supplies modern Pylos, is about 400 m. north of the Kalamata-Pylos road at a point 1.5 km. west of Chandrinon. About 300 m. west-southwest of the spring LH sherds were found thinly spread over a relatively flat area about 130 m. east to west by 80 m. A very low mound about 17 m. in diameter lies some 40 m. to northwest, and another about 15 m. in diameter and 4 m. in height at Ayios Athanasios on the opposite (southeast) side of the road.

F 32 CHANDRINOU: PLATANIA # (*MME* No. 33)
N LH III(A-B) A C

Messenia I 245, *III* 151; *AD* 19 (1964) B 149, 23 (1968) B 156, 24 (1969) B 145.

The Mycenaean habitation site is to the west of the Platania spring at the south edge of Chandrinou. The low mound here now measures about 80 m. east to west by 50 m., but was originally larger. Sherds exposed by a bulldozer here included LH III and later, and a cache of Neolithic celts was found about 700 m. to the northwest. A small tholos tomb at Yenitsari near the village was found empty, but Mycenaean pottery was found around it. A small mound, containing bones, within the village was said to have been destroyed.

F 33 CHANDRINOU: KISSOS * # (*MME* No. 32)
MH? LH I/II-III(A2-B)

PAE (1962) 90, (1966) 120; *Messenia III* 151.

A large mound, about a kilometre east-northeast of Chandrinou, and 300 m. southeast of the Kalamata-Pylos road, contained pithos burials (MH?) in the centre and around them stone enclosures of oval or oblong shape containing burials, and a small cist grave. The pottery contained early and late Mycenaean. The tombs are similar to those in the Gouvalari mounds (F 29 above).

F 34   SOULINARI: TOURLIDHITSA * #
(*MME* **No. 29**)
LH IIIA(1?)   H

PAE (1966) 129; *Messenia III* 151.

A small tholos tomb was excavated here on a low ridge about 900 m. southeast of the Kalamata-Pylos road and 500 m. west of the branch road to Milioti.

F 35   MESOPOTAMOS: CHILIA CHORIA #
(*MME* **No. 28**)
MH?   LH III(A-B)

Messenia I 245, *III* 151; *PAE* (1966) 120.

About a kilometre southwest of Nea Soulinari and 250 m. north of the Kalamata-Pylos road is a Mycenaean site on the level plateau, marked by sherds over an area at least 100 m. north to south by 50 m.

F 36   KATO KREMMIDHIA: FOURTSAVRISI * # (*MME* **No. 34**)
LH I/II-III(A-B)   C   H

Messenia II 233; *Ergon* (1975) 137; *AR* (1975-6) 15.

A few Mycenaean sherds were found near the springs Fourtsavrisi and Malakasa, about 900 m. east-southeast of Kato Kremmidhia. One of the two mounds observed near here has been partly excavated. It contained small tholos type built tombs, mainly of early Mycenaean date, but with pottery extending to LH IIIB in one tomb.

F 37   MESOPOTAMOS: VELEVOUNI # (*MME* **No. 27**)
LH IIIA2-B   H

Messenia I 245, *III* 151; *AD* 22 (1967) B 207.

The village of Mesopotamos lies at the foot of the hill of Velevouni. The top and upper south slope of the hill comprise the Mycenaean settlement site, an area about 150 m. northeast to southwest by 70 m. The surface is heavily eroded, but recognizable sherds include the base of a LH IIIB deep bowl. A tholos tomb at Tourkokivouro about 700 m. to north-northwest, on the north side of the Pylos-Kalamata road, may be the point of origin of some Mycenaean objects, including a bronze cauldron, in the Kalamata museum.

F 38   ROMIRI: AVISOS # (*MME* **No. 31**)
MH?   LH III(A-B)

Messenia II 233.

The site occupies the top and extensive north and east slopes of a spur above a fine spring named Kephalovrisi, about 1.5 km. northwest of Romiri, and near the small fertile valley of Stipata below to the east. Mycenaean sherds are scattered over the top surface (about 80 m. east to west by 50 m.) and the east slopes above the spring, for a total extent of about 120 m. east to west by 80 m.

The settlement seems to have been rather isolated, in rugged country, but the unusually large number of cattle noted in the vicinity in 1962 suggest better than average pasture.

F 39-41

These three sites lie along an alternative route from Chora to the head of the Messenian Gulf, in upland country not as fertile as that of the main plateau (*i.e.* where sites F 29-31 are located).

F 39   CHATZI: BARBERI #   (*MME* No. 26)
MH?   LH III(A-B)   C

AD 22 (1967) B 207; *Messenia III* 151.

About a kilometre to west-northwest of Chatzi, on the west side of the road to Vlachopoulo, is a low hill (a limestone outcrop), overlooking reasonably fertile land to south, west, and north. The enclosed spring of Kamari lies at the northeast foot, beside the road. The fairly level upper surface of the hill (an area about 150 m. northeast to southwest by 120 m.) and the gently sloping south and southeast terraces were covered with sherds, and Bronze Age wares, including LH, were especially plentiful on the terraces, which appear to have been the main area of the Mycenaean settlement here.

**F 40   VLACHOPOULO: AGRILIA and
          DHRAKORACHI * #** (*MME* **No. 25**)
MH?   LH IIIA1-2

PAE (1964) 89; *AD* 20 (1965) B 204; *Messenia III* 152.

The large and prominent limestone hill of Agrilia is about 2.5 km. east-northeast of Vlachopoulo. The headspring of the Karya river lies at the northwest foot. On the flat top surface (about 120 m. north-northeast to south-southwest by 80 m.), and on the upper west and south slopes, LH and other prehistoric sherds were found.

On a lower ridge called Dhrakorachi, about 700 m. to the west and 80 m. east of the Chatzi-Vlachopoulo road, a small and poorly built tomb imitating a tholos had been set into the upper northwest slope. Most of the contents had been lost, but four vases (LH IIIA1-2) and some bronze knives were saved by Professor Marinatos, who believed that there was at least one more tholos tomb in the immediate area.

The Agrilia hill dominates both the upper Karya valley and the Chatzi-Vlachopoulo route to Chora, and the tholos tomb (or tombs?) is further testimony of its importance in Mycenaean times.

F 41   VLACHOPOULO: STAMATI RACHI #
(*MME* **No. 24**)
MH?   LH?

Messenia III 152.

About 2 km. north-northwest of Vlachopoulo, and about 80 m. to east of the road to Metamorphosis, is a conglomerate hill, on whose upper surface (about 110 m. north-northwest to south-southeast by 60 m.) a few prehistoric sherds were found, apparently including both MH and LH types. The spring of Katsibouri, which supplies Vlachopoulo, is about 500 m. to the east.

F 42 METAXADHA: KALOPSANA # (*MME* No. 22)
MH? LH III(A-B)

Messenia III 147.

About a kilometre to south-southwest of Metaxadha, on the west side of a narrow valley within the foothills of Mt. Aigaleon, is the roughly triangular spur Kalopsana, connected by a thin neck to a range of higher hills on the west. The top is not well defined, but the distribution of the sherds indicates that the Mycenaean settlement covered the upper terraces on the south and southeast over an area about 200 m. northwest to southeast by 150 m. Although somewhat high and remote, the site was evidently quite important, since two Mycenaean double axes and a bronze sword in the Chora Museum were found here, and there are reports that bones, beads, and pottery were found in graves on the site.

F 43-44 and F 46-54

A considerable number of Mycenaean sites (*cf. Messenia III* 132 Ill. 3) has been revealed (by surface reconnaissance alone) in the coastal district between Gargaliani and Kyparissia. Most of the important settlements were found on both the east and the west edges of the prominent limestone escarpment which runs along the east side of the coastal plain, extending from east of Filiatra to south of Gargaliani. Sites F 44, F 47, and F 48 were particularly well sited, on a limestone base, but overlooking the more fertile soils of the coastal plain. Sites F 50 and 51 are similarly well placed, on the edge of the broad plateau between the escarpment and the foothills of Mt. Aiglaeon to the east (it should be noted that these foothills, especially in the vicinities of Christiani and Plati, have not themselves been adequately searched). The large site F 48, on the road from Filiatra to Christiani, is well situated to control both the coastal plain and access to the inner plateau, and it may have been the "capital" of the district.

F 43 GARGALIANI: KANALOS # (*MME* No. 15)
MH LH I/II? LH III(A-B) C H

Messenia I 236.

The site is a low spur, one of a series jutting

southwest into the lower Gargaliani plain, about 2.5 km. west-southwest of Gargaliani and 1.5 km. south of the Gargaliani-Marathoupolis road. The hamlet of Kanalos lies about 500 m. to the east. On the south and east flanks of the spur MH and LH and later sherds are scattered over an area about 170 m. northeast to southwest by 110 m. The soil on the site is a rather sandy loose marl, contrasting with the *terra rossa* (locally called "retsinia") of the level plain to west and southwest. About 400 m. to the southeast is a burial mound named "Toumvos tou Kanalou", about 9 m. in diameter and 4 m. high, with a capping of reddish earth, and large stones protruding on the south side. This is presumably a MH or Mycenaean tomb.

F 44 GARGALIANI: KOUTSOVERI # (*MME* No. 16)
LH (III?)

Messenia III 146.

A rounded limestone hill about 30 m. high lies on the northeast side of the Gargaliani-Filiatra road at a point 2.5 km. northwest of Gargaliani. It is an outcrop of the Gargaliani-Filiatra escarpment. The chapel of Ayia Sotira on the top of the hill marks the approximate centre of a prehistoric site about 150 m. westnorthwest to south-southeast by 120 m. Diagnostic sherds were few but included LH.

F 45 (Number not assigned, due to correction of a previous error).

F 46 GARGALIANI: ORDHINES # (*MME* No. 57)
EH II LH I/II? LH III(A-B)

Messenia I 336.

About 4.5 km. northwest of Gargaliani, on the south side of the Langouvardhos river, is a low flat hill about 200 m. north to south by 100 m., overlooking a small coastal plain with a sandy beach. Sherds sparsely scattered over the eroded and rocky surface include EH II and LH III, and the flat loop handle of a goblet may be early LH.

F 47 VALTA: AYIA PARASKEVI # (*MME* No. 60)
MH LH III(A-B)

Messenia III 136.

This low limestone hill is a spur protruding westwards from the Gargaliani-Filiatra escarpment, and overlooking the coastal plain. Valta is 2.5 km. distant to the southeast, on the other side of the escarpment. MH and LH sherds were sparsely distributed over the hill and its south and west terraces, an area about 120 m. east-northeast to west-southwest by 100 m., and some sherds were also found on an adjacent hill to the north.

F 48   FILIATRA: AYIOS CHRISTOPHOROS
(*MME* No. 63)
MH   LH IIIA2-B

Messenia III 135.

This large settlement is on a broad saddle high up on the western edge of the Filiatra-Gargaliani lime-stone escarpment, dominating the coastal plain and controlling the pass from it inland to the plateau between the escarpment and Christiani. Many LH III sherds of good quality were found, and some MH. Concentrations of sherds occurred on a low knoll named Misolakka, about 100 m. to south of the road to Christiani, and on a terraced slope to north of the road. Sherds were found up to about 100 m. back from the edge of the escarpment, under whose cliffs is the chapel of Ayios Christophonos beside a sluggish spring. The total extent of the spread of sherds is about 300 m. north to south by 150 m., indicating a large and important settlement, near the most fertile area in the Filiatra coastal plain, and having good communications with the fertile interior plateau to north of Valta.

F 49   KOROVILEIKA   #   (*MME* No. 62)
LH

Messenia III 135.

Korovileika is a hamlet on the north side of the route from Filiatra to Christiani, on the eastern edge of the limestone escarpment. The site, which is apparently only about 75 m. north to south by 50 m., is on a limestone spur immediately to east of the hamlet, overlooking the fertile plateau to the east and the even more fertile valley to southeast, towards Valta. Surface pottery was sparse, and mainly coarse, but appears to include LH. The position is strategic, controlling the east end of the pass over the escarpment, and the routes to south and east.

F 50   VALTA: AYIOS PANDELEIMON and
KASTRAKI   #   (*MME* Nos. 58-9)
N? MH LH III(A-B) C? H

Messenia III 145.

The village of Valta is situated on a steep lime-stone hill on the east side of the Filiatra-Gargaliani escarpment, on the north side of the Dhipotamo stream, which here cuts through the escarpment. The church of Ayios Pandeleimon on the southwest edge of the village is at the summit of the hill, and marks the centre of a LH and later settlement. Coarse prehistoric sherds were found spread sparsely over an area about 150 m. northwest to southeast by 120 m., on the slopes below the church, especially to south. The settlement may have been larger, since there is much modern debris (making search for ancient sherds difficult); and the village occupies the north end and west slopes of the hill. In an area called Fterolakka, about

150 m. southeast of the church on the southeast side of the road to Gargaliani, road widening seems to have destroyed a LH tholos or chamber tomb. A few Mycenaean sherds were seen here, and vases were reported to have been taken to the Chora Museum.

On the south side of the Dhipotamo stream, and about 300 m. due south of Ayios Pandeleimon, is the small hill or knoll of Kastraki, immediately above the bridge on the Valta-Gargaliani road, at the southwest end of a small ridge. At the northeast end of the ridge is another knoll, in the sides of which large stones and pithos fragments were observed, and there was apparently a pithos burial (or burials?) in the south side of the Kastraki knoll at the southwest end of the ridge. Prehistoric sherds, mainly MH, are spread thickly between the knolls and down the south and west slopes over an area at least 120 m. northeast to southwest by 70 m. To north of the road to Gargaliani, opposite Kastraki, some LH III sherds were found from a destroyed burial mound, probably a tholos tomb.

The evidence for Mycenaean and earlier habitation at Valta suggests a settlement of considerable importance, especially in the LH period. There is good land in the vicinity, and a fine spring called Kopelina about 2 km. to east, which supplies Valta. The Dhipotamo stream itself has a strong flow in early summer.

F 51   FILIATRA: KASTRAKI   #   (*MME* No. 61)
LH   H?

Messenia III 135.

This site is about 5 km. southeast of Filiatra, but only about 2 km. north of Valta. It is an isolated outcrop on the east side of the limestone escarpment, and dominates the fertile valley to north, south, and east, and the interior route from the Valta to the Filiatra areas. A few LH sherds were found with the coarse ware, in an area about 150 m. northwest to southeast by 120 m., comprising the flat top and the gentle northeast slopes. The hill lies above the Evangelistra stream (running in early July) and its associated springs. This stream cuts through the escarpment in the same manner as the Dhipotamo stream (under F 50 above).

F 52   FILIATRA: AYIOS IOANNIS   #   (*MME* No. 64)

Messenia III 135.

About 1.5 km. north of Filiatra the main road descends abruptly from the low plateau of Filiatra to the fertile coastal plain below to north. The road here cuts through a Mycenaean site, separating the smaller east section around the chapel of Ayios Ioannis from the larger west section immediately overlooking the plain. Plentiful sherds, mainly coarse, but including a few LH III, were found over an extent of about 210 m. north-northwest to south-southeast by 130 m., indicating a fairly large, and probably important, settlement on this main north-south route.

F 53 FILIATRA: STOMION # (Fig. 11)
(*MME* No. 65)
LH III(A-B)

Messenia III 133.

The site, about 125 m. in diameter, occupies a low bluff on the south bank of the Filiatra river, beside the river mouth on an inlet named Stomion. It lies about 600 m. west of the main road to Kyparissia, and about 3 km. north-northwest of Filiatra. Surface sherds were mainly coarse, but included a LH III kylix stem. It is possible that the inlet may have served as a harbour in Mycenaean times.

F 54 ARMENIOI: MANNA # (*MME* No. 68)
LH IIIB

Messenia III 133.

About a kilometre to south-southeast of Armenioi is a spring named Manna. A few coarse ware sherds and the base of a LH IIIB deep bowl were found on sloping ground above the spring. It was difficult to gauge the extent of the spread of surface pottery, but the site appeared to be small. It lies near the base of the rugged Ayia Varvara mountain.

The search for prehistoric settlements between Kyparissia and the Filiatra area (*i.e.* between F 53 and F 54) revealed a few indications of Bronze Age habitation near Chalazoni (*Messenia III* 135, no. 22J) and near Farakladha (*Messenia III* 134, no. 22H). Further search is needed, but the district is less fertile than the Filiatra area, and there is no reason to expect a major Mycenaean settlement here.

F 55-F 60

The results of considerable search in the Methoni area have been very disappointing as regards Mycenaean finds, probably due to the high concentration of sites of the historic and mediaeval periods (especially the latter), which may have obscured the prehistoric traces. The only site in the area where Mycenaean occupation has been certainly established is Nisakouli (F 57), now heavily eroded by the sea. Nos. F 55 and F 56 are probably LH, but nothing prehistoric has been certified in the more fertile region between this upland plateau and Methoni. Nos. 58 (Phoinikounta) and 59 by contrast were obviously important Mycenaean settlements, although the land here is in no way superior to that of the Methoni area.

F 55 PALAIONERO: AYIOS KONSTANDINOS # (*MME* No. 74)
MH? LH?

Messenia III 153.

A limestone spur projects westwards from Palaionero, overlooking the highest point in the rocky pass between modern Pylos and Methoni. Coarse ware surface sherds over an area about 60 m. east to west by 50 m. on the spur probably include both MH and LH. There is a fine spring just below the spur, utilized to maintain large flocks of sheep and goats.

F 56 MESOCHORI: KOUTSOVERI # (*MME* No. 75)
MH? LH?

Messenia III 152.

About 300 m. southeast of Mesochori, on the north side of the road to Pidhasos, is a heavily eroded round limestone hill, on which coarse ware of both MH and LH types was found, over an area at least 100 m. in diameter.

F 57 METHONI: NISAKOULI *
MH LH III(A-B)

AAA 2 (1969) 10; *AD* (1969) B 145; *Messenia III* 153; *JFA* 4 (1977) 19.

Nisakouli is now a round islet about 60 m. in diameter and 10 m. high, on the southeast side of the bay of Methoni and 350 m. from the coast. But the water between the islet and the cliffs on the mainland opposite is less than 2 m. deep, so that the islet was probably once part of a promontory. Excavation revealed MH structures, one identified as an altar, and burials. Most of the surface sherds are MH, but a few Mycenaean sherds were found on the top and on the east beach. The top is heavily eroded, and any Mycenaean levels there would have been stripped away.

F 58 PHOINIKOUNTA: AYIA ANALIPSIS # (*MME* No. 79)
EH II MH LH I/II? LH III(A-B) G C H

Messenia I 247; *AD* 22 (1967) B 207.

The church of Ayia Analipsis lies at the centre of a small acropolis hill on the promontory on the west side of Phoinikounta harbour. The level top measures about 75 m. north to south by 60 m. Sherds and medium sized stones here and on the slopes indicate a total area of prehistoric habitation of at least 180 m. north to south by 140 m., to which should be added indications of a further extension to the south, where the original promontory has been eroded by the sea. There were several diagnostic Mycenaean sherds here; and two were found on the Mytika headland, a kilometre to east of the village [at point C on *AJA* 65 (1961) Ill. 12, but cited as D in the text], where there are signs of a probable ruined Mycenaean tholos tomb. A possible MH or LH burial mound was also noted about 500 m. northeast of the village [at point B on *AJA* 65 (1961) Ill. 12, but cited as C in the text]; and a Geometric tomb has recently been found near Phoinikounta (*AD loc.cit.*).

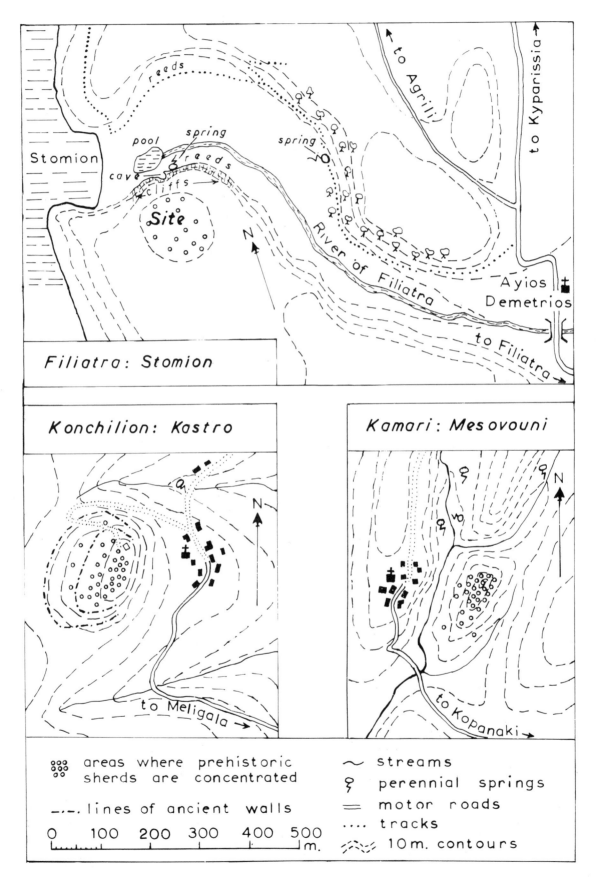

Figure 11

F 59 EXOCHIKON: AYIOS NIKOLAOS
(*MME* No. 78)
MH   LH III(A2-B)

AD 20 (1965) B 208; *Messenia III* 154.

About 1.5 km. west-southwest of Exochikon, and 250 m. west of the road from Kaplani to Lachanadha, is the long conglomerate ridge of Ayios Nikolaos, running north to south, and overlooking the fertile valley of Kambos to east and north. Coarse ware, including MH types and some probably LH, was found on the north part of the summit of the ridge and the upper east and northeast slopes over an area about 100 m. north to south by 80 m.

About 200 m. to east of the ridge is a lower ridge named Mistofolakka, on the top of which are the remains of a destroyed tholos tomb, 7 to 8 m. in diameter. Part of a LH IIIA2 or LH IIIB stirrup-jar brought to the Kalamata Museum was presumably found during the illicit excavation of the tomb.

F 60 KATO AMBELOKIPOI: ASTRAPOKAIMENO
(*MME* No. 77)
LH?

Messenia III 153.

The village of Kato Ambelokipoi is somewhat remote, but lies on the main land route connecting the Methoni-Mesochori area on the west with that of Longa (F 110) on the Messenian Gulf. A high conglomerate spur above the village on its northwest side was sparsely inhabited in the Bronze Age. The surface sherds were all coarse, but are probably contemporary with LH. Their spread indicates an area of habitation of about 150 m. east to west by 50 m., mainly on the southwest slopes.

F 100-F 114

The sites on the west side of the Messenian Gulf appear to fall into two main groups, one in the vicinity of Rizomylo (F 100 to 107, centred on Nichoria, F 100), and the other in the Longa-Koroni coastal area (F 110 to F 114). The Rizomylo group have easy connections both with the Pylos area and with the Lower Pamisos. The Longa-Koroni group are more remote, and may have been of lesser importance (only one tholos tomb has been found in this region, at Charakopio, F 111).

F 100 RIZOMYLO: NICHORIA * # (*MME* No. 100)
N EH II? MH LH I-IIIB LH IIIC? "PG" G A C H

1. The Settlement

Hesperia 41 (1972) 218, 44 (1975) 69; *AAA* 6 (1973) 136 [pumice, *cf. Science* 179 (2/2/1974) 471]; G. Rapp Jr. and S.E. Aschenbrenner (Eds.) *Excavations at Nichoria in Southwest Greece* Vol. I (1978).

The Nichoria ridge is formed of Pliocene deposits, chiefly of conglomerate and marl, adjoining an area of limestone outcrops (a fine source of building material) on higher slopes to the northwest. The ridge is irregular, approximately 500 m. in length from northwest to southeast and 100 m. broad (maximum), flat-topped but cut into by deep gullies on both flanks. It lies above and to west of the important cross-roads of the Kalamata-Pylos and Rizomylo-Koroni highways, rising steeply above the village of Rizomylo at the junction.

The first stratified deposits are of very early MH date, found in the centre of the site. The settlement subsequently expanded to northwest and southeast, and by the LH II period covered about 80% of the ridge, although with varying degrees of density. Remains include a substantial LH IIIA1 building or mansion [*Hesperia* 44 (1975) 100] in the central area, overlying a large LH II complex. The quality of the pottery and other finds suggests that this was a local capital from the beginning of the LH period. Extensive LH III remains include a series of houses in the central area, and a LH IIIB street flanked by poorly preserved houses in the northwest sector. In all areas substantial LH IIIA2 and LH IIIB structures were found, showing constant re-modelling of both houses and of streets and lanes. Some houses have successive floors of the LH IIIA2 and LH IIIB1 periods. But in LH IIIB2 the houses tended to be smaller, and their alignment was usually changed. One LH IIIB2 apsidal building in the northwest sector, for instance, bears no relation to previous alignments in this area.

There seems to have been a break in occupation, but with no signs of any destruction, during LH IIIB2, and only a very few sherds were found (in mixed contexts) which might be assigned to LH IIIC. And these, if indeed LH IIIC, could only be attributed to *later* LH IIIC. When the site was reoccupied early in the Dark Age, the pottery still retained some LH IIIC features.

2. The Tombs

AD 16 (1960) B 108, 17 (1961-2) B 95, 25 (1970) B 179, 26 (1971) B 129, 27 (1972) 262; *AE* (1973) 25; *Hesperia* 44 (1975) 73; *AAA* 9 (1976) 252.

Most of the Mycenaean burials associated with the site are in built tombs, found to northwest of the site, near the limestone outcrops which provided construction material for them. But chamber tombs, dug into the marl, were found to north, west, and southeast. Two of these contained LH IIIA2-B pottery and other goods, but one, which produced much Late Geometric and later pottery, had apparently been cleared of its prehistoric material. A medium-sized tholos tomb (diameter 6.6 m.) of quite good construction was placed at the northwest foot of the ridge. It was used in LH IIIA2-B, although a hoard of bronzes in a pit has earlier parallels. On the east it had partially cut into a curious well-like structure, only 2 m. in diameter, in which the primary burials were associated with three LH IIA vases; several bodies were later flung in carelessly on top, and the reason for this remains a mystery.

The "Veves" tholos tomb, somewhat further to west, was smaller (diameter 5.1 m.) and very poorly preserved; the only finds were vases, ranging from LH I to LH IIIA2, and a few sealstones, gold beads etc. A series of smaller built tombs in the Nikitopoulou field, mostly of tholos shape, contained burials ranging from the end of MH to LH IIIA2-B. Other built tombs, mostly oval or apsidal, are mainly of the Dark Age, although at least one of the apsidal graves in a tumulus close to the Veves tholos contained burials and goods of Mycenaean date.

F 101 VELIKA: SKORDHAKIS # (*MME* No. 112)
MH   LH I/II-III(A-B)

Messenia II 234, *III* 156.

One of the most fertile areas in the vicinity of Rizomylo is the Velika river valley. On a very low hill about 1.5 km. southeast of Velika, on the east side of the valley and 500 m. from the shore, was a small settlement on a very low hill. Sherds, which included a LH I/II cup fragment, were spread over an area about 120 m. north to south by 70 m.

F 102 VELIKA: KOKORA TROUPA # (*MME* No. 113)
N   LH IIIB-C

Messenia II 234, *III* 156.

About 1.5 km. northwest of Velika, in a cliff halfway up the steep east bank of the Velika river, is a cave with a narrow entrance. Some Neolithic and Mycenaean sherds, including one LH IIIC, were found inside not far from the entrance. There is said to be a broad chamber about 300 m. within, but it is now impossible to penetrate more than about 30 m. along a narrow tunnel.

F 103 NEROMILOS: VIGLITSA # (*MME* No. 101)
LH   A

Messenia I 246.

To east of the Kalamata-Pylos road, at a point about 1 km. west-southwest of Neromilos, is a mound about 33 m. in diameter and 5 m. high, almost certainly concealing a Mycenaean tholos tomb (and there are indications of a probable dromos on the west). About 500 m. to southeast, on the south side of the road, a deposit of Archaic pottery was found on the hill at whose west end is the Panayitsa chapel. There are reports of sherds everywhere on the hill below the surface (now occupied by vines) and of a wall "100 m. long". There is a fine spring on the southwest slope,

and signs of a possible second tholos tomb on the south end of a ridge about 300 m. to southwest of Panayitsa.

F 104 DARA: VIGLITSA * # (*MME* No. 114)
MH   LH III(A-B)

Messenia II 234, *III* 156; *Nestor* (1/1/1974) 904; *Hesperia* 44 (1975) 137 n. 55.

Viglitsa is a conical hill in rough country about 600 m. southeast of Dara, on the west side of the road to Daphni. The area strewn with MH and LH sherds (including finer quality LH III) is about 150 m. east to west by 100 m., mainly on the lower north and northwest slopes in cultivated terraces.

A tholos tomb has recently been found (*Nestor* and *Hesperia loc.cit.*) within the territory of Dara but only about 1 km. northwest of Daphni. It lies just to west of the road to Dara and over a kilometre to southeast of Viglitsa. It is not certain whether this tomb (not yet fully published) belongs with the Viglitsa settlement. The contents included evidence of animal sacrifice (horse and deer are represented) as well as much pottery.

F 105 STREPHI: GARALAVOUNI # (*MME* No. 115)
EH II   LH IIA2-B

AD 20 (1965) B 207; *Messenia III* 156.

About 1.5 km. northwest of Strephi, on the east side of the road to Diodia, is a very low rise about 250 m. northwest to southeast by 150 m., some of which appears to be artificial. In the southeast part of this rise is a small knoll of soft white earth, in whose sides LH III fine pottery was found. At the southeast edge of the knoll are clear traces of the dromos of a tholos tomb, whose chamber (collapsed) may have been as much as 8 m. in diameter. In the northwest part of the rise, about 100 m. to northwest of the tomb EH II and LH III pottery of fine quality was observed, over an area about 150 m. northwest to southeast by 100 m. The site lies at the highest point in the fertile plateau between Diodia, Sternes, and Strephi, bounded by tributaries of the Velika river to southwest and northeast.

F 106 PERA: KARKANOS # (*MME* No. 102)
MH?   LH

Messenia III 155.

The spring Kephalovrisi lies at the east foot of a rounded hill named Karkanos, and is now used to irrigate fields and gardens in the valley bottom. The site is about a kilometre north-northeast of Pera and 1200 m. southwest of the larger village of Paniperi. The hill is very rugged and overgrown, so that investigation was difficult, but some LH sherds were found on the gentler south and southeast slopes, which form a terraced semicircular area about 150 m. northeast to southwest by 120 m., above the spring.

F 107 KALOCHORI: AYIOS ILIAS
MH   LH III(A-)B

Messenia II 233.

The site is on a high rocky spur 1.5 km. north of Kalochori, projecting northward over a deep gorge. The road from Kalochori to Paniperi passes over the saddle on the south side. Several LH III sherds were found on the upper area, the saddle, and the gentle east slope, over an area about 120 m. north to south by 90 m. The hill affords a magnificent view to north, west, and east, and together with the mountain above on the south, may have served as an important watchpoint in Mycenaean times.

F 108 MATHIA: PYRGAKI # (*MME* No. 104)
MH?   LH

Messenia II 234, III 155.

Pyrgaki is a conspicuous rounded hill, about 400 m. north-northeast of Mathia, with a fine view to north, east, and south. A few sherds which may be classed as LH, and some possibly MH were found, in very fragmentary condition, mainly on the top, which is only about 50 m. in diameter. But the settlement may have extended over the broad upper terraces also, where search was rendered difficult by thick wheat stubble. The site may have been important strategically, since from it a watch could be kept on land and sea movements along this west side of the Messenian Gulf. And it may also have been important agriculturally, since the surrounding area had a large grain production in 1963.

F 109 VIGLA: AYIOS ILIAS # (*MME* No. 105)
LH III(A-B)

Messenia III 155.

The village of Vigla is high above the coastal plain, and somewhat removed from it. Above the village, and about 300 m. to west, is the chapel of Ayios Ilias, at the eastern end of a long ridge, which is connected by a thin neck on the west to higher hills behind. The Mycenaean settlement occupied the eastern half of the ridge and the terraces to the east below, an extent of about 200 m. east to west by 80 m., as indicated by the spread of sherds, which include LH III of good quality. There is a fine spring-fed well by the church of Ayios Dhimitrios in the village below. There was also some water in early summer in the streams below the ridge on the north and south. The indications are of a medium-sized site with adequate water and good terraces for grain. It also has a magnificent view over the coastal plain.

F 110 LONGA: KAPHIRIO * # (*MME* No. 107)
MH?   LH III(A-B)   "PG"   G?   A?   C   H

Messenia I 248; AR (1960-61) 11.

Kaphirio is a prominent acropolis hill, at the end of a high spur projecting eastwards and overlooking the fertile coastal plain to east and south. It is about a kilometre south-southwest of Longa and 3 km. inland. The Mycenaean settlement extended about 180 m. east to west by 100 m., with sherds concentrated on the north and east slopes. The site was badly eroded, as was shown by the trial excavations, which uncovered scanty remains of Mycenaean and local Protogeometric remains. There was possibly a Mycenaean tholos tomb under the chapel of Ayios Ilias on a connecting ridge about 500 m. to the northwest. Despite the poor condition of the remains, it is clear that this was the most important Mycenaean site in the coastal plain from Longa to Nea Koroni.

F 111 CHARAKOPIO: DEMOTIC SCHOOL * # (*MME* No. 109)
LH I/II?   LH III(A-B)   C   H

PAE (1958) 192; Messenia I 247, II 233.

To south of the Longa coastal plain is an area of dissected marl hills and plateaus, rich in vines and the centre of a flourishing pottery industry. This fertile coastal strip, from Koroni to north of Charakopio, is so heavily cultivated that surface search was extremely difficult. And at Koroni and nearby the debris of various periods from the archaic onwards further contributed to the difficulty.

It was therefore fortunate that a Mycenaean tholos tomb was discovered accidently about 120 m. to northwest of the new Demotic School, about 500 m. north of Charakopio centre. The whole of the north half of the tomb, however, was destroyed by the landowner, and only a part of the contents was recovered, including a bronze cauldron (LH IIIA1 or earlier?), and other bronze objects. Traces of a LH III settlement were found on the low broad hill about 200 m. to south of the tholos, in the course of levelling the playground. Its extent is at least 150 m. east to west by 100 m.

Search of the Charakopio vicinity revealed remains of the Classical and later periods on several hills. And on the western outskirts of Petriadhes, about 1 km. to north of the Charakopio tholos, a grave (or graves) was destroyed. The reported contents included two large pithoi containing bones and ashes, ear-rings, and a bronze pail; and the rounded rim of a bronze vessel and fragments of pithoi were observed near the find-spot. The evidence is not sufficient to establish whether the burials were Mycenaean or of a different period (*e.g.* Geometric).

F 112 FALANTHI: PANORIA # (*MME* No. 108)
LH?

Messenia III 155.

A few coarse ware sherds, probably LH, were found on a low ridge about 200 m. northwest of Falanthi, and to east of the chapel and spring of Ayia Pelayia. The area indicated by the spread of the sherds is about 100 m. north to south by 60 m., on the top and west slopes of the ridge.

F 113 AYIOS ISIDHOROS: LIOFTAKIA # (*MME* No. 110)
MH? LH?

Messenia III 154.

The low ridge called Lioftakia is about 4 km. west of Koroni and 1.5 km. south of Ayios Isidhoros, on the edge of rather infertile country to south. On the south part of the ridge, an area about 100 m. in diameter, coarse ware of MH and LH types were found. The site seems remote and unimportant.

F 114 CHRYSOKELLARIA: AYIOS ATHAN-ASIOS # (*MME* No. 111)
LH   C or H

Messenia III 155.

The village of Chrysokellaria is high above the fertile Koroni-Charakopio coastal area, but has fine springs and good land for grain and olives. The hill of Ayios Athanasios is above the new schoolhouse on the northwest edge of the village. On the summit, and especially on the more sheltered terraces on the south and southwest slopes, several prehistoric sherds, including LH, were found over an area about 150 m. north-northeast to south-southwest by 100 m., indicating a settlement of moderate size.

F 115-F 126

The Mycenaean settlements discovered on the borders of the lower plain of the Pamisos river are fairly evenly spaced, except for a "gap" between Ancient Thouria (F 121) and Kalamata. They are well sited to exploit both the rich lowland pastures and the hill slopes and terraces which are ideal for grain and olive cultivation. The important Mycenaean settlement which occupied part of the territory of the later Ancient Thouria may have been the capital of this whole district.

The present "gap", between this known concentration of Mycenaean sites in the Lower Pamisos valley and the sites (F 100 to F 105) known in the Rizomylo vicinity, may be at least partly due to a selective pattern of search. The *MME* team did visit several of the villages in this low hill country, especially Manesi,

Androusa and Avramiou. In many cases it appeared that the high concentration of later surface remains here, from the Classical to the Mediaeval periods, may have obscured the Mycenaean. The area is full of the Pliocene sediments most favourable to Bronze Age agriculture.

F 115 MADHENA: AYIOS KONSTANDINOS # (*MME* No. 131)
LH III(A2-B)

AD 20 (1965) B 207; *Messenia III* 156.

The chapel of Ayios Konstandinos is on the low hill adjoining Madhena on the southeast. Widening of a track at the northeast foot of the hill ruined a Mycenaean chamber tomb. A few vase fragments recovered, originally assigned to LH IIIC, are almost certainly of the range LH IIIA2-B. Sparse Mycenaean surface sherds on the east slopes of the hill indicate that this may also have been the habitation site, but cultivation and erosion have destroyed nearly all traces. There are good springs and wells in the vicinity.

F 116 MAVROMATI: PANAYIA # (*MME* No. 129)
EH II   LH III(A-B)

Messenia III 158.

The chapel of Panayia stands on a small low ridge which projects eastward almost to the west edge of the road leading north from Messini. It is about 500 m. northeast of Mavromati. Several Mycenaean sherds were found spread over an area only about 90 m. east to west by 50 m.

F 117 KARTEROLI: AYIOS KONSTANDINOS # (*MME* No. 128)
LH III(A-B)

N. Valmin, *Études Topographiques sur la Messénie ancienne* (1930) 64; *BSA* 52 (1957) 246; *Messenia I* 249.

The chapel of Ayios Konstandinos is on a small low hill about 500 m. east-northeast of Karteroli, in the northwest angle between the intersecting main Messini-Meligala road and the branch road to Karteroli. Ruined Mycenaean chamber tombs (seven certain and four probable) were found in the sandy marl of the slopes of the hill, and two more (certain) tombs in the west slope of the hill called Rachi Papalia on the opposite (east) side of the main road. Surface sherds indicate a Mycenaean habitation site centred on Rachi Papalia. The extent is not clear, but the sherds were spread over an area at least 150 m. in diameter.

F 118 EVA: NEKROTAPHEION # (*MME* No. 125)
MH   LH III(A-B)   C

Messenia II 236, *III* 158.

This site is on a very low spur, covered in olive trees, to east of the Messini-Meligala road, and projecting eastward into the Lower Pamisos plain. It is about 300 m. east-southeast of Eva and 100 m. west of the village cemetery. MH and LH sherds were found with later pottery and tile fragments, thinly spread over an area about 150 m. east to west by 100 m. There is a small spring about 600 m. to the east, at the edge of the alluvial plain.

F 119 ARISTODHEMION: PALIAMBELES # (*MME* No. 123)
LH III(A-B)

Messenia II 235.

The village of Aristodhemion is about 200 m. east of the main Messini-Meligala road, on a branch road leading across the Pamisos valley to Plati (F 124). On the south side of the road to Plati, about 500 m. southeast of Aristodhemion, Mycenaean sherds were found on a very low rise, about 90 m. north to south by 35 m., in an olive grove near the border of the alluvial plain. A small mound named Tourko-Skotomeno, about 20 m. in diameter and 5 m. high, in another grove about 200 m. to the southeast, probably conceals a Mycenaean tholos tomb; and there are other possible tholos mounds to north of the village.

F 120 LAMBAINA: TOURKOKIVOURO * # (*MME* No. 122)
EH II LH III(A2-B) G

AD 19 (1964) B 153; *Messenia II* 235, III 157.

About a kilometre east-southeast of Lambaina, on the east side of the Messini-Valyra road, stratified EH, Mycenaean, and Geometric layers were found on the east edge of a clay quarry. About 300 m. to east is a mound named Tourkokivouro, which may conceal a tholos tomb.

F 121 AITHAIA: ELLINIKA (ANCIENT THOURIA) # (Fig. 12) (*MME* No. 137)
EH II MH LH IIIA2-B "PG" G? A? C H

Valmin (1930) 56; *BSA* 52 (1957) 234, 61 (1966) 121; *Messenia I* 250, *II* 239, *III* 158; *AD* 20 (1965) B 207; *PAE* (1975) B 514.

The sketch map (Fig. 12) of Ancient Thouria and its vicinity [reproduced from *BSA* 61 (1966) 122 Fig. 6] is based on intensive survey and study. The high ridge of conglomerate and marl which comprises the site is about 1.8 km. in length north to south, running parallel to, and to east of, the Kalamata-Tripolis road, above the villages of Antheia and and Aithaia. The classical and later town is mainly at the north end. The Mycenaean settlement occupied the central part of the ridge and its upper western slopes, an area at least 400 m. north to south by 150 m. Good quality LH IIIA2 and LH IIIB fine wares were abundant here, especially

on the upper western terraces; and the settlement may have extended further down the west slopes. At least twenty-four Mycenaean chamber tombs, all robbed, were cut into the upper slopes, mainly on the east side, and there is a well constructed tholos tomb on a lower west slope below the Mycenaean settlement. Two artificial mounds, about 10 m. in diameter and 5 m. and 4 m. in height respectively, lie immediately opposite the settlement, across the Xeropotamos gorge on the upper slope of its eastern bank. The clay capping of the northern mound is partly revealed, and near the second mound, about 40 m. to the south, LH III sherds and two obsidian flakes were found. The mounds are therefore probably also Mycenaean tholos tombs.

Ellinika is thus marked as a large and important Mycenaean site, flourishing in the LH IIIA2 and LH IIIB periods. The ridge dominates the east side of the Lower Pamisos valley, affording magnificent views to north, east, and south, and is an excellent natural acropolis, well situated to control a wide territory.

F 122 ARIS: MESOVOUNI # (*MME* No. 126)
MH? LH I/II? LH III(A-B)

Messenia III 158.

The hill Mesovouni, about 10 m. high, lies in the centre of the valley, in low ground about 800 m. east of the Pamisos, and 1.8 km. sotheast of Aris. The hill measures about 350 m. east to west by 100 m. (maximum), but the Mycenaean sherds were found only on the centre and east section, an extent roughly 200 m. east to west by 80 m. The position of the settlement suggests that there was a route (and a ford?) across the Pamisos here, connecting with Karteroli (F 117) on the west, and leading to Thouria (F 121) on the east. Indeed it is likely that this was the most southerly major land route across the Pamisos at this time, and that there was nothing but swamp or marsh to the south [*cf. Science* vol. 195 (11 March 1977) 941].

F 123 PIDHIMA: AYIOS IOANNIS # (*MME* No. 136)
LH I/II LH III(A-B) A? C H

Valmin (1930) 53; *Messenia II* 236.

The site is a broad flat terrace, only 10 m. above the level of the plain, about 100 m. south-southwest of the main Pidhima spring (which supplies the town of Kalamata). The Mycenaean settlement seems confined to the west side of the road, to south and west of the chapel of Ayios Ioannis, which is about 700 m. south of Pidhima village. Plentiful LH sherds cover an area at least 250 m. east to west by 160 m. The higher terraces to east of the road are even more heavily covered in sherds, but mainly Classical and later. The high site in the limestone cleft above the reservoir and spring (Valmin *loc.cit.*) seems to be entirely mediaeval.

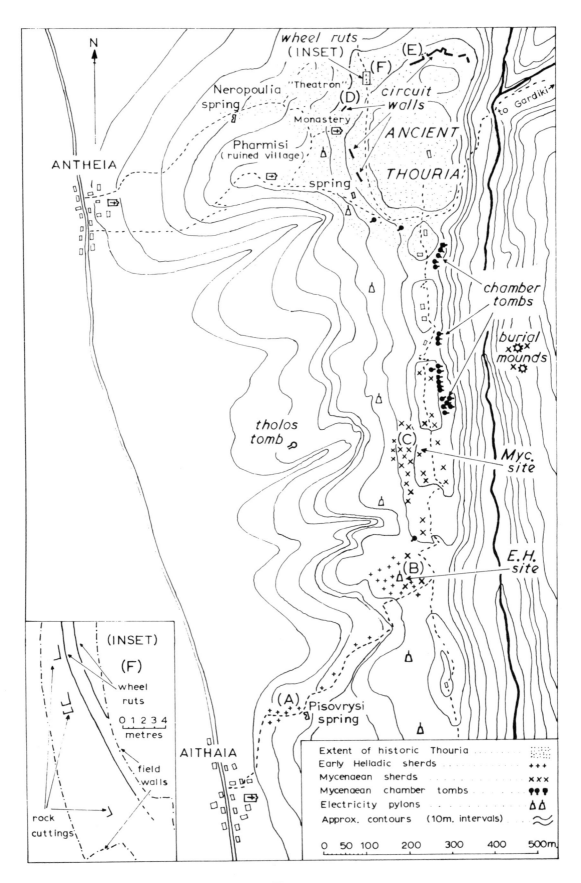

Figure 12

F 124 PLATI: PETROGEPHYRA # (*MME* No. 135)
LH III(A-B)

Messenia II 236.

The road from Aristodhemion (F 119) to Platy crosses the Pamisos on the Petrogephyra bridge. On the east bank the road was cut through a low rise, and a few sherds, including LH III, were found in the sides of the cutting. There are ruins of a Turkish period bridge immediately to north of the Petrogephyra bridge, suggesting that this was the site of a previous ford. There is a spring called Palaiovrysi just to south of the site.

F 125 AYIOS FLOROS # (*MME* No. 134)
MH? LH?

Messenia II 236, III 159.

The springs at Ayios Floros are the main source of the eastern branch of the Pamisos river. The village is on the steep slope on the east of the main road, above the springs. Just above the village, on the west slopes of a rocky limestone knoll, a few coarse Bronze Age sherds were found sparsely strewn over an area about 150 m. east to west by 80 m. MH and LH are probably represented. The site here may have been small, but it is also quite possible that the modern village lies over part or the whole of an ancient settlement.

F 126 AYIOS FLOROS: KAMARIA # (*MME* No. 132)
EH II LH III(A-)B H?

Messenia III 159.

Kamaria is a rocky limestone ridge, which appears as an "island" in the plain, near its northeast edge and the Skala range which separates the Upper and Lower Pamisos valleys. It is about 600 m. north-northwest of the Ayios Floros springs, and 200 m. west of the Kalamata-Tripolis road. The ridge is an irregular oval, about 150 m. north to south by 100 m., with the chapel of Panayia its centre. EH II and LH III, including two sherds certainly LH IIIB, were distributed sparsely over the heavily eroded surface, and mainly near the Panayia chapel.

F 127-F 131

These sites have been recently discovered in southeast foothills of the Kyparissia mountains, and they reveal the extent of Mycenaean penetration into these upland regions. But search here has not been thorough or prolonged; and it would be a mistake to make premature exterpolations as to the *density* of Mycenaean habitation in these areas. There is plenty of good land in the valleys between the three main mountain ridges, and more prehistoric sites probably remain to be found here.

F 127 TRIKORPHO: KAKO KATARRACHI # (*MME* No. 121)
MH LH III(A-B) C

Messenia III 157.

The low hill called Kako Katarrachi is about 2 km. south of Trikorpho, and 200 m. to southeast of the spring Kephalovrysi. It overlooks the fertile Kissos valley which leads southeast towards Manesi, while behind to north is rougher country. The top and the southeast terraces of the hill, an area at least 150 m. northeast to southwest by 120 m., are strewn with Bronze Age sherds, mainly coarse ware, but including at least one LH III piece.

F 128 MANGANIAKO: PALIAMBELA # (*MME* No. 120)
MH? LH IIIA2-B

Messenia III 144.

The prehistoric settlement here occupied three low limestone hillocks and the connecting saddles between them, about 400 m. northeast of the spring in Manganiako village and 150 m. east of the road to Petralona. Some good LH III kylix fragments were found with the coarse ware, and house foundations are visible in at least three places. They average 0.65 m. in width, and the length preserved is at times as much as 6 m., with cross-walls in some cases. The total extent of settlement appears to be about 200 m. northeast to southwest by 130 m., on the top area and the upper east slopes. There is a fine view towards the Messenian Gulf, and good fields of grain and olives and some fruit trees below to south and east.

F 129 DHRAINA: KOUTSOVERI # (*MME* No. 119)
MH LH III(A-B)

Messenia III 144.

On the west side of the road from Dhraina to Koromilea, about a kilometre north-northwest of Dhraina, is a rocky limestone spur projecting westward over a small upland valley. Sherds, mainly of coarse ware, but including LH III, were found on the flat top and upper south slopes, an area about 120 m. northwest to southeast by 80 m.

F 130 MARGELI: KOUTSOVERI # (*MME* No. 116)
MH LH? H

Messenia I 235; *AD* 24 (1969) B 143.

About 500 m. north-northwest of Margeli is a rounded limestone hill, about 40 m. high above the plain. Its slopes are steepest to the northwest above a small plain, and very gradual on the southeast. The upper area, about 150 m. in diameter, is very rocky and uneven, but strewn with local MH sherds, and a few which may be contemporary with LH. The site is on the southeast edge of a small but fertile valley in the rugged interior, in an isolated area probably little affected by Mycenaean culture.

F 131 FLESIADHA: MISORACHI and KOU-PHIERO # (*MME* Nos. 73 and 117)
N   LH I/II?   LH III(A-B)

Messenia I 235, III 145.

A long isolated rocky limestone ridge named Misorachi, oriented roughly east to west, lies about 700 m. north-northeast of Flesiadha, between the village and the mainspring (Kephalovrysi) of the Velika river. At the upper west end of the ridge was a small Mycenaean settlement about 150 m. east to west by 80 m., indicated by a few surface sherds.

About a kilometre east-northeast of Flesiadha and only 600 m. east of Misorachi is a spectacular cave named Kouphiero, high up on the south side of the gorge on whose opposite (northwest) side is the village of Palaio Loutro. The cave is about 40 m. deep and 9 m. wide, and the back part has been converted into a chapel of Ayioi Anaryiroi. Neolithic sherds were found both inside and on the steep slope outside. In a pile of cleared debris just inside the entrance some fine Mycenaean sherds were found together with Neolithic. These may be indicative of a cult here in Mycenaean times.

F 131A CHALVATSOU: KASTRO # (*MME* No. 118) (not marked on Map F)
MH? LH?

Messenia I 235.

This high and bare conical hill stands on the east side of the road from Aristomenis at a point about 2 km. south-southeast of Chalvatsou. On the summit are remains of a mediaeval village. Rough Bronze Age sherds are thinly scattered over the middle and lower west and southwest terraces. The pottery was mainly coarse ware, similar to that from Margeli (F 130), although nothing distinctively MH or LH was found. Two sherds from handles in a softer fabric may be imitating Mycenaean, but the evidence can not be considered sufficient to warrent inclusion of the site on Map F.

F 132-F 140

Most of the Mycenaean settlements on the east side of the Messenian Gulf were placed on limestone outcrops, the spurs or foothills of Mt. Taygetos. Near the head of the Gulf, in the Kalamata area and as far south as Kambos (F 137), there are substantial Pliocene deposits interspersed with the limestone; but to south of Kambos the limestone and the accompanying *terra rossa* predominate. The known settlements are usually near the coast where most of the arable land is situated. The interior plateau of Kambos also appears to have been an important centre, and there may be other sites awaiting discovery in this vicinity, especially near Brinda, where Classical and later sites have been found. It is possible, although less likely, that more Mycenaean settlements may be found in other small fertile areas (such as F 136) among the western slopes of Mt. Taygetos. The main Mycenaean centres in the region appear to have been at Kalamata (F 132), Kambos (F 137), Kardamyle (F 138), and Stoupa (F 139), probably in this order of importance.

F 132 KALAMATA: KASTRO and TOURLES # (*MME* Nos. 141-2)
EH II   MH?   LH III(A2-)B   "PG"?   G A C H

BSA 52 (1957) 242, 61 (1966) 116; *Messenia I* 251, II 237, III 160; *BCH* 83 (1959) 632; *AD* 17 (1961-2) B 96, 23 (1968) B 156.

The mediaeval fortifications on the Kastro hill, on the northern edge of Kalamata, enclose an area about 300 m. northeast to southwest by 150 m. It has been suggested (*BCH loc.cit.*) that parts of the surviving ancient walls (incorporated in the mediaeval fortifications) are Mycenaean. Although this seems unlikely, it does seem that the Kastro was a Mycenaean citadel, since LH III and later sherds were found in its south slope, and it is a natural acropolis.

About 500 m. to northeast of the Kastro, on the north side of the road to Sparta, is a slightly higher hill, composed of sandy marl, named Tourles. LH III sherds and coarse ware were found, together with sherds of various other periods, including EH and local Protogeometric or Geometric, over most of the upper part of the hill and the upper south and east terraces, an area about 200 m. east to west by 100 m. On a south slope were remains of a house wall, apparently prehistoric, and there are remains of chamber tombs, presumably Mycenaean, on the upper southeast terraces and possibly elsewhere on the hill and on the adjacent hill to the northeast [*cf. BSA* 52 (1957) 241 Fig. 5 and *BSA* 61 (1966) 117 Fig. 3].

The archaeological and topographical indications taken together suggest that the Kastro was the centre of the Mycenaean settlement and that the Tourles hill comprised the main part of the outlying "town" beyond the walls. But more evidence is needed as to the extent and density of Mycenaean habitation here.

F 133 PERIVOLAKIA: SOLA # (*MME* No. 140)
MH? LH III(A-B) H?

BSA 61 (1966) 118; *Messenia III* 160.

Perivolakia lies high above the Kalamata plain, at about 600 m. above sea level. On a high limestone spur projecting westward about 300 m. northwest of Perivolakia, is a small Mycenaean site, much eroded. Some worn LH III sherds and coarse ware of LH and possibly MH type were found over an area at most

100 m. northeast to southwest by 80 m. The site is above fertile terraces and has an excellent view over the Kalamata plain. It also lies near an ancient route across Mt. Taygetos.

F 134 VERGA: KASTRAKI # (*MME* No. 143)
MH? LH III(A-B)

Messenia III 160; *BSA* 61 (1966) 116.

The village of Verga (formerly Selitsa) is on the slope of Mt. Kalathion, an outlying spur of Mt. Taygetos. On the limestone ridge adjoining the village on its northwest side, some LH III sherds and Bronze Age coarse ware were found on the upper western terraces, over an area about 100 m. in diameter.

F 135 SOTIRIANIKA: Near 11th km. south of Kalamata
LH I?

AJA 42 (1938) 304; *BSA* 52 (1957) 239; *Messenia III* 160; A. Sakellariou and B. Papathanasopoulos, *National Archaeological Museum A. Prehistoric Collections, a Brief Guide* (1970) 52 (nos. 7381, 7385).

A hoard of gold objects was found in a barren and rocky area (a limestone outcrop) on the east side of the road from Kalamata to Kambos, near the 11th km. mark (from Kalamata), and about a kilometre to north of the side road to Sòtirianika. They were taken to a local goldsmith, and some of the objects were melted down before the police recovered the remainder. The Kantharos, the two smaller mugs, and fragments of a headband or similar ornament have good parallels with the Mycenae Shaft Grave material, and are likely to have come from an important tomb, perhaps a tholos. But the location of the finds strongly suggests a tomb-robbers' cache, ancient or modern, and can not be assumed to indicate the actual location of the tomb.

F 136 PIGADHIA: KOKKINOCHOMATA # (*MME* No. 145)
MH? LH I/II? LH III(A-B) "PG"?

BSA 52 (1957) 240; *Messenia I* 251.

In an area of limestone outcrops, in an upland district about 4 km. northeast of Sotirianika and 4 km. west of Pigadhia, human bones and prehistoric sherds were found in a collapsed cave. They include LH III, indicating Mycenaean habitation in a district fairly high up in the Taygetos foothills.

F 137 KAMBOS: ZARNATA * # (*MME* No 146)
LH (IIB-III) C H

AE (1891) 189; *BSA* 52 (1957) 236, 61 (1966) 114; *Messenia I* 251.

The mediaeval fortress of Zarnata, on a conspicuous limestone acropolis on the west side of the Kambos plateau, about 600 m. west of Kambos, was built on the site of a previous citadel of the Classical or Hellenistic period; and it may also have been the site of a Mycenaean settlement. On the north slope of the hill, in the side of a low ridge, and beside a separate mediaeval tower, is a well constructed tholos tomb (diameter about 7.5 m.). Finds were few, but included characteristic later Mycenaean jewellery, a sealstone, and two lead figurines. The only pottery found near the tomb appears to be LH III, while the quality of the architecture and the style of the jewellery suggest that the tomb was built some time within the LH IIB-IIIA periods.

F 138 KARDAMYLE: KASTRO # (Plate 24a) (*MME* No. 147)
N? EH? MH? LH III(A-B) "PG" G A C H

Valmin (1930) 198, *BSA* 52 (1957) 234, 61 (1966) 114; *BCH* 83 (1959) 639; *Messenia I* 251, *III* 161; *AD* 20 (1965) B 208, 22 (1967) B 206.

The steep acropolis of ancient Kardamyle is the west end of a long limestone spur about 800 m. northeast of modern Kardamyle. Mycenaean sherds were found on the flat summit and the upper western slopes over an area about 250 m. east to west by 150 m. The sherds attributed to Sub-Mycenaean [*AD* 20 (1965) *loc.cit.*] are, however, in fact local Protogeometric; and the polygonal walling on the northwest flank is probably Hellenistic. The extent of fertile land in the vicinity is not large, but the harbour at Kardamyle is one of the best on this west coast of the Mani peninsula.

F 139 STOUPA: ANCIENT LEUKTRA # (Plate 24b) *MME* No. 148)
MH? LH III(A-B) C H

Valmin (1930) 203; *BSA* 52 (1957) 233; *BCH* 83 (1959) 640.

The acropolis of ancient Leuktra is an isolated limestone outcrop about 400 m. east-southeast of the small harbour of Stoupa, on the edge of a plain formed almost entirely of *terra rossa*. A few Mycenaean sherds were found on the hill, but most of the surface pottery was Classical or later. The maximum area of Mycenaean settlement appears to have been 250 m. east to west by 200 m. There is also a partly destroyed Mycenaean chamber tomb at the northeast foot.

F 140 AYIOS DHIMITRIOS: VIGLA # (*MME* No. 149)
LH III(A-B)

Messenia II 237; *BSA* 61 (1966) 113.

On broad terraces sloping down northwards towards the small fishing village of Ayios Dhimitrios, sparse Bronze Age sherds were found, including one LH III fragment. The *maximum* area of settlement indicated is 200 m. north to south by 100 m. The site is on the southern edge of the coastal plain which stretches north to Stoupa (F 139) and beyond.

F 200-205

This group of sites near the mouth of the Kyparissia river together command the main inland routes *via* the Dorion area (F 206-F 223) to the Upper Pamisos valley. Of the sites, Mouriatadha (F 202) and Mirou (F 203) are the most important, and were both fortified. Kyparissia (F 200) also may have been important, although later remains have here obscured the Mycenaean traces.

F 200 KYPARISSIA: KASTRO # (*MME* No. 70)
MH LH (IIIA-B) A C H

Messenia I 232, *III* 133.

The town of Kyparissia occupies the narrow area of the pass here between the Kyparissia mountains and the sea. The acropolis is a limestone spur, above the east edge of the town, connected by a saddle with the mountains to east and southeast. It is very rocky and steep, especially at the north. It completely dominates the small coastal plain, and commands a fine view along the coast to the north. Sparse MH and LH surface sherds were found on the north slope, and a considerable amount of Mycenaean pottery was uncovered during excavation for the foundations of a new house at the west-southwest foot of the Kastro. The acropolis summit (*i.e.* the area within the mediaeval fort) measures about 150 m. north to south by 65 m. (average). But the extent of prehistoric occupation both here and on the slopes can not be estimated, due to the later disturbances on the site. Most of the surface sherds were found near a section of a Classical or Hellenistic wall on the north slope. There is a small harbour at the northwest edge of the town, with a sandy shore, partly protected by a mole from the westerly winds.

F 201 VRYSES: PALAIOPHRYGAS # (*MME* No. 72)
MH? LH (III?)

Messenia III 133.

The village of Vryses, named for its unusually plentiful springs, lies on the upper (southern) route along the south side of the Kyparissia valley. The springs, both called Kephalovrysi, lie on the south side of the road, about 600 m. southwest of Vryses, at the base of the steep Kyparissia mountain. They now provide water for the town of Kyparissia, 3 km. to the west. The limestone spur called Palaiophrygas projects northward, midway between the two springs, over fertile irrigated land. Its top surface is almost denuded, but prehistoric sherds, including LH, were found

thinly scattered on the broad north slopes. The total extent of the site (including the top) was apparently about 100 m. east to west by 90 m.

F 202 MOURIATADHA: ELLINIKO * # (*MME* No. 201)
LH III(B)

PAE (1960) 201; *AD* 16 (1960) B 116; *AJA* (1961) 193, *cf.* Vermeule (1972) 182; *Messenia III* 133.

About 1.5 km. east of Mouriatadha, also along the same route on the northern flank of the Kyparissia mountain, is an imposing acropolis hill. An extensive LH III fortified settlement, about 200 m. north to south by 150 m., was partially excavated here. On the crest of the hill was a large building with many rooms, whose walls had painted plaster, and on the lower south slope, near a tower of the fortification, was a "megaron" containing four column bases, thought to have been possibly a shrine. Remains of other house walls can be seen on the surface on all slopes except the north. The site was heavily eroded, and the excavations produced few finds. The pottery is not described in detail, but is assigned to LH III by the excavator, and by Vermeule (*loc.cit.*) to the thirteenth century B.C. On the south slope of the adjacent hill 200 m. to the northeast was a small tholos tomb (diameter 4.8 m.) which had been largely cleared of its original contents.

This settlement may have been a local capital in the LH IIIB period. It has a commanding position not only along a main route to the east, but also at the head of two passes leading southeast, between the west and east chains of the Kyparissia mountains, to the north shore of the Messenian Gulf. These routes have not yet been properly explored. One leads west of Sellas (F 204), via Kephalovrysi and Aristomenis to Strephi (past F 105) and Rizomylo (F 100). For the other, see under Sellas (F 204).

F 203 MIROU: PERISTERIA * # (*MME* No. 200)
MH LH I-IIIB C H

PAE (1960) 206, (1961) 69, (1962) 90, (1964) 92, (1965) 109; Vermeule (1972) 117; *Messenia III* 133; *SMEA* 3 (1967) 10: *Ergon* (1976) 127, (1977) 118.

Peristeria is another fine acropolis, on the south bank of the Kyparissia river, about 1.5 km. north of Mirou (*alias* Moira or Muron). It is a prominent spur, steep and rocky on the north but with a gentle slope on the south. There is a copious spring at its foot. The site, about 200 m. north to south by 100 m., was apparently first occupied in MH, to judge from the MH tumulus containing pithos burials on Koukirikou hill 500 m. to the west. A fortification wall, about 2.80 m. thick, with casemates attached to it, was preserved for a length of 30 m. on the south slope.

Buildings of early Mycenaean date include the "East House" (apparently LH I), and the earliest burials on the site, in a square built tomb (about 2 m. square) are attributed to the MH/LH transitional period. They were accompanied by a gold vessel, gold jewellery, and various bronzes. The smallest of the tholos tombs, Tomb 3 (diameter 6.9 m), should belong to LH I, to judge from rich goods with similarities to those in the Mycenae Shaft Graves and the two vases found. The finely built tholoi, Tomb 1 (diameter 12.1 m.) and Tomb 2 (diameter 10.6 m), should belong to LH IIA, to judge from the fragments of "palatial" jars found in them. They had been robbed, but contained gold jewellery and fragments of precious vessels of metal and stone. A further tomb to the south resembles a tholos, but was built above ground. It contained pithos burials in addition to ordinary inhumation burials, and the pottery with them appears to be mainly of early LH type (see Addenda).

Material of the LH IIIA-B periods is widespread on the site, although there is no evidence that the great tombs were then still in use. One excavated house contained finds, including figurines, which may be connected with a cult. The pottery in the house is reported to range from the end of LH IIB to LH IIIA2 or later. It is possible, however, that the site declined in importance in the LH III period, especially if the fortification wall is of early Mycenaean date. [It has features resembling the early Mycenaean fortifications at Ano Englianos (F 1).] Thus it is conceivable that the site may have been superseded as a local capital in LH III by Mouriatadha (F 202). On the other hand, it may have remained of greater strategic importance, since it controls the *main* route eastward into the Soulima valley and beyond.

F 204 SELLAS: NEKROTAPHEION # (*MME* No. 202)
MH LH?

Messenia III 133.

The village of Sellas lies on a high route from the northwest to the southwest, through the Kyparissia mountains and *via* Koromilea, Dhraina (F 129), and Trikorpho (F 127). The village cemetery occupies the west end of a high limestone spur projecting westwards over the upper valley of the Peristeria river (which flows northwards to join the main Kyparissia river). The prehistoric site is on the top and upper south terraces, where coarse MH and probably LH sherds are plentiful over an area about 150 m. east to west by 80 m. The pottery, like that of Margeli (F 130), for instance, is of a "provincial" nature, and the site and the valley appear somewhat removed from the main centres of Mycenaean culture in Messenia. The importance of the high routes from the northwest to the southeast (see under F 202 above) should not be exaggerated.

F 205 GLYKORIZI: AYIOS ILIAS # (*MME* No. 239)
N? MH? LH III(A-B)

Messenia III 139.

About 1.5 km. west-southwest of Glykorizi is a conspicuous rounded hill at the south end of a long low ridge. The circular top is about 100 m. in diameter. The surface pottery, which included several examples of LH III fine wares, was concentrated on its sheltered south and east parts and the corresponding upper slopes, over an area about 180 m. northeast to southwest by 120 m. There is a magnificent view from the site over the lower part of the Kyparissia river valley. It may have been important, since its position is strategic, probably complementing sites F 200-F 203 as part of a system of guard-posts at this important northwest point of entry into Messenia.

THE SOULIMA VALLEY
F 206-F 223

The Soulima valley and its environs (Fig. 13) is now one of the most fully investigated areas in Messenia, perhaps second only to the Pylos District in this respect. Many of the Mycenaean settlements found seem neither large nor important, but those found in the more recent surface search in particular help to fill out the pattern of "smaller and satellite" communities.

The more important sites are concentrated in the centre of the valley, near the "bottom land"; and the known tholos tombs in particular, at sites F 209, F 206, F 211, F 217-8, and F 221, are all lined up along the main east to west route between the Upper Pamisos valley and the lower part of the Kyparissia river valley. Particularly interesting are the excavated hill fortress of Malthi (F 217) and the hill of Stylari (F 211). Both are well placed to guard the narrowest defiles on the main route; and it is interesting that both were fortified, Malthi in the MH or early LH period and later, and Stylari in the Hellenistic period, if not before.

The land itself in the valley is perhaps not of the highest quality; much of it being composed of limestone and *terra rossa*, but its fertility would have been greatly enhanced by the higher than average rainfall here and the abundant springs. The pasture land here is also generally good, and in parts excellent.

F 206 ANO KOPANAKI: AKOURTHI * # (*MME* No. 234)
MH LH IIB-III(B) G A C H

Bull Lund (1927-8), 201, 216; Valmin (1930) 79; *Messenia I* 233.

The mounds of three tholos tombs are conspicuous in the flat land of the valley bottom, lying close together to south of the railway line about 1.5 km. west of Ano Kopanaki. The easternmost (A) is about 200 m. south of the line. It was only partly examined.

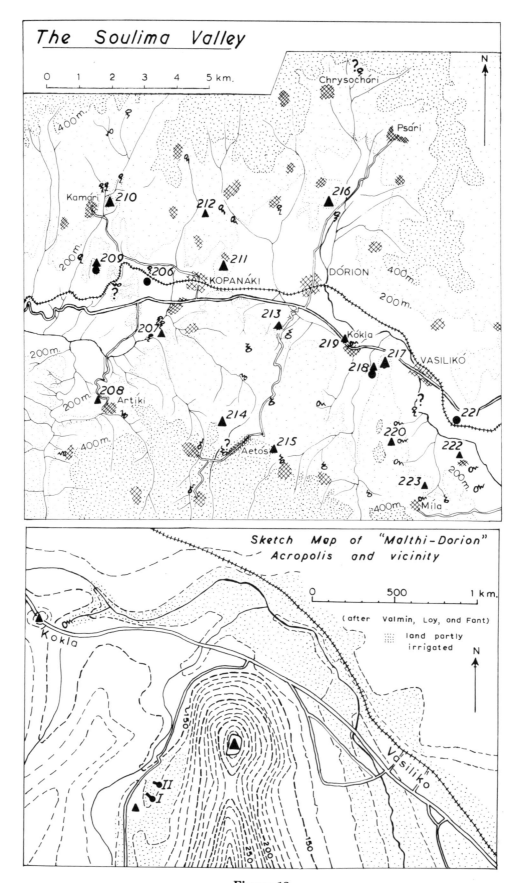

Figure 13

Remains of a wall and MH and LH III sherds were found on its surface. The westernmost tomb (B), 40 m. to west of Tomb A, was fully excavated. It was small (diameter 5.35 m.) and had been robbed. The finds included pottery, some as early as LH IIB. The southernmost tomb has not yet been excavated. No Mycenaean habitation site has been found in the vicinity. The nearest known settlement (F 207) is about 1.5 km. distant, and apparently of insignificant size.

F 207 KATO KOPANAKI: CHALIKIA # (*MME* No. 229)
MH? LH?

Messenia III 140.

About 800 m. southwest of Kato Kopanaki is a thin isolated ridge, on whose highest point is a tall water tower, to which is pumped the water from the spring at the southwest foot of the ridge. And between the ridge and the village is the headspring of the Kyparissia river. Bronze Age sherds, including probable MH and LH, were found with later pottery, over an area about 70 m. northwest to southeast by 40 m., mainly on the upper northeast slopes.

F 208 ARTIKI: RACHI GOURTSIA # (*MME* No. 230)
MH? LH III(A-B)

Messenia III 136.

The village of Artiki is elevated high above the Soulima valley, with an excellent view also over the upper part of the Kyparissia valley. About 200 m. west of the village is a bare, rounded, conglomerate hill, about 90 m. in upper diameter, and heavily eroded. Some very worn potsherds were found on the summit, including some definitely LH III. There is a very fine spring on the slope of the Panayia hill to the southeast, and good land, some of which is irrigated, on the steep slopes to north. There is an easy connection, down a side valley, with the Mouriatadha site (F 202), about 5 km. to the southwest.

F 209 KAMARI: GOUVA # (*MME* No. 236)
LH III(A-B)

Messenia III 137.

On the top of a long isolated ridge, about a kilometer southwest of the Kopanaki-Kamari road, and 1.5 km. south of Kamari, is a large mound whose centre has been completely dug out. From a distance the banks of excavated earth and stone create the impression of two mounds. Several flat stones remain in the "crater", and others in the nearby bushes. Since such stone is "foreign" to this area, there is practically no doubt that this was a large tholos tomb excavated illicitly. Lower down on the ridge to the north, Mycenaean sherds were found, spread over an area about

120 m. north to south by 100 m., mainly on the gentle upper east slope.

F 210 KAMARI: MESOVOUNI # (Fig. 11) (*MME* No. 237)
MH LH III(A-B)

Messenia III 136.

The village of Kamari is at the head of a small side valley to northwest of the main Soulima valley. The Mesovouni hill is opposite the village, on the east side of the stream in the centre of the valley. Sherds, thickly spread over the top and upper slopes, included good representative MH and LH III shapes, and their distribution suggests that the settlement extended at least 130 m. north-northeast to south-southwest by 70 m., and possibly further, down the south slopes. There are excellent springs to north of the site, and good irrigated fields to the south.

F 211 ANO KOPANAKI: STYLARI # (*MME* No. 233)
MH? LH II-III(A-B) C H

Bull Lund (1927-8) 31; Valmin (1930) 79, 101; *Messenia I* 233.

The village of Stylari occupies the top of a prominent hill, an area about 75 m. in diameter, on the north side of the watershed between the Kyparissia and Soulima river valleys. Many Mycenaean sherds, together with later wares, are scattered on the gentle west, south, and southeast slopes, but the Mycenaean settlement appears to have been confined to a smaller area, perhaps about 100 m. in diameter, mainly on the south part. A destroyed tholos tomb was reported on the south slope (Valmin *loc.cit.*) and another at Feretze about 3 km. to the east, but no trace of either could be found in 1960. There is a well preserved section of Hellenistic fortification (including a tower) on the north edge of the hill (Valmin *loc.cit.*).

F 212 ANO KOPANAKI: BAFANO # (*MME* No. 238)
LH

Messenia III 139.

About 2 km. north of Ano Kopanaki, to west of the road to Kephalovrysi, is a low ridge, marked by a limestone outcrop tilting down to the east. The area of LH settlement lay to east of the outcrop, on the northeast, east, and southeast terraces, where LH fine and coarse ware is thinly distributed over an area about 130 m. north to south by 70 m. There is a good view from the site over the Soulima valley.

F 213 AETOS: MOURLOU # (*MME* No. 228)
MH LH III(A-B) LH IIIC?

Messenia III 140.

About 3.5 km. north-northeast of Aetos, on the

west side of the road, and about 700 m. south of the main road to Kyparissia, is a low rounded limestone hill. Sherds spread over the top and upper slopes, over an area about 120 m. east-northeast to west-southwest by 100 m., include MH and LH III. One sherd, formerly attributed to LH IIIA or LH IIIB, may be LH IIIC. There are four springs nearby to south and southwest, and the site is near the good land in the valley centre.

F 214 AETOS: AYIOS DHIMITRIOS (B) # (MME No. 227)
MH? LH III(A-B)

Messenia III 140.

About a kilometre northwest of Aetos is a low ridge which marks the northwest edge of the fertile and well watered Aetos valley. At the northeast end of the ridge is the chapel of Ayios Elias. The Mycenaean site, however, is the slightly lower hill of Ayios Dhimitrios, adjacent to west-southwest. On its upper surface, about 80 m. west-northwest to east-southeast by 50 m., some LH III finer sherds were found with the predominating coarse wares.

F 215 AETOS: PALAIOKASTRO # (MME No. 225)
MH LH

Messenia III 140.

The steep conical limestone hill of Palaiokastro towers above the track from Aetos to Dhrosopiyi. The mediaeval fort on the summit has a commanding view to north, east, and southeast. The upper northeast and east terraces above the track were strewn with mediaeval and Bronze Age sherds over an area about 100 m. northwest to southeast by 80 m. They include MH and LH (the latter should have been mentioned in *Messenia III loc.cit.*).

F 216 DORION: KONDRA # (MME No. 231)
MH? LH I/II? LH III(A-B) H?

Messenia III 139.

The copious spring Koprinitsa lies midway between the villages of Korion and Psari, opposite the chapel of Ayios Konstandinos, above which is a large isolated hill, whose total area is about 600 m. by 500 m. The relatively flat upper area, about 160 m. northeast to southwest by 110 m., is clearly defined by heavy field walls, which may be more or less on the line of (suspected) ancient fortifications. The Bronze Age surface sherds, mainly concentrated in this upper area, include a few recognised as LH III and some which may be MH or LH. The site was certainly larger than Malthi (F 217), and may have been of major importance. The spring at its foot now supplies water for Dorion village and for the irrigation of a considerable area between Dorion and Kokla (F 219).

F 217 VASILIKO: "MALTHI-DORION" * # (Fig. 13) (Plates 23a, 28d) (MME No. 222)
MH LH I-IIIB LH IIIC? "PG" C

Bull Lund (1926-7) 53; N. Valmin, *The Swedish Messenia Expedition* (1938) Part I; *Messenia I* 233, *III* 141.

"Malthi" or "Malthi-Dorion" is the name given by the excavator to the acropolis on the north end of the high limestone ridge of Ramovouni, which lies between the villages of Vasiliko and Kokla, dominating the southwest part of the Soulima valley. The area enclosed within its fortifications is about 140 m. north to south by 80 m. The earliest material from the site (except for a peculiar stone figurine) is MH [*cf. Hesperia* 44 (1975) 111]. It has also become clear that the "Adriatic Ware" reported from all levels is probably MH-LH coarse ware, and that the frequently mentioned tiles are probably Byzantine. Thus much of the excavator's original interpretation must now be discarded. It now appears that, after several phases of scattered buildings a fortified village of integrated plan was established, probably late in the MH period or even early in LH, which survived with few modifications into LH (III?). The finds are not very impressive, particularly after the LH II period.

At the west foot of the acropolis, two tholos tombs (diameters 6.85 m. and 5.75 m.) were dug into the slope of a low hill. The pottery recovered is of LH III date, and some from Tomb 2 may be LH IIIC, but few finds have survived. A single cut grave was also found, in a field to east of the site, and others have been reported here. Whether or not the tholos tombs should be related to a LH III settlement on the acropolis or to the site at Gouves (F 218) is uncertain (see below on Gouves). The question concerning the likelihood of ancient irrigation in the vicinity is deferred to the summary at the end of this chapter.

F 218 MALTHI: GOUVES * # (Fig. 11) (MME No. 223)
MH? LH IIIA2? LH IIIB LH IIIC or "PG" G or A?

OpAth 1 (1953) 29, 2 (1955) 66; *AD* 16 (1960) B 119; *Messenia III* 141.

Part of a LH III settlement was investigated on this very low ridge, about 200 m. north to south by 150 m. (maximum), only 200 m. west of the foot of the "Malthi-Dorion" ridge. It lies less than 100 m. to west of the two Malthi tholos tombs (under F 217). The area investigated was small, and all the finds may belong to a single large building. In one area a lower stratum was reported, which may be prior to LH III. The finds in the main stratum included much LH III pottery, probably mainly LH IIIB, and some unusual stone slabs with incised designs. Some of the pottery may be later than LH IIIB, especially the reported swollen-stemmed kylikes and everted rims; and some surface finds were thought to be Geometric or later. The site may have been the main centre of LH III settlement in the Malthi area; but the excavation was not sufficiently extensive, and the nature and size of the site can not be determined.

F 219 KOKLA: RACHI CHANI # (MME No. 224)
EH? MH LH III(A-B) H

AD (1964) B 154; *Messenia III* 141.

The low rounded hill about 150 m. to the northwest of the great Kokla spring, and at the north end of Kokla villge, was bisected by the cut made for the new road to Kyparissia. A deposit ("apothete"), said to contain many EH and MH sherds, including "Adriatic Ware", was found in one place and some Mycenaean sherds in another. Mycenaean surface sherds indicate a site at least 100 m. in diameter. The sherds salvaged from the road cut have not yet been published.

F 220 MILA: LAKKATHELA on RAMOVOUNI *
EH? MH LH IIIA(2?)-C G A C

AE (1972) *Chronika* 12; *AD* 27 (1972) B 258.

On the east flank of the Ramovouni ridge, about 2 km northwest of Mila and 2 km. south of "Malthi-Dorion" (F 217), is a hollow area named Lakkathela, shaped like an amphitheatre, facing east, between the ridges of Liarameiko and Kriki. Geometric and Archaic levels and structures here overlie a stony Mycenaean level. Part of a Mycenaean building was associated with a floor on which was a deposit of LH IIIC pottery. Some LH IIIA-B pottery and figurines were also found, so that the building may have been built before LH IIIC. Some hand-made dark polished wares, described as EH, were also found and much "Adriatic" ware, presumably MH. The Mycenaean settlement may have been destroyed by fire.

F 221 VASILIKO: XEROVRYSI * # (MME No. 220)
LH IIA A C H

Bull Lund (1927-8) 190, 215; *Messenia I* 234.

The excavated tholos tomb is about 1.5 km. southeast of Vasiliko, on the north side of the railway line. A second tomb (not excavated) lies about 150 m. to southeast of the first and 40 m. south of the line. The excavated tomb (diameter 6.5 m.) was not well built. It had been thoroughly robbed, and fragments of a LH IIA "palatial" jar were the only Mycenaean finds.

F 222 KASTRO: KASTRO TOU MILA # (MME No. 219)
MH? LH?

Messenia III 142.

The Kastro is on a conspicuous conical hill on the north side of the village. The debris of mediaeval and later times obscured most traces of Bronze Age habita-

tion, but enough prehistoric sherds, probably including LH, were found on the north and east slopes to confirm the existence of a Bronze Age settlement, which may have been about 100 m. in diameter, if the area of the mediaeval fort on the top was included.

F 223 MILA: PROFITIS ILIAS # (MME No. 218)
MH? LH

Messenia III 142.

The Profitis Ilias cemetery is about 700 m. north-northeast of Mila on a high limestone spur which projects eastward from the main part of the Ramovouni ridge. Coarse Bronze Age pottery, including a fragment apparently LH, was found thinly spread over the upper north slopes, suggesting an area of habitation about 100 m. east to west by 80 m. (if the area of the modern cemetery was included). There is a good spring in the village, and the site overlooks fertile lowlands to north in the direction of Vasiliko.

F 224-F 226

A small group of sites is now known on the southwest edge of the Upper Pamisos valley, and more are to be expected in this fertile area.

F 224 MELIGALA: AYIOS ILIAS # (MME No. 206)
MH LH III(A-B)

Messenia III 143.

The conspicuous clock tower beside the church of Ayios Ilias is the highest point in the small town of Meligala. The summit of the rounded limestone hill on which it stands has been heavily eroded. Some very worn MH and LH III sherds were identified among the surface pottery which was spread over an area at least 80 m. east to west by 50 m. on the top and the west and southwest slopes, where thick wall foundations, probably ancient, were traced in two places, running down the slopes.

F 225 STENYKLAROS: KATO RACHI # (MME No. 205)
LH III(A-B)

Messenia III 144.

There is a range of low rounded hills to west of Magoula and to southeast of Stenyklaros, on the south side of the road connecting the two villages. At the east end of the range, about 1.5 km. southeast of Stenyklaros, and a kilometre to west of Magoula, some badly worn sherds, including LH III, were distributed over the hilltop, over an area 150 m. in diameter (maximum). The site overlooks good land to northwest, west, and southwest, and is near a crossing over the Mavrozoumenos river and a west to east route across the Pamisos valley.

F 226   NEOCHORI: KOUNOURA   #   (*MME* No. 204)
LH III(A-B)

Messenia III 142.

A low ridge to south of the road from Zerbisia to Neochori, and 800 m. to southwest of Neochori, forms part of the northern foothills of Mt. Ithome. Sherds thinly distributed over an area about 150 m. east to west by 100 m., on the lower northwest slopes, include LH coarse wares and a LH III kylix foot. Despite the extent, the site would seem to have been small and not very important, although it lies not far from the famous ancient bridge (near Neochori) at the confluence of the two branches of the Mavrozoumenos (*cf. MME* index and Plate 4-1).

F 227   KONCHILION: KASTRO   #   (Fig. 11) (Plate 23b)   (*MME* No. 203)
MH   LH III(A-B)   H?

Messenia III 141.

Konchilion lies in the foothills on the east side of the Kyparissia mountains, overlooking fertile terraces to east and south, and a high valley on the west. Kastro is the flat-topped hill immediately above Konchilion on the west side. The upper area, about 150 m. north-northeast to south-southwest by 70 m., is enclosed by the ruins of a thick wall, probably ancient, of large rough boulders and stones. MH and LH III sherds were recognised among the surface pottery within the enclosed area, on the summit and upper west slope. The site is a natural acropolis, resembling "Malthi-Dorion" (F 217) both in its size and its commanding position.

F 228-F 230

These sites lie on the southeast and east edges of the Upper Pamisos valley. More sites are to be expected both here and in the fertile Upper Pamisos plain itself, as is indicated by the discovery of MH burials near Loutro, in the plain about 3 km. northwest of F 230 (*Messenia I* 235, *MME* No. 209).

F 228   KATSAROU: AYIOS ILIAS   #   (*MME* No. 207)
MH?   LH

Messenia II 232.

The chapel of Ayios Ilias crowns a rather steep and rocky isolated limestone hill which rises about 50 m. above the plain. It lies to northeast of the junction formed by the Kalamata-Tripolis road and the branch road to Katsarou, about a kilometre to east-northeast. Ancient occupation was first noted here by

M.S.F. Hood in 1961. Surface sherds in very worn condition, but including LH, and others of Margeli type, were found mainly on the south and southeast slopes. The extent of the site is not clear, but the maximum may be 150 m. east to west by 80 m., although the hill itself extends about 400 m. east to west by about 200 m.

F 229   SIAMOU: PALAIOCHORI   #   (*MME* No. 208)
MH?   LH III(A-B)

Messenia II 231, *III* 143.

In the low foothills and about half a kilometre to north of Siamou village is a small rounded hill on whose top area, barely 50 m. in diameter, were found a few Bronze Age sherds. These included a kylix foot and the handle of a monochrome deep bowl. The coarse ware mainly appeared to be of LH III date also, with some possibly MH. A ruined village occupies much of the west slope of the hill, and at the northwest foot there is a small spring called Kalamaki.

F 230   KALYVIA: PANO CHORIO   #   (*MME* No. 210)
LH III(A-)B

AD 22 (1967) B 206; *Messenia III* 144.

The long flat-topped hill named Pano Chorio or Raches lies above and about 300 m. east of Kalyvia. It is connected by a thin ridge to the higher hills to the east. The top and upper west terraces are strewn with LH fine and coarse wares, including LH III stemmed bowl fragments, over an area roughly 180 m. north to south by 120 m. There is a fine view from the site both over the main Upper Pamisos valley and over its fertile northeast extension.

About 100 m. to south of the village a (chamber?) tomb was destroyed by a bulldozer cutting a road from Kalyvia to Siamou. A piriform jar (LH IIIB), an alabastron, electrum beads, and some gold leaf fragments were rescued. On the northwest slope of the knoll above (on which are situated the chapel and cemetery of Ayios Ilias) a hollow area and many flat shaped stones may indicate a collapsed tholos tomb here.

F 231-F 236

The sites on the north and northwest edges of the Upper Pamisos valley include some quite large settlements, particularly that of Kato Melpia (F 236) in the fertile northwest branch of the plain, and near an exceptionally copious spring.

F 231   POLICHNI: AYIOS TAXIARCHIS   #   (*MME* No. 212)
MH?   LH I?   LH(IIIB)   C

Bull Lund (1928-9) 34; Valmin 1930, 92; *Messenia I* 234.

On a high rounded limestone hill c. 400 m. north of Polichni are the ruins of the mediaeval convent of Ayios Taxiarchis. The site dominates the route connecting the Soulima and Pamisos valleys. The flat hilltop and upper slopes measure about 250 m. south-southeast to north-northwest by 100 m. Coarse Bronze Age and a few Mycenaean sherds were found within this area, including a goblet base which may be MH or LH I. Some LH IIIB sherds from monochrome deep bowls in the Kalamata museum are also apparently from the site. Also in the Kalamata museum is a Mycenaean steatite button said to be from Konstantini, a little to north of Polichni.

F 232 DHIAVOLITSI: LOUTSES # (*MME* No. 214)
MH? LH III(A-)B

AD 19 (1964) B 154; *Messenia II* 231, *III* 143.

This is a low rounded hill of medium size, about 800 m. west-southwest of Dhiavolitsi. The surface sherds were scarce, but found both on the top and on all the slopes, with an apparent concentration on the north side. They included some good LH III fine wares and coarse ware with many grit inclusions. The area of the settlement is not clear, but it must have exceeded 100 m. in diameter. A small LH IIIB chamber tomb was destroyed during construction work near Dhiavolitsi railway station, about 800 m. east-northeast of the settlement site.

F 233 PARAPOUNGION: AYIOS YEORYIOS # (*MME* No. 213)
MH LH III(A-B)

Messenia II 231, *MME* 24 and Pocket Map 2-3.

The site is a high rocky limestone spur about 400 m. northeast of the above Parapoungion, to south of the chapel of Ayios Yeoryios and to north of the railway line. The main concentration of sherds is on the flat top and upper south terraces, an area about 100 m. north to south by 60 m. A few LH III sherds were identified, and many of MH incised ware. The position is both defensible and strategic, dominating the north and northeast sectors of the valley. There is plentiful water from nearby springs. This site was selected for detailed archaeological and environmental studies, as being a typical Later Bronze Age small hill settlement.

F 234 AGRILOVOUNO: AYIOS NIKOLAOS # (*MME* No. 215)
MH LH III(A-)B

Messenia II 231, *III* 143.

The site is on the south tip of a long limestone spur which ends to north of and above Agrilovouno. The top, which measures about 190 m. north to south by 40 m., and the upper parts of the south and east slopes are covered in sherds and medium-sized stones, many of which are clearly from destroyed walls. The surface pottery includes some fine Mycenaean, including LH IIIB, but coarse wares predominate. A stone column base, not *in situ*, seemed to be of typical Mycenaean shape. This important site, resembling Malthi-Dorion both in aspect and position, controls the access to the northwest branch of the Upper Pamisos plain.

F 235 MANDHRA: CHAZNA # (*MME* No. 217)
EH? MH? LH III(A-B)

RE Suppl. VI (1935) 607; *Messenia I* 234, *III* 142.

Karo (*RE loc.cit.*) listed two tholos tombs near Mandhra (formerly Gliata) as reported to him by Valmin. One of these is presumably the ruined tholos tomb about 20 m. southwest of the church of Ayios Yeoryios at the west end of Mandhra village. The circle of stones (exterior diameter about 13 m.) and the line of the dromos (facing east) were still evident in 1960. A small Mycenaean habitation site was subsequently found about 200 m. west-southwest of Mandhra and about 100 m. south of the tholos. Sherds were found only on the south and southeast slopes of a low ridge here, in an area about 100 m. east to west by 50 m. Most were coarse, but two LH III fragments were recognised.

F 236 KATO MELPIA: KREBENI # (*MME* No. 216)
MH? LH IIIA-C A? C H

Messenia I 234, *III* 143.

A large, perhaps major, Mycenaean centre was found on an impressive hill about 400 m. northeast of and above Kato Melpia. It had fine natural defences formed by the precipitous north side of the Venetian Kastro, the deep Langadha gorge on the west (where the fine Koubes spring is located), and steep slopes also on the east and south. The terraces on the southwest, which form the main part of the site, are also high and steep. Classical and Hellenistic walls and sherds are abundant here and cover an extent of about 600 m. east to west by 300 m. Plentiful Mycenaean sherds of good quality were concentrated mostly in the central and upper part, indicating a less extensive, but still considerable, area of habitation, perhaps about 300 m. east to west by 150 m.

F 237-F239

Very little fieldwork has been carried out so far in the hill country between the Soulima and Neda valleys in northern Messenia. Of the three Mycenaean sites discovered the most important is that near Sidherokastro (F 238), in the fertile upland valley of Avlon.

F 237 KEPHALOVRYSI: TSOUKEDHA
(*MME* No. 240)
MH? LH

Messenia III 131.

This site controls the east part of the Avlon valley. It occupies the upper eastern slopes of a small flat-topped rocky hill about 1.5 km. west-northwest of Kephalovrysi. The exposed north and west slopes of the hill were apparently not occupied, and there is little evidence that the small top area, about 40 m. northwest to southeast by 20 m., was inhabited. The surface pottery was confined to the eastern part, and a minimum of about 120 m. northwest to southeast by 80 m. is suggested for the inhabited area. Most of the sherds were coarse, but Mycenaean is certainly represented. There are several fine springs near the site.

F 238 SIDHEROKASTRO: SPHAKOULIA
(*MME* No. 241)
MH LH III(A-)B

Valmin 1930, 82; *Messenia III* 131.

The hill of Sphakoulia is a rocky limestone spur projecting south from the higher ridge in the north side of the Avlon valley, about 1.5 km. north-north-east of Sidherokastro. It dominates the western part of the valley, and the route south to the Kyperissia river valley. The flat top, about 100 m. north-northwest to south-southeast by 70 m., and the upper west and south terraces are strewn with Bronze Age sherds, including MH and LH IIIB. The total extent may be as much as 250 m. north-northwest to south-southeast by 100 m. There are two springs nearby.

F 239 VANADHA: KASTRI # (*MME* No. 242)
MH? LH III(A-B)

Messenia III 131.

The site is the northwest end of the ridge on whose southeast end is the village of Vanadha, about 600 m. distant. Pottery and other material, thinly spread on the small flat summit (about 60 m. in diameter) and on the upper two southeast terraces, includes only a few pieces of Mycenaean fine ware. The total extent is about 100 m. in diameter. A small structure towards the west end of the top may have been a cist grave. This is a small site, but commands striking views in all directions, especially that down the gorge towards Kyparissia to the southwest. It may have been chosen primarily for its strategic position. The surrounding country is rough, but produces fair crops of grain and olives.

F 240 FONISSA: ASPRA LITHARIA # (*MME* No. 243)
MH LH (III?)

Messenia III 130.

About 800 m. southwest of Fonissa the spur of Aspra Litharia projects northward from the hill range on the south side of the Neda valley. The area of ancient settlement appears to have been about 100 m. north to south by 60 m. The top is heavily eroded, and the sherds were found mainly on the west slopes. They include only a few identifiable MH and LH.

So far this is the only reported Mycenaean site in the Neda valley. But reconnaissance currently being carried out by F.A. Cooper in the region of Ancient Phigaleia may alter this picture.

F 241 THOLON: AYIOS DHIMITRIOS
(*MME* No. 244)
LH III(A-B) C or H

Messenia II 130.

The chapel of Ayios Dhimitrios is on a low spur just southeast of the junction of the main north-south coast road and the branch road from Tholon to Lepreon. On a lower knoll about 200 m. east of the chapel some Bronze Age coarse ware and two LH III fragments were found thinly distributed over an area about 60 m. in diameter. Classical and/or Hellenistic potsherds and tile fragments were more abundant, and spread over both the knoll and the spur.

F 242 LEPREON: AYIOS DHIMITRIOS
(*MME* No. 245)
N? EH II MH LH II-III(A-B) C H

AJA 46 (1942) 86; *Messenia I* 231, *III* 130.

This is a spectacular acropolis on a high and steep spur about 200 m. east-southeast of Lepreon, over-hanging a deep and fertile valley. Prehistoric sherds of good quality were found in abundance over the whole hilltop (about 150 m. north to south by 100 m.). They include LH II-III fine wares. Classical and Hellenistic sherds predominate in the south part of the site, and belong to a much larger site (the historic Lepreon) to east and north of the prehistoric acropolis.

APPENDIX TO MAP F: PART I (FIELDWORK)

There is some evidence, albeit inconclusive, that the following sites in Messenia may also have been occupied in Mycenaean times:

Kynigou: Arvanitsa (*Messenia III* 150; *MME* No. 38)
Longa: Palaiokastro (*Messenia II* 234, *III* 155; *MME* No. 106)
Thouria: Ayios Athanasios (*Messenia III* 160; *MME* No. 139)
Chrysochori: Panayia (*Messenia I* 233; *MME* No. 232)
Loutro: Karatsadhes (*Messenia I* 235; *MME* No. 209)

A fuller list of "possible" Mycenaean sites in Messenia is given below.

A MYCENAEAN(?) HIGHWAY IN MESSENIA

AJA 65 (1961) 257 n. 14, 68 (1964) 240; W.A. McDonald, in *Mycenaean Studies* (1964) 217-240; *MME* 25, 142, 244.

Traces of an ancient highway were explored between Pylos and Rizomylo, particularly in the sector from Kazarma to Neromilo [*AJA* 65 (1961) Pl. 70 Fig. 2, *cf. Mycenaean Studies loc.cit.* and *MME* Figs. 2-5 on p. 26]. There is no actual proof that the highway surveyed here is of the Mycenaean period, but its gradients, usually 20%, and averaging 17.8% (*MME* 29), are consistent with use by wheeled traffic, and several sites and tholos tombs are lined up along this route. Mycenaean highways in Messenia are, of course, to be presumed, in view of the evidence from the Pylos Tablets for wheeled chariots and a mobile defence force (see Appendix to Map F: Part II).

RECENT FIELDWORK IN SOUTHWESTERN PELOPONNESE

Some of the work of the Minnesota Messenia Expedition has recently been criticised by J.L. Bintliff [in *Natural Environment and Human Settlement in Prehistoric Greece* (1977) 133-4, 499-520, and 701, *cf. Mycenaean Geography* (1977) *passim*]. The chief accusation made is that the Minnesota team was preoccupied with searching for "prominent acropolis hills . . . that might fit in the Pylos Texts or in Homer", and that they concentrated on locating the "upper hierarchy" of sites, and thereby failed to find the "smaller and satellite" and "low lying" sites. The *MME* survey work was for the most part extensive in nature, and much more remains to be discovered. But the smaller sites were not in fact neglected, and the criticisms stem at least partly from erroneous analyses of the data in the *MME* site register [W.A. McDonald and G.R. Rapp, *The Minnesota Messenia Expedition* (1972) 123-128 and 263-309].

In the hope of obviating any false impression of a (supposed) overall selectivity on the part of the *MME* team, I substitute here a more appropriate analysis, to replace that of Bintliff (*op.cit.* 133-4):

1) The following Mycenaean sites found in Messenia in the course of the Minnesota survey appear to have been settlements which could be classified as either "smaller and satellite" or "low lying" or both:

F 14, F 17 (*MME* No. 47), F 22 (*MME* Nos. 7A to E), F 25, F 28, F 32, F 36, F 41, F 49, F 54, F 55, F 108, F 112, F 116, F 119, F 124, F 136, F 207, F 214, F 224, F 229, F 233, F 235, F 240, F 241.

2) The following sites in Messenia may also have been inhabited in the Mycenaean period, but the evidence is sparse and inconclusive. Some of these may therefore also have been "smaller and satellite" Mycenaean settlements:

MME Nos. 17, 23, 66, 69, 106, 110, 116, 117, 118, 139, 144, 202, 209, 221, 232, 235.

3) The *MME* team also discovered three Neolithic cave sites (*MME* Nos. 113, 117, and 127), and 12 certain and 5 possible Early Helladic sites (*MME* Nos. 6, 7, 57, 79, 115, 124, 129, 130, 132, 137, 141, 145, 147, 217, 246, 305, and 306). These latter constitute exactly half of the total number of Early Helladic sites or possible sites found in the Southwestern Peloponnese. It is suggested by Bintliff (*op.cit.* 507, *cf.* 133), on the grounds of the unpublished EH finds claimed at Kokla (F 219), that many more EH sites await discovery in the Soulima Valley area. Bintliff suggests that the reason they have not yet been found is that the *MME* survey techniques were "specifically directed to the identification of Mycenaean acropolis hills with commanding height". The underlying assumption here is that Early Helladic settlements were principally "low mound" sites. But the real reason for the failure to find Early Helladic sites (if such existed) in the Soulima valley and Upper Pamisos valley may rather have been that typical Early Helladic fine pottery was not much used here, and that we have as yet no means of distinguishing the local Early Bronze Age coarse wares.

Bintliff (*op.cit.* 115 and *passim*) dismisses as being of minor importance the observation made by *MME* that most major prehistoric settlements in Messenia were located near perennial springs. He is here preoccupied with an insistence on the predominant role played by cereal and olive production; and there is indeed room for controversy concerning the amount of land which may have been irrigated in Mycenaean times. Thus Bintliff castigates Loy for an (alleged) exaggeration of the amount of irrigable land then available near Malthi-Dorion (*op.cit.* 504-8, 517-9, *cf.* my Fig. 13 here). But he does not consider the possibility (or probability?) that the springs there in Mycenaean times may have issued at a higher level than at present.

The basis of Mycenaean agriculture in Messenia may indeed have been a combination of cereal and olive production, but both men and livestock need an assured water supply. Where springs are abundant, as in many parts of Messenia, there would be no compelling necessity to dig wells, if the main settlements could be located near the springs, for greater convenience. The modern farmers of Messenia have been quite willing to walk (or ride their donkeys) for considerable distances to their fields, rather than live at the same distances apart from their neighbours. Furthermore, we have no means of guaranteeing that all of the sites assumed to be "smaller and satellite" settlements have been correctly identified as permanent (*i.e.* perennial) residences. In modern Messenia, as elsewhere in Greece, many structures in the countryside are only seasonally occupied, and often only during part of the working *day*, since their owners return to their villages at night.

It would be presumptuous for an archaeologist to attempt to make judgements about rival geographical and geological theories. But Bintliff's fieldwork experience in Messenia has been rather limited. The recent detailed studies by Kraft, Rapp, and Aschenbrenner (1975 and 1977) suggest a much more complex pattern of recent geological history in Messenia (and elsewhere) than that offered by Bintliff's division of the recent depositions into only two periods, *i.e.* those of the "Older Fill" and of the "Younger Fill". The proportionately greater annual rainfall in Messenia also makes it particularly difficult to believe that no alluviation whatsoever took place in Messenia in the interval between the time of the "Older Fill" and that of the "Younger Fill". We must also take into account the considerable increase in man-made disturbances here in the Middle and Late Bronze Age.

[Since this section was written, a further analysis of the Messenian data has been presented by J. Carothers and W.A. McDonald, "Size and Distribution of the Population in Late Bronze Age Messenia: Some Statistical Approaches", in *JFA* 6 (1979) 433-454. In preparation also is an article by J.C. Kraft, G.R. Rapp, and S.E. Aschenbrenner, entitled "Late Holocene Paleogeomorphic Reconstructions in the Area of the Bay of Navarino: Sandy Pylos", intended for the *Journal of Archaeological Science.*]

APPENDIX TO MAP F: PART II
(See Bibliography for Special Abbreviations Used)

THE KINGDOM OF PYLOS 1. THE LINEAR B TABLETS

In several recent essays John Chadwick has reviewed the evidence for the political geography of Mycenaean Pylos in its final year. The evidence is primarily that of the Linear B Tablets themselves, as interpreted chiefly by Michael Ventris and John Chadwick, and to a lesser degree by L.R. Palmer, William F. Wyatt Jr., Cynthia W. Shelmerdine and others.

The main arguments (most recently set out in *MW*, especially pp. 35ff.) are persuasive, and a good case is made out for a logical and *geographical* order of the place names, all of which, it is now argued, probably fall within the area of modern Messenia. The number of place names on the Pylos Tablets is apparently about two hundred (*MW* 40, 68, *cf. DMG* 141-50). Not all of the places are necessarily settlements. From archaeological excavation and survey work we now know the location of about 140 Mycenaen settlements of varying sizes in Messenia. If we assume that about half of the significant Mycenaean settlements in Messenia have already been found, and if we allow that some of the smaller settlements, *i.e.* consisting of hamlets or farms, are mentioned in the tablets, then the figures would correspond reasonably well. As has been emphasized above, some of the larger settlements, and a great many of the smaller ones, have probably disappeared totally or are too difficult to find.

In any case there is now enough information to warrant some kind of a reconstruction, even if all the details can not be worked out (*cf. MW* p.x.). But, in order to demonstrate the *hypothetical* nature of any such reconstruction, an analysis of the methods hitherto employed in the arguments is necessary. This applies also to my own attempt at a reconstruction, which in fact differs only in detail from that proposed by Chadwick, and is, of course, largely based on his work. Indeed the particular suggestions can not be fully understood without reference to the arguments fully set out by Chadwick (see chapter bibliography). In particular, his and Shelmerdine's proposed division of the names in the "Further Province" into four main regions ("southwest", "northeast", and "northwest") is here adopted, and further tentative suggestions are given towards a more precise location of the names. No definitive solutions can now be provided; but it is hoped that these working notes, derived partly from field observations, may at least help to clarify some of the problems, and to stimulate further enquiry.

The only name which can be located with any certainty is Pu-ro, which clearly stands for the Palace at Ano Englianos (*MW* 40), and presumably also the accompanying "lower town" and the immediate environs. It is to be expected that the names reflect a complex pattern (*MME* 102), including names of major towns and/or administrative districts, but also (especially in such contexts as the "coast guard" tablets) some names of smaller places, or even possibly of toponyms denoting specific geographical landmarks. And, if we are right in assuming that some of the land in question was recently acquired (*i.e.* within the LH IIIA2 and LH IIIB periods), then we should expect a mixture of older and newer names. Some of the new names might have been coined by the Pylian bureaucracy, in the manner of names given to English places by the Norman conquerors. And we would expect that old names would at times survive alongside the new (*MME* 102).

Of paramount importance here is the internal evidence of the tablets for the division of the sixteen presumed administrative districts of the "Kingdom" into the "Hither" and "Further" provinces, De-we-ro-a₃-ko-ra-i-ja and Pe-ra-ko-ra-i-ja, composed of nine names and seven (sometimes eight?) names respectively (*MW* 41 ff.). Each district was apparently controlled by a governor, called a Ko-re-te, and a deputy governor, called a po-ro-ko-re-te (*MW* 73, *MME* 105). Since the internal evidence can not by itself provide a means of locating the names with any certainty, all the main steps in the argument must be buttressed to some extent by *external* "checks" or "fixes", for which the main clues are resemblances between the place names on the tablets and names of places or geographical features current in the Greek historical period. The inherent weakness of this method is, of course, obvious; but it is hard to see how any progress could be made otherwise.

The internal evidence demonstrates that an element a(3)-ko-ra-i-ja has been compounded with the prefixes pera- ("beyond") and deuro- ("on this side of"). "Hence we can deduce that the kingdom is divided into two provinces separated by some conspicuous feature" (*MW* 43). Here it must be noted that an element of surmise has already been included in the argument, albeit coupled with some common sense. As to the identification of this presumed landmark, the classical names Akritas (for modern Cape Akritas) and Aigaleon (for modern Mount Ayia or "Haghia") were naturally suggestive; since (if we make allowances for the flexibility of the Linear B spelling rules) they resemble the Linear B element a(3)-ko-ra-i-ja. Of the two alternatives proposed, Chadwick rightly prefers Aigaleon, since this landmark completely dominates the modern Pylos District, and especially Chora and Ano Englianos.

In recent detailed analysis of the "Further Province" by Shelmerdine and Chadwick [*AJA* 77 (1973) 261-278] it is demonstrated that the place names (there called "towns") are divided into "two main groups and four subgroups". It is suggested that the boundary between the two main groups may be the Pamisos river (together with its northern tributary, the Mavrozoumenos), and that the minor boundary might be the Skala range, a row of low hills which divide the Pamisos valley into its upper (northern) and lower (southern) parts [*cf.* Valmin (1930) 64 and *BSA* 52 (1957) 255]. The division of the lower Pamisos valley would have been even more marked in the Mycenaean period, when the shore line at the head of the Messenian Gulf was further to the north, and when more marshy conditions prevailed in the flood plain of the Pamisos [*Geological Society of America Bulletin* 86 (1975) 1191-1208]. The natural divisions in the Upper Pamisos valley are somewhat more complicated. As noted above, the known Mycenaean settlements in the northern plain (F 224-6 and 228-36) fall into three main groups, in the southwest, the east, and the northwest respectively; and these groups correspond roughly with the natural divisions. The main lines of communication in the valley run north to south along both sides of the Pamisos, with an easy route to the Soulima valley on the northwest.

The Pamisos valley and the Soulima valley thus form a natural unit for the "Further Province". Its "capital" was apparently Re-u-ko-to-ro, a prominent place (*MW* 82), which is not listed as one of the "Seven", and is therefore presumed to bear the same relationship to the "Seven" that Pu-ro bears to the "Nine" of the "Hither Province" (*MME* 107). Apart from this clue, there is no further internal evidence as to its location. Chadwick had formerly suggested (*MME* 111) the possibility that it was the name of the settlement at Nichoria, which is now known to have been of considerable size in the LH IIIB period, and which lies on the quickest and easiest route from the Pylos District to the Pamisos valley. But he now prefers (*MME* 111 and *MW* 48) to make Nichoria the candidate for Ti-mi-to-a-ko, the first of the "Seven", and the only one known to be on or near the coast. Here again the internal arguments are buttressed by a resemblance between a name in the tablets and a name (*i.e.* Nedon) of a river of the Greek historical period. In the "coastguard" tablets (*MW* 173 ff.) thirty men stationed at Ti-mi-to-a-ko are apparently being despatched Ne-do-wo-ta-de (*i.e.* "towards Nedwon"). It is not clear, however, whether their destination is a district or merely a geographical feature. Chadwick would prefer to leave the northern Mani (the area marked by sites F 132-140) out of the "Further Province", although the status of Kalamata (F 132), which stands on the Nedon, is not clarified (*MME* 110, *MW* 47). A more natural point of division than the Nedon itself in fact occurs at the point where Mt. Kalathion, a spur of Mt. Taygetos, projects almost to the shoreline, near Almyros, about 6 km. to southeast of Kalamata [*cf. BSA* 61 (1966) 127 n. 108]. The "defile" which occurs here is overlooked by the small site at Kato Verga (F 134).

Throughout the arguments we have seen that it is seldom clear whether the names of the sixteen administrative districts refer to specific centres of administration (*i.e.* "towns") or whether they are primarily district names. Perhaps in the Pylos area, the "heart" of the "Hither Province", the names of some larger and more developed settlements might also have been adopted as the district names. But in the more remote areas of the "Hither Province" and in much of the "Further Province" more of the names might be expected to be purely of district type. In one case two names, E-re-i and E-sa-re-wi-ja apparently overlap [*AJA* 77 (1973) 275 n. 58, 278]; and in another case the names E-ra-to and Ro-u-so are apparently alternatives (*MME* 102). In these and other examples it is possible that both a "town" and a district name occur in the same region. Indeed Chadwick has suggested that E-ra-to might be the principal town in the district of Ro-u-so (*MME* 102, 110), and that Pu-ro itself may lie in the district of Pa-ki-ja-ne. In the case of such compound names as Ti-mi-to a-ke-e (or Ti-mi-to-a-ko, *cf. DMG* 144) and Ro-u-si-jo a-ko-ro ("territory of Lousos"?) we may have yet another category, perhaps related to land holdings (whether contemporary with the tablets or previous) of specific persons (*cf. MME* 102, *MW* 97).

The end result of the combined arguments is a plausible, but also highly speculative, hypothetical reconstruction, whose component parts are of varying degrees of reliability. And, as Chadwick says of the "Further Province" at least, "so far it appears dangerous to press further the identification of these names with actual sites" (*MW* 48). Yet in the same paragraph he also maintains that "The picture which has thus emerged of Pylian geography at the time of the tablets gives us a firm background against which we can set the economic, social and military facts to be won from the documents". In fact, however, it is clear that the order of enquiry has always *begun* with the economic facts (securely based on the numerals and ideograms on the tablets) concerning land-holdings, tax assessments and the like, since it is largely from these that the geography itself is deduced. The size and extent of the provinces and of their sub-divisions must ultimately be gauged from estimates of their agricultural and manufacturing capacity.

In the arguments for the location of individual place names on the tablets, similar external "clues" are often used. Thus Ri-jo, the last name in the list of "Nine" of the "Hither Province", is equated by Chadwick with Rhion and located at modern Koroni because a former town named Rhion was, according to *our* interpretation of a passage in Strabo's geography, apparently in the region of the historic Asine, which was probably on the site of Koroni [*cf. BSA* 61 (1966) 127 n. 111]. But Strabo simply describes Rhion as a city "opposite Tainaron" (Strabo viii. 4, 5-7); and furthermore it is not clear whether Ri-jo in fact refers to a town rather than a district. The name Rhion in classical Greek signifies "promontory".

In addition, no Mycenaean remains have yet been found at Koroni itself. Ka-ra-do-ro, the penultimate name in the list of "Nine," resembles the dual form of the classical Greek word Kharadros, meaning "gully" or "ravine"; and this clue leads Chadwick to place Ka-ra-do-ro at Phoinikous, where gullies are abundant. This further conjecture is, of course, at least partly based on the previous conjecture of the location of Ri-jo at Koroni, which is now assumed to have provided a "fix", on which the next step in the argument depends. Similarly, the northern boundary of the "Hither Province" is placed at or near the river Nedha

(the ancient Neda) again on the basis of internal evidence, common sense, and the clue that "one of the prominent men of the northern area bears a name derived from it, Nedwatas" (*MW* 45). It is noted that the Nedha valley "is apparently bare of Mycenaean sites" and that "it seems to be a natural no-man's land" (*MW* 39). The suggestion (*MW* 45), that the Nedha river and the Tetrazi mountains to south together form some sort of a barrier, is reasonable; but it must be admitted that the valley has not yet been systematically investigated.

Thus, since nearly all of the locations proposed are entirely hypothetical, we can not decide finally which particular clues can be used as definite corner stones in the argument and which must be rejected. For the present, therefore, all reasonable surmises should be considered; and differences of view should be restricted to assessments of the relative weight of the component parts of the evidence. The particular suggestions made below are largely based also on the present known pattern of Mycenaean settlement in Messenia. And, since most of the evidence comes from surface exploration alone, we can seldom be absolutely certain that all the sites in question were in use at the precise time referred to in the tablets. But it is reasonable to assume that most of them were; and by concentrating on *districts* rather than on individual sites, the possibilities of error in this respect may be reduced. The survey and excavation work carried out in Messenia and Triphylia, although considerable and prolonged, has not provided complete, or even uniform coverage; and the most that can now be presented is a working hypothesis. Many of the suggestions have already been made by Chadwick.

"HITHER PROVINCE"   1. PYLOS DISTRICT

Name	Suggested Location	Comment
Pu-ro	The palace at Ano Englianos, together with the "lower town" and immediate environs (F 1).	The name itself may be of the "town" type, or may also denote a district. In any case, it is the only name in the tablets which can be located with any certainty.
Pa-ki-ja-ne	A district probably extending from Chora to Tragana (*i.e.* including sites F 1-13). The "religious centre" was probably at Volimidhia (F 8) (*MME* 109).	One of the "Nine" of the "Hither Province". Apparently also a major "religious" centre, and closely associated with Pu-ro (*MME* 108, *MW* 43, 45, 90-91). But it may also be the name of the district in which Pu-ro lay.
Ro-o-wa	The district between ancient and modern Koryphasion, including the plain to north of Osmanaga Lagoon, *i.e.* roughly comprising the territory of modern Romanou and Koryphasion. (Sites F 3-6 and 19-22 would be included.)	Probably the name of the main port of Pu-ro. It is associated with the "Lawagetas", an official second only to the king, and with other important persons (*MME* 109-110). It is not one of the "Nine", and, like Pu-ro, may have been of special status. It may, however, have been considered part of the district of Pa-ki-ja-ne for some purposes.

Name	Suggested Location	Comment
		The main port of Pu-ro must have been on the north side of the present bay of Pylos, probably on the north shore of the Osmanaga Lagoon. It can hardly have been at Voidhokilia or anywhere else on the exposed west coast to north of modern Palaiokastro (Ancient Koryphasion). Ro-o-wa is a flax-producing area, so that good land, and a good water supply, are also indicated. The centre may have been at the large site of Beyler Bey (F 4).
A-ke-re-wa	The Gialova-Pyla area (sites F 23-7) on the east side of the bay of Pylos. The large site near Gialova (F 23) would be the best candidate for the main centre.	Listed in the "Nine". It was apparently a port of some consequence (*MW* 46, *MME* 110) but must lie to "south" of Ro-o-wa. It can not reasonably be located at modern Pylos, whose harbour is artificial. The beach to south of Gialova is suitable for drawing up ancient ships, and is partly protected by the island of Sphakteria from the prevalent westerly winds. The Gialova-Pyla area also has the sheep pasture and wheat land indicated.
A-pu$_2$	Iklaina-Platanos-Pappoulia region (F 14-18), with centre probably near Iklaina (F 17).	Listed in the "Nine" before A-ke-re-wa, and so might be expected to be further "north". It probably lies away from the coast and a short distance "south" of Pu-ro (*MME* 110). If the identifications proposed above for Pa-ki-ja-ne and Ro-o-wa, and that for Ro-u-so below are correct, then the Iklaina-Platanos-Pappoulia region is the only reasonable candidate. The site near Iklaina (F 17) appears to have been the most important in the group. Substantial buildings were excavated here.
Ro-u-so (E-ra-to)	The "central plateau", comprising roughly the territories of modern Koukounara, Stenosia, Chandrinou, Kremmidhia, and Mesopotamos (*i.e.* including sites F 29-37).	One of the "Nine", and again apparently not coastal. It was the home of wood-cutters, and an important subsidiary centre for "slave" workers (*MW* 45-6). There are residual oak groves in the area between Nea Soulinari and Kremmidhia-Velanidhia (the latter name denotes a type of oak). There are also some large trees in the Koukounara area. It is suggested (*MME* 102, 110) that E-ra-to is the principal town of Ro-u-so. If so, it would probably have been in the Koukounara area (F 29), where some of the tholos tombs were in use in the LH IIIB period.

"HITHER PROVINCE" 2. SOUTHERN AREA

Name	Suggested Location	Comment
Ka-ra-do-ro	Area of Phoinikous and Exochikon (F 58 and 59).	Both Ka-ra-do-ro and Ri-jo (the last two names in the "Nine" are coastal districts. The "gullies" apparently referred to lie between Phoinikous and Exochikon. A district name seems implied here (Ka-ra-do-ro), and the importance of the area is suggested by the tholos tombs at F 58 and F 59.

Name	Suggested Location	Comment
Ri-jo	The coastal area between Koroni and Longa (sites F 110-114).	The Longa plain was clearly an important area, and the low marl hills to south of it, as far as Koroni, are exceptionally fertile. The centre may have been at Charakopeio (F 111), whose importance is indicated by a tholos tomb.
Za-e-to-ro	The Longa site (F 110)?	Ri-jo is omitted from the "coastguard" lists, but Za-e-to-ro (the last name in An 661) might be in the territory of Ri-jo. It could be at Longa, or conceivably at Vigla (F 109), whose name ("sentinel") is suggestive. Za-e-to-ro is the last name in the "coastguard" tablets except for Ti-mi-to-a-ko, and so might adjoin it (*MME* 110).
		Ri-jo may be primarily a district name, denoting the Akritas promontory as a whole.

"HITHER PROVINCE"   3. NORTHERN AREA

Name	Suggested Location	Comment
Pi-swa	The area of modern Sidherokastro, Vanadha and Kephalovrysi (including sites F 237-9).	Both Pi-swa and Me-ta-pa (the first two names in the "Nine") are absent from the "coastguard" tablets, and hence probably inland (*MME* 108-9, *MW* 45). But men from Me-ta-pa are deployed on the coast. In An 218 Me-ta-pa stands in the next line to O-wi-to-no, the "northernmost" coastguard sector. Pi-swa is rich in sheep, and both Me-ta-pa and Pi-swa are in contact with the "Further Province" (*MW* 43). Sheep at Me-ta-pa come from E-ra-te-re-wa in the further province [*AJA* 77 (1973) 276, 278].
Me-ta-pa	The area of modern Mirou, Mouriatadha etc., near the west end of the Kyparissia river valley (including sites F 202-3 and 205).	
		Chadwick's suggestions are here excellent. "If we place Pi-swa well up towards the Soulima valley, and Me-ta-pa nearer the coast to its west, this will satisfy all the details we know about these places" (*MW* 45).
		A good candidate for the administrative centre of the district would be Mirou (F 203) although there are fortifications and a "megaron" of LH IIIB date at Mouriatadha (F 202).
O-wi-to-no	Mouth of the Nedha river? (in vicinity of sites F 240-41).	This is the Headquarters of the most "Northerly" of the "coastguard" sectors (*MME* 108).
Ku-pa-ri-so	Kyparissia? (F 200)	This is presumably a place name. Men from it are found in the "northern" sector of the "coastguard" tablets (*MME* 103-4).
Pe-to-no	The Filiatra-Gargalianoi district (including sites F 43-54).	This is a large district, to judge from the scale of contributions (*MW* 45). It is not in the "coastguard" tablets (*MME* 108). Most of the known sites in the district, and all of the larger ones, are in fact inland. The large site F 48, on the plateau to southeast of Filiatra is well situated to control the region.

"FURTHER PROVINCE" 1. SOUTHERN PAMISOS VALLEY etc.

Name	Suggested Location	Comment
Ti-mi-to-a-ko	The area of the modern Rizomylo, and neighbouring villages, perhaps including sites (F 100-7). The centre would be probably Nichoria (F 100) which was an important site in the LH IIIB period (*MW* 48).	This is the only one of the "Seven" known to be on or near the coast. Men from here are sent to Ne-do-wo (*MW* 47) *i.e.* probably to the river Nedon. It appears to adjoin Za-e-to-ro, which seems to be part of the territory of Ri-jo (the last of the "Nine"). Thus Ti-mi-to-a-ko may be expected to be at one end of the "Further Province". It is indeed first in the list of the "Seven".
Ne-do-wo	The river Nedon and Kalamata (F 132).	The Nedon area may be the southeast boundary of the kingdom (see above).
Re-u-ko-to-ro	Ancient Thouria (F 121).	This is presumed to be the "capital" of the "Further Province". It is not in the list of the "Seven", and is probably a "town" name. Since it was important (*MME* 111), it is likely to have been near a main line of communications. It is presumably *in* one of the "Seven" districts, just as Pu-ro may be in Pa-ki-ja-ne. The site at Ancient Thouria, because of its size and the number of Mycenaean tombs, is the best candidate.
Ra-wa-ra-ta$_2$	On the east side of the Pamisos, from modern Thouria to Ayios Floros (*i.e.* including sites F 121-126).	One of the "Seven". This is placed in the "southeast" sector by Chadwick [*AJA* 77 (1973) 276 and *MW* 46]. It may denote a large district, especially if it included the "capital" (*i.e.* Re-u-ko-to-ro).
Sa-ma-ra	Area of modern Messini, Karteroli, Madena and vicinity (including sites F 115-117).	One of the "Seven". Placed in the "southwest" sector by Chadwick (*AJA loc.cit.*). It presumably adjoined Ti-mi-to-a-ko. There is as yet no good candidate for a major centre, but good chamber tombs have been found at Kasteroli and Madena. The marl and conglomerate hills here are reasonably fertile.
A-sja-ta$_2$	Area of Aristodhemion, Eva, Lambaina, Trikorpho, Manganiako etc. (including sites F 118-120 and 127-129).	One of the "Seven". It is the last name in the "southwest" sector, and should adjoin E-ra-te-re-we of the "northwest" sector (*AJA loc.cit.*). It is of large size and the centre of smiths (*MW* 68). There are also indications of a good wood supply here (*cf. MW* 141).

"FURTHER PROVINCE" 2. NORTHERN PAMISOS VALLEY AND SOULIMA VALLEY

Name	Suggested Location	Comment
E-sa-re-wi-ja (? = e-re-i)	Area of Katsarou, Siamou, Kalyvia, etc., in the eastern part of the Upper Pamisos valley (including sites F 228-30).	One of the "Seven". It is the first name in the "northeast" sector (*AJA loc.cit.*). The largest site known here is Kalyvia (F 230), where LH IIIB chamber tombs have been found.

Name	Suggested Location	Comment
Za-ma-e-wi-ja	Area of Parapoungion, Diavolitsi, Agrilovouno, Mandhra, Kato Melpia etc. (including sites F 231-36).	One of the "Seven". Second name in the "northeast" sector (*AJA loc.cit.*). The largest site here is apparently the furthest from the centre, at Kato Melpia (F 236). The most strategic location for a "capital" of this sector would be at Agrilovouno (F 234).
A-te-re-wi-ja	Meligala and Stenyklaros areas (sites F 224-6) and probably also Konchilion (F 227).	One of the "Seven". First name in the "northwest" sector (*AJA loc.cit.*). It adjoins with A-sja-ta₂ of the "southwest" sector, and has connections with the "Hither Province".
E-ra-te-re-we	The Soulima valley (probably including sites F 208-223).	One of the "Seven". Last name in the "northwest" sector. Has connections with Me-ta-pa of the "Hither Province" (*MV* 48 and see above).

The above notes are intended as a rough estimate only of the probable locations of the districts. It is assumed that the centres of administration for "taxation" purposes would tend to be both large and well situated as regards communications. They would presumably serve as "depots" for the collection of "tribute" from more remote settlements in the inland hill districts, and for the issue of "rations" to them. No attempt has been made here to suggest precise borders between the assumed districts, or to fit the more remote Mycenaean sites into the scheme.

Note: I was not able to read the interesting articles and discussions concerning Pylian Geography in J. Bintliff (Ed.), *Mycenaean Geography* (1977) until after I had written the essay above. I must confess that I am confused by the statistical and computer studies, although the experiments are no doubt valuable for the instruction which they give in methodology. Basically, I believe that the statistical methods employed are too sophisticated for the relatively primitive ancient organisation which is being analysed. I still prefer a more simple approach, one which attempts to fit together *all* the clues, even if on a piecemeal basis and with admitted reliance on a combination of common sense and plain guesswork. So I have decided to leave this essay unaltered, even if its methodology may seem out of fashion.

THE KINGDOM OF PYLOS 2. HOMER THE POET

The tenth chapter of *The Mycenaean World* by John Chadwick is entitled "Homer the Pseudo-historian", and in it a strong case is argued for a total rejection of all "Homeric" geography [similar arguments are presented elsewhere, *e.g. DMG* 415-417 and *Minos* (1973) 55-59]. It is apparent that such an extreme view stems from previous disappointment with the comparative lack of coincidence between the "Homeric" names

and those on the Linear B tablets, especially in the case of the Pylian Kingdom. Although Chadwick here labours the point that Homer was a poet and not an historian, he manages at the same time to chastise him (in retrospect) for faulty political geography. Such treatment appears to imply a lack of sensitivity concerning the complex problems of the oral transmission of the "Homeric" names, especially of those in catalogue form.

In the *Catalogue of the Ships*, and in similar lists of names in the Iliad and the Odyssey, the poet (or poets, according to some pedants) is simply making use of traditional material, while adapting it to his purpose by "story additions" necessary to the plot and by some expansions made for the sake of embellishment. [Attempts made to identify these are discussed in *SMEA* 6 (1968) 39-44.] It is clear that there was a rich stock of such traditional material, and that Homer did not need to invent names of peoples and places. It is also clear that Homer and his audiences shared a profound veneration for their past. And, since the only vehicle for the preservation of their history was poetry, they insisted on recitations of traditional lists which to us appear, despite Homer's embellishments, both lengthy and dull. It is indeed significant that a prayer to *Memory* precedes the recitation [a "tour de force", Beye (1966) 92] of the *Catalogue of the Ships* in the Iliad. The great "creative singer" must here subordinate creativity to memory. Whether or not Homer knew any of the geography at first hand is therefore quite irrelevant (according to many traditions he was blind).

It has been demonstrated that this catalogue as a whole fits Mycenaean Greece too well to be basically a *new* invention by Homer or by poets just before his time (*cf. CSHI* 170), or to be merely the product of "sailor's yarns" (*MW* 186). Such a poetic construction, however, can not be expected to provide a *complete* reflection of Mycenaean Greece, still less an accurate detailed picture. (The exact number of discovered Mycenaean sites is thus immaterial in this context.) Naturally the *numbers* of ships and men, since they are less easy to memorize than names, are more liable to distortion in the process of oral transmission [*CSHI* 161, cf. *SMEA* (1968) p. 40 n. 7]. As for the names, some have presumably dropped out in the process, while all that survive of others appear to be their accompanying epithets. But it would be as ridiculous, for instance, to ask why the Cyclades are "omitted" in the *Catalogue* as to ask why a supposedly Mycenaean Miletus was among the Trojan allies (or to doubt that Argos was "neutral" in the Persian Wars).

With few exceptions (confined to northern Thessaly), the districts into which the *Catalogue* is divided make remarkably good sense geographically, whether or not the particular *political* groupings might be expected. If these groupings in fact mainly reflect the troubled times of the final phase of Mycenaean civilisation (in the LH IIIC period), as has been suggested (*CSHI* 161-4), then, for instance, a division of the Argive plain between the rulers of Mycenae and Argos would be quite intelligible, even if Tiryns (here listed under Argos) had been formerly "the port of Mycenae" (*MW* 187). In a period of general collapse and probably of internal strife, Tiryns and Argos may indeed have been at variance with Mycenae, or strong enough to slip out of her grasp. But many of the actual place names themselves, and especially those of the major centres (*e.g.* Iolkos, Orchomenos, and Pylos), would naturally reflect their importance in the period *before* the collapse. Even some lesser names, *e.g.* Krisa, Dorion, and Eutresis, of this period are recalled (*CSHI* 158. The argument in *Diogenes* 77 p. 10 that the name Dorion is "non-Mycenaean" and "must have been associated with Dorians" seems to be refuted by the occurrence of the forms do-ri-je-we and do-ri-wo in Linear B, cf. *DMG* p. 541). It is quite irrational to expect that a poetic *Catalogue* would be entirely consistent with regard to the periods reflected. Some possible distinction between "past" and "present" is in fact implied by the name Hypothebai ("Sub-Thebes") in the *Catalogue*, which strongly suggests a settlement of squatters at the foot of a destroyed citadel of Thebes. But we should not necessarily expect also a Hypo-Pylos or a Hypo-Sparte, only for the reason that these places were no longer in existence.

To return to Pylian geography, it is of course clear that the "Homeric" picture does not coincide with the hypothetical reconstruction of the "Hither" and "Further" provinces as outlined above. At this point, however, it must be asked whether any such coincidence should ever have been expected [cf. *BSA* 61 (1966) 130]. Although there is no reason to accept the *dramatic* contexts in the *Iliad* at their face value, it is indeed possible that the realm of Nestor in the *Catalogue* and in "Nestor's Tales" (*Iliad* xi. 670-761 and vii. 132-156)

could be a poetic reflection of a loosely controlled and mainly *northern* kingdom of the early years of his reign. The identifiable places concerned, Thryon and Arene, are on or near the Alpheios. Moreover, the actual possibility of such a northern extension of a Messenian Pylos can not in fact be ruled out [*CSHI* 87 n. 50 cf. *BSA* (1966) 128-9]. And the route along the west coast from Pylos to the river Alpheios would be far more easy going for chariots than any route from Pylos to the Pamisos valley. Homer does recall that one of the places, Thryoessa, was "far away on the Alpheios" (*Iliad* xi. 712), which implies some recognition of the distance involved. If Pylos was a naval power, a northward extension would be quite natural. It is indeed conceivable that the realm of Pylos in the tablets represents a *contraction* of the kingdom, when collapse was imminent. The "Seven Cities" (*Iliad* xi. 149-153, 291-5), located near the sea, around the Messenian Gulf [*BSA* 61 (1966) 113-131] might also partly reflect either a similar situation *before* the Pylian expansion into eastern Messenia, or conversely a period of disruption *after* the fall of Pylos.

Of the "Homeric" names, some are clearly of epithet type (specifically Aipy, Antheia, and Aipeia); others (Helos, Arene, Pedasos, and Kyparisseeis) suggest natural features (*cf.* Pylos). All seem to denote specific sites (or "towns") rather than districts. Thus, since the chief names in the "Hither" and "Further" provinces appear to be primarily of districts, there is still less likelihood of a conflict between "Homeric" and Linear B names, even if they are supposed to refer to the same period.

Whether or not these "Homeric" names reflect a period (or periods) different from that of the tablets, there are in fact no cases of direct conflict between *known* locations of names in either category. And, where presumed locations of names in the tablets overlap with *presumed* locations of "Homeric" names, we have no means of deciding whether those in the tablets denote towns or simply districts.

If the possibility of a northern extension at some time of a *Messenian* Pylos is admitted, then Homeric Pylos and Pu-ro may be one and the same. Homeric Kyparisseeis *may* reflect a place in the vicinity of the historic Kyparissia, and Ku-pa-ri-so also seems to be in this region. The place Dorion would fall in the presumed location of the administrative district of E-ra-te-ve-we, *i.e.* the Soulima valley. In the case of the place Pherai, presumed to be at Kalamata, there is no demonstrable clash with Ne-do-wo-ta-de, since this also appears to describe a region or a geographical feature. In all other cases the respective sets of hypotheses concerned are so tentative that there is no possibility of establishing that any contradictions exist.

Furthermore, most of the bureaucratic appellations in the tablets could not be expected to appear in poetry. Many, like the title Lawagetas (*MW* 185), will not scan in hexameter verse. And, as Chadwick rightly insists, bureaucracy and poetry will not mix. So we can not expect, for instance, a poetic record of the details, still less of the numbers, of the contingents on the "coastguard" tablets, or of such matters as the distribution of bronze and bronzesmiths (*MW* 140-1) in the two provinces (*cf. CSHI* 167).

After the holocaust no doubt the descendants of refugees from Kingston will, in the absence of written records, celebrate their point of origin in folk-songs, which will be the only vehicle for the preservation of their history. But the name will probably survive not as "Kingston, of the County of Frontenac, in the Province of Ontario", but either coupled with, or merely in the form of, its current epithet, "The Limestone City". Meanwhile we should indeed continue to remind ourselves that Homer "was a poet not an historian" (*MW* 186, *cf. CSHI* 169). We should accordingly refrain from castigating him for alleged sins which he did not, and could not commit. It would be wise also to remind ourselves constantly of the hypothetical nature of our own reconstructions. We are not here confronted by a "Pseudo-historian", but rather by a pseudo-problem.

THE IONIAN ISLANDS ACARNANIA

WESTERN AETOLIA WESTERN ELIS

MAP G

The sites on this map form various isolated groups, and each group will be discussed separately.

WESTERN ELIS (G 1-6)

This area has never been properly explored. Of the six sites so far located, the three most important are Ancient Pheia (G 1), Chlemoutsi (G 2), and Ancient Teichos Dymaion (G 6), all situated on or near the coast. The other three sites, all on the fringes of the main Elean plain, together with D 49 and D 50, provide an indication of how much more is to be expected in Elis.

G 1 AYIOS ANDREAS: PONTIKOKASTRO (ANCIENT PHEIA) # (Plate 22c) (*MME* No. 304)
N EH II MH LHI/II-IIIB LH IIIC or SMyc PG G A C H

AE (1957) 31; *Messenia I* 224; Desborough (1964) 91.

Ayios Andreas is a small harbour village about a kilometre north of the modern port of Katakolon. Above the harbour is the imposing acropolis of Pontikokastro (about 40 m. high) fortified in mediaeval times, on the northern end of the long ridge which forms the spine of the Katakolon peninsula. The upper part of the acropolis, within the mediaeval fortifications, measures about 115 m. north to south by 55 m. The north slope is precipitous, the east slope steep, and the west slope fairly steep and overgrown. On the south there is a more gentle slope leading to a saddle (Ill. 1 on *Messenia I* p. 224). Mycenaean sherds and other prehistoric pottery were found widely scattered on the top and slopes, over an area about 215 m. north to south by 175 m. They included several LH IIIA-B fine ware pieces with lustrous paint. A vase reported to have come from a cist is either late LH IIIC or SMyc (Desborough *loc.cit.*).

G 2 NEOCHORI: CHLEMOUTSI CASTLE (KASTRO) *
N? MH LH I/II? LH III(A-B) G C

BCH 85 (1961) 123, 88 (1964) 9; *CSHI* 97 and Pl. 9a.

The mediaeval castle of Chlemoutsi occupies the summit of an isolated rounded hill to northeast of Neochori. The site dominates not only the coast but also much of the west part of the plain of Elis. Trial excavations by Servais (*BCH loc.cit.*) have revealed considerable MH deposits, including late MH types which may develop with early Mycenaean. There was also a small amount of LH III pottery, and a Mycenaean tomb was found nearby. The site has been tentatively identified as Ancient Hyrmine (*CSHI* 97).

G 3 ANCIENT ELIS *
EH II MH LH (III) SMyc G A C H

PAE (1961) 180, (1963) 138; *AA* (1962) 215, 263, (1971) 392, 411; Desborough (1972) 74.

Some LH III and Geometric pottery has been reported from the acropolis, and in the area of the theatre 14 pit-graves, probably survivors from a much larger cemetery, have been excavated. The pit-graves have been assigned to the SMyc phase (Desborough *loc.cit.*). Among the contents were two fine swords.

G 4 KAPELETO: STENOULI *
LH IIIA2

AD 21 (1966) B 172.

Four Mycenaean chamber tombs were disturbed by a bulldozer in the slope of a hillock about 500 m. southeast of Kapeleto. A LH IIIA2 jug was recovered.

G 5 KANGADHI: SOTIROULA and MYLOS *
LH IIIA2-C

AR (1955) 17; *BCH* 79 (1955) 252; *AD* 20 (1965) B 223.

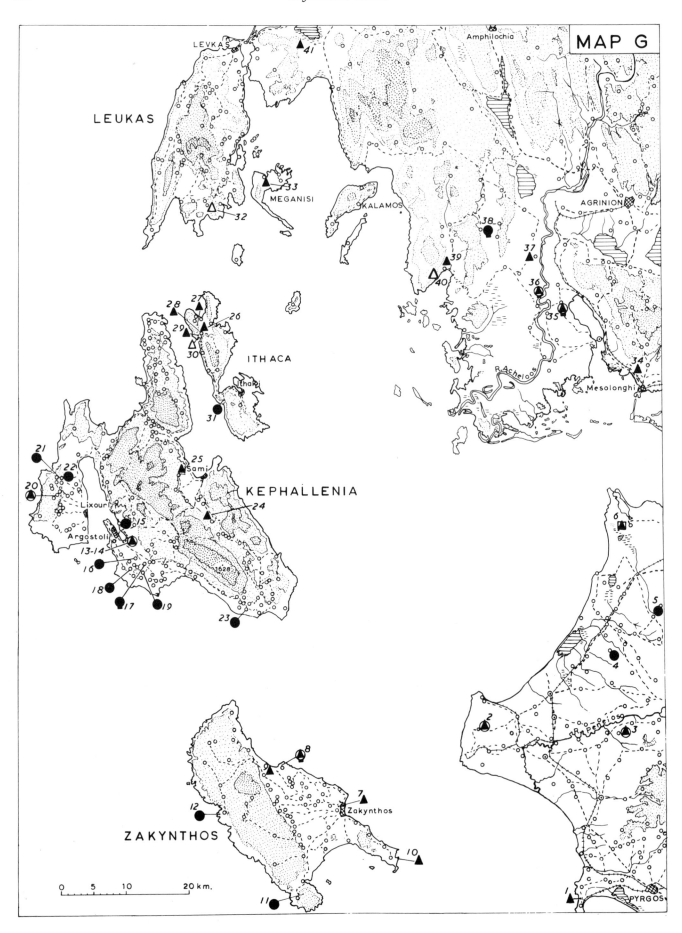

MAP G

LEUKAS

LEVKAS
41

MEGANISI
33
32

Amphilochia

SKALAMOS

AGRINION

38

39
40
37
36
35
R.Achelöos
Mesolonghi
34

28 27
29 26
30
ITHACA
Ithaki
31

25
Sami
KEPHALLENIA
24

21
22
20
Lixouri
Argostoli
15
13-14
16
18
17   19
23
1628

6

5

4

2
R.Peneios
3

ZAKYNTHOS

8
9
7
Zakynthos
12
10
11

1
PYRGOS

0   5   10   20 km.

About 600 m. to north of Kangadhi, during construction of the road to Riolo, chamber tombs were accidently discovered, three at Sotiroula, and two at Mylos. One tomb, divided by stone walls into compartments, contained some pottery which may be contemporary with Sub-Mycenaean.

G 6 ARAXOS: TEICHOS DYMAION * # (Fig. 15)

N EH I-III MH LH IIIB-C G A C H

PAE (1962) 127, (1963) 93, (1964) 60, (1965) 121; *Ergon* (1966) 159; *BCH* 91 (1967) 666; *Archaeology* 15 (1962) 103; *OpAth* 5 (1964) 102, 110; *CHSI* 98.

This fortified Mycenaean acropolis is strategically placed on the Araxos promontory on the northwest tip of the Peloponnese. It was probably a port in Mycenaean times, since the sea would then have come up to the level of the present marshes on the southwest flank. LH III buildings have been uncovered, and a fortification enclosing an area about 190 m. northwest to southeast by 50 m. The circuit walls, ranging in thickness from 4.20 m. to 5.20 m., are extremely well preserved, and there is a main entrance on the southeast, approached by a stairway and flanked by a tower. The fortifications were probably built in the LH IIIB period. The site appears to have been destroyed by fire in the same period, but was occupied again in LH IIIC, and flourished until a second destruction towards the end of this period.

THE IONIAN ISLANDS (G 7-33)

Miss Benton made a spectacular reconnaissance of these islands [*BSA* 32 (1931-2) 213-46], which was followed by extensive excavations by the British School, primarily in Ithaca. The late Marinatos made a valuable contribution on his native island of Kephallenia. Much more remains to be discovered, but the results of excavation and survey already demonstrate the importance of these islands, especially in the LH IIIC period. Miss P.I. Agallopoulou and P.G. Kalligas have reported and discussed the recent Mycenaean finds on Zakynthos and Kephallenia respectively.

ZAKYNTHOS

Zakynthos is by far the most fertile of the Ionian Islands, and it deserves much more search, particularly in the eastern foothills of the main mountain range. Excavations of limited scope were carried out by the British School, under Miss S. Benton, before World War II. Unfortunately, the finds from these were destroyed in the 1953 earthquake, which wrecked the Zakynthos museum. A good summary of recent Mycenaean finds on Zakynthos is given by Miss P.I. Agallopoulou, in *AD* 28 (1973) A 198-214.

G 7 ZAKYNTHOS: KASTRO # (Plate 25a)

LH (III?) A C

BSA 32 (1931-2) 217.

The mediaeval castle of Zakynthos, at the north end of the town, dominates the port, and also overlooks a fine stretch of fertile low hill country to the north and west. It is founded on a hill, steep on all sides, composed of a compact white earth resembling rock. The castle walls enclose an area roughly triangular, with sides about 400 m., 350 m., and 200 m. long respectively. Sherds from the Kastro in the BSA collection include one definitely Mycenaean, with remains of two painted bands on the exterior, and some coarse ware which appears to be Bronze Age. Similar coarse ware was observed on the surface in 1975.

G 8 ALIKANAS: AKROTERION *

LH II-IIIB

BSA 32 (1931-2) 218; *Annual Report of the British School at Athens* (1933-4) 5; *JHS* 54 (1934) 192; *AA* (1934) 161.

The small village of Alikanas lies on the southeast flank of the steep hill of Akroterion, which forms the promontory on the east side of the bay of Alikes. On the hill was a Mycenaean settlement of moderate size. Remains of a house with LH III pottery were found near the top, and on the southeast slope, about 200 m. to east of the house, and about halfway up the hill from Alikanas, was a small tholos tomb. It had apparently been in the use from the LH II to the LH IIIB periods. The most notable of its contents were a necklace of amber (and one faience) beads, and a bronze "violin-bow" fibula, probably LH IIIB. The finds were ruined in the 1953 earthquake.

G 9 KATASTARI: ELEOS

LH III(B?)

BSA 32 (1931-2) 218.

Mycenaean pottery, of fine quality, probably of the LH IIIB period, was found in a well on the property of Eleos, in low ground near the road from Katastari to the sea.

G 10 VASILIKO: KALOGEROS *

LH I-III(A-B) G A

BSA 32 (1931-2) 213; *Annual Report of the British School at Athens* (1933-4) 5; *JHS* 54 (1934) 192; *AA* (1934) 161; Lord William Taylour, *Mycenaean Pottery in Italy and Adjacent Areas* (1958) 21, 186; *AAA* 5 (1972) 65.

The Kalogeros promontory is about a kilometre east of Vasiliko, and immediately east of the taverna at Porto Roma. It is very eroded, and only about 150 m. east to west by 50 m. of top surface remains. Parts of two houses were excavated. The pottery (destroyed by the 1953 earthquake) ranged from LH I (*cf.* Lord

William Taylour *loc.cit.*) to LH III, of which a considerable quantity was found. Not far to south of the site, on the uninhabited Triodi beach on the headland of Yerakas at the farthest southeast tip of Zakynthos, is a ruined structure thought to be the remains of a Mycenaean tholos tomb (*AAA loc.cit.*). If this is so, it would presumably have been connected with the Kalogeros site, since the Yerakas promontory seems too exposed for a settlement.

G 11 KERI: KLAPSIAS *
LH II

AD 21 (1966) B 325, 28 (1973) A Pls. 113-4; *AAA* 5 (1972) 65.

In the course of widening a track, a small built tomb was revealed in the south slope of Klapsias hill, about 1.5 km. east of Keri. It measured 1.50 m. by 0.80 m., and had a crude form of "relieving triangle" over the entrance, and apparently two lintel stones. The only contents reported are two skeletons and two LH II vases.

G 12 KAMBI: VIGLA *
LH IIIA1? LH IIIA2-B LH IIIC?

AAA 5 (1972) 63; *AD* 28 (1973) A 198.

The hill of Vigla rises sheer above the sea about 500 m. west of Kambi. On the east flank of the hill a large cemetery of rectangular slab-covered rock-cut tombs was found. Fourteen tombs were investigated, most of which had been robbed. The evidence from the unrobbed tombs suggests that all had contained several burials each. Most of the pottery was LH IIIA2-B, but alabastra from Tombs 12 and 14 are probably LH IIIA1, and two stirrup-jars from the area might be LH IIIC. Sherds of handmade pottery were found in the fill of some of the tombs.

KEPHALLENIA

Mycenaean sites have been found in the three most fertile areas of Kephallenia, near the principal towns of Argostoli, Lixouri, and Sami. The largest concentration is in the low hill country south of Argostoli, in and around the plain of Kranaia. P.G. Kalligas has recently given a good commentary on this group (G 13-G 19) and other prehistoric sites in Kephallenia, in *AAA* 10 (1977) 116-125. He is probably correct in his view that the main Mycenaean enclave in Kephallenia was the area of Ancient Krane. But neither the north nor the southeast parts of the island have been properly explored.

G 13 ARGOSTOLI: PALAIOKASTRO (ANCIENT KRANE) *
EH or MH? LH III(A-B) C H

P. Kavvadias, *Proistorike Arkhaiologia* (1909) 372; *Comptes Rendus* (1911) 7; *AD* 5 (1919) 83, 24 (1969) B 270; *BSA* 32 (1932-3) 223, *AAA* 10 (1977) 116.

Ancient Krane is about 3 km. east-southeast of Argostoli, at the north end of the plain of Kranaia, and above the southeast end of the Koutavos lagoon. The extensive walled town occupied a high acropolis consisting of three hilltops and the saddles between them. Prehistoric pottery and other finds are reported from two locations on the higher southeast hilltop of Paizoules (which measures about 300 m. northwest to southeast by 200 m.). Monochrome handmade Bronze Age wares predominate, although some of Mycenaean types were observed and a Mycenaean kylix stem was found in the wall of "Building A" (*BSA loc.cit.*). A ruined tholos tomb was also reported on the acropolis slope; and Kalligas (*AAA loc.cit.*) reports that an amygdaloid sealstone, now in the National Museum at Athens, came from the acropolis.

G 14 ARGOSTOLI: DIAKATA and STAROCHORAFA *
LH IIIC

PAE (1912) 117; *AD* 1 (1915) *Parartema* 59, 5 (1919) 92; *AE* (1932) 14, 42 n. 2; *AAA* 10 (1977) 122.

A Mycenaean cemetery was discovered on the south slopes of a ridge about 1200 m. east-southeast of the acropolis of Krane. A large rectangular chamber tomb of the "cave dormitory" type and a small roughly circular tomb were excavated. The pits in them contained many burials, and weapons and fine jewellery in addition to the pottery. Finds included three long pins and a fibula, goods which suggest that the cemetery continued in use until late in the LH IIIC period.

To the south of the tombs, on the lower part of the slope, in a locality named Starochorafa, three walls of a Mycenaean house were uncovered [*AE* (1932) *loc.cit.*]. There was little depth of earth, since the slope is now steep; and only a few Mycenaean sherds were found, together with coarse ware also presumably Mycenaean.

The Diakata tombs, so close to the acropolis of Krane, give further support to the hypothesis that Krane was a major Mycenaean site. The Mycenaean building at Starochorafa is not in itself impressive, but may have been part of a "satellite" settlement, subordinate to that at Krane.

G 15 PROKAPATA: GEPHYRI *
LH IIIB

AD 5 (1919) 114; *BSA* 32 (1931-2) 222.

A small chamber tomb was excavated at Gephyri, described as lying below the main road from Prokapata to Razata. The three fine Mycenaean vases found are assigned by Wardle to the LH IIIB1 period.

G 16-19

This group of important Mycenaean cemeteries,

in low hill country on the south side of the plain of Kranaia, strongly suggests the presence of one or more major Mycenaean centres here, although no traces of Mycenaean habitation sites have yet been found. Fine olive orchards and vineyards are abundant here, among the many prosperous modern settlements.

G 16 KOKKOLATA: KANGELISSES *
MH LH IIIA? LH IIIB(-C?)

Kavvadias 1909, 371; *Comptes Rendus* (1911) 7; *PAE* (1912) 247; *AAA* 10 (1977) 116.

Kangelisses is a small rocky plateau, about 300 m. to southwest of Kokkolata, on the south side of a stream bed, and near the track to Menegata. MH cist tombs were succeeded by two small Mycenaean circular built tombs. Several burial deposits were found, apparently in irregular pits. The pottery from these certainly includes LH IIIB, and may include some LH IIIA and LH IIIC. Jewellery, including several seal-stones, and a few bronze objects were also found.

G 17 MAZARAKATA *
LH IIIA2-C

RA (1900) 128; Kavvadias 1909 , 355, *Comptes Rendus* (1909) 382; *PAE* (1912) 246, (1951) 184; *AAA* 7 (1974) 186, 10 (1977) 122.

A large Mycenaean chamber tomb cemetery occupies the northwest slopes of a low ridge about 500 m. southeast of the small village of Mazarakata. A ruined tholos tomb and sixteen chamber tombs, including eight of the "cave dormitory" type, were excavated here. The pottery has a wide range, in some tombs extending late into LH IIIC. Other finds include gold and glass jewellery, fibulae, at least one long pin, and other bronze objects.

G 18 LAKKITHRA *
LH IIIB-C   C or H

AE (1932) 17; *AAA* 10 (1977) 122.

The Mycenaean cemetery is immediately below the south edge of the long ridge occupied by the village of Lakkithra, at the southwest end, and near the church of Ayios Nikolaos. Four chamber tombs were excavated here; all but the smallest contained burials in pits, often accompanied by gold jewellery and bronze weapons and vessels. A slab which may have been a grave *stele* was found in the smallest tomb. The large tombs all seem to have continued in use until late in the LH IIIC period.

G 19 METAXATA: TA CHALIKERA *
LH IIIB-C   PG   G   A   C   H

AE (1933) 73; *AD* 16 (1960) A 41; *AR* (1960-61) 16; *AA* (1962) 289; *AAA* 7 (1974) 187, 10 (1977) 122.

In the northwest and south slopes of the low hill called Ta Chalikera, about 300 m. to southeast of Metaxata, six chamber tombs have been excavated, four of which are of "cave dormitory" type and two imitate tholoi. The burials, mainly in pits, were accompanied by pottery and other goods, including spearheads and fibulae. Two tombs continued in use until late in the LH IIIC period, and most showed signs of later disturbance. There are indications of ancient settlement in the vicinity, *i.e.* on the hill of Ta Chalikera itself and around it, although no Mycenaean habitation site here is yet confirmed.

G 20-22

The three Mycenaean sites found in the Lixouri peninsula are on the edges of the fertile lowlands in the east part of the peninsula. It is extremely likely that several more Mycenaean settlements existed in the Lixouri area.

G 20 PARISATA *
LH III(A2-B)

PAE (1951) 186.

The site is about 600 m. north-northeast of Parisata, on the saddle where the road to Monopolata begins to wind down from a steep north-south ridge eastward towards the main road from Lixouri to Kontogenada. On the south side of the road is a very fine chamber tomb, imitating a tholos. Its contents had been disturbed, but included pottery, fragments of one or more stone larnakes, and a gold cap which may be from a rivet. On the north side of the road there are traces of a Mycenaean settlement, marked by LH III(B?) sherds, on a small and rather conical hill, about 150 m. north to south by 90 m. on the top, terraced, and with steep east and west sides. The site overlooks both the lower country to the east and the upland valley on the west in which Parisata is situated.

G 21 KONTOGENDA *
LH III(A-B)?   LH IIIC

AE (1933) 70, 77; *PAE* (1951) 186.

Kontogenada lies on the north edge of the valley of Chalikias. At the south foot of the village, at the start of the valley, three chamber tombs imitating tholoi and a small (and probably half-finished) tomb of the same type were excavated. They were close together, and immediately north of "Stous Minous", where there is a deserted village on a low knoll. All but the first of the tombs (Tomb A) had been completely robbed. Tomb A contained some LH IIIC pottery, and the remains of one or more stone larnakes in a pit. These suggest a link with the Parisata tomb (G 20), and accordingly also a date prior to LH IIIC for the construction of the tombs. The area is now ruined by quarrying, but two empty oval rock-cut pit graves, similar to those in the Lakkithra tombs (G 18), were noted in 1975 in the quarry area.

G 22   KONTOGENADA: OIKOPEDA   *
LH II-III(B?)   C or H

AD 6 (1920-1) *Parartema* 175; *AE* (1932) 10; *AAA* 10 (1977) 118.

Oikopeda is an upland plateau to east-northeast of Kontogenada. At the west end of this plateau, about 1 km. from Kontogenada, excavation revealed a large quantity of pottery and other goods, including jewellery and bronze knives. Some of the pottery may be assigned to LH II on the basis of shape, and may thus be the earliest Mycenaean pottery found in Kephallenia. Good LH III shapes and local types were also represented. The curving wall in whose vicinity the Mycenaean finds were discovered may have been a rebuilding of a prehistoric wall, perhaps the perimeter wall of a tumulus (*AAA loc.cit.*). But the Mycenaean finds can not be clearly associated with any structure; and a straight wall found nearby is definitely of classical or later date.

G 23   MAVRATA: KOTRONIA   *
LH IIIC

A Mycenaean chamber tomb was discovered in 1936 at Kotronia near Mavrata. The finds remain unpublished, but many LH IIIC vases found in the tomb are displayed in the Argostoli Museum. The discovery is of special interest, since it demonstrates Mycenaean habitation in the southeast part of Kephallenia.

G 24   KOULOURATA: PALATI
LH III(A-B)   H?

BSA 32 (1931-2) 225.

Mycenaean kylix stems were found by Miss S. Benton on the west side of a hill below a small Hellenic fort along the main route from the plain of Sami to the southeast part of Kephallenia. They provide a further indication of the Mycenaean habitation which may be expected in this region.

G 25   VLACHATA: AYIOI THEODHOROI   *
LH III(A-B)

AE (1964) 23.

The inland village of Vlachata has recently been abandoned, and replaced by the coastal settlement of Karavomilos or "Nea Vlachata". About a kilometre to southeast of Karavomilos, and about 300 m. to southwest of the junction of the roads to Sami from Karavomilos and Roulata, is the northern end of a long limestone ridge which bounds the west side of the plain of Sami. At Ayioi Theodhoroi, on the southern summit of the ridge, about 1.5 km. south of Karavomilos, part of a Mycenaean house was excavated.

ITHACA

There is relatively little cultivable land on this mountainous island, although there are some good upland pastures. The most fertile area is the vicinity of Stavros in the north, where most of the Mycenaean sites have been found (G 26-30). There has been much discussion as to which of the excavated sites was the main Mycenaean centre here. The best commentary on Ithaca (which deals also with the Homeric question) is that of Wace and Stubbings [*CH* 398-407, with illustrations, *cf.* Schoder (1974) 100-103].

G 26   STAVROS: PELIKATA   *
EH II-III   MH   LH III(A2-B)   "PG"?   A?

BSA 35 (1934-5) 1, 44 (1949) 307, 47 (1952) 279.

The low and rounded hill of Pelikata, about 600 m. north of Stavros, has the best position of all the Mycenaean sites in the northern group. It lies on the central height controlling the three northern bays of Ithaca. The site has been severely eroded, and consequently no good structural remains were found in the excavations. There are many traces of a circuit wall of large blocks, but this can not be securely dated. The traces of earlier occupation, especially in the EH II period, were far more numerous than the Mycenaean, which occurred only near the top, where some foundations of a Mycenaean house were traced. Some of the pottery classed as LH III may in fact be Dark Age, and the full extent and the nature of the Mycenaean occupation of the site can not be determined.

G 27   STAVROS: AYIOS ATHANASIOS   *
LH III(A-B)   H

BSA 35 (1934-5) 33.

About 1.5 km. north-northwest of Stavros an ancient spring chamber of the Hellenistic period was investigated, on a terraced slope below the hill of Ayios Athanasios. A few kylix fragments and other LH sherds were found in the spring chamber and the vicinity. On the hill itself later remains may have removed or obscured traces of Mycenaean occupation. The indications suggest only a small Mycenaean settlement here.

G 28   STAVROS VILLAGE   *
EH?   MH?   LH III(A-B)   C

BSA 35 (1934-5) 33, 40-41 (1939-45) 2, 47 (1952) 227, 236.

In Stavros village itself, traces of a Bronze Age settlement were found below a classical cemetery. Some rather poor Mycenaean pottery was found here, and a few Mycenaean sherds also near the Asprosykia fountain on the west side of the village.

G 29   STAVROS: TRIS LANGADHAS   *
MH   LH IIIA1-B

BSA 68 (1973) 1.

The rather poorly preserved remains of some Mycenaean buildings were found on various terraces of a steep hillside above Polis Bay, about a kilometre to southwest of Stavros. Mycenaean pottery, also poorly preserved, was relatively abundant, and generally of better quality than at most sites on Ithaca. It is, however, uncertain whether the quantity and quality of the Mycenaean pottery here should be taken as an indication that this site was more important than Pelikata (G 26), where erosion has removed a proportionately larger amount of the evidence.

G 30   STAVROS: POLIS CAVE   *
EH   MH   LH I/II   LH IIIA(2)-C   "PG"   G   A   C   H

BSA 35 (1934-5) 45, 39 (1938-9) 1, 44 (1949) 307; Desborough (1964) 108; Schoder (1974) 100.

Excavations at this famous cave on the west shore of Polis Bay produced much prehistoric and later material. Most of the Mycenaean pottery belongs to the LH IIIC period, and is of local type. The cave was certainly used as a cult centre in the Geometric period; and the sanctity of the site may have originated in the LH IIIC period or earlier, to judge by the presence in a later context of small spears of LH IIIB-C type, and reports that other bronzes of Mycenaean type were found here [*BSA* 35 (1934-5) 71]. But there may not have been complete continuity here from the Mycenaean to the Geometric periods.

G 31   AETOS   *
LH III(A-B)?   LH IIIC?   PG   G   A

BSA 33 (1932-3) 22, 48 (1953) 255, 267; Desborough (1964) 109, (1972) 243.

A site of unusual type was found on the saddle between the Gulf of Molo and Pisaetos Bay. Groups of stones associated with deposits of greasy black earth were originally thought to be the remains of burial cairns, but they are now interpreted as remains of hearths or industrial installations. Most of the finds were of pottery, and a complete Dark Age range seems to be represented. Some fragments may be Mycenaean, especially sherds from stirrup-jars, and a figurine of LH type was found.

LEUKAS

No actual Mycenaean settlement is yet known on this island, despite the investigations by Dorpfeld [*Alt-Ithaka* (1927)], and the clues provided by the finds from the Choirospilia cave (G 32) and on the nearby island of Meganisi (G 33). Parts of Leukas are extremely fertile, and it is very likely that further search here would be well rewarded.

G 32   LEUKAS CHOIROSPILIA
N   EH III?   MH   LH IIIA2-B   C

W. Dörpfeld, *Alt-Ithaka* (1927) 266, 330; *BSA* 31 (1931-2) 230.

Mycenaean sherds of good quality were found in this cave in the south of Leukas.

G 33   MEGANISI: SPARTOCHORI
N   BA   LH III(A-B)

BSA 32 (1931-2) 230.

Meganisi is a comparatively barren island, and lacking a good water supply. Yet the fields to south of the main settlement at Spartochori were strewn with Bronze Age sherds, including several Mycenaean.

G 34-41

The remaining sites on Map G are too few to be an adequate indication of the true distribution of Mycenaean settlements in western Aetolia and in Acarnania, where there are large tracts of fertile country. The site at Ayios Ilias (G 35) is by far the most important discovered in Aetolia, and may have been a local capital. The Cyclopean walls of Kekropoula (G 41) and its strategic position suggest both that this Acarnanian site was of major importance, and also that it was probably one among many other Mycenaean settlements here. Acarnania, in particular, has not been properly searched.

G 34   MESOLONGHI: GYPHTOKASTRO ("OLD PLEURON")   *
EH?   LH III(A2-B)   "PG"   G   A?   C   H

BSA 32 (1931-2) 239; *AD* 22 (1967) B 300, 26 (1971) B 236.

Gyphtokastro is a low hill, about 300 m. in diameter, in the plain, a short distance to east of the main road at a point about 2 km. north of Mesoionghi. It is strewn with rocks and boulders, and amongst these are plentiful ancient potsherds, tiles, and wall foundations. Remains of ancient walls noted by Miss Benton on the north side are of "Cyclopean" appearance. Their thickness (over two metres) indicates a circuit wall, and part of this can also be traced on the southwest flank, where there are the characteristic small stones used in the interstices. Obsidian flakes and Bronze Age coarse ware sherds were noted on the top surface of the hill, together with some others of finer fabric apparently Mycenaean. Recently some Mycenaean sherds and cists of Protogeometric to Geometric date have been found on the north and northwest sides. A cist grave and five pithos burials noted earlier may also be of the Protogeometric or Geometric periods. The pithoi were found laid on their sides. Most of their contents had been removed, but human bones were observed beside them and a bronze ring (interior diameter 0.20 m.).

G 35   AYIOS ILIAS (ANCIENT ITHORÍA?)   *
(Plate 25 b)
N   MH   LH IIB-IIIC   C   H

PAE (1963) 203; *AD* 19 (1964) B 295; *CSHI* 107.

The village of Ayios Ilias is towards the north end of the long and high ridge which lies between the Acheloos river and the head of the Aetolian Gulf. To south of the village rises the thin acropolis peak, presumed to be the centre of Ancient Ithoria (by Woodhouse, *cf. CHSI loc.cit.*). On the saddle just below the south flank of the acropolis a habitation site has been identified (by K. Wardle), with evidence of Middle Helladic, Mycenaean, and Hellenistic occupation.

Neolithic material has been found in the Kokkini Spilia cave lower down to the southwest. Important Mycenaean tombs were found on the lower slopes of the ridge. A chamber tomb in the village was only partly excavated, but produced a scarab of Amenophis III, much LH IIB-IIIA pottery and one or two fragments possibly LH IIIC. One tholos tomb was found at Seremeti, about 300 m. south of the acropolis, and three others at Marathia, between 300 m. and 500 m. to southwest of it. All were made with fairly regular coursed blocks and all had a dromos roofed with slabs but lacked a stomion. The Seremeti tomb (diameter 5.27 m.) contained much pottery and jewellery, and had apparently been used continuously from the LH IIB to LH IIIC periods. The Marathia tombs (whose diameters were 4.14 m., 4.17 m., and 3.1 m. respectively) had all been robbed, but still contained some LH III pottery. Complete LH IIIC vases were found with several burials in the dromos of Tomb 2. Although the extent of the Mycenaean settlement here has not yet been determined, the rich finds from the tombs demonstrate that this was an important Mycenaean centre over a considerable period of time.

G 36 PALAIOMANINA: MILA *
LH (III?)

AD 22 (1967) B 322; *AR* (1968-9) 21.

A large tholos tomb (diameter 10.7 m.) was excavated at Mila, on the west bank of the river Acheloos, and between the villages of Palaiomanina and Pentalofos. Its construction is similar to that of the tholos tombs near Ayios Ilias (G 35), but no finds are reported.

G 37 PALAIOMANINA: ANCIENT SAURIA
EH MH LH "PG" G

AD 22 (1967) B 322.

At the site of Ancient Sauria near Palaiomanina Bronze Age and other sherds, including Mycenaean, and Protogeometric pithoi were reported.

G 38 CHRYSOVITSA: ANCIENT KORONTA *
LH III(A) A C H

PAE (1908) 100; *BSA* 32 (1931-2) 240.

The site of Ancient Koronta lies between the villages of Chrysovitsa and Prodromos, on a rocky wooded hill. Two small Mycenaean tholos tombs were excavated here. They contained LH III sherds, probably LH IIIA, several bronze knives, and beads.

G 39 ASTAKOS: GRABES * # (Plate 25c)
EH II MH LH IIIA2-C "PG"? C

BSA 32 (1931-2) 243, 33 (1932-3) 219.

The hill of Grabes is about a kilometre northeast of Astakos, high above the west side of the road. On the top surface of the hill (about 160 m. north to south by 100 m.) many EH and LH III sherds were found, and in the fill of the cave on the east flank EH, MH, and LH III material was excavated, including LH IIIC. This Mycenaean settlement presumably commanded a route to the interior of Acarnania from the harbour at Astakos, which would also have provided a good connection with the Ionian Islands.

G 40 ASTAKOS: AYIOS NIKOLAOS *
M LH III(A-B) H

BSA 52 (1947) 156, 173.

In the cave of Ayios Nikolaos, near the shore about 2 km. southwest of Astakos, a single Mycenaean sherd was found with Neolithic material.

G 41 PALAIROS: KEKROPOULA
LH III(A-B) G A C H

LAAA 4 (1912) 133; *AD* 2 (1916) *Parartema* 49; *BSA* 32 (1931-2) 238.

This high acropolis dominates a fertile plain to south and also the route north to the Gulf of Arta. Mycenaean sherds were found in association with Cyclopean walls near the southwest gate of the extensive fortress of the Classical and Hellenistic periods. Finds ranging from the Geometric to Hellenistic periods have recently been reported from the vicinity of Palairos [*AD* 20 (1965) B 344].

APPENDIX TO MAP G

Sites in Elis where Mycenaean habitation is possible, but not yet verified include Ayios Ioannis: Sodhiotissa (*Messenia I* 225), Skaphidhia: Anemomylo (*Messenia I* 225), and Kyllini: Glarentza [*BCH* 85 (1961) 130, especially 160]. Two other sites in Kephallenia, investigated by Miss Benton may also have been Mycenaean, *i.e.* Korneli [*BSA* 32 (1931-2) 220] and Sami: Roupaki [*BSA* 32 (1931-2) 225]. Mycenaean sherds were also claimed at the Ayios Sotiros cave on Leukas, but are not certified [W. Dörpfeld *Alt-Ithaka* (1927) 319, *cf. AM* 59 (1934) 182].

THESSALY   EURYTANIA
THE SPERCHEIOS VALLEY

MAPS H AND J

Most of the Mycenaean settlements known in Thessaly are concentrated in the eastern parts (Map H); and it is likely that Mycenaean civilisation in Thessaly did initially spread inland from the east, principally from the Volos area. Indeed, Ancient Iolkos (H 1) with its palace may have been the most important Mycenaean site in all Thessaly, especially if the two tholos tombs at nearby Dimini (H 3) are connected with it. The cluster of small tholos tombs near Pteleon (H 11-12) may indicate another important centre; but in Thessaly the Mycenaean tholos tombs may not by themselves be a reliable indication of importance, since they may be merely a local alternative for chamber tombs, of which only one group is so far known in Thessaly (H 15). In any case, apart from the tholos tombs in the Volos and Pteleon areas, the only other important Mycenaean tholoi in Thessaly appear to be those at Marmariani (H 27) and Georgikon (J 8). Other important Mycenaean centres are known at the site of Ancient Pherai (H 14) and at Petra (H 16). If the "Cyclopean" circuit walls of Petra are in fact Mycenaean, they would indicate the largest fortified Mycenaean site so far known. Two other sites in Thessaly may have had Mycenaean fortifications, namely Ktouri (H 47) and Pyrgos Kieriou (J 5); and there are some other sites of significant size, such as Gremnos (H 23), Chasambali (H 26), Bounarbashi (H 31), Phalanna (H 35) and Argyropouli (H 38).

In general, the major concentrations of Mycenaean habitation have been found in the Volos, Larisa, and Pharsala areas, and Mycenaean sites are sparse in western and northern Thessaly. No certifiably Mycenaean material has yet been found in the western part of the Spercheios Valley, for instance, although Middle Bronze Age wares have been found at Ayios Demetrios near Karpenision [*AAA* 2 (1969) 358, 4 (1971) 196], and occupation here may have extended into the Mycenaean period.

H 1-4

All the Mycenaean sites found in the Volos area are in or around the small but fertile Volos plain. In view of the even greater fertility of parts of the west and southwest slopes of Mt. Pelion to the east, it is surprising that no Mycenaean settlements have yet been discovered on these, especially since Protogeometric and later tombs have been found there.

H 1 VOLOS: KASTRO (ANCIENT IOLKOS) *
EB I-III MH LH I-IIIC PG G A C H

PAE (1900) 72, (1901) 42, (1956) 118, (1957) 54, (1960) 49, (1961) 45; C. Tsountas, *Hai Proistorikai Akropoleis Dimeniou Kai Sesklou* (1908) 15, 21; *BCH* 45 (1921) 530; *JHS* 49 (1929) 95; *AE* (1906) 211; *AAA* 3 (1970) 198.

The site is of "high mound" type, measuring about 400 m. by 270 m., towards the west end of modern Volos. It seems to have been continuously occupied throughout the Bronze Age, at least until some time within the LH IIIC period. The Mycenaean strata have been partly removed by later terracing, but remains have been found of two successive large Mycenaean buildings, assumed to be palaces. The earlier building, attributed to the LH IIIA period, had stucco and slab floors. The later building, attributed to the LH IIIB period, also had stucco floors and a timber frame; and fresco fragments and two large groups of plain kylikes were associated with it. This building is said to have been burnt in the early part of the LH IIIC period, but no conclusive evidence for this date has been published. There are, however, certainly LH IIIC strata on the site, and these show close links with the earlier LH IIIC phases at Lefkandi (B 67) [*cf. BSA* 66 (1971) 348]. It is not clear whether or not occupation was continuous from the LH IIIC to the Protogeometric periods.

Cist graves have been found both on the Kastro site and at Nea Ionia to the northwest. Those at Nea Ionia are definitely LH IIB-IIIA1, and some of them contained fine bronze weapons. The Mycenaean tholos tomb at Kapakli to the north is large (about 10 m. in diameter), but not especially well built. It contained at least twenty burials and much jewellery. The

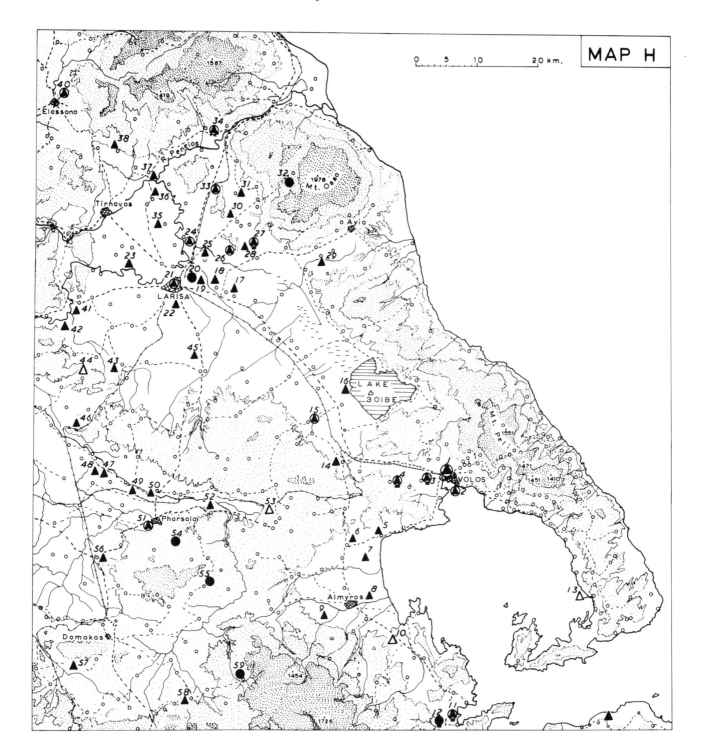

few published vases are LH IIB-IIIA1, but stirrup-jar fragments are also referred to in the report, and some of these might be of later date.

H 2 VOLOS: PEFKAKIA (ANCIENT NELEIA?) *
N EB I-II MH LH I-IIIB PG A C H

AM 14 (1889) 262; *PAE* (1908) 212, (1912) 173, (1916) 31, (1957) 55; *AD* 23 (1968) B 263, 24 (1969) B 221; *BCH* 95 (1971) 711, *AR* (1968-9) 20, (1970-71) 16, F. Stählin *et al.*, *Pagasai und Demetrias* (1934) 162; N.M. Verdelis, *Ho Protogeometrikos Rhythmos tes Thessalias* (1958) 52; V.R. D'A. Desborough, *Protogeometric Pottery* (1952) 133, 153.

The low promontory of Pefkakia forms the southwest arm of the inner bay of Volos, and lies at the northwest end of the later site of the historic Demetrias. There is a considerable depth of prehistoric deposits on the promontory, and occupation seems to have been continuous from the Dimini phase of Late Neolithic. The later phases of Bronze Age settlement are best preserved at the south end of the site, where Middle Helladic houses were succeeded by a cist grave cemetery, enclosed by a wall, which continued in use into the LH II period. Above this were Mycenaean structures of the LH III period, including a large LH IIIB house. Mycenaean houses have also been reported to west of the promontory; and an extensive cemetery, perhaps part of the one previously mentioned, has been found on the face of the hill. This included rectangular built tombs with entrances, and a "tholos" tomb has been reported. A group of LH IIA-IIIA1 vases is reported to have come from these tombs (*AM* and Stählin, *loc.cit.*). The Sub-Mycenaean date suggested for some of these vases (Verdelis, *loc.cit.*) is unacceptable, but two Protogeometric vases come from the area (Desborough, *loc.cit.*).

It is difficult to gauge the exact extent of the Mycenaean settlement at Pefkakia, because of later disturbances from the historic to modern periods, but both the finds made and the strategic position suggest a considerable importance. The promontory itself provides protection for the small harbour here on its north side, and the site may have constituted a major part of the harbour of Mycenaean Iolkos.

H 3 DIMINI: TOUMBA * # (Plate 28c)
N EB I-III MH LH IIA-IIIB

AM 11 (1886) 435, 12 (1887) 136; *PAE* (1901) 37; Tsountas (1908) especially 65, 125, 147; A.J.B. Wace and M.S. Thompson, *Prehistoric Thessaly* (1912) 82 (henceforth abbreviated as *PT*); A. Hunter, *The Bronze Age in Thessaly and its Environs, with Special Reference to Mycenaean Culture* (1953) 23, 36, 38 (henceforth abbreviated as *Hunter*).

The site is a mound on the low spur which projects into the Volos plain about 500 m. northeast of Dimini village. The famous Late Neolithic walled settlement occupies an area only about 110 m. northeast to southwest by 90 m., comprising the top area and the uppermost slopes. Some Mycenaean sherds were

found here (*PT loc.cit.*), but most were found on the lower terraces, suggesting that the Mycenaean settlement was concentrated there, rather than among the ruins of the Neolithic settlement on the top (*Hunter loc.cit.*). Two Mycenaean cist graves of the LH IIIA2 period were found, and the remains of a burial deposit apparently LH IIIA. The two tholos tombs are quite large, and each had a "relieving triangle". The first (diameter c. 8.3 m.) was set into the north side of the spur. The other, at Laminospito 300 m. further north, was dug into the slope of the hillside opposite. Both contained structures set against the chamber wall. They had been robbed, but remains of gold and glass jewellery were found, and some Mycenaean sherds of the LH IIIA2-B periods are reported from the dromos of the Laminospito tomb. Since there is no evidence that the Mycenaean settlement at Dimini was itself of importance, it is quite probable that the tholos tombs are to be connected with Mycenaean Iolkos (H 1).

H 4 SESKLO: KASTRAKI *
N EB I-III MH LH III(A2-B) PG G?

Tsountas (1908), especially 73, 107, 115, 125; *Hunter* 23, 142, 151; *PAE* (1911) 294, (1965) 7, (1971) 18; *Ergon* (1976) 99.

Sesklo is in a small side valley, connected by a narrow pass with the Volos plain. The "high mound" site here is one of the oldest settlements in Greece. Important "preceramic" Neolithic deposits have been found, and by the Middle Neolithic period it was an extensive town. It lies to northeast of Sesklo, on the lower part of the same spur. Its centre is a natural rise between two stream-beds, now measuring about 100 m. northeast to southwest by 45 m., but considerably eroded. Like Dimini (H 3), it was more important in the Neolithic than the Bronze Age. But some Mycenaean sherds were found at the foot of the mound on a lower southwest terrace (*Hunter* 23) and also on the east slope [Tsountas (1908) 73], and a LH III sherd was recently found in Sesklo village. A small Mycenaean tomb of tholos type was excavated in the neighbourhood, and is possibly the source of a LH IIIB pyxis noted as from "T.5" by Hunter (*Hunter* 151, and *cf.* also 142 for another whole vase, presumably from a tomb).

H 5-10

Several Mycenaean settlements have been found in and around the Krokian plain, on the west side of the bay of Volos, and centred on Almyros. But even here it is obvious that many more remain to be found. Little has been done here since the pioneer work of Wace and Thompson.

H 5 NEA ANKHIALOS: ANCIENT PYRASOS *
N EB I EB II? MH LH II-IIIB PG G C H

PT 10; *Hunter* 182; *Thessalika* 2 (1959) especially 59ff.; *AD* 16 (1960) B 170; *PAE* (1968) 31, (1969) 16 (N.B. plan on p. 18).

This "high mound" site, on a rather steep hill above the harbour of Nea Ankhialos, has a top surface measuring about 110 m. north to south by 80 m. A few Mycenaean sherds were found on the hill itself, but the bulk of the Mycenaean finds were from flat ground near the south foot of the hill, where good LH II-IIIB pottery was found in a stratified deposit. More Mycenaean sherds were found in two other areas about 100 m. apart and about 100 m. from the acropolis foot, demonstrating a fairly extensive Mycenaean "lower town".

H 6   MIKROTHIVAI: ANCIENT PHTHIOTIC THEBES *
N MH LH III(A2-B) PG G A C

AM 31 (1906) 5; *PAE* (1907) 166, (1908) 163; *PT* 166; F. Stäh-lin, *Die Hellenische Thessalien* (1924) 171 (with plan).

A few Mycenaean sherds were found in a mixed deposit here, above better stratified Neolithic remains; and some Mycenaean sherds were found on the surface. The Mycenaean settlement appears to have been confined mainly to the east end of the rocky spur of the historic site, where it projects into the northern edge of the Krokian plain. The date of the wall called "Cyclopean" by the excavator [*PAE* (1908) 166] is uncertain (*cf. PT* 166).

H 7   AIDHINIOTIKI MAGOULA *
N EB I-II MH LH III(A-B)

PAE (1907) 171; *PT* 169; *Thessalika* 2 (1959) 60; *AA* (1971) 395.

This mound, about 3 km. from the present shore and 7 km. northeast of Almyros, is high and very large. Trial excavations produced abundant prehistoric material, especially MH, and some Mycenaean has been found on the surface.

H 8   ALMYRIOTIKI MAGOULA
N MH LH III(A-B)

PT 10, 208; *Alin* 145.

This is a low mound about 2.5 km. east of Almyros. A Mycenaean Psi figurine in the Almyros museum is marked as from the site; and some Mycenaean sherds in the museum said to be from the vicinity of Almyros are probably also from the magoula.

H 9   ZERELIA: KASTRAKI *
N EB I(-III?) MH LH I-III(A2-B1) "PG"?

PT 150; *Hunter* 33, 35.

The site is of "high mound" type, set on a hill between two small lakes, in the foothills on the southwest edge of the Krokian plain, about 5 km. west-southwest of Almyros. The top surface measures about 110 m. north-northwest to south-southeast by 70 m. Trial excavations revealed eight strata, of which the lowest six are certainly Neolithic. Most of the Bronze Age material was found in the top layer, where much MH was found, a few LH I-II pieces, and LH III sherds including at least one decorated kylix fragment. A bronze double axe found on the surface (*PT* 166, Hunter catalogue no. 288) is also presumably Mycenaean.

H 10   ANCIENT HALOS *
LH IIIA? PG G C H

BSA 18 (1911-12) 1; *Hunter* 230.

A piriform jar of LH IIIA type described as being from Halos was on display in Volos museum in 1967. Part of a sword hilt, resembling those of Type C but unflanged, is reported to have come from a tomb at Halos (*Hunter loc.cit.*). But the site is most noted for its series of Dark Age graves, at the foot of the historic acropolis.

H 11   PTELEON: GRITSA *
N MH LH IIIA1-C PG C

PAE (1951) 129, (1952) 164, (1953) 120; *Hunter* 11; Desborough (1964) 130.

The importance of this site is demonstrated by the tholos tombs both here and at Ayios Theodoros nearby (H 12). The bay of Pteleon lies at the entrance to the Gulf of Volos, and it has been suggested that Pteleon may have had connections with the south (*i.e.* with Euboea, Locris, Boeotia etc.) especially in the LH IIIC period (Desborough *loc.cit.*). The prehistoric settlement itself is on the rocky hill named Gritsa, of moderate height, at the head of the bay of Pteleon, and about 3 km. to south of the village. Mycenaean and earlier sherds were found on most of the top surface of the hill, about 300 m. north to south by 180 m., and there are remains of MH cist graves, three Mycenaean tholos tombs, and a small LH IIIC tomb of tholos type. The tholos tombs, which range in diameter from about 4.0 m. to over 5.0 m. (Tomb 3) contained vases ranging from LH IIIA1 to LH IIIC. They were placed along the lower spur which runs westward from the hill of Gritsa. The tombs were not very rich in goods, but contained some jewellery and other objects.

H 12   PTELEON: AYIOS THEODOROS *
LH III(A2-B) H

PAE (1951) 150, (1952) 181.

A small tholos tomb (diameter 3.54 m.) was excavated here, about 2 km. northeast of Ayios Theodoros, to north of the road, and overlooking Gritsa and the bay of Pteleon. It contained Mycenaean pottery, bronzes, sealstones, and some jewellery. As was suggested above, this tomb probably belongs with the group at Gritsa (H 11).

H 13 ARGALASTI: KHORTOS
LH III(A2-B) PG?

PT 6 n. 1; *PAE* (1914) 221; *Hunter* 159.

An alabastron, marked "Khortokastron Argalastes", in the Almyros museum was noted by Hunter (*loc.cit.*). It is probably LH IIIA2. A Dark Age tholos tomb was noted near Argalaste (*PAE loc.cit.*), and the head of a double axe from Khortos was seen in the Volos Museum (*PT loc.cit.*). These discoveries are the first indication of the presence of Mycenaeans on the Magnesia promontory, where very little archaeological exploration has been carried out.

H 14-45

These sites are in or around the main eastern plain of Thessaly. There is a major concentration in the Larisa vicinity, but the distribution of known sites elsewhere in the eastern plain may be somewhat misleading. For instance, Mr. and Mrs. D.H. French have found Mycenaean sherds at several of the mound sites near the Volos-Larisa road, *i.e.* in that part of the plain between sites H 16 (Petra) and H 17. The evidence they recovered is in the BSA collection, and publication of the details is in preparation. Elsewhere in the plain, as in all of Thessaly, survey coverage has been rather sporadic and unsystematic. Many more Mycenaean settlements should be expected here, especially since several sites have produced early Mycenaean material (*i.e.* H 15, H 21, H 23, H 26, H 27, H 31, H 34, and H 44).

H 14 VELESTINO (ANCIENT PHERAI) *
N EB MH LH IIIA2-B LH IIIC? PG G A C H

PAE (1907) 160; *BCH* 45 (1921) 529; Y. Béquignon, *Recherches archéologiques à Phères* (1937); *AAA* 10 (1977) 174.

Magoula Bakali, a "high mound" site on the west side of the village of Velestino, appears to have been the centre of the Mycenaean settlement at Velestino. The historic town was much bigger, and its acropolis is now known to have included the hill of Ayios Athanasios immediately southwest of the Magoula. Mycenaean sherds were found on the top surface of the Magoula, which measures about 400 m. northeast to southwest by 100 m., and Mycenaean finds are recorded from the area of the temple, to north of Magoula [continuity of cult here from Mycenaean onwards was argued by Wrede, *AA* (1926) 429]. Recent stratigraphical investigations between the acropolis of ancient Pherai and the Hypereia spring, an area now covered by modern Velestino, have revealed deposits ranging from the Early Bronze Age to Hellenistic; and significant Mycenaean finds are included. In addition, good LH IIIA2-B vases have been found, presumably from tombs (*Hunter*, catalogue nos. 2-3, 31, 40, 78, *cf.*

p. 215) and one which may be LH IIIC [Volos Museum Cat. No. 646, *cf.* Desborough (1964) 132]. Hunter also cites Mycenaean figurines [*cf. BSA* 66 (1971) 184]. There is thus evidence for a substantial Mycenaean settlement here.

H 15 MEGA MONASTIRION: MAGOULA and LIVADHI *
LH IIIA1-B PG

AD 19 (1964) B 225; *AR* (1964-5) 20; *BCH* 91 (1957) 708.

About 1.5 km. east-northeast of Mega Monastirion, in the northwest bank of the torrent which runs past the flank of the Magoula hill, five large rock-cut chamber tombs (the first to be found in Thessaly) have been excavated. They contained much Mycenaean pottery (including a painted toy chariot and two yoked horses), gold and glass jewellery, and fine sealstones. Not far to the west, at Livadhi, were traces of a Mycenaean settlement and a much ruined LH IIIA2 chamber tomb.

H 16 STEPHANOVIKEION: PETRA *
N EB I MH LH IIIA2-B LH IIIC? C

AM 62 (1937) 60 n. 1; *AA* (1955) 221, (1960) 150; *BCH* 80 (1956) 311, 81 (1957) 597, 84 (1960) 764; *AD* 16 (1960) B Pls. 164B, 165, *AD* 18 (1963) B 144.

The site of Petra is formed by three low hills and the saddles and hollows between them, on the western edge of Lake Boibe (now mainly drained). The extensive "Cyclopean" circuit walls, which are up to 5 m. thick, enclosed an area about 1,000,000 m² (nearly 5 km. in circumference) around the three hills, two of which are also ringed by separate circuit walls. Good MH and Mycenaean sherds have been found in many and widely separated parts of the hills and the flatter areas between and around them [*cf.* the plan *AA* (1955) 227, Abb. 22], often associated with cists and the remains of buildings. The Mycenaean material is particularly extensive, and seems to indicate an important site. If the circuit walls are indeed Mycenaean, as is claimed, this would be the largest fortified Mycenaean site yet known.

H 17 PLATIKAMBOS: KARAGATS MAGOULA
N EB I LH G

PT 8 no. 21; *Thessalika* 3 (1960) 47f. and n. 1.

This large double mound is about a kilometre north of Platikambos. Surface sherds include Mycenaean.

H 18 MELISSOCHORI: PALIAMBELA
LH III(A-B)

PT 8 no. 24; *Alin* 140 s.v. "Metiseli"

Mycenaean surface sherds were found at this Magoula, by the 6th kilometre stone at a point about 2 km. north of Melissochori (formerly Metiseli).

H 19   MESIANI MAGOULA   *
N   EB   MH   LH

PT 8 no. 26, 55.

This is a tall conical hillock described as "between the fourth and fifth kilometre stones on the north side of the Larisa-Ayia road". Trial excavations revealed mainly Neolithic material, but some Bronze Age was also found, and there are Mycenaean sherds from here in the National Museum at Athens.

H 20   LARISA: GEDIKI
MH?   LH IIIA2(-B?)

Thessalika 3 (1960) 47; *AR* (1962-63) 24; *AD* 23 (1968) B 269.

Vases and bronze objects from tombs accidentally discovered at Gediki, near Larisa aerodrome, include Mycenaean. The "tholos tomb" mentioned in a newspaper report (*AR loc.cit.*) may be an exaggerated description of a small built tomb of tholos type.

H 21   LARISA: The Acropolis
N   EB   MH   LH IIB-IIIA1   PG   C

Fimmen (1921) 2; *Hunter* 33, 36; *PAE* (1910) 174; *Thessalika* 3 (1960) 47; *AD* 21 (1966) B 254, 26 (1971) B 300.

Prehistoric sherds were found on the acropolis, and fine LH IIB-IIIA1 vases are reported, presumably from tombs in the area. Traces of Mycenaean habitation were also noted behind the hospital, near the right bank of the Peneios river, some distance to northeast of the acropolis.

H 22   AVEROF: MAGOULA
LH

Thessalika 3 (1960) 47.

Some Mycenaean sherds were found on this low mound about 500 m. south of Averof, a village about 3 km. south-southeast of the outskirts of Larisa.

H 23   GREMNOS (ANCIENT ARGISSA)   *#
(Plate 26b)
N   EB I-III   MH   LH I-II   LH IIIB   PG   G   A   C   H

AA (1955) 192, (1956) 221; *AD* 16 (1960) B 186; V. Miløjčič, *Hauptergebnisse der deutschen Ausgrabungen in Thessalien 1953-58* (1960) 3, 21; V. Miløjčič *et.al.*, *Argissa I* (1962) 27; E. Hanschmann and V. Miløjčič, *Argissa III* (1976).

This large high mound (about 350 m. northeast to southwest by 120 m.) stands on the north bank of the Peneios river, which has partly eroded it. The site was first inhabited in Palaeolithic times and again in the early Neolithic period. There is evidence of Mycenaean settlement on the mound itself, but Miløjčič argues that the Mycenaeans here lived mainly in the area surrounding the mound rather than on it. In any case, the widespread distribution of the Mycenaean finds suggests a settlement of considerable size and importance.

H 24   SOUPHLI MAGOULA   *
N   EB I   MH   LH IIB/IIIA1   LH III(A-B)

PT 9 no. 28; *AA* (1957) 53, (1959) 59; *Thessalika* 1 (1958) 78.

The magoula is a low rise on the east bank of the Peneios river, about a kilometre southeast of Koulouri. "Preceramic" Neolithic was found here and a remarkable stele resembling a menhir and somewhat similar to the stelai from Troy. Pottery found in trial excavations near the stele includes at least one LH IIB/IIIA1 fragment [*AA* (1959) 62 Fig. 7]; and a child's cist grave containing an askos and an amber bead is presumably Mycenaean. It is possible that Souphli may be the real provenance of the sherds said to have come from "Suphlar" (Fimmen 1921, 4; *Alin* 142), although the name Suflar or Tsuflar occurs in at least three different places in Thessaly.

H 25   OMORPHOCHORI: KARAGATS MAGOULA
LH (III?)

Thessalika 3 (1960) 57 n. 1.

Mycenaean sherds are reported from this mound (which is apparently *PT* no. 29) on the north side of Omorphochori (formerly Nechali).

H 26   CHASAMBALI (KEPHALOVRYSO?)   *#
N   EB I   MH   LH IIB/IIIA1-B   PG   H

PAE (1910) 185; *Thessalika* 3 (1960), 50, 4 (1962) 35, 73; *Hunter* 10, 40, 198 (Kephalovryso material).

This was noted by Arvanitopoulos (*PAE loc.cit.*) as a very important settlement, on either side of the spring Kephalovryso, on the eastern edge of the Larisa plain, a kilometre to northeast of the village of Chasambali [*cf.* the map, *BSA* (1930-31) 2 Fig. 1], to the east of the quarries on the lower slopes of Mt. Mopsion. Arvanitopoulos claimed that prehistoric settlement was more or less continuous from Chasambali to Eleutherion about 4 km. to east-southeast; and the abundant springs between Chasambali and Marmariani (H 27) further demonstrate that this area could have supported a considerable prehistoric population. At Chasambali excavations uncovered apsidal megara and cists which are probably late Middle Helladic. Mycenaean vases, the earliest of which is LH IIB/IIIA1 [Thessalika 4 (1962) 42 Fig. 8], and some Protogeometric been handed in, and are said to have come from similar tombs.

This site must surely also be the provenance of a fairly large collection of MH and LH IIIA-B sherds marked "Kephalovryso" in the BSA collection; and Hunter reports LH IIIA2-B from both "Chasambali" and "Kephalovryso". Hunter, however, suggested a different provenance for the "Kephalovryso" material (*cf. Alin* 140 s.v. 'Kefalovryso'), namely a location about 10 km. west of Elasson, in remote hill country, from which nothing else has yet been recorded of a prehistoric nature. This alternative location appears unlikely.

H 27 MARMARIANI *
N MH LH IIIA1-B LH IIIC? PG G

PT 53; *BSA* 31 (1930-31) 1; *Hunter* 11, 39.

The mound of Marmariani is about 2 km. southwest of the village of the same name, and lies in the plain near the southwest foot of Mt. Ossa. It was originally a Neolithic site, re-occupied in the MH period. Mycenaean sherds (mainly LH IIIA-B, but including some probably LH IIIC) are plentiful on the lower terraces, especially the southeast. A tholos tomb (of diameter not over 6 m.) on the west edge of the mound contained LH III(A2-B) pottery. Six others, on the east side, smaller and rather irregular in shape, contained Protogeometric and Geometric burials, and some sherds of these periods were found on the site.

H 28 BARA
LH III(A2-B) LH IIIC? PG?

In 1958 a considerable Mycenaean settlement, about 150 m. north to south by 100 m. was located on slopes near a copious spring about 2 km. southeast of the mound of Marmariani (H 27). This discovery is a further indication of the importance of the Chasambali-Marmariani area in Mycenaean times.

H 29 DHOGANI: AYIOS ILIAS
EB or MH LH III(A-B)

Hunter 8.

A prehistoric settlement was discovered by Hunter in the plain at the east foot of the hill of Ayios Ilias, to south of Dhogani. Mycenaean and earlier sherds were identified.

H 30 NESSONIS
N EB I-III MH LH

BCH 82 (1958) 953.

There is a brief report that on three mounds in the area of the Nessonis marsh all prehistoric periods were represented on the surface.

H 31 SIKOURI: BOUNARBASHI *
N EB MH LH IIIA1-B LH IIIC? PG G

AD 19 (1964) B 262, 22 (1967) B 296; *AJA* 74 (1970) 272; V. Miløjčič *et:al., Magulen um Larisa 1966* (1976) 65.

Bounarbashi is a fairly high and rather flat-topped hill, about 350 m. north to south by 250 m., at the north end of a broad valley, and about 3.5 km. northwest of Sikouri. A wide range of prehistoric material was found in trial excavations, which revealed a thick Mycenaean layer. The earliest pieces from this may be LH IIIA1, as is an alabastron handed in [*AD* 19 (1964) B

Pl. 304e), and the latest may be LH IIIC, but the bulk seem to be LH IIIB.

H 32 SPILIA: KAVAKI * # (Plate 26a)
LH IIIA2-B

AAA 2 (1969) 165; *AD* 24 (1969) B 223.

Mycenaean built tombs of tholos type have now been found high up on the west flank of Mt. Ossa. The excavated tomb was small (diameter 2.3 m.), and contained a single adult burial provided with two LH IIIA2-B vases, a knife, a sealstone, and other objects. It lies on the northeast brow of the ridge to southwest of the spring Kavaki, about 2 km. southwest of Spilia. A tomb of similar type but much ruined was found at Kibourli, about a kilometre to west along the same ridge; and, according to local reports, two other tombs, also situated on the ridge and between the two investigated, had been destroyed previously. No traces of a Mycenaean settlement site have yet been found, but one should be expected [*cf.* Arkines (E 9) in Laconia], even if habitation here was only seasonal.

H 33 RACHMANI: MAGOULA *
N EB I-III MH LH IIIA2-B LH IIIC?

PT 25; *Hunter* 12, 41, 182, 198.

This is a conspicuous low mound, measuring 112 m. by 95 m., to east of the Larisa-Tempe road, and near the eastern edge of the Larisa plain. Excavations revealed a deep stratigraphic sequence. As was noted at Dimini (H 3) and Sesklo (H 4), Mycenaean material was more abundant on the slopes, in this case especially the east, and with the exception of the north. This may be partly due, however, to erosion of the centre of the mound here. The Mycenaean sherds are mainly, if not entirely, LH IIIA2-B; LH IIIC has been claimed, but is not certain. A ruined tomb, containing two burials, LH IIIA pottery, and some jewellery, was apparently a small tomb of tholos type.

H 34 GONNOS
N EB MH LH IIIA1-B LH IIIC? G C H

PAE (1910) 241, (1911) 315, (1914) 208; *PT* 207; F. Stählin, *Die Hellenische Thessalien* (1924) 32; *MP* 646; *Alin* 139; *Hunter* 8, 37; B. Helly, *Gonnoi* I (1973) especially 53, and the plan and photos.

Hunter recorded sherds (in the BSA collection) of EB, MH and LH IIIA-C date from the small natural hill of Besik Tepe at the south foot of the acropolis of ancient Gonnos, about 2 km. east-southeast of modern Gonnos (formerly Dereli). On the northwest slope of the acropolis itself there was a tholos tomb, and a Mycenaean to Geometric cemetery is reported near Besik Tepe. One grave here was a cist within a tumulus, and contained a contracted burial, an amber bead, and a sealstone.

Three vases from Gonnos were brought to the Almyros Museum [*PT* 207, Fig. 143, *cf. AM* (1909) 84 and *LAAA* (1908) 133]. They have been attributed (*Alin loc.cit.*) to the vicinity of the neighbouring village of Baba (now re-named Tembi); and Furumark (*MP* 646) regarded the askos as from elsewhere, although a very old label marked "Gonnos" (in Greek alphabet) was seen attached to the vase in the museum in 1958. There seems indeed little doubt that the vases are in fact from Gonnos, although they may have been brought to Baba subsequently. They were classed as LH IIIB [by Desborough (1964) 133], but the high-handled cup with stipple pattern can now be definitely classed as LH IIIA1.

H 35 PHALANNA: TATAR MAGOULA
N EB I-III MH LH III(A-B) C H

PT 9 no. 36; *AA* (1955) 221; *Historia* 4 (1955) 471; *BCH* 80 (1956) 311.

This large high mound lies about 1.5 km. west of Phalanna (formerly Tatar). In 1958 the top knoll was being ploughed away by a bulldozer. Before destruction this knoll measured about 80 m. north to south by 60 m., and the total dimensions of the mound are about 300 m. north to south by 225 m. The abundant Classical sherds in the cutting made by the bulldozer, and inscriptions found on the site previously, show that this was the centre of a Hellenic town, probably ancient Phalanna.

H 36 VRYOTOPOS: TSAIRLI MAGOULA
N LH III(A-)B

AD 21 (1966) B 254; *BCH* 94 (1970) 1049.

Neolithic and Mycenaean sherds were found on the surface of this low mound about a kilometre north of Vryotopos. A "Zygouries type" kylix fragment and a robbed tomb were recorded.

H 37 RODHIA: MAGOULA PERA MACHALA
N EB I-II LH III(A-B)

Hunter 9, 183; *AD* 19 (1964) B 263.

This large "high mound" site lies about 1.5 km. southeast of Rodhia, immediately to north of the junction of the Peneios and Titaresios rivers. Fine Mycenaean surface sherds are reported and robbed cist tombs. Mycenaean sherds were also found in lower ground at the southeast foot of the mound, where there is an extension of the settlement reaching to the west bank of the Peneios.

H 38 ARGYROPOULI: KASTRI # (Fig. 8)
MH? LH IIIA2-C C H

PT 10 no. 81; *CSHI* 146 and Pl. 11.

The village of Argyropouli (formerly Karatsoli)

lies at the northwest edge of the Larisa plain, beneath the foothills of Mt. Olympus, and at the southern entrance to the Melouna pass which leads to the valley of Elasson. To northwest of and above the village is the hill of Kastri, where there are remains of a monastery and a chapel of Ayia Paraskevi. The main part of the Mycenaean settlement lay on the monastery hill, a spur about 250 m. north to south by 100 m., but some sherds here also found on the higher hill above to the northeast. Considerable quantities of fine Mycenaean pottery were found on the site in 1961, especially behind the chapel on the neck of land joining the two hills. Here erosion has created a large pit, in the sides of which Mycenaean deposits nearly three metres thick are revealed, and in one side a Mycenaean house wall preserved to a height of nearly two metres.

H 39 MAGOULA (Near ELASSON)
N? EB? MH? LH?

PT 12 no. 124, 207; *AA* (1959) 84.

The village of Magoula is about 13 km. southwest of Elasson, on a low hill in the Europos river valley. Wace and Thompson recorded monochrome hand-made ware here, and saw four "LM II" vases in private possession in Larisa, reputed to have come from Magoula. There does not seem to be enough evidence to certify a Mycenaean settlement here, however, and the site has accordingly been omitted from the map.

H 40 ELASSON: PANAYIA (Plate 27a)
LH III(A-)B C H

AD 23 (1968) B 269; *CSHI* 147.

Mycenaean vases, including a LH IIIB deep bowl, have been found by chance at Elasson, and are presumably from tombs. And a pyxis in the Almyros Museum marked "Elassona" (in Greek alphabet) is either LH IIIA2 or LH IIIB. The Mycenaean settlement was presumably on the same site as the historic Elasson, *i.e.* the hill of the Panayia monastery on the west side of the modern town [*cf. AA* (1959) 85]. This is the northernmost Mycenaean site in Thessaly, and may also mark the northern limit of Mycenaean penetration here.

H 41 KOUTSOCHEIRON: MAGOULA VRASTERA
N EB LH IIIA2-B

Thessalika 2 (1959) 69; *AD* 16 (1960) B 172.

Mycenaean sherds were reported, together with Neolithic and Early Bronze Age, from a site named as "Magoula Vrastera" and described as being on the right bank of the Peneios river and about 2 km. southwest of Koutsocheiro. The mound in question is, however, locally known as "Magoula Zariba". It is indeed about 2 km. southwest of Koutsocheiro, and only about 150 m. to east of the right bank of the Peneios.

Fine painted Neolithic wares and abundant LH IIIA2-B are visible on the eroded west flank of the site, which is a large low mound about 200 m. east to west by 150 m.

H 42 ALIFAKA: ANCIENT ATRAX
LH III(A-B) PG A C

AA (1960) 173; Stählin 1924, 101; *Alin* 138.

The citadel of ancient Atrax is a conical hill about 500 m. southwest of the village of Alifaka, which is near the south bank of the Peneios river. Some Mycenaean sherds were found here, although later wares were more abundant.

H 43 ANCIENT KRANNON *
N EB LH III(A-B) G A C H

Stählin 1924, 111; *AD* 16 (1960) B 177, 25 (1970) B 279.

Ancient Krannon occupies a large and irregular low plateau, about 400 m. in diameter [*cf. AD* 16 (1960) B 178, Fig. 2], about 2 km. southwest of the modern village of Krannon. The circuit walls of the historic town follow the outer contours of this plateau, within which are two mounds, at the southwest angle and at the south side respectively. That on the southwest is higher, measuring about 150 m. northwest to southeast by 100 m., and appears to have been the main prehistoric centre. Neolithic, Middle Helladic, and abundant Mycenaean sherds have been found here (although the latter are of rather poor quality). On the lower mound (about 150 m. east to west by 120 m.) the only prehistoric sherds seen in 1958 were Neolithic.

H 44 CHABASLAR (modern VOUVAINA)
LH II(B?)

Hunter 33, 36; *Alin* 146.

In the Almyros Museum are a squat alabastron and an askoid jug (Hunter nos. 74 and 103), labelled "Tsiambaslar" (= Chabaslar). Both are of the LH II period. The Mycenaean site from which they came has not yet been closely identified.

H 45 NEAI KARYAI: SARLIKI
N EB LH C H

Thessalika 3 (1960) 47 n. 1; *AD* 16 (1960) B 185.

Neai Karyai is a village about 19 km. south of Larisa. About 3 km. northwest of Neai Karyai is an acropolis hill named Sarliki, steep on the north side and surrounded by ravines. Prehistoric surface sherds here included Mycenaean.

H 46-56

A considerable number of Mycenaean sites have been investigated in the Pharsala district, mainly in the Enipeus valley. The group at Ktouri (H 47-8) may be the most important, lying near the cross-roads of the main east-west and north-south routes of communication in this part of Thessaly.

H 46 PHYLLOS: GIOLI (ANCIENT PHYLLE?)
LH III(A-B)

AD 16 (1960) B 186; *Thessalika* 3 (1960) 47 n. 1, Figs. 8-9.

About 4 km. east of Phyllos, at the north foot of Mt. Dogadzi, is the site named Gioli, thought to be that of ancient Phylle (Stählin 1924, 133). A large Mycenaean settlement and cemetery are reported here, near a marsh and the railway line. No exact details are given, but the sherds illustrated (but not described) appear to include some LH III(A-B).

H 47 KTOURI (ANCIENT EUHYDRION?) *
LH IIIB C H

BCH 55 (1931) 493, 56 (1932) 122; *Alin* 141.

The summit of this high and extensive hill is surrounded by an inner enceinte of fortifications, enclosing a small area only about 80 m. in diameter. An outer enceinte, much lower down on the hill, surrounds an area about 700 m. north to south by 350 m. This is in rough polygonal style, constructed partly of very large blocks, and is about 3.8 m. thick (average). Only one diagnostic sherd (Classical or Hellenistic black-glazed) was found in the trial associated with this outer enceinte. The inner enceinte is built of smaller stones than the outer and is only about 2.5 m. thick [except at the five small towers or buttresses, *cf. BCH* 56 (1932) 127 Fig. 24]. But the masonry is of normal Mycenaean style, with small stones in the interstices and rubble fill. Trial excavations revealed several LH IIIB sherds in close association with the walls of this inner enceinte; and in 1958 a LH IIIB sherd was found *within* the wall. No certain traces of permanent Mycenaean dwellings were found; and, if the inner enceinte is indeed Mycenaean, the site may have been merely a small fort at this time, serving as a lookout and refuge for the main Mycenaean settlement at the Magoula below (H 48). The hill is indeed an excellent point from which to survey the Enipeus valley and the western Thessalian plain.

H 48 KTOURI MAGOULA *
MH LH IIIA2-B PG G A C

BCH 55 (1931) 493, 56 (1932) 137; Desborough (1964) 131; *Alin* 141.

The Magoula lies about 500 m. west-northwest of the foot of Ktouri hill. It is a low mound about 150 m. long, and a fairly large plateau to west of the mound appears to have been an extension of the settlement. Excavation produced prehistoric and later material. None of the Mycenaean pottery need be later than LH IIIB. A fine spring issues from the rock on the northwest side of Ktouri hill, and there are three other small springs in the vicinity of Magoula.

H 49 TSINI
  N   EB?   LH II or LH IIIA1

PT 11 no. 88; *RE* Suppl. VI 611; *Hunter* 19; *Alin* 141.

This is a low mound on the south bank of the Enipeus near the village of Tsini. A fragment from here in the BSA collection is from the neck of an ewer of LH II or LH IIIA1 date. It is presumably the same as the "Mittelmykenische" said by Karo to have been found by Heurtley (*RE loc.cit.*).

H 50 PHARSALA: MYLOS
  N   MH?   LH III(A-B)

PT 9 no. 44, 207.

Some Mycenaean sherds were found by Wace and Thompson on this low mound in the Pharsala plain, near the south bank of the Enipeus and to north of Pharsala railway station.

H 51 PHARSALA: FETIH-TSAMI * #
  N   EB?   MH   LH IIB/IIIA1-B   LH IIIC?   G   A   C
  H

PAE (1952) 195, (1953) 128, (1955) 145; *AD* 16 (1960) B 175, 19 (1964) B 260.

Trials on the northeast slope of the Fetih-Tsami (or Ayia Paraskevi) ridge, southwest of and above modern Pharsala, produced material ranging from Late Neolithic to Mycenaean and later. About 800 m. to the west, at the foot of the ridge is a group of tombs beneath an Archaic structure of tholos type. The group included two rectangular built tombs (with dromoi) and a cist tomb covered by a tumulus. These had been disturbed, but LH III pottery, including a monochrome deep bowl that may be LH IIIC, faience beads, and other goods were found. On show in the Volos Museum in 1967 were three LH IIB/IIIA1 squat jugs said to be from Pharsala.

H 52 AMBELIA (formerly DERENGLI): PALAIO-KASTRO *
  EB   MH   LH IIIA2-B   PG   G   A

BCH 55 (1931) 492, 56 (1932) 82; *RA* (1958:1) 95.

This acropolis hill lies on the south bank of the Enipeus, to north of and below Ambelia. It measures about 170 m. by 120 m. on the top, and occupation extended also over the considerable slopes. Prehistoric material, including Mycenaean, was found in a deep sounding on the site, which the excavator, Y. Béquignon, conjectured to be that of the Old Pharsalos mentioned by Strabo (ix 5,6).

H 53 TSANGLI: KARAMAN TSAIIR MAGOULA
  *
  N   MH   LH III?

PT 9 no. 38, 86, 114.

This mound lies at the east end of the Enipeus valley. It is large (about 200 m. by 200 m.), but mainly important in the Neolithic period. Some MH Grey Minyan was found in the top stratum, and Wace and Thompson saw a LH III sherd supposed to have been found at the site.

H 54 AKHILLION
  LH IIIA1(-B)

AR (1961-2) 14.

Near this village, about 5 km. southeast of Pharsala, a deposit of vases was found. Those on show in the Volos Museum in 1967 included LH IIIA1 jars and later types.

H 55 AYIOS ANTONIOS (formerly KOUTSELI): HOLEVA TRYPA *
  LH IIIA2-B

AD 19 (1964) B 261, 21 (1966) B 253.

Two small Mycenaean built tombs with dromoi were excavated at Holeva Trypa about 1.5 km. northeast of Ayios Antonios. One was rectangular, and the other was of irregular shape. Each contained several burials, LH III pottery, and other goods, including a Type E dagger.

H 56 GYNAIKOKASTRO (ANCIENT PROERNA)
  *
  N   MH   LH III(B)   G   A   C   H

PT 11 no. 104; *AD* 21 (1966) B 252.

Trials on the mound of Tapsi on the acropolis of ancient Proerna produced Mycenaean sherds, said to be of the LH IIIB period.

H 57 PANAYIA: RACHI or PALIOKKLISI
  N   EB   MH   LH IIIA-B

AD 25 (1970) B 244.

On this mound of elliptical shape, near Panayia, about 7 km. southwest of Domokos, surface sherds included several from Mycenaean tall-stemmed kylikes.

H 58 MELITAIA: AYIOS YEORYIOS
  N   MH   LH IIIA?   H

PT 208, Y. Béquignon, *La Vallée du Spercheios* (1937) 135; *Hunter* 10; *Thessalika* 2 (1959) 80.

A prehistoric settlement was found by Hunter about a kilometre to southwest of Melitaia (formerly Avaritsa), and about 500 m. from the west end of the walls of ancient Melitaia. It was revealed in the banks of a small ravine near the east bank of the Avaritso-revma, at the northeast foot of an isolated hill, near the chapel of Ayios Yeoryios. Both on the site and on a small plateau nearby MH pottery was found on the surface. Béquignon mentions an alabastron said to have been found at Avaritsa, and purchased by Stählin at Lamia. It appears to be of LH IIIA date. A broken gem of red carnelian was seen by Wace and Thompson in the possession of a peasant at Avaritsa.

H 59 ANAVRA (formerly GOURA): BADI
LH (III?)

AM 21 (1896) 247; *PT* 208; *Hunter* 16, 232; *Alin* 145.

A small built tomb of the tholos type (diameter 3.55 m. or greater) was found in rough ground a short distance to north of Anavra, and destroyed by peasants who converted it into a lime-kiln. The pottery within was lost, but Wace and Thompson attributed the tomb to the "LM III" period, presumably on the evidence of the conical steatite whorls and bronze tweezers. Hunter commented on the possibility of copper mining in the vicinity in Mycenaean times, and noted the presence of copper ore deposits and disused mine shafts on the slopes of Mt. Othrys, especially near Melitaia (H 58), Anavra, and Pteleon (H 11-12).

APPENDIX TO MAP H

At the following sites, which fall within the territory included in Map H, there are indications that there may have been Mycenaean settlement, although the evidence is so far inconclusive:

NEVESTIKI

JHS 26 (1906) 153; Stählin 1924, 53.

This acropolis on the northeast edge of the fertile plain of Lechonia overlooks the bay of Volos. There are remains of Cyclopean walling on the south side, and prehistoric occupation is indicated by obsidian and coarse ware on the surface. But the recognisable sherds are Classical and Hellenistic. The ancient walls enclose an area about 200 m. by 150 m., and the wide terraces to south and west also bear traces of ancient habitation. There are fine springs on the south side.

AYIOS ANDREAS: PALAIOKASTRO

JHS 26 (1906) 148; *PAE* (1910) 217; Stählin 1924, 54.

The steep hill of Palaiokastro is on a narrow part of the isthmus which connects the peninsula of Trikeri to the main part of Magnesia. There are small harbours to north and south. The summit of this little acropolis measures about 100 m. by 70 m., and is surrounded by a fortification wall of large blocks. Rock-cut graves and cist graves noted in the vicinity were Archaic or later, and the diagnostic sherds on Palaiokastro were Classical or Hellenistic. Nevertheless Mycenaean habitation also seems likely.

ARMENION: TRANI MAGOULA

PT 8 no. 10; *AD* 19 (1964) B 255.

This large Neolithic mound about 2 km. south of Armenion was said to have been inhabited in the Mycenaean period. But, since no details of the finds were given, confirmation is still required.

SOURPI: MAGOULA

PT 10 no. 71.

The high mound of Magoula, about 2 km. south of Sourpi, resembles Zerelia both in form and in situation. MH Minyan ware was reported to be abundant here. Mycenaean habitation also appears likely.

BAKRAINA

PAE (1911) 334; Philippson *GL* I 307 no. 183; *CSHI* 145.

This acropolis, identified as Ancient Gyrtone, was probably occupied in Mycenaean times, although the earliest sherds noted in 1961 were "orientalizing". The site is marked "Mycenaean to Hellenistic" by Kirsten (Philippson *loc.cit.*). It has some strategic significance because of its proximity to the Tempe pass.

ANO DRANITSA

PAE (1911) 351; *RE* Suppl. VI 610; Philippson *GL* I 307 no. 204.

A ruined tholos tomb was found on the south slopes of the acropolis (of Ancient Ktimene?) to southwest of and above the village of Ano Dranitsa. The contents were described as Sub-Mycenaean, but may really belong to the Early Iron Age. Philippson (*loc.cit.*) marks the site as "Mycenaean to Hellenistic", and Geometric pottery was certainly attested. The site is remote, in the hills to south of the western Thessalian plain.

NEZEROS

PT 207; *JHS* 21 (1901) 126 Fig. 16.

A silver statuette, now in the Ashmolean Museum, said to be from Nezeros, in the foothills of Mt. Olympus, has been attributed to the "LM II" period.

J 1 STIRFAKA: KALANTZINA
LH

AD 19 (1964) B 242 n. 2.

A few Mycenaean sherds were found on the surface of this site near Stirfaka, about 12 km. northwest of Lamia, on the north side of the Spercheios valley.

J 2-8

This group of sites, around Kardhitsa in the southern part of the western Thessalian plain, provides a good indication that many more Mycenaean

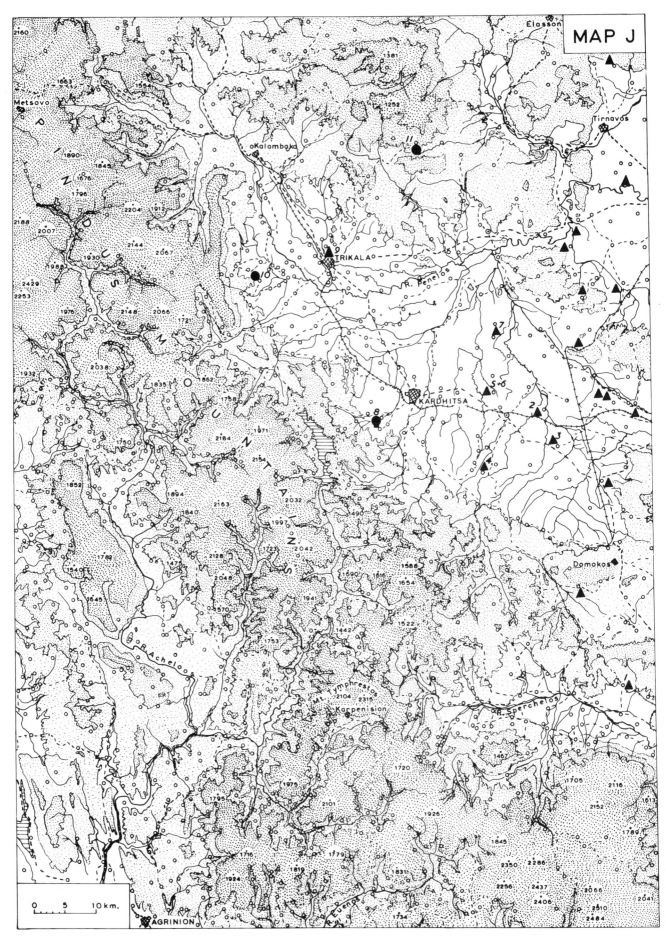

MAP J

Metsovo

oKalambaka

TRIKALA

R. Penelos

KARDHITSA

Domokos

R. Acheloos

Mt. Tymphrestos
Karpenision

R. Sperchelos

R. Evenos

AGRINION

Elasson

Tirnavos

0   5   10 km.

172

sites will be found both in the plain and in the foothills surrounding it. The area has received little attention from archaeologists. The sites at Pyrgos Kieriou (J 8-9) and the tholos tomb at Georgikon (J 12) in particular demonstrate the importance of this area. Early Mycenaean pottery has been found at Palamas (J 7) and in the Sophadhes area (J 3A).

J 2 TSANI MAGOULA *
N EB I-III MH LH III(A2-B)

PT 11 no. 96, 135, 207; *Alin* 142.

This low mound, about 105 m. by 73 m., lies on the north side of the railway line, about 5 km. east of Sophadhes. Above deep Neolithic and Early Bronze Age deposits, some Middle Helladic material and a single Mycenaean plain kylix stem were found in the top stratum.

J 3 SOPHADHES: MAGOULA THEOPHANI
N LH

AD 22 (1967) B 301.

Some Neolithic and Mycenaean sherds are reported from this mound, about 11 km. southeast of Sophadhes, on the north side of the road to Domokos.

J 3A SOPHADHES AREA
LH IIB or LH IIIA1 LH III(A-B)

RE Suppl. VI 611; *Hunter* 19, 159; *Alin* 141; *BSA* 66 (1971) 183.

According to Karo (*RE loc.cit.*), Heurtley found "mittelmykenische" pottery in the Sophadhes area. This presumably refers to a sherd in the BSA collection recorded as from the area. It is a fine alabastron fragment with "Rock Pattern" decoration, and is either LH IIB or LH IIIA1. A Mycenaean animal figurine has also been found in the Sophadhes area (*BSA loc.cit.*).

J 4 PHILIA: THE SANCTUARY OF ATHENA ITONIA *
LH III(A2-B) G A C H

AD 18 (1963) B 138, 20 (1965) B 312, 22 (1967) B 295.

The sanctuary is on a low mound about 1 km. north of the centre of Philia village, at Hamakia about 400 m. east of the Sophadhitikon river. Mycenaean pottery, apparently mainly LH IIIB, and figurines were found here on virgin soil. The earliest material from the later sanctuary above is Late Geometric.

J 5 PYRGOS KIERIOU: ANCIENT ARNE-KIERION
LH III(A-B) G A C H

AA (1955) 229; *BCH* 80 (1956) 311; *Thessalika* 2 (1959) 69.

The citadel of Ancient Kierion is a rocky hill on the west side of and above the village of Pyrgos. A circuit wall of very large blocks (one of which measures about 2.60 m., by 1.35 m. by 1.10 m.) surrounds the summit, enclosing an area about 200 m. north to south by 140 m. The blocks are only roughly hewn, and small stones in the interstices might suggest Cyclopean masonry. Miløjčič (*AA loc.cit.*) indeed argues for a Mycenaean date. But the style appears to differ in some respects from the Mycenaean, and resembles more closely that of the outer enceinte at Ktouri (H 47), which is demonstrably later than Mycenaean. Nevertheless, Mycenaean sherds have been found on the hill (*BCH* and *Thessalika loc.cit.*); and there may have been a small Mycenaean fort here, as at Ktouri, although in both cases the main Mycenaean settlements seem to have been on the mounds at the foot of the citadels (H 48 and J 6 respectively).

J 6 PYRGOS KIERIOU: MAKRIA MAGOULA
N? EB III MH LH III(A-B) C H

PT 11 no. 95; *AA* (1955) 229, (1960) 167.

At the southwest foot of the citadel of Ancient Kierion is a low mound, about 180 m. east to west by 70 m. Prehistoric surface sherds found here in 1958 included a few from Mycenaean stemmed bowls and kylikes. There are signs of (circuit?) walls on the south side.

J 7 PALAMAS
LH IIB

Thessalika 2 (1959) 69; *Alin* 142.

In the Volos museum are some LH IIB vases from Palamas. The site is presumably the settlement mound (*PT* 11 no. 98) "on which stands the southern part of Palamas".

J 8 GEORGIKON: KOUPHIA RACHI *
LH (III?) "PG"?

BCH 44 (1920) 295; *BSA* 31 (1930-31) 11; *AD* 16 (1960) B 171; *Alin* 142.

A large tholos tomb was discovered in the side of a low hill named Kouphia Rachi, about 700 m. west-southwest of Georgikon, and about a kilometre to south of the Kardhitsa-Metropolis road. In the vicinity are three other mounds, probably concealing other tholos tombs. The tholos investigated has a diameter of 8.85 m., and a stomion about 9 m. long, covered with five lintel blocks. It is quite well built, and the dome is preserved (height about 9 m.). It was opened up by Arvanitopoulos (*BCH* and *BSA loc.cit.*), but no finds were reported. It was subsequently reopened by Theochares (*AD loc.cit.*), who found some "Matt-painted" pottery in a robbers' spoil heap in the dromos. This pottery has been dated LH I/II, but could easily be local Protogeometric. But the time of the construction of the tomb must surely lie within the

Mycenaean period, to judge from its size and quality. The different toponyms (*i.e.* "Tsipousi" and "Kouphia Rachi") given for the same tomb have misled some scholars (*e.g. Alin loc.cit.*) to assume (erroneously) that *two* tombs were investigated.

J 9   TRIKKALA: AYIOS NIKOLAOS   *
N? EB MH LH IIIA2-B LH IIIC? PG G C H

PAE (1958) 62; *AD* 16 (1960) B 169, 20 (1965) B 3, 6, 21 (1966) B 247; *CSHI* 140 and Pl. 10(a).

Excavations near the church of Ayios Nikolaos, in the northern part of the town of Trikkala, at some distance from the southeast foot of the Kastro, revealed a large building of the Roman period, which may be associated with the Asklepieion of ancient Trikke. In the lower levels a wide range of prehistoric material was found, including Mycenaean pottery, mainly monochrome. If, as seems probable, the centre of the Mycenaean settlement was the Kastro, then the discovery of Mycenaean pottery at some distance below the Kastro slopes presumably signifies a considerable extent of occupation.

J 10   HEXALOPHOS   *
LH IIIC

AAA 1 (1968) 289; *AD* 23 (1968) B 263.

At the western edge of the plain, at the foot of Mt. Pindus, a tumulus was found, in flat ground about 200 m. south-southeast of Hexalophos, on the north side of the road to Eleftherochorion. The tumulus is quite large (diameter 27 m.) but not very high. It contained at least two cists. One, in the centre, contained the bones of a man. It had been robbed, but a group of weapons and some kylikes were recovered. The other cist tomb, on the periphery of the tumulus, was found intact. It contained kylikes, plain vases of local type, and bronze ornaments. The kylikes are probably to be attributed to a time late in the LH IIIC period. They are similar to LH IIIC types in Kephallenia, Ithaca, and Epirus. This find is of considerable importance, since, together with the discoveries at Trikkala (J 9), it constitutes the first proof that the Mycenaeans had penetrated at least as far as Mt. Pindus and the northwestern Thessalian plain. More Mycenaean sites are surely to be expected here, especially between Trikkala and Kalambaka, and to east of Trikkala along the main road to Larisa.

J 11   AGRILIA: AYIOS ATHANASIOS   *
MH? LH (IIIC?) H

BCH 79 (1955) 272; Desborough (1964) 132; *AAA* 1 (1968) 293.

Agrilia (formerly Smolia) is a village in the Chasian

mountains north of the Thessalian plain. Near the village, at Ayios Athanasios, beside a stream flowing into the modern Titaresios, a group of cist tombs was excavated. Some tombs contained Mycenaean vases, some contained local handmade pottery, and some both. Two small spearheads from Agrilia, of late Mycenaean type, are also probably from these tombs, which are dated "c. 1200 B.C." An apsidal building, attributed to MH, could be contemporary with the tombs or even later. These finds, on the northern fringes of Mycenaean Thessaly, deserve fuller publication, since they may illustrate the relationship between the Mycenaean and the local Bronze Age pottery.

APPENDIX TO MAP J

The question (raised above) concerning possible Mycenaean habitation in the upper (western) part of the Spercheios Valley requires further discussion, of two sites in particular.

LIANOKLADHI: PALAIOMYLOS

PT 171; *AAA* 6 (1973) 395.

This site has not been marked on Map J, but can be easily located on that map, since Lianokladhi village is about 5 km. due south of Stirfaka (J 1). The mound of Palaiomylos is about 2 km. west of Lianokladhi, close to the north bank of the Spercheios river. In the uppermost stratum substantial Middle Helladic buildings were found. No Mycenaean was conclusively identified, although there is a Mycenaean sherd labelled "Paleomylos" among sherds from Lianokladhi in the BSA collection. In 1958 some Hellenistic sherds and lumps of iron slag were found on the surface; and it is possible that these signify later disturbances which may have removed traces of Late Bronze Age levels.

KARPENISION: AYIOS DEMETRIOS

AAA 2 (1969) 358, 4 (1971) 196.

Karpenision lies on a main east-west route, below Mt. Tymphrestos and about midway between the headwaters of the Acheloos and Spercheios rivers. On a hill about 2 km. southwest of Karpenision, much prehistoric material has been found. Rough ware of Minyan type and many stone tools indicate a Middle Helladic settlement, which probably extended into the Late Bronze Age. Some of the painted ware found may be of the Dark Age, and a cist tomb, found in the courtyard of the Karpenision high school, may be of the Geometric period.

THESPROTIA   EPIRUS
MACEDONIA

MAPS K AND L

GENERAL INTRODUCTION

The sites listed under Maps K and L are, with the exception of Parga (K 2), and probably of Xylokastro (K 1), places where Mycenaean finds occur in local Late Bronze Age contexts. Mycenaean pottery, weapons, and tools in Epirus and in Western and Central Macedonia are clearly imports or local copies; and the vases and sherds of Mycenaean style are in any case usually outnumbered by the local Late Bronze Age wares. The position has been well summarised by K.A. Wardle, in his recent paper "The Northern Frontier of Mycenaean Greece", in *BICS* 22 (1975) 206-212 (University of London Mycenaean Seminar). As he says, in Epirus little Mycenaean pottery has been found, and none certainly prior to LH IIIA2. And the local LB pottery in Epirus is hardly affected by the few Mycenaean imports; although numerous swords of Mycenaean type and spearheads of "northern" type have been found in cists in this area.

D.H. French, in his *Index of Prehistoric Sites in Central Macedonia* (1967), lists about fifty sites where Late Bronze Age pottery has certainly been found. Of these at least thirty-six have also produced pottery of Mycenaean type. As might be expected, Mycenaean influences are strongest near the coast, or at sites easily accessible from the coast. In the fertile areas of Central Macedonia, particularly the Axios and Galliko river valleys, the Langadas basin (to north and east of Salonica), and in Chalcidice, many of the mound sites have yielded Mycenaean sherds. With one possible exception (L 18), these apparently begin in the LH IIIA2 period, although most appear to belong to LH IIIB or early LH IIIC. At some sites, particularly at Sedes (L 19), Gona (L 20), Saratse (L 32), and Vardarophtsa (L 45), LH IIIB imported sherds and local imitations are particularly numerous, although they are always accompanied by a higher proportion of the local Late Bronze Age wares. In the main part of Western Macedonia, however, in the interior part of the Haliakmon valley, only three sites (L 13 to 15) have so far yielded finds of Mycenaean type.

K 1 (= L 2)   MESOPOTAMOS: XYLOKASTRO * # (Plate 27b-c)
BA LH(IIIB-C)? PG? C H

PAE (1958) 107, 111, (1963) 91; (1975) A 146; *AD* (1963) B 153; *Antike Kunst* Beiheft 1 (1963) 51; *PPS* 33 (1967) 32; N.G.L. Hammond, *Epirus* (1967) 314, 369; Ergon (1975) 88, (1976) 84, (1977) 68.

The conical hill of Xylokastro is at the north end of the isolated ridge (83 m. a.s.l.) which occupies the angle between the river Acheron (on the south) and the river Kokytos (on the east). At the south end of the ridge, about 600 m. to the south-southeast, is the site of the Classical and Hellenistic Nekyomanteion, on a lower spur around the chapel of Ayios Ioannis Prodromos.

The outer perimeter walls (Plate 27c) enclose an area about 450 m. north-northwest to south-southeast by 100 m. (average). They are of "Cyclopean" style, with the characteristic large unworked stones and smaller stones in the interstices. There are remains of a gateway on the south side, about two metres in width. Traces of two other perimeter walls are preserved on the south side. The innermost, enclosing the summit of jagged rocks, is in a polygonal style common in the Hellenistic period.

A burial-tumulus, placed against the outer (west) face of the outer perimeter wall, contained several burials (including the children's pithos burials found in 1958 which were assigned to the Protogeometric period); and among the goods was a Mycenaean "krateriskos" said to be of the 13th or 12th century B.C. From this it is deduced that the wall is prior to the 12th century. Local Bronze Age coarse ware and fragments from tall-stemmed kylikes are also reported from Xylokastro.

Two children's cist graves found on the site of the

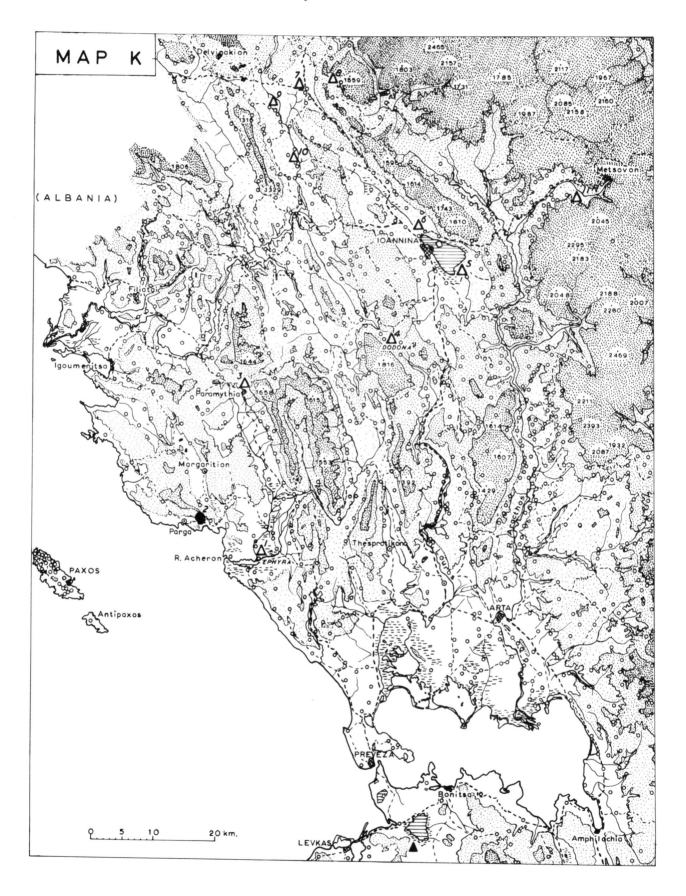

Nekyomanteion contained no closely datable pottery, but are likely to be either LH III or DA. At Likouresi, about 100 m. to the south, a Type F sword was found by chance (*PPS loc.cit.*).

The evidence is not yet sufficient to confirm the existence of a Mycenaean citadel at Xylokastro, and the reports of Mycenaean finds require further confirmation; but, in view of the Mycenaean tholos tomb near Parga (K 2 below), similar coastal penetration by the Mycenaeans at Xylokastro seems very likely.

K 2 (= L 1) PARGA: KIPERI *
LB LH IIIA1? LH IIIA2-B LH IIIC? C H

PAE (1960) 123; *AR* (1960-61) 15, 16 Fig. 14; *BCH* 84 (1960) 733.

The small tholos tomb found here is the furthest to the northwest of all Mycenaean tholos tombs, and one of the most remote. It may be compared to Arkines (E 9) on Mt. Taygetos in Laconia, and to Spilia (H 32) on the slopes of Mt. Ossa in Thessaly. The site is a wooded slope about 3 km. east of Parga, and about 1 km. inland from the beach of the bay of Lignou. It is above the main road, below a rocky spur (on which Classical and Hellenistic sherds were found), and about 200 m. to west of, and above, the Kiperi spring. The tomb (d. 4.5 m.) resembles those of Ayios Ilias in Aetolia (G 35) in that it lacks a stomion, has a chamber of coursed blocks, and a floor of pebbles in both chamber and dromos. The Mycenaean sherds, which are accompanied by local black polished wares, certainly include LH IIIA2-B types, and may include earlier and later.

About 50 m. to east of the tholos tomb is a wall about 2 m. thick, running down the slope, which may be part of a circuit wall surrounding a settlement on the slope and the spur above. But, although some Classical and Hellenistic sherds have been found on the spur, no certain traces of a Mycenaean settlement have yet been found here.

Other LH finds reported from the vicinity are a spearhead found in 1937 [*cf. BSA* 63 (1968) 107], supposedly from the tholos, and another from Ayia Kyriaki near Parga [*AD* 23 (1968) B 293 Pl. 239a].

K 3 (= L 3) PARAMYTHIA *
LH III(B-C)?

AD 20 (1965) B 348; *PPS* 33 (1967) 30 n. 1.

In a pit grave at the north edge of the town a small spearhead and a Type F short sword were found.

K 4 (= L 4) ANCIENT DODONA *
N BA LH IIIA2-C G A C H

PAE (1930) 68, (1931) 85, (1952) 280, (1959) 114, (1967) 39, (1968) 56, (1969) 26, (1972) 97; *AE* (1956) 134, 141; *AJA* 67 (1963) 130; *Antike Kunst* Beiheft 1 (1963) 35; Hammond (1967) 299, 318; Schoder (1974) 60.

A "prehistoric" stratum (only 0.40 m.-0.60 m. thick) underlies most of the excavated area of the later sanctuary, on the relatively flat ground below the theatre hill. There are no traces of any stone foundations in this stratum, but post-holes, a hearth, and an oven have been found. Imported pottery, which is greatly outnumbered by local, includes LH IIIA2-C and LG. LH bronzes, including a Type C sword and a Type F sword, have been found on the site without clear context, and could be dedications made much later than the time of manufacture, and even brought from elsewhere. There is nothing at present to suggest that the site had religious significance in the Bronze Age; and the settlement is clearly outside the main sphere of Mycenaean influence.

K 5 (= L 5) KASTRITSA *
N BA LH III(B-C) "PG"? C H

PAE (1951) 173, (1952) 268; *AD* 19 (1964) B 312, 20 (1965) B 348, 21 (1966) B 288, 23 (1968) B 291; *AE* (1956) 151; *PPS* 33 (1967) 26, 30; Hammond (1967) 314.

Prehistoric material has been found at two locations near Kastritsa. The first is a drainage ditch in the plain on the southeast edge of the Lake Ioannina, at the northeast foot of a long spur, on which is an extensive Classical and Hellenistic fortress. Among native Epirot wares found here were some wheelmade stemmed cups with swollen stems [*PAE* (1951) 182 Fig. 7, and *PAE* (1952) 365 Fig. 3], somewhat resembling LH IIIC examples from Kephallenia or the LH IIIC to "PG" from the Polis Cave on Ithaca [*cf.* Desborough (1964) 105, 109, Pl. 96]. At the second location, a trial excavation between the Asprochaliko cave and the lake shore, prehistoric finds from graves included a stirrup-jar of LH IIIC appearance and a Type F sword.

K 6 (= L 6) IOANNINA: PERAMA
BA LH III (A-B)?

AE (1956) 131; Hammond (1967) 321.

Two swords, of the "local" Type C variety found at Dodona, are reported to be from a grave here, near the north end of Lake Ioannina.

K 7 (= L 7) KALBAKI
BA LH III(B-C)?

AE (1956) 114; *AD* 23 (1968) B 294.

Four cist graves were excavated here, about 100 m. west of the Ioannina-Konitsa road, near the 31.5 km. mark. In one cist were a Type F sword and a spearhead, both likely to be of late date [*cf. BSA* 63 (1968) 96, 107]. Some other goods were also found, with Bronze Age pottery of entirely local type. Recently another Type F sword has been handed in from the area.

K 8 (= L 8) ELAPHOTOPOS *
LH III(B-C)? "PG"?

PPS 33 (1967) 30 n. 1; *AE* (1969) 179.

A Type F sword was reported from Kalyvia Ela-
photopou. Four cists were excavated at the foot of the
hill Konismata, on the east side of a highland plateau.
They contained local pottery, a curved knife, and
jewellery. Traces of a probable settlement were found
nearby. The cists have been attributed to LH IIIB-C,
on the basis of parallels with Kalbaki (K 7), but could
be of considerably later date (*e.g.* c. 1000 B.C., as suggested by Wardle).

K 9 (= L 9) GRIBIANI
LH III(B-C)?

AE (1956) 115, 131.

A spearhead of late type [*BSA* 63 (1968) 107] is
said to have come from a grave here.

K 10 (= L 10) MAZARAKI ZITSAS: PALAIO-
KOULI *
BA LH III(A2-B) LH IIIC?

AE (1969) 191; *AD* 24 (1969) B 252.

Cist graves were found here on the south slope of
the hill Palaiokouli, overlooking the river Thyamas.
The contents of one included an imported stirrup-jar,
a local imitation of an alabastron, and some bronzes,
the finest of which is a Type D sword. A kylix-stem
from the fill of this grave is assigned to LH IIIC.

K 11 (= L 11) METSOVO: between ANTHO-
CHORI and VOTONOSI
BA? LH III(B-C)? A C

AD 23 (1968) B 293; *AE* (1969) 197.

A spear was found in a cist at Pyrgos to north of
Anthochori, on the south bank of the river Arachthos,
about 4 km. southwest of Metsovo, and opposite
Votonosi.

L 12 VOUVALA-LIKOUDHI
N LH III "PG"

PAE (1914) 192; *AD* 18 (1963) B 133, Pl. 170b-c.

Tholos tombs and magoulas with Neolithic pottery
were reported from the area described as between the
villages of Vouvala and Likoudhi. One Mycenaean
and one Protogeometric vase from here are in the Elasson collection.

L 13 GREVENA
LH IIIA?

W.A. Heurtley, *Prehistoric Macedonia* (1939) 102; *AE* (1953-4)
B 120 n. 1.

Two Mycenaean rapiers, one of the horned and
one of the cruciform type, were found near Grevena.
They have been compared (*AE loc.cit.*) with a rapier in
Skopje Museum from the Yugoslavian area of Macedonia.

L 14 KOZANI *
BA LH IIIB-C C

PAE (1950) 281, (1958) 96; *AE* (1953-4) B 113.

During the construction of the Kozani-Verroia
road, a Classical cemetery was discovered, about
150 m. to south of the modern Kozani cemetery. LH
IIIB-C sherds were found in the fill of some of the
Classical tombs, and the apsidal end of a Bronze Age
house was also uncovered.

L 15 PLATANIAS (formerely BOUBOUSTI) *
BA LH III(B-C) "PG"

BSA 28 (1926-7) 158, Heurtley (1939), n. 4; *AE* (1953-4) B 120
n. 2; *BICS* 22 (1975) 210.

The site is a hill between the village of Boubousti
and the Haliakmon river. Most of the pottery here was
of a local Bronze Age type, but one sherd (*BSA* 28 Fig.
29 no. 3) is LH III, and there is some Protogeometric.
A class of the local pottery much resembles that of
Kastritsa (K 5 above).

INTRODUCTION
TO CENTRAL MACEDONIA (L 16-51)

The main sources for Mycenaean finds in this area
are W.A. Heurtley, *Prehistoric Macedonia* (1939), especially pp. 124, 129, and the maps on pp. xxii-xxiii; Ph.
M. Petsas, in *AE* (1953-4) B 113 ff., especially p. 114
n. 1 and p. 120 nn. 1-2; V.R. d'A. Desborough, *The
Last Mycenaeans and Their Successors* (1964), especially
pp. 139 ff.; D.H. French, *Index of Prehistoric Sites in
Central Macedonia* (1967). References to French (1967)
are here given first, and attention is drawn to the fact
that the extremely full and comprehensive references
given in that excellent work are not normally repeated
here. The additional numbers given here after the site
names (*e.g.* "*CM* No. G 11" for L 16 etc.) are those assigned by French. (N.B. *CM* is used as an abbreviation
for Central Macedonia.) The names are usually those
of the modern villages. Former names of villages are
here given in brackets after the current names. The
sites near Salonica are listed first (Nos. L 16 to L 22),
followed by sites in the Chalcidice peninsula (Nos. L
23 to L 29). Next comes the Langadas region (Nos. L 30
to L 34), followed by the Galliko and Axios river valleys (Nos. L 35 to L 51). Other sites, where Mycenaean
sherds have probably or possibly been found, are
listed separately at the end. Some chronological divisions given by French are here omitted, *i.e.* the sub-
divisions of Neolithic and Early Bronze Age, and his
indications "Iron Age and Later" for material later
than LB which can not be securely dated.

Since I have not visited any of these sites, I have
not been able to check any of the topography. For sites
not yet excavated, I have excerpted some of the topographical details given by French. For the topography

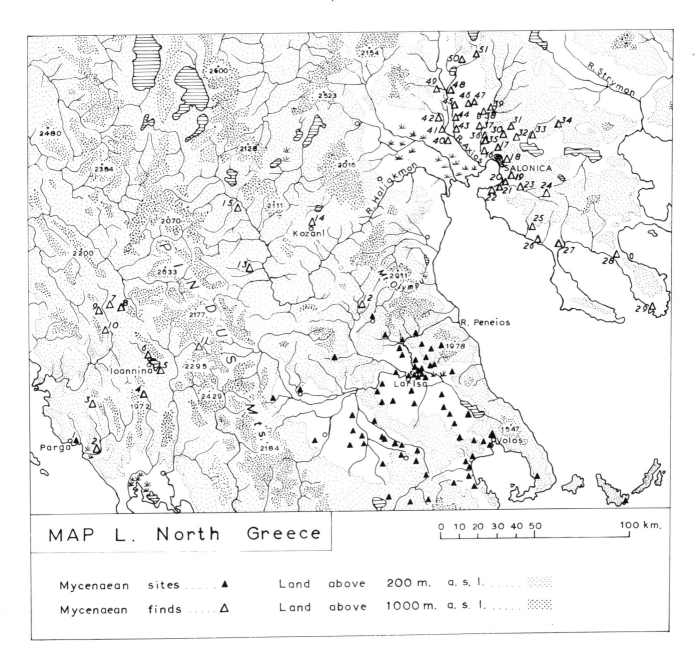

MAP L. North Greece

Mycenaean sites ..... ▲   Land above 200 m. a.s.l. .....

Mycenaean finds ..... △   Land above 1000 m. a.s.l. .....

of excavated sites, readers are referred mainly to the excavation reports (listed by French).

L 16 LACHANOKIPOS (ARAPLI) (CM No. G 11)
LB LH (III)

D.H. French, *Index of Prehistoric Sites in Central Macedonia* (1967) 17, 60.

Arapli is a small low mound on the southwest edge of Lachanokipos, in the plain near the east bank of the river Galliko. A few Mycenaean sherds have been found here, but are outnumbered by the local LB.

L 17 ASPROVRYSI (AKBOUNAR) * (CM No. S 5)
LB LH (III)

French (1967) 6, 57.

This low mound lies in rolling country below foothills, about 1.5 km. southeast of Asprovrysi village. Several Mycenaean surface sherds were found here, but are outnumbered by the local LB.

L 18 KALAMARIA * (CM No. S. 1)
N EB MB LB LH I or II? LH III

French (1967) 13, 59.

This low mound is on sloping ground in a suburb of Salonica. The six Mycenaean surface sherds recorded by French are said to include one of LH I or LH II date. Only one sherd of local LB is listed.

L 19 THERMI TOUMBA (SEDES) * (CM No. V 4)
N EB MB LB LH IIIB "PG"

French (1967) 34, 66; *BCH* 41-3 (1917-9) 248 Pl. 48; Heurtley (1939) 24; V.R. d'A. Desborough, *The Last Mycenaeans and Their Successors* (1964); *BICS* 22 (1975) 208.

Sedes is a large high mound about 1 km. to northeast of the village of Thermi, and about 6 km. to southeast of Salonica. At this important site, Rey (*BCH loc.cit.*) was said to have established the existence of a "Mycenaean stratum" (Heurtley, *loc.cit.*), in which, as at Gona (L 20 below) Mycenaean pottery was termed "the characteristic ware of the Late Bronze Age" (Desborough, *loc.cit.*). But Wardle (*op.cit.*) implies that all Mycenaean pottery in Central Macedonia probably consists either of imports or local imitations.

L 20 GONA * (CM No. V 3)
EB MB LB LH IIIB "PG"

French (1967) 12, 59; *BCH* 41-3 (1917-9) 248 Fig. 46, Pl. 47; Heurtley (1939) 23; Desborough (1964) 140.

Gona is a fairly small low mound about 4 km. to south of Salonica. As at Sedes (L 19), strong Mycenaean influence was observed in the pottery (Desborough, *loc.cit.*).

L 21 LIVADHI (TSAIR) * (CM No. V 5)
EB LB LH III

French (1967) 19, 61; Heurtley (1939) xxiii; Desborough (1964) 140 n. 5.

Some Mycenaean surface sherds were found at Tsair, on a small tumulus in the plain, about 8 km. to south of Salonica.

L 22 EPIVATAI (CM No. V 7)
EB MB? LB LH (III)

French (1967) 11, 59.

This is a small low mound at the edge of a small coastal plain, about 600 m. southwest of Epivatai and about 500 m. from the sea. Two Mycenaean sherds and sixteen of local LB were among the surface finds.

L 23 LOUTRA THERMIS (CM No. V 10)
EB LB LH (III)

French (1967) 20, 61.

The site is a fairly large low mound in the plain, about 2 km. west of the village of Loutra. Among the surface finds are four local LB sherds and one Mycenaean.

L 24 GALATISTA (CM No. V 8)
LB LH (III)

French (1967) 11, 59.

A low mound, about 5.5 km. to southwest of Galatista was discovered by French, who recorded twenty-four sherds of local LB and five Mycenaean.

L 25 NEA SYLLATA (CM No. C 13)
EB MB? LH LH (III) "PG" C or H

French (1967) 24, 63.

This large conical mound, with "table" below, lies in a valley about 2.5 km. northeast of Nea Syllata. Surface finds include seven local LB and three Mycenaean sherds.

L 26 PHLOYITA (CM No. C 5)
N EB LB LH (III)

French (1967) 29, 65.

This large low mound lies on an isolated ridge, about 750 m. from the shore, between the villages of Playia and Phloyita. Surface sherds include one of local LB and four Mycenaean.

L 27 AYIOS MAMAS * (CM No. C 1)
N EB MB LB LH IIIA2? LH IIIB LH IIIC?

French (1967) 8, 57; *BSA* 29 (1927-8) 117; Desborough (1964) 140; *BICS* 22 (1975) 208.

This important site is a fairly large high mound on

the edge of a river-plain, about 1 km. north of Ayios Mamas and about 750 m. to south of the village of Olynthos. Some of the Mycenaean sherds were described by the excavators (Heurtley and Radford) as of Tell-el-Amarna type (LH IIIA2?), and as being of excellent quality technically, contrasting with the local LB, Desborough classes the Mycenaean as probably LH IIIB, "with a few pieces that might be later".

L 28 NIKITA (*CM* No. SI 3)
EB? MB LH (III)

French (1967) 26, 63.

A fairly large low mound was discovered by French on an isolated ridge about 1.5 km. southeast of Nikita. Several sherds of local LB were collected, but only one Mycenaean.

L 29 TORONE (*CM* No. SI 4)
EB MB LB LH (III)

French (1967) 35, 66; *Ergon* for 1976, 68; *BCH* 101 (1977) 606.

The prehistoric site is under the mediaeval fort on the Torone peninsula. Four Mycenaean sherds and two of local LB are among the surface finds recorded. Prehistoric levels are now being investigated on the Lekythos promontory.

L 30 DHRYMOS (*CM* No. L 4)
N EB LB LH (III)

French (1967) 9, 58.

A small mound lies under the northeast part of Dhrymos village. Surface finds here include ten sherds each of Mycenaean and local LB.

L 31 ASSIROS TOUMBA * (*CM* No. L 6)
MB LB LH IIIB-C "PG"

French (1967) 6, 57; AR (1975-6) 19, (1977-8) 44.

The site is a mound of moderate size, about 2 km. to southwest of Assiros village, on the west side of the Salonica-Serres road. Three seasons of excavations conducted here by K.A. Wardle have already revealed an important stratigraphic sequence from c. 2000 to c. 900 B.C. The structures, both of the Bronze Age and of the Iron Age strata contained many fragments of Mycenaean pottery, some imported, but most of local Macedonian manufacture.

L 32 PERIVOLAKI (SARATSE) * (*CM* No. L 5)
EB MB? LB LH IIIA2? LH IIIB LH IIIC? PG

French (1967) 28, 64; BSA 30 (1929-30) 113; Heurtley (1939) 26, 124, 222; Desborough (1964) 140; BICS 22 (1975) 208, 210.

Saratse is a mound of medium size, about 1 km. south of Perivolaki village, in the plain to northeast of Salonica. This inland site produced Mycenaean pottery in relatively large quantity; and Heurtley inferred from this, and from similar evidence at Vardarophtsa

(L 45), that there were actually Mycenaean coastal and riverside trading stations in Macedonia. The Mycenaean sherds and local imitations are mainly LH IIIB, but some may be LH IIIA2 and LH IIIC.

L 33 CHRYSAVYI (*CM* No. L 15)
EB LB LH (III)

French (1967) 16, 60.

This low mound of considerable size lies about 2.5 km. northeast of Chrysavyi village. Many sherds of local LB and almost as many Mycenaean (including local imitations) were found here.

L 34 SOCHOS: TOUMBA TOU OURDHA * (*CM* No. L 16)
LB LH (III)

French (1967) 33, 66.

Survey work and minor excavations have been carried out at this mound on a small knoll about 1.5 km. southwest of Sochos. A few Mycenaean sherds are recorded, but local LB predominated.

L 35 PENTALOPHOS B (*CM* No. G 6)
EB LB LH (III)

French (1967) 27, 64.

A small high mound and a larger "table" are recorded on the edge of the Galliko river plain, about 2 km. southwest of Pentalophos. Surface sherds include seven Mycenaean and eleven local LB.

L 36 PENTALOPHOS A (*CM* No. G 9)
EB LB LH (III) C?

French (1967) 27, 64.

This high mound of moderate size lies in dissected country near the east bank of the river Galliko, about 2 km. west-northwest of Pentalophos. The surface sherds collected include three Mycenaean and ten local LB.

L 37 PHILADELPHIANA TOUMBA (*CM* No. G 5)
EB MB LB LH (III)

French (1967) 29, 64.

The mound is on a high isolated knoll above the Galliko river, about 1.5 km. south of Philadelphiana. Only three sherds of local LB and one Mycenaean were recorded by French, and the Mycenaean sherd was thought to be a local imitation.

L 38 XYLOKERATIA (GIATZILAR) (*CM* No. G 4)
N LB LH (III)

French (1967) 40, 69; Desborough (1964) 140 n. 5.

This small mound lies on an isolated hill about 1.5 km. south of Xylokeratia. Surface finds include several LB and Mycenaean.

L 39 GALLIKO (*CM* No. G 3)
  EB LB? LH (III) H?

French (1967) 12, 59.

This medium sized low mound about 500 m. east of Galliko, lies on the edge of the river plain, not far from the west bank of the Galliko river. One Mycenaean sherd was found, so that LB habitation may be presumed.

L 40 VALTOCHORI (*CM* No. A 16)
  N LB LH (III)

French (1967) 38, 68.

This low mound lies in the plain about 1.5 km. southwest of Nea Chalkidon, and about 1.5 km. east of Valtochori. It is interesting that more Mycenaean surface sherds have been recorded than local LB.

L 41 KOUPHALIA A (*CM* No. A 15)
  N LB? LH III

French (1967) 16, 60.

A Mycenaean kylix fragment was found on a very large mound here about 750 m. north of Nea Chalkidon.

L 42 TOUMBA LIVADHI (*CM* No. A 13)
  MB? LB LH (III)

French (1967) 36, 67.

A mound of uncertain size was discovered by French about 1.5 km. north of Kouphalia. Fifteen LB and four Mycenaean sherds are among the surface finds.

L 43 DOURMOUSLI (*CM* No. A 7)
  EB MB LB LH (III)

French (1967) 10, 58.

On this small low mound near the river Axios at least eleven LB surface sherds and five Mycenaean have been found.

L 44 KASTANIA (KARAOGLOU) (*CM* No. A 6)
  LB LH IIIA? LH IIIB-C "PG" C

French (1967) 15, 60; *BCH* 101 (1977) II 602.

This mound, about 13 m. high, is on the right bank of the Axios river, about 1.5 km. west-southwest of Kastania village. Recent excavations have revealed some Mycenaean pottery and a burnt layer of the period of transition from the Bronze Age to the Iron Age.

L 45 AXIOCHORI (VARDAROPHTSA) * (*CM* No. A 4)
  EB MB? LB LH IIIB-C "PG" G C H

French (1967) 7, 57; *BSA* 27 (1925-6) 1, 28, (1926-7) 195;

Heurtley (1939) 36; Desborough (1964) 140; *BICS* 22 (1975) 206, 208.

This important site, consisting of a mound and a "table" below, is at the south end of the village of Axiochori, on high ground overlooking the Axios river plain. The excavators claimed that of one hundred and fifty Mycenaean fragments found only twelve were imported. They declared that Vardarophtsa was a secondary centre of manufacture and distribution of Mycenaean pottery. The LB deposits were unusually thick; and there is evidence of a destruction at some time during the LH IIIC period. Mycenaean pottery continued in use, however, even after the occupation by northern invaders. Apparently the settlement continued, without further break, into the early Iron Age.

L 46 ANTHOPHYTOS A (SARIBAZAR) (*CM* No. A 5)
  EB LB LH (III)

French (1967) 5, 57.

This is a small low mound about 2.5 km. east of Anthophytos, in the plain on the edge of a river marsh. Only two LB sherds and one Mycenaean sherd are recorded by French.

L 47 ANTHOPHYTOS B (SARIBAZAR) (*CM* No. A 17)
  LB LH (III)

French (1967) 5, 57.

The site is a medium-sized low mound, about 3 km. east-northeast of Anthophytos A, in the plain near a stream. French lists twenty-three LB sherds and only one Mycenaean.

L 48 LIMNOTOPOS (VARDINO) * (*CM* No. A 3)
  N EB LB LH IIIB-C C

French (1967) 18, 61; *LAAA* 12 (1925) 15; Heurtley (1939) 33, 152; *AE* (1953-4) B 114 n. 1; Desborough (1964) 140, 142; *BICS* 22 (1975) 209.

Vardino is a small high mound of conical shape, on a natural hill overlooking the Axios river plain, about 1.5 km. south of Limnotopos. Like Vardarophtsa (L 45), this inland site produced a fair quantity of Mycenaean pottery, apparently of the same range (LH IIIB-C) as that found at Vardarophtsa. The site is, however, neither large nor important.

L 49 TOUMBA PAIONIAS (*CM* No. A 10)
  MB LB LH III(A2-B)

French (1967) 35, 67; *AE* (1953-4) B 113.

The site is on a small isolated knoll, overlooking a tributary of the Axios river, about 1.5 km. north of the village. Only one Mycenaean sherd was found with the local LB surface sherds.

L 50   TSAOUTSITSA   *   (*CM* No. A 2)
LB LH (III)

French (1967) 37, 67; *Archaeologia* 74 (1923-4) 73 Pl. 27, 1, i; *BSA* 26 (1923-5) 1; S. Casson, *Macedonia, Thrace, and Illyria* (1926) 128, 132, 134; Desborough (1964) 140, 142; *BICS* 22 (1975) 208.

At this remote site, some distance to east of the main Axios valley, only one Mycenaean sherd (*Archaeologica loc.cit.*) was found with the local LB in the excavations.

L 51   KALINDRIA (KILINDIR)   *   (*CM* No. A 1)
EB LB LH III(B-C)

French (1967) 14, 59; *AJ* 6 (1926) 59; *RE* Suppl. VI (1935) 611; Heurtley (1939) 31; Desborough (1964) 140; *BICS* 22 (1975) 208.

Kilindir is the northernmost site in Macedonia where Mycenaean pottery has been found. The finds are said to have included a stirrup-jar (*RE loc.cit.*).

APPENDIX TO MAP L

The following are sites in central Macedonia where Mycenaean finds have been claimed, but where the evidence is still not conclusive. In particular the finds are *not* confirmed by Heurtley (1939) or by Petsas [in *AE* (1953-4) B p. 114 n. 1]. The sites are arranged in approximately the same order as the sites (L 16 to L 51) where Mycenaean finds have been clearly demonstrated.

PYLAIA (KAPOUTZIDES)   (*CM* No. S 3)
N? LB LH III?

French (1967) 31, 65; *AE* (1953-4) B 114 n. 1.

Petsas (*AE loc.cit.*) cites Heurtley (1939) as the authority for alleged Mycenaean finds at this mound about 4 km. east of the outskirts of Salonica. But Heurtley records only LB finds here. Further LB surface sherds were also found here by French.

LEMBET   (*CM* No. S 2)
LB LH III?

French (1967) 18, 45, 61; *BSA* 20 (1913-4) 128.

This mound is on the northern outskirts of Salonica, near the road to Serres. Surface sherds included some apparently of Mycenaean type (*BSA loc.cit.*).

VASILIKA B   (*CM* No. V 2)
EB LB? LH III?

French (1967) 38, 68; *BSA* 20 (1913-4) 128; Casson (1926) 134.

This low mound lies in the plain, about 1 km. east of Vasilika, and about 25 km. southeast of Salonica. Casson includes this site in his list of those where "Mycenaean" sherds were said to have been found, following the list made by Wace (*BSA loc.cit.*).

MESIMERIANI TOUMBA   (*CM* No. C 10)
N EB LB LH III?

French (1967) 20, 61; *AA* (1936) 146.

A few LB sherds, and one possible Mycenaean, are recorded from this low mound, about 3 km. north-northwest of Mesimeri, and about 30 km. south of Salonica.

MESIMERI   *   (*CM* No. C 11)
EB LB? LH IIIC?

French (1967) 21, 43, 62; *AA* (1937) 150; *BICS* 22 (1975) 209.

This is a very small mound on the north side of Mesimeri village. The earliest graves in a cremation cemetery here were said to be Mycenaean.

KRITZIANA: TOUMBA MESIMERIATIKI   * (*CM* No. C 3)
LB LH III?

French (1967) 17, 44, 80; Heurtley (1939) 17, 158; *AAA* 7 (1974) 268.

This low mound lies on the coast about 6 km. south-southeast of Epanomi. It is not clear whether or not there were Mycenaean sherds in the LB stratum investigated here by Heurtley. In a valuable note (*AAA loc.cit.*) Th. Pazaras sets in order the topography of the coastal sites between Epanomi and Nea Kallikratia on the east coast of the Thermaic Gulf. His proposed names are here adopted for this site and the following two sites.

TABLE METOCHI KRITZIANA
LB LH III?

French (1967) 43, 44; *BCH* 41-43 (1917-9) 163 no. 2; *RE* Suppl. VI (1935) 611; *AAA* 7 (1974) 268.

According to Karo (*RE loc.cit.*), LH III sherds were found by L. Rey (*BCH loc.cit.*) on this site (named "Apanomi Table A" by French) on the coast about 5 km. south of Epanomi.

TOUMBA NEA KALLIKRATIA   (*CM* No. C 12)
N EB? MB LB LH III? "PG" C H

French (1967) 22, 62; *BCH* 41-43 (1917-9) 166; *AAA* 7 (1974) 268.

This small low mound lies on the east side of Nea Kallikratia. Among the many sherds collected here by French were a few apparently Mycenaean, but these are by far outnumbered by the LB.

NEA TRIGLIA: YILI   (*CM* No. C 14)
N LB? LH III? "PG" C or H

French (1967) 25, 63; *BSA* 20 (1913-4) 128; Casson (1926) 134.

The site is about 4 km. north of Nea Triglia, on a high isolated knoll, inland, and about 10 km. north of Phloyita (L 26). Mycenaean surface pottery was claimed here by Casson, following Wace (*BSA loc.cit.*).

ANCIENT OLYNTHOS   *   (*CM* **No. C 2**)
N   EB   LB?   LH III?   A   C   H

French (1967) 26, 63; *BSA* 20 (1913-4) 128; G.E. Mylonas, *Olynthus I* (1929) *passim*; *AA* (1932) 160; *RE* Suppl. VI (1935) 612.

The prehistoric site was on the natural rock, under part of the ancient city. Mycenaean sherds have been claimed (*RE loc.cit.*). The site is about 3 km. northeast of Ayios Mamas (L 27).

MOLYVOPYRGO   *   (*CM* **No. C 4**)
EB   MB   LB   LH III?

French (1967) 21, 62; *BSA* 29 (1927-8) 156; *RE* Suppl. VI (1935) 611; Heurtley (1939) 10; *BICS* 22 (1975) 208.

This mound lies on a small natural ridge, about 100 m. from the shore, and about 6 km. east of Ayios Mamas (L 27). Mycenaean finds were claimed (*RE loc.cit.*), but no certainly Mycenaean sherds were found in the excavations (*BSA loc.cit.*).

YEPHYRA (TOPTSIN)   (*CM* **No. A 8**)
N   LB?   LH III?   C or H

French (1967) 40, 69; Fimmen (1921) 95; *RE* Suppl. VI (1935) 611; Heurtley (1939) 76, 154, 235.

This very large mound, about 1 km. southeast of Yephyra village, lies near the original mouth of the Axios river, and about 5 km. to southeast of Dourmousli (L 43). Karo (*RE loc.cit.*) claims Mycenaean sherds from this site, referring to Fimmen (*loc.cit.*). But Heurtley does not even report LB from here.

ASPROS TOUMBA   (*CM* **No. A 19**)
EB   MB?   LB   LH III?   "PG"   C?   H

French (1967) 5, 57.

This small low mound overlooks the river plain of the Axios. Among the very few surface sherds col-lected here are two which may be Mycenaean. The site is about 1.5 km. north of the village of Aspros Toumba, and about 3 km. south of Vardino (L 48).

TOUMBA RAKHONA   (*CM* **No. A 12**)
LB   LH III?

French (1967) 36, 67.

A few LB sherds and some possibly Mycenaean were found by French on this mound, which lies on a tributary of the Axios river, about 1 km. northeast of Rakhona.

NEOCHORI   (*CM* **No. P. 2**)
LB   LH III?

French (1967) 25, 63.

This large high mound lies on the edge of hill country, overlooking the coastal plain near the mouth of the Haliakmon river. A few LB sherds and one or two possibly Mycenaean are recorded here by French.

For the following sites the alleged evidence for Mycenaean finds is weak:

SALONICA: AYIOS ILIAS [mentioned by Fimmen (1921) 95, but not confirmed subsequently];

ANKHIALOS (INGILIZ), described by Fimmen (*loc.cit*) as "Am linken Ufer der Galiko" [*cf.* French (1967) 42, 45];

UCHEVLI (now NEOCHORI) in Chalcidice, listed by Casson (1926) 134, citing *BSA* 20 (1913-4) 128;

VERGINA, where, according to Wardle [*BICS* 22 (1975) 209], "The earliest tumuli contained two Mycenaean left-overs . . ." [*cf. AR* (1958) 13]. It is apparent that the vases in question are either imitations made after the Mycenaean period, or survivals which may be out of context and location.

THE NORTHERN SPORADES
SKYROS
THE CYCLADES

MAP M

Since I have visited only a few of these islands, full topographical notes will not be given here. For most details I have relied on the work of K. Scholes, C. Renfrew, and R. Barber. Mr. Barber is currently studying the later periods of the Bronze Age in the Cyclades; and Professor Renfrew and his team are re-investigating Phylakopi on Melos, and are also surveying the island of Melos as a whole. I am greatly indebted to Mr. Barber for details on some of the Late Bronze Age sites.

In general, the pattern of excavation and surface survey work carried out in the Cyclades is uneven, and it is obvious that many more prehistoric sites remain to be found. In contrast to the already numerous Early Bronze Age sites, Middle and Late Bronze Age sites so far discovered are few [cf. Renfrew, The Emergence of Civilisation (1972) Appendix I]. In these later periods there is a tendency towards selection of "acropolis" sites of a defensible nature. By the end of the Early Bronze Age, the rise in eustatic sea level may have diminished considerably the amount of arable land in the islands.

SKOPELOS

CAPE STAPHYLOS *
LH IIA-III(A-B)

KC 3 (1949) 534; BCH 62 (1938) 481.

A rectangular built tomb was found on a hill near Cape Staphylos at the southeast tip of Skopelos. Some objects of bronze (including a rapier) and gold were found, together with several vases, most of which are LH IIB-IIIA1.

SKYROS

KASTRO
N EB MH LH IIIA-C PG G A C H

H. Hansen, "Prehistoric Skyros", in Studies Presented to D.M. Robinson (ed. G.E. Mylonas) I (1951) 54; Archeion Euboikon Meleton 6 (1959) 313; AD (1967) B 287; N.K. Sandars, The Sea Peoples (1978) 130 Ill. 85.

The hill of Kastro on the south side of modern Skyros town was the acropolis of ancient Skyros. Traces of a chamber tomb cemetery have been noted on the lower northeast slope of the hill, and this may be the source of several vases in the museum (cf. AD loc.cit.), the most interesting of which is a LH IIIC stirrup-jar decorated with a ship (Sandars, loc.cit.). Surface finds on the hill include EB and MH, and at Magazia to north the sherds included one Mycenaean.

ANDROS

PALAIOUPOLIS
LH III(A2-B)

BSA 51 (1956) 11, 31.

Palaioupolis is near the southwest coast not far from the centre of the island. Three Mycenaean vases in the Andros museum are given this provenance. They presumably come from a tomb.

EPISKOPIO
LH (III)

BSA 51 (1956) 11, 31.

A Mycenaean alabastron in the Andros museum is said to have come from this village, in the hills behind the bay of Korthi near the south end of Andros.

TENOS

VRYOKASTRO (AKROTERION OURION)
EB III? MB LH III(A-B) G

BSA 51 (1956) 13, 15, 21, 32, 69 (1974) 50; AA (1972) 164.

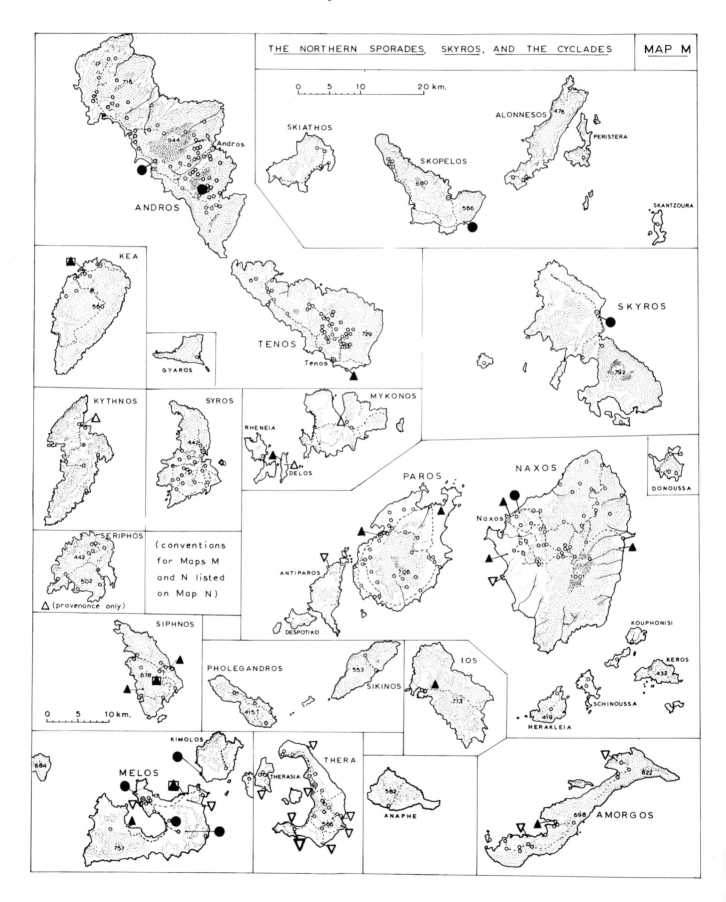

THE NORTHERN SPORADES, SKYROS, AND THE CYCLADES   MAP M

0   5   10   20 km.

ALONNESOS
SKIATHOS
SKOPELOS
PERISTERA
SKANTZOURA

ANDROS
Andros
KEA
GYAROS
TENOS
Tenos
SKYROS

KYTHNOS
SYROS
MYKONOS
RHENEIA
DELOS
DONOUSSA

SERIPHOS
(conventions for Maps M and N listed on Map N)
△ (provenance only)
PAROS
NAXOS
Naxos
ANTIPAROS
DESPOTIKO
KOUPHONISI
KEROS
SCHINOUSSA
HERAKLEIA

SIPHNOS
PHOLEGANDROS
SIKINOS
IOS

0   5   10 km.

KIMOLOS
MELOS
THERA
THERASIA
ANAPHE
AMORGOS

This is a high acropolis at the end of a wide bay at the south tip of the island, about 2.5 km. southeast of the town of Tenos. Occupation was particularly intense in the Middle Bronze Age, to which the fortifications identified may belong (*cf. BSA* 69 *loc.cit.*), since there is relatively little material later than the Bronze Age.

KEA

AYIA IRINI *
N EB II-III MB LB I-II LH IIIA1-C PG G A C H

BSA 51 (1956) 11; *Hesperia* 31 (1962) 266, 33 (1964) 317, 35 (1966) 364, 40 (1971) 359, 41 (1972) 357; *AR* (1972-3) 23, (1973-4) 28, (1974-5) 21, (1975-6) 23; *AJA* 81 (1977) 516, 82 (1978) 349; Schoder (1974) 108.

The site is a low promontory, now partly submerged, projecting into the sheltered bay of Vourkari. It already had a fortification wall and substantial houses in the Middle Bronze Age; and connections with Crete, which began in MM II, grew progressively stronger up to their peak in LM IB. But connections with the Greek mainland were also strong in LB I-II, when almost as much LH I-II as LM IA-B was imported. The town was completely destroyed at a time late in the LM IB period. After this it lost most of its importance. The pottery from LH IIIA1 onwards is purely LH in type and there are progressively fewer buildings. The only material certainly subsequent to LH IIIA2 is that found in the "temple", which was apparently rebuilt after the earthquake and flourished until late in LH IIIC, when another destruction preserved many whole pots very similar to those of the third major LH IIIC phase of Lefkandi (B 67).

SYKAMIAS (not marked on Map M)
N EB LH III(B-C)? PG?

Hesperia 41 (1972) 358.

Some fragments of deep bowls found on this promontory on the northeast coast may be LH IIIB or LH IIIC, or even of the early Dark Age.

KYTHNOS

AYIA IRINI
MB LH I/II

BSA 51 (1956) 12, 21, 30.

There is slight evidence of prehistoric occupation on a low conical hill on a promontory about 200 m. west of Ayia Irini, on the south side of Loutra Bay in the northeast of the island. Finds include a LH I/II "Vapheio" cup base, presumably imported.

A stirrup-jar of LH IIIA2-B date is also said to have come from Kythnos (*MV* 32).

MYKONOS

PALAIKASTRO
EB? MB LB? PG G A C

BSA 51 (1956) 12, 15, 21; *BCH* 88 (1964) 556; Renfrew (1972) 514 (No. 6); *AD* 26 (1971) B 463; Bintliff (1977) 589.

Palaikastro is a small and high acropolis hill about 1.5 km. inland from Panormos Bay. Occupation in the Middle Bronze Age is securely attested, and Barber reports sherds almost certainly of LH type, among the larger quantities of later material.

DELOS

THE TEMENOS *
MB? LH I-II LH IIIA-C PG G A C H

BCH 71-2 (1947-8) 148, 89 (1965) 225, 90 (1966) 100; *BSA* 51 (1956) 11, 22, 27, 30, 34; H. Gallet de Santerre, *Délos primitive et archaïque* (1958); Desborough (1964) 148; Schoder (1974) 53; Bintliff (1977) 595.

The small amount of LB material from the site of the later sanctuary, on flat ground to northwest of Mt. Kynthos, suggests that the LB settlement here may have had a history similar to that of Ayia Irini on Kea and Phylakopi on Melos. The Theke, or "Tomb of the Hyperborean Maidens" appears to have been a LB tomb, from which came a wide range of material, including a probably LM I hole-mouth jar. The Sema may possibly have been a tomb also.

Doubt has been expressed [e.g. Desborough (1964) 44] about the date and nature of the claimed Mycenaean sanctuaries. The famous hoard of ivories and other objects found beneath the Artemision may be considered a foundation-deposit; but it was clearly laid down well after the Mycenaean period, and there is no guarantee that the objects attributable to LH were dedicated at a LH shrine or even found on the island originally [*cf. BCH* Suppl. 1 (1973) 415, where some of the ivories are argued to be of Cypriot origin and of the second half of the 13th century B.C.]. And the hoard is very mixed, including ordinary MB, LH, PG, and G pottery. Nevertheless, the apparent importance of the LB settlement here does require some special explanation, since the island is practically barren. There is no evidence of continuity between the LH IIIC period and the time of the next datable material, i.e. Late Protogeometric.

MT. KYNTHOS *
KS EB III MB? LH

A. Plassart, *Délos XI* (1928) 11, *Délos XV* Pl. I: 1; *BSA* 51 (1956) 11; *AA* (1972) 162.

This rather steep small hill, about 112 m. above sea level, dominates the island. There are remains of a settlement of Keros-Syros type, but Barber does not consider that MB occupation is proved; and the small number of Mycenaean sherds indicates use at this time but not necessarily a habitation site.

NAXOS

This appears to have been the most important island in the Cyclades in Mycenaean times, since far more Mycenaean material has been found here than on any of the other islands. The most productive areas of the island are in the centre and west; and the known Mycenaean settlements are mainly those near the west coast.

GROTTA (with PALATI, APLOMATA, KAMINI) *
GP KS EB III? MB LH I-II LH IIIA-C SMyc PG G A C H

AA (1930) 132, (1968) 374, (1972) 152, 165, (1974) 27 Fig. 47; *BSA* 51 (1956) 12, 15, 27, 30, 32, 34, 69 (1974) 53 n. 187; *PAE* (1949) 112, (1950) 269, (1951) 214, (1958) 228, (1959) 185, (1960) 262, (1961) 191, (1963) 148, (1965) 168, (1967) 112, (1969) 139, (1970) 146, (1971) 172, (1972) 143; *AD* 16 (1960) B 249; Desborough (1964) 149, 228, 232; *Kadmos* 4 (1965) 84; *Ergon* (1976) 154; *BCH* 101 (1977) II 637; A. Kardara, *Aplomata Naxou: Kineta Evrimata Taphon A kai B* (Athens 1977); Schoder (1974) 148.

The Mycenaean settlement at Grotta occupied a considerable area, on the north and northwest environs of the modern town of Naxos; and the Palati promontory may have served as its acropolis. There was a large settlement at Grotta in the early phases of the Early Bronze Age, but little MB-LB II material. The Mycenaean settlement flourished throughout LH III, and there may have been continuity into Protogeometric and Geometric times, although the buildings of these latter periods were on a quite different alignment from the preceding Mycenaean, which include Early and Late Mycenaean houses, and a building of megaron type.

There were extensive Mycenaean cemeteries on Aplomata hill about 2.5 km. to the northeast, and at Kamini about 2 km. to the east (and about a kilometre south of Aplomata). The Aplomata chamber tombs were in use from LH IIIB to SMyc, and pit-graves here in SMyc and PG. The LH IIIC Kamini cemetery and the LH IIIC tombs at Aplomata are particularly rich, and this was clearly one of the major centres of the Aegean at that time.

RIZOKASTELIA
KS? MB LH III(A-)B A

PAE (1910) 272; *BSA* 51 (1956) 12; *AA* (1972) 166; C. Renfrew, *The Emergence of Civilisation* (1972) 518 (no. 11).

This is a high and rocky acropolis about a kilometre southwest of Byblos (formerly Tripodes) and near the west coast. MB and LB sherds have been observed here by Scholes and also by Renfrew and by

Barber, who records a fragment from a LH IIIB/C deep bowl. There are possible traces of fortifications which might belong to MB or LB.

VIGLA
EB MB LB/LH

AD 20 (1965) B 507 n. 4; *BSA* 69 (1974) 50.

This promontory site, on the west coast about 4 km. southwest of Byblos, may also have been fortified. Among the surface finds recorded were sherds of decorated and plain wares of Minoan appearance, including conical cups.

LYGARIDIA (STENO) and KARVOUNOLAKKI *
EB LH IIIC

PAE (1906) 86; *AD* 20 (1965) B 505; *BSA* 69 (1974) 53 n. 186.

At least five EB graves were excavated at Lygaridia, about 2 km. south-southwest of Moutsounas, near the east coast of Naxos. A small built tomb here, and two rooms of a building excavated on the hillside of Karvounolakki above, are assigned to LH IIIC by Barber, who comments that Moutsouna is the only practicable harbour on the east coast.

PAROS

This island is also reasonably fertile, especially the lowland areas around the bay of Naoussa in the north and around Paroikia in the west, near the two main harbours. Further good land is found in the eastern coastal valleys.

PAROIKIA *
GP? KS? Phyl I MB LH IIIA-C PG G H

AM 42 (1917) 1; *BSA* 51 (1956) 12, 14, 20, 32, 34; *AA* (1972) 165.

The small low hill of Ayios Konstandinos in the centre of the modern town of Paroikia seems to have been the main settlement on Paros in the final phase of the Early Bronze Age and in the Middle Bronze Age. Some Mycenaean material has also been found, but remains of this period here have been much disturbed by later occupation.

KOUKOUNARIES * (incorrectly positioned on Map M)
EB MB? LH III(A?-)B PG G A

PAE (1974) 185, (1975) A 197; *Ergon* (1975) 140, (1976) 146, (1977) 144; *BCH* 101 (1977) II 635.

The site is a rocky acropolis on a remote and inaccessible headland on the northwest arm of the bay of Naoussa. The summit appears to have been artificially levelled for a large Mycenaean building, some of whose rooms were supported by a thick wall which may have served as a fortification. Storage pithoi were found in one of these rooms. A thick ash layer indicates a destruction by fire, which is said to have occurred in LH IIIC; but the published pottery all seems to be no later than LH IIIB. A Mycenaean burial was found in a small cave on the site. The recent discovery of this important site is a further dramatic indication of the incomplete nature of exploration for prehistoric sites in the Cyclades.

ANTIPAROS

This island possesses some small but productive cultivable areas. It would have been considerably larger in the Bronze Age, since in Neolithic times it was apparently linked to Paros by an isthmus [*cf.* J.D. Evans and A.C. Renfrew, *Excavations at Saliagos near Antiparos* (1968)].

"NORTHWEST PROMONTORY"
LB I

Renfrew (1972) 524 Fig. (Approx. I.6 no. 15).

On a promontory on the northwest coast of Antiparos, not far from the town of Antiparos, surface sherds were found including one with ripple decoration.

SERIPHOS

The only indication of possible Late Bronze Age habitation here is the single LH IIIA2 stirrup-jar reported to have come from the island [*BSA* 51 (1956) 32].

SIPHNOS

The coasts of Siphnos are mainly steep. The small amount of agricultural land is concentrated mainly in the east central district and around the inhabited bays.

AYIOS ANDREAS *
EB? MB LH IIIB G A C H

AE (1899) 115; *AD* 25 (1970) B 431; *AAA* 6 (1973) 93; *AR* (1972-3) 25, (1975-6) 23; *Ergon* (1975) 152, (1976) 141, (1977) 139; *PAE* (1975) A 235; *BCH* 101 (1977) II 635.

The site is a steep acropolis in a dominant position in the interior of the island, about 2 km. to south of Apollona. Well constructed and well preserved fortifications of the LH IIIB period, including 8 towers, enclose an area about 100 m. north to south by 90 m. There are also remains of a stairway which must have given access to the battlements. A small building of the same date has been found within the walls and another outside on the northeast, and a few traces of earlier habitation (in MB); but most of the excavated buildings are of Late Geometric date. Nevertheless it is probable that this fortified site was the main Mycenaean centre on the island.

KASTRO *
GP? Phyl I MB LH III(A) PG G A C H

BSA 44 (1949) 15, 31, 51, (1956) 12, 15, 32.

Excavations at this small natural acropolis on the east coast revealed sparse prehistoric material, and nothing Mycenaean. But a LH III surface sherd was found, and it is surmised that the later occupation of the site has removed most of the traces of prehistoric habitation here.

TO FROUDHI TOU KALAMITSIOU
LH III(A-B)

D. Fimmen *Die kretisch-mykenische Kultur* (1921) 14; *BSA* 51 (1956) 12, 32; *AAA* 6 (1973) 101.

On this lofty acropolis, on the west coast about 1.5 km. north of Vathy harbour, Mycenaean surface sherds have been found.

AMORGOS

The best land on Amorgos is that around the best harbours in the northwest coast, namely the bays of Katapola, Aigiali, and Kaloteri. Most of the southwest is high and unproductive; and the hills in the centre are a formidable obstacle to land communications between the southwest and northeast villages.

AIGIALE: VIGLI
EB (KS) MB LB/LH? A C

AM 11 (1886) 40; *Kykladika I* 138; *BSA* 51 (1956) 11.

Some material of the Middle Bronze Age and some apparently of the Late Bronze Age has been found at this small acropolis, about 500 m. northwest of Tholaria, near the north tip of the island, and about a kilometre from the sea.

XILOKERATIDI
EB (KS) LH III(A-C?)

CVA British Museum Pl. 484 no. 11; *BSA* 51 (1956) 11, 29, 31, 34; *AR* (1961-2) 22; Desborough (1964) 147.

A Mycenaean sherd has been found at this site, which lies about a kilometre west of Katapola, at the north end of the harbour bay. And some Mycenaean vases and sherds from Amorgos probably came from tombs in the neighbourhood. Indeed a LH III stirrup-jar was purchased at the site by Bosanquet (*CVA loc.cit.*); and a plundered Mycenaean chamber tomb was found near Katapola in 1961.

ARKESINE (KASTRI) *
KS Phyl I MB? LB/LH H

AM 11 (1886) 16; *Kykladika I* 208; E.-M. Bossert, in *Festschrift für Peter Goessler* (1954) 23; *BSA* 51 (1956) 11; *AJA* 71 (1967) 11.

Kastri is a steep-sided acropolis about 1.5 km. north of Vroutsi, on the north coast towards the southwest end of the island. Nearby tombs are the source of a group of weapons of Mycenaean type.

IOS

Ios is hilly and mainly infertile. The most productive area is that round the town and the harbour bay at the west end of the island.

CHORA
EB   MB   LB/LH

BSA 69 (1974) 50.

Sherds were collected by Barber at an un-named hill site about 1.5 km. north-northeast of Chora, the main town of Ios. They include fragments attributed to LB or LH.

KIMOLOS

This island has little water, and only a small amount of productive land, mainly in the south.

ELLINIKA
LH IIIA2-C   G   A   C   H

J.T. Bent, *The Cyclades* (1885) 55; *AM* 69-70 (1954-5) 154; *BSA* 51 (1956) 11, 29, 32; *AD* 20 (1965) B 514, 21 (1966) B 387.

The islet of Ayios Andreas was once joined to this promontory on the southwest coast. Substantial remains of buildings are to be seen on the islet and underwater. A cemetery of rock-cut tombs here appears to be LH, and good LH III pottery has been reported, although no excavations have been made. Vases seen by Moustakas (*AM loc.cit.*) are clearly LH IIIC, according to Barber.

MELOS

The island is the only important source of obsidian in the Aegean. The bay of Melos is an excellent harbour, a natural port between Crete and mainland Greece. The eastern half of the island consists of flat land or low hills, and is mainly cultivable. The west is hilly and much less fertile. The geography of the island is discussed in Bintliff (1977) 521-587; and the archaeological survey by C. Renfrew and J. Cherry is soon to be published.

PHYLAKOPI   *
GP   KS   Phyl I   MB   LB I-II   LH IIIA1-C   G

T.D. Atkinson *et. al.*, *The Excavations at Phylakopi in Melos* (1904); *BSA* 17 (1910-11) 1, 51 (1956) 12, 69 (1974) 1; *AD* 20 (1965) B 513, 22 (1967) B 465; *AA* (1972) 168; *AR* (1974-5) 23, (1975-6) 25; (1977-8) 52, Renfrew (1972) *passim*, especially 138 ff., 186 ff., *AJA* 82 (1978) 349; *Antiquity* 52 (1978) 7.

The site, now greatly eroded, was once a promontory, probably affording shelter to a harbour on its southwest side. Probably only about half of the site has survived; and the sea is continually eating into this remainder. Recent excavations have clarified its history, and especially that of the Late Bronze Age. The "Third City" of the beginning of LB, shows strong signs of Cretan influence. It had fortifications and a substantial building of complex type, suggestive of a Minoan villa. In a phase corresponding to LM IB, Cretan influence was surpassed by Mycenaean; and in the LH IIIA1 period the "Megaron", a prototype of the LH III palaces, was built. The site was still important in the LH IIIB period, when it was again fortified. Two successive shrines near these later fortifications were in use from LH IIIA to well into LH IIIC. Finds include both male and female figurines of unusual types.

KAPARI
Phyl I   MB   LB

Renfrew (1972) 511; *AD* 21 (1966) B 587.

A small settlement is indicated here about a kilometre to southeast of Phylakopi.

AYIOS ILIAS
MB   LB   G   A   C   H

BSA 51 (1956) 12.

Reported traces of MB and LB occupation on the acropolis of ancient Melos, on the southwest edge of modern Melos, are confirmed by Barber.

LANGADA: SOTIRA and TRYPITES
LH IIIA2(-B?)

AD 20 (1965) B 510, 513, 22 (1967) B 465.

A robbed EB cemetery and a ruined Mycenaean chamber tomb were reported at Sotira, about 1.5 km. east of Zephyria in the southeast part of Melos. A Mycenaean chamber tomb was also found at Trypites nearby, further uphill.

KANAVA
LH III(A-B)

A Mycenaean vase in the Melos museum is said to have come from Kanava, on the east side of the bay of Melos.

AYIOS SPIRIDON
LH IIIA2-B2

Bintliff (1977) 550.

Many Mycenaean sherds have been found on the flat summit of a prominent acropolis hill on the west side of the bay of Melos. But the fact that large quantities of kylix fragments were found is not sufficient evidence to demonstrate that the site was a "peak sanctuary" (Bintliff, *loc.cit.*). It was, however, obviously quite an important Mycenaean settlement.

THERA

As is well known, the present island is only a portion (about half) of the original one, whose central volcanic cone was destroyed, and replaced by a deep caldera, by the action of the massive eruption of c. 1500 B.C. The island never regained its former fertility (as Mr. Doumas remarked to me, there is now not enough mud for swallows to build their nests); but there are some moderately productive areas in the northeast and southeast. All the known Late Bronze Age settlement sites are of the LB I period, i.e. contemporary with LM IA. Two later vases, a LM IB flask and a LH IIIA2-B pyxis, are recorded in the photograpic archive of the German Archaeological Institute in Athens [cf. *BICS* 16 (1969) 150 for the former, and *Alt-Ägäis* Pl. 948]. But there are no definite signs of re-occupation until the Geometric period.

The Late Bronze Age sites on Thera are here listed in an order roughly south to north.

AKROTIRI *
EB? MB LBI

H. Mamet, *De Insula Thera* (1874); F. Fouqué, *Santorin et ses Eruptions* (1879) 105; *BSA* 51 (1956) 13, 26; *BCH* 96 (1972) 21; S. Marinatos, *Excavations at Thera I-VII* (1968-1976); *Ergon* (1973) 92; (1975) 145, (1976) 160, (1977) 161; *PAE* (1973) 119, (1975) A 212, (1976) 309; *AAA* 7 (1974) 87, 416; *AE* (1974) 119; *Antiquity* 47 (1973) 50, 48 (1974) 110, 53 (1979) 57.

This extensive site, on flat ground on a low-lying southwest promontory of Thera, was probably the most important on the island. Most of the remains are of the final phase of occupation in LB I, and are exceptionally well preserved under the deep layer of volcanic ash. Some LM IA and LH I pottery was imported at this time, but late MB types were still current. Much Cretan influence is shown in the art of this period, but there are also many individual local features which indicate that this was not simply a Cretan "colony", like Kastri on Kythera and Trianda on Rhodes.

The absence of characteristic LM IB and LH IIA imports argues against any association between the destruction of this site and the destructions of sites in northern Crete which took place during LM IB. But it is not clear whether the abandonment of the Akrotiri site took place *immediately before* the eruption. The site appears to have been deserted suddenly and then partly reoccupied before the final eruption [*Thera* III 7, *Kadmos* 9 (1970) 97]. The length of time between the desertion and the eruption is disputed. Most experts seem to favour as little as a single year for the sequence of events. But it has been claimed that there was a layer of humus between the original ground surface and the volcanic ash above [*Antiquity* 47 (1973) 50]; and a period considerably longer than a year might be needed for the accretion of such a layer [cf. *Antiquity* 48 (1974) 110].

BALOS *
LB I

Fouqué (1879) 107.

A farmhouse or similar building was excavated here, about a kilometre west-northwest of Akrotiri village, and not much further from the Akrotiri site.

EXOMITI
LB I

H. von Gaertringen, *Thera III* (1904) 42; *BSA* 51 (1956) 13.

Exomiti is the southern tip of Thera. A vase of LM IA type was bought here in 1879.

MESAVOUNO and SELLADHA *
LB I G A C H

BSA 51 (1956) 13.

Mesavouno is the site of Ancient Thera, a high ridge which forms the east tip of Thera. This is reported to be the source of LB I vases, including a pithos said to have come from a tomb, possibly on the adjacent ridge of Selladha, on whose northeast slope lay the main cemeteries of Ancient Thera, from the Geometric period onwards.

KAMARA
LB I

H. von Gaertringen, *Thera III* (1904) 39; *BSA* 51 (1956) 13, 26.

Some house remains were excavated here, about 500 m. south of Kamari village, not far to north of Mesavouno.

PHTELLOS *
LB I

AE (1973) 161.

Remains of houses excavated here, about a kilometre south of the modern town of Thera, were destroyed in the same manner as those of the Akrotiri settlement.

AKROTIRI KOLOUMBON
LB I

BSA 51 (1956) 13.

Some vases of LM IA type were reported to have come from tombs here, at the northeast end of Thera.

THERASIA

This island is all that is left of the west part of the original island of Thera. LB I house remains were found on the south coast [Fouqué, *op.cit.* 96; *BSA* 51 (1956) 13, 26]. This site thus forms part of the interesting pattern of scattered smaller LB I sites (presumably all 'satellites" of a main centre at Akrotiri) on the formerly prosperous island.

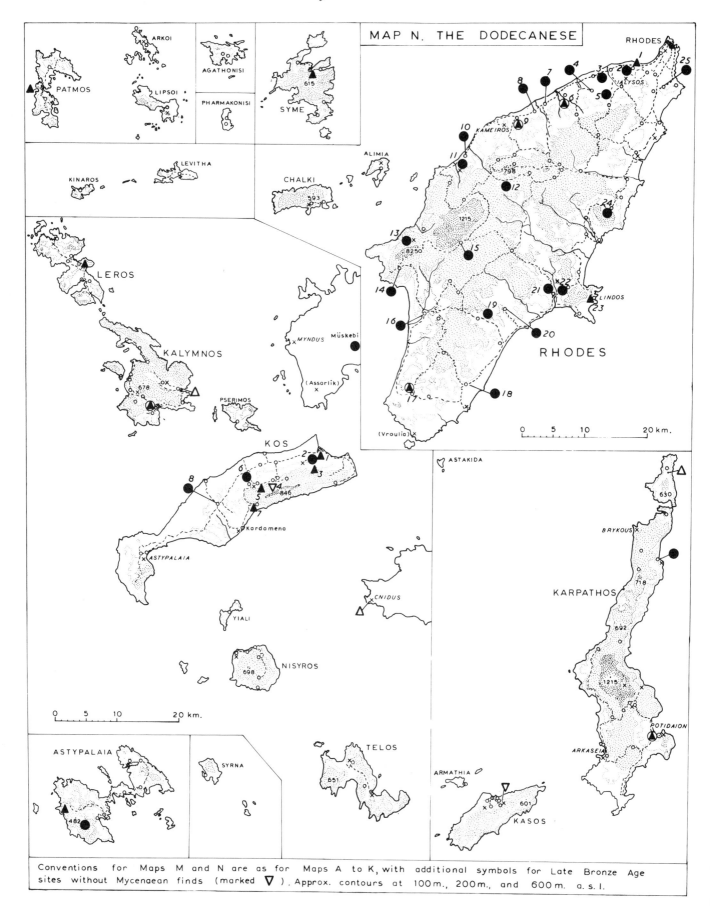

MAP N. THE DODECANESE

ARKOI

AGATHONISI

LIPSOI

PHARMAKONISI

PATMOS

SYME
615

RHODES

1

KAMEIROS
IALYSOS
7 4
8 3
6 5

25

LEVITHA

KINAROS

ALIMIA

CHALKI
593

10

11
798

LEROS

12

24

1215

KALYMNOS

13
8250

15

678

14

22
21

LINDOS
23

PSERIMOS

KOS

MYNDUS Müskebi

16

19

20

(Assarlik)

2 1
6 3
8   4
5   846
7

17

18

RHODES

Kardamena

ASTYPALAIA

(Vroulia)

0   5   10   20 km.

ASTAKIDA

630

CNIDUS

BRYKOUS

YIALI

KARPATHOS
718

NISYROS
698

692

1215

0   5   10   20 km.

POTIDAION

ASTYPALAIA

SYRNA

TELOS

ARMATHIA

ARKASEIA

482

551

601

KASOS

Conventions for Maps M and N are as for Maps A to K, with additional symbols for Late Bronze Age
sites without Mycenaean finds (marked ▽). Approx. contours at 100m., 200m., and 600m. a.s.l.

THE DODECANESE

Most of the Mycenaean finds in the Dodecanese come from the extensive Mycenaean cemeteries on Rhodes and Kos, and from smaller tomb groups of Kalymnos, Karpathos, and Astypalaia. Few sites are known to have been occupied in the earlier periods (LH I-LH IIIA1), and the bulk of the pottery is LH IIIA2-C, with the later phases of LH IIIC poorly represented. The two partly excavated settlement sites, Trianda on Rhodes and the Seraglio on Kos, both exemplify the familiar pattern of Minoan influences gradually surpassed, if not replaced, by Mycenaean. Both are flat sites (or perhaps originally of "low mound" type), in contrast to the known later Mycenaean settlement sites, most of which are of the "acropolis" type. Four of these (i.e. Palaiopyli on Kos, Perakastro on Kalymnos, Kastro on Leros, and Kastro tou Ayiou Ioannou on Astypalaia) later became the sites of mediaeval fortresses.

The Dodecanese, together with the Cyclades and at least part of Eastern Attica, seem to have escaped the disasters which overtook much of the Greek mainland at the end of LH IIIB. The quantity of finds of the earlier phases of LH IIIC in the Dodecanese, especially in the cemeteries of Kos, and their resemblances to the contemporary finds at Perati and on Naxos in particular, give considerable support to the hypothesis [Desborough (1964) 147 ff., 227 ff. and *passim*] that they formed a "miniature Mycenaean *koine*" with the Cyclades and Eastern Attica at this time, reminiscent of the ancient traditions concerning the "Carian Thalassocracy".

RHODES

The northwestern coastal plain of Rhodes is more fertile than most of the rest of the island, and was naturally the best choice for Minoan and Mycenaean expansion, being preferable to both the west and south parts especially. It is indeed clear that it became both the first and the most important Mycenaean en-clave. Elsewhere on Rhodes, the distribution of Mycenaean finds is sporadic, mainly occurring in other relatively fertile districts on or near the coasts, e.g. Koskinou, Archangelos, Pilona-Lardos, Vati-Yenadhi, Lachania, Kattavia, Apollakia, Siana-Monolithos, and Kritinia-Mandhriko. Three other prosperous areas, Afandou, Malona-Massari, and Salakos-Kapi were probably also occupied in Mycenaean times; while the finds from Apollona and Ayios Isidoros indicate that the interior was not neglected. By LH IIIB settlement appears to have spread over most of the island. Rhodes would have provided a balanced agricultural economy, although perhaps of limited potential (*cf. Dodecanese III* 155 n. 168).

A considerable amount of excavation and survey work has been carried out on Rhodes. But, while finds from Mycenaean tombs are quite abundant, discoveries of actual Mycenaean settlement sites are few. Evidently many of the latter have been covered over or obliterated by the widespread Hellenistic and Roman settlements on the same sites. For instance, it is more than likely that there was once a Mycenaean settlement in the vicinity of the town of Rhodes itself.

The Mycenaean sites considered to be more or less firmly verified are here listed first, in a roughly anti-clockwise order, from northwest through west and southeast to east. Some less certain reports also listed here have not been marked on Map N. (*cf. Dodecanese III* 127 for Select Bibliography and abbreviations used and fuller references. It should again be noted that references given here are selective.)

TRIANDA: POTAMYLO and PARASKEVA * # (Fig. 14) (Marked 1 on Map N)
MM III? LM IA-IIIA1 LH IIA-IIIA2 LH IIIB?

Memorie 3 (1938) 57; *Clara Rhodos* 10 (1941) 43; *OpArch* 6 (1950); *BICS* 16 (1969) 1 n. 6; *Dodecanese III* 135, 173.

A settlement of Minoan type, if not an actual Minoan colony, was established here, probably at some time in MM (*BICS loc.cit.*), and flourished in LM

Figure 14

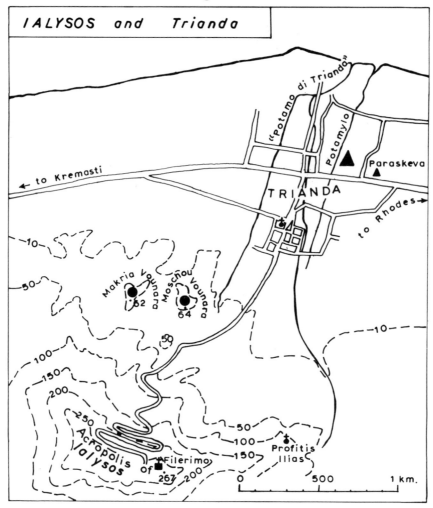

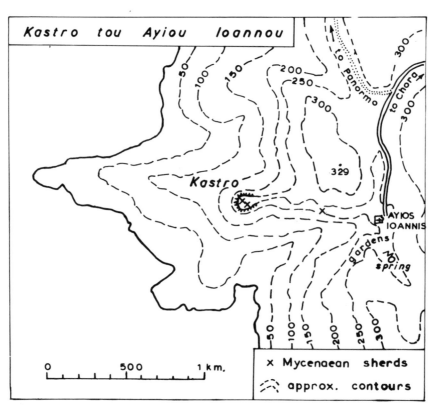

IA-IIIA1. The site, which was discovered beneath later alluvium, was of the open variety, and either flat or originally perhaps a low mound or rise. It was only partly excavated, and was presumably of considerable size, since it consisted of at least the area between trial no. 1 in Paraskeva village and trials nos. 2-6 about 200 m. distant on the east bank of the Potamylo stream (see Fig. 14). It is about 500 m. from the present shore.

Three main strata were recognized, called Trianda I, IIA and IIB. The beginning of the last of these, Trianda IIB, is marked by extensive rebuilding, apparently following an earthquake. During this phase (LM IIIA1) the fine pottery at Trianda became increasingly more Mycenaean in style. It was assumed that the settlement was abandoned at some time in this period. But some LH IIIA2 sherds were found both in the Paraskeva trial and the Potamylo excavations, and one sherd from Paraskeva may even be as late as LH IIIB1 (*Dodecanese III loc.cit.*). It is not clear whether these indicate continuity of occupation or a re-occupation.

TRIANDA: MOSCHOU VOUNARA and MAKRIA VOUNARA * # (Marked 2 on Map N) (Fig. 14 and Plate 29b)
LH IIB-IIIC

MV 1; *BMCat* A 39 nos. 801-970; *Ann.* 2 (1916) 271, 6-7 (1923-4) 86, 13-14 (1930-1) 254, 344; *Clara Rhodos* 1 (1928) 56; *Dodecanese III* 135, 173.

The main Mycenaean cemetery in the Ialysos area in LH IIIB-IIIC was on the two small low conglomerate hillocks of Moschou Vounara and Makria Vounara below the acropolis of the historical Ialysos. The Mycenaean chamber tombs excavated in the slopes of these hills are numerous and large, and especially rich in finds. It is also possible that Moschou Vounara in particular marks the centre of a habitation site, occupied before and/or during the period of its use as a cemetery, since in addition to Mycenaean fine wares there is a considerable amount of prehistoric coarse pottery on the hill, and some traces of rough walls have been observed, including a corner. Similar coarse sherds are spread over a wide area at the north foot and on the lower slopes, and also on the flatter ground between the hill and Makria Vounara. The coarse wares appear to be mainly of LH type. The LH fine wares found in the same area may, of course, be either from a settlement or spilled out from robbed or excavated tombs (*Dodecanese III loc.cit.*).

It is possible, however, that the main centre of Mycenaean habitation was in fact on the acropolis of Ialysos itself. Nothing Mycenaean has ever been found here, but the extensive later construction work here may have removed all traces of LH occupation. Although the size of the acropolis (about 600 m. by 200 m.) and its height would perhaps make it an unusual choice for a normal Mycenaean habitation site, it would have constituted an excellent fortress, especially since it possessed a natural water supply near the top (*Dodecanese III* 137).

PARADHISI: ASPROVILO and KOURI ect. * # (Marked 3 on Map N)
LH IIIA2

Ann. 1 (1914) 369; *Boll. d'Arte* 10 (1916) 87; *Ann.* 6-7 (1923-4) 252; *MP* 645, 749 (s.v. "Korou"); *Dodecanese III* 138.

Some rock-cut chamber tombs were found on the north slopes of Paradhisi hill, in various locations to east of Paradhisi village (formerly Villanova). Three vases of early LH IIIA2 date were recovered from two of the tombs, one at Asprovilo and one at Kouri. In 1968 two of the tombs were re-discovered about 400 m. to east of Paradhisi, and sherds of prehistoric coarse ware were found on a flat spur above and to west of the gully into whose sides the tombs were cut. But the sherds were not widespread, and a more likely position for the Mycenaean centre indicated here would be at Kouri about 200 km. to the east of the tomb, near three fine springs. A small ancient settlement was previously recorded here, and in 1968 some Late Roman surface sherds were found.

A "tholos micenea" was also recorded [*Memorie* 2 (1938) 49, 51] at a place named "Zuccalades", described as "fra Peveragno e Villanova", from which came two vases apparently LH IIIA2. The location is not clear, but a position to east of Paradhisi is indicated, and possibly in the same general vicinity as the Asprovilo-Kouri tombs.

DAMATRIA: "ACROSCIRO-CALOPETRA" (Marked 4 on Map N)
LH

Memorie 2 (1938) 51; *Dodecanese III* 138.

There have been various reports of Mycenaean finds near Damatria, and a report of two Mycenaean tombs at a place "Acrosciro-Calopetra", described as "Fra i villagi di Tolo e Damatria".

MARITSA: KAPSALOVOUNO * # (Marked 5 on Map N)
MB? LH III(A-B)

Boll. d'Arte series 2 no. 6 (1926-7) 331; *Memorie* 2 (1938) 51; *Dodecanese III* 139.

In a region of low conglomerate hills, about 2 km. northwest of Maritsa, and overlooking the plain of Rhodes airport to the northeast, are the remains of a chamber tomb on the eastern edge of a prominent hill named Kapsalovouno. Mycenaean sherds were found near the tomb in 1968, and from local information it was deduced that this is probably part of the cemetery of "Coccala", where three chamber tombs with dromoi were excavated in 1926. The tombs were said to have contained vases similar to those from the Mycenaean cemeteries of Ialysos. No signs of a Mycenaean habitation site have yet been found on or near the hill.

TOLON: AYIOS IOANNIS THEOLOGOS * # (Marked 6 on Map N)
LH IIIA1   LH III(A-B)   A   H

Clara Rhodos 6-7 (1933) 44; *Dodecanese III* 140.

The ruined chapel of Ayios Ioannis Theologos lies at the northwest tip of the low and broad triangular conglomerate ridge of Anemomylos, about a kilometre to southwest of Tolon. On the broad and flat eroded terraces of the ridge, Mycenaean and perhaps other prehistoric sherds were thinly spread over an area about 120 m. east to west by 90 m. The coarse ware closely resembles the surface pottery from Moschou Vounara, and is also probably mainly LH. Two LH IIIA1 vases were recovered from a ruined chamber tomb in this vicinity.

SORONI   #   (Marked 7 on Map N)
LH (III)   H

Memorie 2 (1938) 51; *Dodecanese III* 140.

Some Mycenaean cist graves were found in 1932 to south of Soroni. They were said to have contained "materiale miceneo tardo". Many Hellenistic sherds were found in 1970 on the long conglomerate ridge which extends to south from the village outskirts, and this area is probably also the site of the cist graves.

FANES   #   (Marked 8 on Map N)
LH III(A2-B)   LH IIIC   C?   H

Ann. 6-7 (1923-4) 253; *CVADanemark* Pl. 53 no. 11, Pl. 62 no. 2; *Dodecanese III* 141.

Two LH III vases from Fanes were brought to the Rhodes Museum (*Ann. loc.cit.*) and a stemmed cup and a stirrup-jar from Fanes in the Copenhagen Museum are attributed to LH IIIA2/B and LH IIIC1 respectively. Tombs of the 4th century B.C. are also recorded; and sporadic traces of Hellenistic and later settlement found in 1970 on the long and broad plateau above and southeast of Fanes suggest that this is the main centre of ancient settlement here. The plateau stretches for about 500 m., as far as the hill of Malla Vouno, where the ridge ends. The ancient sherds were found on the lower (northern) part of the plateau.

KALAVARDA: ANIFORO * # (Marked 9 on Map N)
MB?   LH IIIA2-C   G   C   H

JdI 1 (1886) 133; *MV* 17, 18; *Ann.* 1 (1914) 369, 6-7 (1923-4) 252; *Boll. d'Arte* 9 (1915) 284, 297; *Clara Rhodos* 6-7 (1933) 11, 133; *Memorie* 2 (1938) 49; *Dodecanese III* 141.

Eight Mycenaean chamber tombs have been excavated in the area to south of Kalavarda, at locations variously described as "Tzitzo", "Kaminaki Lures"

and "Aniforo", including one with a double dromos. Their contents range from LH IIIA2 to LH IIIC. On the broad and heavily eroded conglomerate terraces immediately below the thin ridge of Aniforo, c. 500 m. south of the village, prehistoric and later sherds were found scattered over an area about 150 m. east to west by 90 m. They include LH III(A2-B), and some which appear to be MB of Middle Minoan character. The impression given by the spread of the sherds and the predominance of coarse wares is that this was a settlement site as well as a cemetery. All but two of the chamber tombs have apparently been obliterated by erosion and/or cultivation.

Most, if not all, the Mycenaean finds in the Kameiros area may have come from the vicinity of Aniforo. But it is possible that some of the Mycenaean vases from the Kalavarda vicinity now in the Louvre museum in fact came from Papa-Lures, the main cemetery of nearby Kameiros (*Dodecanese III* 143 with refs.).

MANDHRIKO: MELISSAKI   #   (Marked 10 on Map N)
LH III(A2-B)   H

Ann. 6-7 (1923-4) 252; *Dodecanese III* 144.

On the hill of Melissaki, to northeast of Mandhriko, a chamber tomb with dromos was discovered, from which came two Mycenaean vases. The site is apparently the small hillock to northeast of Mandhriko, where Hellenistic and Late Roman sherds were found in 1970.

KRITINIA: KASTRAKI etc.   #   (Marked 11 on Map N)
LH IIIB-C   G   C   H

Ann. 1 (1914) 365, 6-7 (1923-4) 252; *Boll. d'Arte* 8 (1914) 230; *CVADanemark* Pl. 46 no. 11; *Dodecanese III* 145.

Kastraki is a small but prominent limestone outcrop on the south edge of the small coastal plain of Liros, about 3 km. northwest of Kritinia (formerly Castellos). Remains found at Kastraki are of the Classical and Hellenistic periods, and include a fine section of polygonal walling. Copious Mycenaean, Geometric, and Classical sherds were said to have been found in the vicinity of chamber tombs on the hills to the northeast, on the east side of the bay. No signs now remain of the dromoi reported, but some rock chambers filled with brush were observed in 1970, on lower slopes about 400 km. to northeast of Kastraki, and near these were some small worn sherds, including a fragment of a LH IIIB deep bowl handle.

Kritinia is given as the provenance of two Mycenaean vases, in the Rhodes Museum and the Copenhagen Museum, attributed to LH IIIB and LH IIIC respectively. And some other Mycenaean vases in the Copenhagen Museum are said to be from either Castellos (i.e. Kritinia) or Siana (*Dodecanese III* 145 with refs.).

APOLLONA: LELOS * # (Plate 29c) (Marked 12 on Map N)
LH IIIA2-B

Ann. 2 (1916) 298, 6-7 (1923-4) 248; *Dodecanese III* 144.

The thin spur named Lelos projects southward from Mt. Profitis Ilias at a point about 4 km. west-southwest of Apollona, to south of a bend in the modern highway. Seven Mycenaean chamber tombs were excavated here, and two others were found empty. The tombs are all in the upper part of the spur, and most were clearly visible in 1968. The vases recovered are of the LH IIIA2 and LH IIIB periods.

It is probable that a group of LH IIIB vases from a site described as "Cariones" (*ILN* 20/5/1933) in fact came from the vicinity named "Scariones" [*Ann.* 2 (1916) 300] about a kilometre to northeast of Lelos, where there is a fortified Classical settlement.

SIANA: AYIOS FOKAS and KYMISALA * # (Marked 13 on Map N)
N or EB? LH IIIA2-C A C H

JdI 1 (1886) 133; *Ann.* 1 (1914) 365, 2 (1916) 285, 6-7 (1923-4) 252; *Clara Rhodos* 1 (1928) 83; *CVADanemark* Pl. 39 no. 3 and Pl. 50 no. 1; *Dodecanese III* 146.

Ayios Fokas was the centre of a considerable settlement in the Classical and Hellenistic periods, despite its elevated and remote situation. There is good water at the Stelies fountain nearby, and good arable land (now partly abandoned) both here and in the plains of Kymisala to the east and Vasilika to northwest. At both Ayios Fokas and Vasilika substantial remains include fortifications, probably Hellenistic. There were extensive ancient cemeteries, mainly Archaic to Hellenistic, on the northern edge of the Kymisala plain, both on the slopes of Ayios Fokas on the northeast and on Mesa Vouno on the northwest. Some Mycenaean vases were collected from Kymisala (*JdI* and *Ann.* 6-7 *loc.cit.*). Others in the Copenhagen Museum are said to be from "Siana" (*CVADanemark loc.cit.*) of from "Siana ou Kastellos" (see on Kritinia above). Some at least of these probably came from the Kymisala vicinity. The only signs of a possible prehistoric habitation site are a few coarse sherds found in 1970 on Ayios Fokas, including part of a lug of a type resembling Late Neolithic or Early Bronze Age examples (*Dodecanese III loc.cit.*).

MONOLITHOS (Marked 14 on Map N)
LH (III)?

Memorie 2 (1938) 51; *Dodecanese III* 147.

A Mycenaean burial was recorded here "in localita imprecisata" (*Memorie loc.cit.*), and Mycenaean tombs were claimed both at Chimaria and Palaiochora to north of Monolithos. The reports require confirmation, but the general location seems probable, especially since it borders on the Kymisala area.

AYIOS ISIDOROS (Marked 15 on Map N)
LH III (B)?

BMCat A no. 1025; *Dodecanese III* 147.

A Mycenaean vase in the British Museum is said to be from here.

APOLLAKIA (Marked 16 on Map N)
LH IIIA2-C A

CVADanemark Pls. 39-63 (*passim*); *Ann.* 6-7 (1923-4) 253; *Dodecanese III* 147.

The many Mycenaean vases attributed to this area may have come from Chimaro, about 2 km. to southwest of the village, where later tombs were found.

KATTAVIA: AYIOS MINAS # (Marked 17 on Map N)
LH IIIA1? LH IIIA2-B A

K.F. Kinch, *Fouilles de Vroulia* (1914) 2-4; *JdI* 26 (1911) 249; *Dodecanese III* 147.

The chapel of Ayios Minas is on a thin limestone spur to northwest of, and above, the village of Kattavia. Some Mycenaean chamber tombs were plundered on the slopes below, between the chapel and the village. Only three vases were recovered from the illicit excavations. They appear to range from LH IIIA2 to LH IIIB, and include an ox-head rhyton (*JdI loc.cit.*). Sherds collected in 1970 from the area below the tombs are all LH IIIA2 or LH IIIB, except one fragment from a stemmed cup (*Dodecanese III* 148, Pl. 39a 1) which is probably LH IIIA1. The Mycenaean settlement seems to have been centred on the spur of Ayios Minas, where some coarse ware of LH type occurred with finer sherds including LH III.

KATTAVIA: KARAVI # (Not Marked on Map N)
LH (III)? H

Kinch (1914) 3; *Dodecanese III* 148.

According to Kinch, there was another Mycenaean cemetery at Karavi, described as "en 1908 encore intacte". Karavi is about 2.5 km. east-southeast of Ayios Pavlos church. The northern part of the site is a knoll of soft limestone about 150 m. east-west by 100 m.; and there are remains of a ruined chamber tomb and signs of possible others at the north foot. The only other signs of ancient habitation here were some sherds, including Hellenistic, on the saddle on the south side of the knoll.

LACHANIA (Marked 18 on Map N)
LH IIIA2-B

Ann. 6-7 (1923-4) 253; Fig. 157; *Dodecanese III* 149.

Some Mycenaean vases were recovered from the area of this village. They appear to be of the range LH IIIA2-B.

YENADHI: AYIA SOTIRA (Not Marked on Map N)
LH (III)? H

Ann. 6-7 (1923-4) 253; *Dodecanese III* 149.

Finds of Mycenaean pottery from chamber tombs with dromoi were reported "in localita imprecisata" (*Ann. loc.cit.*); it was conjectured later that this lay at Ayia Sotira about 4 km. to southwest of Yenadhi. The chapel crowns a low hillock about 200 m. in length, where there are plentiful traces of Late Hellenistic to late Roman settlement. There are no visible signs of chamber tombs here, although the white soil and soft "kouskouras" rock here appears suitable for them.

VATI: APSAKTIRAS etc. * # (Marked 19 on Map N)
LH IIIA2-C

Kinch (1914) 2-4; *Ann.* 6-7 (1923-4) 253, 255 Fig. 158; *CVADanemark* Pls. 39-63 (*passim*); *Dodecanese III* 150; S. Dietz and S. Trolle, *Arkaeologens Rhodos* (1974) 27.

The low eastern spur of the hill of Apsaktiras, about 1.5 km. east of Vati, was the centre of an important Mycenaean cemetery. The area is now partly covered by bushes, but some hollows in the conglomerate rock show the position of two or more of the tombs. A thin scatter of worn sherds in the vicinity may indicate a settlement site in addition to the necropolis. Some details from Kinch's unpublished report are given in a recent publication of the Copenhagen Museum (S. Dietz and S. Trolle *loc.cit.*). Fine vases ranging from LH IIIA2 to LH IIIC were recovered and some weapons and ornaments.

A further Mycenaean cemetery was claimed at Anghio Vouno, a much higher hill over a kilometre to the east. But the finds have not been published, and the location is not confirmed (*Dodecanese III* 150 n. 137).

VATI: PASSIA * (Not Marked on Map N)
LH IIIA2-C

S. Dietz and S. Trolle (1974) 27.

A cemetery of chamber tombs was also investigated by Kinch at Passia, about 3 km. west of Vati, near the road to Apollakia, and about mid-way between the west and southeast coasts. A sketch of one of the tombs and drawings of unpublished finds from this tomb and another are given by S. Dietz and S. Trolle (*loc.cit.*), from Kinch's unpublished manuscripts.

ASKLIPIO (Marked 20 on Map N)
LH IIIA2/B1

CVADanemark Pl. 40 n. 5, Pl. 42 no. 5; *MP* 645 (s.v. "Askle-peio"), *cf.* 590; *Dodecanese III* 150.

Two vases in the Copenhagen Museum said to be from Asklipio have been assigned to the transitional period from LH IIIA2 to LH IIIB.

LARDOS: TROULLO VOUNO (Marked 21 on Map N)
LH IIIA2-C

Ann. 6-7 (1923-4) 253, 255, Figs. 159-60; *Dodecanese III* 150.

An extensive Mycenaean and later cemetery to north of Lardos was almost entirely looted in illicit excavations. The seven vases recovered by archaeologists, including an interesting "ostrich-egg" rhyton dated LH IIIA2, appear to range from LH IIIA2 to LH IIIC1. The nucleus of the cemetery appears to have been on the lower slopes of Troullo Vouno, behind the school on the north edge of Lardos. On these slopes rock-cut shafts and the remains of one chamber tomb are visible. This site is quite separate from that of the important Geometric cemetery of Exochi [K.F. Johansen, in *Acta Archaeologica* 28 (1958)] which lies about 1.5 km. to northeast of Lardos (*cf. Dodecanese III* 151 n. 145).

PILONA: AMBELIA * # (Marked 22 on Map N)
LH IIIB-C

Ann. 13-14 (1930-31) 335; *Historia* 5 (1931) 468; *Memorie* 2 (1938) 15; *Dodecanese III* 151.

In the course of road works in 1929, a large Mycenaean chamber tomb was found at Ambelia, about a kilometre to southwest of Pilona. The tomb was evidently part of a cemetery of (mainly plundered) chamber tombs on the lower slopes of the ridge of Plakoto on the north side of the road, where some can still be seen. The vases from the excavated tomb appear to range from LH IIIB to LH IIIC1.

LINDOS (Plate 29a) (Marked 23 on Map N)
LN? EB (I? III?) LH IIIB-C PG G A C H

C. Blinkenberg, K.G. Kinch, and E. Dyggve, *Lindos. Fouilles et Recherches 1902-1914* (1931); *Ann.* 6-7 (1923-4) 252; *Dodecanese III* 151; *Acta Archaeologica* 45 (1974) 133, 135, 143; Schoder (1974) 129.

Some objects from Lindos acropolis are certainly of the Early Bronze Age and others are either EB or late Neolithic. There is no direct evidence for occupation in the Middle Bronze Age, although this is certainly probable. Few Mycenaean sherds were found in the Lindos excavations, but the Mycenaean levels may have been largely destroyed by the extensive later constructions on the acropolis. The Mycenaean pottery (*Lindos* 1 68-79 nos. 29-40) appears to range from LH IIIB to LH IIIC1. The site is a fine natural fortress, dominating an important harbour.

ARCHANGELOS: ANAGROS and MALA * # (Marked 24 on Map N)
N? EB? LH IIIA2-C

AD 18 (1963) A 135; *Dodecanese III* 152.

Two chamber tombs were found at Mala, about

400 m. to south of Archangelos. One was fully excavated, from which came several vases of the LH IIIA2 to LH IIIC1 periods. The tombs were at the foot of the steep hills on the south side of the Archangelos plain.

Signs of prehistoric settlement, including sherds apparently Neolithic and Early Bronze and two possibly Mycenaean, were found on the hill of Anagros, a conspicuous limestone outcrop on the northeast side of Archangelos. Prehistoric sherds and obsidian were spread over the upper terraces here, over an extent of about 150 m. north to south by 100 m.

KALLITHIES: EREMOKASTRO # (Not Marked on Map N)
EB? LH?

RA 18 (1868) 153; *Ann.* 6-7 (1923-4) 564; *Memorie* 2 (1938) 51; *Dodecanese III* 154.

Eremokastro, as the name suggests, is a relatively high and remote citadel, on a limestone outcrop about 3 km. southeast of Kallithies, overhanging the precipitous east coast. Its walls, which average about 1.70 m. in thickness, are in a very rough polygonal style, somewhat resembling Cyclopean, and they enclose an area about 150 m. northeast to southwest by 75 m. On the overgrown upper surface the only ancient finds noted in 1968 were an obsidian chip and a single coarse ware sherd, apparently prehistoric. There is no confirmation of the Mycenaean finds claimed here or of the supposed Mycenaean cemetery at Trauni on the southwest slopes.

Some traces of disturbed Classical and Hellenistic tombs were observed at the northeast fort of the hill of Vigla opposite, but there was nothing to substantiate the Mycenaean burials claimed here (*Dodecanese III loc.cit.*).

KOSKINOU (Marked 25 on Map N)
LH IIIA2-C

AD 18 (1963) A 133; *Dodecanese III* 155.

A collection of LH IIIA2-C vases was recovered from the vicinity of Koskinou. They were thought to have come from one tomb. No Mycenaean habitation site has yet been found here, but search has not yet been sufficiently thorough. The terrain, with its soft marl and conglomerate rocks, is very appropriate.

Other areas on Rhodes where there are indications of probable Mycenaean settlement include the following:

Salakos (*Dodecanese III* 143)

Kapi (*Dodecanese III* 144)

Glifadha near Siana (*Dodecanese III* 147)

Plimmiri near Lachania (*Dodecanese III* 149)

Malona-Massari district (*Dodecanese III* 152)

Kolimbia (*Dodecanese III* 154)

Ayios Ilias near Afandou (*Dodecanese III* 154)

Mesonos near Kallithies (*Dodecanese III* 155)

KARPATHOS

This island is formed mainly of high mountains, which form a more or less continuous chain from the north to the south, broken only by a lowland belt in the south between the Arkasa and the Pigadhia areas, where there are small coastal plains. Elsewhere, cultivation is mainly on hill terraces, many of which, however, have been recently abandoned.

PIGADHIA: XENONA
EB? LM IA? LH IIIA2-B

Dodecanese I 160, II 68.

On a low rise by the shore on the western outskirts of Pigadhia, abundant LH III sherds were found, concentrated over an area about 130 m. north to south by 100 m., inland from the Xenona building. The sherds also extend, although more sparsely for about 100 m. further to the south, where part of a conical cup, probably of LM IA date, was also found.

PIGADHIA: MAKELLI *
LH/LM IIIA1-B

Dodecanese I 159, II 69; *AD* 17 (1961-2) A 32.

A chamber tomb on a terrace about 400 m. to south of Pigadhia harbour contained some bronze weapons and other metal objects, and over ninety vases, mainly Minoan in style, the latest of which are of the LH IIIA2/B transitional phase. There are indications of other chamber tombs in the vicinity. In particular a small group of LM/LH IIIA vases in private possession was seen in 1960, said to have been found in a field about 700 m. to west of Makelli and about 500 m. to south of the Xenona site.

The Makelli tomb lies about 400 m. to southwest of the acropolis of ancient Potidaion, a walled acropolis of the Classical and Hellenistic period. But no traces of Mycenaean habitation have yet been found here; and the tomb (or tombs) are probably to be connected with the Xenona site, less than a kilometre distant.

YIAFANI
LH/LM IIIA2(-B?) A? C or H

JHS 8 (1887) 449; *BSA* 9 (1902-3) 201; *BMCat* A 971-7; *CVA British Museum* 5 Pl. 10, 8-14; *Dodecanese I* 161, III 173.

Seven Mycenaean vases were said to have been found "on the eastern slope of the island above Yiafani" (*BSA loc.cit.*), near the northeast end of Karpathos. Some of the vases are similar to specimens from Rhodes [especially a bull's-head rhyton [*cf. JdI* 26 (1911) 259, 261]]. But other vases may be Late Minoan. The mixture of Minoan and Mycenaean influences is to be expected on this island mid-way between Crete and Rhodes. The vases may be tentatively associated with a site at Kambi on terraces to south of Yiafani, where some Classical or Hellenistic and later material was found.

No certain evidence of Mycenaean habitation has yet been found elsewhere on Karpathos; but at the sites of ancient Brykous and Arkaseia, some sherds possibly LH were found, and at Arkaseia some obsidian chips (*Dodecanese I* 161, *II* 69).

SARIA

TA PALATIA etc.
EB? LB C H?

JHS 17 (1897) 64; *BSA* 9 (1902-3) 201; *Dodecanese I* 167.

Implements found on Saria include a dagger blade of LH type and a bronze chisel. There is little arable land on this small island to north of Karpathos, and no prehistoric site has yet been identified, although Classical and later remains have been noted at Ta Palatia near the north end of the island.

KASOS

Apart from the small plain in the northern and central part of Kasos, there is very little fertile land on Kasos. Occupation, both ancient and modern, is concentrated in this area.

POLIN: KASTRO
EB LB LH III? G A C H

Dodecanese I 168, *II* 69.

The main ancient settlement was on the Kastro above Polin. The top surface of this small acropolis hill, about 60 m. east to west by 40 m., and its south and west slopes are strewn with sherds, which include three of Late Bronze Age type, which may be Mycenaean of local kind.

There is no confirmation of the Middle Mincan and Mycenaean sherds alleged to have been found in the cave of Ellinokamara near Arvanitochori (*Dodecanese II* 71 and refs.).

SYME

The small area of agricultural land on Syme is mainly concentrated around the town of Syme and its satellite villages in the north part of the island. Another, even smaller, fertile area is around the Panormiti monastery near the south tip.

SYME: KASTRO
EB I LH III(A-B) A? C H

Dodecanese I 168, *II* 63, *III* 170.

The Kastro commands both the main harbour and the main area of agricultural land. The ancient walls enclosed an area about 80 m. east to west by 30 m., and there are signs of ancient habitation also on the upper slopes below the walls. On the north slopes some EB sherds and at least one Mycenaean were found with sherds of later periods.

KOS

The northeast half of the island is reasonably fertile, and has extensive plain land, sufficient water, and cultivable mountain and hill slopes. The southwest half, however, has little water and considerable areas of poor soil ("bad-lands"). The distribution pattern of ancient settlements, particularly the prehistoric, as revealed by recent excavation and survey work, coincides well with the distribution pattern of the good agricultural land. The recent surface survey work has been both successful and relatively thorough, especially in the northeast sector (from Antimachia and Kardhamena to the environs of Kos town).

KOS: THE SERAGLIO * # (Marked 1 on Map N)
EB III MMII? MM III LM IA-B LH IIIA-C PG G A C H

Boll. d'Arte 25 (1950) 320; *RA* 39 (1952) 103; *PAE* (1959) 195; *Dodecanese I* 171 n. 157, *II* 55, *III* 173; *Ann.* 43-44 (1965-6) 306; Desborough (1964) 153, 227, 253; Schoder (1974) 124.

The Seraglio is a low mound or rise c. 300 m. by 250 m., near the south side of the town of Kos. Apart from some EB sherds, the main habitation here begins in MM III-LM IA, when Minoan influences are strong. In the LH IIIA period or before, Mycenaean influence seems to have supplanted Minoan. The settlement continued to flourish until well into the LH IIIC period (Desborough *op.cit.* 153). The total size of the Mycenaean site is not known, but it appears to have been important, and was probably large. The most recent excavations (*PAE loc.cit.*) revealed substantial remains of LH III buildings, including part of an apsidal house, in the level below the Geometric necropolis.

KOS: LANGADHA * # (Marked 2 on Map N)
LH IIB-IIIC PG G

Boll. d'Arte 35 (1950) 316; *Ann.* 43-44 (1965-6) 5; *Dodecanese II* 55, *III* 173 and n. 287.

A large Mycenaean cemetery was excavated at Langadha (and at Eleona nearby), about a kilometre to southwest of the Seraglio site, with which the cemetery must surely be connected. Burials began in LH IIB and continued well into LH IIIC. The quantity and quality of the LH IIIC vases is striking.

KOS: ASKLUPI * # (Marked 3 on Map N)
EB I EB III LH III(A-B)

Boll. d'Arte 35 (1950) 324; *Ann.* 43-44 (1965-6) 306; *Dodecanese II* 57, *III* 170.

The hill of Asklupi lies about 3 km. to south of Kos town, on the southern edge of the coastal plain. The backbone of the hill is a thin limestone ridge, about 100 m. in length, running approximately north to south. On the extensive terraces of the east slopes, a thin scatter of Bronze Age sherds, including EB I and LH III, was found over an area about 150 m. north to south by 120 m. The EB III burials were found about 200 m. to northeast of, and below, the hill.

ZIA: MISONISI # (Marked 4 on Map N)
EB LB

Dodecanese II 58.

Immediately above and to northwest of the mountain village of Zia is a long, thin, and steep limestone spur named Misonisi, projecting from the mountains on the south. The much eroded top surface, about 150 m. northwest to southeast by 40 m., and the steep terraces on the northeast side are sparsely covered with small and worn prehistoric sherds, which include EB and LB types. The latter, although lacking in distinctive shapes are of a fabric comparable to that of the LH from Asklupi and Palaiopyli (below). The position of the site is magnificent, and there is a fine spring above the village, and not far from the site; and the terraces here are covered in fine vineyards and fruit trees.

AMANIOU: PALAIOPYLI # (Plate 30a-b) (Marked 5 on Map N)
EB I MB? LH III(A-B) H

Dodecanese II 59, *III* 171, 173.

The mediaeval fortress of Kastro or Palaiopyli lies about 1.5 km. southeast of Amaniou, on one of the foothills of Mt. Dymaion. No remains earlier than mediaeval were found within the walls of the Kastro itself, but on the north slope, near walls of "Cyclopean" style (Plate 30b), there was a considerable spread of prehistoric sherds (over at least 70 m. by 70 m.) including several Mycenaean. This site, like Zia, is in a strategic position, dominating the lower foothills to the north. There is a fine spring on the saddle to south, near the ruins of a Metochi.

PYLI: AYIA PARASKEVI and LINOPOTIS PIYI # (Marked 6 on Map N)
EB? MB? LH III(A2-B) LH IIIC?

Dodecanese II 60.

Near the chapel of Ayia Paraskevi, about 1.5 km. north of Pyli, a ruined Mycenaean tomb was found. The four vases certainly include LH IIIA2 or LH IIIB, and two may be as late as LH IIIC. The site is about a kilometre to south of the pool known as Linopotis Piyi at the turning to Pyli. About 300 m. to east of the pool is a low hill, the most western of a group here on the south edge of the northern coastal plain. The top of this hill (about 120 m. northeast to southwest by 90 m.) is covered in stone heaps. A few prehistoric sherds were found on the top surface, but most were on the southern flank. All phases of the Bronze Age appear to be represented.

ELEONA # (Marked 7 on Map N)
LH III(A-B) C

Dodecanese I 171, *II* 62.

About a kilometre to west of the small hamlet of Eleona, to right of the main road from Kradhamena to Pyli, some Mycenaean and later sherds were found, concentrated on a hill terrace about 100 m. broad, not far from a spring. Some cuttings in the conglomerate rock on the sides of the plateau appear to be the remains of chamber tombs. A Mycenaean settlement of moderate size is indicated, on this northwest edge of the small and relatively fertile Kardhamena plain.

ANTIMACHIA (Marked 8 on Map N)
LH IIIB?

MV 33; Fimmen (1921) 16; *BMCat* A 978 and 979; Stubbings (1951) 22; *Dodecanese I* 171.

Antimachia is given as the provenance of a vase in the British Museum (Fimmen *loc.cit.*). Stubbings (*loc.cit.*) attributes two vases (*BMCat loc.cit.*) from Kos to the LH IIIB period. It is not clear whether the two reports refer to the same vase (or vases), and no Mycenaean site is known at Antimachia.

THE ASKLEPIEION * # (Marked, but not numbered, on Map N)
LH III(A?)

Boll. d'Arte 35 (1950) 327; *Dodecanese I* 171 n. 157; Schoder (1974) 126.

Some Mycenaean weapons and vases were found in excavations at the edge of the sanctuary. They are presumably from a tomb.

THE ASPRIPETRA CAVE * (Not Marked on Map N)
N EB I? LH III(B) C H

Ann. 8-9 (1925-6) 235, 310; *PPS* 22 (1956) 193; *Dodecanese I* 171, *II* 62, *III* 170.

The Aspripetra cave lies about 3 km. south-south-east of Kephalos, near the southwest tip of Kos. Mycenaean sherds from the cave [*Ann.* 8-9 (1925-6) Fig. 60] include one from a deep bowl, presumably LH IIIB.

KOS: ADDENDUM

The sites of ancient Halasarna (near Kardhamena), and of ancient Astypalaia (to south of Kephalos) near the southwest tip of the island were thoroughly searched, but no Mycenaean remains were found, although a Mycenaean site at Astypalaia is very likely.

KALYMNOS

The island consists mainly of mountain ranges, and most of the agricultural land is concentrated in two narrow valleys, that of Pothia near the south end, and the Vathy valley on the east.

POTHIA: PERAKASTRO # (Plate 31a-b)
N LH IIIA2-C PG G A C H

JHS 8 (1887) 446; *BMCat* A 1001-24; *CVA British Museum* 5 Pl. 8; 22-28, Pl. 9; *Dodecanese I* 172, *III* 174.

The hill of Perakastro on the west side of the port of Pothia dominates both the harbour and the valley. The mediaeval fort on the top, enclosing an area about 80 m. northeast to southwest by 40 m., has obscured the traces of ancient settlement here; but abundant Mycenaean sherds were found on the upper terraces below the limestone cliffs, especially on the east side, indicating an area at least 120 m. northeast to southwest by 100 m. From tombs in the torrent bed below on the east, on the south side of the road from Pothia to Sykia, about 30 LH IIIB-C vases were recovered, most of which are in the British Museum. In the Ayia Varvara cave, about 400 m. to northeast of Perakastro, Neolithic and LH IIIB-C sherds have been found. Other Mycenaean and later vases in the Pothia Museum are probably also mainly from the Perakastro vicinity.

RINA: DASKALIO *
N EB I EB III MB LH III(A-B)

Clara Rhodos 1 (1928) 110; *PPS* 22 (1956) 188, 193; *Dodecanese I* 172, *III* 170.

Finds from the Daskalio cave above the small harbour at Rina, at the mouth of the Vathy valley, included EB, MB of "Kamares" style, and Mycenaean sherds. So far, however, there is no certain indication of a Bronze Age habitation site in the Vathy valley.

LEROS

Leros is more low-lying than Kalymnos, and has a considerable amount of good agricultural land, especially in the central areas near the two ports of Lakki and Ayia Marina.

AYIA MARINA: KASTRO
MB? LH III(A-B) LH IIIC? A C H

Dodecanese II 53.

The high limestone acropolis of Kastro above Ayia Marina was the main citadel of Leros both in ancient and Mediaeval times. And it appears to have been the Mycenaean centre also. Several Mycenaean sherds were found on the upper northwest slopes, outside the castle walls, over an area about 120 m. north to

south by 80 m. Elsewhere the extensive area outside the castle walls has been disturbed by the mediaeval remains, especially by the giant cisterns.

PATMOS

This relatively low island is of only moderate fertility. Only one ancient centre has so far been found on Patmos.

SKALA: KASTELLI # (Plate 31c)
MB LH III(A-B) G A C H

Dodecanese II 48.

The hill of Kastelli, on the isthmus above the harbour of Skala in the centre of the island, was the ancient acropolis, fortified in the Hellenistic period. A few Mycenaean sherds were found here on the central limestone ridge; and it is likely that the Mycenaean settlement occupied about the same area as that enclosed by the fortification, i.e. about 200 m. northwest to southeast by 70 m. (maximum).

ASTYPALAIA

Apart from some very small patches of productive land on the south coast of the island, especially around Livadhia bay, Astypalaia is largely barren. The interior has suffered considerably from deforestation and erosion.

ARMENOCHORI: PATELLES *
LH III(A2-B) C H

Dodecanese III 161; *AAA* 6 (1973) 120, 124; *AD* 26 (1971) B 549; *AR* (1975-6) 33.

In the southern part of the interior is a small plateau named Armenochori. Two Mycenaean chamber tombs have been excavated on the slope of the saddle of Patelles which forms the west side of the plateau. Over a hundred vases, and several bronze implements were found. The finds are not fully published, but the three fine vases illustrated appear to be LH IIIA2 or LH IIIB. The Mycenaean habitation site here has not yet been discovered, but Classical and Hellenistic sherds were found on nearby sites.

KASTRO TOU AYIOU IOANNOU # (Plate 32a-b; Fig. 14)
EB I MB LH III(A2-B) G? C or H

Dodecanese III 162; *AD* 26 (1971) B 551.

The steep limestone crag of Kastro forms the tip of a high spur overlooking the small bay of Ayios Ioannis in the centre of the west coast. Two Mycenaean sherds were among the few finds observed within the ruined mediaeval walls, which enclose an area about 100 m. east to west by 70 m.

Another Mycenaean sherd was found in an area of fallen boulders between the Kastro and the chapel of Ayios Ioannis, where there is a spring with fruit trees and vegetable gardens on terraces below it.

APPENDIX TO MAP N

CHALKI, CASTELLORIZO, TELOS, NISYROS, LIPSOI

Some search has been carried out in these smaller islands for prehistoric settlement. Signs of Bronze Age settlement were found on Telos (*Dodecanese II* 66), Nisyros (*Dodecanese I* 169, *III* 171), and possibly also on Lipsoi (*Dodecanese II* 51). But there are no positive indications of Mycenaean presence in these cases.

ADDENDUM

Since the completion of this section of the Dodecanese, C.B. Mee, formerly Assistant Director of the British School of Archaeology at Athens, has completed his Doctoral thesis, which includes an important review of Mycenaean finds in the Dodecanese. This review will both augment, and partially supersede the discussion here when the substance of the thesis is presented in published form.

MAP O. THE AEGEAN
AND ASIA MINOR

Mycenaean sites.....▲
Mycenaean finds....△

*(Some ancient names here
printed in italics)*

△TROY

LEMNOS

1767

Antissa△

Thermi△

LESBOS

Pitane△ *Elaia*△

④△

Larisa△

R. *Hermos*

Sardis

1260   1295

SKYROS

PSARA

CHIOS

Erythrai

Smyrna△

Clazomenai△

1510   2157   ③△

R. Cayster

Colophon△

△*Ephesus*
②

R. *Maeander*

1792

EUBOEA

ANDROS

KEA

TENOS

MYKONOS

Delos

SYROS

KYTHNOS

SERIPHOS

PAROS

Antiparos

SIPHNOS

Kimolos

MELOS

SIKINOS

Sikinos

Pholegandros

THERA

Anaphe

NAXOS

Donoussa

Keros

IOS

AMORGOS

Levitha

ASTYPALAIA

Syrna

IKARIA

Fournoi

Patmos

SAMOS

MILETUS

1367

Mylasa
1373

Stratonicea

1892

Lipsoi

LEROS

KALYMNOS

①

KOS

KOS

Yiali

Cnidus

Nisyros

Telos

Syme

Chalki

Ialysos

1215

RHODES

Saria

KARPATHOS

1215

KASOS

Land above 200 m. a.s.l. ....
Land above 1000 m. a.s.l. ....
0 10 20 30 40 50   100 km.

204

THE AEGEAN
WESTERN ASIA MINOR

MAP O

The extent of Mycenaean penetration of mainland Asia Minor is still uncertain, despite the recent considerable increase in the volume of Mycenaean finds. At Miletus a Mycenaean style of pottery succeeds a Minoan early in the LH period [French (1969) 73 Fig. 7]. But elsewhere, especially at Iasos, Müskebi, and Ephesus, the earliest Mycenaean finds are those assigned to LH IIIA1; and the bulk belong to the LH IIIA2-B "Koine" period. During this phase of expansion, the islands of Samos, Chios, and Psara were probably dominated by the Mycenaeans; and there appear to have been Mycenaean settlements or "colonies" at Miletus, Iasos, and Müskebi. The vases from Ephesus and the small built tomb of tholos type at Colophon also suggest (but do not prove) actual Mycenaean settlements at these places. Elsewhere, however, and especially from Smyrna northwards, as well as in the interior, the sporadic Mycenaean finds are set against a background of native Anatolian cultures.

The interesting question of the relations between Mycenaeans and Hittites (the evidence for which has been recently summarised by Jakar, 1976) will not be discussed here. But it still appears that direct contact was relatively limited, presumably due mainly to geographical factors. The geographical "unit", formed by the Dodecanese Islands and western Asia Minor, is separated, both by distance and by rugged terrain, from the Anatolian interior. Mycenaean trade depended largely on sea communications, and the Dodecanese Islands are well placed on the main route to the Levant.

It seems likely, indeed, that the Islands were of greater importance to the Mycenaeans than the mainland opposite; and the pattern of Mycenaean finds in Asia Minor suggests that Mycenaean penetration inland was slight. The sporadic nature of Mycenaean imports and local imitations on Lesbos, in northwest Asia Minor, and in the interior of western Anatolia, indicate that these areas were either on or beyond the fringes of Mycenaean civilisation. Eastern Anatolia and the Levant are outside the scope of this study. But the recently discovered Mycenaean vases from Maşat Hüyük near Zile (found in a Hittite level provisionally dated c. 1300 B.C.), about 120 km. east-northeast of Boghazköy, are a remarkable example of the distance that Mycenaean exports could travel.

The Mycenaean settlements of Samos, Chios, and Psara are here listed first, followed by the mainland sites in western Asia Minor shown on Map O, together with those on the island of Lesbos, following an order roughly south to north. The sites on the Turkish mainland are only briefly described here, and references given are selective, since good summaries have already been given elsewhere, especially by M.J. Mellink annually in the *American Journal of Archaeology* and by J.M. Cook and others in *Archaeological Reports*.

ADDENDUM

Since this section was compiled, two new publications have appeared concerning Asia Minor. The first is a survey by C. Mee, "Aegean Trade and Settlement in Anatolia in the Second Millenium B.C.", in *AS* 28 (1978) 121-155, based on thorough fieldwork and study. This detailed summary of all Mycenaean finds in Asia Minor largely supersedes my brief and partial notes here, but I consider that the latter are still necessary, if only as an accompaniment to my map. There is now also a new review of recent discoveries, entitled "Mycenaeans in Asia Minor", by S. Mitchell and A.W. McNicoll, in *AR* (1978-9) 64-4, and 59-90 *passim*.

SAMOS

Much of Samos is still covered by forest, and most of the agriculture is concentrated in the lowland plains, especially the main southeast plain, where the three known Mycenaean sites are located. Exploration for prehistoric remains on Samos, however, has so far been limited.

TIGANI: KASTRO　*
N　EB (I?)　MB　LH I (-II)　LH III(A-B)　PG　G　A　C　H

AM 54 (1929) 7, 60-61 (1935-6) 165, 190; *OpArch* 6 (1950) 200;
G.L. Huxley, *Achaeans and Hittites* (1960) 21; Schoder (1974)
187.

The low hill of Kastro dominates the only natural
harbour in the southeast coastal plain in Samos. The
contents of a pit included decorated sherds of LM IA
style, and plain wares of MM III-LM I type, together
with local wares (*OpArch loc.cit.*). LH III surface sherds
have also been found (Huxley, *loc.cit.*).

THE HERAION　*
EB II-III　MB　LB I-II?　LH III(A-B, C?)　PG　A　C　H

AM 72 (1957) 35, 74 (1959) 1; V. Miløjčič, *Samos I* (1961); *AD*
18 (1963) B 286, 19 (1964) B 403; *AA* (1964) 226, 495; *Archaeology* 26 (1973) 170; Schoder (1974) 190.

The Heraion site, now barely 100 m. from the
shore, apparently lay at or near the mouth of the ancient Imbrasos river, in the coastal plain about 7 km.
west of Tigani. There was an important fortified LH III
settlement here, on flat ground. A built chamber tomb
beneath a tumulus has been dated to LH IIIA.

Some fragments of animal figurines were found
in a LH level (*AA loc.cit.*), but these can not be considered as evidence for a cult here in Mycenaean times.
And there is no evidence for continuity of occupation
here from the Bronze Age to the Iron Age in any case.

MYLOI　*
LH IIIA

AD 16 (1960) B 249; *BCH* 85 (1961) 839.

A small circular chamber tomb was found at the
western end of the coastal plain, not far to northwest
of the Heraion. No other tombs were found in a brief
search of the vicinity.

CHIOS

The most fertile parts of Chios are the south and
the southeast, roughly from Chios town southwards,
and it is here that most of the modern population is
concentrated. The north and northwest parts are
rugged and mountainous. The island has not yet been
thoroughly explored for prehistoric settlements.
Those discovered lie mainly near the coast.

EMPORIO　*
N　EB I-II　EB III?　MB　LH IIIA?　LH IIIB-C　G　A　C　H

AR (1954) 20, (1955) 35; Desborough (1964) 158; M.S.F.
Hood, in *Sixth International Congress of Prehistoric and Proto-
historic Sciences II* (1965) 224; J. Boardman, *Excavations in
Chios 1952-55: Greek Emporio* (1967).

The site lies on the southeast coast, near the south
tip of the island. The centre of Mycenaean settlement
was the low hill on the southwest side of a small bay,
the first good harbour to south of Chios town. The hill
was previously occupied in the EB period (when it was
fortified) and in MB, and was later the site of a Roman
fort. The Mycenaean occupation seems to have begun
in LH IIIB, which is represented by sherds from the
hill and vases from a cist-grave on a hill opposite. But
the three building periods identified appear all to be
LH IIIC. The site was destroyed by fire; and the next
occupation of the area, in the Geometric period, was
centred on the much higher acropolis of Profitis Ilias,
to north of the harbour and further inland.

VOLISSOS:　LEFKATHIA　#
LH III(A-)B　A　C

BSA 41 (1940-45) 38; J. Boardman, *The Greeks Overseas* (1964)
52.

The site is a low hill on a promontory on the west
coast, on the south side of the harbour of Limnos and
about 2 km. southwest of Volissos. The upper surface
of the hill (about 150 m. east to west by 125 m.) was in
1960 seen to be sparsely covered in ancient sherds.
These were mainly A and C (as Boardman had previously recorded); but there were also several LH III,
including parts of LH IIIB deep bowls, especially on
the southern terraces.

KATO PHANA (PHANAI)　*　(Not Marked on Map O)
LH III(A-B)　PG (or Sub PG)　G　A　C　H

BSA 35 (1934-35) 157; V.R. d'A. Desborough, *Protogeometric
Pottery* (1951) 15, 27; Boardman (1967) 250, n. 3.

The main finds at this sanctuary site were of Geometric and later periods. But fragments of a kylix and a
"skyphos" (deep bowl?) and a dagger-pommel of Mycenaean date were reported by Boardman to be in the
Chios Museum. Since it is not certain whether these
finds represent an actual Mycenaean site, it has not
been marked on the map.

FRANKOMACHALA (CHIOS TOWN)　*　(Not Marked on Map O)
LH III(A-B)　A　C　H

Boardman (1967) 250, n. 3.

A kylix foot from this site was reported to be in the
Chios museum. The rest of the material is Archaic and
later. It is uncertain whether there is a Mycenaean site
here, and the earliest levels have not yet been investigated.

PSARA

This is a small, bare and rugged island to northwest of Chios. The main modern settlement, the village
of Psara, lies on the isthmus at the southwest end,
where Geometric to Hellenistic sherds have been
found.

ARCHONTIKI *
LH III(A-)B

AD 17 (1961-2) B 266; *BCH* 86 (1962) 878; *AR* (1961-2) 23.

On the shore of Archontiki bay, on the west coast about 3 km. to north of Psara village, a cemetery of LH cist graves was found. The graves, built with large slabs, were exposed in a row for an extent of about 100 m. along the beach. A large number of LH III(A-)B sherds were collected on the surface here, and a jar of local Grey ware and a bronze spearhead were retrieved from one of the graves.

CNIDUS *
MM LM I LH? A C H

AS 19 (1969) 18; *AJA* 73, (1969) 241; *AR* (1970-71) 53; *AJA* 82 (1978) 321; *AR* (1978-79) 63, 82.

It has been reported that some sherds from Cnidus were identified as Mycenaean by Akurgal. Further confirmation appears needed. Middle Minoan and Late Minoan I pottery has been recently found near the harbour.

MÜSKEBI * (Marked 1 on Map O)
EB (III?) LH IIIA1-C A C H

AJA 67 (1963) 352, 68 (1964) 157, 69 (1965) 140; *Archaeology* 17 (1964) 244; *AR* (1964-5) 55, (1970-71) 48; *TAD* 13 part 2 (1964) 31, 14 (1965) 123; *Belleten* 31 (1967) 67; *Anadolu* 11 (1967) 1, 31, 45, 15 (1971) 63; Y. Boysal, *Katalog der Vasen im Museum in Bodrum I. Mykenisch-Protogeometrisch* (1969); *BSA* 68 (1973) 173, 178.

The village of Müskebi is about 7 km. west of Bodrum. In the side of a low hill to north of the village about fifty chamber tombs have been found. The cemetery is some distance inland, in a reasonably fertile district. All the pottery from the tombs is Mycenaean, mostly LH IIIA2-B, with relatively little LH IIIA1 and LH IIIC. It has close affinities to Mycenaean pottery on Rhodes and Kos. Search for the (presumed) actual Mycenaean settlement site has not so far been successful. But an Early Bronze Age site was found to south of Müskebi (at a depth of about nine metres below ground), covering a wide area close to the sea. A discussion of these latter finds and a map of the Müskebi valley is given in *Archaeology (loc.cit.)*.

IASOS *
EB MB MM II-III LM I-II LH IIIA-C PG G A C H

Ann. 39-40 (1961-2) 505, 43-4 (1965-6) 401, 45-6 (1967-8) 539, 47-8 (1969-70) 461; *AR* (1964-5) 53, (1970-71) 46; *AJA* 77 (1973) 177, 78 (1974) 114; *AS* 26 (1976) 41.

Ancient Iasos occupied a promontory about 900 m. in length (north to south) by 500 m. (*maximum* width). It had a sheltered harbour, and lay at the head of an easy route to the interior. Remains of prehistoric settlement have been found both on the promontory and inland (the EB cemetery). The Mycenaean settlement appears to have covered all or most of the northern part of the promontory at least [*cf. AR* (1970-71) map on P. 46]. LH III sherds were found just above the rock in excavations to south of the theatre i.e. on the upper slopes of the hill in the centre of the promontory. Part of a Mycenaean wall and abundant Mycenaean pottery were found on the site of the later sanctuary of Artemis Astias on the northwest side, near the promontory neck. A Mycenaean stratum nearly a metre thick was found in the area of the basilica by the east gate. Two Mycenaean rooms excavated here were apparently on either side of a street.

Substantial remains of several Mycenaean buildings were found below the Protogeometric necropolis beneath the agora. In the centre of the agora, a little to east of the necropolis, a large rectangular building of the Middle and Late Bronze Age was found, with a door on its north side, opening onto an adjacent cobbled street. The stratigraphy here revealed a familar pattern of Minoan influences superseded by Mycenaean. In stratum I, MM II-III imported wares were found with the local MB, which includes local imitations of polychrome Kamares ware. In stratum II, imported LM I-II sherds and local imitations were found, and, in Stratum III, LH IIIA-C wares and imitations.

In general, much of the Mycenaean pottery from Iasos is of good quality, and seems to be the dominant fine ware of the period here. The evidence of the large buildings, the cobbled streets, and the apparent extent (approximately 300 m. by 300 m. *minimum*) of the Mycenaean period settlement, clearly demonstrates its importance.

MYLASA (MILÂS) *
LH IIIB C H

AM 12 (1887) 230 Fig. 10; F.H. Stubbings, *Mycenaean Pottery from the Levant* (1951) 23; Desborough (1964) 161; *AJA* 52 (1948) 140; *AR* (1964-5) 44.

A piriform jar from Mylasa (*AM loc.cit.*) is ascribed to LH IIIB by Stubbings and Desborough. But reports of further Mycenaean pottery from the Swedish excavations (*AJA loc.cit.*) have met with scepticism (*AR loc.cit.*).

STRATONICEA (ESKIHISAR)
LH III(B-C) H

AJA 72 (1968) 51; *AS* 19 (1969) 74 Fig. 7.

A stirrup-jar and a carinated bowl in the Eskihisar museum are presumably from the site of Stratonicea. They have been assigned to LH IIIC by some (*AJA loc.cit.*) and by others to LH IIIB (*AS loc.cit.*).

MILETUS *
MM III LM I LH I-IIIC SMyc PG G A C H

Ist. Mitt. 7 (1957) 102, 9-10 (1959-60) 1, 18 (1968) 87, 144, 19-20 (1969-70) 113, 25 (1975) 9; C. Weickert, in *Neue Deutsche Ausgrabungen im Mittelmeergebiet und im Vorderen Orient*

(1959) 181; Desborough (1964) 161; G. Kleiner, *Alt-Milet* (1966) 11; G. Kleiner, *Die Ruinen von Milet* (1968) 9, 24, 125; *AR* (1964-5) 50, (1970-71) 44; *AJA* 78 (1974) 114, 79 (1975) 207, 80 (1976) 270.

If the evidence of the pottery finds is a reliable guide, at Miletus a Minoan settlement in MM III and LM IA was succeeded by a Mycenaean settlement in LH II-IIIC, centered on the peninsula to south of Theatre bay. Here a substantial house and a pottery kiln of the LH IIIA2 period were followed in LH IIIB by a massive fortification wall, over four metres thick, with towers at intervals, enclosing an area roughly 450 m. by 150 m. (author's calculations). The fortifications most closely resemble those of Enkomi in Cyprus. They rest on a thick burnt level and are covered by another. The two destructions indicated have been attributed by Kleiner to the Hittites and to the "Sea Peoples" respectively. On Stadium Hill, the highest point within the Mycenaean fortifications, a megaron and remains of a residential complex with central court have recently been found.

The Mycenaean settlement may have extended beyond the limits of the fortifications, since Mycenaean sherds were found to north of the southern cross-wall of the Hellenistic and Roman city, although not in stratified contexts. The Mycenaean necropolis lay some distance further to the southwest, on Değirmentepe. The excavations indicate that Miletus is the largest and most important Mycenaean settlement so far discovered in Asia Minor.

EPHESUS *
LH IIIA A C H

AR (1964-5) 44, 49, (1970-1) 43; *TAD* 13 part 2 (1964) 125; *AJA* 68 (1964) 157; *Anadolu* 11 (1967) 31; *AS* 19 (1969) 74 Fig. 7.

Remains of a disturbed tomb were found in front of "The Gate of the Persecution" on the Byzantine citadel (Ayasoluk) at Ephesus. The Mycenaean vases found have been attributed to the LH IIIA1 or LH IIIA2 period. No Mycenaean settlement site has yet been found here, but the citadel itself appears to be the likeliest candidate.

KUŞADASI   (Marked 2 on Map O)
LH

AS 14 (1964) 30; *AR* (1964-5) 44.

A Mycenaean sherd was found at Yilanci Burun, a peninsula near Kuşadasi.

COLOPHON *
LH III(B-C) G A C H

AJA 27 (1923) 67; *Hesperia* 13 (1944) 91, 94, 43 (1974) 264; G.L. Huxley, *Achaeans and Hittites* (1960) 39.

A small built tomb of tholos type (diameter 3.87 m.) was found to west of ancient Colophon, in the area of the modern village (Değirmendere). Only a few bits of

pottery and scattered bone fragments were left by the ancient tomb robbers. According to Huxley, the excavator (Miss Goldman) dated the tomb as LH IIIB or LH IIIC. Some unusual features of construction are considered to indicate the work of "local builders" (*Hesperia* 43 *loc.cit.*). No trace of a settlement of the Mycenaean period has yet been discovered here.

OLD SMYRNA (BAYRAKLI) *
EB MB LB LH IIIA2-B PG A C H

BSA 53-4 (1958-9) 9; *AS* 19 (1969) 74 Fig. 7; Desborough (1964) 161; *AJA* 77 (1973) 178.

Only a few Mycenaean sherds were found in the excavations, and these are classed as LH IIIA2-B (*AS loc.cit.*). Other Mycenaean sherds were found recently "in peripheral areas of the mound" (*AJA loc.cit.*). Although the LB levels have not been properly investigated, it is already apparent that Mycenaean was not the predominant ware here at the time.

CLAZOMENAE *
LH IIIA2-B G A C H

M.B. Sakellariou *La Migration Grecque en Ionie* (1958) 506; Desborough (1964) 161; *AD* 19 (1969) 74 Fig. 7.

A few Mycenaean sherds from Clazomenae in the National Museum at Athens have been classed as LH IIIA2-B (*AS loc.cit.*).

ERYTHRAI AREA
LH (III)

AJA 72 (1968) 134; *AR* (1970-1) 41.

Akurgal reported Mycenaean surface sherds from a small peninsula 8 km. distant from Erythrai, between the villages of Sifne and Reisdere. He apparently also found a Mycenaean settlement closer to Erythrai.

LARISA ON THE HERMOS *
LH (III) A C H

Desborough (1964) 161.

Only one certainly Mycenaean sherd was found in the Larisa excavations.

ÇERKES SULTANIYE   (Marked 4 on Map O)
LB LH III(A-B)

Anadolu 11 (1967) 48, Pl. 22; *AJA* 72 (1968) 52; *AS* 19 (1969) 52, 73; *AR* (1970-71) 41.

A Mycenaean piriform jar, thought to be of Rhodian manufacture, was found in a local LB pithos burial at Çerkes Sultaniye near Manisa, on the northern edge of the Hermos valley and about 50 km. inland. It is suggested that this site may be the cemetery for the settlement at Egriköy, where two possibly Mycenaean sherds were found. The jar (now in the Manisa Museum) has been attributed by some to LH IIIB and others (*AS loc.cit.*) to LH IIIA1.

SARDIS. *
LB LH III(B-C) PG G A C H

AJA 66 (1962) 83; *AR* (1964-5) 39, 44 (1970-1) 39 with refs.; Desborough (1964) 161; *AS* 19 (1969) 73 n. 16; G.M.A. Hanfmann and Jane C. Waldbaum, in *Essays in Honor of Nelson Glueck* (1970) 308.

A few late Mycenaean and rather more Protogeometric sherds, together with much larger amounts of plain local ware, were found associated with a rubble wall, floors, and pits. Mycenaean shapes were said to include kraters, deep bowls and several types of cup. But some sherds found earlier, originally thought to be Mycenaean, are not now generally accepted as such (*AS loc.cit.*).

GÂVURTEPE (Marked 3 on Map O)
MB LB LH IIIA2

Anadolu 11 (1967) 46; *AJA* 74 (1970) 166; *AR* (1970-1) 41.

Further east up the Hermos valley, two Mycenaean sherds of LH IIIA date (one is LH IIIA2) have been found on the surface of the mound of Gâvurtepe near Alaşehir, together with other material of the second millenium B.C. The site is almost 110 km. inland (from Smyrna), on a main route to the interior.

PITANE (ÇANDARLI): KOCABAĞLAR
EB? LB LH IIIC

AJA 67 (1963) 189; Desborough (1964) 161; *AR* (1964-5) 36, 44; *BSA* 68 (1973) 174.

The LH IIIC stirrup-jar from Pitane, which is said to be of Dodecanesian origin (Desborough *loc.cit.*), is now thought to have come from a necropolis to east of Pitane. This appears to have been on the rocky spur to northeast of the prehistoric site of Kocabağlar, 2 km. to east of Çandarli. At Kocabağlar itself fragments of Trojan face urns have been found, and some EB vases found earlier may also have come from here. A Mycenaean settlement "further to the east" was apparently claimed (*AJA loc.cit.*); but this supposed report has been neither re-iterated nor verified.

ELAIA
LH (III) C H

AS 18 (1968) 188.

One Mycenaean sherd has been reported from Elaia.

LESBOS

Much of Lesbos is rugged and mountainous. The west appears rather barren, but the eastern part has fairly dense vegetation on lower slopes and the alluvial plains at the heads of the gulfs of Kalloni and Yera.

Mycenaean finds on Lesbos are few, and it is clear, from the overwhelming preponderance of the local Red and Grey wares in the two excavated sites, that the Mycenaean pottery is intrusive, although there are also some local imitations of it.

THERMI *
EB MB LB LH IIIA

W. Lamb, *Excavations at Thermi in Lesbos* (1936) 142, Fig. 42; F.H. Stubbings, *Mycenaean Pottery from the Levant* (1951) 22; Desborough (1964) 60.

The site is near the east coast, to north of the Gulf of Yera. Two at least of the Mycenaean sherds are probably LH IIIA, and the remainder probably are also. There are also some imitations, in local ware, of LH II cups (Stubbings, *loc.cit.*). The site was destroyed before the LH IIIB period, in a colossal conflagration.

ANTISSA *
LB LH III(A-B) LH IIIC? PG G A C H

A. Furtwaengler and G. Loeschke, *Mykenische Vasen* (1886) 33, 83; *BSA* 31 (1930-1) 161, 166; Desborough (1964) 160.

In the western half of the island, on the north coast, excavations at Antissa also produced a few Mycenaean sherds, and local imitations, and a small stirrup-jar from the site was recorded by Furtwaengler and Loeschke. The range of the Mycenaean pottery is probably LH IIIA-B, and contact with the Mycenaean world may have been maintained into LH IIIC, although this can not yet be proved (Desborough, *loc.cit.*).

MAKARA (Not Marked on Map O)
LH?

AD 17 (1961-2) B 266.

At the western entrance to the Gulf of Kalloni cist tombs were found of a type similar to those at Psara (above).

LISVORI (Not Marked on Map O)
EB MB LB LH (III)

AD 26 (1971) B 457; *AR* (1975-6) 28.

A Bronze Age settlement has been found at Lisvori on the shore of the Gulf of Kalloni. Surface finds include Mycenaean sherds.

TROY *
EB MB LB LH I-IIIC A C H

C.W. Blegen, J.L. Caskey *et al.*, *Troy I-IV* (1950-56); C.W. Blegen, "Troy VI" in *CAH* II-1 pp. 683-5 and "Troy VII" in *CAH* II-2 pp. 161-4; Desborough (1964) 163.

Some LH I and LH II sherds were found in the middle sub-periods of Troy Settlement VI, and LH IIIA sherds are fairly numerous in the later sub-periods, with some LH IIIB before the end of the final phase. Some LH IIIA still occurs in Troy VIIa, but the bulk can be attributed to LH IIIB: and it is at this period that pottery of Mycenaean style is relatively most abundant. It is noted, however, that the number of actual Mycenaean "imported" pieces now declines, and there is a corresponding increase in the number of imitations in local Trojan fabric. The destruction of Troy VIIa came at a time when LH IIIB wares and imitations were common, and apparently before the beginning of LH IIIC. In the succeeding settlement, Troy VIIb 1 (considered to be an immediate reoccupation of the site, presumably by survivors of the disaster), there are some pieces still in LH IIIB style, but most apparently LH IIIC. The next stratum, Troy VIIb 2, features the arrival of a new people who introduced the "Buckelkeramik" or "Knobbed Ware", which is accompanied by a few sherds of later LH IIIC of the "Granary Style". The site was subsequently abandoned for some three centuries. It should be emphasised that the wares of Mycenaean style, which are most frequent in Troy VIIa, never form a high proportion of the pottery in any of the periods in question.

ADDENDA
RECENT DISCOVERIES

Because of other commitments, the composition of the text of this book has been spread over a number of years. For practical reasons, it has not been possible to incorporate some recently published discoveries before going to press. The additions made below are confined to excavated sites where significant new evidence has been obtained.

ORCHOMENOS (C 1)

The Mycenaean "palace" recently identified is now said to belong both to the LH IIIA and LH IIIB periods. Its destruction seems to have occurred at the end of the LH IIIB period [AD 28 (1973) B 258; AR (1978-9) 23].

THE MENELAION (E 1)

Supplementary excavations at three points on the hills immediately to south of the Menelaion have provided further conformation of the size of the Mycenaean settlement. They have also yielded the first evidence for occupation of the site in the early part of the LH IIIC period. On the south flank of Aetos hill, debris, including large limestone blocks, from a destruction horizon of the LH IIIB2 or early LH IIIC period, strongly suggests that the building with which it was originally associated was of monumental quality. A flat slab with carefully dressed edges is interpreted as a stair-tread fallen from an upper floor [AR (1978-9) 19, cf. AR (1977-8) 31]. More early Mycenaean material was found on the slope of the North Hill [AR (1978-9) 20, cf. AR (1976-7) 33].

AYIOS STEPHANOS (E 14)

Recent excavations have uncovered more Middle Helladic and Mycenaean buildings and graves. There is now evidence for a Mycenaean street and for a stepped ramp of early Mycenaean date. A fragment of a clay crucible with a scrap of bronze adhering to it provides evidence for metal-working on the site [AR (1977-8) 31].

Further details of work undertaken by G.S. Korres in Western Messenia are published in PAE (1976). The reports are preliminary, and the summary here is entirely provisional, pending fuller reports. Attention is drawn in particular to the important new evidence from Peristeria (F 203).

KORIFASION: CHARATSARI (F 5)

The tholos tomb was cleared and re-examined. It is discussed in connection with other tombs of the MH/LH I transitional period in Messenia [PAE (1976) A 270].

TRAGANA: VIGLITSA (F 6)

The two tholos tombs were cleared and measured, and an important new examination was made of the technique of their construction [PAE (1976) A 265].

TRAGANA: VOROULIA (F 7)

The important LH I pottery from this site has now been mended and studied in comparison with similar pottery from sites in Messenia and elsewhere [PAE (1976) A 271].

MYRSINOCHORI: ROUTSI (F 13)

The Mycenaean pottery from the two tholos tombs has been partly mended and studied, and attention is drawn to the first phase (LH I/IIA) of the use of the tombs [PAE (1976) A 281].

PETROCHORI: VOIDHOKOILIA (F 21)

The Mycenaean tholos tomb is now known to have been inserted into a Middle Helladic tumulus containing numerous pithos burials. Beneath the tumulus are Early Helladic settlement remains [*PAE* (1976) A 254, *cf. Ergon* (1977) 128]. Excavations are continuing here, and further study will be necessary before the exact date of the construction of the tholos tomb can be established.

MIROU: PERISTERIA (F 203)

In recent work Korres has established that the "southeast house" was occupied from the LH IIB to the LH IIIA2 periods. Tests on the north side of the hill have revealed parts of an extensive building associated with LH III material. The small MH/LH I tomb has now been completely excavated, and the LH IIA date of Tholos 1 is further documented. Tholos 3 is now known to have been destroyed and its stomion filled in during the LH II period. Further work has been carried out on the "circle", on the perimeter wall of Tholos 1, on Tholos 2, in the "west house", and at several other points. The importance of Peristeria, especially in early Mycenaean times, is now even more firmly established [*PAE* (1976) B 469, *cf. Ergon* (1977) 118].

Since 1974 the Phokis-Doris Expedition of Loyola University of Chicago, under the direction of E.W. Kase, has been exploring the natural mountain corridor which runs between the Malian Gulf in the north and the Corinthian Gulf in the south. In antiquity the end points of this route would have been at Vardhates and Itea. Some of the results obtained by the Phokis-Doris Expedition were reported by P.W. Wallace, in *Symposium on the Dark Ages in Greece* (1977) 51-57 (see above under C 63A, C 63B, C 73A, and C 73B). I am most grateful to N.C. Wilkie and E.W. Kase for the following further preliminary reports of the expedition's surface exploration and limited trial excavations.

LILAIA (C 63A)

On the small conical hillock to northeast of the village of Lilaia the expedition collected surface sherds in 1977 and excavated three trial trenches in 1978. One of the trenches was located on a broad terrace directly adjacent to the modern cemetery. The other two trenches were on an upper terrace inside the polygonal circuit wall which runs along the north and east ends of the site. The earliest habitation appears to have been in the EH I period. The EH II period is repre-

sented by large quantities of material including fragments from Urfirnis sauceboats and Yellow Mottled Wares. A few EH III sherds were recovered, and MH Grey and Yellow Minyan wares were found. Mycenaean material, mainly LH III, was found, but only in small quantities. The upper levels of the trenches also produced Classical and later material.

OITI: PANAYIA

The site of Panayia, near the village of Oiti, was first occupied in the Early Neolithic period. Only a few Mycenaean sherds were found, together with wares which may be of the Early and Middle Helladic periods. Sherds of the Late period were abundant, both on the surface and in the trial trenches.

RAKHITA (C 72)

Surface investigation in 1977 and a single trial trench in 1979 produced evidence of occupation in Middle Helladic times and later. MH Grey Minyan and Matt-painted wares were found in the lowest levels of the trench. Mycenaean sherds, including LH IIIA2, LH IIIB, and early LH IIIC, came from the intermediate levels, followed by a clear break separating the prehistoric from the late Classical and Hellenistic material. Core drilling was also undertaken in the plain immediately below the site in order to determine the location of the shoreline during antiquity.

DHIOVOUNA: DHEMA (C 73A)

Dhema is located near the village of Dhiovouna, at the northern entrance of the pass which connects Malis with Doris. The site was discovered by the expedition in 1975 (*cf.* P.W. Wallace, *op.cit.* 55). Its strategic location is emphasised by a massive fortification wall, perhaps of the period of Justinian, which effectively closed off the pass for some time in late antiquity. A number of trial trenches excavated in 1977 produced large quantities of prehistoric material. The earliest occupation of the site seems to have been in the EH I period. The EH II and EH III periods are only sparsely represented. MH Grey Minyan, Yellow Minyan, and Matt-painted wares were found. Of the Mycenaean sherds a few could be LH I or LH II, but the majority seem to LH IIIA and LH IIIB, and a few are apparently LH IIIC.

SUMMARY

MYCENAEAN GREECE:
THE SETTLEMENT PATTERN

When we consider our present "map" of Mycenaean Greece, we are bound to ask to what extent the known distribution of sites gives a reliable indication of the *actual* pattern of Mycenaean settlement. I began by outlining some of the more obvious limitations inherent in both excavation and survey work. The considerable progress already made has opened our eyes both to new possibilities and to new difficulties. It has been deduced by some (*e.g.* Bintliff 1977) that we have failed so far to discover the "lower hierarchy" of sites, *i.e.* the smaller settlements which are believed to be everywhere interspersed among the larger centres, which are more easily discovered. Thus there has been a growing movement towards favouring "intensive" rather than "extensive" surveys. But the former require much increased resources in terms of time, funds, and trained personnel.

Since in practice it is usually only possible to cover rather small areas in intensive surveys, there is a natural temptation to assume that such areas can be treated as valid "samples", which can (supposedly) be used as guides for exterpolation to larger areas. But such arguments should be regarded with great caution. Among the limiting factors is the condition of the surface artefacts themselves. In the eastern parts of Mainland Greece, and especially in the Argolid, Attica, Boeotia, and Euboea, the surface potsherds are usually in a much better state of preservation, and the Mycenaean pottery is generally of better quality than in the western provinces. Thus, for instance, the Mycenaean surface material in the eastern Argolid is usually far more diagnostic than that in southwestern Peloponnese. It follows that it will probably be easier to detect any "smaller and satellite" settlements in the eastern Argolid than in the southwestern Peloponnese. Another difficulty regarding the interpretation of survey data is that in all surveys a proliferation of small "scatters" of surface potsherds is encountered in many parts of Greece. It can not be assumed that all such scatters represent actual sites at the locations where they are observed. The differential factors of erosion and/or deposition and other disturbances must always be considered.

Since surface surveys are intrinsically subject to such limitations, it follows that stringent control should be placed on any exterpolations made from surveys alone. It is, for instance, likely that the "sampling strategy" being used on Melos may be a reasonably useful guide for "retrodiction" as regards ancient sites in the remainder of Melos. But it can not, and should not, be used as a guide for other parts of Greece. I have recently been engaged in an "intensive" survey of the Kommos area in South Crete, an area which borders in the Ayiofarango valley intensively surveyed previously (Branigan *et al.* 1977). There were great differences between these two contiguous areas both as to the actual survey data and as to the problems involved in their interpretation. We conclude that the results will have to be assessed separately, mainly because the surface conditions differ so greatly. This is not the place to discuss the details, but this example should serve as a warning to hopeful theorists, especially to those with access to computers. For the most part, it is neither possible nor desirable to construct hypotheses for one area solely on the basis of survey results from another area.

It would also be erroneous to assert that the relative density of Mycenaean settlement was everywhere proportionate to the relative fertility of the soil. The geographical "determinism" argued by some (*e.g.* Bintliff 1977) is only one of the factors which affected the positioning of ancient settlements. For example, the mediaeval and later population of the Mani far exceeded the agricultural potential of the district (Wagstaff, 1975). The unusually high concentrations of population at Mycenae and Tiryns in the Mycenaean period were similarly due mainly to political reasons.

There are, of course, many cases in recorded history where people have made choices which may appear absurd to geographers. There is little point in trying to make all the evidence fit a pre-conceived pattern. In general, we are still very much at the stage of recording the "raw data", and computer simulations and the like are premature.

On the other hand, there is a need for more guidance and planning with regard to survey work. Our "extensive" coverage of Greece is still very uneven, and there are many "gaps", especially for the prehistoric periods.

MAP A

Even in areas well served by excavation, such as the Argolid, there are obviously many more Mycenaean sites to be found. In this case a combination of the results of the previous extensive survey work and of the new intensive survey in the eastern Argolid probably would furnish a reliable indication of the density to be expected elsewhere in the Argolid where similar terrain and conditions exist. Particularly good subjects for further intensive survey in this province would be the Inachos valley, and the neighbourhoods of Asine and Troizen. But, even in this relatively well explored province, there is still a need for more extensive coverage also, as has been revealed by "rescue" and other recent excavations and chance discoveries. The area in the immediate vicinity of ancient Corinth has been well searched, but little or no work has been undertaken in districts to the south and west of Corinth, for example. There is some quite fertile land between Corinth and Nemea, for instance, in foothills to south of the coastal plain. Elsewhere on Map A, we may observe a paucity of sites in the Megarid (contrasting oddly with a fairly high number between Loutraki and Perachora), and Aegina is also still mainly unexplored.

MAP B

There are similar "gaps" on Map B. The eastern and central parts of Attica have received much attention, but the Eleusis plain in the west has been neglected. Eleusis itself is so far the only Mycenaean site known here. And there should be more sites between the Marathon area and Oropos, for instance. There is also probably considerably more to be found in Euboea, even in the relatively well searched central portion.

MAP C

It is probable that most of the important Mycenaean settlements in Boeotia have already been located, and in this province the need is mainly for intensive survey, such as that already being undertaken by the Cambridge, Bradford, and Ohio University teams in the vicinity of ancient Thisbe and Thespiai. But one major task which should be undertaken promptly, is a full survey of Lake Copais, including full mapping and photographing (especially from the air) of the ancient roads, dykes, and fortifications. These monuments are being steadily removed by agricultural and other modern disruptions. We await the full publication of the results of the recent survey work in Phocis and Doris, but East Locris, and in particular the plain of Molos to east of Thermopylae, has not received even extensive coverage. Some reconnaissance has been carried out in Malis and northern Euboea, but much more fieldwork is needed here also.

MAP D

Howell's excellent survey has opened up eastern Arcadia, but northern and western Arcadia are seldom even visited by archaeologists. In particular we should expect many more sites along the Alpheios and Ladon river valleys. Nor has a single prehistoric site yet been found in the Megalopolis area. In Achaea most of the Mycenaean sites discovered are those easily accessible from Patras or Aigion. The present "gap" between Aigion and Derveni is surely illusory. The concentration of known sites in the Olympic area is also due mainly to the disproportionate amount of attention given to it by archaeologists based at Olympia. It almost certainly is not a reflection of the true distribution of Mycenaean sites in Elis. The results of the "rescue" survey in the Peneios Barrage district provide a good indication of what may be expected in the main Elean plain and the surrounding foothills. And there should be many more sites in Triphylia, between the Alpheios and Neda rivers. Aetolia and western Locris have hardly been searched at all. The Naupactos and Agrinion districts in particular should prove rewarding.

MAP E

The Laconia survey is by no means complete. There are still several large "blanks" in the extensive coverage, especially in the eastern part, which consists of Mt. Parnon and its foothills. The upper part of the Vardhounia valley, inland to northwest of Gythion, may perhaps have still been largely forest or woodland in Mycenaean times, since the agricultural terracing in this district appears to be relatively recent. But further search is needed. Perhaps we should not expect much more from the southern part of the Mani (south of Areopolis), but the coastal plains to southwest of Gythion should yield results. The Vatika plain in southeast Laconia would be a good subject for intensive survey, since the site at Pavlopetri (E 33) was obviously large, and probably important. The marl soils around this plain would have been particularly easy to cultivate. More sites obviously await discovery in and around the Molaoi plain also. Surprisingly also, archaeologists have generally neglected the area immediately to north of Sparta itself.

MAP F

Messenia has received more attention than most provinces, but even here some further extensive work is needed, particularly in the Kyparissia mountain district (to south and southeast of Kyparissia), in the Neda valley, and in the western foothills of Mt. Taygetos. And the undulating low hill country to west of the Pamisos plain has not been searched thoroughly enough. Good subjects for further intensive work have been revealed, especially in the Pylos district and in the Pamisos and Soulima valleys. It should, however, be borne in mind that adverse soil and other conditions in the southwest Peloponnese may continue to make diagnosis of the surface pottery here especially difficult.

MAP G

As was said above, much more work is needed in Elis and Aetolia. Acarnania has scarcely been touched. Much has already been found in Ithaca and Kephallenia, but it should be noted that no Mycenaean site has yet been found in *northern* Kephallenia, and Leukas is an almost complete "blank" also. In Zakynthos both extensive and intensive work would be well repaid.

MAPS H AND J

Most of the Mycenaean sites found in Thessaly are in the east, particularly in the vicinities of Larisa, Volos, and Pharsala. And the emphasis has been on collecting sherds from the many obvious mound sites. Little attention has been paid to the villages in the foothills, especially those on the eastern flanks of the Pindus Mountains. The relative lack of exploration in western Thessaly in general may be giving us a somewhat distorted picture of the distribution. There are other obvious gaps in extensive coverage, *i.e.* the whole of the Pindus range itself and the cantons of the Pelion and Ossa mountain ranges. The tombs of tholos type found near Spilia (H 32), high up on the west flank of Mt. Ossa itself, provide a spectacular clue in this respect. It remains likely that the Mycenaeans did not in fact penetrate as thoroughly into western Thessaly as into eastern Thessaly. But much fuller extensive exploration of all of Thessaly, and also of the upper (western) part of the Spercheios valley, is needed before this major question can be resolved. As for intensive survey in Thessaly, the natural "units" (*i.e.* the plains and the surrounding hills) are almost all very large. And the landforms and the terrain in general are so diverse that "sampling strategies" would seem inappropriate.

MAPS K AND L

The finds from the tholos tomb at Parga (K 1) show that some Mycenaeans at least had reached Thesprotia. Whether they arrived by land or sea must remain uncertain, since the district to southeast, which includes the large plain of Arta and the lower reaches of the Louros and Acheloos rivers, has never been properly searched. It remains uncertain whether the site at Mesopotamos (K 2) is of Mycenaean or local Late Bronze Age type.

In Epirus the few and widely scattered Mycenaean finds mainly consist of weapons from tombs. The Mycenaean material from the partly excavated settlement sites of Dodona (K 4) and Kastritsa (K 5) is far outweighed by that of local Late Bronze Age type. It therefore remains probable that all Mycenaean finds in Epirus were imported. The same is probably true also for western Macedonia, although here too there has been little excavation or survey work.

In Central Macedonia more of the Late Bronze Age settlements have been excavated, so that we are here in a better position to estimate the strength of Mycenaean influence. The record shows that here also the Mycenaean wares are greatly outnumbered by those of local Late Bronze Age type. As in Thessaly, the excavation and survey work in Central Macedonia has been concentrated on sites of the "mound" variety. It is possible that "intensive" survey, especially of *selected* strips of the coastline and riverside, might reveal the presence of Mycenaean settlements, perhaps of a different (and smaller?) kind. It is conceivable that Mycenaean settlers existed here, but were only tolerated in separate trading posts, and excluded from the local Late Bronze Age sites, *e.g.* at Sedes (L 19), Gona (L 20), Assiros Toumba (L 31), Saratse (L 32), and Vardarophtsa (L 45).

MAPS M, N, AND O

Mycenaean settlements have been found on most of the major islands in the Aegean, and include some sites of considerable size and importance. But at some of the more remote sites the Late Bronze Age wares found are either purely or mainly of local type. Some of the Mycenaean settlements were fortified, *i.e.* Ayia Irini on Kea, Ayios Andreas on Siphnos, Koukounaries on Paros, and the Heraion on Samos. A considerable amount of reconnaissance work has taken place in the Aegean, but the only fully intensive survey is that carried out recently on Melos, by C. Renfrew, J.F. Cherry, and others, which is to be published shortly. It is clear that intensive work on some other islands would be particularly rewarding. But in other cases, as on Rhodes for instance, later habitation, particularly in the Hellenistic and Roman periods, has evidently obscured the traces of prehistoric occupation. This is true also of Western Asia Minor, where the amount of excavation and survey work has been considerable, but the Mycenaean finds (with the notable exceptions of Miletus, Müskebi, and Iasos) still relatively few. The current position in Asia Minor as a whole has been well assessed recently by C.B. Mee (1978).

GENERAL SUMMARY

Only when we have taken into account all the limitations outlined above, and the considerable deficiencies in our fieldwork, can we turn to the present map of Mycenaean Greece, and try to draw a few tentative conclusions. All distribution maps tend to present a simplified picture, and fail to reflect adequately the subtle changes in the development of cultures. And, partly because potsherds of the earlier Mycenaean periods (LH I-IIIA1) are more rarely diagnosed on the surface, the map of Mycenaean Greece is, in general, a truer reflection of the "koine" period (LH IIIA2-B) than of any other Mycenaean period. Besides this, the major criterion for dating, the pottery, is neither of uniform type nor of uniform quality. In Epirus, Macedonia, Lesbos, and parts of Western Asia Minor, for instance, we may be able to classify the Mycenaean pottery as imported. But even in parts of Greece known to be under Mycenaean bureaucratic control, such as Messenia, much of the pottery is of poor quality and of "local or "provincial" appearance. Conversely, in some areas where the pottery is of Mycenaean appearance, as in some parts of the Cyclades and the Dodecanese, it is difficult to estimate the degree of Mycenaean *political* influence. (The extent of Mycenaean control over Crete in the Late Helladic period is even more difficult to gauge.)

I hope that the discussion above concerning the "gaps" in our fieldwork and other difficulties of interpretation will serve to discourage scholars from drawing too many "negative" conclusions from the distribution map of Mycenaean settlements. On the other hand, I must repeat the warning against the facile assumption that all fertile areas in Mainland Greece and the islands were fully settled in the Mycenaean period. Mycenaean culture was still relatively primitive. The Mycenaeans achieved some outstanding feats of structural engineering, but there is as yet no convincing proof that they possessed an overall network of roads for wheeled traffic or any overall systems of drainage or irrigation. Even within provinces, communications with outlying settlements in fringe areas, especially the mountain districts and the remote islands, were probably not well developed. This seems to be indicated, for instance, by the provincial nature of the Mycenaean pottery on many sites in Arcadia and Achaea. Here, as at Thermon in Aetolia, and at Emporio on Chios, it is often difficult to judge whether the pottery is truly Mycenaean, or merely a local imitation. And, of course, no *political* conclusions can be drawn in these cases. The distribution map should not be understood as representing any evidence of uniformity, still less of political unity. Strong and convincing arguments have been adduced (*e.g.* Thomas, 1970) against the probability of such a unity.

The rugged terrain of Greece, with its numerous mountain barriers, was obviously a major factor in the development of the numerous separate city-states of the historical period. Such divisions almost certainly existed in Mycenaean Greece, and there is sufficient evidence to warrant at least a tentative identification of some of these. The system of roads in the Argolid, and perhaps also in Corinthia (pp. above), together with the evidence for a fortification wall across the Isthmus of Corinth, provide the best argument for a political unity of some kind in this central area during the LH IIIA2-B periods. Attica, on the other hand, may at this time have been divided into several small "kingdoms". The tholos tombs at Menidi and Marathon may provide some indication of this, when combined with the legend of the Synoecism of Attica by Theseus. It was argued above that Orchomenos was the main beneficiary of the Lake Copais drainage system. And ancient tradition also gives support to the argument that Thebes and Orchomenos were separate powers. If the place names in the Pylos tablets have been more or less correctly located in general, this would be our best case of all for a Mycenaean political unit, comprising most, if not all, of Messenia. Elsewhere there are few clues as to the identification of any further large units or "states". Indeed the evidence usually tends to indicate many separate centres, with even smaller territories than those of the minor city states of the historic period. Thus it appears likely that large units under centralised bureaucratic control were the exception rather than the rule.

While it is possible that future fieldwork may provide further substantial clues, it is not likely that we will obtain any definitive resolutions of the outstanding historical problems, both political and social. Almost all of the obvious major Mycenaean centres have been more or less fully excavated; and we have now no reason to expect much explicit documentary evidence from any "new" hoard of Linear B tablets which may be discovered. Most of the information we now possess is derived from the LH IIIB destruction levels at the major sites; and it provides more questions than answers. Recent debate (especially in *Antiquity* 1974 and 1976) has focussed on the decline of Mycenaean civilisation at the end of the LH IIIB period. Most scholars now attribute this decline to a collapse of the bureaucratic systems in the central areas, due principally to the destructions of the major sites. The consensus of opinion is that these destructions were mainly the work of the Mycenaeans themselves. They would have resulted in a breakdown of systems for the distribution of any surpluses (primarily of food) to non-productive members of communities. It is, of course, probable that most of their livestock, and stores of grain etc., would have been seized. The survivors would thus have been faced with a sudden need to consume any livestock that remained, and probably also the seed grain (Betancourt, 1976). The suggestion (Carpenter, 1966) that the decline of Mycenaean civilisation was due to a disastrous drought has been strongly refuted, especially by Wright (1968) and by Bryson *et al.* (1974). But the theory that the population had outstripped the carrying capacity of the land (Betancourt 1976) also seems most unlikely. Even in Messenia it has been calculated (*MME* 245 ff.) that only about one third of the land at present cultivated would have been needed for food production in Mycenaean times, and that probably a maximum of 25% of the land surrounding each Mycenaean settlement here was intensively cultivated.

It is not yet possible, however, to make a reliable overall estimate of the population of Mycenaean Greece. Even if the whole of Messenia, for instance, were to be intensively surveyed (by enormous numbers of trained archaeologists with almost unlimited time available), the data obtained still could not supply anything more than a slightly better basis for guesswork. The limitations of survey *data* in this respect, and even of that derived from excavation, should be obvious. Indeed most of our attempts to estimate prehistoric populations resemble an infant's attempt to run before it can walk. The chief duty of the present generation of archaeologists is to collect and record the data, not to indulge in premature speculation, however much we may enjoy this exercise. On the other hand, there is a need at least to summarise the results of major survey and excavation work, and to point out trends and unanswered questions. The authors of *MME*, for instance, were well aware of the hypothetical nature of their tentatively expressed conclusions. Their object was simply "to make available to interested scholars the present state of our thinking" (*MME* 254).

Similarly, in an attempt to forestall any misguided criticism from reviewers, I have used appropriate expressions of caution and verbal qualifications, when summarising the present state of our knowledge of Mycenaean Greece. I hope that the attempts I have made here to predict (or retrodict?) where further Mycenaean sites are to be found, and consequently where fieldwork is needed, will be understood as entirely conjectural. Their only value is that they are based on experience gained in the field. Of one thing, however, I am completely certain—there is an immense amount of work still to be done, and, because of the rapid pace of modernisation, little time left in which to discover and record the remains.

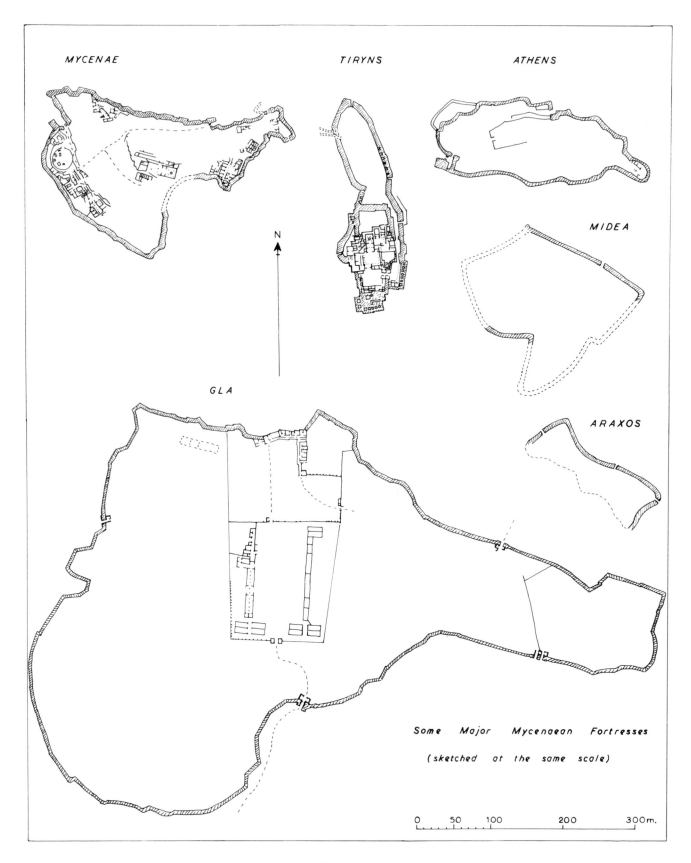

MYCENAE

TIRYNS

ATHENS

MIDEA

ARAXOS

GLA

N

Some Major Mycenaean Fortresses

(sketched at the same scale)

0   50   100   200   300m.

Figure 15

SELECT BIBLIOGRAPHY

ABBREVIATIONS FOR PERIODICALS AND SERIALS

AA	*Archäologischer Anzeiger: Beiblatt zum Jahrbuch des Deutschen archäologischen Instituts*
AAA	*Athens Annals of Archaeology*
AD	*Archaiologikon Deltion*
AE	*Archaiologike Ephemeris*
AJA	*American Journal of Archaeology*
AM	*Mitteilungen der Deutschen archäologischen Instituts: athenische Abteilung*
Ann.	*Annuario della scuola italiana di Atene e delle missioni italiani in oriente*
AR	*Archaeological Reports* (by the Society for the Promotion of Hellenic Studies in conjunction with the British School at Athens)
Arch.Zeit.	*Archäologischer Zeitung*
AS	*Anatolian Studies*
BCH	*Bulletin de correspondance hellénique*
BICS	*Bulletin of the Institute of Classical Studies of the University of London*
Boll. d'Arte	*Bolletino d'Arte del Ministero della pubblica Istruzione*
BSA	*Annual of the British School at Athens*
Bull. Lund	*Bulletin de la société royale de lettres de Lund*
Clara Rhodos	Clara Rhodos: *studi e materiali pubblicati a cura dell'Instituto storico archaeologico di Rodi*
CVA	*Corpus Vasorum Antiquorum*
Ergon	*To Ergon tes Archaiologikes Etaireias*
GRBS	Greek, Roman, and Byzantine Studies
ILN	*Illustrated London News*
Ist. Mitt.	*Istanbuler Mitteilungen*
JdI	*Jahrbuch des deutschen archäologischen Instituts*
JFA	*Journal of Field Archaeology*

219

JHS	*Journal of Hellenic Studies*
KC	*Kretika Chronika*
LAAA	*Liverpool Annals of Archaeology and Anthropology*
Memorie	*Memorie dell'Instituto storico archaeologico di Rodi*
OpArch	*Acta Instituti Romani Regni Sueciae: Opuscula Archaeologica*
OpAth	*Acta Instituti Atheniensis Regni Sueciae: Opuscula Atheniensia*
OJh	*Jahreshefte des Österreischischen archäologischen Instituts*
PAE	*Prakitka tes Archaiologikes Etaireias*
PPS	*Proceedings of the Prehistoric Society*
PZ	*Praehistorische Zeitschrift*
RA	*Revue Archeologique*
REG	*Revue des Etudes Grecques*
SIMA	*Studies in Mediterranean Archaeology*
SMEA	*Studi micenei ed egeo-anatolici*

Other periodicals such as *Euphrosyne, Hesperia* (Journal of the American School of Classical Studies at Athens), *Mnemosyne* etc., will be referred to either by their usual abbreviated titles or in full.

ABBREVIATIONS FOR FIELD SURVEYS

Arcadia	R.J. Howell, "A Survey of Eastern Arcadia in Prehistory", in *BSA* 65 (1970) 79-127.
CG	D.H. French, *Notes on Prehistoric Pottery Groups from Central Greece* (circulated typescript, 1972).
CM	D.H. French, *Index of Prehistoric Sites in Central Macedonia* (circulated typescript, 1967).
Dodecanese I, II, III	R. Hope Simpson and J.F. Lazenby, "Notes from the Dodecanese", in *BSA* 57 (1962) 154-75, 65 (1970) 44-77, 68 (1973) 127-79.
Euboea	L.H. Sackett *et al.*, "Prehistoric Euboea: Contributions Towards a Survey", in *BSA* 61 (1966) 33-112.
Hunter	A. Hunter, *The Bronze Age in Thessaly and its Environs, with Special Reference to Mycenaean Culture* (B. Litt. thesis, Oxford 1953).
Laconia I, II	H. Waterhouse and R. Hope Simpson, "Prehistoric Laconia, Part I (II)", in *BSA* 55 (1960) 67-107, 56 (1961) 221-60.
Messenia I, II, III	W.A. McDonald and R. Hope Simpson, "Prehistoric Habitation in the Southwestern Peloponnese", in *AJA* 65 (1961) 221-60, "Further Explorations in Southwestern Peloponnese (1962-3) (1964-8)", in *AJA* 68 (1964) 229-45, 73 (1969) 123-78.
MME	W.A. McDonald and G. Rapp Jr. (eds.), *The Minnesota Messenia Expedition*, Minneapolis 1972.
PT	A.J.B. Wace and M.S. Thompson, *Prehistoric Thessaly*, Cambridge 1912.

1. GENERAL SURVEYS AND STUDIES, AND SPECIAL ABBREVIATIONS

Alin   P. Ålin, *Das Ende der mykenische Fundstätten auf der griech-ischen Festland* (*SIMA* vol. 1), Lund 1962.

                         J.L. Bintliff (ed.), *Mycenaean Geography* (Proceedings of the Cambridge Colloquium September 1976), Cambridge 1977.

Bintliff (1977)   J.L. Bintliff, *Natural Environment and Human Settlement in Prehistoric Greece* (British Archaeological Reports Supplementary Series no. 28), Oxford 1977.

                         R.A. Crossland and A. Birchall, *Bronze Age Migrations in the Aegean*, Park Ridge, New Jersey 1974.

BMCat. A   J. Forsdyke, *Catalogue of the Greek and Etruscan Vases in the British Museum*, vol. I, Part 1, London 1925.

CAH   *The Cambridge Ancient History* Volume II (Third Edition, revised), Cambridge 1970-75.

CH   A.J.B. Wace and F.H. Stubbings (eds.), *A Companion to Homer*, London 1962.

CMP   A. Furumark, *The Chronology of Mycenaean Pottery*, Stockholm 1941.

                         G. Christopoulos (ed.), *History of the Hellenic World I: Prehistory and Protohistory*, Athens 1970 (in Greek) and 1974 (English translation).

CSHI   R. Hope Simpson and J.F. Lazenby, *The Catalogue of the Ships in Homer's Iliad*, Oxford 1970.

Desborough (1964)   V.R. d'A. Desborough, *The Last Mycenaeans and Their Successors*, Oxford 1964.

Desborough (1972)   V.R. d'A. Desborough, *The Greek Dark Ages*, Oxford 1972.

                         O.T.P.K. Dickinson, *The Origins of Mycenaean Civilisation* (*SIMA* vol. 49), Göteborg 1977.

DMG   M. Ventris and J. Chadwick, *Documents in Mycenaean Greek* (Second edition), Cambridge 1973.

Fimmen (1921)   D. Fimmen, *Die Kretisch-mykenische Kultur*, Leipzig and Berlin 1921.

Frazer, *Pausanias*   J.G. Frazer, *Pausanias' Description of Greece*, London 1898.

                         J.G. Frazer and A.W. Van Buren, *Graecia Antiqua* (Maps Plans to Illustrate Pausanias' Description of Greece), London 1930.

                         R. Hope Simpson and O.T.P.K. Dickinson, *A Gazetteer of Aegean Civilisation in the Bronze Age, Vol. I: The Mainland and Islands* (*SIMA* vol. 52), Göteborg 1979.

                         D. Leekley and N. Efstratiou, *Archaeological Excavations in Central and Northern Greece*, Park Ridge, New Jersey 1980.

                         D. Leekley and R. Noyes, *Archaeological Excavations in the Greek Islands*, Park Ridge, New Jersey 1975.

                         D. Leekley and R. Noyes, *Archaeological Excavations in Southern Greece*, Park Ridge, New Jersey 1976.

MMA   G.E. Mylonas, *Mycenae and the Mycenaean Age*, Princeton, New Jersey 1966.

MP	A. Furumark, *Mycenaean Pottery, Analysis and Classification,* Stockholm 1941.
	A. Furumark, "The Settlement of Ialysos and Aegean History 1550-1400 B.C.", in *OpArch* 6 (1950) 150-271.
MT II, III	E.L. Bennett *et al., The Mycenae Tablets II,* Philadelphia 1958.
	J. Chadwick *et al., The Mycenae Tablets III,* Philadelphia 1963.
MV	A. Fürtwängler and G. Löschcke, *Mykenische Vasen,* Berlin 1886.
MW	J. Chadwick, *The Mycenaean World,* Cambridge 1976.
MycCon I	*Atti e memorie del primo congreso internazionale di micenologia* Vol. I (1968).
	W.A. McDonald, *Progress into the Past: The Rediscovery of Mycenaean Civilisation,* New York 1967.
Philippson *GL*	A. Philippson, *Die Griechischen Landschaften* (ed. E. Kirsten), Frankfurt am Main 1950-59.
Pritchett (1965)	W.K. Pritchett, *Studies in Ancient Greek Topography* Part I, Berkeley, California 1965.
Pritchett (1969)	W. K. Pritchett, *Studies in Ancient Greek Topography* Part II (Battlefields), Berkeley, California 1969.
RE	*Real-Enkyklopädie der klassischen Altertumswissenschaft* (eds. Pauly, Wissowa, and Kroll) especially "Mykenische Kultur" by G. Karo in Suppl. VI (1935).
Renfrew (1972)	C. Renfrew, *The Emergence of Civilisation: The Cyclades and the Aegean in the Third Millenium* B.C., London 1972.
	N.K. Sandars, *The Sea Peoples,* London 1978.
	N.C. Scoufopoulos, *Mycenaean Citadels* (*SIMA* vol. 22), Göteborg 1971.
Schoder (1974)	R.V. Schoder, *Ancient Greece from the Air,* London 1974.
	F. Schachermeyr, *Die Ägäische Frühzeit 2: Die Mykenische Zeit und die Gesittung von Thera,* Wien 1976.
	A.M. Snodgrass, *The Dark Age of Greece,* Edinburgh 1971.
	K.T. Syriopoulos, *He Proistoria tes Peloponnesou,* Athens 1964.
	K.T. Syriopoulos, *He Proistoria tes Stereas Hellados,* Athens 1968.
	Lord William Taylour, *The Mycenaeans,* New York 1964.
	C. Tsountas, *Mykenai kai Mykenaios Politismos,* Athens 1893.
	C. Tsountas and J.I. Manatt, *The Mycenaean Age,* London 1897.
	E. Vermeule, *Greece in the Bronze Age* (1972).
	A.J.B. Wace, *Mycenae. An Archaeological History and Guide,* Princeton 1949.

2. THE GEOGRAPHY OF ANCIENT GREECE

The following are recommended as a general introduction to the geographical background:

> M. Cary, *The Geographic Background of Greek and Roman History,* Oxford 1949.

N.G.L. Hammond, *A History of Greece to 322* B.C., Oxford 1959.

N.G.L. Hammond (ed.), *Atlas of the Greek and Roman World in Antiquity*, Park Ridge, New Jersey 1981.

J.L. Myres, *Geographical History in Greek Lands*, Oxford 1953.

C. Vita-Finzi, *The Mediterranean Valleys*, Cambridge 1969.

For specialized studies of the geology of Greece, its soils, and vegetational history etc., the most recent general bibliography is that given by J.L. Bintliff, *Natural Environment and Human Settlement in Prehistoric Greece* (1977). Items of special importance include the following:

J.C. Kraft, *A Reconnaissance of the Geology of the Sandy Coastal Areas of Eastern Greece and the Peloponnese*, Delaware 1972.

W.A. McDonald and G. Rapp (eds.), *The Minnesota Messenia Expedition*, Minneapolis 1972.

cf. also J.C. Kraft, S.E. Aschenbrenner, and G. Rapp, "Paleographic Reconstructions of Coastal Aegean Archaeological Sites", in *Science* 195 (1977) 941-7.

3. MYCENAEAN SITES AND DISTRICTS
(listed by Map)

MAP A

J.L. Angel, *Lerna II: The People*, Princeton 1971.

P. Äström, "Das Panzergrab von Dendra: Bauweise und Keramik", in *AM* 82 (1967) 54-67.

J.M. Balcer, "The Mycenaean Dam at Tiryns", in *AJA* 78 (1974) 141-9.

J.L. Bintliff, *Natural Environment and Human Settlement in Prehistoric Greece* (1977) 173-356 and *passim*.

C.W. Blegen, "Corinth in Prehistoric Times", in *AJA* 24 (1920) 1-13.

C.W. Blegen, *Korakou, A Prehistoric Settlement near Corinth*, Boston and New York 1921.

C.W. Blegen, *Zygouries, A Prehistoric Settlement in the Valley of Cleonae*, Cambridge, Mass., 1928.

C.W. Blegen, "Gonia", in *Metropolitan Museum Studies* 3 (1930) 55-86.

C.W. Blegen, *Prosymna, The Helladic Settlement Preceding the Argive Heraeum*, Cambridge, Mass., 1937.

O. Broneer, "The Cyclopean Wall on the Isthmus of Corinth", in *Hesperia* 35 (1966) 346-62 and 37 (1968) 25-35.

J.L. Caskey, preliminary reports of excavations at Lerna, in *Hesperia* 23 (1954) 3-30, 24 (1955) 25-49, 25 (1956) 147-73, 26 (1957) 142-52, 27 (1958) 125-44, 28 (1959) 202-6.

P. Courbin, "Discoveries at Ancient Argos", in *Archaeology* 9 (1956) 166-74.

J. Deshayes, "Les Vases mycéniens de la Deiras (Argos)", in *BCH* 77 (1953) 59-89.

J. Deshayes, *Les Fouilles de la Deiras* (1966).

J. Deshayes, "Les Vases Vollgraff de la Deiras", in *BCH* 93 (1969) 574-616.

O. Frödin and A.W. Persson, *Asine, Results of the Swedish Excavations, 1922-1930*, Stockholm 1938.

K. Gebauer, "Forschungen in der Argolis", in *AA* (1939) 268-94.

N.G. Gejvall, *Lerna I: The Fauna* (1969).

P. Gercke *et al.*, *Tiryns Forschungen und Berichte V* (1971).

I. and R. Hägg, *Excavations in the Barbouna Area of Asine I*, Uppsala 1973.

R. Hägg, "Research at Dendra 1961", in *OpAth* 4 (1962) 79-102.

R. Hägg, *Die Gräber der Argolis I* (1974).

J.P. Harland, *Prehistoric Aigina*, Paris 1925.

S. Hiller, "Mykenische Keramik", in *Alt-Ägina* (ed. H. Walter) vol. IV part 1, Mainz 1975.

S. Iakovidis, *Guide to Argos, Tiryns, and Nauplia*, Athens 1978.

U. Jantzen, *Führer durch Tiryns*, Athens 1975.

G. Karo, "Die Perseia von Mykenai", in *AJA* 38 (1934) 123-6.

G. Karo, *Die Schachtgräber von Mykenai*, Munich 1930-33.

A.D. Keramopoullos, "Mykenaikoi taphoi en Aiginei kai en Thebais", in *AE* (1910) 172-209.

J.C. Kraft, S.E. Aschenbrenner, and G. Rapp, "Paleographic Reconstructions of Coastal Aegean Archaeological Sites", in *Science* 195 (1977) 941-7.

H. Lehmann, *Argolis*, Athens 1937.

K. Müller, *Tiryns III: die Architektur der Burg und des Palastes*, Augsburg 1930.

K. Müller *et al.*, *Tiryns VIII*, Mainz 1975.

G.E. Mylonas, *Ancient Mycenae: The Capital City of Agamemnon*, Princeton 1957.

G.E. Mylonas, "He Akropolis ton Mykenon", in *AE* (1958) 153-207, (1962) *passim*.

G.E. Mylonas, *Mycenae and the Mycenaean Age*, Princeton 1966.

G.E. Mylonas, *Mycenae's Last Century of Greatness*, Sydney 1968.

G.E. Mylonas, *The Cult Centre of Mycenae*, Princeton 1972.

G.E. Mylonas, *Mycenae, a Guide to its Ruins and its History*, Athens 1973.

G.E. Mylonas, *Ho Taphikos Kyklos B ton Mykenon*, Athens 1973.

H. Payne *et al.*, *Perachora I*, Oxford 1940.

A.W. Persson, *The Royal Tombs at Dendra near Midea*, Lund 1931.

A.W. Persson, *New Tombs at Dendra near Midea*, Lund 1942.

G. Rodenwaldt, *Tiryns II: die Fresken des Palastes*, Augsburg 1912.

G. Säflund, *Excavations at Berbati 1936-7*, Stockholm 1965.

H. Schliemann, *Mycenae: A Narrative of Researches and Discoveries at Mycenae and Tiryns*, New York 1880.

H. Schliemann and W. Dörpfeld, *Tiryns. The Prehistoric Palace of the Kings of Tiryns*, New York 1885.

H.B. Siedentopf *et al.*, *Tiryns Forschungen und Berichte VI*, Mainz 1973.

H. Steffen, *Karten von Mykenai*, Berlin 1884.

C. Tsountas, "Anaskaphai taphon en Mykenais", in *AE* (1886) 136-58.

N.M. Verdelis, "Neue Geometrische Gräber in Tiryns", in *AM* 78 (1963) 1-62.

N.M. Verdelis, "Neue Funde von Dendra", in *AM* 82 (1967) 1-53.

W. Vollgraff, "Fouilles d'Argos", in *BCH* 28 (1904) 364-99, 30 (1906) 5-45, 31 (1907) 139-44.

A.J.B. Wace *et al.*, "Excavations at Mycenae", in *BSA* 24 (1919-21) 185-209, 25 (1921-3) *passim*.

A.J.B. Wace, *Chamber Tombs at Mycenae* (*Archaeologia* vol. 82), Oxford 1932.

A.J.B. Wace, *Mycenae: An Archaeological History and Guide*, Princeton 1949.

A.J.B. Wace *et al.*, preliminary reports of excavations at Mycenae in *BSA* 45 (1950) 203-28, 48 (1953) 3-29, 69-83, 49 (1954) 231-53, 266-91, 50 (1955) 175-237, 51 (1956) 103-22.

H. Wace, E. French, and C.K. Williams, *Mycenae Guide*, Meriden, Connecticut 1971.

G. Walberg, "Finds from Excavations in the Acropolis of Midea 1939", in *OpAth* 7 (1967) 161-75.

G. Welter, *Aigina*, Berlin 1938.

G. Welter, *Troizen und Kalaureia*, Berlin 1941.

MAP B

M. Benzi, *Ceramica Micenea in Attica*, Milan 1975.

O. Broneer, "Excavations on the North Slope of the Acropolis", in *Hesperia* 2 (1933) 329-72.

O. Broneer, "A Mycenaean Fountain on the Athenian Acropolis", in *Hesperia* 8 (1939) 317-433.

O. Broneer, "Athens in the Late Bronze Age", in *Antiquity* 30 (1956) 9-18.

J.A. Bundgaard, *The Parthenon and the Mycenaean City on the Heights* (National Museum of Denmark Arch.-Hist. Series vol. 17), Copenhagen 1976.

W.G. Cavanagh, *Attic Burial Customs ca. 2000-700 B.C.* (Ph.D. thesis, London 1977).

D.H. French, *Notes on Prehistoric Pottery Groups from Central Greece* (circulated typescript 1972).

V. Hankey, "Late Helladic Tombs at Khalkis", in *BSA* 47 (1952) 49-95.

H.D. Hansen, "The Prehistoric Pottery on the North Slope of the Acropolis", in *Hesperia* 6 (1937) 539-50.

E.J. Holmberg, *Aten*, Göteborg 1975.

S. Iakovidis, *He Mykenaike Akropolis ton Athenon*, Athens 1962.

S. Iakovidis, *Perati: To Nekrotapheion I-III*, Athens 1970.

S.A. Immerwahr, *The Athenian Agora XIII: The Neolithic and Bronze Ages*, Princeton 1971.

W. Kraiker and K. Kübler, *Kerameikos: Ergebnisse der Ausgrabungen I*, Berlin 1939.

H.F. Mussche, J. Bingen, J. Servais *et al.*, *Thorikos I* (1963) 27-46, *III* (1965) 20-24, *V* (1968) 21-102.

G.E. Mylonas, *Proistorike Eleusis*, Athens 1932.

G.E. Mylonas and K. Kourouniotis, "Excavations at Eleusis, 1932", in *AJA* 37 (1933) 271-86.

G.E. Mylonas, "Eleusiniaka", in *AJA* 40 (1936) 415-31.

G.E. Mylonas, *Aghios Kosmas*, Princeton 1959.

G.E. Mylonas, *To Dytikon Nekrotapheion tes Eleusinos*, Athens 1975-6.

M. Pantelidou, *Hai Proistorikai Athenai* (doctoral thesis, Athens, 1975).

G.A. Papavasileiou, *Peri ton en Euboiai archaion taphon*, Athens 1910.

M.R. Popham and L.H. Sackett, *Excavations at Lefkandi, Euboea 1964-66*, London 1968.

L.H. Sackett *et al.*, "Prehistoric Euboea: Contributions Towards a Survey", in *BSA* 61 (1966) 33-112.

T. Spyropoulos, preliminary reports of excavations at Tanagra, in *PAE* (1969) 5-15, (1970) 29-36, (1971) 7-14, (1973) 11-21, (1974) 9-33, *Ergon* (1975) 17-26, (1976) 8-14, *cf.* also *AAA* 2 (1969) 20-25, 3 (1970) 184-95.

B. Stais, "Proistorikoi synoikismoi en Attikei kai Aiginei", in *AE* (1895) 193-263.

F.H. Stubbings, "The Mycenaean Pottery of Attica", in *BSA* 42 (1947) 1-75.

D.R. Theochares, preliminary reports of excavations at Raphina and Asketario, in *PAE* (1951) 77-92, (1952) 129-51, (1953) 105-18, (1954) 104-13, (1955) 109-17.

D.R. Theochares, "Asketario", in *AE* (1953-4) III 59-76.

D.R. Theochares, "Ek tes proistorias tes Euboias kai Skyrou", in *Arkheion Euboikon Meleton* 6 (1959) 279-328.

MAP C

Y. Béquignon, *La Vallée du Spercheios*, Paris 1937.

H. Bulle, *Orchomenos I: die alteren Ansiedlungsschichten*, Berlin 1907.

L. Dor *et al.*, *Kirrha, Étude de préhistoire phocidienne*, Paris 1960.

J.M. Fossey, "The End of the Bronze Age in the Southwest Copaic", in *Euphrosyne* 6 (1973-4) 7-21.

D.H. French, *Notes on Prehistoric Pottery Groups from Central Greece* (circulated typescript, 1972).

R. Hope Simpson and J.F. Lazenby, "The Kingdom of Peleus and Achilles", in *Antiquity* 33 (1939) 102-5.

J. Jannoray and H. van Effenterre, "Fouilles de Krisa", in *BCH* 61 (1937) 299-326, 62 (1938) 110-47.

U. Kahrstedt, "Die Kopaissee in Altertum und die "Minyschen Kanäle, in *AA* (1937) 1-19.

M.L. Kambanis, "Le dessèchement du Lac Copais par les anciens", in *BCH* 16 (1892) 121-37 and 17 (1893) 322-42.

J.A. Kenny, "The Ancient Drainage of the Copais", in *LAAA* 22 (1935) 189-206.

A.D. Keramopoullos, "He Oikia Kadmou", in *AE* (1909) 57-122.

A.D. Keramopoullos, "Mykenaikoi taphoi en Aiginei kai en Thebais", in *AE* (1910) 209-52.

A.D. Keramopoullos, "Thebaika", in *AD* 3 (1917) *passim.*

A.D. Keramopoullos, "Biomekhanai kai Emporion tou Kadmou", in *AE* (1930) 29-58.

S. Lauffer, "Topographische Untersuchungen in Kopaisgebiet", in *AD* 26 (1971) 239-45.

F. Noack, "Arne", in *AM* 19 (1894) 405-85.

A. de Ridder, "Fouilles de Gla", in *BCH* 18 (1894) 271-310, and 446-52.

A. de Ridder, "Fouilles d'Orchomène", in *BCH* 19 (1895) 137-224.

L.H. Sackett, *et al.*, "Prehistoric Euboea: Contributions Towards a Survey", in *BSA* 61 (1966) 33-112.

S. Symeonoglou, *Kadmeia I. Mycenaean Finds from Thebes, Greece* (*SIMA* vol. 35), Göteborg 1973.

I. Threpsiades, preliminary reports on excavations at Gla, in *PAE* (1955) 121-4, (1956) 90-93, (1957) 48-53, (1958) 38-42, (1959) 21-25, (1960) 23-38, (1961) 28-40.

C. Vatin, *Médéon de Phocide*, Paris 1969.

Various authors, preliminary reports on excavations in Thebes in *AD* 19 (1964) B and following, to present, *cf.* also *AAA* 3 (1970) 322-7 (T. Spyropoulos), 7 (1974) 162-73, 8 (1975) 25-8, 86-90 (K. Demakopoulou).

MAP D

P. Äström, "Mycenaean Pottery from the Region of Aigion, with a List of Prehistoric Sites in Achaea", in *OpAth* 5 (1964) 89-110.

W. Dörpfeld, "Alt-Pylos I. Die Kuppelgräber von Kakovatos", in *AM* 33 (1908) 295-317.

W. Dörpfeld, *Alt-Olympia*, Berlin 1935.

E.J. Holmberg, *The Swedish Excavations at Asea in Arcadia*, Lund 1944.

R.J. Howell, "A Survey of Eastern Arcadia in Prehistory", in *BSA* 65 (1970) 79-127.

L. Lerat, *Les Locriens de l'Ouest*, Paris 1952.

K. Müller, "Alt-Pylos II. Die Funde aus den Kuppelgräbern von Kakovatos", in *AM* 34 (1909) 269-328.

A.J. Papadopoulos, *Excavations at Aigion—1970* (*SIMA* vol. 46), Göteborg 1976.

L. Parlama, summary of Mycenaean finds in Elis, in *AD* 29 (1974) A 25-28.

K. Romaios, reports of excavations at Thermon, in *AD* 1 (1915) 225-79, 2 (1916) 179-89.

J. Sperling, "Explorations in Elis 1939", in *AJA* 46 (1942) 77-89.

E. Vermeule, "The Mycenaeans in Achaea", in *AJA* 64 (1960) 1-21.

F. Weege, "Einzelfunde aus Olympia 1907-9 I: die Funde aus Wohnhauserschicht", in *AM* 36 (1911) 163-85.

N. Yalouris, "Mykenaikos Tymbos Samikou", in *AD* 20 (1965) A 6-40.

N. Yalouris, "Trouvailles mycéniennes et prémycéniennes de la Région de Sanctuaire d'Olympie", in *MycCon I* 176-82.

N. Zafeiropoulos, preliminary reports of excavations in the Pharai area, in *PAE* (1952) 398-400, (1956) 173-207, (1957) 114-7, (1958) 167-76.

Reports of surveys and test excavations in the area of the Peneios river dam in Elis, in *AD* 23 (1968) B 174-94.

MAP E

J.L. Bintliff, *Natural Environment and Human Settlement in Prehistoric Greece* (1977) 371-497 and *passim*.

J.N. Coldstream and G.L. Huxley (eds.), *Kythera: Excavations and Studies*, Park Ridge, New Jersey 1972.

K. Demakopoulou, "Mykenaika angeia ek thalamoeidon taphon periokhes Hagiou Ioannou Monemvasias", in *AD* 23 (1968) A 145-94.

A. Harding *et al.*, "Pavlopetri, an Underwater Bronze Age Town in Laconia", in *BSA* 64 (1969) 113-42.

J.B. and S.H. Rutter, *The Transition to Mycenaean*, Los Angeles 1976.

Lord William Taylour, "Excavations at Ayios Stephanos", in *BSA* 67 (1972) 205-70.

C. Tsountas, "Erevnai en tei Lakonikei kai ho taphos tou Vapheiou", in *AE* (1889) 129-72.

H. Waterhouse and R. Hope Simpson, "Prehistoric Laconia (Parts I, II)", in *BSA* 55 (1960) 67-107, 56 (1961) 221-60.

MAP F

C.R. Beye, *The Iliad, The Odyssey, and the Epic Tradition,* New York 1966.

J.L. Bintliff, *Natural Environment and Human Settlement in Prehistoric Greece* (1977) 499-520 and *passim.*

C.W. Blegen, M. Rawson *et al., The Palace of Nestor at Pylos in Western Messenia* vols. I and III, Princeton 1966-73.

A. Choremis, "Mykenaikoi kai protogeometrikoi Taphoi Karpophoras Messenias", in *AE* (1973) 25-72.

R. Hope Simpson, "Identifying a Mycenaean State", in *BSA* 52 (1957) 231-59.

R. Hope Simpson, "The Seven Cities Offered by Agamemnon to Achilles", in *BSA* 61 (1966) 113-31.

Th. Karageorga, "Anaskaphe periokhes arkhaiou Doriou", in *AE* (1972) *Chronika* 12-20.

G.S. Korres, preliminary reports of excavations in Messenia, in *PAE* (1974) 139-62, *Ergon* (1975) 132-9, (1976) 127-40, (1977) 118-135.

J.C. Kraft, G. Rapp, and S.E. Aschenbrenner, "Late Holocene Paleography of the Coastal Plain of the Gulf of Messenia, Greece, and its Relationships to Archaeological Settings and Coastal Change", in *Geographical Society of America Bulletin* v. 86 (1975) 1191-1208.

J.C. Kraft, S.E. Aschenbrenner, and G. Rapp, "Paleographic Reconstructions of Coastal Aegean Archaeological Sites", in *Science* 195 (1977) 941-7.

J.C. Kraft and S.E. Aschenbrenner, "Paleographic Reconstruction in the Methoni Embayment in Greece, in *JFA* 4 (1977) 19-44.

M. Lang, *The Palace of Nestor at Pylos in Western Messenia II: The Frescoes,* Princeton 1969.

W.G. Loy, *The Land of Nestor: A Physical Geography of the Southwest Peloponnese* (Office of Naval Research Report No. 34), Washington 1967.

S. Marinatos, preliminary reports of excavations in Messenia, in *PAE* (1952) 473-96, (1953) 238-50, (1954) 299-316, (1955) 245-55, (1956) 202-6, (1957) 118-20, (1958) 184-93, (1959) 174-9, (1960) 195-209, (1961) 169-76, (1962) 90-98, (1963) 114-21, (1964) 78-95, (1965) 102-20, (1966) 119-32.

S. Marinatos, "Palaipylos", in *Das Altertum* 1 (1955) 140-163.

S. Marinatos, "Problemi archeologici e filologici di Pilo", in *SMEA* 3 (1967) 7-18.

W.A. McDonald, "Overland Communications in Greece during LH III, with special Reference to Southwest Peloponnese", in E.L. Bennett (ed.) *Mycenaean Studies* (1964) 217-240, Madison 1964.

W.A. McDonald and R. Hope Simpson, "Prehistoric Habitation in the Southwestern Peloponnese", in *AJA* 65 (1961) 221-60.

W.A. McDonald and R. Hope Simpson, "Further Explorations in the Southwestern Peloponnese (1962-3, 1964-8)", in *AJA* (1964) 229-45, 73 (1969) 123-78.

W.A. McDonald and G. Rapp (eds.), *The Minnesota Messenia Expedition,* Minneapolis 1972.

W.A. McDonald *et al.*, "Excavations at Nichoria in Messenia (1969-71, 1972-3)" in *Hesperia* 41 (1972) 218-73, 44 (1975) 69-141.

W.A. McDonald and J. Carothers, "Size and Distribution of the Population in Late Bronze Age Messenia: Some Statistical Approaches", in *JFA* 6 (1979) 433-54.

C.W. Shelmerdine and J. Chadwick, "The Pylos Ma Tablets Reconsidered", in *AJA* 77 (1973) 261-278.

N.S. Valmin, *Études topographiques sur la Messénie Ancienne*, Lund 1930.

N.S. Valmin, "Continued Exploration in Eastern Triphylia", in *Bull. Lund* (1927-8) 1-54.

N.S. Valmin, *The Swedish Messenia Expedition*, Lund 1938.

N.S. Valmin, "Malthi-Epilog", in *OpAth* 1 (1953) 29-46.

MAP G

P.I. Agallopoulou (Mycenaean sites on Zakynthos), in *AD* 28 (1973) A 198-214.

S. Benton, "The Ionian Islands", in *BSA* 32 (1931-2) 213-46.

S. Benton, "Excavations in Ithaka III", in *BSA* 39 (1938-9) 1-16.

S. Benton and H. Waterhouse, "Excavations in Ithaka: Tris Langadas", in *BSA* 68 (1973) 1-24.

W. Dörpfeld, *Alt-Ithaka*, Munich 1927.

W.A. Heurtley, "Excavations in Ithaka II", in *BSA* 35 (1934-5) 1-44.

P.G. Kalligas, "Kephalleniaka 3", in *AAA* 10 (1977) 116-125.

S. Marinatos, reports of excavations in Kephallenia in *AD* 5 (1919) 82-122, 6 (1920-21) 175-7, *AE* (1932) 10-47, (1933) 70-97.

E. Mastrokostas, preliminary reports of excavations at Teikhos Dymaion, in *PAE* (1962) 127-33, (1963), 93-8, (1964) 60-67, (1965) 121-36, *Ergon* (1966) 156-65.

E. Mastrokostas, "Anaskaphe Hagiou Ilia—Mesolongion (Ithorias)", in *AD* 19 (1964) B 295-300.

J. Servais, "Le site helladique de Khlemoutsi et l'Hyrminè homérique", in *BCH* 88 (1964) 9-50.

K. Wardle, *The Greek Bronze Age West of the Pindus* (Ph.D. thesis, London, 1972).

MAPS H AND J

Y. Béquignon, reports of excavations in the Pharsala area, in *BCH* 55 (1931) 492-3, (1932) 89-119, 122-191.

Y. Béquignon, *Recherches archéologiques à Phères*, Paris 1937.

E. Hanschmann and V. Miløjčič, *Argissa III*, Bonn 1976.

B. Helly, *Gonnoi* (vols. I and II), Amsterdam 1973.

A. Hunter, *The Bronze Age in Thessaly and its Environs, with Special Reference to Mycenaean Culture* (B.Litt. thesis, Oxford 1953).

K. Kourouniotes, "Anaskaphe tholotou taphou en Voloi", in *AE* (1906) 211-40.

V. Miløjčič, *Hauptergebnisse der deutschen Ausgrabungen in Thessalien 1953-58*, Bonn 1960.

V. Miløjčič *et al.*, *Argissa I*, Bonn. 1962.

V. Miløjčič *et al.*, *Magulen um Larisa 1966*, Bonn 1976.

F. Stählin, *Die Hellenische Thessalien*, Stuttgart 1924.

D.R. Theochares, preliminary reports of excavations at Volos and Pefkakia, in *PAE* (1956) 119-30, (1957) 54-69, (1960) 49-59, (1961) 45-54.

D.R. Theochares "Iolkos, whence sailed the Argonauts", in *Archaeology* II (1958) 13-18.

C. Tsountas, *Hai Proistorikai Akropoleis Dimeniou kai Sesklou*, Athens 1908.

A.J.B. Wace and M.S. Thompson, *Prehistoric Thessaly*, Cambridge 1912.

MAPS K AND L

I.P. Bokotopoulou, "Neoi kibotioschemoi taphoi tes YE IIIB-Γ periodou ex Epeirou", in *AE* (1969) 179-207.

S.I. Dakaris, "Proistorikoi taphoi para to Kalbaki-Ioanninon", in *AE* (1956) 114-53.

S.I. Dakaris, "Das Taubenorakel von Dodona und das Totenorakel bei Ephyra", in *Antike Kunst* Beiheft 1 (1963) 35-56.

S.I. Dakaris, "A Mycenaean IIIB Dagger from the Palaeolithic Site of Kastritsa, Epirus, Greece," in *PPS* 33 (1967) 30-36.

D.H. French, *Index of Prehistoric Sites in Central Macedonia* (circulated typescript, 1967).

N.G.L. Hammond, *Epirus*, Oxford 1967.

W.A. Heurtley, *Prehistoric Macedonia*, Cambridge 1939.

P.M. Petsas, "Mykenaika ostraka ek Kozanis kai Paionias", in *AE* (1953-4) B 113-120.

K.A. Wardle, *The Greek Bronze Age West of the Pindus* (Ph.D. thesis, London, 1972).

K.A. Wardle, "The Northern Frontier of Mycenaean Greece", in *BICS* 22 (1975) 206-212.

MAPS M AND N

T.D. Atkinson *et al.*, *The Excavations at Phylakopi in Melos* (*JHS* suppl. 4), London 1904.

R. Barber, "Phylakopi 1911 and the History of the Later Cycladic Bronze Age", in *BSA* 69 (1974) 1-53.

J.L. Bintliff, *Natural Environment and Human Settlement in Prehistoric Greece* (1977) 521-604.

J.L. Caskey, "Investigations in Keos", in *Hesperia* 40 (1971) 358-96, 41 (1972) 357-401.

S.I. Charitonides, "Thalamoeides taphos Karpathou", in *AD* 17 (1961-2) A 32-76.

R.M. Dawkins and J.P. Droop, "The Excavations at Phylakopi in Melos", in *BSA* 17 (1910-11) 3-22.

A. Furumark, "The Settlement at Ialysos and Aegean History 1550-1400 B.C.", in *OpArch* 6 (1950) 150-271.

H. Gallet de Sanṭerre, *Délos primitive et archaique*, Paris 1958.

H.D. Hansen, "Prehistoric Skyros", in *Studies Presented to David M. Robinson*, vol. I, St. Louis 1951.

R. Hope Simpson and J.F. Lazenby, "Notes from the Dodecanese", in *BSA* 57 (1962) 154-75, 65 (1970) 47-77, 68 (1973) 127-79.

G. Jacopi, "Nuovi Scavi nella Necropoli Micenea di Jaliso", in *Ann.* 13-14 (1930-31) 253-345.

A. Maiuri, "Jalisos-Scavi della Missione Archeologica Italiana a Rodi (Parte I e II)", in *Ann.* 6-7 (1923-4) 83-341.

S. Marinatos, *Excavations at Thera I-VII,* Athens 1968-74.

G. Monaco, "Scavi nella zona micenea di Jaliso", in *Clara Rhodos* 10 (1941) 41-185.

L. Morricone, "Eleona e Langada: Sepolcreti della Tarda Eta del Bronzo a Coo", in *Ann.* 43-44 (1965-6) 5-311.

L. Morricone, "Coo: Scavi e Scoperte nel 'Serraglio' e in Localita Minori (1935-1943)", in *Ann.* 50-51 (1972-3) 139-396.

N. Platon, "Ho taphos tou Staphylou kai ho Minoikos apoikismos tes Preparethou", in *KC* 3 (1949) 534-73.

C. Renfrew, *The Emergence of Civilisation,* London 1972.

O. Rubensohn, "Die praehistorische und frühgeschichtliche Funde aus dem Burghügel von Paros", in *AM* 42 (1917) 1-72.

K. Scholes, "The Cyclades in the Later Bronze Age: A Synopsis", in *BSA* 51 (1956) 9-40.

F.H. Stubbings, *Mycenaean Pottery from the Levant,* Cambridge 1951.

C. Tsountas, "Kykladika", in *AE* (1898) 137-212, (1899) 73-134.

MAP O

G. Bass, "Mycenaean and Protogeometric Tombs in the Halicarnassus Peninsula", in *AJA* 68 (1963) 353-61.

C.W. Blegen *et al.* Troy I-IV, Princeton 1950-56.

Y. Boysal, *Katalog der Vasen im Museum in Bodrum: I-Mykenisch-Protogeometrisch,* Ankara 1969.

R. Bridges, "The Mycenaean Tholos Tomb at Kolophon", in *Hesperia* 43 (1974) 264-6.

J.M. Cook, "Old Smyrna, 1948-51", in *BSA* 53-54 (1958-9) 1-34.

J.M. Cook, "Greek Archaeology in Western Asia Minor", in *AR* (1959-60) 27-57.

J.M. Cook and D.J. Blackman, "Greek Archaeology in Western Asia Minor", in *AR* (1964-5) 32-62.

J.M. Cook and D.J. Blackman, "Archaeology in Western Asia Minor" in *AR* (1970-71) 33-62.

V.R. d'A. Desborough, *The Last Mycenaeans and Their Successors* (1964) 158-166 and *passim.*

D.H. French, "Prehistoric Sites in North-west Anatolia I-The Iznik Area", in *AS* 19 (1969) 4-98.

J. Jakar, "Hittite Involvement in Western Anatolia", in *AS* 26 (1976) 117-28.

G. Kleiner, *Alt-Milet,* Wiesbaden 1966.

G. Kleiner, *Die Ruinen von Milet,* Berlin 1968.

D. Levi, preliminary reports of excavations at Iasos, in *Ann.* 39-40 (1961-2) 505-71, 43-44 (1965-6) 401-546, 45-46 (1967-8) 537-90, 47-48 (1969-70) 461-532.

C.B. Mee, "Aegean Trade and Settlement in Anatolia in the Second Millenium B.C.", in *AS* 28 (1978) 121-55.

J. Mellaart, "Anatolian Trade with Europe and Anatolian Geography and Culture Provinces in the Late Bronze Age", in *AS* 18 (1968) 187-202.

M.J. Mellink, "Archaeology in Asia Minor", in *AJA* 60 (1956) 369-84, 63 (1959) 73-85,
64 (1960) 57-69, 65 (1961) 37-52, 66 (1962) 71-85, 67 (1963) 173-90, 68 (1964) 149-66, 69
(1965) 133-49, 70 (1966) 139-59, 71 (1967) 155-74, 72 (1968) 125-47, 73 (1969) 203-27, 74
(1970) 157-78, 75 (1971) 161-81, 76 (1972) 165-88, 77 (1973) 169-93, 78 (1974) 105-30, 79
(1975) 201-22, 80 (1976) 261-89, 81 (1977) 298-321, 82 (1978) 315-338, 83 (1979) 331-44.

V. Miløjčič, *Samos I: Die prähistorische Siedlung unter dem Heraion*, Bonn 1961.

S. Mitchell and A.W. McNicoll, "Archaeology in Western and Southern Asia Minor
1971-78", in *AR* (1978-9) 59-90.

W. Schiering, "Die Ausgrabung beim Athena-Tempel in Milet 1957-I: Sudabschnitt",
in *Ist. Mitt.* 9-10 (1959-60) 4-30.

W. Schiering, "Die Minoisch-Mykenische Siedlung in Milet vor dem Bau der Grossen
Mauer", in *Ist. Mitt.* 25 (1975) 9-15.

F.H. Stubbings, *Mycenaean Pottery from the Levant*, Cambridge 1951.

W. Voigtlander, "Die Mykenische Stadtmauer in Milet und Einzelne Wehranlagen der
Spaten Bronzezeit", in *Ist. Mitt.* 25 (1975) 17-34.

C. Weickert, "Grabungen in Milet 1938", in *Bericht über den VI internationalen Kongress
für Archäologie*, Berlin 1940.

C. Weickert, "Die Ausgrabung beim Athena-Tempel in Milet 1955", in *Ist. Mitt.* 7
(1957) 102-32.

C. Weickert, "Neue Ausgrabungen in Milet", in E. Boehringer (ed.), *Neue Deutsche
Ausgrabungen im Mittelmeergebiet und im Vorderen Orient*, Berlin 1959, pp. 181-96.

C. Weickert, "Die Ausgrabung beim Athena-Tempel in Milet 1957-III: Der Westab-
schnitt", in *Ist. Mitt.* 9-10 (1959-60) 63-6.

4. SPECIAL BIBLIOGRAPHY FOR SUMMARY

P. Betancourt, "The End of the Greek Bronze Age", in *Antiquity* 50 (1976) 40-45.

R.A. Bryson *et al.*, "Drought and the Decline of Mycenae," in *Antiquity* 48 (1974) 46-
50, 228-30.

R. Carpenter, *Discontinuity in Greek Civilisation*, Cambridge 1966.

E.B. French, "Mycenaean Problems 1400-1200 b.c.", *BICS* 24 (1977) 136-8.

N.K. Sandars, *The Sea Peoples*, London 1978.

C.G. Thomas, "A Mycenaean Hegemony? A Reconsideration," in *JHS* 70 (1970) 184-92.

J.M. Wagstaff, "A Note on Settlement Numbers in Ancient Greece", in *JHS* 95 (1975)
163-83.

H.E. Wright, "Climatic Change in Mycenaean Greece", in *Antiquity* 42 (1968) 123-7.

5. MYCENAEAN POTTERY AND CHRONOLOGY

O.T.P.K. Dickinson, "Late Helladic IIA and IIB: Some Evidence from Korakou", in
BSA 67 (1972) 103-12.

O.T.P.K. Dickinson, "The Definition of Late Helladic I", in *BSA* 69 (1974) 109-20.

O.T.P.K. Dickinson, *The Origins of Mycenaean Civilisation* (*SIMA* vol. 49), Göteborg
1977.

E. French, "Pottery Groups from Mycenae: A Summary", in *BSA* 58 (1963) 44-52.

E. French, "Late Helladic IIIA1 Pottery from Mycenae", in *BSA* 59 (1964) 241-61.

E. French, "Late Helladic IIIA2 Pottery from Mycenae", in *BSA* 60 (1965) 159-202.

E. French, "A Group of Late Helladic IIIB1 Pottery from Mycenae", in *BSA* 61 (1966) 216-38.

E. French, "Pottery from Late Helladic IIIB1 Destruction Contexts at Mycenae", in *BSA* 62 (1967) 149-93.

E. French, "A Group of Late Helladic IIIB2 Pottery from Mycenae", in *BSA* 64 (1969) 71-93.

E. French, "The First Phase of L.H. IIIC", in *AA* (1969) 133-6.

A. Furumark, *Mycenaean Pottery, Analysis and Classification*, Stockholm 1941.

A. Furumark, *The Chronology of Mycenaean Pottery*, Stockholm 1941.

A. Furumark, "The Mycenaean IIIC Pottery and its Relation to Cypriote Fabrics", in *OpAth* 3 (1944) 194-265.

V. Hankey and P.M. Warren, "The Absolute Chronology of the Aegean Late Bronze Age", in *BICS* 21 (1974) 142-52 (with references).

R. Hope Simpson and O.T.P.K. Dickinson, *A Gazetteer of Aegean Civilisation in the Bronze Age, Vol. I: The Mainland and Islands* (*SIMA* vol. 52), Göteborg 1979.

S. Iakovidis, "The Chronology of LH IIIC, in *AJA* 83 (1979) 454-62.

P.A. Mountjoy, "Late Helladic IIIB1 Pottery Dating the Construction of the South House at Mycenae", in *BSA* 71 (1976) 77-111.

M. Popham and E. Milburn, "The Late Helladic IIIC Pottery of Xeropolis (Lefkandi), A Summary", in *BSA* 66 (1971) 333-49.

J.B. Rutter, "Ceramic Evidence for Northern Intruders in Southern Greece at the Beginning of the Late Helladic IIIC period", in *AJA* 79 (1975) 17-32, *cf. AJA* 80 (1976) 186-8.

J.B. and S.H. Rutter, *The Transition to Mycenaean*, Los Angeles 1976.

F.H. Stubbings, "The Mycenaean Pottery of Attica", in *BSA* 42 (1947) 1-75.

N.M. Verdelis, E. and D.H. French, "Tiryns: Mykenaike epikhosis exothen tou Dytikou Teikhous tes Akropoleos", in *AD* 20 (1965) A 137-52.

A.J.B. Wace *et al.*, "Prehistoric Cemetery: A Deposit of L.H. III Pottery", in *BSA* 52 (1957) 207-19.

E.B. Wace, "The Cyclopean Terrace Building and the Deposit of Pottery Beneath It", in *BSA* 64 (1954) 267-91.

K.A. Wardle, "A Group of Late Helladic IIIB1 Pottery from Within the Citadel at Mycenae", in *BSA* 64 (1969) 261-97.

K.A. Wardle, "A Group of Late Helldic IIIB2 Pottery from Within the Citadel at Mycenae", in *BSA* 68 (1973) 297-348.

6. LINEAR B (MAJOR PUBLICATIONS OF MATERIAL FROM SITES ON THE GREEK MAINLAND)

E.L. Bennett and A.J.B. Wace, "The Mycenae Tablets", in *Proceedings of the American Philosophical Society* 97 (1953) 422-70.

E.L. Bennett, *The Pylos Tablets: Texts of the Inscriptions Found 1939-54*, Princeton 1955.

E.L. Bennett, "The Mycenae Tablets II", in *Transactions of the American Philosophical Society* 48 (1958) 1-122.

E.L. Bennett, *The Olive Oil Tablets of Pylos: Texts of Inscriptions Found, 1955* (Minos September 2, 1958).

E.L. Bennett, and J.-P. Olivier, *The Pylos Tablets in Transcription*, Rome 1973.

H.W. Catling and A. Millett, "A Study of the Inscribed Stirrup-Jars from Thebes", in *Archaeometry* 8 (1965) 3-85.

J. Chadwick *et al.*, "The Mycenae Tablets III", in *Transactions of the American Philosophical Society* 52 (1963) 1-76.

J. Chadwick, "Linear B Tablets from Thebes", in *Minos* 10 (1970) 115-37.

J. Chadwick, *The Thebes Tablets II* (*Minos Suppl.* 5), 1975.

J.-P. Olivier, *The Mycenae Tablets IV*, Leiden 1969.

L.R. Palmer, *The Interpretation of Mycenaean Greek Texts*, Oxford 1963.

C.W. Shelmerdine, "The Pylos Ma Tablets Reconsidered", in *AJA* 77 (1973) 261-75.

M. Ventris and J. Chadwick, *Documents in Mycenaean Greek*, Cambridge 1973.

W.F. Wyatt, "The Ma Tablets from Pylos", in *AJA* 66 (1962) 21-41. (See also Chadwick, *The Mycenaean World*, Cambridge 1976, especially references on pp. 195-6.)

REFERENCES

References to books and periodicals are necessarily selective, and preference is given to *primary* sources. Thus, when a primary account has appeared in *Archaiologikon Deltion (AD)*, for instance, *later* references to that account in other periodicals (such as *AR* and *BCH*) are not normally given. It is assumed that most interested scholars will be aware of the reviews of discoveries which appear regularly in *AJA, AR, BCH,* and other periodicals. References to general surveys and studies are similarly selective. Many of the books and articles listed in the Select Bibliography above are not cited in the text subsequently. Nevertheless, many of the conclusions and judgements made in the text have been greatly facilitated by the combined work of all the scholars listed.

SITE INDEX

This site index includes all types of sites, and various districts and islands either known to be, or alleged to be, the provenance of Mycenaean finds. The index is, however, selective, and does not include all of the toponyms cited in the Gazetteer. The site names and names of alleged provenances are given in boldface capital letters. The relevant district names (ancient) or island names (modern) are given after the site names. Sites listed on Maps A to L are also identified by their numbers (in brackets) or by the relevant Map or Appendix to each Map (abbreviated Appx.). The primary references (i.e., to the discussions of the sites themselves) are given first. Primary page references to sites are given first and are in boldface.

Several names of districts, islands, and geographical features (usually mountains, rivers, or plains) are also given in the index, in regular print.

PARTIAL INDEX TO
CERTAIN SPECIAL FEATURES

This selective index is confined to prominent features at sites known to be Mycenaean or considered to be probably Mycenaean. Features at sites on Maps A to L are usually indexed only by their map and number. Features at sites on Maps M to O are indexed by their place names and page numbers. A question mark after a site number or a place name indicates that either the identification or the date of the feature is uncertain.

(A) MAJOR BUILDINGS ON MYCENAEAN SETTLEMENT SITES

Palaces (Major) A 1, 10; B 1?; C 1?, 22; F 1; H 1; generally 4
"Mansions" and Other Large Buildings (Other Than Major Palaces) A 1, 6?, 8?, 10, 51, 63; B 1?, 14?; C 1, 7, 22, 51; E 1; F 1, 17, 30, 100, 202, 203, 218; H 1; Ayia Irini (Kea), 187, Phylakopi (Melos), 190

(B) FORTIFICATIONS

Fortresses (Major) A 1, 8, 10, 14?; B 1; C 7, 22?, 39, 51; F 1?; G 6; H 17?; Phylakopi (Melos), 190
Fortified Settlements (Other Than Major Fortresses) (Note: In most cases where a question mark is added in this category, walls of "Cyclopean" style but undetermined date have been found.) A 11?, 13?, 25, 33, 47, 51, 59, 61, 89?; B 6?, 16?, 32?, 33?, 51?, 53; C 2?, 3?, 6?, 9, 10, 11, 16?, 20?, 41?, 42?, 43?, 47?, 56?, 82?; D 9?, 10?, 21?, 25?, 68?, 70?, 71?; E 14?, 16?; F 132, 202, 203, 217; G 26?, 34?, 41?; H 47?; J5?; K 1?, 2?; Ayia Irini (Kea), 187, Ayios Andreas (Siphnos), 189, Koukounaries (Paros), 188-189; Eremokastro? (Rhodes), 199, Amaniou? (Kos), 201; The Heraion (Samos), 206, Miletus (Asia Minor), 207-208
Minor Forts or "Watchtowers" (Note: This category *excludes* sites where evidence suggests a "permanent" habitation site.) A 1 (Mt. Profitis Ilias), A 14 (The Larisa?), A 54 (Acrocorinth?), A 35A?, Mt. Ptoon? (Boeotia), 64, Megalovouno? (Boeotia), 64
The Mycenaean Wall at the Isthmus of Corinth A 61; generally 4, 11, 33

(C) SHRINES AND OTHER CENTRES OF "CULT" ACTIVITY

A 1, 24, 30?, 48?, 64?; B 3?, 14?, 43?; C 52; E 1?, 5, 56; F7?, 131?, 202?, 203?; G 30?; H 14?; Ayia Irini (Kea), 187, The Temenos? (Delos), 187, Phylakopi (Melos), 190; The Heraion? (Samos), 206

(D) TOMBS

Tholos Tombs A 1, 6, 7, 9, 10, 14?, 28; B 10, 22, 41, 51?, 74; C 1, 27?; D 38?, 42, 70; E 4, 9, 58; F 1, 5, 6, 13, 17, 18?, 21, 27, 29, 32, 34, 37, 50?, 58, 59, 100, 104, 105, 110, 111, 121, 137, 202, 203, 206, 209, 211, 217, 221, 230, 235; G 8, 10?, 13?, 17, 35, 36, 38; H 1, 2, 3, 11, 12, 20, 27, 34; J 8; K2; generally 2, 4, 5, 9, 41, 143, 161
Built Tombs of Tholos Type B 22, 72, 76, 77; C 49; D 5; E 9, 48; F 29, 36, 40; G 11; H 4, 20, 32, 33, 59; Colophon (Asia Minor), 208
Other Built Tombs A 14; B 22; C 49, 73; D 66; E 13, 50, 51; F 29, 100; G 16, 22; H 2, 51, 55; The Temenos (Delos), 187, Lygaridia (Naxos), 188; The Heraion (Samos), 206
Chamber Tombs (Cut in Rock or Earth) A 1, 2, 4, 5, 6, 7, 9, 10, 11, 14, 15, 20, 24, 29, 31, 32, 33, 38, 47, 52, 53, 69, 76; B 1, 3, 4, 9, 14, 17, 18, 19, 20, 21, 27?, 28, 29, 30, 32, 33, 35, 37, 40, 46, 50, 52, 54, 57, 59, 61, 66, 69, 71, 74, 77, 78; C 1, 5, 13, 22, 27, 30, 35, 43, 45, 52, 61, 62, 69, 72, 75, 83, 85; D 17, 22, 23, 24, 27, 28, 29, 30, 31, 32, 33, 35, 36, 37, 38, 39, 40, 41, 43, 44, 45, 46, 49, 51, 53, 55, 58, 62, 63, 67, 73?, 76, 78, Akrata? (Achaea), 97, Diakofto: Kastron? (Achaea), 97, Mamousia? (Achaea), 97, Kouloura: Palaiokamares? (Achaea), 98, Vovoda? (Achaea), 98, Krini? (Achaea), 98, Damiza? (Elis), 98, Kalliani? (Arcadia), 98; E 5, 6, 19, 30, 33, 36, 37, 42, 48, 53, 54; F 1, 2, 8, 9, 50?, 100, 117, 121, 132, 139, 232; G 4, 5, 14, 15, 17, 18, 19, 20, 21, 23, 35; H 17; Kastro (Skyros), 185, Grotta, etc. (Naxos), 188, Ellinika (Kimolos), 190, Phylakopi (Melos), 190, Sotira (Melos), 190, Trypites (Melos), 190; Trianda: Moschou Vounara and Makria Vounara (Rhodes), 195, Paradhisi (Rhodes), 195, Damatria (Rhodes), 195, Maritsa (Rhodes), 195-196, Tolon (Rhodes), 196, Fanes? (Rhodes), 196, Kalavarda: Aniforo, etc. (Rhodes), 196, Apollona (Rhodes), 197, Mandhriko (Rhodes), 196, Kritinia (Rhodes), 196, Siana? (Rhodes), 197, Ayios Isidhoros? (Rhodes), 197, Apollakia? (Rhodes), 197, Kattavia: Ayios Minas (Rhodes), 197, Kattavia: Karavi? (Rhodes), 197, Yenadhi (Rhodes), 198, Vati: Passia (Rhodes), 198, Vati: Apsaktiras (Rhodes), 198, Asklipio? (Rhodes), 198, Lardos: Troullo Vouno (Rhodes), 198, Pilona: Ambelia (Rhodes), 198, Archangelos: Mala (Rhodes), 198-199, Koskinou? (Rhodes), 199, Pigadhia: Makelli (Karpathos), 199, Yiafani? (Karpathos), 199-200, Kos: Langadha and Eleona (Kos), 200, Pyli: Ayia Paraskevi (Kos), 201, Eleona? (Kos), 201, Antimachia? (Kos), 201, The Asklepieion? (Kos), 201, Pothia (Kalymnos), 202, Armenochori: Patelles (Astypalaia), 202, Myloi (Samos), 206, Müskëbi (Asia Minor), 207, Miletus (Asia Minor), 207; generally 5
Chamber Tombs Imitating Tholos Tombs D 17; E 46; F 8; G 19, 20, 21
Tumuli and Burial Mounds (Note: This category includes some "tholos mounds" provisionally identified by *survey alone*. These are marked here with an asterisk.) B 41; C 1; D 1; D 54, 64, 68; F 12*, 23*, 29, 30, 32, 33, 36, 43*, 50, 58*, 103*, 119*, 120*, 121*; G 22*; H 34, 51; J 10; K 1; L 12.

Plate 1a.   Mycenae: Citadel from northeast

Plate 1b.   Mycenae: Citadel from east

Plate 2a. Mycenae: Citadel from southwest, with Mt. Profitis Ilias above

Plate 2b. Mycenae: Bridge over Chavos ravine from west

Plate 3a.   Mycenae: "Treasury of Atreus" from east

Plate 3b.   Mycenae: Sally-port in northeast extension, from outside

Plate 3c.   Mycenae: Vaulted passage to Perseia spring-chamber

Plate 4a.   Midea: Acropolis from west

Plate 4b.   Midea: Walls on northeast side of acropolis

Plate 5a.   Asine from northwest

Plate 5b.   Argos: The Aspis from the Larisa

Plate 6a.   Agrilovounaki: Mycenaean road from east at point C

Plate 6b.   Agrilovounaki: Bridge at Lykotroupi (point F) from east

Plate 7a. Ancient dam near Tiryns from northeast (points B and C indicated by arrows)

Plate 7b. Dam from north, showing line of original stream

Plate 7c. Remains of outer wall of dam at points C and D (indicated by arrows)

Plate 7d. Outer wall of dam at point C

Plate 8a.   Kasarma from southwest, with Arkadiko bridge in foreground

Plate 8b.   Arkadiko bridge from northeast

Plate 9a.   Arkadiko bridge from southeast

Plate 9b.   Arkadiko bridge:
Interior of culvert

Plate 9c.   Arkadiko bridge from northwest

Plate 10a. The Corinthian plain from Acrocorinth

Plate 10b. Sikyon (Vasiliko) from northeast

Plate 11a.   Korakou from west

Plate 11b.   Megara and Palaiokastro from south

Plate 11c.   Brauron: The acropolis from northeast

Plate 12a. Orchomenos: "Treasury of Minyas" from above

Plate 12b. "Treasury of Minyas": Door to side chamber

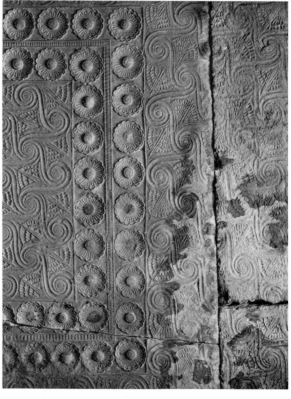

Plate 12c. "Treasury of Minyas": Part of carved ceiling of side chamber

Plate 13a.   Gla from north

Plate 13b.   Ayia Marina from Gla

Plate 13c.   Pyrgos (Aspledon?) from east

Plate 14a.   Gla: South gate from outside

Plate 14b.   Gla: South gate from inside

Plate 14c.   Gla: "Guardrooms" in the southeast gate

Plate 14d.   Gla: Outside walls of "palace" on the north side

Plate 15a.   To west from Ayia Marina to Topolia and Stroviki
(Arrows indicate dyke remains at point A.)

Plate 15b.   South retaining wall of dyke at point A, from east

Plate 15c.   Outer (north) face of retaining wall at point A, with Gla behind

Plate 16a. Thisbe from southeast

Plate 16b. Eretria: The acropolis from southwest

Plate 16c. Pyrgos (Kynos?) from northwest

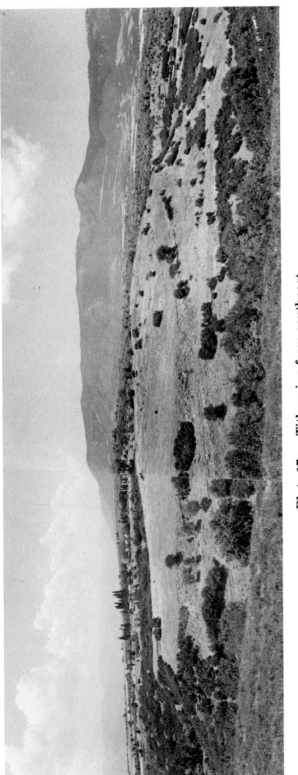

Plate 17a.　Tithronion from southeast

Plate 17b.　The Kephissos valley, from Ayioi Anargyroi near Amphikleia

Plate 18a.   Krisa and Itea, from below Delphi

Plate 18b.   Thermon: Temple of Apollo from south

Plate 19a.   Pheneos: The Asklepieion site from south

Plate 19b.   Nestane from west

Plate 19c.   Palaiopyrgi from north

Plate 20a. Mt. Taygetos and the Sparta Plain, from the Menelaion

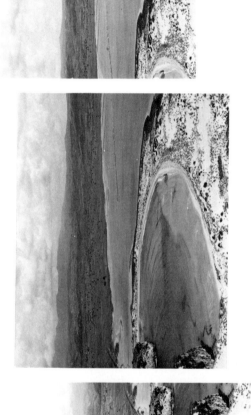

Plate 20b. Osmanaga Lagoon from "Nestor's Cave" on Palaiokastro

Plate 21a.   Lekas and Ayios Stephanos from north

Plate 21b.   Epidaurus Limera from south

Plate 21c.   Goulas from southwest, and the Molaoi plain

Plate 22a.   The Island of Cranae

Plate 22b.   Klidhi (Arene?) from northeast

Plate 22c.   Pontikokastro (Ancient Pheia) from west

Plate 23a. "Malthi-Dorion" from east

Plate 23b. Konchilion from southeast

Plate 24a.   Kardamyle: Citadel from west

Plate 24b.   Leuktro from north

Plate 25a. Zakynthos town and Kastro above

Plate 25b. Profitis Ilias (Aetolia) from southwest

Plate 25c. Astakos from northeast

Plate 26a. Kavaki ridge near Spilia from northeast

Plate 26b. Gremnos (Ancient Argissa) from east

Plate 27a. Elasson from south

Plate 27b. Xylokastro (Ephyra?) from south

Plate 27c. Xylokastro: "Cyclopean" walls on the southwest side

Plate 28a. Mycenae: "Tomb of the Genii"

Plate 28b. The Menidi tholos tomb

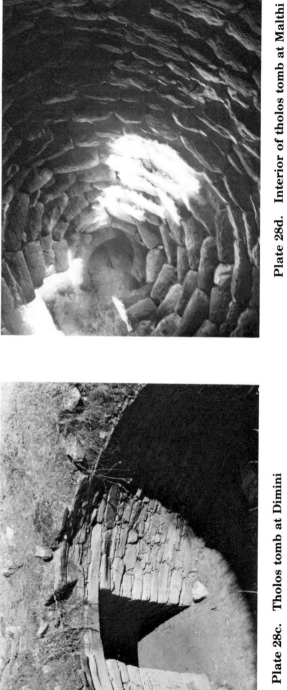

Plate 28c. Tholos tomb at Dimini

Plate 28d. Interior of tholos tomb at Malthi

Plate 29a.   Lindos from northwest

Plate 29b.   Moschou Vounara from northeast, with Ialysos acropolis behind

Plate 29c.   Lelos and Mt. Attaviros from northeast

Plate 30a.   Kos: Palaiopyli from north

Plate 30b.   Palaiopyli: Walls on north side

Plate 31a. Kalymnos: Perakastro from southeast

Plate 31b. Perakastro from east

Plate 31c. Patmos: Kastelli from east

Plate 32a.   Astypalaia: Kastrou tou Ayiou Ioannou from southeast

Plate 32b.   Kastro tou Ayiou Ioannou from east